STUDENT'S GUIDE TO THE
Supreme Court

Student's Guides to the U.S. Government Series

Volume 1: Student's Guide to
Elections

Volume 2: Student's Guide to
Congress

Volume 3: Student's Guide to
the Presidency

Volume 4: Student's Guide to
the Supreme Court

STUDENT'S GUIDE TO THE

★ ★ ★ ★ ★ ★ ★ ★ ★ ★ ★ ★ ★ ★

Supreme Court

ADVISORY EDITOR

Bruce J. Schulman, Ph.D.

Boston University

CQ PRESS

A Division of SAGE

Washington, D.C.

Developed, Designed, and Produced by

DWJ BOOKS LLC

CQ Press
2300 N Street, NW, Suite 800
Washington, DC 20037

Phone: 202-729-1900; toll free, 1-866-4CQ-PRESS (1-866-427-7737)

Web: www.cqpress.com

Cover design: Matthew Simmons/www.MyselfIncluded.com

Photo acknowledgments for the Primary Source Library: The Granger Collection, New York: pp. 278; Library of Congress, Prints and Photograph Division: p. 286; Collection of the Supreme Court of the United States: p. 287; AP Photo: p. 292; AP Photo, J. Scott Applewhite: p. 312; AP Photo, Supreme Court, HO: p. 326.

♾ The paper used in this publication exceeds the requirements of the American National Standard for Information Sciences—Permanence of Paper for Printed Library Materials, ANSI Z39.48–1992.

Printed and bound in the United States of America

12 11 10 09 08   1 2 3 4 5

Library of Congress Cataloging-in-Publication Data

Student's guide to the Supreme Court/advisory editor, Bruce J. Schulman.
    p. cm. — (Student's Guides to the U.S. Government Series; v. 4)
  ISBN: 978-0-87289-553-9
  1. United States. Supreme Court. I. Schulman, Bruce J. II. Title. III. Series.

KF8742.S78 2010
347.73'26—dc22   2010012525

CONTENTS

List of Illustrations ... viii
Reader's Guide ... x
About the Advisory Editor ... xiii
Preface ... xiv
Historical Milestones of the U.S. Supreme Court,
1787–2009: A Timeline ... xvi

Part One: ESSAYS

The Supreme Court: The Weakest or Strongest
Branch of Our Government? ... 1
How Does the President Nominate a
Supreme Court Justice? ... 17
How Does the Supreme Court Affect
Citizens Today? ... 27

Part Two: THE SUPREME COURT A TO Z

Abortion, Constitutional Debate on ... 34
Affirmative Action ... 36
Aliens, Protection of ... 37
Alito, Samuel A. (1950–) ... 38
Appellate Jurisdiction ... 40
Articles of Confederation ... 40
Associate Justices ... 41
Automobile Searches ... 43
Bail ... 45
Baker v. Carr (1962) ... 45
Bankruptcy and Bankruptcy Laws ... 47
Bill of Rights ... 47
Bills of Attainder ... 50
  Spotlight: The Twenty-Seventh Amendment
Brandeis, Louis D. (1856–1941) ... 51
Brennan, William Joseph Jr. (1906–1997) ... 53
Breyer, Stephen (1938–) ... 54
Brown v. Board of Education (1954) ... 55
  Justice for All: Linda Brown and the
  Brown Foundation
Burger, Warren E. (1907–1995) ... 59
Burr, Aaron, Trial of ... 60
  Justice for All: Treason and the
  Letter of the Law
Bush v. Gore (2000) ... 61

  Spotlight: Extraordinary Circumstances:
  1876 and 2000
Censorship ... 65
Checks and Balances ... 66
Chief Justice of the United States ... 67
Child Labor ... 69
Circuit Court of Appeals ... 71
Citizenship and Naturalization ... 73
  Spotlight: Washington, D.C., and Citizenship
Civil Rights Act of 1964 ... 75
Civil Rights and the Supreme Court ... 75
Civil Rights Cases (1883) ... 78
Confessions ... 78
Confirmation of Justices and Judges ... 79
  Decision Makers: The Importance of
  Senatorial Courtesy
Congress and the Supreme Court ... 83
Constitution of the United States ... 90
Contempt of Court ... 91
Cruel and Unusual Punishment ... 91
Cruzan v. Missouri Department of Health (1990) ... 92
Dartmouth College v. Woodward (1819) ... 94
Death Penalty Cases ... 95
  Spotlight: Is Lethal Injection Cruel and Unusual
  Punishment?
Declaratory Judgments ... 98
Double Jeopardy ... 98
Dred Scott v. Sandford (1857) ... 99
  Spotlight: The Fourteenth Amendment
Due Process ... 102
  Justice for All: Due Process for Delinquents
Electronic Eavesdropping ... 104
Eminent Domain ... 105
Engle v. Vitale (1962) ... 105
  Spotlight: School Prayer and
  Congressional Backlash
Equal Employment Opportunity ... 107
Equal Protection of the Law ... 110
Escobedo v. Illinois (1964) ... 110
Exclusionary Rule ... 112
Ex Parte Milligan (1866) ... 113
Ex Post Facto Laws ... 113

Fair Housing — 114

Federalism — 115

Field, Stephen Johnson (1816–1899) — 116

Fiscal and Monetary Power and the Supreme Court — 117

  Spotlight: The Tomato: Fruit Or Vegetable?

Flag Burning — 120

Foreign Affairs and the Supreme Court — 120

Frankfurter, Felix (1882–1965) — 121

Freedom of Assembly — 122

  Justice for All: A Right to Loiter?

Freedom of Association — 124

  Justice for All: Private Clubs

Freedom of Religion — 126

  Justice for All: Jehovah's Witnesses

Freedom of Speech — 128

  Spotlight: Fighting Words and Hate Crimes

Freedom of the Press — 133

Freedom to Petition — 135

Gag Rules — 136

Gibbons v. Ogden (1824) — 136

Gideon v. Wainwright (1963) — 139

  Justice for All: The Right to Refuse Counsel

Ginsburg, Ruth Bader (1933–) — 141

Grandfather Clauses — 142

Griswold v. Connecticut (1965) — 143

Harlan, John Marshall I (1833–1911) — 144

Harlan, John Marshall II (1899–1971) — 145

Hazelwood School District v. Kuhlmeier (1988) — 146

Heart of Atlanta Motel v. United States (1964) — 147

Hill, Anita (1950–) — 149

Holmes, Oliver Wendell Jr. (1841–1935) — 150

Hughes, Charles Evans (1862–1948) — 152

Impeachment of Justices — 153

Implied Powers — 153

Injunctions — 154

Interstate Relations — 155

Jay, John (1745–1829) — 156

Judicial Restraint — 157

Judicial Review — 158

Judiciary Act of 1789 — 159

Jurisdiction of the Supreme Court — 161

Juveniles, Rights of — 163

Kennedy, Anthony M. (1936–) — 164

Korematsu v. United States (1944) — 164

Legislative Veto — 166

Libel — 167

Line Item Veto — 168

Loving v. Virginia (1967) — 169

Loyalty Oaths — 170

Mapp v. Ohio (1961) — 171

Marbury v. Madison (1803) — 172

Maritime and Admiralty Law — 174

Marshall, John (1755–1835) — 175

Marshall, Thurgood (1908–1993) — 176

McCulloch v. Maryland (1819) — 177

Miranda v. Arizona (1966) — 179

New Deal and the Supreme Court — 181

New York Times v. Sullivan (1964) — 182

  Spotlight: Group Libel

Obscenity — 184

O'Connor, Sandra Day (1930–) — 187

One Person, One Vote — 189

Opinions — 189

Pentagon Papers — 191

Plessy v. Ferguson (1896) — 193

Powell v. Alabama (1932) — 195

Presidency and the Supreme Court — 197

  Spotlight: The Solicitor General

Probable Cause — 200

Race and Redistricting — 201

Rehnquist, William H. (1924–2005) — 202

Ricci v. DeStefano (2009) — 203

Right to a Jury Trial — 204

Right to a Public Trial — 205

Right to a Speedy Trial — 205

  Spotlight: Enemy Combatants at Guantanamo

Right to Die — 207

Right to Legal Counsel — 207

  Point/Counterpoint: Privacy for Consenting

  Adults: *Lawrence v. Texas* (2003)

Right to Privacy — 210

Right to Vote — 210

Roberts, John G. (1955–) — 211

Roe v. Wade (1973) — 213

Roosevelt's 1937 Court Reform Plan — 214

Salaries and Benefits of the Justices — 218

Scalia, Antonin (1936–) — 218

School Prayer and Bible Readings — 219

Search Warrants — 220

Self-Incrimination — 221

  Justice for All: Private Search

Sex Discrimination — 222

Sit-Ins — 223

  Spotlight: Women in the Military

Slaughterhouse Cases (1873) — 224

Slavery Issues — 225

  Spotlight: The *Amistad*

Sotomayor, Sonia (1954–) — 226

Souter, David (1939–) — 228

Speech, Unprotected — 228

Stevens, John Paul (1920–) 229
Stop-and-Frisk Searches 230
Story, Joseph (1779–1845) 230
Sturges v Crowninshield (1819) 231
Supreme Court, History of the 232
 Spotlight: Mandatory Retirement?
Supreme Court, Traditions of the 237
 Point/Counterpoint: Should Supreme Court
 Hearings Be Televised?
Swann v. Charlotte-Mecklenburg County Board
 of Education (1971) 242
Symbolic Speech 243
Taft, William Howard (1857–1930) 244
 Decision Makers: Taft and the
 Supreme Court Building
Taney, Roger B. (1777–1864) 246
 Spotlight: A Right To Travel
Term of the Supreme Court 248
Thomas, Clarence (1948–) 248
 Decision Makers: Senate Judiciary Committee
 Spotlight: Anti-War Protests
Tinker v. Des Moines (1969) 251
United States v. Nixon (1974) 252
University of California Regents v. Bakke (1978) 254
U.S. District Courts 255
Wallace v. Jaffree (1984) 256
War Power and the Supreme Court 257
Warren, Earl (1891–1974) 258
 Spotlight: The Court, Congress, and Cambodia
White Primaries 259
Writ of Habeas Corpus 260
Writ of Mandamus 261

Part Three: PRIMARY SOURCE LIBRARY

Judiciary Act, Chapter XX, Sections 1–4, 9,
 11, 14, 1789 262
Marbury v. Madison, 1803 264
Dartmouth College v. Woodward, 1819 269
McCulloch v. Maryland, 1819 273
Sturges v. Crowninshield, 1819 276
Supreme Court Chamber, 1860–1935 278
Gibbons v. Ogden, 1824 279

Circuit Court of Appeals Act, Sections 2, 3,
 and 4, 1891 280
Plessy v. Ferguson, 1896 282
 Point/Counterpoint: Plessy (1896) and
 Brown (1954)
Uncle Sam Anti-Alien Cartoon, 1918 286
The Justices and the Building, 1929 287
Korematsu v. United States, 1944 288
Brown v. Board of Education, 1954 290
The Supreme Court and the Communist
 Threat, 1951 292
Ad from The New York Times, 1960 293
Baker v. Carr, 1962 294
Gideon v. Wainwright, 1963 295
Escobedo v. Illinois, 1964 297
New York Times v. Sullivan, 1964 299
Miranda v. Arizona, 1966 301
Loving v. Virginia, 1967 303
Tinker v. Des Moines, 1969 305
From the Harry A. Blackmun Papers, 1970 307
Swann v. Mecklenburg County Board of
 Education, 1971 307
Roe v. Wade, 1973 310
Hazelwood School District v. Kuhlmeier, 1988 313
George W. Bush, et. al., petitioners, v.
 Albert Gore Jr., et. al., 2000 315
Lawrence v. Texas, 2003 318
Memorandum of Associate Justice
 Antonin Scalia, 2004 322
Associate Justice Ruth Bader Ginsburg on
 Brown v. Board of Education, October 21, 2004 324
Associate Justice Sandra Day O'Connor's
 Letter of Resignation, July 1, 2005 326
President George W. Bush Nominates Judge John
 Roberts as Chief Justice, September 5, 2005 327
Judge Sonia Sotomayor on Her Nomination
 to the Supreme Court, May 26, 2009 328

Using Primary Sources 331
Glossary 335
Selected Bibliography 339
Supreme Court Case Index 343
General Index 347

LIST OF ILLUSTRATIONS

Charts/Graphs

Associate Justices' Salaries 41

Foreign-Born Justices 42

Landmark Decision Highlights: *Baker v. Carr* (1962) 46

Landmark Decision Highlights: *Brown v. Board of Education* (1954) 55

Landmark Decision Highlights: *Bush v. Gore* (2000) 64

Chief Justices' Salaries 68

Landmark Decision Highlights: *Civil Rights Cases* (1883) 78

Supreme Court Nominations Not Confirmed by the Senate 80

Significant Acts of Congress Struck Down as Unconstitutional 85

Landmark Decision Highlights: *Cruzan v. Missouri Department of Health* (1990) 92

Landmark Decision Highlights: *Dartmouth College v. Woodward* (1819) 94

Landmark Decision Highlights: *Dred Scott v. Sanford* (1857) 101

Landmark Decision Highlights: *Engle v. Vitale* (1962) 107

Standards of Review: Equal Protection Claims 109

Landmark Decision Highlights: *Escobedo v. Illinois* (1964) 111

Public Speech on Private Property: The First Amendment Restricted 130

Landmark Decision Highlights: *Gibbons v. Ogden* (1824) 137

Landmark Decision Highlights: *Gideon v. Wainwright* (1963) 141

Landmark Decision Highlights: *Hazelwood School District v. Kuhlmeier* (1988) 146

Landmark Decision Highlights: *Heart of Atlanta Motel v. United States* (1964) 148

How a Case Reaches the Supreme Court 162

Landmark Decision Highlights: *Korematsu v. United States* (1944) 165

Landmark Decision Highlights: *Loving v. Virginia* (1967) 169

Landmark Decision Highlights: *Mapp v. Ohio* (1961) 171

Landmark Decision Highlights: *Marbury v. Madison* (1803) 173

Landmark Decision Highlights: *Miranda v. Arizona* (1966) 180

Landmark Decision Highlights: *New York Times v. Sullivan* (1964) 184

Landmark Decision Highlights: *Plessy v. Ferguson* (1896) 194

Landmark Decision Highlights: *Powell v. Alabama* (1932) 197

Landmark Decision Highlights: *Roe v. Wade* (1973) 213

Landmark Decision Highlights: *Swann v. Charlotte-Mecklenburg County Board of Education* (1971) 242

Landmark Decision Highlights: *Tinker v. Des Moines* (1969) 251

Landmark Decision Highlights: *United States v. Nixon* (1974) 252

Landmark Decision Highlights: *University of California Regents v. Bakke* (1978) 254

Tables

Cases Incorporating Provisions of the Bill of Rights into the Due Process Clause of the Fourteenth Amendment 49

Chief Justices of the United States, 1789–2005 68

Justices Who Served in Congress 88

Major Acts of Congress Relating to the Supreme Court 89

Key Provisions of the Judiciary Act of 1789 160

Obscenity: An Elusive Definition and a Changing Standard 185

Amendments That Extended Voting Rights 211

Changes in the Size of the Supreme Court 233

Meeting Locations of the Supreme Court 240

Maps

United States Circuit Courts (1789) 71

United States Circuit Courts (2009) 72

Photos

Supreme Court building 6
The Justices today 18
Citizens protesting in front of Supreme Court building 29
Cartoon: Affirmative Action 36
Samuel A. Alito 39
Police searching car 44
Stephen Breyer 54
Linda Brown in class 56
Cartoon: Censorship 1889 66
John Jay 67
Child labor 70
Sotomayor testifies before Congress 84
Execution chamber 96
Dred Scott 99
Present-day currency coming off the presses 119
Civil rights protestors praying, 1963 122
Ku Klux Klan 129
Ogden 137
Gibbons 137
Gideon's handwritten petition 140
Ruth Bader Ginsburg 142
Owner of Heart of Atlanta Motel 148
Oliver Wendell Holmes Jr. 150
Japanese internment camp in United States 165
Chadha and family 167
President Clinton signing Line Item Veto Act 169
President Adams appoints "midnight judges" 172
William Marbury 173
John Marshall 175
Thurgood Marshall 177
Miranda warning card 179
Warren Burger swears in Sandra Day O'Connor 188
Daniel Ellsberg 192
Run-down, segregated school 193
Scottsboro Boys 196
President Barack Obama announces retirement of Justice David Souter 198
William H. Rehnquist 202
Justice John G. Roberts swears in President Barack Obama, January 20, 2009 212
The Court in 1932 215
The Court in 1940 216
Cartoon: Court packing 217
Cartoon: FDR and Supreme Court 217
Sit-in at lunch counter 224
The Court in 1865 232
Supreme Court exterior 241
William Howard Taft 244
Roger B. Taney 246
Cartoon: Nixon and Supreme Court gavel 252
Earl Warren 259
Old Supreme Court chamber restored 278
Cartoon: Anti-alien 286
The Justices and the Supreme Court model 287
Eugene Dennis 292
The New York Times ad 293
Jane Roe and attorney 312
Sandra Day O'Connor's letter of resignation 326

READER'S GUIDE

The list that follows is provided as an aid to readers in locating articles on related topics. The Reader's Guide arranges all of the A–Z entries in the *Student's Guide to the Supreme Court* according to seven key concepts of the curriculum in American Government: Civil Rights and Civil Liberties; Constitutional Issues; Laws; People; Principles of Government; Supreme Court Cases; and Supreme Court Procedures and Processes. Some articles appear in more than one category.

Civil Rights and Civil Liberties

Affirmative Action
Aliens, Protection of
Automobile Searches
Bail
Bill of Rights
Brown v. Board of Education (1954)
Capital Punishment (*See* Death Penalty)
Child Labor
Civil Rights Cases (1883)
Contempt of Court
Cruel and Unusual Punishment
Cruzan v. Missouri Department of Health (1990)
Death Penalty Cases
Declaratory Judgments
Double Jeopardy
Dred Scott v. Sandford (1857)
Due Process
Eighth Amendment (*See* Cruel and Unusual Punishment)
Electronic Eavesdropping
Equal Employment Opportunity
Equal Protection of the Law
Fair Housing
Flag Burning
Freedom of Assembly
Freedom of Association
Freedom of Religion
Freedom of Speech
Freedom of the Press
Freedom to Petition
Grandfather Clauses
Juveniles, Rights of
Korematsu v. United States (1944)
Loving v. Virginia (1967)
Loyalty Oaths

Race and Redistricting
Right to a Jury Trial
Right to a Public Trial
Right to a Speedy Trial
Right to Die
Right to Legal Counsel
Right to Privacy
School Prayer and Bible Readings
Search Warrants
Self-Incrimination
Sex Discrimination
Slavery Issues
Stop-and-Frisk Searches
White Primaries

Constitutional Issues

Affirmative Action
Aliens, Protection of
Appellate Jurisdiction
Automobile Searches
Bail
Bill of Rights
Brown v. Board of Education (1954)
Burr, Aaron, Trial of
Bush v. Gore (2000)
Capital Punishment (*See* Death Penalty)
Child Labor
Confessions
Congress and the Supreme Court
Constitution, The U.S.
Cruel and Unusual Punishment
Dartmouth College v. Woodward (1819)
Death Penalty Cases
Dred Scott v. Sandford (1857)
Due Process
Electronic Eavesdropping

Eminent Domain
Equal Employment Opportunity
Equal Protection of the Law
Federalism
Flag Burning
Foreign Affairs and the Supreme Court
Freedom of Religion
Freedom of Speech
Freedom of the Press
Freedom to Petition
Gag Rules
Impeachment of Justices
Implied Powers
Injunctions
Interstate Relations
Judicial Restraint
Judicial Review
Jurisdiction of the Supreme Court
Juveniles, Rights of
Legislative Veto
Libel
Line Item Veto
Marbury v. Madison (1803)
New Deal and the Supreme Court
Obscenity
One Person, One Vote
Original Jurisdiction
Pentagon Papers
Presidency and the Supreme Court
Probable Cause
Race and Redistricting
Right to Vote
Roosevelt's 1937 Court Reform Plan
Self-incrimination
Sit-ins
Slavery Issues
Speech, Unprotected
Stop-and-Frisk Searches
Symbolic Speech
War Power and the Supreme Court
Writ of Habeas Corpus
Writ of Mandamus

Laws

Articles of Confederation
Associate Justices
Automobile Searches
Bail
Bankruptcy and Bankruptcy Laws
Bill of Rights

Bills of Attainder
Brown v. Board of Education (1954)
Burr, Aaron, Trial of
Child Labor
Circuit Court of Appeals
Congress and the Supreme Court
Constitution, The U.S.
Court-packing Plan (*See* Roosevelt's 1937 Court Reform Plan)
Cruel and Unusual Punishment
Ex Post Facto Laws
Fiscal and Monetary Power and the Supreme Court
Judiciary Act of 1789
Juveniles, Rights of
Legislative Veto
Line Item Veto
Loyalty Oaths

People

Aliens, Protection of
Alito, Samuel A.
Associate Justices
Brandeis, Louis D.
Brennan, William Joseph, Jr.
Breyer, Stephen
Burger, Warren E.
Burr, Aaron, Trial of
Clinton, William J. (*See* Impeachment, Role in)
Dred Scott v. Sandford (1857)
Field, Stephen Johnson
Frankfurter, Felix
Ginsburg, Ruth Bader
Harlan, John Marshall I
Harlan, John Marshall II
Hill, Anita
Holmes, Oliver Wendell Jr.
Hughes, Charles Evans
Jay, John
Jehovah's Witnesses (*See* Freedom of Religion)
Johnson, Andrew (*See* Impeachment, Role in)
Kennedy, Anthony M.
Marshall, John
Marshall, Thurgood
O'Connor, Sandra Day
Rehnquist, William H.
Roberts, John G.
Scalia, Antonin
Sotomayor, Sonia
Souter, David
Stevens, John Paul

Story, Joseph
Taft, William Howard
Taney, Roger B.
Thomas, Clarence
Warren, Earl

Principles of Government

Appellate Jurisdiction
Bill of Rights
Checks and Balances
Circuit Court of Appeals
Congress and the Supreme Court
Constitution of the United States
Equal Protection of the Law
Federalism
Implied Powers
Interstate Relations
Judicial Review
Judiciary Act of 1789
Jurisdiction of the Supreme Court
Presidency and the Supreme Court
War Power and the Supreme Court

Supreme Court Cases

Baker v. Carr (1962)
Brown v. Board of Education (1954)
Burr, Aaron, Trial of
Bush v. Gore (2000)
Civil Rights Cases (1883)
Cruzan v. Missouri Department of Health (1990)
Dartmouth College v. Woodward (1819)
Dred Scott v. Sandford (1857)
Engle v. Vitale (1962)
Escobedo v. Illinois (1964)
Ex Parte Milligan (1866)

Gibbons v. Ogden (1824)
Gideon v. Wainwright (1963)
Hazelwood School District v. Kuhlmeier (1988)
Heart of Atlanta Motel v. United States (1964)
Korematsu v. United States (1944)
Loving v. Virginia (1967)
Mapp v. Ohio (1961)
Marbury v. Madison (1803)
McCullough v. Maryland (1819)
Miranda v. Arizona (1966)
New York Times v. Sullivan (1964)
Plessy v. Ferguson (1896)
Powell v. Alabama (1932)
Roe v. Wade (1973)
Slaughterhouse Cases (1873)
Sturges v. Crowninshield (1819)
Swann v. Mecklenburg County Board of Education (1971)
Tinker v. Des Moines (1969)
United States v. Nixon (1974)
University of California Regents v. Bakke (1978)
Wallace v. Jaffree (1984)

Supreme Court Procedures and Processes

Appellate Jurisdiction
Associate Justices
Circuit Court of Appeals
Confirmation of Justices and Judges
Impeachment of Justices
Salaries and Benefits of the Justices
Supreme Court, History of
Supreme Court, Traditions of
Supreme Court Building
Term of the Supreme Court

ABOUT THE ADVISORY EDITOR

Bruce J. Schulman is The William E. Huntington professor of History at Boston University, a position he has held since 2007. Dr. Schulman has also served as the Director of the American and New England Studies Program at Boston University. Prior to moving to Boston University, Dr. Schulman was associate professor of History at the University of California, Los Angeles. Dr. Schulman received his Ph.D. and M.A. from Stanford University; he received his B.A., Summa Cum Laude with Distinction, in history from Yale University.

Since the 1980s, Dr. Schulman has been teaching and writing about the political face of the United States. He has taken an active role in education at the high school level as well as serving as the Principal Investigator for the Teaching American History Grant program with the Boston Public Schools. He also worked with the History Alive program, a curriculum-based interactive instructional program. In addition, Dr. Schulman served as director of The History Project in California, a joint effort of the University of California and the California State Department of Education to improve history education in the public primary and secondary schools.

Dr. Schulman is the author of several award-winning and notable books that combine his interest in history and politics. Among them are: *From Cotton Belt to Sunbelt: Federal Policy, Economic Development, and the Transformation of the South, 1938–1980; Lyndon B. Johnson and American Liberalism; The Seventies: The Great Shift in American Culture, Politics, and Society;* and *Rightward Bound: Making America Conservative in the 1970s* (co-edited with Julian Zelizer). Dr. Schulman's published books and numerous essays have examined and scrutinized the fabric of America's political and socioeconomic life and its direct impact on today's citizens.

PREFACE

As British Prime Minister Winston Churchill once remarked, "It has been said that democracy is the worst form of government except for all those others that have been tried." In CQ Press's new series, *Student's Guides to the U.S. Government,* librarians, educators, students, and other researchers will find essential resources for understanding the strange wonder, alternately inspiring and frustrating, that is American democracy.

In the *Student's Guide to the Supreme Court,* the fourth volume in the *Student's Guides* series, both young and experienced researchers, especially students and teachers, will find all they need to know about America's highest court and its far-reaching decisions—the constitutional provisions and legal procedures, the pivotal cases and the contentious debates, the key players and the watershed policy changes—the mystery and controversy of the American judicial system. Part aristocracy (the black-robed justices head the only unelected branch of government), and part democracy (all Americans can access the legal system and they do so with vigor), this most dynamic and scrutinized branch of the federal government has always been a mass of contradictions. As the Supreme Court developed from an institution without clear purpose (and even without its own building) into the unchallenged arbiter of the nation's most pointed and vexing controversies, its principal actors and their decisions have become sources of fascination and conflict. Critics have seen danger in the unchecked power of judges shielded from the will—and the votes—of the ordinary citizens. However, partisans of justice the world over also have hailed the Supreme Court as a beacon of hope, a symbol of the rule of law—an institution that makes even the most powerful leader subject to the same rules as the lowliest striver. Justice Hugo Black captured the judiciary's essential role when he explained that, "No higher duty, or more solemn responsibility rests upon this Court than that of translating into living law and maintaining this constitutional shield . . . for the benefit of every human being subject to our Constitution."

The *Student's Guide to the Supreme Court* unravels the historical development of the American judicial system—the ways the Supreme Court has changed over the past two-and-a-half centuries as well as its current status—unlocking the mysteries surrounding such contemporary issues as affirmative action, the qualifications for the nation's highest court, the death penalty, school prayer, and the separation of powers. Each of the three parts of the *Student's Guide to the Supreme Court* takes a unique approach to enhancing users' understanding of the high court. Part One features three essays, each of which addresses a provocative issue or question about America's highest court: "The Supreme Court: The Weakest or the Strongest Branch of Our Government?"; "How Does the President Nominate a Supreme Court Justice?"; and "Do They Matter? How Supreme Court Decisions Affect Modern American Life."

Part Two features more than 160 A–Z entries spanning everything from the constitutional debate surrounding abortion to operation of war powers. Not only do entries address the major decisions the Court has handed down, the issues it has tackled, and the doctrines it has developed, but also the ways in which the judicial branch has been organized, the contributions of key justices, and the relationship between the Supreme Court and other institutions—including Congress, the president, political parties, the states, and the federal bureaucracy. Special features within Part Two abound: "Point/Counterpoint" highlights opposing views on the same issue using primary evidence and concludes with a thought-provoking "Document-Based Question." "Spotlight" focuses on unique situations and events. "Decision Makers" takes a closer look at notable individuals, and "Justice for All" examines important moments in the long journey to extend the fundamental rights of citizens to all Americans.

Part Three contains a "Primary Source Library" of key documents, including laws, excerpts from landmark Supreme Court rulings, photos, and political cartoons that are essential to understanding the history of the American Supreme Court—from its earliest days through its development as a truly coequal and powerful branch within the nation's system of checks and balances. These documents complement the information highlighted in both the essays in Part One and the A–Z entries in Part Two. Part Three also includes guidelines for using the Primary Source Library and for general research. The guidelines offer direction on Researching with Primary and Secondary Sources, Developing Research Questions, Identifying Sources of Information, Planning and Organizing research for use in a paper or report, Documenting Sources for the Bibliography, and Citing Sources.

Other helpful tools include a List of Illustrations, a Reader's Guide that arranges material thematically according to the key concepts of the American Government curriculum, and a timeline of Historical Milestones of the U.S. Supreme Court. The *Guide* concludes with a Glossary of political and judicial terminology, a Selected Bibliography, a Case Index, and a General Index.

An eye-catching, user-friendly design enhances the text. Throughout, numerous charts, graphs, tables, maps, cross-references, sources for further reading, and images illustrate concepts.

The Student's Guides to the U.S. Government Series

Additional titles in the *Student's Guides to the U.S. Government* series include the *Student's Guide to Elections*, the *Student's Guide to Congress*, and the *Student's Guide to the Presidency*. Collectively, these titles offer indispensable data drawn from CQ Press's collections and presented in a manner accessible to secondary level students of American history and government. The volumes place at the reader's fingertips essential information about the evolution of American politics from the struggles to create the United States government in the late eighteenth century through the ongoing controversies and dramatic strides of the early twenty-first century.

For study in American history, the *Student's Guides to the U.S. Government* collect a treasury of useful, often hard-to-find facts and present them in the context of the political environment for easy use in research projects, answering document-based questions, and writing essays or reports.

The *Student's Guides* offer valuable tools for civics education and for the study of American politics and government. They introduce young people to the institutions, procedures, and rules that form the foundations of American government. They assemble for students and teachers the essential material for understanding the workings of American politics and the nature of political participation in the United States. The *Guides* explain the roots and development of representative democracy, the system of federalism, the separation of powers, and the specific roles of legislators, executives, and judges in the American system of governance. The *Guides* provide immediate access to the details about the changing nature of political participation by ordinary Americans and the essential role of citizens in a representative democracy.

At the heart of the *Student's Guides to the U.S. Government* is the conviction that the continued success of the American experiment in self-government and the survival of democratic ideals depend on a knowledgeable and engaged citizenry—on educating the next generation of American citizens. Understanding American government and history is essential to that crucial education process, for freedom depends on knowing how our system of governance evolved and how we are governed.

By learning the rudiments of American government—the policies, procedures, and processes that built the modern United States—young people can fulfill the promise of American life. By placing at hand—in comprehensive essays, in easily recovered alphabetical format, and in pivotal primary source documents—the essential information needed by student researchers and all educators, the *Student's Guides to the U.S. Government* offer valuable, authoritative resources for civics and history education.

Bruce J. Schulman, Ph.D., Advisory Editor
William E. Huntington Professor of History
Boston University

1787: Delegates at the Constitutional Convention include an independent Supreme Court in the proposed new U.S. government.

1788: Nine of thirteen states ratify the Constitution, making it the Supreme Law of the Land.

1789: Congress passes the Judiciary Act of 1789, establishing the structure of the Supreme Court and other subordinate courts.

1791: The first ten amendments, known as the Bill of Rights, are added to the Constitution; these amendments guarantee Americans many civil rights and protections.

1793: In *Chisholm v. Georgia,* the Court rules that citizens of one state have the right to sue another state in federal court, without the consent of the defendant state. The ratification of the Eleventh Amendment in 1795 reverses this ruling, barring such suits from federal court unless the defendant state consents.

1801: John Marshall is appointed the fourth Chief Justice of the United States.

1803: In *Marbury v. Madison,* the Supreme Court establishes the principle of judicial review, asserting its right to declare laws passed by Congress unconstitutional.

1819: In *Maryland v. McCulloch,* the Supreme Court rules that the "necessary and proper" clause of the Constitution grants Congress the power to charter a national bank. Observing that the "power to tax involves the power to destroy," the Court also held that the national bank was immune to state taxation.

1819: In *Dartmouth College v. Woodward,* the Supreme Court confirms the sanctity of contracts by ruling that the states cannot alter or repeal private corporate charters, such as that between New Hampshire and the trustees of Dartmouth College establishing that institution.

1819: In *Sturges v. Crowninshield,* the Supreme Court rules that the Constitution's grant of power to Congress to enact a uniform bankruptcy law does not deny states the power to pass such laws, at least until Congress enacts a bankruptcy law.

1824: The Supreme Court defines the power of Congress to regulate interstate commerce in *Gibbons v. Ogden.*

1832: In *Worcester v. Georgia,* the Court rules that federal jurisdiction over Indian affairs is exclusive, leaving no room for state authority. States lack any power to pass laws affecting Indians living in Indian Territory within their borders. The Court reverses the conviction, under Georgia law, of two missionaries who had failed to comply with a state law requiring the licensing of all white persons living in Indian Territory.

1833: The Supreme Court rules in *Barron v. Baltimore* that the Bill of Rights was added to the Constitution to protect persons only against the action of the federal, not state, government.

1857: In *Dred Scott v. Sandford,* the Supreme Court rules that blacks are not, and cannot become, citizens of the United States.

1865: The Thirteenth Amendment, outlawing slavery, is ratified.

1868: The Fourteenth Amendment, defining citizenship and guaranteeing due process of law, is ratified. The amendment also guarantees equal protection of the law.

1870: The Fifteenth Amendment, guaranteeing African American males the right to vote, is ratified.

1870: In *Hepburn v. Griswold* (First Legal Tender Case), the Court declares unconstitutional acts of Congress that substituted paper money for gold as legal tender for the payment of debts contracted prior to adoption of the first Legal Tender Act in 1862. The law was enacted to help the Union finance the Civil War (1861–1865), but the Court holds it an improper exercise of Congress's implied powers under the "necessary and proper" clause.

1871: *Knox v. Lee, Parker v. Davis* (Second Legal Tender Case) overturns *Hepburn v. Griswold.* The Court now holds that Congress had exercised its implied powers properly when it made paper money legal tender for the payment of debts.

1875: In *Minor v. Happersett,* the Court rules that the privileges and immunities clause of the Fourteenth Amendment does not guarantee women the right to vote. A state therefore does not violate that amendment's guarantee when it denies a woman the right to vote. "[T]he Constitution of the United States does not confer the right of suffrage on anyone," the Court said.

1877: In *Munn v. Illinois*, the Court rules that the state police power includes the right of states to regulate private business.

1883: In the *Civil Rights Cases*, the Court rules that neither the Thirteenth Amendment nor the Fourteenth Amendment empowers Congress to enact a law barring discrimination against blacks in privately owned public accommodations. The Fourteenth Amendment prohibits only state-sponsored discrimination, not private discriminatory acts, the Court holds. Private discrimination does not violate the Thirteenth Amendment because "such an act of refusal has nothing to do with slavery or involuntary servitude."

1886: In *Wabash, St. Louis and Pacific Railway Co. v. Illinois*, the Court determines that states may not regulate the rates charged by railroads that form part of an interstate network, even if the state regulates only for the intrastate portion of a trip. Such state regulation infringes upon the federal power to regulate interstate commerce.

1889: In *Chae Chan Ping v. United States* (Chinese Exclusion Case), the Supreme Court rules that the power of Congress over the entry of aliens, derived from the need to preserve the nation's sovereign status, is exclusive and absolute. The Court upholds an act of Congress that barred the entry of Chinese aliens into the United States.

1895: In *In re Debs*, the Court rules that a federal court injunction that was intended to break the 1894 Pullman strike was valid, as was Eugene V. Debs's conviction. A lower court upheld the validity of the injunction under the Sherman Antitrust Act (1890), and the Court affirms the validity on the broader grounds of national sovereignty, which the Court says gave the federal government authority to remove obstructions to interstate commerce and transportation of the mails.

1896: In *Plessy v. Ferguson*, the Supreme Court upholds the concept of "separate but equal" facilities for whites and African Americans.

1908: The Court decides in *Twining v. New Jersey* that the Fourteenth Amendment does not automatically extend the Fifth Amendment privilege against compelled self-incrimination—or other provisions of the Bill of Rights—to state defendants.

1911: In *Standard Oil Co. v. United States,* the Court rules that only unreasonable combinations and undue restraints of trade are illegal under the federal Antitrust Act. In this decision, which resulted in the breakup of the Standard Oil monopoly, a majority of the Court for the first time adopted the so-called "rule of reason." Previously, the Court had held that any combination that restrained trade, whether "reasonable" or "unreasonable," was a violation of the federal statute.

1914: In *Weeks v. United States,* the Court rules that a person whose Fourth Amendment rights to be secure against unreasonable search and seizure are violated by federal agents has the right to demand that evidence obtained in the search be excluded from use against him in federal courts. This was the Court's first decision adopting the so-called exclusionary rule.

1915: The Court rules in *Guinn v. United States* that an Oklahoma "grandfather clause" for voters was an unconstitutional evasion of the Fifteenth Amendment guarantee that states would not deny citizens the right to vote because of their race. Oklahoma law imposed a literacy test upon potential voters but exempted all persons whose ancestors voted in 1866. The Court rules that although race, color, or previous servitude were not mentioned in the law, selection of a date prior to adoption of the Fifteenth Amendment was intended to disenfranchise blacks in "direct and positive disregard" of the amendment.

1918: Ruling in the *Selective Draft Law Cases,* the Court determines that Congress is authorized to institute a compulsory draft of persons into the armed forces under its power to raise armies and under the necessary and proper clause. Moreover, service in the military is one of the duties of a citizen in a "just government." Compulsory conscription is not involuntary servitude in violation of the Thirteenth Amendment.

1919: In *Schenck v. United States,* its first decision dealing with the extent of the First Amendment's protection for speech, the Court sustains the Espionage Act of 1917 against a challenge that it violated the guarantees of freedom of speech and press. The First Amendment is not an absolute guarantee, the Court says. Freedom of speech and press may be constrained if "the words used are used in such circumstances and are of such a nature as to create a clear and present danger that they will bring about the substantive evils that Congress has a right to prevent."

1925: In *Gitlow v. New York*, the Court rules that the First Amendment prohibition against government abridgment of the freedom of speech applies to the states as well as to the federal government. The freedoms of speech and press "are among the fundamental personal rights and 'liberties' protected by the due process clause of the Fourteenth Amendment from impairment by the states," the Court asserts—even though it rejected Gitlow's free speech claim. This ruling was the first of a long line of rulings holding that the Fourteenth Amendment extended the guarantees of the Bill of Rights to state, as well as federal, action.

1928: The Court rules in *Olmstead v. United States* that wiretaps do not violate the Fourth Amendment's prohibition against unreasonable searches and seizures where no entry of private premises occurred.

1930: In *Patton v. United States*, the Court rules that the three essential elements of a jury trial required in federal courts by the Sixth Amendment are a panel of twelve jurors, supervision by a judge, and a unanimous verdict.

1931: In *Near v. Minnesota*, the Court rules that a state law that bars continued publication of a newspaper that prints malicious or defamatory articles is a prior restraint of the press in violation of the First Amendment. This decision marks the first time the Court specifically enforced the First Amendment's guarantee of freedom of the press to strike down a state law because it infringed too far on that freedom.

1932: In *Powell v. Alabama* (known as the "First Scottsboro Case"), the Court rules that, under the particular circumstances of this case, in which a number of young black men charged with raping two white women were tried in a hostile community atmosphere, the failure of the trial court to provide the defendants the effective aid of an attorney for their defense constitutes a denial of due process.

1935: In *Norris v. Alabama* (known as the "Second Scottsboro Case"), the Court sets aside the conviction of the black defendant because blacks had been consistently barred from service on both the grand jury and trial jury in this case.

1935: The Court holds its first session in the new Supreme Court building.

1937: In *National Labor Relations Board v. Jones & Laughlin Steel Corp.*, the Court rules that the federal power to regulate interstate commerce permits Congress to regulate intrastate matters that directly burden or obstruct interstate commerce. In this case, the Court finds that a dispute between management and labor that threatened to close down a Pennsylvania steel factory directly affected interstate commerce because the factory was in a stream of commerce. This decision, in which the Court finally abandoned its narrow

view of the federal power to regulate interstate commerce, sustained the constitutionality of the National Labor Relations Act of 1935.

1937: In *DeJonge v. Oregon*, the Court rules that the First Amendment guarantee of freedom of assembly prohibits a state from making it a crime to organize and participate in a meeting at which no illegal action was discussed, even if the meeting was held under the auspices of an association that had as its goal the forcible overthrow of the government. For the first time, the Court recognizes that the right of assembly is on an equal footing with the rights of free speech and free press, and that the First Amendment guarantee of freedom of assembly is applicable to the states through the due process clause of the Fourteenth Amendment.

1942: In *Betts v. Brady*, the Court rules that the Fourteenth Amendment's due process clause does not require states to supply defense counsel to defendants too poor to employ their own attorney. This decision was overturned by *Gideon v. Wainwright* in 1963.

1943: The Court determines in *West Virginia State Board of Education v. Barnette* that the First Amendment guarantee of the free exercise of religion protects the right of persons to remain silent and forbids the government to compel them to participate in a symbolic display of patriotic unity that conflicts with their religious beliefs. The Court upholds the right of Jehovah's Witnesses' children to refuse to participate in compulsory flag salute ceremonies in public schools.

1944: In *Korematsu v. United States*, the Court upholds the removal of Japanese Americans to relocation centers at inland camps away from the West Coast. It holds that the removal program was within the combined war powers of the president and Congress. In this case, for the first time, a majority of the Court says it would give classifications by race increased attention to ensure that racial antagonism does not lie at the base of the classification. In this instance, however, the Court holds that military necessity warrants the racial classification.

1952: In *Youngstown Sheet and Tube Co. v. Sawyer* (also known as the "Steel Seizure Case"), the Court rules that President Harry S. Truman (1945–1953) exceeded his power in seizing the nation's steel mills to prevent a strike. The president had based the seizure order on his general powers as commander in chief and chief executive. The Court holds he could not take such action without express authorization from Congress.

1954: In *Brown v. Board of Education*, the Court holds that segregation of the races is unconstitutional, overturning its ruling in the *Plessy* case (1896).

1961: In *Mapp v. Ohio*, the Court rules that evidence obtained in violation of the Fourth Amendment guarantee against unreasonable search and seizure must be excluded from use at state as well as federal trials.

1962: The Court rules, in *Engel v. Vitale*, that public school officials may not require pupils to recite a state-composed prayer at the beginning of each school day, even though the prayer is denominationally neutral and pupils who so desire may be excused from reciting it. Official state-sanctioned prayers, the Court holds, are unconstitutional attempts by government to establish religion.

1962: In *Baker v. Carr*, the Court rules for the first time that constitutional challenges to the maldistribution of voters among legislative districts might properly be resolved by federal courts. The Court rejects the doctrine set out in *Colgrove v. Green* (1946) that all such apportionment challenges are "political questions" beyond the proper reach of the federal courts.

1963: In *School District of Abington Township v. Schempp*, the Supreme Court rules that state-ordered recitation of the Lord's Prayer and the reading of the Bible in the public school system as a devotional exercise violates the establishment clause.

1963: In *Gideon v. Wainwright*, the Court unanimously determines that the due process clause of the Fourteenth Amendment extends to state as well as federal defendants the Sixth Amendment guarantee that all persons charged with serious crimes will be provided the aid of an attorney. *Betts v. Brady* (1942) was overruled. States are required to appoint counsel for defendants who cannot afford to pay their own attorneys' fees.

1964: In *Heart of Atlanta Motel v. United States*, the Court rules that the commerce power may be used to prohibit racial discrimination in privately owned public accommodations. This decision effectively overturns the Court's 1883 *Civil Rights Cases* and sustains Title II of the Civil Rights Act of 1964. That section prohibited discrimination, on the basis of race, religion, or national origin, in accommodations that catered to interstate travelers or that served food or provided entertainment, a substantial portion of which was shipped through interstate commerce.

1964: The Court determines in *New York Times Co. v. Sullivan* that the First Amendment guarantee of freedom of the press protects the press from libel suits for defamatory reports on public officials unless the officials prove that the reports were made with actual malice. Actual malice is defined as "with knowledge that it [the defamatory statement] was false or with reckless disregard of whether it was false or not." Until this decision, libelous statements were not protected by the First Amendment.

1964: In *Escobedo v. Illinois*, the Court expands a suspect's right to counsel under the Sixth Amendment, holding that confessions obtained by police who had not advised the suspect of his right to counsel—or acceded to his requests for counsel—are inadmissible as evidence.

1964: In *Reynolds v. Sims*, the Court rules that the equal protection clause of the Fourteenth Amendment requires application of the "one person, one vote" apportionment rule to both houses of a state legislature.

1966: The Court determines in *Miranda v. Arizona* that the due process guarantee requires that suspects in police custody be informed of their right to remain silent, that anything they say may be used against them, and that they have the right to counsel—before any interrogation can permissibly take place.

1967: The Supreme Court determines in *In re Gault* that juveniles have some—but not all—due process privileges in juvenile court proceedings. The privilege against self-incrimination and the right to counsel do apply.

1967: In *Loving v. Virginia*, the Court unanimously decides that a state law punishing persons who enter into interracial marriages violates both the equal protection and due process clauses of the Fourteenth Amendment. "Under our Constitution, the freedom to marry or not marry a person of another race resides with the individual and cannot be infringed by the state," the Court declares. This decision is the first in which the Court explicitly holds classifications by race "inherently suspect" and justifiable only by compelling reasons.

1969: In *Tinker v. Des Moines Independent Community School District*, the Court determines that students have the right to engage in peaceful nondisruptive protest, recognizing that the First Amendment guarantee of freedom of speech protects symbolic as well as oral speech. The wearing of black armbands to protest the Vietnam War is "closely akin" to the "pure speech" protected by the First Amendment, the majority says, and therefore a public school ban on this form of protest, which did not disrupt the school's work or offend the rights of others, violates these students' rights.

1970: The Court rules in *In re Winship* that the Fourteenth Amendment guarantee of due process requires that juveniles, like adult defendants, be found guilty "beyond a reasonable doubt." The Supreme Court forbids states to use a lesser standard of proof in juvenile proceedings.

1971: In *Swann v. Charlotte-Mecklenburg County Board of Education,* the Court unanimously determines that busing, racial balance ratios, and gerrymandered school districts are all permissible interim methods of eliminating the vestiges of state-imposed segregation from Southern schools. There are limits to the remedies that might be used to eliminate the remnants of segregation, the Court says, but no fixed guidelines setting such limits can be established. The Court acknowledges that there might be valid objections to busing when so much time or distance is involved as to risk the children's health or to impinge significantly on the education process.

1971: In *New York Times Co. v. United States, United States v. The Washington Post,* (known as the Pentagon Papers Case), the Court denies the federal government's request for a court order barring continued publication in the *New York Times* and the *Washington Post* of articles based on classified documents detailing the history of U.S. involvement in Indochina, popularly known as the Pentagon Papers.

1973: In *Roe v. Wade,* the Court determines that the right to privacy, grounded in the Fourteenth Amendment's due process guarantee of personal liberty, encompasses and protects a woman's decision whether or not to bear a child. This right is impermissibly abridged by state laws that make abortion a crime. During the first trimester of pregnancy, the decision to have an abortion should be left entirely to a woman and her physician. The state can forbid abortions by non-physicians. During the second trimester, the state may regulate the abortion procedure in ways reasonably related to maternal health. During the third trimester, the state may, if it wishes, forbid all abortions except those necessary to save the mother's life.

1974: In *United States v. Nixon,* the Court rules that neither the separation of powers nor the need to preserve the confidentiality of presidential communications alone can justify an absolute executive privilege of immunity from judicial demands for evidence to be used in a criminal trial. The Court holds that President Richard M. Nixon (1969–1974) comply with a subpoena for tapes of certain White House conversations, sought for use as evidence against White House aides charged with obstruction of justice in regard to the investigation of the break-in at the Democratic National Headquarters in the Watergate Office Building in June 1972.

1977: In *Coker v. Georgia,* the Court determines that the death sentence for the crime of rape is an excessive and disproportionate penalty forbidden by the Eighth Amendment ban on cruel and unusual punishment.

1978: In *Regents of the University of California v. Bakke,* the Court decides that a special state medical school admissions program under which a certain number of slots were set aside for minority group members, and white applicants were denied the opportunity to compete for them, violates Title VI of the 1964 Civil Rights Act. Title VI forbids exclusion of anyone, because of race, from participation in a federally funded program. Admissions programs that consider race as one of several factors involved in the decision to admit an applicant are not unconstitutional in and of themselves.

1983: In *Immigration and Naturalization Service v. Chadha, United States House of Representatives v. Chadha, United States Senate v. Chadha,* the Court finds the "legislative veto" unconstitutional. The one-house legislative veto, under which Congress claimed the power to review and veto executive branch decisions implementing laws, is unconstitutional. It violates the separation of powers between executive and legislative branches, and it runs counter to the "single, finely wrought, and exhaustively considered procedure" the Constitution prescribes for the enactment of legislation: approval by both chambers and signature of the president.

1984: In *United States v. Leon,* the Court rules that illegally obtained evidence may be used by the prosecution at trial if the police officers who seized it were acting on a search warrant and believed they were acting legally. This ruling is the Court's first adoption of a "good faith" exception to the exclusionary rule it adopted seventy years earlier in *Weeks v. United States,* which had barred all use of such evidence at trial.

1985: The Court rules in *Wallace v. Jaffree* that moment-of-silence laws intended to restore prayer to the nation's public schools are unconstitutional. The Court strikes down an Alabama law that permits a moment of silence for prayer or meditation at the beginning of each school day. The history of the law made clear that it was intended as an endorsement of religion, to encourage students to pray.

1986: In *Wygant v. Jackson Board of Education,* the Court determines that an affirmative action plan voluntarily adopted by a school board, under which white teachers with more seniority were laid off to preserve the jobs of newly hired black teachers, is unconstitutional—a denial of the white teachers' right to equal protection of the law. The primary flaw was that the plan was adopted without any evidence showing that the school board had previously discriminated against black teachers.

1987: In *Edwards v. Aguillard,* the Court rules that a Louisiana law requiring public schools that teach the theory of evolution also teach "creation science" violates the establishment clause, because the state legislature enacted it for the purpose of promoting religion.

1988: The Court rules in *Thompson v. Oklahoma* that it is unconstitutional for a state to execute a capital defendant who was younger than sixteen at the time of his offense, if his sentence was imposed under a law that does not set a minimum age at which defendants are subject to the death penalty.

1989: In *Stanford v. Kentucky,* the Court determines that the imposition of the death penalty upon a defendant convicted of a capital crime committed when he or she was sixteen or seventeen years old does not violate the ban on cruel and unusual punishment simply because of the defendant's youth.

1989: In *Texas v. Johnson,* the Court rules that the First Amendment guarantee of freedom of expression precludes a state from punishing someone for desecrating the American flag in the course of a peaceful political demonstration.

1990: In *Cruzan v. Director, Missouri Department of Health,* the Court determines that states may stop the family of a comatose patient from disconnecting life support systems unless the family shows clear and convincing evidence of the patient's previously expressed wish to die under such circumstances. Because the choice between life and death is a personal decision of overwhelming finality, the Court says, a state may require clear and convincing evidence of that personal choice.

1991: The Court rules in *Arizona v. Fulminante* that the use of a coerced confession at trial does not automatically taint a conviction that results. If there is other evidence sufficient to convict the defendant, use of a compelled confession may be a harmless error, and therefore not require a new trial. With this decision, the Court reverses a 1967 decision, *Chapman v. California,* which established the rule that due process is always denied when a forced confession is used against a defendant.

1992: In *Planned Parenthood of Southeastern Pennsylvania v. Casey,* the Court affirms the central holding of *Roe v. Wade* (1973), which established a constitutional right to abortion, and said states may not prohibit abortions at least until a fetus becomes viable.

1995: In *United States v. Lopez,* the Court rules that Congress exceeded its authority to regulate interstate commerce when it passed a law banning guns within one thousand feet of a school. The Court says the statute had "nothing to do with commerce or any sort of economic enterprise." The simple possession of a gun in or near a school is an essentially local, noncommercial activity that does not have a substantial effect on interstate commerce, the Court said.

1995: The Court rules in *U.S. Term Limits, Inc. v. Thornton* that states may not set a limit on the number of terms their representatives serve in Congress. The Constitution sets three qualifications for members of Congress: age, citizenship, and residency. To allow states to adopt term limits would create a patchwork of tenure qualifications and undermine the uniform national character of Congress sought by the Founders, the Court concludes.

1996: In *Romer v. Evans,* the Court rules that an amendment to the Colorado state constitution prohibiting local laws that protect homosexuals from discrimination violates the federal Constitution's guarantee of equal protection. The amendment, adopted by voters in 1992, barred any legislative, executive, or judicial action designed to protect Coloradans based on their "homosexual, lesbian or bisexual orientation, conduct, practices or relationships." The Court says the amendment lacked a rational relationship to any legitimate state interest. Indeed, it "seems inexplicable by anything but animus [animosity] toward the class that it affects," the majority says.

1997: The Court determines in *Clinton v. Jones* that a president is not immune from being sued and forced to stand trial for alleged private wrongdoing. In *Nixon v. Fitzgerald* (1982), the court ruled that a president is forever shielded from being sued over "official acts," but the justices refused to extend that shield of immunity to the president's private life.

1998: In *Clinton v. City of New York,* the Court rules that the Line Item Veto Act of 1996 is unconstitutional because it allows the president to amend laws passed by Congress. Justice John Paul Stevens notes that the Constitution gives the president an all-or-nothing choice when presented with a bill passed by the House and Senate—sign it into law, or veto it. Passed as a reform favored by Republicans as well as Democrats, the Line Item Veto Act authorized the chief executive to "cancel" select items in large spending bills.

1999: The Court rules in *City of Chicago v. Morales* that a city cannot arrest suspected gang members for "loitering" simply because they fail to disperse when told to do so by a police officer. Such a law gives police too much authority over persons who may be standing innocently on a street corner. The Court says: "Freedom to loiter for innocent purposes is part of the 'liberty' protected by . . . the 14th Amendment."

2000: In *Bush v. Gore,* the Court stops the recount of presidential ballots in Florida, noting that the Florida Supreme Court's recounting methods deny citizens equal protection of the law. Florida's twenty-five electoral votes are awarded to Republican Texas Governor George W. Bush, making him the forty-third president of the United States and ending the dispute between Bush and Democrat Al Gore, who had won the popular vote.

2002: In *Atkins v. Virginia,* the Court rules that the death penalty for a mentally retarded defendant is cruel and unusual punishment and is therefore prohibited. Persons who have an I.Q. of less than 70 are more likely to act on impulse and less likely to consider the consequences, Stevens notes.

2003: The Court determines in *Lawrence v. Texas* that state laws that criminalize private sexual conduct between consenting adults are unconstitutional. The ruling struck down a Texas sodomy law as well as similar laws in twelve other states. It also overrules *Bowers v. Hardwick* (1986), which had upheld a Georgia sodomy law.

2003: The Court decides in *Grutter v. Bollinger* that a "compelling interest" in racial diversity validates a college's or university's use of a minority student's race as a "plus factor" in admissions. The decisions affirm the rule set in *Regents of the University of California v. Bakke* (1978), which allowed a limited use of race. The Court upholds the admissions policy at the University of Michigan Law School because officials "engage in a highly individualized, holistic review of each applicant's file." However, it strikes down the undergraduate admissions policy at the university because all minority applicants received twenty bonus points.

2003: In *Ewing v. California* and *Lockyer v. Andrade,* the Court determines that it is not cruel and unusual punishment to sentence a repeat offender to decades in prison even if such a long sentence is triggered by a petty crime. The pair of rulings upholds California's "three strikes and you're out" law. Although the law was enacted in response to the highly publicized kidnapping and murder of 12-year-old Polly Klass by a paroled kidnapper, the statute may be triggered by a minor crime if the offender has prior felonies. Gary Ewing had a long record of thefts and was given a twenty-five-year term for trying to steal golf clubs from a pro shop. Leandro Andrade had two burglary convictions and received a fifty-year sentence for stealing videotapes from a Kmart.

2003: In *Nevada Department of Human Resources v. Hibbs,* the Court rules that state agencies can be sued for damages by employees who are denied the right to take unpaid leave to care for a sick relative. Chief Justice Rehnquist rejects the state's claim that it had a "sovereign immunity" from the federal Family and Medical Leave Act of 1993. This law "aims to protect the right to be free from gender-based discrimination in the workplace," he says, and under the Fourteenth Amendment, Congress has the authority to remedy race and sex discrimination by states.

2003: In *Virginia v. Black,* the Court rules that the blanket banning of cross burning violates the First Amendment's protection for freedom of speech. States, however, can make it a crime to burn a cross with an intent to intimidate if prosecutors prove that the action was meant as a threat and not solely as symbolic speech.

2003: In *United States v. American Library Association, Inc.,* the Court rules that public libraries must install software filters on computers to prevent juveniles from viewing sexually explicit materials on the Internet. The Court rules that the Children's Internet Protection Act of 2000 is a constitutional exercise of Congress's spending powers and does not impose unconstitutional conditions on public libraries or free expression. Chief Justice Rehnquist notes that adults could request that filters be removed while they use the computers.

2004: In *McConnell v. The Federal Election Commission,* the Court upholds major aspects of the 2001 law intended to thwart corruption—or the appearance of corruption—in political elections. The Court rules that the ban on unlimited donations to political parties, known as soft money, does not violate free speech.

2004: In *Locke v. Davey,* the Court upholds the provisions of Washington State's Promise Scholarship program, which offers taxpayer-funded scholarships to low-income college students enrolled in secular studies. The justices rule that the states do not violate the First Amendment's guarantee of religious freedom if they choose not to subsidize students studying for the ministry.

2004: In *Rasul v. Bush,* the Court rules that foreign detainees held at the U.S. naval base in Guantánamo Bay, Cuba, are legally entitled to file petitions for writs of habeas corpus when they believe they are being held illegally because the base falls under the jurisdiction of federal courts. The Court notes that Guantánamo Bay is "territory over which the United States exercises exclusive jurisdiction and control."

2004: In *Missouri v. Seibert,* the Court rejects the police tactic of questioning suspects twice, first before advising them of their *Miranda* rights—with the intention of eliciting a confession—and again after. The Court determines that the strategy intentionally avoids informing suspects of their right to remain silent before questioning and undermines *Miranda.*

2005: In *Roper v. Simmons,* the Court rules that executing people who commit crimes before they turn eighteen constitutes cruel and unusual punishment, a violation of the Eighth Amendment to the U.S. Constitution.

2005: In *Van Orden v. Perry,* the Court rules that, taken in historical context, the six-foot-tall monument of the Ten Commandments on display on the grounds of the Texas capitol in Austin does not violate the Establishment Clause. The monument, which has been up for about forty years without causing controversy, is one of seventeen in the twenty-two-acre park. Chief Justice Rehnquist notes, "Simply having religious content or promoting a message consistent with a religious doctrine does not run afoul of the Establishment Clause."

2005: In *Jackson v. Birmingham Board of Education,* the Court decides that the federal law, known as Title IX, which forbids sex discrimination in schools and colleges also protects third-party "whistleblowers" who file such complaints. Justice Sandra Day O'Connor notes that, "The statute is broadly worded: it does not require that the victim of the retaliation must also be the victim of the discrimination that is the subject of the original complaint."

2005: In *Cutter v. Wilkinson,* the justices unanimously determine that the Religious Land Use and Institutionalized Persons Act, a federal law that requires prison officials to accommodate inmates' religious requirements, does not violate the Establishment Clause of the First Amendment.

2005: In *Gonzales v. Raich,* the Court upholds the right of Congress to prohibit the use of medical marijuana as well as to prosecute those who violate the law, even in the eleven states that have passed initiatives legalizing marijuana for medical purposes.

2006: In *Rumsfeld v. Forum for Academic and Institutional Rights,* the Court upholds a federal law that says colleges and universities must grant military recruiters the same access to students as other potential employers or else lose federal financing. A group of law schools challenged the law, called the Solomon Amendment, saying it violated their First Amendment right to free speech and association. The law schools objected to the military's presence on college campuses because of its policy of excluding openly gay men and women.

2007: In *Winkleman v. Parma City School District,* the Court concludes that parents do indeed have enforceable rights under the Individuals with Disabilities Education Act (IDEA). The case arose from a situation in which Jeff and Sandee Winkelman contested the adequacy of the Parma City School District's Individual Education Plan for their eight-year-old autistic son, Jacob. In its decision, the Court reviewed the IDEA statute, noting both specific instances in which it anticipated parents initiating and participating in administrative proceedings, as well as pointing to the language that presumes and affirms parents' rights under the Act. The Court reverses the ruling of the Sixth Circuit.

2007: In *Brendlin v. California,* the Court rules that a passenger in a car that was detained in an unwarranted traffic stop was "seized" under the terms of the Fourth Amendment and may thus challenge the seizure. Bruce Edward Brendlin was a passenger in the car that was stopped for expired license tags. Upon verifying that Brendlin was a parole violator, the officers formally arrested him and searched him, the driver, and the car, finding, among other things, methamphetamine paraphernalia. Charged with possession and manufacture of that substance, Brendlin moved to suppress the evidence obtained in searching his person and the car, arguing that the officers lacked probable cause or reasonable suspicion to make the traffic stop, claiming it was an unconstitutional seizure of his person. In a 9-0 decision, Justice David Souter clearly notes: "When a police officer makes a traffic stop, the driver of the car is seized within the meaning of the Fourth Amendment. The question in this case is whether the same is true of a passenger. We hold that a passenger is seized as well and so may challenge the constitutionality of the stop."

2008: In *District of Columbia v. Heller,* the Court overturns the District of Columbia's handgun ban; the Court rules that the Second Amendment protects the individual right to own a gun for private use — not only in connection with service in a militia.

2008: In *Kennedy v. Louisiana,* the Court strikes down as unconstitutional a Louisiana statute that allowed the death penalty for the rape of a child in which the victim did not die. The Court holds that all such laws, where the crime against an individual involved no murder, were not in keeping with the national consensus restricting the death penalty to the worst offenses.

2009: Associate Justice David Souter announces his resignation from the Court; President Barack Obama (2009–) selects Sonia Sotomayor as his first nominee to the Court. She is confirmed by the Senate in August 2009 and becomes the first Hispanic justice to serve on the Court.

2009: In *Ricci v. Stefano,* the Court rules that the City of New Haven, Connecticut, discriminated against ten white firefighters who passed a promotional exam but were subsequently denied promotions because no minority candidates passed the same exam.

2010: In *Kiyemba v. Obama,* the Court remands the case back to the United States Court of Appeals for the District of Columbia Circuit, because most of the Guantánamo detainees involved in the case have been offered resettlement in another country. The Supreme Court notes that the Court of Appeals should determine, in the first instance, what further proceedings in that court or in the District Court are necessary and appropriate for the full and prompt disposition of the case in light of the new developments.

2010: In *Citizens United v. Federal Election Commission,* the Court overturns key provisions of the Bipartisan Campaign Reform Act of 2002, often called the McCain-Feingold Act, and determines that corporations and unions may establish political action committees (PACs) for express advocacy or electioneering communications purposes and that the government may not ban political spending by corporations in candidate elections. The Court notes that the decision supported the First Amendment's most basic free speech principle—that the government has no business regulating political speech.

PART ONE

Essays

The Supreme Court: The Weakest Or Strongest Branch of Our Government?

Although the modern U.S. Supreme Court is undoubtedly one of the most influential forces in American politics and society, it took the institution many years to grow into and assume its powerful role. In the early days of the nation, it appeared as if Alexander Hamilton was correct in his claim that the Supreme Court would be the weakest of the branches of government. Over time, however, the Court has broadened its *jurisdiction* and assumed greater authority relative to the *executive* and *legislative* branches of government.

Today, some critics claim that the Supreme Court has become too powerful, particularly because its members are not elected by the public, and because they hold office for life. Does that mean the "weakest" branch is actually the strongest?

Constitutional Roots of the Question

The individuals who met in Philadelphia in 1787 to draft a constitution for the United States were keenly aware of the difficulties of devising a workable governing structure for the new nation. Longtime English subjects, the Framers adopted many aspects of the English system of government when framing the Constitution. Principal among these was the notion of separating the government into three branches: a single executive officer sharing power with an elected legislature and with a judiciary composed of judges appointed by the executive.

While the Framers rejected a hereditary monarch in favor of an elected president, they modeled the executive and legislative branches of the new nation closely after their British counterparts. The new nation's leaders generally admired the British system of government; in fact, many were genuinely saddened to break with the English king and Parliament. This affection, however, did not extend to the judiciary. During the **colonial** era, British judges wielded near-absolute authority, often harshly and—in the minds of many colonists—unjustly. The Framers were wary of a powerful judiciary, and this attitude is reflected in the Constitution.

1

Provisions of the Constitution

Articles I and II of the Constitution set out at considerable length the powers and prerogatives of Congress and of the executive branch. By contrast, Article III simply sketches the outline of a federal judiciary. One scholar, Julius Goebel Jr., suggests that, at least for some delegates to the Constitutional Convention, "provision for a national judiciary was a matter of theoretical compulsion rather than of practical necessity . . . more in deference to the maxim of separation [of powers] than in response to clearly formulated ideas about the role of a national judicial system and its indispensability." At any rate, with little discussion and even less debate, the Constitutional Convention approved that

66 *According to the Framers:*

The judicial Power of the United States, shall be vested in one supreme Court, and in such inferior Courts as the Congress may from time to time ordain and establish.

Section 1 provides that federal judges will hold their posts during "good behavior" and that their salaries may not be diminished during their terms in office. Article II provides that the members of the Supreme Court be appointed by the president with the advice and consent of the Senate and that judges, along with all other civil officers of the national government, "shall be removed from office on Impeachment for, and Conviction of, Treason, Bribery, or other high Crimes and Misdemeanors." Section 2 of Article III describes the reach of federal judicial power. The Supreme Court would have original jurisdiction—the power to hear initial arguments—in cases involving foreign dignitaries and in those involving states. In all other cases, the Court's jurisdiction would be appellate, meaning that it would hear appeals of rulings of lower courts.

There ended the Constitution's description of the nation's judicial branch. The remaining sections of Article III deal with jury trials, the place of trials, and the crime of treason. The brevity of the constitutional description left to Congress and to the Court the task of filling in much of the substance and all of the details of the new judicial system. One early observer commented, "The convention has only crayoned in the outlines. It is left to Congress to fill up and colour the canvas."

The Case for an Independent Judiciary

Despite, or perhaps because of, the Constitution's vague treatment of the judiciary, many still worried about granting too much power to an appointed judiciary that served for life. Writing in the *The Federalist #78*, Alexander Hamilton tried to calm fears about the proposed Supreme Court by arguing that the judiciary was actually the weakest branch of government.

66 *Hamilton argued:*

Whoever attentively considers the different departments of power must perceive, that, in a government in which they are separated from each other, the judiciary, from the nature of its functions, will always be the least dangerous to the political rights of the Constitution; because it will be least in a capacity to annoy or injure them. The Executive not

★ ★

Essays

only dispenses the honors, but holds the sword of the community. The legislature not only commands the purse, but prescribes the rules by which the duties and rights of every citizen are to be regulated. The judiciary, on the contrary, has no influence over either the sword or the purse; no direction either of the strength or of the wealth of the society; and can take no active resolution whatever. It may truly be said to have neither FORCE nor WILL, but merely judgment; and must ultimately depend upon the aid of the executive arm even for the efficacy of its judgments.

Like Hamilton, the delegates to the Constitutional Convention generally accepted the concept of a separate and relatively independent judiciary. At the time, six of the original thirteen states had independent judicial branches. Delegates, however, disagreed over whether Congress or the president should appoint the members of the Supreme Court, and whether the Court should try impeachments. A compromise resulted in giving the president the power to name the Court's members, but with the advice and consent of the Senate. The compromise also gave the Senate the power to try impeachments. To safeguard judicial independence, the "good behavior" and salary provisions were added. Alexander Hamilton wrote of this in the *Federalist Papers*.

Hamilton wrote:

The standard of good behavior for the continuance in office of the judicial magistracy is certainly one of the most valuable of the modern improvements in the practice of government. In a monarchy it is an excellent barrier to the despotism of the prince; in a republic it is a no less excellent barrier to the encroachments and oppressions of the representative body. And it is the best expedient which can be devised in any government to secure a steady, upright, and impartial administration.

The First Court: Was Hamilton a Prophet?

"The status of the federal judiciary in the 1790s," wrote political scientist Robert G. McCloskey, "was ambiguous and . . . comparatively minor. . . . The paramount governmental tasks were legislative and executive." The record of the Supreme Court's first decade bears out that statement. Only three of the six justices were present for the Court's opening session February 1, 1790. There was no business, however, aside from organizational matters, chief among which was the appointment of a clerk. After several days of admitting attorneys to practice before it, the Court **adjourned** its first term on February 10, 1790. The second term lasted two days.

In 1791, the capital and the Court moved to Philadelphia, where the Court shared, with the mayor's court, a room in the new City Hall. The Court decided no cases in 1791 or 1792. As Hamilton suggested, the Court was a bit player in the business of government, and an appointment to the Court held little of the prestige and importance attached to such a position today. In 1791, Justice John Rutledge resigned his seat on the Court to take a state judgeship, and two of the men offered his seat declined, preferring to retain their seats

Essays

in state legislatures. In 1792, Chief Justice John Jay, who described his Court post as "intolerable," campaigned unsuccessfully from the bench for the post of governor of New York.

On February 18, 1793, the Court announced its decision in *Chisholm v. Georgia,* its first major case. In *Chisholm,* the Court upheld the right of citizens of one state, South Carolina, to bring original suits in the Supreme Court against another state, Georgia. The states were shocked, seeing in this decision the potential for their economic ruin. In response, Congress proposed an amendment to the Constitution declaring that states could not be sued, without their consent, in federal courts by citizens of another state. In 1798, the Eleventh Amendment was ratified, effectively overturning the first major Court decision. Political historian Julius Goebel Jr. wrote of the first Court, "Its posture toward acts of Congress, except for a few instances of individual critique, was one of respect." Hamilton seemed to be right: lacking the formal powers granted to Congress and the president, the Court had the least power of all government branches to influence constitutional debate.

Establishing Power

In 1801, the United States began a new century with a new president, Thomas Jefferson (1801–1809), and a new chief justice, John Marshall. That same year, the government moved to a new permanent home, Washington, D.C. The Capitol was under construction as the seat of Congress, and a residence was planned for the president, but no one had thought to provide a place for the Supreme Court to meet. At the last minute, it was given a small room in the unfinished Capitol, where it met for its February 1801 term.

Marbury v. Madison *(1803) and Judicial Review*

That same year, Congress passed an act that would open the door to the Court's first major assertion of constitutional powers. The act created a number of positions for justices of the peace for the new capital, and on March 2, outgoing President John Adams (1797–1801) appointed political allies to fill these posts. Congress confirmed the appointments the following day, and the commissions were drafted and signed. However, John Marshall, who was the outgoing secretary of state as well as the sitting chief justice, failed to deliver commissions to all the nominees before the Adams administration officially ended on the night of March 3. President-elect Thomas Jefferson did not appoint all of these men to their posts.

One of the nominees whom Jefferson refused to appoint, William Marbury, asked the Supreme Court to order the new secretary of state, James Madison, to deliver his commission. Marbury filed an original suit with the Court, asking that the justices use the authority granted them by the Judiciary Act of 1789 and issue an order called a writ of mandamus to Madison. Such a writ compels an officer of the government to perform one of his or her official duties—in this case, delivering a commission to an appointed official.

Although the Court rebuked Jefferson for not delivering Marbury's commission, it ruled that it was powerless to order Madison to deliver the commission. The majority argued that the section of the Judiciary Act of 1789 that authorized the Court to issue writs of mandamus was an impermissible expansion of

the Court's original jurisdiction. That provision was thus unconstitutional and void. In a single ruling, the Court had claimed, exercised, and justified its power to review and nullify acts of Congress that it found to conflict with the Constitution. This was the first of several landmark decisions under John Marshall's leadership that would establish the Court as a co-equal with the other branches of government.

McCulloch v. Maryland *(1819): Limiting the States*

In *Marbury v. Madison,* the Court first successfully asserted its power in relation to Congress. Sixteen years later, in *McCulloch v. Maryland,* it would demonstrate its authority to limit the power of state governments. The case, which revolved around the founding of the proposed Bank of the United States, posed two questions: Could Congress **charter** a national bank? And could states tax the bank's operations? When the state of Maryland imposed a stiff tax on notes issued by the Bank, the Bank's director in Maryland, John McCulloch, refused to pay. The Maryland Supreme Court upheld the tax, as well as the state's argument that the Bank was unconstitutional because the Constitution did not specifically authorize Congress to create such a bank. The case was then appealed to the Supreme Court.

The Court found unanimously in favor of McCulloch and against the states. Congress, the justices declared, has broad power under the "necessary and proper" clause of the Constitution to decide the means by which it implements its powers. "Let the end be legitimate, let it be within the scope of the Constitution," Marshall wrote, "and all means which are appropriate . . . which are not prohibited are constitutional." The Court ruled that the Bank of the United States was a useful instrument for national economic stability, so Congress was properly authorized to charter it. Furthermore, states could not hamper the exercise of this power. They could not tax the Bank, for by taxing it they could destroy it and frustrate the congressional purpose in chartering it. The ruling in *McCulloch v. Maryland* greatly expanded federal power at the expense of the states and established the Supreme Court as the principal arbiter of disputes between state and federal government.

By 1825, the Court had nullified as unconstitutional at least one law from each of ten states. These rulings set off an effort to remove or to at least restrict this power. Although none of these proposals was approved by Congress, the reaction to the Court's growing role in government showed clearly that it was not the "weakest branch."

Presidential Power and the Civil War

The growing influence and power of the Court in the first half of the nineteenth century faced a severe test during the Civil War. When the war began in April 1861, Congress was not in session and did not meet until midsummer. In the interim, President Abraham Lincoln (1861–1865) called for troops, imposed a blockade on Southern ports, and in some circumstances authorized military commanders to suspend the writ of habeas corpus. The writ, which compels authorities to produce a prisoner and state the charges against him or her, is considered one of the most basic constitutional safeguards of civil liberties. These actions were the most dramatic

The U.S. Supreme Court building, located in Washington, D.C., is a powerful symbol of the nation's judicial system. Article III, Section 1, of the U.S. Constitution vests all judicial power "in one Supreme Court, and in such inferior courts as the Congress may from time to time ordain and establish." (AP Photo, Pat Benic)

expansion of executive power up to that point in the nation's history. Not surprisingly, many critics challenged them as exceeding the president's constitutional authority.

Chief Justice Roger Taney was among the first to declare Lincoln's actions unconstitutional. A month after war had broken out, a military commander in Baltimore refused to comply with an order to produce in court John Merryman, a civilian imprisoned by the Union army for anti-Union activities. The commander cited, as grounds for his refusal, Lincoln's instructions allowing him to suspend the privilege of the writ of habeas corpus. Taney responded with an opinion, which he sent to Lincoln himself, declaring that only Congress could suspend this privilege, and that Lincoln's actions were unconstitutional. Lincoln, nevertheless, maintained suspension of the writ throughout the war. Only after the war had ended did the Supreme Court, in *Ex parte Milligan* (1866), uphold Taney's position.

The war also raised another constitutional question that the Court failed to address at the time: Can a president in wartime replace the nation's civilian courts with military courts-martial, to which civilians as well as military personnel are subject? During the war, Lincoln instituted trial by military commission for civilians in areas where the war was not being fought, the regular civil courts continued to function. In April 1866, a year after the war ended, the Court finally ruled this practice unconstitutional. Like the decision in *Ex parte Milligan,* however, this ruling came after the fact and did nothing to limit Lincoln's use of military tribunals in wartime. The Court, during the

Civil War, established a pattern of deference to presidential authority during times of war and national emergency that would be repeated down to the present day.

The Postwar Balance of Power

Postwar developments quickly led to a restoration of much of the power that the Court had ceded to the executive. Concern for the states as effective functioning units of the federal system was paramount in the minds of the justices; therefore, to enhance state power, the Court began to curtail federal authority. The Court wielded its power of judicial review concerning acts of Congress with new vigor. Between 1803 and 1873, the Court held as unconstitutional ten acts of Congress; six of the ten were struck down between 1870 and 1873.

The Civil War Amendments

No better example of the Court's influence on the scope and exercise of state and federal power can be found than its rulings interpreting the so-called Civil War **amendments.** In 1865, the Thirteenth Amendment formally abolished slavery. Three years later, the Fourteenth Amendment gave added protection to the rights and liberties of persons threatened by state action. In 1870, the Fifteenth Amendment guaranteed blacks the right to vote. Congress intended these amendments to act as instruments of change. However, the Court interpreted them so narrowly that they were virtually useless for most of the ensuing century. The effect of these Court rulings was to preserve state power over the rights of individuals by denying any expansion of federal authority in that area.

The Court was reluctant to acknowledge either that the Civil War Amendments had expanded federal power to enforce individual rights, or that the amendments had expanded the list of federally protected rights. Illustrating that view, the Court in 1876 voided portions of laws that Congress had passed to ensure the Fifteenth Amendment's guarantee of the right to vote and the Thirteenth Amendment's abolition of slavery. The Court declared that Congress had overreached in enacting a broad statute penalizing persons who used violence to deny blacks the right to vote. That right, the Court reiterated, came from the states; only the right to be free of racial **discrimination** in voting came from the U.S. Constitution. These rulings left Congress powerless to protect the newly enfranchised black Americans.

Protection for Business

The Court of the late 1800s not only effectively blocked Congress's attempts to enlarge the scope of Americans' personal freedoms, it also frustrated Congressional action to regulate business and defended the interests of property against federal power and organized labor. In 1890, Congress passed the Sherman Antitrust Act, aimed at breaking up large monopolies under its power to regulate interstate commerce. In January 1894, however, the Court held that the Sherman Antitrust Act did not outlaw manufacturing monopolies. The Court reasoned that manufacturing was not commerce, so it was not reachable under the federal commerce power, upon which the Sherman Act was based. The monopoly remained intact, and the antitrust law lay virtually useless.

In May 1895, the Court struck down an act of Congress that imposed the nation's first general peacetime tax on personal income. In *Pollock v. Farmers' Loan and Trust Co.* (1895), the Court overturned a century-old precedent and declared the income tax a direct tax. Because the Constitution requires that direct taxes be apportioned among the states according to population, the Court declared the tax unconstitutional. The ruling resulted in the Sixteenth Amendment to the Constitution in 1913, which lifted the apportionment requirement for income taxes.

Preserving the Social Status Quo

In the 1890s, the position of the Court concerning social issues was no more liberal than its views on economic matters. The case of *Plessy v. Ferguson* (1896) drove home this point when the Court upheld a Louisiana law requiring railroads operating in the state to provide separate cars for white and black passengers. This law was not a violation of the Fourteenth Amendment's equal protection clause, declared the majority, but a reasonable exercise of the state police power to preserve the public peace and public order. The majority argued that social equality of the races could not be accomplished by laws that conflicted with general community sentiment. The government can secure its citizens equal legal rights and equal opportunities, but it can and should go no further.

66 *In Plessy, the Court ruled:*

Legislation is powerless to eradicate racial instincts or to abolish distinctions based upon physical differences, and the attempt to do so can only result in accentuating the difficulties of the present situation. If the civil and political rights of both races be equal, one cannot be inferior to the other civilly or politically. If one race be inferior to the other socially, the Constitution of the United States cannot put them upon the same plane.

The Court also demonstrated its continuing willingness to leave to the states questions regarding the vote, even if the states effectively denied blacks that right. In *Williams v. Mississippi* (1898), the Court found no constitutional flaw in a law that required voters to pass a literacy test before being allowed to cast their ballot. Decisions such as these flew in the face of congressional efforts to remove barriers to political participation, especially in the South, where state legislatures passed various measures such as poll taxes to discourage or prevent blacks from voting. By refusing to rule such practices unconstitutional, the Supreme Court frustrated the will of Congress and, by extension, the will of the voters who elected its members.

The Court would retain this essentially conservative outlook throughout the early 1900s. The Great Depression of the 1930s, however, brought national challenges that required drastic government actions, actions that directly conflicted with the Court's conservative philosophy. This set up a showdown between the justices and President Franklin D. Roosevelt (1933–1945), whose aggressive New Deal policies challenged the economic status quo.

Essays

The Court and FDR

The Court is almost never a really contemporary institution. The operation of life tenure in the judicial department, as against elections at short intervals of the Congress, usually keeps the average viewpoint of the two institutions a generation apart. The judiciary is thus the check of a preceding generation on the present one; a check of conservative legal philosophy upon a dynamic people, and nearly always the check of a rejected regime on the one in being.

According to Attorney General Robert H. Jackson:

In 1941, Jackson was an active participant in the New Deal battles between the Court and the White House, and later a member of the Court. Never was Jackson's point more dramatically made than by the events of 1935, 1936, and 1937. A Court made up of men born in the mid-nineteenth century looked with distaste upon the radical legislative measures espoused by President Franklin D. Roosevelt and the Congress elected in the midst of the Great Depression.

The Court's Opposition

The Court's first decision on a New Deal measure was in *Panama Refining Co. v. Ryan* (1935). In this case, the Court struck down part of the National Industrial Recovery Act (NIRA) because in it Congress had delegated power to the executive without setting specific standards for its use. In May 1935, the Court struck down the comprehensive retirement system Congress had set up for railroad employees. In *Railroad Retirement Board v. Alton Railway Co.* (1935), the Court held that the commerce power did not provide a sufficient basis for such a system.

Three weeks later, a unanimous Court handed Roosevelt three major defeats. In *A.L.A. Schechter Poultry Corp. v. United States* (1935), the Court held invalid other major provisions of the NIRA, finding them an unconstitutional delegation of power from Congress to the president. The Court also held the Federal Farm Bankruptcy Act in violation of the **due process** guarantee, and in a third decision the justices sharply limited the president's removal power, which it had envisioned as virtually unlimited only nine years earlier.

Several cases testing the validity of New Deal legislation were still pending, and the justices were clearly divided. In its October 1935 term, the Court struck down several more pieces of legislation aimed at helping American workers and the unemployed. At the same time, the Court once again wielded the due process guarantee to strike down a state minimum wage law in *Morehead v. New York ex rel. Tipaldo* (1936).

As the justices recessed for the summer of 1936, the Court, the president, and the country stood at a crossroads. The Great Depression maintained its grim grip on the nation's factories and farms. For his part, President Roosevelt was committed to using the levers of government to prop up prices and wages, and he had behind him the support of a solidly Democratic Congress. The Court, however, stood in the way, insisting that the Constitution did not allow the government to regulate the everyday

transactions of workers and their employers or of sellers and their customers.

66 *Declared Chief Justice Charles Evans Hughes:*

Extraordinary conditions do not create or enlarge constitutional power.

Roosevelt's Reaction

Frustrated by the Court's unwillingness to support New Deal legislation, Roosevelt made a daring move. He proposed a bill that would allow the president to appoint a new Supreme Court justice for every sitting member of the Court over 70½ years of age. Roosevelt portrayed this as a way to relieve the workload on the Court, but his real goal was to "pack" the Court with supporters to force approval of his policies. The proposal outraged many, but, in the end, it was an unnecessary measure.

Unknown to any but the justices themselves, the Court had begun to change on its own as 1937 dawned. While Roosevelt's Court-packing proposal was mired in a Senate committee, the Court announced a major surprise in *West Coast Hotel Co. v. Parrish* (1937). Chief Justice Charles Evans Hughes, who had earlier declared that "extraordinary conditions" do not alter the Constitution, pointed to the "recent period of depression" as a justification for new laws that protect against "the exploitation of a class of workers who are in an unequal position with respect to bargaining power and are thus relatively defenseless against the denial of a living wage." Justice Owen Roberts, who had voted with Hughes to uphold Washington's minimum wage law, after having voted to strike down New York's the year before, said nothing—but his change in position was popularly described at the time as "the switch in time that saved the Nine." The switch of Justice Roberts's vote likely kept Roosevelt's proposal to increase the number of justices from nine to fifteen from moving forward in Congress.

War Powers Revisited

In late 1941, the United States entered World War II, and for the next several years issues of personal liberty and governmental power dominated the Court's work. In July 1942, the Court called a special session to consider the constitutionality of trying accused Nazi saboteurs by a military commission rather than in civilian courts. In *Ex parte Quirin* (1942), the Court upheld the president's actions as within the scope of the authority delegated to him by Congress.

In three other decisions, in 1943 and 1944, the Court also upheld the forcible internment of persons of Japanese descent ordered by the president and Congress. The Court conceded the odious nature of ethnic distinctions but found them justified in this particular wartime situation. In one of these cases, however, *Korematsu v. United States* (1944), the Court for the first time declared that "all legal restrictions which curtail the civil rights of a single racial group are immediately suspect . . . [T]he Courts must subject them to the most rigid scrutiny." Thus, even in condoning severe infringements of personal liberty and individual rights in the war years, the Court laid the foundation for later decisions expanding those rights.

★ ★

Civil Liberties and Civil Rights

The philosophical shift evident in the decisions of 1937 was reinforced by the rulings of the succeeding terms. Not only did the Court redirect its efforts away from matters of property rights and toward issues of personal rights, it began also to develop different standards for the two types of cases. When faced with regulations of business or property, the justices deferred to Congress or the states and upheld the laws. They became more willing, however, to strike down federal and state laws that infringed upon civil rights and liberties. This new set of standards—plus the extension of the guarantees of the Bill of Rights to the states begun with *Gitlow v. New York* (1925)—formed the foundation for the civil rights revolution to come.

Brown v. Board of Education (1954)

In the early 1950s, a series of cases came before the Supreme Court that challenged the Court's infamous ruling in *Plessy v. Ferguson* (1896). In that case, the Court had refused to strike down state laws providing for racial segregation of public accommodations. In *Brown v. Board of Education* (1954), the unanimous Court reversed *Plessy v. Ferguson* and found the segregation of the Topeka, Kansas, public school system to be unconstitutional.

> **W**e conclude that in the field of public education the doctrine of "separate but equal" has no place. Separate educational facilities are inherently unequal.

In his first major opinion, Chief Justice Earl Warren said: ❞

Although the Court had carefully limited its opinion to the subject of schools, it was clear that *Brown* spelled the end for all forms of state-sanctioned segregation. The Court, however, made almost no rulings on segregation during the remainder of the 1950s. Instead, it instructed lower courts to reconsider such cases in light of *Brown*. Resistance to these rulings was fierce and was soon felt in Congress. The period from 1954 to 1960, writes historian William Swindler, was one of "tension between the high tribunal and Congress unparalleled even by the early years of the 1930s." The roles, however, were reversed: the Court was the champion of change and Congress the seat of resistance.

The Due Process Revolution

Involving itself in still another area traditionally left to state control, the Court in the 1960s accelerated the step-by-step application of due process requirements to state law enforcement and criminal procedures. By 1969, the Court had required states to abide by virtually every major provision of the Bill of Rights. The first major ruling in this "due process revolution" came in a 5-4 vote in *Mapp v. Ohio* (1961), in which the Court held that evidence obtained in violation of the Fourth Amendment guarantee of security against unreasonable search and seizure must be excluded from use in state, as well as federal, courts.

A year later, the Court for the first time applied the Eighth Amendment ban on cruel and unusual punishment to strike down a state law. In *Robinson v. California* (1962), the Court held that a state could not make narcotics addiction a crime. After that, the Court declared in *Gideon v. Wainwright* (1963)

that states must provide legal assistance for all defendants charged with serious crimes. If defendants are unable to pay for an attorney, the state must provide one for them. In June 1964, the Court ruled that states must observe the Fifth Amendment privilege against compelled self-incrimination. A week later, in *Escobedo v. Illinois* (1964), the Court held that suspects have a right to legal assistance as soon as they are the focus of a police investigation.

Perhaps the Court's most controversial criminal law ruling came the following term in June 1966. In *Miranda v. Arizona* (1966), the Court held that police may not interrogate suspects in custody unless they have been informed of their right to remain silent, of the fact that their words may be used against them, and of their right to have the aid of a lawyer. Statements obtained in violation of this rule may not be used in court. Chief Justice Earl Warren wrote the majority opinion; dissenting were Justices Tom C. Clark, John Marshall Harlan II, Potter Stewart, and Byron White. The next term, as criticism of the Court mounted in Congress and in statehouses across the nation, the Court extended to state defendants the right to a speedy trial, enlarged the due process guarantees for juvenile defendants, and brought wiretapping and electronic surveillance under the strictures of the Fourth Amendment warrant requirement.

This step-by-step process of applying the Bill of Rights against state as well as federal action was nearly complete by the end of the decade. The Court's actions in this regard had resulted in historic changes in American society and placed it at the center of heated debate about the proper role of government. Supporters saw the Court's rulings as finally fulfilling the promise of freedom and equality to all Americans, and as protecting the rights and liberties of the most vulnerable citizens. Opponents criticized the Court for "legislating from the bench"—overturning the laws passed by elected state and federal representatives and imposing its will and its social and moral standards on the nation.

Roe v. Wade *and the Right to Privacy*

Arguably the Court's most controversial decision of the twentieth century came early in the following decade. In January 1973, the Court, in *Roe v. Wade* (1973), overturned state rules criminalizing abortion, ruling that a woman had a right to privacy that prevented the state from intervening in her decision to carry a pregnancy to term. The Court placed restrictions on that right, ruling that the state could restrict abortion in the final three months of pregnancy to safeguard the health of the mother.

The ruling in *Roe* touched off a firestorm of protest. In addition to the outrage among many observers who were opposed to abortion, conservative legal scholars criticized the justices for finding new rights where, they argued, none existed. Critics denounced the Court's pronouncement of a "right to privacy" not specifically mentioned in the Constitution. As with the controversy over extending due process, the Court's detractors accused it of overstepping its authority and trying to create, rather than interpret and apply, the law.

Conservative Backlash

In 1981, Ronald Reagan (1981–1989) became president and brought with him the conviction that he had a mandate from the American people to change the

way government related to the governed. The Supreme Court was a major focus of his campaign for change. Reagan disagreed with the substance of many of the modern Court's liberal decisions and with the judicial activism that informed them. He believed federal judges were intruding into controversial matters that, in a democracy, should be left to elected officials. The phrase *judicial restraint* was his administration's shorthand for the belief that courts should leave most major controversies to legislatures and elected officials to resolve. Reagan used his appointments and his administration's power of argument to move the Court in that direction. For eight years he tried to bring about a change of direction in the Supreme Court. Despite four appointments and innumerable arguments, that change did not take place until after he left the White House.

Reversing the Liberal Tide

The Court's October 1988 term brought Reagan's campaign for change closer to fruition. By the end of the term, even the most cautious observers were calling it a watershed in the Court's history. "Rarely has a single Supreme Court term had such an unsettling effect on the political landscape," declared *The New York Times*.

The first signal of the Court's conservative shift came in January 1989, when the justices struck down a Richmond, Virginia, minority contractor set-aside program. The city's plan required that 30 percent of city funds granted for construction projects go to firms with minority owners. The Court, 6-3, ruled that the set-aside, challenged by a white contractor, was too rigid and that the city had not sufficiently justified it with specific findings of past discrimination. For the first time, a majority of the Court ruled that government programs that discriminate against whites are to be viewed with the same "strict scrutiny" as programs that discriminate against blacks. This conclusion cast doubt on most "affirmative action" approaches by state and local agencies.

On questions of criminal law, the Court took a tough stand, refusing to find it unconstitutional for a state to execute criminals who were juveniles at the time of their crime, or to execute a mentally retarded defendant.

In the most closely watched case of the term, the Court gave states power to regulate abortions more thoroughly than at any time since *Roe v. Wade*. The Court's willingness to uphold a ban on abortions in publicly funded hospitals and tests for fetal viability was widely viewed at the time as a step toward the eventual overturn of *Roe*. In *Webster v. Reproductive Health Services* (1989), Chief Justice William H. Rehnquist wrote the opinion without mentioning the right of privacy—the basis of *Roe* and a right he had stated previously he had never located in the Constitution.

As the Court's second century thus came to an end, the rulings upholding increased state regulation of abortions, narrowing the reach of federal antidiscrimination laws, and strengthening prosecutors' hands in criminal cases all indicated the Court's new conservative bent.

The Court in the 1990s

As the new term began, liberals feared the Court would move sharply to the right. Eight of the nine justices were Republican appointees, and the only remaining Democrat, Justice Byron White, voted with conservatives and supported overruling *Roe v. Wade*. In spring 1992, the Court faced challenges to

its ban on school-sponsored prayers as well as a test of abortion rights. However, the term ended with two surprising defeats for the conservatives. In *Lee v. Weisman* (1992), a 5-4 majority prohibited clerics from delivering invocations at graduation ceremonies, affirming the principle of the separation of church and state. In *Planned Parenthood of Southeastern Pennsylvania v. Casey* (1992), the majority upheld the "essential holding" of *Roe*: Pregnant women have a right "to choose to have an abortion before viability and to obtain it without undue interference from the State." The rulings stressed the importance of adhering to a precedent, even one that remained in great dispute.

A Second Wind for Conservatives

In 1995, the Court announced a new agenda for itself. Since joining the Court in 1972, Chief Justice Rehnquist had been instrumental in reviving the original Constitution's vision of limited power for Congress as well as an independent role for the states. Since the New Deal era, the Court had deferred to Congress when it exercised its powers for regulating commerce, usually at the expense of state power. That era of deference came to an end with the ruling in *United States v. Lopez* (1995). The 5-4 decision struck down the Gun-Free School Zones Act of 1990 because "the possession of a gun in a local school zone is in no sense an economic activity," Rehnquist wrote. If the Court were to uphold such broad reaching federal measures, "there never will be a distinction between what is truly national and what is truly local. This we are unwilling to do." A year later, the Court took up another obscure dispute—rules for gambling on Indian lands—to announce a broad principle of law: States have a "sovereign immunity" that shields them from being sued by persons whose rights under federal law have been violated. In *Seminole Tribe of Florida v. Florida* (1996), the Court said that Congress does not have power under the Commerce Clause to violate this immunity.

The Rehnquist Court also moved to stop affirmative action and other measures intended to benefit minorities. In *Adarand v. Pena* (1995), the Court stated, "All racial classifications, imposed by whatever federal, state, or local governmental actor, must be analyzed . . . under strict scrutiny." In *Missouri v. Jenkins* (1995), the Court called a halt to a long-running and costly desegregation plan for the Kansas City schools and signaled that federal judges elsewhere should step back from supervising public schools. The Court also struck down black-majority congressional districts in Georgia and North Carolina.

Rehnquist and his colleagues also moved to strengthen the free speech rights of religious activists and church groups. Since the 1960s, when the Court struck down state-sponsored school prayers, the Court's opinion in religion cases had stressed the First Amendment's ban on "an establishment of religion" by public officials. Beginning in the mid-1990s, the Rehnquist Court stressed the free speech rights of Christian students in schools and colleges. A key decision came in 1995, when the Court ruled that Christian students who published a campus magazine with an evangelical theme at the University of Virginia were entitled to the same university support as other campus publications. The Constitution requires "government neutrality" toward religion and does not permit "disfavored treatment" for those who

Essays

espouse religious views, the 5-4 majority said in *Rosenberger v. University of Virginia* (1995).

In 1996, the Court for the first time struck down a jury award of punitive damages as "grossly excessive" and unconstitutional. For more than a decade, the justices had been troubled by multimillion-dollar jury verdicts intended to punish corporations and insurers. In a series of false starts, however, they had failed to agree on when such verdicts become so extreme as to be unconstitutional. In *BMW v. Gore* (1996), the Court said such verdicts punished the company unfairly and violated its right not to be deprived of property without due process of law.

The Court in the Twenty-First Century

The Court's rulings during the 1990s signaled its belief that the federal government—particularly Congress—had become too powerful. As the twenty-first century dawned, however, the issues facing the Court would focus on the president rather than Congress.

The Election of 2000

In fall 2000, the power of the Court emerged as a key issue in the presidential race. Trailing by 327 votes in the battle for Florida's crucial twenty-five electoral votes, Vice President Al Gore, a candidate for president, asked county courts in Florida for a hand recount of paper ballots that were not tallied by the tabulating machines. Although he won a pair of victories in the Florida Supreme Court, George Bush's lawyers filed an **appeal** to the Supreme Court asking for the recount to be halted on the ground that Bush would suffer "irreparable harm" if the state went ahead with a "standardless recount." In a 5-4 vote, the Court stopped the recount at midday on December 9 with an emergency order to the teams recounting to suspend their work. On December 12, the Court ended the Florida recount by the same 5-4 vote. Many observers considered the Court's controversial intervention in presidential politics an unconstitutional interference with the states' power to administer elections.

The War on Terror

Four years after the decision that ensured George W. Bush's election, the Court demonstrated a rare willingness to stand up to the executive branch in matters of national security. Following the terrorist attacks of September 11, 2001, President Bush had ordered an aggressive war against terrorists and those who harbored them. U.S. troops invaded Afghanistan to topple the Taliban regime that had protected Osama bin Laden, the Saudi-born financier of the al Qaeda network. Hundreds of suspected terrorists and Taliban fighters were captured and eventually imprisoned at the now controversial U.S Naval base at Guantanamo Bay, Cuba. Bush and Secretary of Defense Donald Rumsfeld designated these prisoners as "unlawful enemy combatants." As such, they were neither prisoners of war protected by the Geneva Conventions nor criminals who would face charges and a trial. Even more controversial was the administration's decision to apply this designation to American citizens who were being held in the United States.

In spring 2004, the Court rejected the administration's approach. "We hold that . . . due process demands that a citizen held in the United States as an enemy combatant be given a meaningful opportunity to contest the factual basis for that detention before a neutral decision-maker," Justice Sandra Day O'Connor wrote for a six-member majority. The majority also found that the foreign prisoners held at Guantanamo had the right to seek relief from a judge.

Striking a Balance

The Court's rulings in the 2000 Florida recount and the cases resulting from the war on terror reveal the Court's potential for exercising significant power vis-à-vis the states as well as the other branches of the federal government. Hamilton's assertion that the Court would be toothless without the power of the sword or purse has proven to be mistake. At the same time, however, history has shown that the Court is also strongly influenced by the other branches of government. Presidential appointments to the Court typically are made with an eye to imposing a particular political or judicial philosophy on the Court. Just as Franklin Roosevelt's appointees took the Court in a liberal direction, those of Ronald Reagan and George W. Bush resulted in a conservative shift. In the final analysis, the Court cannot be said to be either the weakest or the strongest of the branches. It is the balance between the branches—a balance that the Court attempts to maintain—that remains the strength of the U.S political system.

See also: *Bush v. Gore* (2000); Checks and Balances; Congress and the Supreme Court; Due Process; Judicial Activism; Judicial Restraint; Judicial Review; *Marbury v. Madison* (1803); *McCulloch v. Maryland* (1819); New Deal and the Supreme Court; Presidency and the Supreme Court; Right to Privacy; *Roe v. Wade* (1973); Roosevelt's 1937 Court Reform Plan; Separation of Powers; War Power and the Supreme Court.

Further Reading

Baum, Lawrence. *The Supreme Court.* Washington, D.C.: CQ Press, 2009.

Crawford, Jan Greenburg. *Supreme Conflict: The Inside Story of the Struggle for Control of the United States Supreme Court.* New York: Penguin, 2008.

Irons, Peter. *A People's History of the Supreme Court: The Men and Women Whose Cases and Decisions Have Shaped Our Constitution.* New York: Penguin, 2005.

Essays

How Does the President Nominate a Supreme Court Justice?

 Choosing Supreme Court justices is one of the most powerful tools available to the president of the United States to shape the country's long-term political and social landscape. The nomination process is also one of the most visible examples of the principles of separation of powers and checks and balances built into the American political system.

Although Supreme Court justices do not have to face election (or reelection), they owe their positions to the presidents who nominate them, and a president's choice of nominee typically is constrained by larger political considerations. Among the more important of these is awareness of how members of Congress will react to the nominee. For while the president can nominate any candidate for the Court, the Senate has the power to confirm or reject the president's selection.

The president's need to satisfy several different interest groups—both within and outside of government—makes the nomination process a tricky business. The president hopes to pick a candidate who will please the administration's political allies, while offering his political opponents as little as possible to criticize. However, despite going to great lengths to determine how a nominee will rule once he or she is appointed, many justices defy the expectations of those who appointed them to the Court.

Constitutional Requirements

Article II, Section 2, of the U.S. Constitution provides that:

. . . [The president] shall nominate, and by, and with the advice and consent of the Senate, shall appoint ambassadors, other public ministers and consuls, judges of the Supreme Court, and all other officers of the United States, whose appointments are not herein otherwise provided for, and which shall be established by law . . .

Advice and Consent

Senate consent to executive appointments was a unique innovation incorporated into the Constitution. The original idea of Senate participation in the selection as well as confirmation of nominees never materialized, however. President George Washington (1789-1797) collided with the Senate over approval of an Indian treaty and subsequently refused to consult it on appointment matters, except to send up nominations for approval.

Senate consent to an executive appointment came to mean simply that a majority of the Senate approves the president's nomination. Presidents customarily have consulted individual senators of their own political party on matters

Essays

Since the Supreme Court first met in 1789, its powers have grown significantly. Through its power of judicial review, for example, the Court can rule that laws passed by Congress and signed by the president are unconstitutional and therefore void. (AP Photo, Charles Dharapak)

of appointments related to their home states. Policy and political considerations, however, often take precedence over the practice of senatorial courtesy, and failure of the president to extend this courtesy to the appropriate senators usually has not alone resulted in a nominee's rejection.

Once the Senate has approved a nominee, it cannot reverse its decision. At one time, however, Senate rules permitted the recall of a confirmation resolution within two days after its passage. This practice ended after the administration of President Herbert C. Hoover (1929–1933) challenged the Senate's recall of George O. Smith, a Hoover appointee to the Federal Power Commission. Hoover, who had already delivered Smith's commission, refused to return it. The Senate then took the matter to court to test Smith's right to continue in office. When the case came before the Supreme Court, the Court upheld Smith's right to the post.

Recess Appointments

The Constitution authorizes the president to fill vacant offices during a Senate break, or recess. A recess is considered to mean a period longer than a holiday break or a brief and temporary adjournment.

❝ *The Constitution states:*

The President shall have Power to fill up all Vacancies that may happen during the Recess of the Senate, by granting Commissions which shall expire at the End of their next Session.

Fifteen men have been nominated to the Supreme Court while the Senate was not in session and have received "recess" appointments. These appointments

permit the individual to be sworn in and to take part in the Court's work be-fore the nomination is confirmed. Once the Senate returns, the president must then formally nominate the individual, who is then subject to confirmation. If confirmed, he or she is sworn in a second time.

Only five of the 15 Supreme Court justices who received such appointments took their seats on the bench before Senate confirmation. Four were eventually confirmed: Benjamin R. Curtis, appointed and confirmed in December 1851; Earl Warren, appointed as chief justice in September 1953 and confirmed in March 1954; William J. Brennan Jr., appointed in October 1956 and confirmed in March 1957; and Potter Stewart, appointed in October 1958 and confirmed in May 1959. The Senate rejected the fifth, John Rutledge, who had served as an associate justice from 1790 to 1791. President George Washington gave Rut-ledge a recess appointment as chief justice in the summer of 1795. Although Rutledge presided over the Court's August 1795 term, at which two cases were heard and decided, the Senate eventually refused to confirm him.

Choosing a Nominee

George Washington, as the first president, had the responsibility of choosing the original six justices of the Supreme Court. The type of men he chose and the reasons he chose them foreshadowed the process of selection carried out by his successors.

Political Loyalties

In naming the first justices, Washington paid close attention to their politics, which at that time primarily meant loyalty to the new Constitution. Of the six original appointees, three had attended the Philadelphia convention that drafted the Constitution, and the other three had supported its adoption. John Jay, the first chief justice, was coauthor, with Alexander Hamilton and James Madison, of *The Federalist Papers,* a series of influential essays published in New York sup-porting ratification of the Constitution. During his two terms of office, Washington had the opportunity to make five additional Supreme Court appointments. All were staunch supporters of the Constitution and the new federal government.

As political parties became an established fact of American political life, the major parties sought to promote the appointment to the Court of members who supported their view of the proper role of the federal government. As Washington had appointed supporters of the new Constitution, so most presi-dents have selected nominees with whom they felt comfortable, both philosoph-ically and politically.

It is the exception when a president goes to the opposite political party to find a nominee. The first clear-cut instance of a president of one party appointing a member of the other to the Supreme Court was Republican Abraham Lincoln's (1861–1865) selection of Democrat Stephen J. Field of California in 1863. President John Tyler (1841–1845), who was elected vice president as a Whig in 1840, appointed Democrat Samuel Nelson to the Court in 1845. By that time, however, Tyler was no longer identified with either major political party.

After Lincoln's example, Republican presidents occasionally appointed Democrats to the Court. President Benjamin Harrison (1889-1893) selected

Howell Jackson of Tennessee in 1893; Warren G. Harding (1921–1923) appointed Pierce Butler in 1922; Herbert Hoover appointed Benjamin Cardozo in 1932; Dwight D. Eisenhower (1953–1961) appointed William J. Brennan Jr. in 1956; and Richard Nixon (1969–1974) appointed Lewis F. Powell Jr. in 1971 (1969–1974). Republican William Howard Taft (1909–1913) was the only president to appoint more than one member of the opposite party to the Court. Three of his six nominees to the Court were Democrats: Edward D. White, whom he elevated from associate justice to chief justice, and Horace Lurton and Joseph R. Lamar, Southern Democrats appointed in 1909 and 1910, respectively.

The only two Democrats ever to appoint Republicans to the Supreme Court were Franklin D. Roosevelt (1933–1945) and Harry S. Truman (1945–1953). Roosevelt elevated Justice Harlan Stone, a Republican, to chief justice in 1941. Truman appointed Republican Senator Harold H. Burton of Ohio, an old friend and colleague from Truman's Senate days, in 1945.

Geographical Balance

Another of Washington's major considerations was geography. The new states were a disparate group that barely had held together during the fight for independence and the early government under the Articles of Confederation during the 1780s. To bind them more closely together, Washington consciously tried to represent each geographical area of the country in the nation's new Supreme Court.

His first six appointees were three Northerners—Chief Justice John Jay from New York and Associate Justices William Cushing of Massachusetts and James Wilson of Pennsylvania—and three Southerners—John Blair of Virginia, James Iredell of North Carolina, and John Rutledge of South Carolina. The five later appointees were Oliver Ellsworth of Connecticut, Thomas Johnson and Samuel Chase of Maryland, William Paterson of New Jersey, and Rutledge, appointed a second time. By the time Washington left office, nine of the original thirteen states had achieved representation on the Court.

The tradition of weighing geographic factors in appointing justices continued for more than a century. It was reinforced by the justices' duty under the Judiciary Act of 1789 to ride around the country and preside over circuit court sessions. Presidents not only strove for geographic balance in their appointments but also considered it important that each justice be a native of the circuit over which he presided. Congress ended the burdensome circuit-riding requirement in 1911.

In its heyday, the geographic factor was frequently the deciding factor among potential nominees. The longest-lasting example, which endured from 1789 to 1932, was the so-called New England seat, usually occupied by an appointee from Massachusetts. There was also a seat for a New Yorker from 1806 to 1894, and a Maryland-Virginia seat from 1789 to 1860.

Geography had strong political implications as well, especially for the South. With the growth of sectional differences, particularly over the slavery issue before the Civil War (1861–1865), the South felt itself to be on the defensive. One of the ways it sought to protect its interests was to gain a majority on the Supreme Court. Indeed, five of the nine justices in 1860 were from slaveholding states.

Essays

With the coming of the Civil War, the sectional balance of power shifted. Four of the five Southern justices died between 1860 and 1867, and another, Justice John A. Campbell of Alabama, resigned to join the Confederate cause. Not one of these justices was replaced by a Southerner, and by 1870 every Supreme Court seat was held by a Northerner or Westerner.

With the gradual decline of bitterness over the war, Southerners again began to reappear on the Court. President Rutherford B. Hayes (1877–1881), who sought to reconcile relations between the North and South, made the first move by appointing William B. Woods of Georgia in 1880. Woods was not a native Southerner; he had moved South after the Civil War. Despite his "carpetbagger" background, he was never identified with the corruption associated with the Reconstruction era. As a federal judge for the Fifth Circuit, located in the Deep South, he gained the respect of his neighbors for his fairness and honesty.

The first native Southerner appointed to the Court after the Civil War was Woods's successor, Lucius Q.C. Lamar of Mississippi, appointed by President Grover Cleveland (1885–1889, 1893–1897) in 1888. Lamar had personally drafted the ordinance of secession for Mississippi in 1861 and had served the Confederacy both as a military officer and as a diplomatic envoy to Europe. His appointment to the Court was an even more significant symbol of reconciliation than Woods's appointment eight years earlier.

Since the early twentieth century, geography has become a less important consideration in Court nominations. As recently as 1970, however, President Richard M. Nixon made an issue of the Senate's refusal to confirm Southerners Clement Haynsworth Jr. and G. Harrold Carswell to the Court. Nixon, who claimed the Senate would not confirm a conservative Southerner, eventually nominated Harry A. Blackmun of Minnesota instead, and he was confirmed by the Senate on May 12, 1970.

Popular Pressure

Before a president finally decides on a nominee, a process of balancing and sifting usually goes on, sometimes involving many participants and sometimes only a few. Occasionally, however, overwhelming pressure for a particular nominee all but forces the president's choice.

One of the more dramatic instances of this process occurred in 1853, when President Franklin Pierce (1853–1857) nominated John A. Campbell of Alabama for a seat on the Court. Campbell was a forty-one-year-old lawyer who had such a brilliant reputation that the justices decided they wanted him as a colleague. The entire membership of the Court wrote to Pierce requesting Campbell's nomination. To emphasize their point, two justices delivered letters in person. Pierce complied, and the Senate confirmed Campbell within four days.

In 1862, President Lincoln was looking for a new justice from the Midwest. The Iowa congressional delegation began pressing for the appointment of Samuel Miller, a doctor and lawyer who had helped form the Iowa Republican Party and who had a strong reputation for moral and intellectual integrity. The movement grew rapidly until 129 of 140 House members and all but four senators had signed a petition for Miller's nomination. With such massive and unprecedented congressional support, Miller received Lincoln's approval despite his lack of any judicial experience. He became the first justice from west of the Mississippi River.

In 1932, a strong national movement began for the appointment of Benjamin Cardozo, chief judge of the New York Court of Appeals, to the Supreme Court. Cardozo was a Democrat, while the president who was to make the appointment, Herbert C. Hoover, was a Republican. Furthermore, Cardozo was Jewish, and there was already one Jew on the Court, Louis D. Brandeis. Under these circumstances, it was considered unlikely Hoover would make the nomination.

Cardozo's record was so impressive, however, that it created a groundswell of support. Deans and faculty members of the nation's leading law schools, chief judges of other state courts, labor and business leaders, and powerful senators all urged Hoover to choose Cardozo. Despite his desire to appoint a Western Republican, Hoover finally yielded and nominated Cardozo, who was confirmed without opposition.

Judicial Surprises

Presidents hope to choose nominees who will support the president's political views from the bench. However, they can never be certain how the individuals they appoint to the Court will rule when the Court is faced with a challenge to the exercise of presidential power.

Thomas Jefferson (1801–1809) made several appointments to the bench whom he hoped would counteract Chief Justice John Marshall's control over the Court's decisions, but Jefferson's effort to reduce Marshall's effectiveness failed. President Lincoln appointed Salmon P. Chase to the bench to deflect Chase's presidential ambitions and to harness his legal talents for the administration. Chase, who had advocated passage of the Legal Tender Act as treasury secretary, later opposed the Lincoln administration in the first of the *Legal Tender Cases, Hepburn v. Griswold* (1870), holding those acts unconstitutional.

Two of the four justices Harry Truman appointed to the bench, Justices Tom C. Clark and Sherman Minton, were close friends of the president. When Truman tried to use federal power to take control over the steel industry, however, Clark joined with the majority to oppose the move; he was joined by two other Truman appointees. President Richard Nixon appointed Warren E. Burger chief justice in part because Burger had been outspoken in his criticism of the Court's previous rulings limiting prosecutors' efforts to convict criminals. In an ironic turn of events, Burger wrote the Court opinion in *United States v. Nixon* (1974), which left Nixon with the option of resigning as president or facing impeachment and a trial.

The individual whom Burger succeeded as chief justice, Earl Warren, represents one of the most dramatic cases of a Supreme Court nominee defying the political expectations of the nominating president. In 1952, Warren was considered a leading candidate for the Republican nomination for president, but he withdrew from the race to support the candidacy of Dwight D. Eisenhower. Warren was said to have offered to support Eisenhower's campaign in return for an appointment to the Supreme Court at the first possible opportunity.

In 1953, Eisenhower nominated Warren to be Chief Justice of the United States. Eisenhower wanted a conservative justice and commented that "(Warren) represents the kind of political, economic, and social thinking that I believe we need on the Supreme Court . . . He has a national name for integrity, uprightness, and courage that, again, I believe we need on the Court."

However, Warren turned out to be far more liberal than Eisenhower could have imagined. Warren presided over many landmark cases that dramatically changed the social and political fabric of the country, moving it in a much more liberal direction. These included *Brown v. Board of Education* (1954), which desegregated public schools; *Loving v. Virginia* (1967), which legalized interracial marriage; and *Gideon v Wainwright* (1963) and *Miranda v. Arizona* (1966), which greatly expanded the rights of criminal defendants. When asked later to name his greatest mistake as president, Eisenhower is supposed to have remarked, "Earl Warren."

The Confirmation Process

The choice of a nominee is only the first step on the path to a Supreme Court appointment. Before the candidate can take a seat on the Court, he or she must first win approval by the Senate, a process that takes place in two stages: hearings by the Senate Judiciary Committee, followed by a vote of the entire Senate.

Committees are subgroups of senators who share expertise or interest in a particular topic. The party that holds the most seats in the Senate chairs all committees and chooses all committee members. Committees usually are composed of senators from both parties, with the party controlling the Senate typically holding a slight majority on most committees. All proposed legislation starts out by being considered in the appropriate committee, as do the names of potential presidential appointees.

The Judiciary Committee holds hearings in which both supporters and opponents may testify for or against a Supreme Court nominee. During this time, the committee members gather information about the nominee's background, judicial experience, legal philosophy, and other biographical information that might factor into their decision to approve or reject the nominee. Committee hearings occasionally produce some new revelations about the nominee, but in most cases they serve as a forum to review the nominee's known record and views.

If a majority of the members approve of the nominee, the committee will "report" the nomination, or send it to the full Senate for a vote. If the committee opposes the nominee, however, its members can refuse to report the nomination, allowing it to "die" in committee without ever reaching a floor vote in the Senate. Some observers criticize this process, arguing that the president's nominee deserves an "up or down vote." Supporters of the current practice counter that the committee process works the same for Supreme Court justices as it does for every bill before Congress. They contend that the process is intended to weed out nominees who are unqualified or who were chosen for obviously partisan reasons without regard to judicial competence.

The Judiciary Committee reports most nominations to the Senate, where a simple majority of senators present must vote to confirm the nominee. Once there, confirmation is many times a formality. Most nominees win confirmation by large margins; eight have been confirmed by voice vote alone, without the need for an actual tally. A number of votes, however, have been decided by slim margins. The narrowest victory belongs to Stanley Matthews, who in 1881 won confirmation by a single vote, 24-23. More recently, in 1991, Clarence Thomas received the support of just 52 percent of the Senate, the smallest margin of victory since the Matthews confirmation. The closest vote to reject a nominee came in 1861, when the Senate voted down Jeremiah S. Black 25-26.

Controversial Nominees

Some amount of sniping and opposition from the president's political foes is part of almost every Supreme Court nomination. For most nominees, opposition is generally slight, and the president's choice moves quickly through the confirmation process. In some cases, however, the president's choice raises serious concerns, even among the president's supporters and fellow party members. In some cases, this opposition is sufficiently widespread to lead the Senate to reject the president's choice, or force the president to withdraw the name from consideration.

Early Battles

The first controversy surrounding a Supreme Court nominee occurred early in the Court's history. When John Jay retired as the first chief justice in 1795, President George Washington nominated former associate justice John Rutledge to succeed him. Rutledge, however, was something of a political maverick whose views alienated many members of the ruling Federalist Party. Rutledge, for example, supported slavery and believed that only property owners should have the right to hold political office. Washington granted Rutledge a recess appointment in August 1795, but the Senate refused to confirm him when it reassembled, and Rutledge's term expired in December of that year.

Continuing sectional rivalries following the Civil War led to controversy surrounding the nomination of Lucius Quintus Cincinnatus Lamar in 1887. President Grover Cleveland selected Lamar, his secretary of the interior, to fill the vacancy caused by the death of Associate Justice William Woods. Lamar, however, was also a divisive figure. A former member of Congress from Georgia, he had resigned his office in 1861 to join the Confederate cause. In fact, Lamar personally drafted the state's resolution of secession from the Union. Many Republican senators were bitterly opposed to naming a prominent former Confederate to the Court. Other Republicans, however, argued that rejecting Lamar's nomination on the basis of his service with the Confederacy would be seen as a ban on political service for all Confederate veterans. Lamar eventually won confirmation and served five years on the Court.

Twentieth Century Controversies

After 125 years of operation, the Court continued to be composed entirely of white, Christian males. That tradition ended only after a prolonged struggle over President Woodrow Wilson's nomination of Louis D. Brandeis in 1916. Brandeis drew opposition from conservative politicians not only because he was Jewish, but also because of his support for organized labor against big business. One critic called Brandeis a "business-baiter, stirrer up of strife, litigious lover of hate and unrest, destroyer of confidence, killer of values, commercial coyote, spoiler of pay envelopes." Another wrote, "There is only one redeeming feature in the nomination and that is that it will assist to bury Mr. Wilson in the next presidential election."

The Senate debated the nomination for four months but could find no substantive reason for opposing Brandeis. One of his supporters put it bluntly when he said that the opposition was based solely on the fact that "Mr. Brandeis is an outsider, successful, and a Jew." In the end, Brandeis won confirmation by a vote of 47-22 and became one of the most prominent voices on the Court during his twenty-three-year tenure as associate justice.

Essays

Before 1900, the Senate had rejected twenty-five presidential nominees for associate justiceships, but only one for chief justice—John Rutledge. In 1968, Abe Fortas became the second nominee for chief justice to fail to win confirmation. Fortas had served as an associate justice on the Court for three years at the time President Lyndon B. Johnson (1963–1969) nominated him to replace retiring Chief Justice Earl Warren. The nomination raised charges of "cronyism" by political foes of Johnson, who was a close friend of Fortas and who had named Fortas to the Court in 1965. Accusations of financial irregularities also arose surrounding money Fortas had accepted for a series of university seminars he taught while serving on the Court. Under extreme pressure, Johnson withdrew the nomination. Although Fortas continued to serve as an associate justice, he resigned from the Court a year later amid rumors of additional financial violations that Fortas denied.

Recent Appointment Showdowns

Three of the most heated confrontations over Supreme Court nominees have occurred in the past twenty-five years. The debates over these nominees focused on a wide variety of factors including ideology, race, sex, and basic competence. All gained additional fury from the sharp ideological battles that have raged in Washington since the 1980s.

The first of these struggles occurred late in the second term of the presidency of Ronald Reagan (1981–1989). In 1980, Reagan and the Republican Party ended decades of Democratic political control in Washington by winning the presidency and a majority in the Senate. This helped Reagan win easy approval for his first two nominees to the Court, Sandra Day O'Connor and Antonin Scalia. By the time Reagan nominated Robert Bork in 1987, however, Democrats had recaptured the Senate, and they met the nomination with fierce resistance. Democratic Senators found Bork's strongly conservative views—particularly on abortion and civil rights—unacceptable, and swiftly rejected the nomination. By contrast, the Senate approved Reagan's alternate choice, the moderate jurist Anthony Kennedy, by a vote of 97-0.

Four years later, the nomination of Clarence Thomas by Reagan's successor George H.W. Bush (1989–1993) touched off one of the bitterest fights ever over a Supreme Court appointment. Bush named the staunchly conservative Thomas to replace Thurgood Marshall, the nation's first African American Supreme Court justice, who retired in 1991. The nomination of Thomas, who also was African American, raised immediate opposition from the president's liberal political foes. Thomas's conservative views, and particularly his opposition to affirmative action, were clearly at odds with the views of the justice he was replacing. Many critics called the nomination a cynical move to replace Marshall with a black justice acceptable to conservatives. Thomas's relative lack of experience—he had been an appeals court judge for only a year and had never argued a case before the Supreme Court as a lawyer—also was cited as a reason for opposing his nomination.

During the Senate Judiciary Committee hearings, only one witness testified against Thomas—but that testimony produced a bombshell. Anita Hill, who had formerly worked for Thomas at two government agencies, accused Thomas of having made crude sexual remarks and unwanted advances toward her. Under questioning from senators, she reported explicit details of alleged sexual

harassment by Thomas. The nominee condemned the proceedings as "a high-tech lynching for uppity blacks." Although another former female employee of Thomas's refused to testify, she signed a written statement also accusing him of sexual harassment. Other former employees and co-workers testified in Thomas's favor. In the end, the committee split 7-7 but reported the nomination to the full Senate. The final vote of 52-48 in favor of confirmation was one of the closest ever and was largely along party lines. Only eleven of fifty-seven Democrats voted for Thomas; only two of forty-three Republicans voted against him.

The most recent Senate showdown over a Supreme Court appointment involved President George W. Bush's nomination of Harriet Miers in 2005. The storm of opposition the nomination whipped up was based on both considerations of political ideology and basic qualifications. Miers, who served as White House counsel at the time of nomination, was a longtime friend and confidante of the president, having served as his personal lawyer for many years. It was not, however, simply the long personal relationship between the two that raised concerns, but the fact that Miers had no judicial experience at any level. The fact that Bush had passed over many highly qualified candidates in favor of Miers intensified the charges of cronyism leveled against him. Ironically, many of the president's political allies also opposed the nomination on the basis that Miers's political views were not sufficiently conservative. Intense opposition from both sides of the political spectrum scuttled the nomination, and Bush named Samuel Alito instead. Like Anthony Kennedy, Alito too was confirmed by a unanimous vote of the Senate.

Ideological differences between the major political parties have always made Court nominations a balancing act. Today, Democrats and Republicans differ over issues such as abortion, affirmative action, and same-sex marriage, but past controversies over states' rights, slavery, and the right to vote generated just as much passion in their day. The choice of a nominee is never an easy or clear-cut decision and, even after more than two hundred years of practice, presidents still find it at best an inexact science.

See also: Alito, Samuel A.; Associate Justices; Burger, Warren E.; Checks and Balances; Chief Justice of the United States; Confirmation of Justices and Judges; Congress and the Supreme Court; Due Process; Hill, Anita; Jay, John; Judicial Activism; Judicial Restraint; Kennedy, Anthony M.; Marshall, Thurgood; O'Connor, Sandra Day; Presidency and the Supreme Court; Scalia, Antonin; Separation of Powers; Thomas, Clarence; Warren, Earl.

Further Reading

Phelps, Timothy M., and Winternitz, Helen. *Capitol Games: Clarence Thomas, Anita Hill, and the Story of a Supreme Court Nomination.* New York: Hyperion, 1992.

Rutkus, Denis Steven, ed. *Supreme Court Nominations 1789–2005: Actions (Including Speed) by the Senate, the Judiciary Committee, And the President.* Hauppauge, NY: Nova Science Publishers, 2006.

Simon, Paul. *Advice and Consent: Clarence Thomas, Robert Bork and the Intriguing History of the Supreme Court's Nomination Battles.* Washington, D.C.: National Press Books, 1992.

How Does the Supreme Court Affect Citizens Today?

 By the early 1800s, most American citizens understood something that the drafters of the U.S. Constitution had clearly intended: that this new document established a much stronger federal government for the nation than had the old Articles of Confederation, the young country's first government, which was in force between 1781 and 1789. The new government under the Constitution was invested with its own authority to govern and did not have to rely upon powers borrowed from the state governments. The federal government under the Articles of Confederation failed, in part, because the nation could not act if all thirteen states could not agree on an issue.

Under the Constitution, the federal government responded directly to the people of all the states who sent elected representatives to the nation's capital in Washington, D.C. By 1803, many of the present-day functions of the *executive* and *legislative* branches of the new government had been clearly established.

The third branch of the new government, the **judicial,** was perhaps the least certain in its powers in 1803. In that year, however, the Supreme Court firmly established its role. Chief Justice John Marshall wrote an opinion in a case called *Marbury v. Madison*. The case had to do with an appointment to a minor public office, but Chief Justice Marshall used the facts of the case to establish the Court as the final interpreter of the U.S. Constitution. The powers and limits of each of the three branches of government became much clearer. As Marshall described the role of Congress, "The powers of the Legislature are defined, and limited; and that those limits may not be mistaken, or forgotten, the constitution is written." The heart of constitutional government comes from limiting the power of each branch. The Court recognized that it could overturn congressional and presidential actions only under certain circumstances, but it asserted that it could and would undo unconstitutional actions.

The decisions of the Court are often extremely important because they reshape the law and therefore reshape the way that the language of the Constitution affects everyday aspects of society. Many legal scholars believe that constitutional rights are not, and have never been, static and unchangeable. The Constitution provides a framework, but the Supreme Court constantly applies that framework, aided by the weight of precedent, to an ever-expanding number of situations. This process continues today and even continues to clarify the meaning of the original Bill of Rights.

Therefore, the Supreme Court, through its ruling in *Marbury v. Madison*, established its power and authority over the other two branches of government,

as well as over all people living in the United States—both citizens and non-citizens. Over the centuries, the Court's power has grown and, through various rulings, its decisions have affected all aspects of American life—from rulings on commerce, to what defines cruel and unusual punishment, to civil rights, to the power of local law enforcement officers to search a person's home.

Hearing Appeals and the Weight of Precedent

The Supreme Court functions most of the time as a **court of appeals.** There are a few types of cases that it hears for the first time, but these are very limited. Most of the time, the Court is making a decision that will impact the rights of citizens by either affirming or overturning an earlier decision made by another court.

Some of these cases will have started out in the federal judicial system. Or the parties involved are from different states, and trying the case in federal court means neither one has a home-state advantage. Other cases start out in state courts. On state law, the state's Supreme Court is the highest authority. Often, though, a case may come to court under state law but involve a federal constitutional question. In such a case, the U.S. Supreme Court is the highest authority for resolving such questions.

By the time any **appellate case** reaches the Court, it may have been argued several times. A case that begins with a trial in a U.S. District Court will be appealed to a U.S. Circuit Court of Appeals before it reaches the Supreme Court. On appeal, each side focuses its arguments on the specific issues of the appeal. Lawyers for each side submit briefs, which are written documents containing the facts of the case, transcripts of testimony at the trial, and other information the appellate judges may find useful in deciding. Oral arguments are also often heard. Standing before the panel of judges, each lawyer shapes the facts and circumstances of the case at hand and compares them to earlier cases. By using the **precedent** of earlier cases, lawyers provide judges with assurance that their arguments have the force of established law.

Precedent is incredibly important in law. While a lawyer must do an effective job of telling the story of the present case, she or he absolutely must find earlier cases that support the new argument. The law uses prior cases to guide decisions in current cases. Sometimes the phrase "a line of cases" is used to describe a set of old decisions that point toward how a court should rule. Imagine that each case draws the line out a little farther. Some cases add more than others; some bend the line in unexpected directions. When lawyers argue before the Supreme Court, they argue for how the facts of the story they are telling match the end of the existing line, and why decisions in their favor draw the line in the proper direction. Part of making a good argument, of course, is in explaining why the opposing lawyer's argument would draw out the line of precedent in the wrong direction.

It is the weight of precedent that comes with a Supreme Court decision that makes the decision influential and often controversial. Sometimes the justices take an old decision and apply it in an unexpected way. In other cases, a more recent past case may get minimized, as the majority looks further back to an older decision. "Distinguishing" an old opinion also can be very important; this requires the justice writing the opinion to recognize that an older

The decisions handed down by the nine justices of the U.S. Supreme Court affect everyone in the country. Through the years, the Court has ruled on subjects as varied as trade between the states, voting rights, and marriage laws. (Kevin Dietsch, UPI, Landov)

case represents good law but to then find sufficient differences in the facts of the present case to prevent the earlier decision from forcing an outcome.

The Exclusionary Rule as an Example

The U.S. Constitution is a very compact document. In a short space it establishes the three branches of the federal government, lists the powers of each, and provides an impressive list of rights guaranteed to citizens. The Constitution uses very broad language to accomplish these tasks.

For example, the Fourth Amendment, added as a part of the Bill of Rights in 1791, notes that police and other authorities must have good reasons for searching a home or arresting a person. Post-Revolutionary Americans had recent memories of British authorities harassing and threatening Americans. They intended the Fourth Amendment to prevent any repeat of such bullying.

The Fourth Amendment states: 🙶

The right of the people to be secure in their persons, houses, papers, and effects, against unreasonable searches and seizures, shall not be violated, and no Warrants shall issue, but upon probable cause, supported by Oath or affirmation, and particularly describing the place to be searched, and the persons or things to be seized.

The text of the amendment, however, raises more questions than it answers. What makes a search "unreasonable"? What exactly is "probable cause"? Do all searches require warrants to be legal? What happens if an "unreasonable

search" produces evidence of a person's guilt? None of these questions can be answered by the text of the Constitution alone. The document must be interpreted by the Supreme Court to arrive at answers that impact the rights of all citizens.

In 1913, the Court provided an answer to the question of what to do with evidence found during an unreasonable search. The Court created what became known as the "exclusionary rule" in the case *Weeks v. U.S.* The Court found that if illegally obtained evidence could be used, then the protection stated in the Fourth Amendment "is of no value, and . . . might as well be stricken from the Constitution."

Creating an exclusionary rule leads to cases about when the rule applies and when it does not. The first such issue concerned the application of the exclusionary rule to police acting under state authority. *Weeks* concerned the actions of a federal marshal, but in 1961, *Mapp v. Ohio* held that the exclusionary rule applies to municipal police (who take their authority from state government). The Court reasoned that the Fourth Amendment applied to the states through the due process clause of the Fourteenth Amendment, and that the exclusionary rule goes with it.

Further Clarification

By 1968, the exclusionary rule again needed clarification. In *Terry v. Ohio,* the Court held that police may perform investigative stops when they have reasonable suspicion of criminal activity but not probable cause for an arrest.

In the next case regarding the exclusionary rule, *United States v. Calandra,* the Court held that the purpose of the rule is to cause police to avoid future illegal searches and seizures. The Court rejected the idea that the rule is a personal constitutional right of the victim. It would only allow the rule to operate in situations where it really could convince police to avoid future Fourth Amendment violations.

The exclusionary rule cases of the 1970s and 1980s continued to limit the rule's use. These decisions gave more room for police to operate without the exclusion of evidence. One case established that an honest mistake by police in believing that an arrest warrant was valid, when it in fact was not, did not require exclusion of the evidence obtained under the warrant. In the 1960s, the Court had expanded the rule, and primarily expressed concern for protecting the privacy of individual citizens. In the 1970s and 1980s, the Court became more **conservative** in its politics and followed a general trend in American society to concern itself with personal safety and the prevention of crime.

The Court's change in emphasis, following changes among the justices, is important. The Court is not a political branch of the government. It does not need to follow opinion polls and take positions based upon the chances of reelection. However, the Court still tends to follow general trends of society, particularly to the extent that the justices share the politics of the presidents who appoint them.

The Herring Case

This process continues today. In 2009, the case of *Herring v. United States* built upon the exclusionary rule precedents already mentioned and allowed Chief Justice John Roberts to build upon the good faith exception to the rule.

Essays

Bennie Dean Herring wished to retrieve items from his impounded pickup truck at the Coffee County, Alabama, Sheriff's Department. One of the department's investigators learned of Herring's presence. He asked the county warrant clerk to check for any outstanding warrants against Herring. When Coffee County's records produced no outstanding warrants, the investigator asked the clerk to call the warrant clerk for neighboring Dale County. A check of the Dale County database returned a record of an outstanding arrest warrant.

Within minutes, the Coffee County investigator, aided by a deputy, took Herring into custody on the Dale County warrant and searched his person, resulting in the discovery of methamphetamine, an illegal drug. A search of Herring's pickup truck yielded a pistol, which Herring, as a convicted felon, could not legally possess.

Meanwhile, the Dale County warrant clerk searched the paper files for a physical copy of the warrant to fax to Coffee County. This search instead led to the discovery that the freshly executed warrant for Herring's arrest had been recalled five months earlier. Still, Herring was indicted in federal court for illegal possession of the gun and of the drugs. Herring moved to suppress the evidence taken from his person and truck on grounds of an illegal arrest. A magistrate judge recommended denying this motion, the district court adopted that recommendation, and the circuit court of appeals **affirmed.** The Eleventh Circuit held that the Coffee County officers were innocent of wrongdoing, and the Dale County law enforcement official who had failed to update the records did so negligently rather than intentionally. This simple negligence, distanced from the actual arrest, meant that the exclusionary rule would have no future deterrence effect. The evidence was admissible under the good faith rule.

Further Definition
Writing for the majority, Chief Justice John Roberts affirmed the Eleventh Circuit's opinion, thus upholding Herring's convictions. However, the majority accepted the parties' assumption that Herring did suffer a violation of his Fourth Amendment rights.

The majority opinion rested upon four main points. First, an unreasonable search or arrest in violation of the Fourth Amendment does not necessarily lead to exclusion of evidence thus obtained. The exclusionary rule is not an individual right, but is instead enforced to applications resulting in **appreciable deterrence,** or preventing law enforcement officials from ignoring the Constitution's requirements without risking suppression of evidence discovered after an unreasonable entry. The benefits of deterrence must outweigh its costs, holding that the exclusionary rule will not apply when police act "in objectively reasonable reliance" upon a subsequently invalidated warrant.

The majority's second main point is that the extent to which the exclusionary rule is justified by the principles of deterrence varies with the guilt of the conduct of law enforcement. Flagrant misconduct would go against the good faith exception. Here, the chief justice factually distinguishes the flagrant conduct at issue in *Weeks* and *Mapp.* This discussion leads into the third main point of the opinion: triggering of the exclusionary rule requires sufficiently

deliberate police conduct such that exclusion can meaningfully deter it, as well as guilt great enough to justify the systemic costs of exclusion. The chief justice stated that exclusion serves to deter deliberate, reckless, grossly negligent, and occasionally systemically negligent conduct, none of which is met by the simple negligence at issue in *Herring*.

Finally, the majority's fourth point is that some police recordkeeping errors might trigger the exclusionary rule. Reckless recordkeeping, or intentional falsification of records, would justify exclusion should either scenario result in a Fourth Amendment violation. Reckless reliance by police upon a system routinely creating errors could also form a basis for exclusion. However, no such showings are made in the *Herring* case. The majority concluded that the marginal deterrence created by exclusion arising from negligent mistakes did not exceed the social costs weighed against it.

In her **dissent,** Justice Ruth Bader Ginsburg starts with the assertion that Herring was arrested and searched despite the lack of a warrant outstanding against him or probable cause to believe that he was engaged in criminal activity. This dissent refers to "a more majestic conception" of the Fourth Amendment and the exclusionary rule. This concept demands, in part, negligence liability to ensure proper and accurate recordkeeping. For example, computer data base error risks rise in step with the proliferation of data bases themselves, which have become the "nervous system of contemporary criminal justice operations," and the suppression of evidence resulting from data base error provides the previously insufficient incentive to ensure accuracy.

Evolving Protections

The *Herring* case demonstrates the ability of the law to change and evolve, even as the Constitution remains unchanged. Over the course of almost a century, the Supreme Court began with the idea that something besides the text of the Fourth Amendment had to protect personal privacy, and then undertook a long and continuing process of not merely identifying that extra protection as the exclusionary rule but slowly building up case law to explain exactly when that rule will operate, and when it will not.

Chief Justice Roberts wrote for a majority of only five justices in the *Herring* case; four justices disagreed. This 5-4 split in the Court is not uncommon. The Court often deals with "close questions," cases that could go either way because precedent exists on both sides. Many of the most famous Court decisions are exactly this sort of question. Many are decided upon a 5-4 vote.

Ongoing Interpretations

The Fourth Amendment is one of the many issues before the Court. In 2008, the Court decided on issues related to the First, Second, Eighth, and Fourteenth Amendments. The topics in these cases ranged from limitations on the amounts of money individuals may donate to political campaigns, to the constitutionality of the death penalty. One case reaffirmed the right of an individual to own a gun for lawful purposes, while another held that a state may require voters to present photo identification before they are permitted to cast a ballot.

Other issues before the Court came from federal statutes or regulations rather than the Constitution itself. Cases involving preemption, the idea that federal statute overrides state law on a particular subject, often comes before the Court. In the past few years, federal regulation of prescription drugs and medical devices, for example, has led to several important preemption cases. In another case, the Court decided that investors could not use a federal Securities and Exchange Commission (SEC) rule to sue a company the investors believed had cheated them on a stock price.

American society has become extremely complex and very diverse. Competing interests give rise to very different views of difficult questions. Some of these questions can seem very narrow and technical. Others require interpretation of basic constitutional rights. The sweeping questions that come before the Court tend to gain the most news coverage, but the Court also routinely settles issues that are basic and vital to American society and the economy. In all cases, the basic function of the Court as final interpreter of the Constitution, and the federal laws made under it, has remained the same for more than two hundred years. In molding past precedent to fit new circumstances, the Court continually affects the lives of citizens by ensuring that the Constitution remains a living and evolving framework for a nation grounded in basic principles—but forever changing.

Further Reading

Greenburg, Jan Crawford. *Supreme Conflict: The Inside Story of the Struggle for Control of the United States Supreme Court.* New York: Penguin, 2008.

Toobin, Jeffrey. *The Nine: Inside the Secret World of the Supreme Court.* New York: Anchor, 2008.

Trachtman, Michael G. *The Supremes' Greatest Hits: The 34 Supreme Court Cases That Most Directly Affect Your Life.* Sterling Publishers, 2006.

A–Z

Abortion, Constitutional Debate on

Fundamental issues surrounding an individual's right to terminate a pregnancy prior to birth. Abortion has been one of the most hotly debated constitutional issues since the landmark case of *Roe v. Wade* (1973) recognized a woman's constitutional right to abortion. In the years since *Roe*, the Supreme Court has considered frequent challenges to that decision.

Constitutional Issues

The question of the constitutionality of abortion turns on two basic issues: the right to privacy, and a legal concept known as substantive due process. Differences in opinion over how to interpret these issues are at the heart of the constitutional debate over abortion.

Right to Privacy

Pro-choice advocates argue that the decision to end a pregnancy is a private matter to be decided solely by the mother; the state should have no say in the decision. They hold that a basic right to privacy shields women from government interference in that decision. Abortion opponents counter that the Constitution contains no specific guarantee of a right to privacy. Indeed, whether such a right exists has been the subject of a number of Supreme Court cases.

The Court generally has considered the Fourteenth Amendment to guarantee a fairly broad right of privacy. That amendment's due process clause

provides that "No State shall . . . deprive any person of life, liberty, or property, without due process of law." The Court has used that clause to make rulings on a wide range of subjects, from marriage to child rearing to medical care. The landmark privacy case was *Griswold v. Connecticut* (1965), in which the Court struck down a state law banning the sale of contraceptives to married couples. The justices who voted with the majority offered various legal justifications for their decision, but the effect was to create a general expectation of a right to privacy.

Substantive Due Process

The due process clause of the Fourteenth Amendment addresses what are known as "procedural" rights—rights that specify the procedures by which a government can lawfully deprive a person of "life, liberty, or property." These rights do not prevent the individual's liberty from government infringement; they simply set limits on how the government may go about infringing upon them.

The Court, however, has developed the notion of "substantive due process," which holds that the due process clause guarantees that the state may not deprive a person of life, freedom, or property without appropriate justification. The Court has in effect decided that the due process clause addresses not only procedural rights but also substantive rights—general rights such as freedom of speech and religion. Substantive due process gives the Court great freedom to decide what rights are protected by due process and how far that protection extends. It can then compel states to change their laws to comply with these rights. Some members of the Court cited substantive due process as part of their reasoning in *Roe v. Wade*, as well as later cases touching upon abortion rights.

Landmark Cases

The first Supreme Court case to challenge an anti-abortion law was *United States v. Vuitch* (1971). In this case, opponents of existing District of Columbia laws tried to have the laws overturned on the grounds that the wording was too vague to be enforceable. In *Vuitch*, the Court never considered the issues of privacy or substantive due process that would become the key to the most important abortion case, *Roe v. Wade* (1973).

Roe v. Wade *(1973)*

In 1970, Norma McCorvey (alias "Jane Roe") and her lawyer, Sarah Weddington, brought suit in state court to overturn a Texas law that prohibited all abortions except to save the mother's life. *Roe* became one of a number of **test cases**—lawsuits filed to determine the courts' position on a matter of law—considered by the Court at the time that challenged existing abortion laws. It was the only one the Court chose to hear. The Court actually was forced to hear the case twice due to the retirements of ailing Justices Hugo Black and John Marshall Harlan II during the initial deliberations. The second hearing took place after Lewis Powell and William Rehnquist filled the vacant seats on the court in late 1971.

By a vote of 7-2, the Court struck down not only the Texas abortion law but abortion laws of almost every state. The Court declared abortion an absolute constitutional right during the first three months of pregnancy, and permissible during the second three months to protect the health of the mother. Six months into a pregnancy, the Court ruled that a state could regulate or ban abortion to protect the fetus. More significantly, the Court ruled that the right to privacy includes the right to abortion, and that a state must show it that has a "compelling interest" in having an anti-abortion law. The justices also concluded that the unborn are not "persons" as defined in the Fourteenth Amendment. This means that they are not entitled to the protections of the due process clause.

The decision in *Roe* has been the subject of nearly continuous controversy and debate since

the Court handed it down in 1973. Rehnquist and Byron White, the two dissenters from the majority opinion, continued to oppose the decision throughout their careers on the Court. The ruling in *Roe* stood unchallenged for more than a decade, but in 1989, Rehnquist and White joined a majority that broke with the 1973 ruling.

Webster v. Reproductive Health Services *(1989)*

In this case, the Court refused, by a 5-4 vote, to overturn a Missouri law stating that human life began at conception. The law also prohibited the use of state property for abortions and requiring women seeking later-term abortions to test for the viability of the fetus. However, the justices refused to completely overturn the decision in *Roe*, or to rule that the state had a "compelling interest" in protecting the unborn throughout pregnancy. *Roe* stood, even though the Court chose not to follow it in its ruling in *Webster*. It seemed that the Court was losing its commitment to retaining the *Roe* decision.

Planned Parenthood v. Casey *(1992)*

This case has replaced *Roe* as the basis for modern abortion law in the United States. The organization Planned Parenthood challenged a Pennsylvania law that required any woman who sought an abortion to undergo a twenty-four-hour waiting period and sign an informed consent form. The law also required minors seeking abortions to obtain parental consent, and wives to notify their husbands, before the procedure. In a 5-4 vote, the Court upheld all provisions of the law except the one requiring spousal notification.

In the majority opinion, centrist Justices Sandra Day O'Connor, Anthony Kennedy, and David Souter kept the basic ruling of *Roe v. Wade* but discarded the trimester (three-month) framework for determining the state's interest. Justice O'Connor also outlined a new "undue burden" standard to decide when the state was justified in intervening in the decision to have an abortion. This test asks courts to consider whether the law in question places an undue burden on a woman's right to choose an abortion. The state no longer needs to demonstrate a "compelling interest," as the Court ruled in *Roe v. Wade,* to pass regulations on abortion.

A - Z

Only a few justices were completely pleased with the final ruling. Justices Harry Blackmun and John Paul Stevens dissented with parts of the decision, arguing to retain much more of the original structure of *Roe v. Wade.* Chief Justice Rehnquist, along with Justices White, Antonin Scalia, and Clarence Thomas, joined in a dissenting opinion that argued for overturning *Roe* completely and returning to the previous standard when upholding the law.

More Recent Cases

Two later cases have focused on the more specific issue of late-term abortions—so-called "partial birth abortions." In *Stengberg v. Carhart* (2000), the Court overturned a Nebraska law that banned the procedure, declaring the law "an undue burden" on a woman's right to an abortion. Seven years later, however, in *Gonzales v. Carhart* (2007), the Court upheld a similar federal law banning the same procedure. It did not, however, rule out challenges to the law from individual women who argue that the procedure is necessary to preserve their health.

See also: Due Process; O'Connor, Sandra Day; Right to Privacy; *Roe v. Wade* (1973).

Further Reading

Friedman, Leon. *Abortion.* New York: Facts On File, 1995.

Rubin, Eva R., ed. *The Abortion Controversy.* New York: Praeger, 1993.

Affirmative Action

Measures taken by the federal government since the 1960s to benefit African Americans and other minorities in order to achieve greater equality. The phrase "affirmative action" originated in 1961 with an executive order issued by President John F. Kennedy (1961–1963). Setting the goal of achieving "equal opportunity" in federally funded projects, Kennedy said contractors should "take affirmative action" to make sure the hiring of workers was free of racial bias.

Most scholars, however, credited the concept of affirmative action to Kennedy's successor,

President Lyndon B. Johnson (1963–1969). The year after winning passage of the Civil Rights Act of 1964, Johnson told the graduating class at Howard University that ending discrimination was not enough. Advocates for minority rights took up Johnson's call for "equality as a fact and as a result." They insisted on "goals and timetables" that would measure racial progress in numbers. This triggered a backlash, particularly among white conservatives, who argued that the law demanded equal treatment for individuals, not equal results for groups.

In a series of lawsuits that reached the Supreme Court, the justices grappled with the practical meaning of equality in the law and in society. In a nation whose history includes black slavery and blatant racial bias, is it acceptable for employers and colleges to give qualified black applicants an edge in order to achieve overall equality, or does that system of advantages for some violate the rights of whites who lose out?

The Court found itself as divided and uncertain as the nation. The justices were unable to agree on clear, decisive rulings that either allowed the "affirmative" use of race, or rejected it entirely. In the most significant opinions, however, the Court left the door open for employers and colleges to make a limited use of affirmative action.

VIEWPOINTS

A political cartoonist expresses the view that, because the Supreme Court ruled that affirmative action policies are subject to strict examination, African Americans and other minorities still face discrimination, much as they did before the Civil War (1861–1865). (Mike Peters. Reprinted by permission: Tribune Media Services)

Regents of the University of California v. Bakke

One of the earliest cases to test the boundaries of affirmative action was the Court's 1978 ruling in *Regents of the University of California v. Bakke*. To ensure diversity as well as minority representation in the student body, the university had set aside sixteen seats for minority applicants in each medical school class of one hundred students. Allan Bakke, a thirty-eight-year-old white engineer, was twice denied admission to the medical school at the University of California at Davis. In each year his application was rejected, the school had accepted some minority applicants with qualifications inferior to his. Bakke argued that he would have been admitted had it not been for the university's rigid preference system.

On one point, the Court, in a 5-4 vote, told state universities that they may not set aside a fixed quota of seats in each class for minority group members, denying white applicants the opportunity to compete for those places. On a second point, a different five-justice majority held that admissions officers do not violate the equal protection guarantee when they consider race as one of many factors that determine which applicant is accepted and which is rejected. The Court ruled that colleges and universities may use a black applicant's race as a "plus factor" in admissions.

More Recent Cases

In the late 1990s, the Center for Individual Rights, a Washington-based law firm that opposed affirmative action, sued on behalf of two white women who had been rejected for admission by the University of Michigan. Each year the school enrolled about 350 new students, and school officials said they sought a "critical mass" of minority students who made up roughly 15 percent of the class. Barbara Grutter, a white student, applied to the law school in 1996 and was rejected, although her grades and test scores were better than most of the minority students who were accepted. In 1997 she sued Lee Bollinger, who was then dean of the law school, alleging she was denied the equal protection of the laws. During the trial, an expert for the law school testified that if a "race-blind admissions system" had been used, the percentage of minority students would have fallen from 14.5 percent to 4 percent in the entering law class of 2000.

Jennifer Gratz, a white student who applied in 1995 to the University of Michigan campus in Ann Arbor, would have won admission if she had been a minority applicant. The admissions office ranked applicants based on a 150-point index, and all minority applicants were awarded twenty bonus points. After Gratz was rejected, she too sued Bollinger, who had become the university president. A 5-4 majority upheld the law school's admissions policy in *Grutter v. Bollinger* (2003), while a 6-3 majority in *Gratz v. Bollinger* (2003) struck down Michigan's undergraduate admissions policy because of its point system.

Since affirmative action's inception, its underlying rationale has shifted considerably. At first, its proponents said "goals and timetables" were needed to stop discrimination. Like President Johnson, they said it was unfair and illogical to ignore centuries of oppression of blacks by whites. By the late 1980s, however, the Court had rejected past "societal discrimination" as a rationale for continuing affirmative action. Rather, advocates switched the focus to "diversity." Education officials argued that having students from rural as well as urban backgrounds, from small towns and big cities, from blue-collar homes as well as from those of highly paid professionals, makes for a richer experience for all. In 2003, the Court endorsed diversity as a "compelling" justification for affirmative action in colleges and universities.

See also: Equal Employment Opportunity; Racial Equality; Reverse Discrimination; *University of California Regents v. Bakke* (1978).

Further Reading

Curry, George. *The Affirmative Action Debate*. New York: Basic Books, 1996.

Kowalski, Kathiann M. *Affirmative Action (Open for Debate*. New York: Benchmark Books, 2006.

Aliens, Protection of

Court rulings that safeguard the rights of persons who reside in the United States but were born in another country and who have not become U.S. citizens. The Supreme Court has traditionally allowed the federal government to treat U.S. citizens and aliens differently. Because the

Constitution gives Congress absolute authority over immigrants' admission to the United States, as well as over their **naturalization,** the Court requires Congress only to present some rational basis for making a distinction between citizen and alien, or between some aliens and other aliens.

In *Yick Wo v. Hopkins* (1886), the Court declared that the Fourteenth Amendment protects persons, not just citizens. The justices required states to show more than a merely rational basis for a legal distinction between aliens and citizens. In later years, however, the Court would declare alienage, like race, a "suspect" category justifiable only by a compelling government interest.

By the early twentieth century, the country was growing suspicious of and hostile toward immigrants from certain countries. Congress established immigration quotas, based on national origin, which heavily favored the immigrants of northwestern Europe. In 1924, it passed a law that effectively barred most immigration from Asia. Following World War II (1939–1945), the Court took a more sympathetic stance toward the rights of aliens. A series of cases in the 1940s upheld the right of aliens to own and inherit property in the United States, and to earn a living.

Questions of discrimination against aliens did not come before the Court again until the 1970s. At that time, the Court ruled that states could not deny certain welfare benefits to aliens who pay state and federal taxes. Over the next few years, the Court struck down a variety of state laws barring aliens from certain types of employment and eligibility for state financial aid for higher education.

In 1982, the Court ruled that, regardless of their illegal status, aliens may not be denied the right to a free public education. This decision has sparked a great deal of controversy at the state and local level. Many citizens see this as an unnecessary drain on public funds and resources, which they feel should be reserved for U.S. citizens. Some state legislatures, including those of Virginia (in 2003) and Maryland (in 2007), have since attempted to pass laws barring aliens from admission to institutions of higher education.

See also: Citizenship and Naturalization; Education, Schools, and the Supreme Court; Equal Protection of the Law; *Korematsu v. United States* (1944).

Alito, Samuel A. (1950–)

Associate justice of the U.S. Supreme Court, appointed by President George W. Bush (2001–2009) and confirmed by Congress on January 24, 2006. Alito is the 110th justice to serve on the Court and the second Italian American to do so. Most observers consider him fairly conservative but less so than fellow Associate Justices Antonin Scalia and Clarence Thomas.

Alito was born in Trenton, New Jersey, in 1950, and graduated from Princeton University in 1972. He later attended Yale University Law School, earning his law degree in 1975. Between 1976 and 1990, Alito served in a series of positions in the U.S. Attorney's office, arguing twelve cases before the U.S. Supreme Court during this time. In 1987, he was appointed U.S. Attorney for the District of New Jersey. Three years later, President George H.W. Bush (1989–1993) nominated Alito for a position as judge on the U.S. Court of Appeals for the Third Circuit. The Senate unanimously confirmed the appointment.

When Associate Justice Sandra Day O'Connor announced her retirement from the Supreme Court in 2005, President George W. Bush first nominated White House Counsel Harriet Miers to fill the vacant seat. Miers later withdrew from consideration after widespread criticism that she was unqualified to hold the post; Bush then nominated Alito.

Although Alito was universally seen as qualified for the seat, many senators opposed his views on abortion, presidential powers, and **reapportionment.** As an appellate judge, Alito voted to uphold a law that required that a husband be notified when his wife sought an abortion. The Court later rejected Alito's reasoning. Critics also noted that Alito claimed that he had been motivated to go to law school by conservative writings criticizing the Court's decisions in the areas of criminal procedure, the **establishment clause,** and reapportionment. Alito's views led the American Civil Liberties Union (ACLU) to formally oppose his nomination, only the third Supreme Court nominee to be opposed by the group.

Samuel A. Alito, nominated to the Supreme Court by President George W. Bush (2001–2009), takes his oath as he prepares to testify at his Senate hearing in early 2006. After being confirmed by the Senate, Alito was sworn in as the 110th justice of the Supreme Court on January 31, 2006. (Reuters, Chuck Kennedy, Pool, Landov)

After his confirmation hearing, the Senate Judiciary Committee voted 10-8 to allow the full Senate to vote on the appointment. The committee vote was along party lines, with all ten Republican committee members voting in favor and all eight Democrats opposed. The vote in the full Senate was also close—58-42—and largely along party lines.

See also: Associate Justices; Circuit Court of Appeals; Confirmation of Justices and Judges; Nomination of Justices and Judges; O'Connor, Sandra Day; Scalia, Antonin; Thomas, Clarence.

A–Z

Appellate Jurisdiction

Power granted to certain courts to review and reverse decisions reached by lower courts. The term *jurisdiction* refers to the area in which a court may exercise its authority. Trial courts have what is known as "original jurisdiction"; that is, they are authorized to try a case when it is first introduced into the justice system. A party that loses a case in a trial court may file an appeal, or challenge, with a higher court that has appellate jurisdiction. Such a court is known as an appellate court or a court of appeals.

The U.S. Supreme Court is primarily an appellate court; it has original jurisdiction in only a limited number of cases specified by the Constitution. The Court may review decisions made by federal and state courts, as well as laws passed by other branches of the federal government. However, it may rule only on judgments that involve a question of constitutional law or federal **statutory law.**

Article Three of the Constitution gives the government power to create "such inferior Courts as the Congress may from time to time ordain and establish." Using this authority, Congress has created hundreds of federal trial courts (known as district courts) spread among 89 separate judicial districts. These districts are grouped into twelve geographical regions, or circuits. Each judicial circuit also contains a court of appeals, or circuit court, that has appellate jurisdiction over the district courts in its circuit. In general, parties have an automatic right to appeal the orders of a district court to a circuit court.

Appellate courts focus on issues of law. They may overturn a lower court decision if the lower court misapplied the facts to the law or applied the wrong legal standard. Appellate courts typically do not rule on decisions made by the trial court concerning the facts of a case. When they do review issues of fact, they usually look for cases of "clear error." In general, appellate courts defer to the original findings of the trial judge and jury, who saw the evidence and observed witnesses' testimony firsthand. An appellate court may also review some of the decisions a lower court judge made during a trial, such as refusing to allow evidence.

See also: Circuit Court of Appeals; Circuit Court of Appeals Act of 1891; Jurisdiction of the Supreme Court; Original Jurisdiction.

Articles of Confederation

The original governing document of the United States of America, which was later replaced by the U.S. Constitution. The Articles of Confederation was drafted in 1777, during the early years of the American Revolution (1775–1783). The aspiring nation adopted the form and function of the federal government outlined in the Articles but did not **ratify,** or formally approve, the document until 1781. Just six years later, dissatisfied with the relative powerlessness of the federal government, representatives of the states met to amend the Articles. They would ultimately write an entirely new governing document, the Constitution.

The Articles called for a confederation, or loose alliance, between the various states. They gave the federal government the power to make war, to negotiate treaties, to mint coins and borrow money, and to deal with issues concerning the Western territories of the United States. The Articles also created a "perpetual" union between the states, each of which was required to abide by the terms of the Articles.

While the Articles proved to be sufficient to govern the country during the Revolution, their weaknesses became apparent after the war was won. Two of the main shortcomings of the Articles were the fact that they gave the federal government no control over commerce between the states and, perhaps more important, no power to raise taxes from the states. As a result, the federal government had little effective power. Another major weakness of the Articles was their failure to provide for a federal court system.

These problems were brought home in 1786 when a group of Massachusetts farmers, struggling under large debts and heavy local taxes, formed an army and attacked a federal armory. The initial response by the government to the uprising, known as Shays's Rebellion, was slow and hesitant. Although the rebellion was soon put down, many citizens and lawmakers saw the incident as a warning that the Articles left the central government too weak to perform its duties.

Later that year, representatives of several states called for a convention to meet and address the problems with the federal government. This meeting produced little in the way of concrete action, but by early 1787 momentum was gathering to amend the Articles. That summer, representatives from the states met at the Second Constitutional Convention in Philadelphia to take up that task. The Articles, however, did not survive the convention, whose delegates instead adopted the Constitution, which provided for a much more robust central government.

See also: Constitution, U.S.; Constitutional Convention.

Associate Justices

In the U.S. Supreme Court, the eight members who serve in addition to the chief justice. In most ways, associate justices exercise the same power

Associate Justices' Salaries

Years	Salary	Years	Salary
1789–1819	$3,500	1982–1983*	96,700
1819–1855	4,500	1984	100,600
1855–1871	6,000	1985–1986	104,100
1871–1873	8,000	1987	110,000
1873–1903	10,000	1990	118,600
1903–1911	12,500	1991	153,600
1911–1926	14,500	1992	159,000
1926–1946	20,000	1993–1998	164,100
1946–1955	25,000	1999	167,900
1955–1964	35,000	2000	173,600
1964–1969	39,500	2001	178,300
1969–1975	60,000	2002	184,400
1975	63,000	2003	190,100
1976*	66,000	2004	194,300
1977	72,000	2005	199,200
1978*	76,000	2006	203,000
1979*	81,300	2007	203,000
1980*	88,700	2008	208,100
1981*	93,000	2009	208,100

*A cost-of-living adjustment equal to 5 percent of regular salary.

As with other federal officials, the salaries of associate justices have increased over time. Associate justices make slightly less than the chief justice.

A–Z

Foreign-Born Justices

- **James Wilson,** born on September 14, 1742, in Caskardy, Scotland. Wilson grew up in Scotland and was educated at St. Andrews University in preparation for a career in the ministry. But in 1765 he sailed for America, where he studied law and became a land speculator. A signer of the Declaration of Independence, Wilson also was a member of the 1787 Constitutional Convention and its Committee of Detail, which was responsible for writing the first draft of the Constitution. In 1789, President George Washington appointed Wilson one of the original members of the Supreme Court.

- **James Iredell,** born on October 5, 1751, in Lewes, England. Iredell was born into an old English family allegedly descended from Oliver Cromwell's son-in-law. Through family connections, Iredell received an appointment as colonial comptroller of customs at Edenton, North Carolina, at age seventeen. After six years, he was promoted to collector of the port of Edenton. But Iredell identified with the colonial cause and resigned his job as collector in 1776. While serving in his colonial offices, Iredell had studied law and began practice in 1770. By 1788, he had become a strong supporter of the new federal Constitution and worked for its ratification by North Carolina. President Washington appointed him a Court justice in 1790.

- **William Paterson,** born on December 24, 1745, in County Antrim, Ireland. Paterson emigrated to America with his parents when he was only two years old. He received his education at the College of New Jersey (now Princeton University) and then read law, opening his own law practice in 1769. Paterson was active in New Jersey affairs during the Revolutionary and Confederation periods, and he served as a delegate to the Constitutional Convention in 1787. He was a member of the First Senate from 1789 to 1790 and, as a member of the Judiciary Committee, helped to write the Judiciary Act of 1789. Later, he codified the laws of the state of New Jersey and, in association with Alexander Hamilton, laid out plans for the industrial city of Paterson. He was appointed to the Supreme Court by President George Washington in 1793.

- **David Brewer,** born on June 20, 1837, in Smyrna, Asia Minor, where his father was serving as a Congregational missionary. Brewer's mother was the sister of Justice Stephen J. Field (1863–1897) and Cyrus W. Field, promoter of the first Atlantic cable. The family returned to the United States soon after Brewer's birth. Brewer sought his fortune in Kansas and spent most of his career in the Kansas court system and lower federal courts. He was elevated to the Supreme Court by President Benjamin Harrison in 1890.

- **George Sutherland,** born on March 25, 1862, in Buckinghamshire, England. Sutherland's father converted to Mormonism about the time of George's birth and moved his family to the Utah Territory. Although the senior Sutherland soon deserted the Mormons, the family remained in Utah, where George was educated at Brigham Young Academy (now Brigham Young University). When Utah entered the Union as a state in 1896, Sutherland was elected to the state legislature. In 1900, he won a seat in the U.S. House and served two terms in the U.S. Senate (1905–1917) before being defeated in a bid for reelection. While in the Senate, he formed a close friendship with a fellow senator, Warren G. Harding of Ohio. When Harding became president, he appointed Sutherland to the Court.

- **Felix Frankfurter,** born on November 15, 1882, in Vienna, Austria. Frankfurter came to the United States with his parents in 1894 and grew up on the Lower East Side of New York City. He had a brilliant academic record at City College and Harvard Law School, after which he practiced law for a time in New York City. In 1914, he joined the Harvard Law faculty and remained there, with time out for government service during World War I, until his appointment to the Court by President Franklin D. Roosevelt in 1939.

The Constitution does not require that Supreme Court justices be native-born Americans. Therefore, presidents are free to name foreign-born persons to the Court. To date, six Supreme Court justices have been born outside the United States, one the son of an American missionary abroad. Of the remaining five, four were born in the British Isles. Only one, Felix Frankfurter, was born in a non-English-speaking country, Austria. President George Washington appointed three of the foreign-born justices. The others were selected by Presidents Benjamin Harrison, Warren G. Harding, and Franklin D. Roosevelt.

as the chief justice, because each justice casts a single vote in cases that appear before the Court. The chief justice, however, does have additional duties and responsibilities that set the office apart as "first among equals" on the Court.

Article III of the U.S. Constitution established the Supreme Court but did not specify its structure or composition. Article II mentions the office of chief justice, but only to note that that officer presides over presidential impeachment trials. The Constitution makes no specific mention of associate justices. Even the total number of justices was not established until passage of the Judiciary Act of 1789. That act called for a court consisting of a chief justice and five associate justices.

Congress has periodically changed the number of associate justices on the Court. It added a justice in 1807 in response to population growth in what was then the Western frontier. In 1869, Congress added two more associate justices after the Court struck down a law by a 4-3 vote. The Court reheard the case after the new justices were seated and reversed the earlier decision by a vote of 5-4. During the 1930s, President Franklin D. Roosevelt (1933–1945) unsuccessfully attempted to add associate justices to the Court who would be sympathetic to his legislative proposals, which a majority of the sitting justices had ruled to be unconstitutional. This was the last serious attempt to alter the composition of the court.

Surprisingly, there are no written qualifications for serving on the Court. The Constitution specifies no age limits, does not require that justices be native-born citizens, and does not even require them to have a legal background. The president may nominate anyone to fill a vacancy on the Court. The Senate Judiciary Committee then holds hearings to determine whether to allow the full Senate to vote on the nominee. The support of a simple majority of senators is required to approve the nomination. Of the 150 Supreme Court nominees since the founding of the nation, only twenty-eight have been rejected by the Senate.

Although all associate justices are theoretically equal, they are ranked according to seniority. Justices who have served on the Court longer are more senior than more recently appointed justices. Seniority plays some role in their actions and duties. For example, when the Court reaches a decision, the senior justice among those in the majority writes the opinion for the Court, unless the chief justice specifically assigns the task to another justice. In addition, when deliberating cases, justices customarily offer their arguments in order of seniority.

See also: Chief Justice of the United States; Confirmation of Justices and Judges; Judiciary Act of 1789; Nomination of Justices and Judges; Roosevelt's 1937 Court Reform Plan.

Automobile Searches

Supreme Court rulings that outline acceptable and unacceptable procedures that authorities may use when searching an automobile. The Fourth Amendment prohibits "unreasonable" searches and seizures, and this prohibition extends to automobiles, including to their drivers and passengers. However, it is considerably less strict when compared to the rule governing searches of homes and other private spaces.

Police officers generally do not need warrants to stop cars and to search a vehicle or its passengers and luggage. An officer who has "reasonable suspicion" that a driver is intoxicated or otherwise violating the law may pull the vehicle to the side of the road and investigate further. The officer may look inside for a weapon in plain sight, and may search the car if he or she sees evidence of illegal drugs or alcohol. When a driver gets behind the wheel and takes a car on the public roadways, the balance of what is considered an "unreasonable" search tips in favor of the government. The Court holds that the privacy interests of individuals must be balanced against the government's interest in enforcing the law.

The landmark case in this area is *Carroll v. United States* (1925). George Carroll was convicted of transporting liquor for sale in violation of a federal law at the time that prohibited the manufacture and distribution of alcohol. Federal agents, acting without a search warrant, had taken the liquor from his car used it as evidence against him. The Court rejected Carroll's argument

Although the Fourth Amendment prohibits unreasonable searches and seizures of a person's property, the Supreme Court has ruled that law enforcement officials have wide latitude when stopping and searching vehicles. These officers are searching a car in the driveway of a home where five suspects were arrested on charges of drug possession. (AP Photo, Imperial Valley Press, Todd Kraninin)

against that this seizure violated his Fourth Amendment rights.

Subsequent rulings have clarified the scope of exceptions to the requirement to obtain a warrant to search an automobile. In 1949, the Court ruled that warrantless searches of automobiles are reasonable if police have probable cause to believe the cars were involved in illegal activity. That is still the standard used today. In *Rakas v. Illinois* (1978), the Court extended search exceptions to passengers. It held that passengers do not have the right to challenge the warrantless search of the vehicle in which they are riding or the use of evidence seized in that search against them.

On a few occasions, the Court has ruled that the police went too far in stopping or searching a car for no specific reason. Rarely, however, has it rejected searches and seizures on highways when the police could furnish a specific reason for their actions. Moreover, the reason cited by an officer for stopping a car need not be the true reason. The Court ruled unanimously in *United States v. Whren* (1996) that officers may stop cars for minor traffic violations as a "pretext" to search for drugs.

See also: Probable Cause; Search Warrants; Unreasonable Search and Seizure.

★ ★ ★ B ★ ★ ★

Bail

Money or property pledged by an accused person to guarantee his or her appearance at trial. The Eighth Amendment states that "[e]xcessive bail shall not be required." Throughout U.S. history, federal law has provided that persons arrested for noncapital offenses—those not punishable by death—shall be granted the right to post bail and win release to participate in preparing their defense. The Court has held that a presumption in favor of granting bail exists in the Bill of Rights.

The Federal Rules of Criminal Procedure provide that the courts determine the amount of bail based on the nature and circumstances of the offense, the weight of the evidence, the defendant's ability to pay, and his or her general character. Under the 1966 Bail Reform Act, almost all persons charged with noncapital federal offenses are able to obtain release on personal recognizance or unsecured bond.

The leading Supreme Court decision on the question of excessive bail is *Stack v. Boyle* (1951). In this case, the government **indicted,** or formally charged with a crime, twelve communist leaders in California for conspiracy under the Alien Registration Act of 1940. The court set bail at $50,000 for each defendant. The defendants argued that the amount of bail was excessive and in violation of the Eighth Amendment. The Court agreed.

The following spring, however, the Court held that the Eighth Amendment did not guarantee an absolute right to bail. Authorities had detained certain alien communists prior to a hearing on their deportation. The attorney general, acting under provisions of the Internal Security Act of 1950, denied the defendants' application for bail. In *Carlson v. Landon* (1952), the Court rejected the defendants' argument that bail should be granted. Justice Stanley F. Reed, writing for the

majority, stated that the Eighth Amendment does not guarantee everyone detained by federal authority the right to be released on bail.

Twice in the 1980s, the Supreme Court approved the denial of bail to certain suspects. In 1984, it upheld the denial to dangerous juveniles, and, in 1987, to organized crime figures. In *United States v. Salerno* (1987), Chief Justice William H. Rehnquist discussed the Eighth Amendment guarantee, pointing out that it "says nothing about whether bail shall be available at all." The primary function of bail, he acknowledged, "is to safeguard the courts' role in adjudicating the guilt of innocence of the defendants [by preventing flight]." The Eighth Amendment does not, however, deny the government the opportunity to regulate pretrial release for other reasons. "We believe," Rehnquist concluded, "that when Congress has mandated detention on the basis of a compelling interest other than prevention of flight, as it has here, the Eighth Amendment does not require release on bail."

See also: Constitution of the United States.

Baker v. Carr (1962)

Supreme Court case that established the principle that **reapportionment** of seats in state legislatures was an issue that fell within the **jurisdiction** of the Court. Reapportionment involves the periodic redistribution of seats in a legislature based on changes in population.

Basis of the Case

The case centered on complaints by residents in urban areas of Tennessee that they were underrepresented in the state legislature. By 1962, despite a dramatic shift in population from rural to urban areas in the early to mid-twentieth century, the Tennessee legislature had not reapportioned

Landmark Decision Highlights: *Baker v. Carr* (1962)

Issue: Whether the Supreme Court has jurisdiction over questions of legislative apportionment

Opinion: Citing past examples, the Court determined that it has jurisdiction to intervene to correct violations in matters pertaining to state administration. The Court concluded that the Fourteenth Amendment equal protection issues, which Baker and others raised in this case, merited judicial evaluation.

itself for sixty years. Legislative districts in rural areas held nearly twice as many seats as they would have been entitled to by apportionment on a population basis alone. For example, one of the worst instances of malapportionment was the Alabama state legislature's refusal to reapportion either the House or Senate from 1901 until 1972. As a result, by 1960, 25 percent of the state's population controlled the majority of the seats in a legislature dominated by white legislators from rural areas. A similar degree of imbalance existed with respect to congressional districts.

Appeals to the legislature to reapportion itself were futile. A suit brought in state court was rejected on the grounds that state courts, like federal courts, should stay out of such legislative matters. The city dwellers who brought the state suit then appealed to the federal courts, charging that the "unconstitutional and obsolete" apportionment system denied them the equal protection of the laws promised by the Fourteenth Amendment.

The Court's Ruling

In *Baker v. Carr*, the Court abandoned the view that such claims were political questions outside the competence of the courts. It ruled, 6-2, that constitutional challenges to legislative malapportionment were "justiciable"—that is, suitable to be decided by the courts. The Court stopped there, refusing to address the question of whether the current apportionment in Tennessee was unconstitutional.

In his majority opinion, Justice William J. Brennan Jr. argued that the case fell within the federal judicial power as defined in Article III: "An unbroken line of our precedents sustains the federal courts' jurisdiction of the subject matter of federal constitutional claims of this nature." Turning to the question of the voters' **standing,** or legal right, to bring the case, Brennan explained that they did have standing because they had been deprived of an interest they sought to defend.

Brennan also asserted that the suit did not present a "political question" outside the proper scope of the Court's consideration:

> [T]he mere fact that the suit seeks protection of a political right does not mean it presents a political question . . . It is argued that apportionment cases, whatever the actual wording of the complaint, can involve no federal constitutional right except one resting on the guaranty of a republican form of government, and that complaints based on that clause have been held to present political questions which are nonjusticiable.
>
> We hold that the claim pleaded here neither rests upon nor implicates the Guaranty Clause and that its justiciability is therefore not foreclosed by our decisions of cases involving that clause.

The guaranty clause to which Brennan refers is in Article IV, Section 4, of the Constitution: "The United States shall guarantee to every State in this Union a Republican Form of Government." *Luther v. Borden* (1849), which resulted in one of the first major examinations of the "political question" doctrine, involved this guarantee. In that case, the Court held the clause's enforcement to be a political question outside judicial competence and one best left to the political branches— Congress and the president. *Baker v. Carr* rendered the guaranty clause virtually useless.

Dissent and Aftermath

In a dissenting opinion, Justice John Marshall Harlan II argued that the Constitution does not require proportional representation in legislative districts. "Nothing in the Equal Protection Clause or elsewhere in the Federal Constitution," he wrote, "expressly or impliedly supports the view that state legislatures must be so structured as to reflect with approximate equality the voice of every voter . . . In short, there is nothing in the Federal Constitution to prevent a State, acting not irrationally, from choosing any electoral legislative structure it thinks best suited to the interests, temper, and customs of its people."

Baker v. Carr opened the doors of federal courtrooms across the country to individuals challenging state and congressional apportionment systems. However, it provided no standards to guide federal judges in determining whether the challenged systems were valid. In 1963 and 1964, the Court created a standard, known as the "one man, one vote" or "one person, one vote" rule, by which to evaluate apportionment plans.

See also: 📖 *Baker v. Carr*, 1962, in the **Primary Source Library;** Jurisdiction of the Supreme Court; One Person, One Vote.

Further Reading

Graham, Gene S. *One Man, One Vote: Baker v. Carr and the American Levellers*. New York: Little Brown, 1972.

Bankruptcy and Bankruptcy Laws

The legal declaration that an individual is unable to pay his or her debts, and the laws establishing the legal rights and responsibilities of a person who declares bankruptcy. A person or business that declares bankruptcy is relieved of paying much of their debt but often must surrender assets to satisfy creditors. In the United States, there are several forms of bankruptcy, whose terms vary depending upon whether an individual or a firm is involved. and according to the specific circumstances of each case.

The Constitution says little about the subject except to authorize Congress to make "uniform Laws on the subject of Bankruptcies." Congress enacted bankruptcy laws in 1800, 1841, and 1867 to meet specific economic crises, but each of these laws was repealed a few years after passage.

In its first bankruptcy law, Congress extended coverage to bankers, brokers, commodities agents, and insurance underwriters, as well as to tradespeople. The Court has since given its implicit approval to laws extending bankruptcy coverage to almost every class of person and corporation. The Court also has approved federal laws to rehabilitate the debtor as well as to provide appropriate relief to creditors.

In 1982, the Court for the first time struck down a federal bankruptcy law because it violated the constitutional standard of uniformity. The Court ruled a 1980 law passed to protect the employees of the Rock Island Railroad to be invalid because it gave the employees protection not available to people who worked for other bankrupt railroads. The same year, the Court sent Congress back to the drawing board in its effort to reform the nation's bankruptcy laws. The Court held that a comprehensive reform law passed in 1978 violated Article III, which provides that federal judicial power be exercised only by federal judges whose independence is assured. The law would have created a new corps of bankruptcy judges with broad powers but without the guarantees of life tenure and fixed compensation that federal judges enjoy.

In 2005, Congress passed the Bankruptcy Abuse Prevention and Consumer Protection Act, which significantly amended the federal bankruptcy code. Under the new law, Americans who have the ability to pay will be required to pay back at least a portion of their debts. Those who earn less than their state's median income will not be required to repay their debts. The law also imposes limits on debt relief for individuals who declare bankruptcy more than once. In addition, the law makes it more difficult for people struggling primarily with consumer debts (such as credit cards) to qualify for financial relief under Chapter 7 of the Bankruptcy Code.

Bill of Rights

The first ten amendments to the U.S. Constitution, which guarantee basic civil rights. As written, the Bill of Rights protects people only against actions taken by the federal government. Early in the nation's history, the Supreme Court refused to extend those protections to civil rights threatened by state action. In the mid-1920s, however, the Court began using the Fourteenth Amendment's guarantee of due process to protect certain of those individual rights against infringement by a state.

Freedoms Guaranteed by the Bill of Rights

The First Amendment forbids Congress to restrict freedom of religion, speech, the press, peaceable assembly, and petition. The Second Amendment ensures the right of the states to maintain militias. In connection with that state right, it also protects the right of the people to keep and bear arms. The Third Amendment restricts the government's power to quarter soldiers in people's homes. The Fourth Amendment protects individuals against unreasonable searches or seizures.

The Fifth Amendment requires **indictment,** or the filing of a formal charge, against anyone accused of a capital or otherwise serious crime. It forbids trying a person twice for the same offense or compelling a person to testify against himself or herself. The due process clause of the amendment states that no one should be deprived of life, liberty, or property without "due process of law," and it protects private property from being taken for public use without just compensation.

The Sixth Amendment guarantees a speedy and public jury trial for all persons accused of crimes, with an impartial jury selected from the area where an alleged crime occurred. It also guarantees defendants the right to be notified of the charges against them, to confront witnesses testifying against them, to compel witnesses to testify in their favor, and to have the aid of an attorney in their defense.

The Seventh Amendment provides for a jury trial in all common-law suits involving more than twenty dollars. The Eighth Amendment forbids excessive bail, excessive fines, and cruel and unusual punishment. The Ninth and Tenth Amendments do not guarantee specific rights. The Ninth declares that the mention in the Constitution of certain rights should not be interpreted as denying or disparaging other rights retained by the people. The Tenth reserves to the states, or to the people, all powers not specifically granted by the Constitution to the national government nor prohibited by the Constitution to the states.

The Struggle for Incorporation

An early case that tested the applicability of the Bill of Rights to state actions was *Barron v. Baltimore* (1833). In this case the city had dumped tons of debris from its street paving operation into Baltimore's harbor. This obstructed part of the harbor, making it unusable. John Barron, the co-owner of a wharf on the harbor, sued the city for damages resulting from loss of business, but lost his case. He then appealed to the Supreme Court, claiming that dumping amounted to taking his private property without compensation, a violation of his rights under the Fifth Amendment. The Court, however, rejected his argument.

Ratification of the Fourteenth Amendment in 1868 marked the first move toward applying the Bill of Rights to state actions. The amendment states, in part, "No state shall make or enforce any law which shall abridge the privileges or immunities of citizens of the United States; nor shall any state deprive any person of life, liberty, or property, without due process of law; nor deny to any person within its jurisdiction the equal protection of the laws." Nevertheless, for many years afterward the Court continued to issue rulings that indicated the amendment did not give citizens the full protections of the Bill of Rights against state actions.

Extending the Bill of Rights

It was not until the 1920s that the Court began to incorporate protections guaranteed by the Bill of Rights into the Fourteenth Amendment's due process clause. The first major case in this area was *Gitlow v. New York* (1925), in which the Court overturned a state law that forbade the publication of materials advocating the overthrow of government. The Court agreed that the Fourteenth Amendment's due process clause included the First Amendment guarantee of freedom of the press.

Over the following years, the Court incorporated other Bill of Rights guarantees into the Fourteenth Amendment's due process clause. Then, in the mid-twentieth century, that amendment's equal protection guarantee came into use as the effective guarantor of individual rights that its authors had intended it to be. Using the equal protection clause as a measure, the Court struck down state laws requiring racial segregation in public schools, on public transportation, and in public accommodations, setting off a civil rights

Cases Incorporating Provisions of the Bill of Rights into the Due Process Clause of the Fourteenth Amendment

Constitutional Provision	Case
First Amendment	
Freedom of speech and press	Gitlow v. New York (1925)
Freedom of assembly	DeJonge v. Oregon (1937)
Freedom of petition	Hague v. CIO (1939)
Free exercise of religion	Cantwell v. Connecticut (1940)
Establishment of religion	Everson v. Board of Education (1947)
Fourth Amendment	
Unreasonable search and seizure	Wolf v. Colorado (1949)
Exclusionary rule	Mapp v. Ohio (1961)
Fifth Amendment	
Compensation for the taking of private property	Chicago, Burlington and Quincy R. Co. v. Chicago (1897)
Self-incrimination	Malloy v. Hogan (1964)
Double jeopardy	Benton v. Maryland (1969)
When jeopardy attaches	Crist v. Bretz (1978)
Sixth Amendment	
Public trial	In re Oliver (1948)
Due notice	Cole v. Arkansas (1948)
Right to counsel (felonies)	Gideon v. Wainwright (1963)
Confrontation and cross-examination of adverse witnesses	Pointer v. Texas (1965)
Speedy trial	Klopfer v. North Carolina (1967)
Compulsory process to obtain witnesses	Washington v. Texas (1967)
Jury trial	Duncan v. Louisiana (1968)
Right to counsel (misdemeanor when jail is possible)	Argersinger v. Hamlin (1972)
Cruel and unusual punishment	Louisiana ex rel. Francis v. Resweber (1947)
Ninth Amendment	
Privacy*	Griswold v. Connecticut (1965)

* The word *privacy* does not appear in the Ninth Amendment (or elsewhere in the Constitution). In *Griswold*, several members of the Court viewed the Ninth Amendment as guaranteeing (and incorporating) that right.

NOTE: The Court has not incorporated the following provisions: Second Amendment right to keep and bear arms; Third Amendment right against quartering soldiers; Fifth Amendment right to a grand jury hearing; Seventh Amendment right to a jury in civil cases; and Eighth Amendment right against excessive bail and fines.

For more than a century after ratification of the Bill of Rights, the Supreme Court held that its protection of individual rights did not extend to persons threatened by state action. In the early twentieth century, however, the Court, on a case-by-case basis, began to federalize several of these protections. The justices did so by applying the due process guarantee of the Fourteenth Amendment to those rights deemed to be "fundamental." This process of selective incorporation unfolded over a number of years.

The Twenty-Seventh Amendment

Can Congress extend the deadline for ratification of a proposed constitutional amendment? Opponents of the Equal Rights Amendment (ERA) posed that question in their challenge to a 39-month extension that was approved by Congress in October 1978. The proposed amendment, which would have given men and women equal rights under the law, originally provided seven years for ratification, with an expiration date of March 22, 1979. The 1978 extension moved the deadline to June 29, 1982. At the time Congress passed the extension, thirty-five states had ratified the amendment, so three more states were needed for the ERA to become the Twenty-seventh Amendment.

Debate on the extension centered on its constitutionality, an issue that the Supreme Court had never considered. In *Dillon v. Gloss* (1921) the Court had ruled that Congress has the authority to set a reasonable time period in which the states must ratify a proposed constitutional amendment, and in *Coleman v. Miller* (1939) the Court held that the question of what constitutes a reasonable time period was a political matter for Congress to determine. A related issue concerning ERA ratification was whether states that had ratified the amendment could subsequently rescind (take back) ratification. As of July 1979, Idaho, Nebraska, South Dakota, and Tennessee had done just that. In *Coleman*, the Court had written that the matter "should be regarded as a political question pertaining to the political departments, with the ultimate authority in the Congress in the exercise of its control over the promulgation of the adoption of the amendment."

revolution that continues today. Black citizens were not the only beneficiaries of equal protection rulings; during the second half of the twentieth century, the Court found a similar rationale useful for discarding laws that discriminated against women and aliens as well.

See also: Aliens, Protection of; Constitution of the United States; Due Process; Equal Protection of the Law; Freedom of Assembly; Freedom of Association; Freedom of Religion; Freedom of the Press; Freedom to Petition; *Slaughterhouse Cases* (1873); Unreasonable Search and Seizure.

Bills of Attainder

A legislative act that inflicts punishment without a judicial trial. Article I of the Constitution forbids federal and state legislatures to enact bills of attainder or ex post facto laws—laws that punish past actions or declare an action a crime after it has been committed. The Court has declared only three acts of Congress to be bills of attainder and only one to be an ex post facto law.

In 1867, the Court struck down an 1865 law that barred attorneys from practicing before federal courts unless they had sworn an oath that they had remained loyal to the Union throughout the Civil War. Persons taking the oath falsely could be charged with and convicted of perjury. A.H. Garland of Arkansas had been admitted to practice law before the federal courts during the 1860 Supreme Court term. When Arkansas subsequently seceded, Garland went with his state, becoming first a representative and then a senator in the Confederate Congress.

In 1865, Garland received a full pardon from the president for his service to the Confederacy. His case, *Ex parte Garland*, came to the Court two years later, when he sought to practice in federal

SPOTLIGHT

In 1981, a federal judge in Idaho ruled that Congress had exceeded its power in extending the ERA ratification deadline. The ruling declared that states could rescind their approval of the amendment if they acted during the ratification period. Early in 1982, the Court agreed to hear an appeal on these rulings, but after the ratification period expired on June 30, the Court dismissed the case, leaving the issues unresolved. The proposed ERA died.

Ironically, the Twenty-seventh Amendment that was ratified and added to the Constitution in 1992 had the longest period of consideration by the states— more than 202 years. The Twenty-seventh Amendment was originally proposed in 1789 by James Madison as a part of the Bill of Rights. However, it was not ratified in 1791, when the Bill of Rights was approved and added to the Constitution. A few states ratified the proposed amendment later in the 1800s, but it was largely forgotten. In 1982, the languishing amendment was discovered by a student at the University of Texas at Austin. He began a push for the proposal's ratification. Then, on May 5, 1992, Alabama became the 38th state to ratify the amendment, thus making it a part of the U.S. Constitution. The new amendment states:

> No law, varying the compensation for the services of the Senators and Representatives, shall take effect, until an election of Representatives shall have intervened.

courts without taking the required loyalty oath. The Court reasoned that lawyers who had served with the Confederacy could not take the oath without perjuring themselves. The act thus constituted a bill of attainder because it punished former Confederates without benefit of a trial.

The second instance occurred in 1946, when Congress passed an act that blocked the **appropriation,** or setting aside of money, to pay the salaries of three government employees. Democratic Representative Martin Dies of Texas sponsored the act, declaring that the employees were affiliated with communist front organizations. The Court struck down this law, declaring, "Legislative acts, no matter what their form, that apply either to named individuals or to easily ascertainable members of a group in such a way as to inflict punishment on them without a judicial trial are bills of attainder."

In *United States v. Brown* (1965), the Court again found that Congress had enacted a bill of attainder when it approved a provision of the Labor Management and Reporting Act of 1959. This act declared it a crime for a present or former member of the Communist Party to serve as an officer or employee of a labor union. The Supreme Court, however, found this provision unconstitutional, because it punished individuals for their former associations. As such, the Court considered not only a bill of attainder but also an ex post facto law.

See also: Ex Post Facto Laws.

Brandeis, Louis D. (1856–1941)

Highly influential Supreme Court justice whose opinions favored the common people as opposed to special interest. The first Jewish justice, Louis D. Brandeis was nominated by President Woodrow Wilson (1913–1921) on January 28, 1916, to replace Joseph R. Lamar, who had died. Brandeis was confirmed by the Senate on June 1, 1916, by a 47-22 vote and took the judicial oath on June 15, 1916.

Louis Dembitz Brandeis was the son of Adolph and Fredericka Dembitz Brandeis, Jews who had emigrated from Bohemia after the unsuccessful democratic revolts of 1848. His father was a prosperous grain merchant who provided his family with comfort, education, and culture. Having completed two years of preparatory studies in Dresden, Germany, but without a college degree, Brandeis enrolled at Harvard Law School when he was eighteen years of age. He graduated in 1877 with the highest average in the law school's history. After eight months practicing law in St. Louis, Missouri, Brandeis returned to Cambridge, Massachusetts, and with Bostonian Samuel D. Warren Jr., who ranked second in their law school class, opened a one-room law office.

The late 1800s and early 1900s marked the rapid growth of corporate monopolies—the "curse of bigness," as Brandeis described it. He chose to protect the rights not of special interest groups but of the general public, and usually without a fee for his services. Brandeis initiated sliding scale gas rates in Boston, which lowered consumer costs while raising corporate dividends, and instituted savings bank insurance policies, another reform later implemented in the rest of the country. He defended municipal control of Boston's subway system and opposed the monopolistic practices of the New Haven Railroad. He arbitrated labor disputes in New York's garment industry and established the constitutionality of state maximum hour and minimum wage statutes. For thirty-seven years, Brandeis devoted his time, energy, and talents to a host of public causes. He called himself an "attorney for the situation," but the press adopted the popular title "people's attorney."

President Wilson respected Brandeis and often sought his opinion. Wilson nominated him associate justice of the Supreme Court on January 28, 1916, to fill the vacancy left by Justice Joseph Lamar's death. However, vicious opposition to his appointment ensued. One particularly offensive critic described Brandeis as a "business-baiter, stirrer up of strife, litigious lover of hate and unrest,

destroyer of confidence, killer of values, commercial coyote, spoiler of pay envelopes."

Factory owners paying higher wages, New Haven Railroad stockholders, moguls in the Boston transit system, insurance and gas industries—in short, all the losers in court—united to voice their objections to the appointment. Among those seeking satisfaction for past injuries was a former president, William Howard Taft (1909–1913). His administration had been embarrassed by an investigation led in part by Brandeis of the conservation practices of Secretary of the Interior Richard A. Ballinger.

The former president, ambitious for a justiceship himself, described the nomination as "one of the deepest wounds that I have had as an American and a lover of the Constitution" and spoke of the "indelible stain" on the Wilson administration that confirmation would bring.

Another critic, Clarence W. Barron, editor and publisher of the *Wall Street Journal*, also felt the choice was unwise: "There is only one redeeming feature in the nomination and that is that it will assist to bury Mr. Wilson in the next Presidential election." The president viewed the political climate differently. He believed Brandeis was a smart choice who would attract the needed **Progressive** vote.

During four months of bitter debate over his appointment, Brandeis quietly pursued his legal practice. He went to the office every day and did not resort to personal attacks against his opponents. The hearings in the Senate Judiciary Committee turned up no valid grounds for rejection. According to Senator Thomas J. Walsh of Montana, Brandeis's only "real crime" was that "he had not stood in awe of the majesty of wealth." One of his supporters from the Harvard Law School, Arthur Hill, attributed the opposition to the fact that "Mr. Brandeis is an outsider, successful and a Jew." Brandeis was confirmed by the Senate on June 1, 1916, by a vote of 47-22, becoming the first Jewish justice.

His pro-labor positions led to many dissents in cases favoring employers' rights over those of workers. A staunch believer in the rights of the individual, Brandeis also dissented when the Court upheld the government's right to wiretap. He said the Founding Fathers had included in the Constitution the "right to be let alone."

At eighty-two, Brandeis resigned from the Court, but not from public service. After twenty-two years on the bench, he devoted the last two years of his life to the Zionist movement and a boycott of German products. As *The New York Times* noted upon his retirement in 1939, "the storm against him . . . seems almost incredible now."

See also: Right to Privacy; Taft, William Howard.

Brennan, William Joseph Jr. (1906–1997)

Long-serving liberal Supreme Court justice nominated as a recess appointment by President Dwight D. Eisenhower (1953–1961) on October 16, 1956, to replace Sherman Minton, who had resigned. Brennan was then nominated again by President Eisenhower on January 14, 1957, and was confirmed by the Senate on March 19, 1957, by a voice vote. He served until his retirement on July 20, 1990.

William J. Brennan Jr. was the second of eight children of Irish parents who immigrated to the United States in 1890. Young William showed impressive academic abilities early in life. He was an outstanding student in high school, an honors student at the University of Pennsylvania's Wharton School of Finance, and in the top 10 percent of his Harvard Law School class in 1931.

After law school, Brennan returned home to Newark, New Jersey, where he joined a prominent law firm. Following passage of the Wagner Labor Act in 1935, Brennan began to specialize in labor law. With the outbreak of World War II (1939–1945), Brennan entered the Army, serving as a manpower troubleshooter on the staff of the undersecretary of war, Robert B. Patterson. At the conclusion of the war, Brennan returned to his old law firm. As his practice grew, however, Brennan, a dedicated family man, began to resent the demands it placed on his time.

A desire to ease the pace of his work was one of the reasons Brennan accepted an appointment to the newly created New Jersey Superior Court

in 1949. Because Brennan had been a leader in the movement to establish the court as part of a large program of judicial reform, it was not a surprise when Republican Governor Alfred E. Driscoll selected him, even though he was a registered Democrat, to serve on the court.

During his tenure on the superior court, Brennan's use of pretrial procedures to speed up the disposition of cases brought him to the attention of New Jersey State Supreme Court Justice Arthur T. Vanderbilt. It was reportedly at Vanderbilt's suggestion that Brennan was moved first in 1950 to the appellate division of the superior court and then in 1952 to the state supreme court. Late in 1956, when President Eisenhower was looking for a justice to replace Sherman Minton, Vanderbilt and others strongly recommended Brennan for the post, and Eisenhower gave him a recess appointment in October. There was some criticism that Eisenhower was currying favor with voters by nominating a Roman Catholic Democrat to the bench so close to the 1956 presidential election, but Brennan's established integrity and nonpolitical background minimized the impact of the charges.

In his time on the Court, thirty-four years and nine months, it was hard to find an area of American life that Brennan did not affect. Among his most important opinions is *Baker v. Carr* (1962). Ruling that federal courts could consider cases of disproportionate voting districts, he said that states that fail to reapportion may be in violation of the equal protection clause. In the area of free speech, Brennan ruled in *New York Times v. Sullivan* (1964) that to sue for libel public figures had to prove actual malice on the part of the media. Brennan also influenced thinking on the right to privacy. In *Eisenstadt v. Baird* (1972), Brennan wrote the opinion in which the Court expanded on its ruling in *Griswold v. Connecticut* (1965). *Eisenstadt* said that a ban on distribution of contraceptives to unmarried persons was unconstitutional.

Even after his many years on the Court, it was with reluctance that Brennan retired July 20, 1990. He had suffered a small stroke and was advised that the combination of his medical condition and his age, eighty-four at the time, would make it difficult to keep up his rigorous Court schedule. In the years immediately after his retirement, Brennan continued to go to his office every

A–Z

day. He kept busy with federal appeals court work, law school lectures, and speeches.

See also: Baker v. Carr (1962); *New York Times v. Sullivan* (1964); Right to Privacy.

Breyer, Stephen (1938–)

Associate justice of the U.S. Supreme Court, appointed by President Bill Clinton (1993–2001) and confirmed by Congress on August 3, 1994. Justice Breyer is the 108th justice to serve on the Court.

Breyer was born on August 15, 1938, in San Francisco, California, in a middle-class Jewish home. His father was a lawyer for the San Francisco Board of Education, and his mother was a volunteer for the Democratic Party and for the League of Women Voters. As a youth, Breyer attained the rank of Eagle Scout and later was named by his high school classmates as "most likely to succeed." He attended college at Stanford, earning a Marshall Scholarship to attend Oxford University. Breyer later studied law at Harvard and served as editor of the Harvard Law Review, a student-run legal journal.

After graduating from Harvard Law School in 1964, Breyer served as a clerk for Supreme Court Justice Arthur Goldberg. He worked for several years in the Justice Department, then took a position teaching regulatory law at Harvard. After serving briefly as an aide to prosecutor Archibald Cox in the 1973 Watergate hearings, following the political scandal that forced President Richard M. Nixon (1969–1974) to resign in 1974, Breyer served as legal counsel to the Senate Judiciary Committee. In 1980, President Jimmy Carter (1977–1981) appointed Breyer to a federal judgeship on the First Circuit Court of Appeals. From 1985 to 1989, Breyer also served on the U.S. Sentencing Commission, playing a major role in reforming federal criminal sentencing procedures

Associate Justice Stephen G. Breyer makes a point during a conference. In general, Justice Breyer sides with the liberal wing of the Court, which includes Justices John Paul Stevens and Ruth Bader Ginsburg. (AP Photo, Hessoon Yim)

and creating more uniform federal sentencing guidelines for criminal trials.

In 1993, President Bill Clinton considered Breyer to fill the Supreme Court seat vacated upon the retirement of Justice Byron White. Clinton instead chose Ruth Bader Ginsburg, but the following year he selected Breyer to replace retiring Justice Harry Blackmun. Breyer, who had gained Senate supporters from both political parties during his time on the Appeals Court, won easy confirmation. The final Senate vote was 87-9.

Observers call Breyer's judicial style "pragmatic," noting that he considers the intent of the law and consequences of legal interpretations as well as history, tradition, and **precedents**—earlier legal decisions used as guides for future cases. Breyer himself has noted that this is what distinguishes his judicial style from that of justices who favor a stricter, more conservative interpretation of the Constitution, such as Justice Antonin Scalia.

See also: Associate Justices; Circuit Court of Appeals; Confirmation of Justices and Judges; Ginsburg, Ruth Bader; Nomination of Justices and Judges; Scalia, Antonin.

Brown v. Board of Education (1954)

Landmark Supreme Court ruling in which the Court declared segregated public school systems (those that required black and white students to attend different schools) to be unconstitutional. The ruling in *Brown* not only affected educational practice in the United States but also challenged the entrenched system of legalized racial segregation in the South.

Background

At the time of the *Brown* decision, the United States was a society deeply divided—both emotionally and physically—by race. This was particularly true throughout the South, where so-called Jim Crow laws codified racial discrimination by establishing separate public facilities for blacks and whites. Blacks and whites were forced to stay in separate hotels, use separate restrooms, drink at separate water fountains, and—at the heart of the *Brown* case—attend separate schools.

In 1896, the Supreme Court upheld this policy in the case of *Plessy v. Ferguson*. Homer Plessy, an African American, was jailed for refusing to leave a "whites only" car on the East Louisiana Railroad. Plessy sued, claiming that the state of Louisiana had denied him his constitutional rights under the Thirteenth and Fourteenth amendments. These amendments granted freedom and citizenship to former slaves and extended to them the constitutional freedoms guaranteed in the Bill of Rights. After losing in state court, Plessy appealed to the Supreme Court to overturn the original ruling. The Court, however, ruled by a 7-1 vote that segregation of public facilities was constitutional as long as the facilities provided for both races were "equal." This "separate but equal" doctrine remained the legal standard until *Brown*.

Basis of the Case

As with many of the key Court cases concerning civil rights, *Brown* was a **test case**—a lawsuit filed to determine the Court's position on a matter of law. In 1951 the Topeka, Kansas, branch of the National Association for the Advancement of Colored People (NAACP) recruited thirteen Topeka parents to file suit in Kansas court challenging the state's segregated public school system.

Landmark Decision Highlights: *Brown v. Board of Education* (1954)

Issue: Does the segregation of children in public schools solely on the basis of race deprive minority children of the equal protection of the laws guaranteed by the Fourteenth Amendment?

Opinion: Racial segregation in public education clearly has a detrimental effect on minority children because it is interpreted as a sign of inferiority. The long-held doctrine that separate facilities were permissible provided they were equal was unanimously rejected by the Court. "Separate but equal" is inherently unequal in the context of public education.

A – Z

This 1953 photograph shows the segregated classroom of Linda Brown (front row, right) in Topeka, Kansas. Until the landmark Supreme Court ruling *Brown v. Board of Education* (1954), racially segregated classrooms were legal, as long as the facilities were equal to those provided for white students. In reality, however, facilities for African American students were typically inferior to those of white students. In a unanimous decision, the Court ruled "that, in the field of public education, the doctrine of 'separate but equal' has no place. Separate educational facilities are inherently unequal." (Photo by Carl Iwasaki, Time & Life Pictures, Getty Images).

The families filed a **class action suit,** a lawsuit brought by one or a few individuals on behalf of an entire class of people. The suit named the Board of Education of the city of Topeka, Kansas, as the defendant.

The **plaintiff**—the person who formally brings a case to court—was a railroad employee named Oliver Brown, whose daughter, Linda, attended a segregated black school in Topeka. Although the Browns lived just seven blocks from a whites-only school, Linda was forced to attend a segregated school much farther away from her house. In his suit, Brown asked the Court to overturn the state's segregated educational system.

After losing his case in state court, Brown appealed the decision to U.S. District Court. The District Court also ruled against him, citing *Plessy v. Ferguson* as a **precedent**—an earlier legal decision used as a guide for deciding future cases. Although the court found Topeka's segregation detrimental to black children, it ruled that the segregated system was constitutional because the black and white schools were substantially equal with respect to buildings, curricula, transportation, and teachers.

At the same time that *Brown* was being argued in Kansas, a number of similar lawsuits were brought to court in several other states.

These suits also challenged racially segregated school systems on a variety of legal grounds, including the Fourteenth Amendment's **equal protection clause,** which guarantees equal protection under the law to all persons. In each case, the lower courts ruled against the plaintiffs on the grounds that the education offered to black and white students was substantially equal, or soon would be.

Supreme Court Arguments

Brown appealed the District Court decision to the U.S. Supreme Court, which requested in 1953 that the parties reargue the case. Because the lower courts found the educational accommodations for blacks and whites essentially equal, the Court was left to consider whether public school segregation itself was unconstitutional, regardless of the comparative quality of education offered. The Supreme Court asked the attorneys to address three main questions:

- What historical evidence was there that the framers of the Fourteenth Amendment intended it to apply to segregation in public schools?

- If the answer to the first question was inconclusive, was it within the power of the Court to abolish segregation?

- If school segregation was found unconstitutional, what approach should the Court take to end it?

Answering the Court's Questions

The lead attorneys opposing each other in the case were Thurgood Marshall, director of the NAACP Legal Defense Fund, and John W. Davis, a former U.S. representative from West Virginia and the 1924 Democratic presidential nominee. Davis was also an experienced attorney who had served as solicitor general and had argued more cases before the Supreme Court than any other lawyer of his era. Marshall, then forty-five, was a rising star who would later become the first African American Supreme Court justice. By contrast Davis, at age eighty, was making his final appearance before the Court.

Davis was first to present an answer to the Court's three questions. He argued that the

Fourteenth Amendment was never intended to bar segregation in the nation's public schools. In addition to examining the history surrounding enactment of the amendment, Davis also named the states, both North and South, which continued to segregate schools after the amendment was ratified. Several of those same states had voted to ratify the amendment. Davis reminded the Court that both the lower courts and the Supreme Court itself earlier had upheld the "separate but equal" doctrine. Thus the doctrine had become part of the law of the land. Davis also said he did not believe the courts had the power to tell the states how to desegregate their schools. "Your Honors do not sit, and cannot sit, as a glorified Board of Education for the State of South Carolina or any other state. Neither can the District Court," he declared.

Marshall's Response

Marshall's response to Davis the following day illustrated the difference between the two men's styles and philosophies:

> I got the feeling on hearing the discussion yesterday that when you put a white child in a school with a whole lot of colored children, the child would fall apart or something. Everybody knows that is not true . . . They can't take race out of this case. From the day this case was filed until this moment, nobody has in any form or fashion . . . done anything to distinguish this [segregation] statute from the Black Codes, which they must admit, because nobody can dispute . . . the Fourteenth Amendment was intended to deprive the states of power to enforce Black Codes or anything else like it.
>
> . . . [T]he only way that this Court can decide this case in opposition to our position, is that there must be some reason which gives the state the right to make a classification that . . . for some reason Negroes are inferior to all other human beings . . .
>
> It can't be because of slavery in the past, because there are very few groups

JUSTICE FOR ALL

Linda Brown and the Brown Foundation

Linda Brown, a third-grader in Topeka, Kansas, is often credited with single-handedly bringing down segregation in the United States. The truth is far more complicated.

In the 1950s, the Browns were just one of thirteen African American families recruited in Topeka by the National Association for the Advancement of Colored People (NAACP). In 1950, the national civil rights group was working to enlist plaintiffs nationwide in preparation for a legal assault on the "separate but equal" Supreme Court ruling that had permitted segregation in the nation's schools since the 1896 *Plessy* ruling.

In the fall of 1950, the Browns and twelve Topeka families were asked by the NAACP to try to enroll their children in their neighborhood white schools, with the expectation that they would be rejected. The NAACP then filed a lawsuit against the Board of Education in Topeka. That lawsuit and others brought on behalf of plaintiffs in Virginia, South Carolina, Delaware, and Washington, D.C., were presented together on appeal to the U.S. Supreme Court. By alphabetical accident, because Brown's name started with a "B," the landmark 1954 decision that ended legalized segregation in America went down in history as *Brown v. Board of Education*.

In 1988, The Brown Foundation for Educational Equity, Excellence, and Research was established as a tribute to the attorneys and plaintiffs in the landmark case. The Brown family and community leaders in Topeka established the foundation to commemorate the activities involved in this historic Court case. In 1990, for example, the former Monroe Elementary School, which was once one of four segregated schools for African American children in Topeka, stood empty and was up for sale. The building was to be auctioned by an owner who was unaware of its significance. The Brown Foundation saw an opportunity to intercede and save the unwanted property.

Throughout 1991 and 1992, the Brown Foundation worked with the National Park Service, members of Congress, and the Trust for Public Lands to save and acquire the school. In July 1992, legislation to establish Monroe School as a National Historic Site was introduced in the U.S. Senate. After passing the Senate, the bill was approved by the House of Representatives. On October 26, 1992, President George H.W. Bush (1989–1993) signed the Brown v. Board of Education National Historic Site Act of 1992 into law.

in this country that haven't had slavery some place back in the history of their groups. It can't be color because there are Negroes as white as the drifted snow, with blue eyes, and they are just as segregated as the colored man.

The only thing [it] can be is an inherent determination that the people who were formerly in slavery, regardless of anything else, shall be kept as near that stage as possible, and now is the time, we submit, that this Court should make it clear that that is not what our Constitution stands for.

The Decision

On May 17, 1954, Chief Justice Earl Warren read the Court's unanimous decision in *Brown v. Board of Education*, finding in favor of the plaintiff. The opinion, described by many as the most socially and ideologically significant decision in the Court's history, was just thirteen paragraphs long.

Warren quickly disposed of the Court's first question—whether the framers of the Fourteenth Amendment intended it to bar school segregation. He said the evidence was inconclusive. The chief justice then turned to the "separate but equal" doctrine. Because children attending the segregated public schools in these cases were, or soon would be, receiving substantially equal treatment, he said, the Court must look at the "effect of segregation itself on public education." "Only in this way," wrote Warren, "can it be determined if segregation in public schools deprives these plaintiffs of the equal protection of the laws."

The Court found that education was "perhaps the most important function" of state and local government. Education, wrote Warren, was the foundation of good citizenship and the basis for professional training and adjustment to society. He declared that where the state had chosen to make education available, it must be available to all on equal terms. Warren then posed this question: "Does segregation of children in public schools solely on the basis of race, even though the physical facilities and other 'tangible' factors may be equal, deprive the children of the minority group of equal educational opportunities?" The Court's answer: "We believe that it does." The

Court ruled, "Separate educational facilities are inherently unequal. Therefore, we hold that the plaintiffs and others similarly situated for whom the actions have been brought are, by reason of the segregation complained of, deprived of the equal protection of the laws guaranteed by the Fourteenth Amendment."

See also: Associate Justice Ruth Bader Ginsburg on *Brown v. Board of Education*, October 21, 2004, in the **Primary Source Library;** Bill of Rights; *Brown v. Board of Education*, 1954, in the **Primary Source Library;** Civil Rights and the Supreme Court; Education, Schools, and the Supreme Court; Equal Protection of the Law; Marshall, Thurgood; *Plessy v. Ferguson* (1896); Precedent; Racial Equality; Segregation; Warren, Earl.

Further Reading

Fireside, Harvey, and Sarah Fuller. *Brown v. Board of Education: Equal Schooling for All.* Berkeley Heights, NJ: Enslow Publishers, 1994.

Gold, Susan Dudley. *Brown v. Board of Education: Separate But Equal?.* New York: Benchmark Books, 2004.

Martin, Waldo. *Brown v. Board of Education: A Brief History with Documents.* New York: St. Martin's Press, 2007.

Burger, Warren E. (1907–1995)

Chief Justice of the United States, appointed by President Richard M. Nixon (1969–1974) and confirmed by the Senate on June 23, 1969. Burger was an outspoken "law and order" judge during the turbulent days of the late 1960s. When Nixon chose Burger, he gave the new chief justice a mission: halt or reverse the liberal activism of the Court that occurred under the previous chief justice, Earl Warren.

Burger was born September 17, 1907, in St. Paul, Minnesota, and grew up on a farm at the edge of town. He later attended the University of Minnesota before enrolling at what is now the

A–Z

William Mitchell College of Law. After receiving his law degree in 1931, Burger went into private practice and later taught law at the school where he earned his degree. During this time he met and befriended Harry Blackmun, who would later serve on the Court with Burger as an associate justice.

In 1953, incoming President Dwight D. Eisenhower appointed Burger to the post of assistant attorney general in charge of the Civil Division of the Justice Department. While serving in that position, Burger argued several cases before the Supreme Court on behalf of the U.S. government. In 1956, Eisenhower named Burger to a vacant seat on the U.S. Court of Appeals for the District of Columbia.

In 1968, aging Chief Justice Warren announced his retirement from the Court. President Johnson initially nominated Associate Justice Abe Fortas to succeed Warren as chief justice. The Senate, however, rejected the nomination. Nixon then turned to Burger, whose conservative judicial philosophy matched Nixon's own views. The Senate approved Burger's nomination, making him the fifteenth Chief Justice of the United States.

Burger's mission to impose judicial restraint on the court faced obstacles from the start. Unlike Warren, Burger did not have a group of like-minded justices who were prepared to follow him. He inherited a solid core of liberal justices, including William O. Douglas, William J. Brennan, and Thurgood Marshall, who were determined to maintain the Court's progressive agenda.

Although he won praise for improving and modernizing the federal court system and day-to-day operations at the Supreme Court, many considered Burger a failure as chief justice. He had a pompous demeanor that alienated some of his colleagues, and his presentations in their closed-door conferences were criticized as rambling and unpersuasive. Rather than lead a conservative revival, the Burger Court was best known for liberal advances such as the recognition of women's rights, the 1973 *Roe v. Wade* ruling that confirmed a woman's right to an abortion, and the 1978 decision in *Board of Regents of the University of California v. Bakke* that upheld affirmative action in colleges and universities.

See also: *Roe v. Wade* (1973); Chief Justice of the Supreme Court; Warren, Earl.

Burr, Aaron, Trial of

In 1807, the trial in which the administration of President Thomas Jefferson (1801–1809) charged former Vice President Aaron Burr with **treason.** The case represented an early test of the relative powers of the Supreme Court and the executive branch of government.

The matter began when Burr refused to concede defeat in the disputed presidential election of 1800. A compromise among the electors assured Jefferson enough electoral votes to win, but Jefferson remained angered by Burr's failure to acknowledge him as the legitimate winner. Looking to revive his political fortunes, Burr traveled west and assembled a small force of men on the upper Ohio River. They later moved down the Mississippi River to New Orleans, and rumors circulated that Burr intended to separate the Southwest from the Union. In 1806, Jefferson issued an order for Burr's arrest. Burr fled but was captured and returned to Richmond, Virginia, for trial.

Early in 1807, the Court held that there was insufficient evidence for the government to prosecute two of Burr's accomplices for treason. Jefferson regarded this ruling as another deliberate attack by the Court upon his executive authority, while Jefferson's opponents viewed it as "a noble example of the judicial safeguards to individual liberty." After the Court's term ended, Chief Justice Marshall traveled to Richmond to preside personally, as circuit judge, over Burr's trial.

Marshall's rulings as presiding judge thwarted Jefferson's hopes that Burr would be convicted. Marshall upheld Burr's request to obtain from Jefferson certain letters that Burr claimed he needed to provide an adequate defense. Marshall ruled that the evidence sought was relevant to the case and issued a **subpoena,** or court order, seeking delivery of the letters to the court in Richmond. Jefferson refused to appear at court or to furnish the documents without certain portions deleted. He did agree to provide transcripts of portions of the letters.

The main issue in the case was Marshall's definition of treason. Burr's attorneys maintained that treason consisted of an actual "levying of war" against the United States. This drew a

JUSTICE FOR ALL

Treason and the Letter of the Law

Article III of the Constitution defines treason against the United States as consisting "only in levying War against them, or in adhering to their Enemies, giving them Aid and Comfort. No Person shall be convicted of Treason unless on the Testimony of two Witnesses to the same overt Act, or on Confession in open Court." The Supreme Court has reviewed only three charges of treason, all arising from incidents during World War II. Two of these decisions left interpretation of part of the law in some doubt; the third added little to the discussion.

In *Cramer v. United States* (1945), the Court held that that merely associating with the enemy did not constitute "giving aid and comfort" and thus was not considered treason. The ruling in *Haupt v. United States* (1947) held that sheltering the enemy was an overt act that gave aid and comfort. In *Kawakita v. United States* (1952), the Court ruled that charges of treason could be brought against an American citizen who had committed a treasonous act against the United States in a foreign country.

distinction between the act of war and the advising of it. The prosecution argued that anyone who contemplated treason was engaging in the act itself. They maintained that Burr was guilty because he advised assembling an armed force and moving it down river to New Orleans. Marshall, however, ruled that the prosecution failed to meet the burden of proving the charge of treason because it could not produce two witnesses to the act. In the end, Burr was acquitted of the charge.

Bush v. Gore (2000)

A controversial Supreme Court ruling that prevented a recount of the disputed Florida popular vote in the 2000 presidential election. The case marked the first time that the Court involved itself in a presidential election. As a result of the decision, Republican candidate George W. Bush was awarded Florida's twenty-five electoral votes, which provided him with the narrow margin of victory in a hard-won contest with Democratic candidate Al Gore Jr., who had won the popular vote by 539, 947 votes.

Background

The 2000 presidential race was one of the most closely contested elections in the nation's history, and one of the most controversial. The drama that played out revealed aspects of the American electoral system that surprised and dismayed many voters.

Counting the Votes

The 2000 election showed that the process of counting votes is neither as uniform nor as exact as many people might have assumed. Different states, different counties—even neighboring precincts—use different means of counting votes. That difference can determine the likelihood that a vote will be counted.

In Florida, some precincts used paper card ballots that were punched out by the voter and counted by a tabulating machine. Others used more modern computer scanning systems. The older punch card system does not count as high a percentage of ballots as more modern systems, and in a close election such a difference alone can be vital. Associate Justice John Stevens pointed out that 3.9 percent of the punch card ballots—nearly four hundred out of every ten thousand—were not counted as votes. By contrast, Florida's optical scanners failed to count only 1.4 percent of the ballots. Those differences in the ballot-counting systems proved crucial to the outcome in the Florida election, but they did not figure in the Court's rulings.

An even bigger problem in Florida was the design of the ballot in Palm Beach County. Rather than list all the candidates in a single column, election officials decided to spread them across two pages that opened to the voter, rather like the wings of a butterfly. The punch holes ran down the middle of the two-page ballot, dubbed the "butterfly ballot."

The result was confusion. Republicans George W. Bush and Richard Cheney were listed first on the left side of the ballot, and underneath them were Democrats Al Gore and Joseph Lieberman. Across the page on the right side was Reform Party candidate Patrick Buchanan, whose punch mark was second in the middle column, between Bush and Gore. Many elderly Democratic voters, seeing Gore and Lieberman listed below Bush, punched the second hole. They had voted unwittingly for the conservative Buchanan. Some tried to correct their mistake by punching a second hole next to Gore's name. Nearly twenty thousand ballots in Palm Beach were declared invalid because they displayed a double vote.

Election Results

On election night, the television networks first called Gore the winner in Florida but later changed the call to Bush. By early the next morning, the race was still too close to call. Outside of Florida, Gore had won 267 electoral votes, just short of the 271 needed for victory; Bush had 246. Florida's twenty-five electoral votes would determine the winner.

On election night, Bush had a lead of 1,784 votes in Florida, but his margin decreased to 327 votes after the mandatory machine recount. Gore and his lawyers, convinced a majority of Floridians had voted Democratic, decided to challenge the outcome in court. Bush's advisers said the Texas governor had won narrowly but fairly, and the election was over.

State Court Hearing

Gore's legal team faced an uphill fight from the start. Gore could not ask for a statewide recount

under Florida law—he had to get recounts in individual counties. Florida state law held that a losing candidate can file written requests for recounts in counties where he or she suspects an error was made in counting the votes that "could affect the outcome" of an election. Gore's lawyers argued the failure of the machines to count thousands of punch card ballots could affect the outcome, so they asked for manual recounts in four Democratic-leaning counties. Bush's lawyers went to federal court seeking to block the recounts.

Florida Secretary of State Katherine Harris, an elected Republican, denied the request for a recount. She also stated that her office would enforce a one-week deadline for the counties to submit their final election tallies. Florida Attorney General Robert Butterworth, a Democrat, disagreed with Harris's interpretation of the law and said a manual recount was required.

Fearing that Harris would ignore the recounts, Gore's lawyers appealed to state circuit court Judge Terry Lewis, but lost. The Florida Supreme Court then stepped in to resolve the legal conflict, voting 7-0 in favor of Gore and the county officials. Their decision, handed down on November 21, extended the time for the counties to recount ballots for five more days.

Supreme Court Intervention

The next day, lawyers representing Bush asked the U.S. Supreme Court to intervene. On November 24, to the surprise of most legal analysts, the Court announced that it would hear the Republicans' challenge to the Florida court's decision. It was not clear what constitutional matters were at issue or whether the extended deadline made much difference. Two days later, on November 26, Harris's office declared Bush the winner in Florida by a total of 537 votes.

On December 4, the Court handed down a brief, unanimous, and unsigned opinion that decided very little. The justices set aside the Florida Supreme Court's ruling, stating that they wanted a clearer explanation of the basis for its decision. State judges are required to interpret laws, but they are not free to change them after the election. The justices could not decide whether the Florida court had interpreted the law or changed it. The Court sent the matter back to Florida for clarification. In a 4-3 vote, the Florida Supreme

SPOTLIGHT

Extraordinary Circumstances: 1876 and 2000

The 2000 election was not the first time that the Supreme Court had involved itself in the outcome of a presidential election. However, it was the first time the Court had decided a case based on one.

In 1877, the Supreme Court was thrust into the election process when a dispute arose about the outcome of the 1876 presidential election between Republican Rutherford B. Hayes and Democrat Samuel J. Tilden. The electoral vote count stood at 184-165 in favor of Tilden, with an additional twenty votes in four separate states uncounted. Each party claimed its candidates had won the states in question. To resolve the problem, Congress created a special electoral commission that included five Supreme Court justices. Each House of Congress also chose five members, the Democratic House selecting five Democrats and the Republican Senate five Republicans.

Politically, the five justices were supposed to be divided evenly, two Democrats and two Republicans, plus independent David Davis. Davis, however, withdrew from consideration because he had been elected a U.S. senator from Illinois. Justice Joseph Bradley, a Republican, was substituted for Davis, making the overall lineup on the commission eight to seven in favor of the Republicans. The three Republican justices supported Hayes's claims, and the two Democratic justices backed Tilden, resulting in the election of Hayes. Justice Nathan Clifford, the chairman of the commission, was so contemptuous of the outcome that he called Hayes an illegitimate president and refused to enter the White House during his term.

Court ordered a hand recount of all the remaining uncounted ballots in Florida by December 12.

The recount started again on December 9, but at midday it was halted by a surprise order from the U.S. Supreme Court. In a 5-4 vote, the justices had granted an emergency motion filed by Bush to block the Florida court's ruling from taking effect. The order signaled the end of the fight for Florida and a final victory for George Bush.

Bush's Challenge

Under the Court's rules, emergency stay orders are hard to obtain and rarely granted. Ordinarily, the Court reviews cases that are finally decided by lower courts. It avoids intervening in matters that are still before those courts. To obtain an emergency stay order, a party must show he or she will suffer "an irreparable harm" unless the Court intervenes. In most cases, this is quite difficult.

Bush's motion claimed the Texas governor would suffer an irreparable harm if the Floridians conducted a "standardless" recount. Five members of the Court agreed: Chief Justice Rehnquist, and Justices O'Connor, Scalia, Kennedy, and Thomas. During the oral argument, the justices who voted to grant the stay—notably Justices Kennedy and O'Connor—seemed to struggle for the right legal reason for Bush to win, but they left no doubt the Texas governor would prevail.

A–Z

Landmark Decision Highlights: *Bush v. Gore* (2000)

Issue: Two issues were involved in this case: Do standardless manual recounts violate the equal protection and due process clauses of the Constitution? Did the Florida Supreme Court violate Article II, Section 1, Clause 2, of the U.S. Constitution by making new election law?

Opinion: The majority of the Court determined that the equal protection clause of the Fourteenth Amendment guarantees individuals that their ballots cannot be devalued by "later arbitrary and disparate treatment." The Court held that the Florida Supreme Court's scheme for recounting ballots was unconstitutional. Even if the recount was fair in theory, it was unfair in practice, because different standards were applied from ballot to ballot, precinct to precinct, and county to county. Because of those and other procedural difficulties, the Court held that no constitutional recount could be fashioned in the time remaining. Chief Justice William H. Rehnquist, in a concurring opinion joined by Justices Antonin Scalia and Clarence Thomas, argued that the recount was also unconstitutional because the Florida Supreme Court's decision made new election law, which only the state legislature may do. Thus, Florida's twenty-five electoral votes—and the presidency—were awarded to George W. Bush on December 12, 2000.

The Court's Ruling

On December 12, the Court handed out copies of its decision in *Bush v. Gore* (2000). It was an unsigned opinion and labeled a "per curiam," or opinion of the court. This usually refers to a unanimous and uncontroversial ruling, but this decision was anything but. Attached were four separate dissents by Justices Breyer, Ginsburg, Souter, and Stevens. In addition, Justices Scalia and Thomas joined in a concurring opinion written by Chief Rehnquist. That meant that the

authors of the decisive opinion were the two unnamed members of the Court, Justices Kennedy and O'Connor. During the oral argument, Kennedy in particular spoke about the equal protection problem, and he is credited as being the opinion's primary author.

Bush's appeal had raised two questions: whether the Florida courts had violated federal election law by establishing "new standards" for resolving the disputed election, and whether the "use of standardless manual recounts violates the Equal Protection and Due Process Clauses" of the Fourteenth Amendment. The majority of the justices found a violation of the equal protection clause, arguing that a selective recount would, "by later arbitrary and disparate treatment, value one person's vote over that of another."

The four dissenters said the Court had no business blocking the state's effort to count all of its votes in a very close election. Justice Stevens characterized the Court's intervention as unwise and partisan and an affront to the state judges in Florida. Justice Ginsburg faulted the conservative majority for turning its back on its customary stand of deferring to the states. Justice Breyer pointed out that the Twelfth Amendment and the Electoral Vote Count Act state that state courts and Congress are charged with resolving disputes in presidential elections. The law "nowhere provides for involvement by the United States Supreme Court," he said. If ever there was a case for "judicial restraint," this was it, he added.

See also: Judicial Activism; Judicial Restraint; Jurisdiction of the Supreme Court; One Person, One Vote; Presidency and the Supreme Court.

Further Reading

Sergis, Diana G. *Bush v. Gore: Controversial Presidential Election Case.* Berkeley Heights, NJ: Enslow Publishers, 2003.

Slusher, Heather, et. al. *Bush v. Gore: Understanding the American Legal System*. Upper Saddle River, NJ: Prentice Hall, 2001.

Toobin, Jeffrey. *Too Close to Call: The Thirty-Six Day Battle to Decide the 2000 Election.* New York: Random House, 2002.

Capital Punishment

See Death Penalty Cases.

Censorship

The suppression of speech or other forms of communication. The First Amendment to the U.S. Constitution guarantees, among other rights, freedom of speech and of the press. The nation's Founders considered the ability to share information freely one of the cornerstones of an effective democracy. In fact, the Supreme Court has struck down most laws that have intended to impose restraints on the press.

Prior Restraint

Near v. Minnesota (1931) was the first Supreme Court ruling to touch on the issue of prior restraint— that is, attempting to prevent publication of certain types of material. The case concerned a state law that prohibited publication of malicious, scandalous, and defamatory newspapers, magazines, and other publications. The publisher could cite the truth of the charges as a defense only if they were made with "good motives" and for "justifiable ends."

A weekly periodical in Hennepin County, Minnesota, charged that county officials were sympathetic to a Jewish gangster who ran gambling, bootlegging, and racketeering operations in Minneapolis. The articles named the police chief, a member of the grand jury investigating the rackets, and the county attorney as among those whose actions prevented authorities from stopping the vice operations.

Citing the state law, a court issued an order forbidding continued publication of the newspaper.

J.M. Near, the manager of the paper, appealed the ruling to the Supreme Court. In a 5-4 vote, the Court overturned the lower court's order, holding that the Minnesota statute was an unconstitutional prior restraint on the press in violation of the First and Fourteenth Amendments. The Court did acknowledge that freedom of the press from prior restraint was not absolute. It suggested four exceptional situations in which government censorship might be permissible: publication of crucial war information; obscene publications; publications inciting "acts of violence" against the community or violent overthrow of the government; and publications that invade "private rights."

Sixty years later, the Court cited *Near* when it struck down a New York law that denied criminals the right to proceeds from any book or article written about their crimes; the law instead required that such profits be directed to a victims' fund. In the case of *Simon & Schuster Inc. v. Members of New York State Crime Victims Board* (1991), the Court held that this "Son of Sam" law was too broad in its sweep and thereby violated the First Amendment.

Restrictive Taxation

The Supreme Court prohibited the use of a more traditional kind of prior restraint in *Grosjean v. American Press Co.* (1936). The Louisiana legislature, under the direction of Governor Huey Long, had placed a state tax on the gross receipts of newspapers that sold advertisements and had circulation in excess of twenty thousand copies per week. The tax was promoted as a tax on the privilege of doing business, but it had been calculated to affect only nine big city newspapers opposed to the Long regime.

The papers asked a federal district court to stop enforcement of the law on the grounds that the tax violated freedom of the press. It also claimed that, because smaller newspapers were exempt from the tax, it denied them equal protection.

A–Z

VIEWPOINTS

An 1889 cartoon shows President Benjamin Harrison (1889–1893) placing padlocks on various newsmen as he tries to muzzle the press. The U.S. Supreme Court has overturned most laws that attempted to restrict freedom of speech, a key protection listed in the First Amendment to the U.S. Constitution. (Library of Congress, Prints and Photographs Division)

order preventing *The New York Times* from publishing the material.

The *Times* appealed the case to the Supreme Court, which announced its decision June 30, 1971. By a 6-3 vote, the Court ruled that the government had failed to meet "the heavy burden of showing justification" for restraining further publications of the Pentagon Papers. Each of the nine justices wrote a separate opinion in the case. Several indicated that they believed the newspapers might be subject to criminal penalties for publishing classified government documents, but the question never arose.

See also: Freedom of the Press; Libel; Obscenity; Pentagon Papers.

The federal district court agreed with the papers, and a unanimous Supreme Court upheld that decision solely on First Amendment grounds. The tax "operates as a restraint in a double sense," wrote Justice George Sutherland. "First, its effect is to curtail the amount of revenue realized from advertising, and, second, its direct tendency is to restrict circulation." He went on to state, "The tax here involved is bad . . . because, in the light of its history and of its present setting, it is seen to be a deliberate and calculated device in the guise of a tax to limit the circulation of information to which the public is entitled . . ."

National Security

In the 1971 *Pentagon Papers Case*, the administration of President Richard M. Nixon (1969–1974) attempted to prevent the publication of a series of newspaper articles based upon a classified history of U.S. involvement in Vietnam. The government claimed the articles would cause "irreparable injury to the defense interests of the U.S." A district court judge granted a temporary restraining

Checks and Balances

Provisions in the U.S. Constitution that allow the various branches of government to place limits on each other's power. When the nation's Founders drafted the Constitution in 1787, they created a system of government that featured three separate branches: the executive (the president), the legislative (Congress), and the judiciary (the Supreme Court). In order to prevent any one branch from exercising too much authority and dominating the others, the Founders reserved certain powers to each branch. By doing so, they ensured that the three branches had to work together to pass laws and set government policy.

Under the system established by the Constitution, the legislature has the sole authority to make laws, collect and distribute revenue, declare war, approve or reject treaties, and confirm certain presidential nominees. The president, in turn, may veto laws passed by Congress, oversees congressional spending, acts as commander in chief of the armed forces, makes treaties, and appoints judges with the advice and consent of the Senate. Thus, the powers of the legislative and executive branches complement and balance one another. Neither branch can act effectively in any area of governing without the cooperation of the other.

Compared to the executive and the legislative branches, the judiciary appears to have little constitutional authority. Indeed, early political observers believed that the Supreme Court was the weakest of the three branches. The Court has no say over policymaking, collection or expenditure of revenues, declaring or conducting war, dealing with foreign nations, or appointments to any branch of government. Its main power lies in the process of judicial review—that is, the Court's power to review laws passed by the other branches and determine whether or not those laws are constitutional.

Interestingly, the Constitution does not specifically grant to the Court the power of judicial review. Instead, the principle was established as result of the legal case of *Marbury v. Madison* (1803). In that case, the Court refused to compel the administration of President Thomas Jefferson (1801–1809) to honor a political appointment made by Jefferson's predecessor, John Adams (1797–1801). The Court actually ruled that the appointee, Thomas Marbury, had a right to occupy the office he sought. However, it held that it was unconstitutional for the Court to issue the kind of order Marbury wished it to use to force Jefferson to honor the appointment. The ruling was the object of criticism at the time, and even modern legal scholars debate the logic the Court used in reaching its decision. Nevertheless, the principle of judicial review established by the case has become a central and accepted part of the checks and balances in the federal government.

See also: Judicial Review; *Marbury v. Madison* (1803).

Chief Justice of the United States

The head of the **judicial** branch of the U.S. government and the person who presides over sessions of the Supreme Court. The Constitution mentions the position only once: "When the President of the United States is tried, the Chief Justice shall preside."

It makes no other distinction between the chief justice and the other members of the Court, nor does it confer upon the chief justice any authority over the other justices. Yet because of

John Jay served as the first Chief Justice of the United States, sitting from 1789 until 1795. The most famous ruling of the Jay Court, *Chisholm v. Georgia* (1793), was overturned by the ratification of the Eleventh Amendment in 1795. This amendment forbids a state from being sued in federal court by a person from another state or a foreign country. (Library of Congress, Prints and Photographs Division)

A – Z

Chief Justices of the United States, 1789–2005

John Jay	1789–1795
John Rutledge*	1795
Oliver Ellsworth	1795–1800
John Marshall	1801–1835
Roger B. Taney	1835–1864
Salmon P. Chase	1864–1873
Morrison R. Waite	1874–1888
Melville W. Fuller	1888–1910
Edward D. White	1910–1921
William Howard Taft	1921–1930
Charles Evans Hughes	1930–1941
Harlan Fiske Stone	1941–1946
Frederick M. Vinson	1946–1953
Earl Warren	1963–1969
Warren Burger	1969–1986
William H. Rehnquist	1986–2005
John G. Roberts	2005–

*President George Washington appointed Rutledge on July 1, 1795, during a Congressional recess; Rutledge was later rejected by the Senate on December 15, 1795.

Since 1789, seventeen men have served as Chief Justice of the United States. Chief Justice John Marshall served the longest term—almost thirty-four years.

Chief Justices' Salaries

Years	Salary
1789–1819	$4,000
1819–1855	5,000
1855–1871	6,500
1871–1873	8,500
1873–1903	10,500
1903–1911	13,000
1911–1926	15,000
1926–1946	20,500
1946–1955	25,500
1955–1964	35,500
1964–1969	40,000
1969–1975	62,500
1975	65,625
1976*	68,800
1977	75,000
1978*	79,100
1979*	84,700
1980*	92,400
1981*	96,800
1982–1983*	100,700
1984	104,700
1985–1986	108,400
1987	115,000
1990	124,000
1991	160,600
1992	166,200
1993–1998	171,500
1999	175,400
2000	181,400
2001	186,300

tradition, popular perception of the office, and other intangible factors, the chief justice is widely perceived as more than "first among equals."

Over time, the chief justice has assumed certain duties, although none of these is mandated by law. The chief justice administers the oath of office to the president, presides when the Court is in public and private sessions, and has the duty of assigning the writing of most of the opinions of the other justices. The chief justice is also the chief administrative officer of the Court.

Chief Justices' Salaries, *continued*

Years	Salary
2002	192,600
2003	198,600
2004	203,000
2005	208,100
2006	212,100
2007	212,100
2008	217,400
2009	217,400

*A cost-of-living adjustment equal to 5 percent of regular salary

Over the years, the salary of the Chief Justice of the United States has increased to keep pace with increased costs and the salaries of other federal government officials.

In addition to duties on the Supreme Court, the chief justice serves as chair of the Judicial Conference of the United States, the body that governs administration of the federal judicial system. The chief justice also chairs the Federal Judicial Center, the research, training, and planning arm of the federal judiciary, and supervises the Administrative Office of the U.S. Courts.

Congress has given chief justices many additional tasks in addition to heading the Supreme Court and the federal judicial system. For example, Congress has made the chief justice a member of the board of regents of the Smithsonian Institution and a member of the board of trustees of the National Gallery of Art and of the Joseph H. Hirshhorn Museum and Sculpture Garden.

The chief justice has special perquisites, or benefits, that come with the office. In addition to an annual salary of $217,400 (in 2009) and the attention and respect that surrounds the office, the chief justice may have up to four law clerks, three secretaries, and a messenger. The chief justice also is provided with a car and driver, paid for by the government.

In 1972, Congress authorized the chief justice to appoint an administrative assistant but said nothing about the functions and duties of such a position. The chief justice determines how and in what areas the assistant will work. Chief Justices Warren Burger and William Rehnquist had their administrative assistants operate in areas outside the chief justice's judicial functions. The administrative assistants provided research and analysis for the justices' speeches, monitored literature and developments in judicial administration, and helped with internal matters such as preparation of the court budget.

See also: Associate Justices; Burger, Warren E.; Hughes, Charles Evans: Jay, John; Marshall, John; Rehnquist, William H.; Roberts, John G.; Taft, William Howard; Taney, Roger B.; Warren, Earl.

Child Labor

The practice of businesses employing minors, and Supreme Court rulings touching upon that subject. Twice in the early 1900s, the Court struck down laws that attempted to restrict or forbid child labor. Only in 1941 did the Court reverse itself and uphold federal laws banning child labor.

In *Hammer v. Dagenhart* (1918), the Court struck down a 1916 act of Congress that sought to discourage employment of children. The law prohibited the shipment across state lines of any products made in factories or mines that employed children under age fourteen or allowed children ages fourteen to sixteen to work more than a limited number of hours per week. By a 5-4 vote, the Court declared the law unconstitutional. It ruled that Congress could prohibit interstate commerce only if the articles being shipped were harmful in themselves. The Court also said that mining and manufacture were subject only to state regulation.

Four years later, the Court struck down a second effort to discourage child labor, this time through the use of the taxing power. This case centered on a law that imposed a high tax rate on the profits of companies that employed child labor. The law aimed to end the practice of child labor by making it prohibitively expensive to employ underage workers.

Chief Justice William Howard Taft, speaking for the majority in *Bailey v. Drexel Furniture Co.*

A - Z

A 1913 photograph shows the harsh and crowded conditions under which young boys labored, separating slate from coal in a Pennsylvania coal mine. In the early 1900s, Congress passed laws to restrict child labor, but these laws were declared unconstitutional by the Supreme Court. Finally, in 1941, the Court upheld the Fair Labor Standards Act, which prohibited child labor. (The Granger Collection, New York)

(1922), set out the same objections that the Court had voiced in *Dagenhart*:

> **G**rant the validity of this law, and all that Congress would need to do hereafter, in seeking to take over to its control any one of the great number of subjects of public interest . . . would be to enact a detailed measure of complete regulation of the subject and enforce it by a so-called tax. . . . To give such magic to the word "tax" would be to break down all constitutional limitation of Congress and completely wipe out the sovereignty of the states.

These two rulings stood until 1941, when the Court overruled *Hammer v. Dagenhart*. In doing

so, the Court upheld the Fair Labor Standards Act, which, among other provisions, included a provision prohibiting child labor. The case bringing this landmark opinion was *United States v. Darby* (1941). Writing for the Court, Justice Harlan Fiske Stone declared that:

> **T**he power of Congress over interstate commerce . . . extends to the activities intrastate which so affect interstate commerce or the exercise of the power of Congress over it as to make regulation of them appropriate means to the attainment of a legitimate end, the exercise of the granted power of Congress to regulate interstate commerce.

See also: Commerce Power of the Supreme Court.

Circuit Court of Appeals

Federal system of courts that are empowered to hear appeals from U.S. district courts. The circuit courts of appeal were established in 1891 to reduce the workload of the Supreme Court. Before that time, the Court was virtually the only federal appeals court in the United States, and it was becoming overwhelmed by the number of cases appealed to it.

District Courts and Circuit Courts

Article III of the Constitution states that the "judicial power of the United States, shall be vested in one Supreme Court and in such inferior courts as the Congress may from time to time ordain and establish." Congress first exercised this power with passage of the Judiciary Act of 1789, which established a system of federal district and circuit courts. The former were originally meant to hear admiralty and maritime cases. In 1875, Congress expanded the jurisdiction of district courts, allowing them to hear cases involving constitutional matters, federal laws, and treaties.

Circuit courts, by contrast, heard cases involving disputes between residents of different states, between aliens and the United States, and cases where more than $500 was at stake. They also had limited power to hear appeals from district courts. For many years, Supreme Court justices were required to "ride circuit," with two justices sitting with a district judge on circuit courts. This often required the justices to travel thousands of miles each year to discharge their circuit court duties. In the days before quick and easy transportation, the requirement of circuit riding often represented a significant hardship on the justices.

Revising the Court System

This system prevailed until passage of the Circuit Court of Appeals Act of 1891, in which Congress created an appeals court for each of the nine federal judicial districts then in existence. Judicial districts are geographic regions of the nation, each of which is served by a single federal district court. A separate court of appeals was created for the District of Columbia in 1893. In 1911, Congress abolished the system of circuit courts, finding them unnecessary and redundant in light of the existence of the circuit courts of appeal.

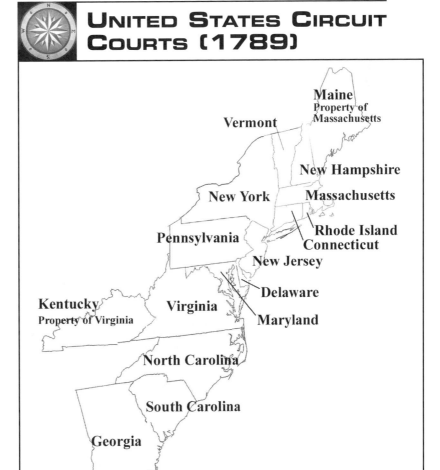

UNITED STATES CIRCUIT COURTS (1789)

The Judiciary Act of 1789 established the first judicial circuit courts in the United States. The act also required the justices of the Supreme Court to "ride circuit," or hear cases, in the circuit courts during each year.

UNITED STATES CIRCUIT COURTS (2009)

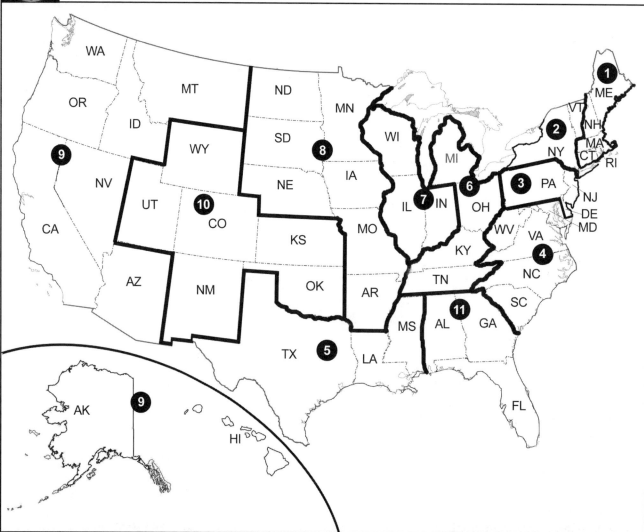

Today, the United States is organized into twelve judicial circuits, which includes the District of Columbia Circuit Court. The circuit with the smallest number of appellate judges is the First Circuit, and the one with the largest number of appellate judges is the vast and populous Ninth Circuit in the far West. The number of judges that the Congress authorizes for each circuit is established by law.

Currently, there are 11 numbered judicial districts in the United States, as well as the District of Columbia, each of which is served by its own circuit court of appeals. There is also a federal circuit court with **jurisdiction,** or authority, over all appeals dealing with certain subjects. This court also hears appeals from specialized courts such as patent courts. Finally, a separate circuit court of appeals hears cases involving active members of the armed forces.

Jurisdiction and Procedure

Because the courts of appeal possess only appellate jurisdiction, they do not hold trials. Instead,

they review decisions made by trial courts to determine if the lower courts made any errors in interpreting or applying the law. This means circuit courts consider only the records and arguments presented in the original trial; they do not consider any evidence or arguments not introduced at that time. Lawyers for the parties involved, however, may present oral arguments before the appeals judges. In most cases, a three-judge panel, randomly selected from judges in the circuit, hears appeals. In some cases, however, all of the judges assigned to the court may hear the appeal; this is known as an "en banc" hearing.

Decisions reached by a circuit court of appeals are considered **precedents,** or decisions used as guides for deciding future cases. As such, they become a permanent part of the law that other courts in that circuit must follow for guidance when considering how to rule in similar cases.

At one time, parties to certain types of cases before circuit courts of appeal had an automatic right to appeal the decision to the Supreme Court. This right of automatic appeal no longer exists. Today, a party who wishes to appeal a case to the Court may ask for a **writ of certiorari**—an order issued by an appeals court to a lower court to review that court's findings. The Court rejects the vast majority of requests for writs of certiorari.

See also: Appellate Jurisdiction; Circuit Court of Appeals Act of 1891; Judicial System, U.S.; Judiciary Act of 1789; Maritime and Admiralty Law; Original Jurisdiction; Precedent.

Further Reading
Drewry, Gavin, et. al. *The Court of Appeal.* Oxford, UK: Hart Publishing, 2007.
Keursten, Ashlyn. *Decisions on the U.S. Courts of Appeals.* London: Routledge, 2001.

Citizenship and Naturalization

Membership in a state or political community and the process by which one becomes a citizen. Although the U.S. Constitution refers to "citizens" in several instances, nowhere does the original document define who is a citizen and how one acquires citizenship. At the time the Constitution was written, a citizen was assumed to be a person who was born in the country and who remained under its **jurisdiction** and protection.

Defining Citizenship
In the 1857 *Dred Scott v. Sandford* decision, the Court adopted an extremely narrow definition that excluded blacks, even native-born free blacks, from citizenship. It also held that national citizenship was dependent on and resulted from state citizenship. This ruling led ultimately to the Fourteenth Amendment, ratified in 1868. Its first sentence states, "All persons born or naturalized in the United States and subject to the jurisdiction thereof, are citizens of the United States and of the State wherein they reside."

The Court confirmed and further defined citizenship in the case of *United States v. Wong Kim Ark* (1898). Here, the Supreme Court declared that, under the Fourteenth Amendment, children born in the United States to resident alien parents were citizens even if their parents were barred from becoming citizens. The Court made several exceptions, including "children of foreign sovereigns or their ministers, or born on public ships, or of enemies within and during hostile occupation of part of our territory, and . . . children of members of the Indian tribes . . ." This last exception was eliminated in 1925, when Congress granted citizenship to Indians living in tribes.

Naturalization
The Court has allowed Congress to establish whatever conditions it deems necessary for citizenship through naturalization. "Naturalization is a privilege, to be given, qualified or withheld as Congress may determine and which the alien may claim as of right only upon compliance with the terms which Congress imposes," the Court said in 1931. The Court has held that Congress even may exclude an entire class or race of people from eligibility for citizenship, and may expel aliens from the country. Wong Kim Ark's parents could not become citizens because Congress in 1882 specifically prohibited citizenship by naturalization to Chinese.

Exclusions
After ratification of the Fourteenth Amendment, Congress enacted laws limiting naturalized citizenship to whites and to blacks of African descent. It also extended citizenship to the residents of some, but not all, of the U.S. territories. The residents of Hawaii became citizens in 1900, those of Puerto Rico in 1917, and those of the Virgin Islands in 1927. Not until passage of the 1952 Immigration and Nationality Act did Congress bar the use of race as a reason for denying citizenship.

Other conditions set by Congress have excluded from naturalization anarchists, members of the Communist Party, and others who advocate

A - Z

A – Z

SPOTLIGHT

Washington, D.C., and Citizenship

The Framers of the Constitution decided that the capital of the new nation should be located outside the control of any state. In 1790, Congress approved a site selected by President George Washington (1789–1797) along the Potomac River, and the site was named the District of Columbia, after Christopher Columbus. Since that time, the city has grown and spread. Today, Washington, D.C., and the District of Columbia are one and the same. The site that was chosen more than two hundred years ago as the nation's capital is now home to almost six hundred thousand people—the vast majority of them U.S. citizens.

Under the Constitution, Congress has final legislative authority over the District of Columbia. Thus, Congress makes laws for the district's citizens. In its early history, the district enjoyed limited self-government, electing a mayor and a council. This arrangement ended in 1874. For the next one hundred years, the district was governed by a board of three commissioners appointed by the president. All the while, the citizens of the district continued to push for home rule. Finally, in 1973, Congress passed the Home Rule Act. The district approved the act, and, in 1975, an elected mayor and council took office.

The home-rule campaign was accompanied by a movement to give the district's citizens the right to vote. The Twenty-third Amendment (1961) gave the district three electoral votes in presidential elections. However, its residents still had no representative in Congress. In 1970, Congress granted the district the authority to elect a nonvoting delegate to the House of Representatives. Therefore, despite being U.S. citizens, District of Columbia residents have no voting representation in Congress.

the violent overthrow of the government. To qualify for naturalization, an alien must have been a resident of the country for five years and be of "good moral character." The latter phrase has been interpreted to exclude drunks, adulterers, polygamists, gamblers, convicted felons, and homosexuals. The Court has generally sustained these exclusions.

Denaturalization

As early as 1824, the Court declared that there was no difference between a naturalized citizen and one who was native born. Aside from not being qualified to run for the presidency,

naturalized citizens enjoy the same rights, privileges, and responsibilities as do native-born citizens. The exception is that naturalized citizens may be denaturalized.

The Immigration and Nationality Act of 1952 contained a long list of circumstances under which a citizen would lose his or her citizenship. These included voting in a foreign election, being convicted for desertion during time of war and being discharged from the armed services, and leaving or remaining outside the country to avoid military service. The question was whether performing any of these actions amounted to voluntarily giving up one's citizenship. If not, then their validity turned on whether Congress had the power to revoke citizenship.

In a series of rulings, the Court rejected the idea that Congress has "any general power, express or implied, to take away an American citizen's citizenship without his assent. . . . 'All persons born or naturalized in the United States . . . are citizens of the United States. . . .' There is no indication in these words of a fleeting citizenship, good at the moment it is acquired but subject to destruction by the government at any time." The Court did make an exception for those who obtained their naturalization through fraud.

See also: Aliens, Protection of; *Dred Scott v. Sandford* (1857).

Civil Rights Act of 1964

The first federal law prohibiting job discrimination. The Civil Rights Act of 1964 prohibited employers, unions, union hiring halls, and employment agencies from discriminating on the grounds of race, color, religion, sex, or national origin in the hiring, classification, training, or promotion of anyone. The act also created the Equal Employment Opportunities Commission (EEOC) to hear complaints and seek compliance with the law.

The Court first fully discussed the scope of Title VII of the Civil Rights Act of 1964 in *Griggs v. Duke Power Co.* (1971). Black employees charged that the company had unfairly discriminated when it required them to have a high school diploma or pass a generalized intelligence test as a condition for employment or promotion. The black workers claimed that neither requirement was related to successful job performance. They also argued that that the requirements disqualified a substantially higher number of blacks than whites, and that the jobs in question were filled by whites under the company's former longstanding policy of racial preference. The Court ruled that under those circumstances the job qualification requirements were discriminatory.

Later cases tested the circumstances under which an employer might challenge a claim of racial discrimination. A unanimous Court held in

McDonnell Douglas Corp. v. Green (1973) that the Civil Rights Act of 1964 did not require a company to rehire a black employee who had engaged in deliberate unlawful protests against it. However, neither was the company permitted to use the protests as a reason for refusing to rehire the employee because of his race. In *Furnco Construction Corp. v. Waters* (1978), the Court ruled that a firm may cite the hiring of a substantial number of black workers to support a claim that it is not guilty of discrimination. However, the Court ruled "a racially balanced work force cannot immunize an employer from liability for specific acts of discrimination."

The Court has upheld the authority of lower federal courts to award back wages and retirement benefits to persons who have suffered illegal job discrimination. In *Albemarle Paper Co. v. Moody* (1975), the Court ruled that back pay was a proper remedy for past job discrimination, even in cases where the employer had acted in good faith to end discrimination. In *Franks v. Bowman Transportation Co. Inc.* (1976), the Court also upheld the authority of federal courts to award retroactive seniority rights and benefits to persons denied employment or promotion by biased policies.

See also: Civil Rights and the Supreme Court; Equal Employment Opportunity; Racial Equality.

Civil Rights and the Supreme Court

Supreme Court rulings that deal with the basic protections ensured by the U.S. Constitution, protections such as freedom of belief, speech, and association. Although the Constitution grants these and other civil rights to U.S. citizens, the federal government has not always been willing or able to safeguard them against infringement by states or individuals. Until the early-to-mid-twentieth century, the Court accepted this situation, repeatedly striking down federal laws intended to protect individual rights. Since then, however, the Court has tended to take a broader view of the federal government's power to ensure that all citizens can exercise their civil rights.

A – Z

Post-Civil War Developments

Civil rights first became a central issue in American politics following the Civil War (1861–1865). In December 1865, eight months after the war's end, the Thirteenth Amendment to the Constitution abolished slavery. Three years later, the Fourteenth Amendment granted citizenship to "[a]ll persons born or naturalized in the United States, and subject to the jurisdiction thereof." It also stated: "[n]o State shall make or enforce any law which shall abridge the privileges or immunities of citizens of the United States; nor shall any State deprive any person of life, liberty, or property, without due process of law; nor deny to any person within its jurisdiction the equal protection of the laws."

The Civil War amendments were aimed at granting full citizenship to former slaves, but the concepts of due process and equal protection mentioned in the Fourteenth Amendment would become the focus of a broad array of civil rights arguments before the Court. Ultimately, the question the Court would be called upon to answer was whether the due process clause of the Fourteenth Amendment meant that the freedoms guaranteed in the Bill of Rights applied to the states as well as the federal government. For many years after **ratification,** or formal approval of the Fourteenth Amendment, the Court refused to endorse this position, known as incorporation.

Early Setbacks

The first case to test the incorporation doctrine involved not former slaves but white butchers in the city of New Orleans. In the *Slaughterhouse Cases* (1873), the state of Louisiana had granted one firm the exclusive right to operate a slaughterhouse in the New Orleans city limits. Other local butchers argued that this deprived them of their right to carry on doing business, which the Fourteenth Amendment guaranteed.

The Court voted 5-4 against the butchers, with the majority arguing that the Fourteenth Amendment applied only to actions of the federal government. In their ruling, the justices found that citizenship in the nation and citizenship in a state were distinct from one another. It was left up to the individual states to protect the civil rights of their citizens; the federal government had no authority to intervene.

Two years later, Congress responded by passing the Civil Rights Act of 1875. This act provided full federal protection of civil rights for individuals in all states, but it proved short-lived. In a collection of lawsuits known as the *Civil Rights Cases* (1883), the Court struck down the act as unconstitutional. The cases involved several instances in which owners of public accommodations, including inns, hotels, railroads, and theaters, denied equal access to blacks. Writing for the 8-1 majority, Justice Joseph P. Bradley found the reason simple: The Fourteenth Amendment forbids state action, not "individual invasion of individual rights."

Protecting Segregation

In 1896, the Court issued one of its most infamous decisions in the highly charged case of *Plessy v. Ferguson.* Four years before, Homer Plessy, an African American, boarded a whites-only railroad car on the East Louisiana Railroad. By this time every Southern state had passed so-called Jim Crow laws that imposed racial segregation throughout every aspect of society. When a railroad official ordered Plessy to move to a blacks-only car, Plessy refused and was arrested.

Plessy argued that, by forcing him to sit on a segregated car, the railroad had violated his rights granted by the Thirteenth and Fourteenth amendments. After losing at the state level, Plessy appealed his case to the Supreme Court, which ruled against him by a vote of 7-1. The majority concluded that the Louisiana segregation law did not violate Plessy's constitutional rights. Furthermore, the Court denied that "the enforced separation of the two races stamps the colored race with a badge of inferiority. If this be so, it is not by reason of anything found in the act, but solely because the colored race chooses to put that construction upon it." The verdict in *Plessy* effectively gave judicial approval to the practice of government-imposed racial segregation.

Twentieth Century Progress

For the next thirty years, the Court continued to reject arguments applying Fourteenth Amendment protections to the states. The cases it heard involved a variety of matters, including voting rights, poll taxes, and maximum work-hour laws. In the 1920s and 1930s, however, the Court began to move toward a broader view of civil rights protection.

Securing Incorporation

The first break in the wall of anti-incorporation rulings came in the 1925 case of *Gitlow v. New York*. Benjamin Gitlow was convicted of violating a New York law that forbade the publication of documents advocating forcible overthrow of the government. He claimed that the law deprived him of his First Amendment guarantees of freedom of speech and the press. The Court agreed with Gitlow that the Fourteenth Amendment's due process clause did apply the First Amendment's protections to persons threatened by state actions. However, it also ruled that the New York law did not violate those rights, and so refused to overturn his conviction. Nevertheless, the ruling established the principle of incorporation and opened the door to expanded protection of civil rights.

In *Palko v. Connecticut* (1937), the Court declined to rule that the Fourteenth Amendment's guarantee of due process of law automatically extended the guarantees in the Bill of Rights to protect persons against state and local officials as it did against the federal government. Only those rights essential to a scheme of "ordered liberty"—that is, elements of the first ten amendments protecting against extreme and arbitrary government actions—were binding upon the states. Over the next 30 years, however, the justices would place almost all the guarantees of the Bill of Rights in this "essential" category.

Setting the Stage

After 1937, the Court directed its efforts toward issues of personal rights and began also to develop different standards for different types of cases. When faced with regulations of business or property, the justices deferred to Congress or the states and upheld the laws. They became more willing, however, to strike down federal and state laws that infringed upon civil rights and liberties.

This change was illustrated in *United States v. Carolene Products Co.* (1938). In it, the Court upheld a federal law barring the interstate transportation of certain milk products. In the majority opinion, Justice Harlan Fiske Stone set out a double standard for constitutional cases. When a law was challenged as impinging upon economic rights, he said, the Court would presume the law to be valid, unless the challenger could prove otherwise. If a law was challenged as impinging upon

personal liberties protected by the Bill of Rights, the Court might be less inclined to assume the law's validity. This new set of standards, plus the extension of the guarantees of the Bill of Rights to the states begun with *Gitlow*, set the stage for the civil rights revolution to come.

Brown and After

Perhaps the high-water mark in the Court's rulings on civil rights occurred with the case *Brown v. Board of Education* (1954). The case involved a challenge to the racially segregated public school system in Topeka, Kansas. Earlier cases had upheld the constitutionality of segregated schools as long as the facilities provided to each race were "substantially equal." In his first major opinion, new Chief Justice Earl Warren said, "We conclude that in the field of public education the doctrine of 'separate but equal' has no place. Separate educational facilities are inherently unequal."

The ruling in *Brown v. Board of Education* reversed the ruling in *Plessy* and set off a long overdue revolution in civil rights. After *Brown*, however, the Court played only a secondary role in the accelerating civil rights movement. In 1964, Congress at last reasserted its power to implement the promises of the Civil War amendments through legislation. Passage of the comprehensive 1964 Civil Rights Act was followed in 1965 by the Voting Rights Act, and in 1968 by the Fair Housing Act. The modern Supreme Court, unlike the Court of the 1870s and 1880s, reinforced congressional action, finding these revolutionary statutes clearly constitutional.

See also: Bill of Rights; *Brown v. Board of Education* (1954); Civil Rights Act of 1964; *Civil Rights Cases* (1883); Constitution, Rights Guaranteed by: Due Process; Equal Protection of the Law; *Plessy v. Ferguson* (1896); Segregation; States, Citizens, and the Supreme Court; Warren, Earl.

Further Reading

Davis, Abraham L., and Barbara L. Graham. *The Supreme Court, Race, and Civil Rights: From Marshall to Rehnquist.* Belmont, CA: Sage, 1996.

Savage, David G. *The Supreme Court and Individual Rights.* Washington, DC: CQ Press, 2009.

A–Z

Civil Rights Cases (1883)

Supreme Court cases that struck down the Civil Rights Act of 1875. That act made it a crime to deny equal access and enjoyment of public accommodations to black persons. The rulings in these cases made it much more difficult to enforce the fundamental civil rights guaranteed to blacks by the Thirteenth and Fourteenth Amendments.

In the *Civil Rights Cases* (1883), the Court very narrowly interpreted the Fourteenth Amendment's protection for black citizens. This narrowing process consisted of two elements: a limited category of federally protected rights, and an insistence that the Fourteenth Amendment applied only to state, not private, action. In the *Civil Rights Cases*, the Court struck down the Civil Rights Act of 1875 as beyond the power granted to Congress by the Fourteenth Amendment. There were five such cases grouped under the title of the *Civil Rights Cases* and decided together by the Court.

In *United States v. Stanley* and *United States v. Nichols,* the defendants were charged with refusing to allow blacks equal access to inns and hotels. In *United States v. Ryan* and *United States v. Singleton,* the defendants had refused to allow black people to sit in a certain part of theaters in

San Francisco and New York. *Robinson v. Memphis and Charleston Railroad Co.* resulted from a railroad conductor's refusal to allow a black woman to ride in the "ladies'" car on the train. The Court voted 8-1 to strike down the Civil Rights Act. Writing for the majority, Justice Joseph P. Bradley found the reason simple: The Fourteenth Amendment forbids state action, not "individual invasion of individual rights."

Justice John Marshall Harlan II dissented in strong terms. Harlan felt that the Thirteenth and Fourteenth Amendments authorized Congress to pass legislation barring private racial discrimination:

> If, then, exemption from discrimination, in respect of civil rights, is a new constitutional right . . . and I do not see how this can now be questioned . . . why may not the Nation, by means of its own legislation of a primary direct character, guard, protect and enforce that right? It is a right and privilege which the nation conferred.

It would be more than seventy years before the Court finally declared racial segregation an unconstitutional infringement on the rights of black Americans. In the 1954 case of *Brown v. Board of Education,* the Court declared that separate facilities for whites and blacks were "inherently unequal."

See also: *Brown v. Board of Education* (1954); Civil Rights and the Supreme Court; Harlan, John Marshall II; Racial Equality; Segregation.

Landmark Decision Highlights: *Civil Rights Cases* (1883)

Issue: Whether the Civil Rights Act of 1875 violated the Tenth Amendment of the Constitution, which reserves all powers not granted to the national government to the states or to the people.

Opinion: The Court determined that Fourteenth Amendment restrains only state action. In addition, the fifth section of the amendment empowers Congress only to enforce the prohibition on state action. Private acts of racial discrimination were private wrongs which the national government had no power to correct.

Clinton, William J.

See Presidency and the Supreme Court.

Confessions

Supreme Court rulings concerning how confessions may be obtained or used by law enforcement authorities. The Fifth Amendment to the U.S.

Constitution protects individuals against self-incrimination: no one "shall be compelled in any criminal case to be a witness against himself." No one may be forced to confess, required to testify, or provide evidence that could convict them.

The Court has ruled that only confessions given voluntarily are admissible as evidence. This requirement has long been the rule in federal courts; since 1936, the same rule has applied to state courts. The question is how to determine when a confession is voluntary. In 1884, the Court said that an involuntary confession is one that "appears to have been made . . . because of a threat or promise . . . which, operating upon the fears or hopes of the accused . . . deprive him of that freedom of will or self-control essential to make his confession voluntary within the meaning of the law."

Delay in charging a suspect with a crime is a significant factor in determining if a confession is admissible. In *McNabb v. United States* (1943), the Court held that confessions obtained after "unnecessary delay" in a suspect's arraignment could not be used as evidence in federal court.

The Court has also determined that the Sixth Amendment's right to counsel applies to confessions. In *Massiah v. United States* (1964), the justices declared that an indicted person could not properly be questioned or persuaded to make incriminating remarks in the absence of a lawyer. That same year, in *Escobedo v. Illinois*, the Court ruled that, in the absence of a lawyer, police must warn suspects of their "absolute constitutional right to remain silent." Any statements made by a person not so warned are not admissible as evidence. In such a case, the Court considers that the accused has been denied counsel in violation of the Sixth Amendment.

Two years after *Escobedo*, the Court, in *Miranda v. Arizona*, (1966) set out "concrete constitutional guidelines" for interrogation practices of state and local police. It forbade prosecutors from using incriminating statements obtained from suspects during interrogation unless strict safeguards had been followed to guarantee that the suspect was aware of his or her rights to remain silent and to have the aid of an attorney. "The presence of counsel," stated Chief Justice Earl Warren, writing for the majority, was "the adequate protective device" to "insure that

statements made in the government-established atmosphere are not the product of compulsion."

See also: Constitution, Rights Guaranteed by; *Escobedo v. Illinois* (1964); Fifth Amendment Protections; *Miranda v. Arizona* (1966); Right to Legal Counsel; Self Incrimination.

Confirmation of Justices and Judges

Power granted to the U.S. Senate by the Constitution to approve or reject nominees for federal judgeships, including seats on the Supreme Court. Article 2 of the Constitution states that the president shall appoint Court justices by and with the advice and consent of the Senate. However, the advisory role usually occurs after the fact as the Senate considers whether or not to confirm the president's choice. A majority of senators must vote to approve the nominee to confirm the appointment. Of the 148 individuals nominated to a seat on the Supreme Court, twenty-eight—nearly one-fifth—have failed to win confirmation.

Selection and Rejection

Individual senators or representatives, particularly those who are personally close to the president, may wield some unofficial influence in the selection process. Presidents also usually take care to ensure that their choice will not be objectionable to senators from the nominee's state. In general, however, the president has a great deal of freedom when nominating someone for the Court.

Qualifications

Surprisingly, the Constitution sets no requirements for Supreme Court justices. In fact, justices do not even need to have a legal background. Pressure from the legal community and the increasing complexity of the law, however, have made experience on the bench an important consideration in the selection of nominees. Proposals to establish qualifications for the Court have been made throughout the nation's history, but few have received more than passing attention in Congress.

Only two Court nominees have gone unconfirmed primarily on the grounds that they were

A - Z

Supreme Court Nominations Not Confirmed by the Senate

Nominee	President	Date of Nomination	Senate Action	Date of Senate Action
William Paterson	Washington	February 27, 1793	Withdrawn[i]	
John Rutledge[ii]	Washington	July 1, 1795	Rejected (10–14)	December 15, 1795
Alexander Wolcott	Madison	February 4, 1811	Rejected (9–24)	February 13, 1811
John J. Crittenden	J. Q. Adams	December 17, 1828	Postponed	February 12, 1829
Roger Brooke Taney	Jackson	January 15, 1835	Postponed (24–21)[iii]	March 3, 1835
John C. Spencer	Tyler	January 9, 1844	Rejected (21–26)	January 31, 1844
Reuben H. Walworth	Tyler	March 13, 1844	Withdrawn	
Edward King	Tyler	June 5, 1844	Postponed	June 15, 1844
Edward King	Tyler	December 4, 1844	Withdrawn	
John M. Read	Tyler	February 7, 1845	Not acted upon	
George W. Woodward	Polk	December 23, 1845	Rejected (20–29)	January 22, 1846
Edward A. Bradford	Fillmore	August 16, 1852	Not acted upon	
George E. Badger	Fillmore	January 10, 1853	Postponed	February 11, 1853
William C. Micou	Fillmore	February 24, 1853	Not acted upon	
Jeremiah S. Black	Buchanan	February 5, 1861	Rejected (25–26)	February 21, 1861
Henry Stanbery	A. Johnson	April 16, 1866	Not acted upon	
Ebenezer R. Hoar	Grant	December 15, 1869	Rejected (24–33)	February 3, 1870
George H. Williams[ii]	Grant	December 1, 1873	Withdrawn	
Caleb Cushing	Grant	January 9, 1874	Withdrawn	
Stanley Matthews	Hayes	January 26, 1881	Not acted upon[i]	
William B. Hornblower	Cleveland	September 19, 1893	Rejected (24–30)	January 15, 1894
Wheeler H. Peckham	Cleveland	January 22, 1894	Rejected (32–41)	February 16, 1894
John J. Parker	Hoover	March 21, 1930	Rejected (39–41)	May 7, 1930
Abe Fortas	L. Johnson	June 26, 1968	Withdrawn	
Homer Thornberry	L. Johnson	June 26, 1968	Not acted upon	
Clement F. Haynsworth Jr.	Nixon	August 18, 1969	Rejected (45–55)	November 21, 1969
G. Harrold Carswell	Nixon	January 19, 1970	Rejected (45–51)	April 8, 1970
Robert H. Bork	Reagan	July 1, 1987	Rejected (42–58)	October 23, 1987

[i] Later nominated and confirmed
[ii] Nominated for chief justice
[iii] Later nominated for chief justice and confirmed

In the more than two centuries since 1789, the Senate has rejected Supreme Court nominees twenty-eight times. One nominee, Edward King, twice failed to win Senate confirmation. A dozen have been rejected outright, and the remainder have been withdrawn or allowed to lapse when Senate rejection seemed imminent. Three were renominated later and confirmed.

not professionally qualified. In 1873, President Ulysses S. Grant's (1869–1877) nominee for chief justice, George H. Williams, asked that his name be withdrawn from consideration when the Senate showed signs of balking at the nomination. Although Williams had served as chief justice of the Oregon Territory, his record was undistinguished. Nearly one hundred years later, Congress rejected President Richard M. Nixon's (1969–1974) 1970 appointment of G. Harrold Carswell because of Carswell's defense of racial segregation and his opposition to women's rights.

More recently, President George W. Bush (2001–2009) withdrew the nomination of White House Counsel Harriet Miers to succeed the retiring Sandra Day O'Connor in 2007. The nomination drew criticism from both conservative and liberal observers, who cited Miers's absence of judicial experience and questioned her intellectual rigor, as well as her personal ties to Bush. Three weeks after choosing Miers, Bush withdrew the nomination, proposing Samuel Alito for the vacant seat instead. The Senate approved Alito's nomination after two months of deliberation.

Partisan Politics

By far, most Senate rejections of Supreme Court nominees have been grounded in political considerations. A primary factor in the rejection of fourteen nominees was the **"lame-duck"** status of the nominating president, or the fact that the party in control of the Senate was confident that its presidential candidate would win the next election. A "lame duck" refers to a president who fails to win reelection, or who is ineligible for reelection.

Both of these problems afflicted the Court nominations of President John Tyler (1841–1845), who has the dubious distinction of having more nominees rejected than any other president. The Senate confirmed only one of his six nominations. One nominee was rejected because his politics offended the party ruling the Senate. Two appointments were killed because the Senate anticipated correctly that Tyler would not be his party's candidate for president in the next election. Senators wanted to hold the vacancies open to be filled by the incoming president. Two others were rejected after the election of 1844, which Tyler's Whig Party lost to the Democratic candidate James K.

Polk (1845–1849). The Senate preferred to let Polk elect a nominee after he assumed office.

In 1987, the Senate defeated Ronald Reagan's nomination of Robert H. Bork after one of the most heated confirmation battles in history. Bork's rejection stemmed largely from his well-known conservative views and the fact that he had been named to replace Justice Lewis F. Powell Jr., a moderate judge who did not take consistently conservative or liberal positions.

One nominee was denied the position of chief justice because the Senate could not decide what his political views were. In addition to being seventy-four years old at the time of his nomination in 1874, Caleb Cushing had been a Whig, a Tyler Whig, a Democrat, a Johnson Constitutional Conservative, and a Republican. Those shifting allegiances gained him so many political enemies that Senate opposition forced President Ulysses S. Grant to withdraw the nomination.

Perhaps the most pointed political rejection of a nominee was the treatment of Henry Stanbery, President Andrew Johnson's (1865–1869) attorney general. Stanbery was well liked, but the president was not. To deny Johnson any opportunity to make appointments to the Court, Republicans in Congress engineered the passage of legislation that reduced the number of justices from ten to seven as vacancies occurred. The seat to which Stanbery had been appointed in 1865 was thus abolished, and his nomination was never considered.

Controversial Confirmations

The Senate has refused to confirm only five nominees as associate justices and one as chief justice in the twentieth century, compared with a total of twenty-two appointees rejected in the nineteenth century. Several other nominations, however, have faced stiff opposition.

Early Twentieth Century

In 1916, the Senate delayed action on the nomination of Louis Brandeis as the Senate Judiciary Committee pondered the nominee's "radical views." Although opposition to the nomination centered on Brandeis's liberal economic, political, and social posture, there is evidence that much of it was motivated by anti-Semitism.

When Harlan Fiske Stone was nominated to the Court in 1925, he was an attorney general in

DECISION MAKERS

The Importance of Senatorial Courtesy

Senatorial courtesy is the practice by which the president of the United States consults with a state's senior senator before nominating anyone from that state to a federal office. Even today, the practice is strictly observed in connection with the appointment of federal judgeships and U.S. attorneys. Senatorial courtesy is generally observed only when the president and the senator are of the same political party. In rare cases, the president extends this courtesy to a senator from the opposition party.

Although it is an unwritten political custom, senatorial courtesy can have a significant impact on a nominee's confirmation. For example, a feud between a president and a senator prompted the only two rejections made solely on the grounds of senatorial courtesy. When Justice Samuel Blatchford died in 1893, President Grover Cleveland (1885–1889, 1893–1897) sought to replace him with another New Yorker. Senator David B. Hill of New York made several suggestions, but Cleveland ignored his recommendations and nominated New York attorney William B. Hornblower. Hill prevailed upon his colleagues, and the Senate rejected the nomination.

Cleveland then proposed another New Yorker, Wheeler Peckham. Again, Hill objected, and again the Senate followed his wishes. To Hill's surprise, Cleveland abandoned his intention to nominate a New Yorker and instead named Edward D. White of Louisiana, then serving as the Senate's Democratic majority leader. He was confirmed the same day he was nominated.

the midst of prosecuting Burton Wheeler, an influential Democratic senator, for fraud. Wheeler was eventually acquitted of the charges and fought Stone's nomination so vigorously that the Senate sent the nomination back to the Judiciary Committee for investigation. Stone then personally appeared before the committee, something no previous Court nominee had done. Subjected to hostile questioning, Stone's performance was impressive, and he was eventually confirmed by the full Senate.

Charles Evans Hughes's nomination as chief justice in 1930 was attacked primarily because the country was entering the Great Depression, and his views were considered too conservative for the times. Seven years later, Hugo Black encountered difficulties because he had once been a member of the Ku Klux Klan.

Recent Controversies

When Chief Justice Warren Burger announced his retirement in 1986, President Ronald Reagan made no secret of his desire to shape a more conservative Court. Reagan, who believed federal judges had become too activist and were interfering with civil rights and social policy that should be controlled by legislators, nominated William H. Rehnquist to succeed Burger. At the time, Rehnquist was an associate justice and the Court's most conservative member. Although the Senate overwhelmingly confirmed his nomination fifteen years earlier, the Senate debated his appointment as chief justice for more than three months before he won confirmation. Civil rights groups mounted an all-out effort to defeat his nomination.

Five years later, Clarence Thomas was confirmed to the Court by the slimmest margin ever. Thomas, selected by President George H.W. Bush (1989–1993), was narrowly confirmed, 52-48, after months of controversy over Thomas's conservative record and unprecedented last-minute hearings into a former employee's allegations of sexual harassment.

The disclosure of the allegations, and the failure of the committee to investigate them thoroughly, touched off a storm of criticism and demands for more hearings. The Judiciary Committee's awkward handling of the allegations, and the lack of resolution of the charges, prompted an outpouring of public anger and scorn. For several years afterward, Thomas's name continued to be associated with the sexual harassment issue, although nothing was ever proven.

See also: Burger, Warren E.; Hughes, Charles Evans; Nomination of Justices and Judges; O'Connor, Sandra Day; Presidency and the Supreme Court; Rehnquist, William H.; Scalia, Antonin; Thomas, Clarence.

Further Reading

Neubauer, David W., and Stephen S. Meinhold. *Battle Supreme: The Confirmation of Chief Justice John Roberts and the Future of the Supreme Court.* New York: Wadsworth, 2005.

Pickering, Charles W. *Supreme Chaos: The Politics of Judicial Confirmation & the Culture War.* Macon, GA: Stroud and Hall, 2006.

Silverstein, Mark. *Judicious Choices: The Politics of Supreme Court Confirmations, Second Edition.* New York: W.W. Norton, 2007.

Congress and the Supreme Court

Supreme Court rulings that set limits on the exercise of power by Congress, the nation's **legislative** body, made up of the House of Representatives and the Senate. The U.S. Constitution grants the legislature most of the power necessary to govern. It also, however, places specific limits on Congress's exercise of power. The First Amendment, for example, prohibits Congress from interfering with the free exercise of speech, the press, assembly, or religion. However, the Constitution says nothing about who would enforce the limitations on Congress. Was Congress to police itself, or would the judiciary—the Supreme Court in particular—take on this role? Eventually, the Court would assume it, but not without resistance from Congress.

Judicial Review

Most constitutional scholars agree that the framers expected the Supreme Court to assume the watchdog role over Congress. However, the Court did not have a chance to test its power to nullify an act of Congress until 1803. In the case of *Marbury v. Madison*, the majority ruled that Congress violated its authority under the Constitution by passing a law expanding the Court's original **jurisdiction,** or area of authority. Chief Justice John Marshall wrote, "It is, emphatically, the province and duty of the judicial department, to say what the law is."

Scholars have questioned the legal reasoning in *Marbury*, but not its significance. The nation might have survived if the Court had not claimed this power to review and declare invalid acts of Congress. Without the power of **judicial** review, however, there would have been no clear check on the exercise of legislative power. This might well have led to a Congress that had unlimited power over both the federal government and the states.

The Commerce Power

Even as the Court established the supremacy of the Constitution over acts of Congress, it was careful to protect congressional power from encroachment by the states. This point was made forcefully in *Gibbons v. Ogden* (1824), in which the Court ruled that a federal permit overrode a state-granted monopoly. Navigation between two states was interstate commerce, Marshall wrote, and state action would not be permitted to limit Congress's power to regulate interstate commerce. The congressional power over commerce, the Court emphasized in *Gibbons*, was not limited to transportation but extended to all commercial intercourse affecting two or more states. The only commerce Congress could not legislate, Marshall

A – Z

A–Z

Sonia Sotomayor, who was nominated to the Supreme Court by President Barack Obama in May 2009, makes a point as she testifies before the Senate Judiciary Committee in July of that year. Sotomayor was confirmed by the full Senate on August 6, becoming the first Hispanic and 111th justice to serve on the Court. (AP Photo, Pablo Martinez Monsivais)

said, was that wholly within one state not affecting any other state.

In the late nineteenth century, Congress exercised this power to regulate not only the railroads but also the huge trusts that monopolized many of the nation's major industries. Although some of the railroads and many of the trusts operated within single states, Marshall's definition of interstate commerce left room for Congress to regulate them, because they affected more than one state.

The Court, sympathetic to business interests, temporarily narrowed Marshall's definition. It held that Congress only could regulate intrastate matters that directly affected interstate commerce. Intrastate matters affecting interstate commerce indirectly were for the states to regulate. It was for the Court to determine which effects were direct and which indirect.

Social Regulation

During this same period, Congress began to use its commerce and tax powers for social as well as economic purposes, developing a federal "police" power used to protect public health and morals. In 1903, for example, the Court upheld a congressional prohibition on the interstate sale and shipment of lottery tickets. In subsequent terms, the Court made additional use of this new federal power. Encouraged, Congress exercised this power to bar from interstate commerce goods made by child labor.

In 1918, however, the Court returned to the narrow view of the commerce power and struck down the child labor law. Congress, the Court ruled, had attempted to regulate manufacturing, not commerce. In addition, the Court said that while lottery tickets were harmful in themselves, goods made by children were not. For several

Significant Acts of Congress Struck Down as Unconstitutional

Missouri Compromise of 1820

In *Scott v. Sandford* (1857), the Court declared unconstitutional the recently repealed Missouri Compromise of 1820, which prohibited slavery in the Louisiana territories lying north of Missouri's southern boundary. Chief Justice Roger B. Taney wrote that slaves were property and that Congress had no authority to regulate local property rights. Taney also held that even free blacks were not citizens of the United States and could not become citizens. The opinion seriously damaged the Court's prestige, and, rather than settling the slavery issue, the decision probably hastened the onset of the Civil War. The *Scott* decision was overturned by the Thirteenth Amendment, ratified in 1865, prohibiting slavery, and by the Fourteenth Amendment, ratified in 1868, making citizens of all persons born in the United States.

Test Oath Law of 1865

The Court in 1867 declared invalid an 1865 act that required attorneys, as a condition for practicing in federal courts, to swear that they had never engaged in or supported the Southern rebellion against the Union. In *Ex parte Garland* (1867), the Court said that the statute was an unconstitutional bill of attainder because it punished persons by prohibiting them from practicing their professions. The Court also held the statute to be an ex post facto law because it was enacted after the commission of the offense. The Court's opinion in this case and other cases originating in the states indicated that it would not review other federal Reconstruction legislation favorably. To avoid this possibility, Congress removed from the Court's jurisdiction cases arising under certain of those laws. It is the only time in the Court's history that Congress specified a group of laws the Court could not review.

Legal Tender Acts of 1862 and 1863

The Legal Tender Acts, enacted in 1862 and 1863, made paper money a substitute for gold as legal tender in the payment of public and private debts. In *Hepburn v. Griswold* (1870), the Court ruled that Congress had exceeded its authority by making paper money legal tender for the payment of debts incurred before passage of the laws. The outcry from debtors and the potential economic repercussions from this decision were so great that within fifteen months the Court—with two new members—reconsidered, and, in *Knox v. Lee* (1871), overturned its earlier decision, thus establishing paper money as legal currency.

Civil Rights Act of 1875

The Civil Rights Act of 1875—one of several federal statutes enacted in the first decade after the Civil War to end discrimination against blacks—barred discrimination in privately owned public accommodations, such as hotels, theaters, and railway cars. The Court held that neither the Thirteenth Amendment nor the Fourteenth Amendment gave Congress the power to act to bar private discrimination of this type. The decision was one in a series that vitiated Congress's power to enforce effectively the guarantees given to blacks by the two amendments. It would be almost a century before Congress and the Court would effectively overturn this series of rulings.

Federal Income Tax

The Court's decision in *Pollock v. Farmers' Loan and Trust* Co. (1895) struck down the first general peacetime income tax enacted by Congress. The Court held that the section of the statute taxing income from real estate was a direct tax and violated the Constitution's requirement that direct taxes be apportioned among the states. This defect, the Court held, was inseparable from the rest of the tax provisions, so as a result they were all struck down. The ruling was overturned in 1913 with the ratification of the Sixteenth Amendment specifically exempting income taxes from the apportionment requirement.

(continued on next page)

Significant Acts of Congress Struck Down as Unconstitutional, *continued*

"Yellow-Dog" Contracts

Exhibiting an antipathy toward organized labor, the Court, in *Adair v. United States* (1908), declared unconstitutional a section of the 1898 Erdman Act making it unlawful for any railway employer to require as a condition of employment that employees not join a labor union. The act was an infringement on property rights guaranteed by the Fifth Amendment, the Court said. Congress had exceeded its authority under the commerce clause, the Court added, because labor relations were not part of interstate commerce and did not directly affect it. It was not until 1930 that the Court sanctioned a federal law guaranteeing railway employees collective bargaining rights and not until 1937 that the Court acknowledged that labor relations affected interstate commerce.

Child Labor Laws

The Court, in *Hammer v. Dagenhart* (1918), struck down a 1916 law that sought to end child labor by prohibiting the shipment via interstate commerce of any goods made by children under a certain age who had worked more than a specified number of hours. The majority said that Congress was not regulating commerce but manufacture, an authority it did not possess. Congress then passed a second statute placing a heavy tax on any goods made by children. The Court struck down this statute, as well, in *Bailey v. Drexel Furniture Co.* (1922), declaring that the tax was not intended to raise revenue but to penalize employers of children. *Hammer v. Dagenhart* was finally reversed in *United States v. Darby* (1941), in which the Court upheld a federal minimum wage and maximum hour law that applied to children and adults

Agricultural Adjustment Act of 1933

Designed to restore farm prices and farmers' purchasing power, the Agricultural Adjustment Act of 1933 levied an excise tax on seven basic food commodities and used the revenue to pay benefits to farmers who reduced their production of the commodities. Striking down the act in *United States v. Butler* (1936), the majority held that Congress had no constitutional authority to regulate agricultural production. The following year, after President Franklin D. Roosevelt's Court-packing threat, the majority approved similar tax benefit schemes when it upheld federal Social Security and unemployment compensation legislation in *Helvering v. Davis* (1937) and *Steward Machine Co. v. Davis* (1937). In 1938, Congress passed a second Agricultural Adjustment Act, which substituted marketing quotas for the processing tax and production quotas of the first act. This second act was upheld in *Mulford v. Smith* (1939).

National Industrial Recovery Act of 1933

The centerpiece of President Franklin D. Roosevelt's economic recovery program, the National Industrial Recovery Act (NIRA) authorized the president to approve industry-wide fair competition codes containing wage and hour regulations. In *Panama Refining Co. v. Ryan* (1935), the Court struck down as an unconstitutional delegation of legislative power a section that authorized the president to prohibit from interstate commerce so-called "hot oil," produced in violation of state regulations controlling production. The Court held that Congress had not drawn specific enough standards to guide the president in exercising such discretionary authority. *Panama* was followed quickly by the "sick chicken case"—*A.L. A. Schechter Poultry Corp. v. United States* (1935)—in which a unanimous Court struck down the entire NIRA, because it gave the president too much discretion in establishing and approving fair competition codes, and because it exceeded congressional power by applying to intrastate as well as interstate commerce.

Since the first declaration that an act of Congress was unconstitutional—in *Marbury v. Madison* (1803)—the Court has found more than 150 particular federal laws to be in violation of the Constitution. Only a handful of the laws struck down, however, have been of major significance for the country.

years, the Court struck down child labor laws while upholding other uses of the federal police power. Only against labor unions did the Court maintain a consistently conservative stance. It ruled repeatedly that many strikes and boycotts were illegal restraints of trade under the antitrust laws.

The Depression and New Deal

During the Great Depression of the 1930s, President Franklin D. Roosevelt (1933–1945) proposed—and Congress enacted—economic recovery laws that regulated business to an unprecedented degree. The Supreme Court struck down several key laws, ruling that Congress did not have the broad power necessary to cope with the national crisis. A majority of the Court during this era refused to acknowledge that Congress had the authority, through its commerce and tax powers, to try to relieve local economic conditions.

In 1937, frustrated with the Court's opposition to his policies, Roosevelt proposed adding a new justice to the Court for each sitting justice over the age of 70½. He hoped in this way to balance the votes of the older, more conservative justices with those of his new appointees. Apparently responding to the president's "Court-packing" threat, the Court returned to Marshall's broad view of the commerce power. The Court upheld a series of acts of Congress banning unfair labor practices and regulating wages and hours and agricultural production. It also approved federal laws establishing the Social Security pension system and the federal-state unemployment compensation system.

Recent Interpretations

Only twice in the next fifty years did the Court declare an act of Congress an unconstitutional exercise of the commerce power. During the same period, it upheld use of the commerce power as a tool to prohibit racial discrimination in public places, and to guarantee the right to travel within the United States.

In 1995, the Court seemed to return to a narrower view when it struck down a 1990 act of Congress banning guns near schools. The majority declared that this law was an impermissible and unjustified intervention in local affairs. Congress had made no explicit connection between interstate commerce and the dangers of guns on school grounds, nor had it distinguished the law from state gun-control statutes applicable to school grounds. To uphold this law in the face of those facts, wrote Chief Justice William H. Rehnquist, would convert Congress's commerce power to a general police power.

States and Citizens

Questions of citizenship in the United States and its territories have posed continuing problems for the Court. In its most infamous opinion, the *Scott v. Sandford* (1857) decision, the Court declared that blacks were not and could not become citizens. The Civil War reversed that decision, and ratification of the Fourteenth Amendment (1868) made citizens of all persons born in the United States and subject to its jurisdiction.

Congressional control over citizenship is extensive. In addition to setting conditions for naturalization, Congress, with the Court's approval, has prohibited several categories of people from entering the country or applying for citizenship. It was Congress that wrote the Fourteenth Amendment, the first definition of citizenship to appear in the Constitution. Following that language, the Court has sustained the citizenship of any person born in the United States, even if the child's parents were not and could not become citizens. Not fully resolved by the Court, however, is the question of whether Congress may revoke the citizenship of a native-born or naturalized citizen against his or her will. The ruling case holds that Congress may not revoke citizenship.

Additional Powers

In most other areas of constitutional authority, the Court has upheld the vast majority of laws passed by Congress. The Court has overturned only three congressional decisions concerning taxes, spending, and currency. In each case, Congress passed subsequent laws that essentially invalidated the Court rulings. The Court has not challenged a law in this area since 1936.

The Court also has taken little part in defining congressional powers in the field of foreign

A–Z

Justices Who Served in Congress

Justice	Congressional Service	Court Service
Senate		
William Paterson	1789–November 13, 1790	1793–1806
Oliver Ellsworth	1789–March 8, 1796	1796–1799
Levi Woodbury	1825–1831; 1841–1845	1845–1851
David Davis	1877–1883	1862–1877
Salmon P. Chase*	1849–1855; March 4–6, 1861	1874–1873
Stanley Matthews	March 21, 1877–1879	1881–1889
Howell E. Jackson	1881–April 4, 1886	1894–1895
Edward D. White*	1891–March 12, 1894	1894–1921
Hugo L. Black	1927–August 19, 1937	1937–1971
Harold H. Burton	1941–September 30, 1945	1945–1958
Sherman Minton	1935–1941	1949–1956
House		
John Marshall*	1799–June 7, 1800	1801–1835
Joseph Story	May 23, 1808–1809	1811–1845
Gabriel Duvall	November 11, 1794– March 28, 1796	1812–1835
John McLean	1813–1816	1829–1861
Henry Baldwin	1817–May 8, 1822	1830–1844
James M. Wayne	1829–January 13, 1835	1835–1867
Philip B. Barbour	September 19, 1814–1825	1836–1841
Nathan Clifford	1839–1843	1858–1881
William Strong	1847–1851	1870–1880
Joseph McKenna	1885–1892	1898–1925
William H. Moody	November 5, 1895–May 1, 1902	1906–1910
Mahlon Pitney	1895–January 10, 1899	1912–1922
Fred M. Vinson*	January 12, 1924–1929; 1931–May 12, 1938	1946–1953
Both Chambers		
John McKinley	S: November 27, 1826–1831; H: 1833–1835	March 4–April 22, 1837 1837–1852
Lucius Q.C. Lamar	H: 1857–1860; 1873–1877 S: 1877–March 6, 1885	1888–1893
George Sutherland	H: 1901–1903 S: 1905–1917	1922–1938
James F. Byrnes	H: 1911–1925 S: 1931–July 8, 1941	1941–1942

* Denotes a chief justice

Twenty-seven of the Supreme Court justices have served in the Senate, the House, or both before appointment to the bench. Only one justice, David Davis, left the Court to serve in Congress, in 1877, when the Illinois legislature elected him to the Senate. Davis had served on the Court since 1862.

Major Acts of Congress Relating to the Supreme Court

Judiciary Act of 1789	Provided basic appellate jurisdiction Created a three-tier judiciary staffed by Supreme Court justices and district court judges Required Supreme Court justices to ride circuit Mandated that the Court consist of a chief justice and five associate justices, any four of whom would be a quorum
Judiciary Act of 1807	Set the number of justices at seven
Judiciary Act of 1837	Divided the country into nine circuits Brought the number of justices to nine Expanded the Court's jurisdiction to include appeals from new states and territories
Judiciary Act of 1863	Added a tenth justice
Judiciary Act of 1866	Allowed the Court to fall to seven members
Judiciary Act of 1869	Increased the size of the Court to nine members Allowed federal judges to retire at full pay at seventy (changed to sixty-five in 1954) if they had at least ten years of service
Act of 1873	Formally fixed October as the start of the Court's term
Judiciary Act of 1891	Established nine Circuit Courts of Appeals (renamed Courts of Appeals in 1948) Broadened Court review of criminal cases Provided for limited discretionary review via writs of certiorari
Judicial Code of 1911	Created general right of appeal from criminal convictions to the circuit court of appeals, with ultimate review lying with the Supreme Court
Judiciary Act of 1925	Greatly extended the Court's discretionary jurisdiction by replacing mandatory appeals with petitions for certiorari
Act to Improve the Administration of Justice (1988)	Eliminated virtually all of the Court's nondiscretionary jurisdiction, except for appeal in reapportionment cases and suits under the Civil Rights Act, the Voting Rights Act, antitrust laws, and the Presidential Election Campaign Act

Article III of the Constitution broadly outlines the exercise of the federal judicial power, but it was Congress's task to fill in the details of the new judicial system. The Judiciary Act of 1789 was Congress's first statutory measure to that effect. Much of the legislation since passed concerning the Supreme Court spells out the number of justices and the scope of the Court's jurisdiction.

A – Z

affairs. In many instances, the Court has refused even to review a foreign affairs or war powers issue, describing it as a political question, the answer to which the political branches of government must decide. In cases the Court has agreed to hear, it generally has upheld exercise of the power in question.

The Court has never questioned the right of Congress to investigate its own members for possible misconduct. Nor has it denied the use of such power to examine issues so that Congress might legislate more effectively. The Court has upheld the right of Congress to compel witnesses to testify and to punish those who refuse. The Court has even been reluctant to curb Congress' investigatory power in order to protect constitutionally guaranteed individual rights.

The Constitution gives Congress powers over its own internal affairs. These include judging the qualifications of members, punishing members for misconduct, regulating federal elections, and establishing rules of procedure. In 1969, the Court held that Congress did not have the authority to add to the Constitution's list of qualifications for membership in the House and Senate. In 1995, the Court cited those qualifications when it ruled that neither Congress nor the states could impose term limits on members of Congress.

See also: Checks and Balances; Citizenship and Naturalization; Commerce Power and the Supreme Court; Fiscal and Monetary Power and the Supreme Court; Foreign Affairs and the Supreme Court; Jurisdiction of the Supreme Court; *Marbury v. Madison* (1803); New Deal and the Supreme Court; Roosevelt's 1937 Court Reform Plan; Separation of Powers; War Power and the Supreme Court.

Further Reading

Fisher, Louis. *The Supreme Court and Congress: Rival Interpretations*. Washington, DC: CQ Press, 2008.

Quirk, William. *Courts and Congress: America's Unwritten Constitution*. Piscataway, NJ: Transaction Publishers, 2008.

Warren, Charles. *Congress, the Constitution, & the Supreme Court*. Buffalo, NY: William S. Hein, 1994.

Constitution of the United States

The governing document of the United States since 1788, which outlines the basic laws of the nation. One of the most important functions of the Supreme Court is to determine whether laws passed by Congress or the states violate the Constitution. The Court is charged with striking down laws that it finds unconstitutional. However, the Constitution was designed to be flexible enough to adapt to changing times and circumstances. As a result, what the Court defines as constitutional has also evolved over time.

The U.S. Constitution consists of an introduction, or preamble, followed by seven Articles that outline the basic structure and functions of the federal government. It also contains twenty-seven **amendments,** or additions, which define the basic rights of citizens and clarify some of the governmental powers and procedures set forth in the Articles.

Article 3 of the Constitution concerns the judicial branch of the government. It places the federal judicial power "in one Supreme Court, and in such inferior Courts as the Congress may from time to time ordain and establish." It provides for lifetime tenure for federal judges, but also empowers Congress to impeach and remove judges from office. Article 3 establishes the **jurisdiction,** or area of authority, of federal courts, and provides that all trials, except for impeachments, be jury trials. The last section of the article defines treason and its punishment.

The first ten amendments to the Constitution are known as the Bill of Rights. These amendments guarantee individuals certain basic freedoms and privileges that the government may not deny them. They include freedom of speech, religion, assembly, and petition; freedom of the press; the right to bear arms; freedom from unreasonable search and seizure; the right to a trial by jury; the right to legal counsel; and freedom from excessive bail or cruel and unusual punishment. The Ninth Amendment gives to the people any rights not specifically mentioned in the Constitution. The Tenth Amendment reserves to the states any powers not specifically granted to the federal government.

After the Civil War (1861-1865), Congress felt compelled to protect the rights of newly freed slaves from government interference in the former Confederate states. The Thirteenth Amendment (1865) abolished slavery; the Fourteenth Amendment granted citizenship (1868) to all native-born individuals and prohibited states from taking actions that denied or restricted their citizens' constitutional rights. Over time, the Court has issued a number of rulings incorporating the Fourteenth Amendment's protections into all the amendments that make up the Bill of Rights.

Virtually all of the remaining amendments deal with voting rights, elections, or presidential succession. Of these issues, the Court has dealt most frequently with voting rights, particularly questions relating to state interference with exercising the right to vote.

See also: Articles of Confederation; Constitution, Rights Guaranteed by; States, Citizens, and the Supreme Court.

Contempt of Court

A court ruling that finds that an individual has shown disrespect to the court or its powers. The contempt power was reinforced by the Judiciary Act of 1789, which authorized the new federal courts "to punish by fine or imprisonment, at the[ir] discretion . . . all contempts of authority in any cause or hearing before the same."

The essential characteristic of contempt is obstructiveness, blocking the proper judicial functions of the court. Little question has been raised about judicial power to maintain peace in the courtroom through the use of the contempt power. In 1970, the Court affirmed the power of a judge to keep peace in the courtroom, even at the cost of having a defendant bound and gagged or physically removed.

A judge may punish individuals summarily for contempt committed in his or her presence; this is known as direct contempt. Indirect contempt involves punishing an individual not in the court's presence, usually for disobeying a court order. As early as 1821, the Supreme Court urged restraint in the exercise of the contempt power. At least one judge, James H. Peck, disregarded this advice and in 1830 was impeached for using the contempt power to disbar and imprison a man who had published an article criticizing one of his opinions. Peck was acquitted, but the event resulted in an 1831 law limiting the use of the contempt power.

Contempt may be civil or criminal in nature, and it is sometimes difficult to distinguish between the two. The test developed by the Court in *Gompers v. Buck's Stove and Range Co.* (1911) ruled that civil contempt consists of refusing to act as the court commands and being punished by imprisonment until one obeys. Criminal contempt consists of committing an act forbidden by the Court and being punished for a definite term.

In 1925, the Supreme Court reinforced the distinction between civil and criminal contempt, ruling that the president's power of pardon extended to allow pardons of persons convicted of criminal (but not of civil) contempt. In 1947, the Court muddied somewhat the distinction between civil and criminal contempt by ruling that the same action could be both. The Court upheld the conviction of the United Mine Workers of America and its president, John L. Lewis, on both types of contempt as a result of his and the union's disobedience of a court order forbidding a strike.

See also: Judiciary Act of 1789.

Court-Packing Plan

See Roosevelt's 1937 Court Reform Plan.

Cruel and Unusual Punishment

The use of penalties that are inhumane or out of proportion to the offense being punished. The Eighth Amendment to the U.S. Constitution prohibits "cruel and unusual punishments," but it does not define the key words. It requires the justices to decide for themselves what is meant by the phrase *cruel and unusual.* Whether the Court is bound by the original understanding of these words when they were drafted, a contemporary standard, or some other meaning is not clear.

Like other provisions of the Bill of Rights, the Eighth Amendment had little practical effect until the Court decided it applied to state and local governments as well as to Congress and the federal government. The first victory for an Eighth Amendment claim came in 1910, when the Court overturned a sentence of fifteen years at hard labor given to a Coast Guard officer for falsifying documents. The Court said "the punishment for crime should be graduated and proportioned to the offense." In the mid-twentieth century, the Court quietly began applying the ban to states, but not until 1962 did it strike down a state-imposed punishment as a violation of the Eighth Amendment.

Since 1976, the Court has held that the Eighth Amendment forbids the "unnecessary and wanton infliction of pain" on prisoners. This includes not only directly inflicting abusive punishment, but also withholding needed medical treatment and deliberately exposing inmates to the risk of serious injury. Conservative justices—most notably Clarence Thomas—have dissented from many of these rulings. Thomas argues that abuse by individual prison guards is not necessarily unconstitutional since it is committed by individuals, not imposed by the courts. Justice David H. Souter, taking a different stance, wrote, "The Constitution does not mandate comfortable prisons, but neither does it permit inhumane ones."

The Constitution was written with the idea that death was the proper punishment for some crimes. There are, however, limits to this practice. In the late 1960s, civil rights lawyers broadly challenged the death penalty as violating basic notions of due process of law and equal protection, as well as the ban on cruel and unusual punishment. In *Furman v. Georgia* (1972), the Court ruled that death penalty laws were unconstitutional because they left too much discretion to juries to impose this ultimate sentence. Four years later, in *Gregg v. Georgia,* the Court refused to declare the death penalty unconstitutional in all circumstances. The majority ruled to retain capital punishment, but

the justices continue each term to review closely the administration of the death penalty.

See also: Death Penalty Cases.

Cruzan v. Missouri Department of Health (1990)

Supreme Court case that raised the question of whether an individual has a constitutional right to die. As Justice Antonin Scalia put it, medical advances are capable of keeping the "human body alive for longer than any reasonable person would want to inhabit it." As a result, a growing movement formed around the concept of "death with dignity." Its proponents argue that dying persons have the right to decide to hasten their death.

Background and Majority Opinion

Nancy Beth Cruzan had suffered irreversible brain damage as a result of an auto accident. For seven years, she had been in what doctors called a "persistent vegetative state," with some motor reflexes but no other brain activity. Her condition

---

Landmark Decision Highlights:
Cruzan v. Missouri Department of Health **(1990)**

Issue: In 1983, Nancy Beth Cruzan was involved in a severe automobile accident that left her in a "persistent vegetative state." Did the due process clause of the Fourteenth Amendment permit Cruzan's parents to refuse life-sustaining treatment on their daughter's behalf?

Opinion: The Court held that while individuals enjoy the right to refuse medical treatment under the due process clause, incompetent persons are not able to exercise such rights. The Court found the State of Missouri's actions designed to preserve human life to be constitutional.

was hopeless. Her parents, Lester and Joyce Cruzan, said their daughter would not want to exist this way, so they asked state hospital officials to remove the water and feeding tube that kept her alive. The officials refused, citing Missouri's strong "right to life" policy.

The Cruzans sought a court order to remove the life-sustaining tubes. A trial judge ruled for the parents, citing statements that Nancy had made before her accident indicating that she would not want to be kept alive in such a fashion. The Missouri Supreme Court reversed that decision, holding that the state must have clear and convincing proof of a hospitalized person's wishes before it could act to end her life.

The Court took up the Cruzans' appeal, and in a 5-4 decision upheld the ruling by the Missouri courts. The ruling was not, however, a total loss for advocates of the right to die. "We assume the United States Constitution would grant a competent person a constitutionally protected right to refuse lifesaving hydration and nutrition," said Chief Justice William H. Rehnquist in *Cruzan v. Missouri Department of Health* (1990). If so, a dying or disabled person may choose to die by starvation and dehydration.

All nine justices agreed that there was a basic right to refuse unwanted medical treatment. The Court split, however, on whether one person or persons—in this case, Nancy's parents—could decide for another to end his or her life. "We do not think the Due Process clause (of the Fourteenth Amendment) requires the State to repose judgment on these matters with anyone but the patient herself," the chief justice said. Therefore, Missouri may "require clear and convincing evidence of the patient's wishes . . . (and) choose to defer only to those wishes, rather than confide the decision to close family members." Justices Byron White, Sandra Day O'Connor, Anthony Kennedy, and Scalia agreed.

Other Opinions

In a concurring opinion, Justice O'Connor said patients and others who are in good health should consider drawing up a "living will" so their views

on such end-of-life matters will be known. She also said that states had the freedom to rethink their laws in this area. "No national consensus has yet emerged on the best solution for this difficult and sensitive problem. Today, we decide only that one state's practice does not violate the Constitution; the more challenging task for crafting appropriate procedures for safeguarding incompetents' liberty interest is entrusted to the laboratories of the states," she said.

In another concurring opinion, Justice Scalia expressed his wish that the court would have closed the door to further legal disputes. "I would have preferred that we announce, clearly and promptly, that the federal courts have no business in this field," he wrote. The answers to these end-of-life questions "are neither set forth in the Constitution nor known to the nine justices of this Court any better than they are known to nine people picked at random from the Kansas City telephone book."

The four dissenters—Justices William Brennan, Thurgood Marshall, Harry Blackmun, and John Paul Stevens—said the Cruzans' request should have been honored. "Nancy Cruzan has dwelt in [a] twilight zone for six years," Brennan noted, even though she had told friends she would wish to forgo medical treatment in such a situation. Rather than honor her rights and her wishes, Missouri officials have "determined that an irreversibly vegetative patient will remain a passive prisoner of medical technology—for Nancy, perhaps for the next 30 years." After the Court's ruling, Nancy's parents went back to the trial judge and presented more evidence of Nancy's wishes. The judge granted the order to remove her feeding tube, and in December 1990, Nancy died.

See also: Right to Die.

Further Reading

Colby, William H. *Long Goodbye: The Deaths of Nancy Cruzan.* Carlsbad, CA: Hay House, 2003.
Perl, Lila. *Cruzan v. Missouri: The Right to Die.* Tarrytown, NY: Marshall Cavendish, 2007.

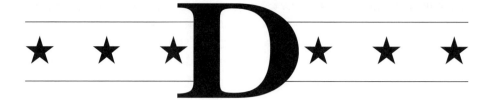

Dartmouth College v. Woodward (1819)

Supreme Court ruling that prevented states from altering or repealing a private corporate charter—a document that sets forth the basic structure and rules of an organization. The ruling encouraged business by limiting the power of the states to interfere with private contracts. Opponents have criticized it for improperly extending individual contract rights to corporations.

Background

Dartmouth College, in New Hampshire, was established by a royal charter from Great Britain's King George III in 1769, six years before the start of the American Revolution (1775–1783). After the

---

Landmark Decision Highlights:
Dartmouth College v. Woodward (1819)

Issue: In 1816, the New Hampshire legislature attempted to change Dartmouth College—a private institution—into a state university. Did the New Hampshire legislature unconstitutionally interfere with Dartmouth College's rights under the contract clause of the U.S. Constitution?

Opinion: The Court held that the college's corporate charter qualified as a contract between private parties, and the legislature could not interfere with this contract. Chief Justice John Marshall's opinion emphasized that the term *contract* referred to transactions involving individual property rights, not to "the political relations between the government and its citizens."

United States established its independence, the agreement with the king became an agreement with the state of New Hampshire. In 1816, the state legislature passed several laws amending the college's charter to convert it into a university, to enlarge the number of its trustees, and otherwise to revise the means and purpose of its operations. The trustees of the college resisted, charging that these amendments impaired the obligation of the contract implicit in the original charter.

In 1818, the case came to the Court, with the famous attorney and lawmaker Daniel Webster arguing the college's case. The state defended the changes in the charter by contending that the school was a public corporation subject to such legislative action. Webster, however, was more convincing. In 1819, the Court ruled for the college, finding the amendments an unconstitutional impairment of the contract obligation. Chief Justice John Marshall wrote the Court's opinion. Assuming a much-debated point, Marshall stated that the charter incorporating the private college was a contract within the protection of the Constitution:

> It is a contract made on a valuable consideration. It is a contract for the security and disposition of property. It is a contract, on faith of which real and personal estate has been conveyed to the corporation. It is then a contract within the letter of the constitution, and within its spirit also.

The Court's Reasoning

Marshall conceded that this application of the contract clause probably never occurred to the men who wrote it into the Constitution: "It is more than possible that the preservation of rights of this description was not particularly in the view of the framers of the constitution when the clause under consideration was introduced into that instrument."

Regardless, the chief justice found no good reason to except these contracts from constitutional protection:

It is probable that no man ever was, and that no man ever will be, the founder of a college, believing at the time that an act of incorporation constitutes no security for the institution; believing that it is immediately to be deemed a public institution, whose funds are to be governed and applied, not by the will of the donor, but by the will of the legislature. All such gifts are made in the . . . hope, that the charity will flow forever in the channel which the givers have marked out for it. If every man finds in his own bosom strong evidence of the universality of this sentiment, there can be but little reason to imagine that the framers of our constitution were strangers to it, and that, feeling the necessity and policy of giving permanence and security to contracts, of withdrawing them from the influence of legislative bodies, whose fluctuating policy, and repeated interferences, produced the most perplexing and injurious embarrassments, they still deemed it necessary to leave these contracts subject to those interferences.

In his concurring opinion, Justice Joseph Story made clear the avenue by which states could retain the power to make modifications in such charters without violating the Constitution. "If the legislature means to claim such an authority, it must be reserved in the grant," Story wrote. Most charters granted by the states since that time have contained language reserving to the state the power to repeal or modify them.

For the half-century following the *Dartmouth College* decision, the contract clause produced more litigation than any other part of the Constitution. Charles Warren, historian of the Court during this period, wrote that this ruling came at a "peculiarly opportune" time:

[B]usiness corporations were for the first time becoming a factor in the commerce of the country, and railroad and

insurance corporations were, within the next fifteen years, about to become a prominent field for capital. The assurance to investors that rights granted by state legislatures were henceforth to be secure against popular or partisan . . . change of legislative policy, greatly encouraged the development of corporate business.

See also: 📖 *Dartmouth College v. Woodward,* 1819, in the **Primary Source Library**.

Death Penalty Cases

Supreme Court cases dealing with administration of capital punishment. The Constitution was written with the idea that death was the proper punishment for some crimes. There are, however, limits to this practice. The Fifth Amendment requires that a person facing death must be **indicted,** or formally charged, by a grand jury. The Fourteenth Amendment holds that a state shall not "deprive any person of life . . . without due process of law." In the late 1960s, however, civil rights lawyers argued that the death penalty violated basic notions of due process of law, equal protection under the law, and the ban on cruel and unusual punishment.

Abolishing Capital Punishment

During the nineteenth century, several Midwestern and Northeastern states abolished the death penalty. Southern states, by contrast, not only retained capital punishment but also used it for crimes such as rape and robbery. As of 1954, rape was still punishable by death in sixteen states, and robbery could result in a death sentence in eight states.

The system gave white prosecutors and jurors wide discretion to impose the death penalty, and blacks were on the receiving end of a disproportionate percentage of death sentences. Of 771 persons who were executed for rape between 1870 and 1950, 701 of them were black. This number does not include men killed in the mob **lynchings** throughout the South in the early decades of the twentieth century. A rape or robbery in a small southern town, particularly when committed by a

A – Z

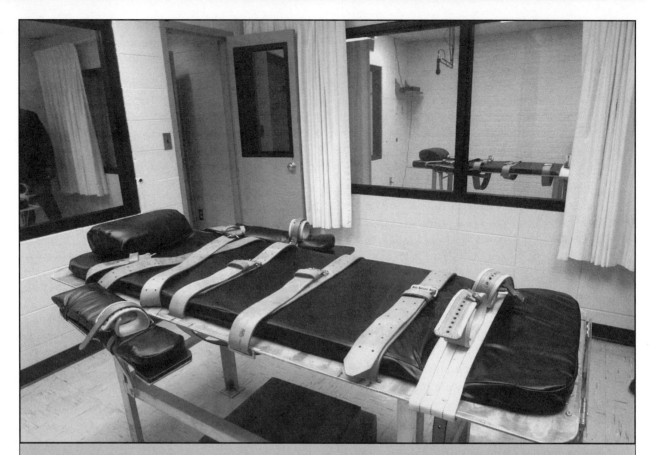

The lethal injection chamber in a Mississippi State prison shows the gurney where criminals convicted of capital offenses receive injections of chemicals that induce death. Capital punishment is very controversial in the United States. Opponents believe it should be outlawed because of the Eighth Amendment's prohibition of cruel and unusual punishment. Supporters contend that the death penalty helps deter crime. (AP Photo, Rogelio Solis)

black person, might result in a death sentence, although a conviction for the same crime elsewhere in the nation would yield only a few years in prison.

Several of the justices had signaled that they had doubts about the death sentencing system across the states. When the justices voted in 1972 to take up the case of *Furman v. Georgia*, however, it seemed that only Justices William J. Brennan Jr. and perhaps Thurgood Marshall were absolutely opposed to capital punishment. It turned out that Brennan and Marshall were not alone. A majority agreed, although for different reasons, that the system as it existed could not stand. The Court found that current state laws left too much discretion to juries to impose the death penalty. The result was a "wanton and freakish" pattern of its use that violated the Eighth Amendment ban on cruel and unusual punishment.

Reimposing the Death Penalty

The *Furman* decision effectively struck down all existing death penalty laws, but it did not close the door to enacting new measures to replace them. A close reading of the various opinions in the case suggested the states had two options for restoring capital punishment. First, they could remove almost all jury discretion from the decision by making death the mandatory punishment for certain crimes. Alternately, they could provide a two-stage procedure in capital cases: a trial to determine guilt or innocence, and, for those persons found guilty, a second proceeding to determine whether to impose a sentence of death.

After the *Furman* decision, thirty-five states passed new death penalty statutes. Ten chose the mandatory route, while the other twenty-five preferred the two-stage procedure. By 1976, both types of laws were back before the bench for the

SPOTLIGHT

Is Lethal Injection Cruel and Unusual Punishment?

In an effort to comply with the Eighth Amendment prohibition on "cruel and unusual punishment," states have over the years changed the method by which they execute convicted felons. Hanging was once the most common form of capital punishment, although some states also used firing squads. The harnessing of electricity in the late 1800s led to the widespread use of the electric chair. By the late twentieth century, most states that instituted capital punishment did so using "the chair."

In the late 1970s, physicians began to propose the use of a lethal combination of drugs as a more humane form of execution for criminals. Texas carried out the nation's first execution by lethal injection in 1982. Since that time, most states have abandoned the use of the electric chair in favor of lethal injection.

Some observers, however, have questioned whether lethal injection is really as humane as its supporters claim. The matter came before the Supreme Court in 2008 in the case of *Baze v. Rees*. Baze, a prisoner on Kentucky's death row, had filed suit in 2005 to prevent his execution by lethal injection, claiming that such a death was far from pain free and thus constituted cruel and unusual punishment. On April 16, 2008, the Court voted 7-2 to uphold the state's use of lethal injection. The ruling reflected general public opinion on the matter. A May 2004 Gallup poll found that 75 percent of Americans did not consider lethal injection to be cruel or unusual punishment.

Court to again determine whether death in and of itself was a cruel and unusual punishment for any crime in the United States. In *Gregg v. Georgia* (1976) and two companion cases, *Proffitt v. Florida* and *Jurek v. Texas*, the Court refused to overrule the judgment of state legislatures and declare capital punishment as unconstitutional in all cases.

Last Chance for Opponents

For opponents of capital punishment, the best hope for ending the death penalty came before the Court in 1987. A study of homicides in Georgia between 1974 and 1979 showed a clear pattern of racial bias based on the race of the victim. Local prosecutors sought the death penalty often when the victims were white but only rarely when they were black.

NAACP Legal Defense Fund lawyers brought the study before the Court in the case of Warren McCleskey. The defendant was a black man who was sentenced to death for shooting a white police officer during the robbery of a furniture store. His lawyers urged the Court to overturn Georgia's system of capital punishment as unconstitutional because it was infected with a racial bias. If McClesky's attorneys were successful, the death penalty in other states would be vulnerable to the same challenge and possibly swept aside.

The Court rejected McClesky's attorneys' argument in *McCleskey v. Kemp* (1987) in a 5-4 vote. The majority ruled that the statistics did not prove that prosecutors deliberately discriminate based on race when they bring their cases. "There can be no perfect procedure for deciding which cases" merit a death sentence. According to legal historian Stuart Banner, "Fifteen years after *Furman*, the Court had given up hope of eliminating the racism and the arbitrariness that had once been the motors of constitutional change. Racism and irrationality were facts of life, and that was that."

See also: Cruel and Unusual Punishment.

Further Reading

Foley, Michael A. *Arbitrary and Capricious: The Supreme Court, the Constitution, and the Death Penalty.* New York: Praeger, 2003.

Steffoff, Rebecca. *Furman v. Georgia: Debating the Death Penalty.* New York: Benchmark Books, 2007.

Declaratory Judgments

Ruling in which a federal court sets forth the duties, rights, obligations and status of parties to a lawsuit without ordering any action or awarding damages to either party. A declaratory judgment is considered a less severe form of an injunction, which is an order compelling a party to discontinue an activity that causes harm that cannot be remedied by a lawsuit.

The Court initially wavered in its view of declaratory judgments. It faced the issue after a number of states adopted laws early in the twentieth century authorizing their courts to issue such judgments. When some cases decided in this way found their way to the Supreme Court, the question arose as to whether they were actual "cases and controversies" as required by the Constitution. Congress eventually resolved the issue by passing the Federal Declaratory Judgment Act of 1934. The act authorized federal courts to issue declaratory judgments in "cases of actual controversy." The Court upheld the constitutionality of the Declaratory Judgment Act three years later.

Unlike an injunction, a declaratory judgment may be issued even though another adequate remedy for the dispute exists and even though there are other pending state or federal suits concerning the same matter. The presence of other pending suits may, however, affect the Court's decision whether to grant the judgment. The Supreme Court is generally reluctant to disrupt ongoing legal procedures, and it has tended to limit the use of declaratory judgments, particularly when their use would leave a state law unenforceable.

Although the Court has insisted that "case or controversy" requirements are applied just as strictly to cases seeking declaratory judgments as to other cases, it has hesitated to approve resolution of major constitutional questions through such judgments. Federal courts thus have broad discretion in deciding whether to grant requests for such judgments. The judgment is available as a remedy in all civil cases except those involving federal taxes.

The Court appears to have adopted a broader view of the power of federal judges to issue declaratory judgments against state laws that violate the First Amendment. In *Zwickler v. Koota* (1967), the Court ruled that federal judges had a duty to hear constitutional challenges to such state laws. The Court allowed courts to escape this duty only in special circumstances.

See also: Injunctions.

Discrimination

See Sex Discrimination.

Double Jeopardy

Standing trial more than once for the same offense. The Fifth Amendment to the U.S. Constitution states that no person shall be "subject for the same offense to be twice put in jeopardy of life or limb."

A defendant is placed in jeopardy at the time a jury is sworn in. However, if a mistrial is declared under certain circumstances, or if the jury fails to agree on a verdict, the double jeopardy clause does not forbid a retrial. If convicted, the defendant may forego protection against double jeopardy to seek a new trial or appeal the verdict to a higher court. If the conviction is set aside for a reason other than insufficient evidence, the defendant may be tried again for the same offense. If acquitted, the double jeopardy clause protects the defendant from any further prosecution for that crime, even if the acquittal results from error.

The Supreme Court has held that the double jeopardy guarantee protects an individual against multiple prosecutions for the same offense, as well as against multiple punishments for the same crime. It also protects an individual who successfully appeals a conviction on a lesser charge from being retried on the original charge. In *Grady v. Corbin* (1990), the Court broadened the double jeopardy provision to bar multiple prosecutions whenever the two offenses charged involved the same conduct. In this case, a driver was ticketed for driving while intoxicated and failing to keep right of the median. Prosecutors later sought to try the driver for the death of a motorist he allegedly hit in the oncoming lane. The Court ruled that a defendant should be protected from repeated government attempts to convict him for a single action. Three years later, the Court reversed the 1990 ruling, holding that multiple prosecutions are permitted if the two offenses contain different elements.

The double jeopardy guarantee protects only against repeated prosecutions by a single sovereign government. Thus, it is not violated when a person is tried on state as well as federal charges arising from a single offense. Until the late 1960s, the double jeopardy clause applied only to federal prosecutions. Then the Court, in *Benton v. Maryland* (1969), held that the due process guarantee of the Fourteenth Amendment extended this protection to persons tried by states as well.

The Court has extended the double jeopardy guarantee to issues of sentencing. In *Bullington v. Missouri* (1981), the Court forbade a state from seeking the death penalty in both the original trial and in a retrial after a successful appeal. The defendant in the case had been convicted of murder and sentenced to death, but successfully appealed the verdict to a higher court. At the retrial, the state again sought the death penalty, but the Court declared this a violation of the double jeopardy clause.

Dred Scott v. Sandford (1857)

Landmark Supreme Court ruling that declared slaves were not citizens entitled to constitutional protections and that Congress could not prohibit the extension of slavery into the Western territories.

One of the most controversial decisions in the Court's history, the ruling's effects eventually were overturned by passage of the Thirteenth and Fourteenth Amendments following the Civil War (1861–1865).

Background

Dred Scott was a slave owned originally by a Missouri family named Blow. In 1833, the Blows sold Scott to an army surgeon, Dr. John Emerson of St. Louis. The next year, Emerson was transferred to Rock Island, Illinois, and later to Fort Snelling in the Wisconsin Territory. Scott accompanied Emerson throughout this period, returning with him to St. Louis near the end of 1838. After Emerson died some years later, his widow moved to New York and left Scott in the care of his original owners, the Blows.

Although a slave owner himself, Blow opposed extending slavery into the Western territories.

An engraving from the late 1850s shows Dred Scott shortly after he was freed. Scott was the subject of the 1857 landmark Supreme Court case in which it was declared that African Americans were not and could not become American citizens. The Court also ruled that the 1820 Missouri Compromise, which forbade slavery in certain U.S. territories, was unconstitutional. (Library of Congress, Prints and Photographs Division)

A-Z

SPOTLIGHT

The Fourteenth Amendment

It took a constitutional amendment to overturn the Supreme Court's ruling, in *Dred Scott v. Sandford* (1857), that blacks were not and could not be citizens under the Constitution. In early 1865, Congress passed the Thirteenth Amendment, abolishing slavery. However, this failed to end state-sponsored racial discrimination in the South. In April 1866, Congress proposed what would become the Fourteenth Amendment. With few changes, the five-part piece of legislation was submitted to the states for **ratification,** or formal approval, in June 1866.

The Fourteenth Amendment directly overruled the *Scott* decision by declaring that all persons born or naturalized in the United States and subject to its jurisdiction are citizens of the United States and the state in which they live. It also prohibited the states from making any law that abridged the privileges and immunities of citizens of the United States, deprived any person of life, liberty, or property without due process of law, or denied anyone equal protection of the laws.

The amendment also penalized any state that abridged the right of its citizens to vote for federal or state officers. Offending states would lose a number of representatives in the House of Representatives proportional to the number of people denied the vote. In addition to ensuring blacks the right to vote, this language was intended to dilute the strength of the southern states and Democrats in Congress. It did not, however, specifically give blacks the right to vote. Moderate Republicans feared that such an outright grant might jeopardize ratification of the amendment in those northern states that still restricted black voting rights. As a result, the southern states ignored this section of the amendment. The subsequent need to protect black voting rights led quickly to adoption of the Fifteenth Amendment in 1870.

Blow helped Scott sue for his freedom in court, arguing that the time Scott lived on free soil in Illinois and Wisconsin made him a free man. A lower state court found in favor of Scott, but in 1852, the Missouri Supreme Court reversed the decision, holding that under Missouri law, Scott remained a slave.

In the years following the reversal, regional tensions over slavery became even more inflamed, and more people began to look to the Court for a solution to the slavery question. A Court settlement of the issue was clearly what those around Dred Scott were seeking. In 1854, Mrs. Emerson arranged for the sale of Scott to her brother, John F.A.

Sanford (misspelled in the court records as Sandford), and Scott's attorney sued for Scott's freedom in the federal circuit court for Missouri. The circuit court held that Scott, as a black slave, was not a citizen of Missouri and therefore did not have the right to bring suit in federal court. Scott appealed to the Supreme Court.

Supreme Court Hearing

Faced with a civil war in Kansas over the issue of slavery in the territories, a Congress unable to find a political solution, and mounting demands for a final judicial solution, the Court agreed to accept the case. Newly elected President James Buchanan

(1857–1861) also put some pressure on the Court to decide the territorial slavery issue. He urged the Court to take up the issue so that at his inauguration he might say that the issue was "a judicial question, which legitimately belongs to the Supreme Court . . ."

On March 6, 1857, two days after Buchanan's inauguration, the Court announced its decision. By a 7-2 vote, the Court ruled against Scott. Writing for the majority, Chief Justice Roger Taney ruled that slaves "are not, and that they are not included, and were not intended to be included, under the word 'citizens' in the Constitution, and can, therefore, claim none of the rights and privileges which that instrument provides for and secures to citizens of the United States." Slaves, he said, were "regarded as being of an inferior order, and altogether unfit to associate with the white race, either in social or political relations; and so far inferior, that they had no rights which the white man was bound to respect." According to Taney, even the words "all men are created equal" in the Declaration of Independence did not encompass the black race.

Taney's Opinion

Taney also touched on the question of whether a person declared a citizen by one state was automatically a citizen of the United States. He concluded that this was not so since the Constitution gave the federal government exclusive control over naturalization. He stated that no state was bound to recognize as a citizen someone granted citizenship by another state. Taney wrote:

> **E**ach state may still confer [citizenship rights] upon an alien, or anyone it thinks proper . . . yet he would not be a citizen in the sense in which the word is used in the Constitution . . . nor entitled to sue as such in one of its courts, nor to the privileges and immunities of a citizen in the other States.

Taney also cited pre-Revolutionary War laws in the states to show that slaves, far from being citizens, were actually considered property. This also was reflected in the only two provisions of the Constitution that specifically mentioned slaves, he argued. These provisions, Taney said, "treat them as property, and makes it the duty of the government to protect it; no other power, in relation to this race, is to be found in the Constitution."

Taney felt it necessary to discuss whether Scott's residence in the Wisconsin Territory made him a free man. In this way he could address the question of whether Congress had the constitutional authority to bar slavery in the states. He declared that Congress did not have that power under Article 4, Section 2, of the Constitution. This language, he said, allowed Congress to make rules and regulations only for the territories held at the time the Constitution was ratified. "It applied only to the property which the States held in common at that time and has no reference whatever to any territory or other property which the new sovereignty might afterwards itself acquire."

Taney noted that the Fifth Amendment provided that no persons should be deprived of life, liberty, or property without due process of law. Since slaves were property, the law that prohibited slavery in the northern portion of the Louisiana Purchase was void. Therefore, Dred Scott had not been freed by his residence there. Scott's residence in Illinois was also

Landmark Decision Highlights: *Dred Scott v. Sanford* (1857)

Issue: Was Dred Scott, an enslaved African American who had lived for several years in the free states of the North, free or enslaved?

Opinion: Dred Scott was a slave. Under Articles III and IV of the Constitution, argued Chief Justice Roger B. Taney, no one but a citizen of the United States could be a citizen of a state, and that only Congress could confer national citizenship. Taney reached the conclusion that no person descended from an American slave had ever been a citizen for Article III purposes. The Court then held the Missouri Compromise unconstitutional, hoping to end the slavery question once and for all.

rejected as ground for a claim to freedom. Taney said that:

> Scott was a slave when taken into the State of Illinois by his owner, and was there held as such, and brought back in that character, his status, as free or slave depended on the laws of Missouri, and not of Illinois.

Other Opinions and Reactions

Justices Robert Grier and James M. Wayne for the most part concurred with Taney's opinion. Justices Peter V. Daniel, John A. Campbell, and John Catron, using different reasoning, all agreed that Congress had no authority to prohibit slavery in the territories. The dissenters, John McLean and Benjamin Curtis, filed lengthy opinions setting out their opposition to the majority. It was Taney's opinion that, in historian Bruce Catton's words, "reverberated across the land like a thunderclap."

Northern papers were quick to criticize the decision and the Court. Northern abolitionists particularly scored Taney's statement that blacks were so inferior to whites "that they had no rights which the white man was bound to respect." Taney had said this, but in the context that this was the general belief at the time the Constitution was written. He also stated that the accuracy or inaccuracy of the belief was not a question before the Court.

Legal scholars and constitutional historians generally agree that Taney's opinion was questionable in several respects. He made no mention of the fact that Congress had been prohibiting slavery in territories for 70 years. Nor did he acknowledge that Missouri courts had accorded citizenship rights to several blacks considered citizens by other states.

By modern standards of judicial restraint, Taney erred badly. He decided on the constitutionality of a federal law when it was not strictly necessary to do so. His opinion applied the law more broadly than was required by the facts of the case. The Court also could have observed the rule that no matter how grave the constitutional questions, the Court will try to interpret federal law in a way that will make it valid. It also seems apparent that the justices allowed their political persuasions to influence their decisions.

Rather than calming the controversy over slavery, the ruling inflamed it, perhaps hastening the onset of civil war. An editorial in the *North American Review* of October 1857 stated:

> The country will feel the consequences of the decision more deeply and more permanently in the loss of confidence in the sound judicial integrity and strictly legal character of their tribunals, than in anything beside; and this, perhaps, may well be accounted the greatest political calamity which this country, under our forms of government, could sustain.

See also: Citizenship and Naturalization; Slavery Issues; Taney, Roger B.

Further Reading

Cromwell, Sharon. *Dred Scott v. Sandford: A Slave's Case for Freedom and Citizenship.* Mankato, MN: Compass Point Books, 2009.

Finkelman, Martin. *Dred Scott v. Sandford: A Brief History with Documents.* New York: Bedford/St. Martin's, 1997.

Herda, D.J. *The Dred Scott Case: Slavery and Citizenship.* Berkeley Heights, NJ: Enslow Publishers, 1994.

Due Process

The principle that government must respect all of the rights guaranteed to an individual by the law. The Fifth Amendment to the U.S. Constitution states, "No person shall . . . be deprived of life, liberty, or property, without due process of law. . . ."

Procedural and Substantive Due Process

There are two types of due process: procedural and substantial. Procedural due process refers to the guarantee that no one is deprived of "life, liberty, or property" without a fair hearing or trial. It includes one's right to be informed of pending legal charges or proceedings, the right to a swift trial, to call witnesses on one's behalf, and the guarantee that legal procedures will be fair, unbiased, and applied equally to all parties. In 1934, the Court held that due process is violated when "a practice or rule offends some principle of justice so rooted in the traditions and conscience of our people as to be ranked as fundamental."

Substantive due process refers to guarantees of fundamental rights that are not specifically mentioned in the Fifth Amendment but are "implicit in the concept of ordered liberty." Because those rights are not clearly defined, they have been the subject of long-running debate. So has the Court's power to enforce those rights under the due process clause. Today, substantive due process centers on issues including the rights of the accused, restrictions on the political process (voting rights and freedom of speech and association), and minority rights.

Applicability

Before the Civil War (1861–1865), the Court held that the Fifth Amendment guarantee of due process applied only to actions of the federal government, not to state or individual actions. It was not until **ratification**, or formal approval, of the Fourteenth Amendment in 1868 that the due process clause applied to state action as well. Until well into the twentieth century, however, the Court held to a strictly procedural view of due process and was unwilling to apply it broadly to state actions.

In the late nineteenth and early twentieth centuries, the due process clause that was enacted to protect individuals was instead turned into a shield for property. In *Allgeyer v. Louisiana* (1897), the Court held that due process protected a citizen's right to do business with out-of-state as well as in-state insurance companies. Eight years later, in *Lochner v. New York* (1905), the Court struck down New York's maximum hours law for bakers as violating the freedom of contract and, hence, due process. *Lochner* was the first in a long series of rulings in which the Court used this theory to strike down state efforts to set maximum hours or minimum wages for workers.

JUSTICE FOR ALL

Due Process for Delinquents

The Supreme Court has ruled that juveniles possess some but not all of the due process rights assured to adults by the Fifth Amendment's due process clause and the Sixth Amendment. Juvenile court proceedings are considered civil, not criminal, hearings.

In *In re Gault* (1967), the Court held that juveniles charged with violating the law did have the right to confront and cross-examine persons presenting evidence against them. Furthermore, juveniles have the same rights as adults to notice, aid of counsel, and protection against self-incrimination.

Juveniles must be found delinquent by proof beyond a reasonable doubt rather than by any lesser standard, the Court held in *In re Winship* (1970). The following year, however, in *McKeiver v. Pennsylvania* and *in re Burrus* (1971), the Court refused to extend the right to trial by jury to juvenile court proceedings. Four years later, the Court extended the Fifth Amendment protection against double jeopardy to minors, ruling that a defendant found in juvenile court to have violated the law could not subsequently be tried for the same act as an adult.

Incorporation

The first crack in the Court's refusal to apply the Bill of Rights to protect individuals against state action came quietly and with little argument. In *Gitlow v. New York* (1925), the Court ruled that the Fourteenth Amendment's due process clause *does* apply First Amendment protections to persons threatened by state action.

In a series of rulings over the next five decades, the Court would more fully embrace the doctrine of incorporation—applying protections in the Bill of Rights to the states using the Fourteenth Amendment's due process clause.

See also: Bill of Rights; *Dred Scott v. Sandford* (1857); Equal Protection of the Law; *Gideon v. Wainwright* (1963); *Mapp v. Ohio* (1961).

Education, Schools, and the Supreme Court

See Tinker v. Des Moines (1969); *Hazelwood School District v. Kuhlmeier* (1988).

Eighth Amendment

See Cruel and Unusual Punishment.

Electronic Eavesdropping

Supreme Court rulings on the constitutionality of using electronic equipment to conduct surveillance of individuals. The basic questions facing the Court are whether and when electronic surveillance constitutes a violation of the Fourth Amendment guarantee of security against unreasonable search and seizure.

From 1928 until 1967, the Court held firmly that the Fourth Amendment applied only when there was physical entry and seizure; it did not

apply to overheard conversations. This rule was set out in *Olmstead v. United States* (1928). In this case, police used wiretaps to gather evidence against a bootlegging operation. The defendants argued that this method of obtaining evidence violated their Fourth Amendment rights. The Court, with Chief Justice Taft writing its opinion, rejected that claim:

The Amendment does not forbid what was done here. There was no searching. There was no seizure. The evidence was secured by the use of the sense of hearing and that only. There was no entry of the houses or offices of the defendants . . . Congress may, of course, protect the secrecy of telephone messages by making them, when intercepted, inadmissible in evidence in Federal criminal trials . . . But the courts may not adopt such a policy by attributing an enlarged and unusual meaning to the Fourth Amendment.″

In 1967, the Court forbade electronic surveillance of all types as a violation of the Fourth Amendment. In *Katz v. United States* (1967), government agents obtained evidence by placing a listening device on the outside of a public telephone booth. The information from the telephone conversations led to the prosecution of individuals involved in illegal bookmaking activities. Justice

Potter Stewart explained, "What a person . . . seeks to preserve as private, even in an area accessible to the public, may be constitutionally protected." The Court ruled that Katz did not surrender his right to privacy simply because he made calls from a public place.

More recently, the Court in 1986 upheld the use of low-flying aircraft to search fields and backyards for marijuana or narcotics. In 1989, the Court also upheld backyard drug searches by helicopters hovering at four hundred feet. In both instances, police used their own eyes from a public vantage point to look for drugs. "What a person knowingly exposes to the public, even in his home or office, is not a subject of Fourth Amendment protection," the Court ruled. The justices, however, drew a line at sensing devices that can look into a house. Obtaining by "sense-enhancing technology any information regarding the interior of the home" crosses the line protected by the Fourth Amendment, said Justice Antonin Scalia, writing for a 5-4 majority.

See also: Right to Privacy; Unreasonable Search and Seizure.

Eminent Domain

The power of government to seize private property for public use. The Fifth Amendment to the U.S. Constitution sets forth limitations on the power of eminent domain, stating private property shall not be taken for public use without "just compensation."

One of the significant early cases in this area was *Charles River Bridge v. Warren Bridge* (1837). In 1785, the Massachusetts legislature chartered a company to build a bridge across the Charles River to Boston, to operate it, and to collect tolls from passengers. The bridge quickly became profitable. Decades later, in 1828, the legislature chartered another company to build a second bridge across the Charles. This would be a toll bridge only until its costs were paid, or for six years, whichever was shorter.

The Charles River Bridge Company, realizing that its business would disappear once it was in competition with a free bridge, challenged the law authorizing the second bridge. This law, the

company said, impaired the contract in its charter and destroyed the value of its franchise by preventing it from earning the tolls it was authorized to collect. The company argued that this amounted to a pubic seizure without just compensation.

The Court disagreed, stating that the original bridge company charter did not grant the company an exclusive right to operate a bridge over the river. Without an explicit grant of exclusive privilege in the original charter, none was assumed to exist to limit the state's power to authorize construction of another bridge.

The broad power of eminent domain gained further recognition in 1848 in *West River Bridge Company v. Dix*. The state of Vermont had taken possession of a privately owned toll bridge and converted it into a free bridge. Although compensated by the state, the bridge owners protested that this impaired their charter and the contract obligation it contained. In 1848, the Supreme Court rejected this claim, upholding a broad state power of eminent domain over contract rights.

In 2005, the Court went even further, upholding the use of eminent domain to transfer property from one private owner to another to promote economic development. In *Kelo v. City of New London*, the Court ruled that such a seizure was constitutional because the community benefited from the economic growth caused by redevelopment. A 5-4 majority argued that this qualified as "public use" under the Fifth Amendment. The decision was widely criticized as a violation of property rights that favored wealthy business interests over private citizens.

Engle v. Vitale (1962)

Supreme Court case that declared the recital of prayers in public school to be a violation of the First Amendment to the U.S. Constitution. The First Amendment begins, "Congress shall make no law respecting an establishment of religion. . . ." That is, Congress cannot designate an official state religion nor pass laws that favor one set of religious beliefs over any other. *Engle v. Vitale* raised the question of whether that prohibition extended school prayer.

School Prayer and Congressional Backlash

"The Supreme Court has made God unconstitutional," declared Senator Sam Ervin, D-N.C., after the Court's rejection of school prayer in *Engel v. Vitale* (1962). Members of Congress, governors, even a former president all spoke out in opposition to the decision.

Although the ruling was greeted favorably by the Jewish community and many Christian leaders, several members of the clergy expressed dismay. Francis Cardinal Spellman said, "The decision strikes at the very heart of the Godly tradition in which America's children have for so long been raised."

The Court's 1963 decision opposing Bible reading in schools generated equally adverse and outspoken criticism. Most major religious organizations opposed a constitutional amendment to overturn the rulings. Nevertheless, mail advocating such an amendment began to pour into congressional offices in the days and months after the Court rulings.

Representative Frank J. Becker of New York proposed an amendment in 1962. It provided that nothing in the Constitution should be interpreted to bar "the offering, reading from, or listening to prayer or Biblical scriptures, if participation therein is

Background

The case involved a recommendation by the New York State Board of Regents that school districts adopt a specified nondenominational prayer to be repeated voluntarily by students at the beginning of each school day. The brief prayer read: "Almighty God, we acknowledge our dependence upon Thee, and we beg Thy blessings upon us, our parents, our teachers, and our country." The school board of New Hyde Park adopted the recommended prayer.

Parents of ten pupils in the school district, with the support of the New York Civil Liberties Union, sued the district. They claimed that the prayer was contrary to their religious beliefs and practices, and that its adoption and use violated the establishment clause. The state courts upheld the prayer because no student would be compelled to participate.

Supreme Court Ruling

By a vote of 6-1, the Supreme Court reversed the state courts, ruling that this use of the prayer was "wholly inconsistent with the Establishment Clause." In the majority view:

> [T]he constitutional prohibition against laws respecting an establishment of religion must at least mean that in this country it is no part of the business of government to compose official prayers for any group of the American people to recite as a part of a religious program carried on by government.

The fact that the prayer was nondenominational did not free the prayer "from the limitations of the Establishment Clause." Nor did the fact that students who did not wish to participate could remain silent or leave the room. Justice Potter Stewart, the sole dissenter, remarked, "I cannot see how an 'official religion' is established by letting those who want to say a prayer say it." Stewart compared the regents' prayer to other state-sanctioned religious exercises, such as the reference to God in the pledge to the flag, in

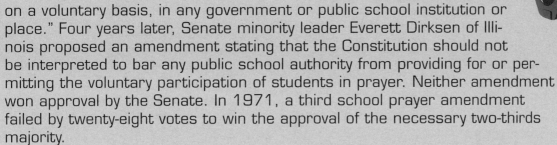

SPOTLIGHT

on a voluntary basis, in any government or public school institution or place." Four years later, Senate minority leader Everett Dirksen of Illinois proposed an amendment stating that the Constitution should not be interpreted to bar any public school authority from providing for or permitting the voluntary participation of students in prayer. Neither amendment won approval by the Senate. In 1971, a third school prayer amendment failed by twenty-eight votes to win the approval of the necessary two-thirds majority.

A decade later, President Ronald Reagan's (1981–1989) support for a constitutional amendment on school prayer revived efforts to win congressional approval. In 1984, the Senate fell eleven votes short of approving the administration's amendment. In October 1994, Congress passed legislation that included a provision withholding federal funds from any public school that willfully violated a court order to allow constitutionally protected voluntary prayer. Many new proposals for a constitutional amendment permitting organized school prayer were offered after the Republicans had won majorities in the House and Senate. None has been adopted.

A – Z

the president's oath of office, and in the formal opening of each day's session of the Court itself.

See also: Freedom of Religion; School Prayer and Bible Readings.

Landmark Decision Highlights: *Engle v. Vitale* (1962)

Issue: Whether the reading of a nondenominational prayer at the start of the school day in New York State violates the "establishment of religion" clause of the First Amendment

Opinion: The Court ruled that by providing the prayer, the State of New York officially approved religion. This was the first in a series of cases in which the Court used the establishment clause to remove all sorts of religious activities, which had traditionally been a part of public ceremonies.

Equal Employment Opportunity

Efforts by Congress and the Supreme Court to prevent job discrimination against African Americans. Although the Civil War (1861–1865) ended slavery, it did not eliminate prejudice against blacks, particularly in the South. Widespread discrimination remained, a situation that limited not only blacks' freedoms but their economic progress as well.

Labor Conditions

Following the Civil War, most of the Southern states enacted Black Codes restricting the kinds of jobs blacks could hold. These laws limited blacks' ability to compete with whites and forced blacks to continue as farm and plantation workers. In some places, the only jobs that blacks could obtain without a license were as farm workers or servants. Licenses were issued by judges who decided whether the black applicants were skilled and morally fit for the work.

Blacks also were required to sign labor contracts with their employers. In many Southern states, failure to fulfill the labor contract was a crime. A black worker could avoid a jail term only by agreeing to work off the original contract, his or her fine for defaulting, and court costs. The Supreme Court struck down such laws as unconstitutional in the early 1900s.

Despite rapid industrialization in the late 1800s and early 1900s, blacks remained relegated to low-paying, unskilled jobs that promised little, if any, advancement. Even if blacks qualified for a better job, they were often passed over in favor of white employees. Until the enactment of state fair employment laws in the mid-1940s, the employer-employee relationship was considered outside the protection of the Fourteenth Amendment. Private employers and labor unions could discriminate against blacks with impunity and many of them did.

Early Rulings

The first employment discrimination case came before the Court in 1938. A federal court ordered blacks to cease picketing outside a District of Columbia grocery to force the owner to hire blacks. The picketers charged that the order violated the Norris-LaGuardia Act, which prohibited federal courts from issuing injunctions in legal labor disputes. The issue was whether picketing to force someone to hire blacks was a legal labor objective within the meaning of the law. By 7-2, the Court held that it was. The Court modified this position in 1950 when it held that picketing to demand that a store owner increase the number of blacks he employed constituted discrimination against already-hired white clerks.

The first case involving union discrimination came in 1944 with *Steele v. Louisville and Nashville Railroad Co.* The Brotherhood of Locomotive Firemen, which represented train firemen of twenty-one railroad companies, agreed with the railroad companies to amend the work contract to end all employment of blacks as firemen. Steele, a black fireman, was reassigned and his job given to a white man with less seniority and no more qualifications.

The Court ruled that the Railway Labor Act of 1930 compelled the exclusive bargaining agent for an entire class of employees to represent all those employees fairly "without hostile discrimination" against any of them. The Court reached a similar conclusion in *Brotherhood of Railroad Trainmen v. Howard* (1952).

Black workers won another measure of job protection in 1945, when the Court upheld the validity of state fair employment laws. The question later arose as to whether a state fair employment practices act placed an impermissible burden on interstate commerce in *Colorado Anti-Discrimination Commission v. Continental Airlines* (1963). A black man named Marion Green applied for a job as a pilot with the interstate airline, which had its headquarters in Denver. He was rejected solely because of his race. The Colorado Anti-Discrimination Commission found the company had violated state law and ordered it to give Green the first opening in its next training course. A state court overruled the order because the law unduly burdened interstate commerce. The Supreme Court reversed the trial court and upheld the commission's order.

Civil Rights Act of 1964

In 1964, Congress enacted the first federal law prohibiting job discrimination. Title VII of the Civil Rights Act of that year prohibited unions representing more than twenty-five workers as well as employers with that same number of employees, union hiring halls, and employment agencies from discriminating on the grounds of race, color, religion, sex, or national origin in the hiring, classification, training, or promotion of anyone. The act also created the Equal Employment Opportunities Commission (EEOC) to hear complaints and seek compliance with the law. In 1972, Congress extended coverage to employers and unions with fifteen or more employees or members, state and local governments, and educational institutions. The 1972 act also authorized the EEOC to go into federal courts to enforce the law.

See also: Affirmative Action; Civil Rights Act of 1964.

Standards of Review: Equal Protection Claims

Standard of Review	Definition	Classification	Key Cases
Rational basis (also referred to as the "traditional standard" or "minimum scrutiny")	The government need only show that the challenged classification is rationally related to serving a legitimate government interest	Economic interests and non-suspect classifications	*Lindsley v. Natural Carbonic Gas Co.* (1911) *Kotch v. Board of River Port Pilot Commissioners,* (1947) *Williamson v. Lee Optical of Oklahoma,* (1955) *McGowan v. Maryland,* (1961)
Intermediate scrutiny (also referred to as "middle-tier scrutiny" or "heightened scrutiny")	The government must show that the challenged classification serves an important government interest and that the classification is at least substantially related to serving that interest	Quasi-suspect classifications including gender and illegitimacy	*Plyler v. Doe,* (1982) *Craig v. Boren,* (1976) *Central Hudson Gas & Electric Co. v. Public Service Commission of New York,* (1980)
Exceedingly persuasive justification (also referred to as "skeptical scrutiny")	The government must show an "exceedingly persuasive justification" for the challenged classification	Quasi-suspect classifications including gender	*Mississippi University for Women v. Hogan,* (1982) *United States v. Virginia et al.,* (1996)
Strict scrutiny (also referred to as the "active standard," the "modern standard," or "rigid scrutiny")	The government must show that the challenged classification serves a compelling government interest and that the classification is necessary to serve that interest	Suspect classifications, based on race, national origin, alienage, and classifications affecting fundamental rights	*United States v. Carolene Products Co.,* (1938) *Skinner v. Oklahoma,* (1942) *Korematsu v. United States* (1944) *Loving v. Virginia,* (1967) *Wygant v. Jackson Board of Education,* (1986)

The Equal Protection Clause of the Fourteenth Amendment forbids a state to "deny to any person within its jurisdiction the equal protection of the laws." The clause has been applied by the Supreme Court to prevent states from enforcing laws that discriminate on the basis of race, creed, gender, and national or ethnic origin. The Court applies a multi-tiered system of review to cases involving equal protection claims. The standard it applies depends on how the victim is classified and whether the government has a reasonable basis or a compelling state interest to act. The Court's standards follow, arranged from the most permissive government classification to the strictest.

A – Z

Equal Protection of the Law

Guarantee contained in the Fourteenth Amendment to the U.S. Constitution intended to protect individual rights from interference by states. The Court, however, has never interpreted this clause to require that all persons and all groups are treated in exactly the same way. The question the Court must answer is whether or not the legal classifications made by states are permissible or the result of a distinction that is unacceptable.

Under the first standard it developed, the Court was satisfied that a classification was valid if a state could show that it had a reasonable basis. This traditional standard still applies to certain cases today. Using this standard, the Court upheld few challenges to laws on equal protection grounds. The Court noted in 1927 that the clause had become no more than "the usual last resort of constitutional arguments."

In the late 1930s, the Court shifted its focus from property rights to individual rights, which led it to develop a stricter standard for evaluating charges of denial of equal protection. Under this so-called active standard, some classifications require a greater degree of justification for their existence than simple rationality. A state must prove not only that it has a compelling governmental interest for making the challenged classification but also that the classification is narrowly tailored to achieve that interest.

The development of this modern standard came in distinct stages. In 1944, the Court declared race to be a suspect category requiring heightened judicial scrutiny. It later applied this standard of equal protection in *Brown v. Board of Education* (1954), which called for an end to school segregation. Classifications by **alienage**, or being from a foreign country, came under heightened review as early as 1948, but not until 1971 did the Court explicitly describe alienage as a suspect category.

As early as 1942, the Court indicated that the equal protection clause protected all individuals from state deprivation of certain fundamental rights. However, the development of the modern equal protection standard began after Congress passed the Civil Rights Act of 1964. The act prohibited discrimination on the grounds of race, color, national origin, or religion in most privately owned public accommodations. It also prohibited job discrimination on these grounds and on the basis of sex. In 1965, Congress authorized federal action to enforce the rights of blacks to vote, and in 1968, Congress barred discrimination in the sale and rental of housing.

As a result of these federal laws, minorities and other groups traditionally victimized by discrimination brought increasing numbers of lawsuits charging a denial of equal protection. In reviewing these cases, the Court moved away from the traditional "reasonable basis" standard. So far, however, race and alienage are the only two categories to which the Supreme Court has accorded suspect status.

See also: Brown v. Board of Education (1954); Civil Rights Act of 1964; Due Process.

Escobedo v. Illinois (1964)

Supreme Court ruling that linked the Fifth Amendment privilege against self-incrimination with the Sixth Amendment right to counsel. In *Escobedo*, the Court established the principle that even voluntary confessions are not admissible as evidence if the accused has been denied the right to counsel.

Background

In 1958, the Court ruled that confessions obtained from a suspect who was denied legal counsel during interrogation could still be considered voluntary and used in court. A few years later, however, it reversed that view. In *Massiah v. United States* (1964), the justices declared that a person charged with a crime could not properly be questioned or otherwise persuaded to make incriminating remarks in the absence of a lawyer. Later that year, in *Malloy v. Hogan*, the Court extended the Fifth Amendment privilege against self-incrimination to state defendants. This ruling laid the groundwork for *Escobedo*.

Landmark Decision Highlights: *Escobedo v. Illinois* (1964)

Issue: Whether an arrested individual has the right to remain silent

Opinion: In his majority opinion, Justice Arthur Goldberg spoke for the first time of "an absolute right to remain silent." The individual in this case, Danny Escobedo, had not been adequately informed of his constitutional right to remain silent rather than to be forced to incriminate himself.

A week after *Malloy*, the Court announced its decision in the case of Danny Escobedo, who was convicted of murder in Illinois on the basis of his own words. In *Escobedo v. Illinois* (1964), the Court adopted a new standard for determining the admissibility of confessions. It moved away from an approach that looked at the "totality of the circumstances" and instead concentrated on the procedures police followed in obtaining a confession.

Supreme Court Hearing

Escobedo repeatedly asked for and was denied the opportunity to see his attorney during his interrogation by police. Incriminating statements he made during this time were used as evidence against him. He challenged his conviction as a denial of his right to counsel. The Court agreed, ruling that defendants have a right to remain silent rather than be forced to incriminate themselves. If police do not warn a suspect of the "absolute constitutional right to remain silent," said the Court, the suspect has been denied "the assistance of counsel" in violation of the Sixth Amendment.

The year before, the Court had declared in *Gideon v. Wainwright* (1963) that the Sixth Amendment required that every person accused of a serious crime be provided the aid of an attorney. Justice Arthur Goldberg reasoned in *Escobedo* that the right guaranteed in *Gideon* would be a hollow one if it did not apply until after police obtained a confession:

W e have . . . learned . . . that no system of criminal justice can, or should, survive if it comes to depend for its

continued effectiveness on the citizens' abdication through unawareness of their constitutional rights. No system worth preserving should have to fear that if an accused is permitted to consult with a lawyer, he will become aware of, and exercise, these rights. If the exercise of constitutional rights will thwart the effectiveness of a system of law enforcement, then there is something very wrong with that system.

We hold, therefore, that where, as here, the investigation is no longer a general inquiry into an unsolved crime but has begun to focus on a particular suspect, the suspect has been taken into police custody, the police carry out a process of interrogations that lends itself to eliciting incriminating statements, the suspect has requested and been denied an opportunity to consult with his lawyer, and the police have not effectively warned him of his absolute constitutional right to remain silent, the accused has been denied "the Assistance of Counsel" in violation of the Sixth Amendment . . . and that no statement elicited by police during the interrogation may be used against him at a criminal trial.

The dissenting opinion criticized the majority's ruling that any incriminating statement made by an arrested suspect who was denied the opportunity to see his lawyer was inadmissible:

B y abandoning the voluntary-involuntary test . . . the Court seems driven by the notion that it is uncivilized law enforcement to use an accused's own admissions against him at his trial. It attempts to find a home for this new and nebulous rule of due process by attaching it to the right of counsel guaranteed in the federal system by the Sixth Amendment and binding upon the States by virtue of the due process guarantee of the Fourteenth Amendment. . . . The right to counsel now not only entitles the accused to counsel's advice and aid in preparing for trial but stands as an impenetrable barrier to any interrogation once the accused has become a suspect.

See also: Confessions; 📖 *Escobedo v. Illinois*, 1964; *Gideon v. Wainwright* (1963), in the **Primary Source Library;** Right to Legal Counsel; Self-Incrimination.

Exclusionary Rule

Legal guidelines developed by the Supreme Court which serve to determine when to prohibit the use in federal courts of evidence seized by federal agents in violation of the Fourth Amendment ban against unreasonable search and seizure. The Court announced the controversial rule in *Weeks v. United States* (1914). It subsequently applied the rule to forbid use of evidence taken in violation of other constitutional rights, in particular the Fifth Amendment privilege against self-incrimination and the Sixth Amendment right to counsel. Not until *Mapp v. Ohio* (1961), however, did the Court extend the exclusionary rule to apply also to state trials.

Applying the Rule

Application of the exclusionary rule has been the subject of continuing legal controversy. By denying prosecutors the use of certain evidence, the rule can cause the collapse of the government's case and allow a guilty person to go free. As Benjamin Cardozo wrote before he sat on the Court, "The criminal is to go free because the constable has blundered." Some, including Chief Justices Warren E. Burger and William H. Rehnquist, believed that such an outcome is too high a price for society to pay for inadvertent violations of constitutional guarantees.

In *Silverthorne Lumber Co. v. United States* (1920), the Court made clear that the exclusionary rule announced in *Weeks* forbade *all* use of illegally obtained evidence in federal courts. In 1954, however, the Court held that narcotics illegally seized by federal officials, while not admissible as evidence at trial, could be used to impeach a defendant's credibility after he or she has testified

that he or she has never used them. In other decisions, the Court made clear that only the person whose rights are violated by the search and seizure can invoke the exclusionary rule.

The Court, in *Weeks v. United States,* announced two rules of evidence for federal courts. One was the exclusionary rule: federal prosecutors could not use evidence obtained by federal agents in violation of the Fourth Amendment protection against unreasonable search and seizure. The second rule became known as the "silver platter" doctrine: federal prosecutors *could* use evidence obtained by *state* agents through unreasonable search and seizure if that evidence was obtained without federal participation and was turned over to the federal officials—in other words, handed to them on a silver platter.

The Court extended the exclusionary rule to the states in *Mapp v. Ohio.* In this case, the Court finally declared that "the exclusionary rule is an essential part of both the Fourth and Fourteenth Amendments." The Court held, however, that the *Mapp* decision would not be retroactively applied to overturn state criminal convictions that had occurred before the new standard was devised. The Court in the 1970s limited the use of the exclusionary rule to overturn convictions, reflecting the lack of enthusiasm of some members of the Court for the rule.

The Court subsequently refused to forbid prosecutors to use illegally obtained evidence when questioning witnesses before grand juries. It also declined to direct federal judges to release persons challenging their state convictions if obtained with illegally seized evidence. So long as the state has provided an opportunity for a full, fair hearing of the defendant's challenge to that evidence, held the Court, there is no constitutional obligation for federal courts to use the writ of habeas corpus to enforce the exclusionary rule.

Exceptions to the Rule

In the 1980s, the Court approved several exceptions to the exclusionary rule. A "good faith" exception permits the use of illegally obtained evidence at trial if the police who seized it had a search warrant and thought they were acting legally only to find that because of some "technical" flaw, their search was in fact illegal. In such a case, the exclusion of valid evidence has no deterrent effect and exacts too high a price from society. The same year, the Court also permitted evidence taken in violation of a defendant's rights to be used at trial if the prosecutor can show that the evidence ultimately would have been discovered by lawful means.

In 1995, the Court extended the good faith exception to mistakes made by judicial personnel. The case of *Arizona v. Evans* (1995) involved a courthouse computer mistake, which led a police officer to believe that a warrant that actually had been quashed still was valid. After the officer arrested the individual involved, he discovered a bag of marijuana in the man's car. The Court ruled 7-2 that errors made by clerical employees resulting in an unconstitutional arrest do not invoke the exclusionary rule and that the drug evidence need not be suppressed.

See also: Mapp v. Ohio (1961); Search Warrants.

Ex Parte Milligan (1866)

Supreme Court case dealing with the president's ability to suspend the writ of habeas corpus during wartime. Habeas corpus is a legal protection built into Article I of the U.S. Constitution. It requires the government to bring a prisoner before a court to determine whether the prisoner is being held legally. If the court determines that the detention is illegal, it can order the prisoner to be released. The writ of habeas corpus is one of the most basic safeguards against wrongful imprisonment.

Article I, Section 9, of the Constitution states, "The Privilege of the Writ of Habeas Corpus shall not be suspended, unless when in Cases of Rebellion or Invasion the public Safety may require it." During the Civil War (1861–1865), President Abraham Lincoln (1861–1865) used this provision to suspend the privilege of the writ in parts of the country where Union forces were combating Southern sympathizers. In March 1863, Congress retroactively authorized the suspension of the writ at the president's discretion.

In 1864, a man named L.P. Milligan was tried by a military commission in Indiana and convicted of conspiracy. He was sentenced to die for plotting to release and arm rebel prisoners for an invasion of Indiana. Following the war, President Andrew Johnson (1865–1869) commuted Milligan's sentence to life in prison. Milligan, nevertheless, appealed to the Supreme Court, challenging his trial and conviction. In 1866, the Court unanimously ordered his release, holding that the president had no power to require that civilians be tried by military courts in areas where regular courts continued to function.

The Court divided 5-4 on whether Congress had the power to authorize military trials under such circumstances. However, the decision established that martial law must be confined to "the theater of active military operations":

> . . . Martial law cannot arise from a threatened invasion. The necessity must be actual and present; the invasion real, such as effectually closes the courts . . . Martial rule can never exist where the courts are open, and in the proper and unobstructed exercise of their jurisdiction. It is also confined to the locality of actual war.

The assumption of broad presidential powers in a wartime emergency ended—temporarily—with Lincoln's death and the end of the war. The issue would arise repeatedly in the coming decades as the United States took a greater role in world affairs.

See also: Writs of Habeas Corpus.

Ex Post Facto Laws

Laws that criminalize an action that was legal when it was originally committed. An ex post facto law makes illegal an act that has already taken place, or it makes the punishment greater than it was at the time of the act.

In *Calder v. Bull* (1798), the earliest Supreme Court discussion of ex post facto laws, the Court held that the constitutional prohibition did not apply to civil statutes but only to criminal laws. In *Ex parte Garland* (1866), the Court applied the notion of ex post facto laws to loyalty oaths. The case involved one of the nation's leading attorneys, Southerner Augustus H. Garland, who had practiced before the Court prior to the Civil War (1861–1865). When Arkansas, his home state, joined the Confederacy, he served in the Confederate Congress.

In 1865, Congress passed an act that required all attorneys who wished to practice in the Supreme Court and other federal courts to take an oath that they had not aided the Confederate cause by word or deed. Under the "test oath" requirement imposed by the 1865 law, Garland was forever disqualified from resuming his legal practice before the federal courts.

In July 1865, however, President Andrew Johnson (1865–1869) pardoned Garland for all offenses committed during the Civil War. Garland cited the pardon and asked for permission to practice in federal court. However, he was still unable, due to his service to the Confederacy, to take the test oath. Garland argued that the act of Congress was unconstitutional. Beyond that, he argued that even if the act was constitutional, the pardon released him from compliance with its provisions.

The Court ruled for Garland on both points. For the first time, the Court struck down an act of Congress by the narrow margin of 5-4. It found the test oath law unconstitutional as both a bill of attainder and an ex post facto law. It argued that to prohibit an attorney from practicing before federal courts without taking the oath was to punish him for past acts not defined as illegal at the time they were committed.

In other instances, however, the Court has upheld a number of statutes against charges they were ex post facto laws. These include laws that denied polygamists the right to vote in a territorial election, laws that deported aliens for criminal acts committed prior to the deportation law's enactment, and laws that revoked naturalization papers obtained fraudulently before passage of the law.

See also: Bills of Attainder; Loyalty Oaths.

Fair Housing

Supreme Court rulings that deal with the right of citizens to inherit, purchase, lease, sell, and convey property. The Civil Rights Act of 1866 gave blacks the same property rights as whites. Nevertheless, many states and cities adopted laws segregating blacks and whites, actions that undermined the fundamental property rights of blacks. As a result, the Court was forced to step in on a number of occasions to protect those rights.

In one of the earliest fair housing cases, *Buchanan v. Warley* (1917), the Supreme Court struck down a city ordinance that forbade members of one race to buy, reside on, or sell property on streets where a majority of the residents were of the other race. The Court subsequently upheld several lower court decisions invalidating similar laws.

Restrictive Covenants

In response, many communities replaced forced segregation with private **restrictive covenants**. Under such covenants, white residents of an area agreed to refuse to sell or lease their homes to blacks. The Court upheld the use of such covenants in *Corrigan v. Buckley* (1926), arguing that Congress had no authority to protect individuals from private discrimination.

Eventually, however, the Court nullified restrictive covenants by forbidding states to enforce them. *Shelley v. Kraemer* (1948) arose when a black couple bought property to which a restrictive covenant applied. A white couple in the neighborhood sued to stop the Shelleys from taking possession of the property. The trial court ruled that the covenant was not ineffective, but the State Supreme Court of Missouri reversed the decision. It ruled the covenant effective and not a violation of the Shelleys' Fourteenth Amendment rights.

The Shelleys appealed to the U.S. Supreme Court, which repeated its earlier opinion that the Fourteenth Amendment does not reach "private conduct, however discriminatory or wrongful." However, by forcing the trial court to enforce the covenant, the Missouri State Supreme Court action used the state's power unconstitutionally to deny the Shelleys' equal protection of the laws. The U.S. Supreme Court struck down the state court's ruling.

Housing Referenda

In 1964, California passed a constitutional amendment barring the state from interfering with the right of any person to sell or refuse to sell his property to anyone for any reason. The amendment effectively nullified several state fair housing laws. When a family named the Mulkeys sued Neil Reitman for refusing to rent them an apartment solely because they were black, Reitman asked the court to dismiss of the complaint, based on the 1964 amendment. The California Supreme Court, however, held that the amendment acted "to make private discriminations legally possible" and thus had violated the Fourteenth Amendment's equal protection clause. Reitman appealed to the Court, which upheld the state court ruling in *Reitman v. Mulkey* (1967).

Individual Discrimination

Despite these rulings, blacks and other minorities still had little protection from housing discrimination by individual home and apartment owners until the late 1960s. In 1968, Congress passed the Fair Housing Act, the first federal fair housing law. Three weeks later, in *Jones v. Alfred H. Mayer Co.* (1968), the Supreme Court ruled that the 1866 Civil Rights Act barred individual as well as state-backed discrimination in the sale and rental of housing.

The following year, the Court held that the 1866 act also prohibited a community recreational

club from refusing membership to a black man who received membership as part of his lease of a home in the neighborhood. In *Tillman v. Wheaton-Haven Recreation Association* (1973), the justices also ruled that a community recreation area violated the 1866 Civil Rights Act when it limited membership in its swimming pools to white residents of the community and their white guests.

Remedies for Discrimination

The Court has heard only one case dealing with remedies for housing discrimination. In *Hills v. Gautreaux* (1976), it unanimously upheld the power of a federal judge to order a metropolitan area-wide remedy for segregated public housing in Chicago. In *Hills*, the Chicago Housing Authority (CHA) was found guilty of discrimination in placing most of the city's public housing in black ghettoes. The Court ruled that the remedy for racial discrimination in public housing need not be confined to the city in which the discrimination occurred, but could include the surrounding metropolitan area.

The following year, the Court seemed to limit the potential impact of *Hills*. In *Village of Arlington Heights v. Metropolitan Housing Development Corporation* (1977), the Court upheld the village's refusal to rezone property to permit building of a housing development for low- and moderate-income persons of both races. The Court ruled that the rezoning did not show a "discriminatory motive" and therefore did not violate the Fourteenth Amendment.

See also: Equal Protection of the Law.

Federalism

System of government in which political power is divided between a central government and a number of individual political units. In the United States, the individual political units, or states, are bound together under a common national government yet still retain significant authority over internal state matters. The Court has often been called upon to determine the limits of federal authority over state affairs.

Article 4 of the U.S. Constitution describes the relationship between the states and the federal government, as well as among the individual states. Article 6 states that the Constitution, and any laws and treaties made under it, are the supreme law of the land. It also specifies that the states' constitutions and laws should not conflict with the federal Constitution. In cases of conflict, the federal laws and constitution take precedence. The Tenth Amendment grants to the states any powers the Constitution does not give specifically to the federal government or prohibit the states from exercising.

In the early landmark cases of *McCulloch v. Maryland* (1819) and *Gibbons v. Ogden* (1824), the Court upheld the federal government's power to pass laws that are binding on the states. In the former, the Court ruled that the state of Maryland could not tax a federally established bank operating in its borders. In the latter, the Court upheld the federal government's power to regulate interstate commerce. These rulings significantly expanded the power of the federal government in relation to the states.

Following the Civil War (1861–1865), the Thirteenth and Fourteenth Amendments further extended federal authority. These amendments granted federal and state citizenship to ex-slaves, and guaranteed their constitutional rights of **due process** and equal protection of the laws against infringement by the states. Even so, throughout the late 1800s and early 1900s, the Court consistently upheld state laws denying equal protection to some citizens.

Not until the 1920s and 1930s, did the Court begin to extend Fourteenth Amendment protection to all of the rights guaranteed under the Constitution. By the mid-1900s, however, the pendulum had swung from judicial support for state rights to support for a strong federal government. During this time, the federal government used its power to regulate interstate commerce to strike down many state laws that discriminated against certain classes of citizens. Between 1938 and 1995, the Court did not once rule against this practice.

The Court finally broke with this tradition in *United States v. Lopez* (1995), striking down a federal law forbidding possession of a gun near school. It ruled that such possession is not an economic activity that has a substantial effect on interstate commerce. This ruling reflected a movement called "New Federalism," initiated by President Ronald Reagan (1981-1989) in the 1980s, which is characterized by a gradual return of power to the states.

See also: Due Process: Equal Protection of the Law; *Gibbons v. Ogden* (1824); Interstate Relations; *McCulloch v. Maryland* (1819).

Field, Stephen Johnson (1816–1899)

Supreme Court justice nominated by President Abraham Lincoln (1861–1865) on March 6, 1863, for a newly created seat on the Court. Field was confirmed by the Senate on March 10, 1863, by a voice vote. He took the judicial oath of office on May 20, 1863, and retired on December 1, 1897.

Born on 1816 in Haddam, Connecticut, Stephen Johnson Field was the son of Submit Dickinson Field and David Dudley Field, a New England Congregational clergyman. Field studied law with John Van Buren, son of President Martin Van Buren (1837–1841), and was admitted to the New York bar in 1841. For the next seven years, he practiced law in partnership with his brother, Dudley. In 1849, after a trip to Europe, he decided to strike out on his own and moved to California. Settling in Marysville, in the heart of the gold fields, Field lived the rough-and-tumble life of a frontier entrepreneur.

Field was elected to the California Assembly, the lower house of the legislature, in 1850, and during his year of service was the chief drafter of the civil and criminal codes for the new state. After being defeated in a bid for the state senate in 1851, he resumed his legal career for a time and then was elected to the California State Supreme Court as a Democrat in 1857.

In 1863, Congress authorized an additional seat on the U.S. Supreme Court, partly to gain a new justice who would support the Civil War measures of the federal government, and partly because there was a need for a new circuit for the West Coast. Many cases concerning land and mineral issues were coming to the Court from California, and Westerners wanted someone familiar with those issues.

Lincoln, a Republican, crossed party lines to appoint Field to the new seat. The California and Oregon congressional delegations unanimously recommended him, even though he was a Democrat. Field had staunchly supported the Union cause and was an acknowledged expert in land and mining issues.

During his term on the Court, Field served, in 1877, on the electoral commission that decided the contested presidential election in favor of Republican Rutherford B. Hayes (1877–1881). Field voted on the losing Democratic side on all questions.

Field's name was mentioned for the Democratic presidential nomination in 1880 and 1884, but his candidacy did not advance very far. He aspired to be chief justice in 1888, when Morrison Waite died, but President Grover Cleveland (1885–1889, 1893–1897) picked Melville W. Fuller instead.

In the 1890s, Field's mental powers were noticeably declining, and he was taking an increasingly smaller part in Court proceedings. Finally, the other justices strongly hinted that he retire. Ironically, Field had been part of an effort to get an aging justice, Robert C. Grier, to retire in 1877. Field finally quit the Court in late 1897, but only after he had surpassed Chief Justice John Marshall's record of thirty-four years and five months of service.

Fifth Amendment

See Freedom of Assembly; Freedom of Religion; Freedom to Petition; Self-Incrimination.

Fifth Amendment Protections

See Double Jeopardy; Due Process; Self-Incrimination; Writ of Habeas Corpus.

Fiscal and Monetary Power and the Supreme Court

Supreme Court rulings that deal with the government's power to raise and spend money and collect taxes. Congress and the Court have both liberally interpreted the government's taxing and spending power. Historian C. Herman Pritchett notes, "In almost every decision touching the constitutionality of federal taxation, the Supreme Court has stressed the breadth of congressional power and the limits of its own reviewing powers."

Only three times has the Court disapproved a major act of Congress involving its fiscal and monetary powers. In each case, the Court's decision was eventually overturned. The Court ruled in 1870 that paper money could not be substituted for gold as legal tender; fifteen months later, it reversed that decision. The Court's 1895 decisions barring a federal income tax were nullified by adoption of the Sixteenth Amendment in 1913. Forty years later, the Court attempted to limit the power of Congress to spend for the general welfare, but eventually reversed itself.

Direct Taxation
The Supreme Court wrestled for a century with the definition of direct taxes. As early as 1796, the government asked the Court to define direct taxes in a test case concerning a federal tax on carriages. The Court found the carriage tax an indirect use tax, ruling that only head taxes and taxes on land were direct taxes. This definition remained in place until the Court in 1895 struck down an income tax as unconstitutional on the grounds that it was a direct tax not levied proportionately among the states.

A federal tax on personal income was first imposed during the Civil War (1861–1865) to meet the need for additional revenue. The Court upheld the tax as an indirect tax. In the 1890s, with the nation's economic base shifting from wealth based on land to wealth based on earnings, there was increasing pressure for an income tax. In 1894, Congress passed a tax of 2 percent on personal and

SPOTLIGHT

The Tomato: Fruit Or Vegetable?

The Supreme Court has declared that the tomato is a vegetable, not a fruit. The question arose in a nineteenth century tariff case because fruits could be imported duty free under an 1883 tariff act, but importers of vegetables were required to pay a duty equal to 10 percent of their value. Maintaining that tomatoes were fruits, an importer sued the New York port collector to recover back duties. The Court, in *Nix v. Hedden* (1893), held that tomatoes were vegetables. Delivering the opinion of the Court, Justice Horace Gray wrote:

> Botanically speaking, tomatoes are the fruit of a vine, just as are cucumbers, squashes, beans and peas. But in the common language of the people, whether sellers or consumers of provisions, all these are vegetables, which are grown in kitchen gardens, and which, whether eaten cooked or raw, are, like potatoes, carrots, parsnips, turnips, beets, cauliflower, cabbage, celery and lettuce, usually served at dinner in, with, or after the soup, fish or meats which constitute the principal part of the repast, and not, like fruits generally, as dessert.

corporate incomes in excess of $4,000. In *Pollock v. Farmers' Loan and Trust Co.* (1895), the Court ruled the tax unconstitutional.

Dissatisfaction with the decision resulted eighteen years later in enactment of the Sixteenth Amendment, which established a federal income tax. It also cost the Court prestige. The *Pollock* decision, Pritchett wrote, "earned the Court a popular reputation as a tool of special privilege which was not dispelled for forty years."

The Power to Spend

From the early days of the Union, the power to spend money for internal improvements has been justified by the authority given Congress over war, interstate commerce, territories, and the mails. Use of the spending power rarely has been challenged, partly because the Court, by finding that neither a taxpayer nor a state has standing to sue the federal government, has made it extremely difficult to bring a challenge.

Article I of the Constitution gives Congress the power "to provide for the common defense and general welfare." This power has been more widely debated. Some argued that it applied only to spending for purposes connected with the powers specifically mentioned in the Constitution. Others argued that it gave the government spending power independent from those specified powers. This broad interpretation eventually came to be the accepted view. In the case of *United States v. Butler* (1936), the majority concluded that "[T]he power of Congress to authorize is not limited by the first grants of legislative power found in the Constitution."

The Currency Powers

With one exception, the Court has ruled that the power "[to] coin Money, regulate the Value thereof, and of foreign Coin, and fix the Standard of Weights and Measures" gives Congress complete

Because the power to coin money is noted in the U.S. Constitution, the Supreme Court has upheld Congress's power to regulate the value of currency and pay debts in paper currency. (Jim Young/Reuters /Landov)

control over the nation's currency. For example, the Court upheld creation of a national bank, established largely to give some stability to the various state and foreign currencies in use during the Union's early history.

A national currency did not exist until the Civil War (1861–1865), when Congress authorized the printing of paper money. In *Veazie Bank v. Fenno* (1869), the Court upheld a federal tax that was intended to drive state bank notes out of circulation and leave a single uniform national currency. The following year, in

Hepburn v. Griswold (1870), the Court struck down a law making paper currency legal tender to pay debts contracted prior to 1862. However, the Court soon reversed itself, in *Knox v. Lee* (1871), stating that refusing to accept paper money "must cause, throughout the country, great business derangement, widespread distress, and the rankest injustice." The Court reaffirmed this ruling in a series of cases in the 1930s in which it upheld Congress's power to regulate the value of currency and pay debts in paper currency rather than gold.

Flag Burning

Supreme Court decisions regarding the use of the American flag to symbolize opposition to government policy. In five modern cases, the Court reversed the convictions of persons who used the American flag in this manner.

Street v. New York (1969) concerned a man who protested the shooting of civil rights activist James Meredith by publicly burning a flag. He was convicted under a New York law that made it illegal to mutilate a flag or to cast contempt upon it either by words or conduct. Overturning the conviction, the Court said the statute was too broad because it permitted the punishment of words, which were protected by the First and Fourteenth Amendments.

In *Smith v. Goguen* (1974), the Court overturned the conviction of a man who wore a small flag on the seat of his pants. He was arrested under a Massachusetts law that made contemptuous treatment of the flag a crime. The Court ruled that the law was unconstitutionally vague because it "fails to draw reasonably clear lines between the kinds of non-ceremonial treatment [of the flag] that are criminal and those that are not." Later that year, in *Spence v. Washington* (1974), the Court ruled that a student flying a flag upside down, on which he had superimposed a peace symbol, was a form of symbolic speech protected under the First Amendment.

In 1989, the Court set off a storm of protest when it struck down laws that made it a crime to burn an American flag. In 1984, Gregory Johnson went to the Republican National Convention in Dallas to protest the policies of the Reagan administration. Standing outside the city hall, he set a flag on fire and was later convicted for violating the Texas law against flag desecration. The Texas Court of Criminal Appeals overturned his conviction on free speech grounds, and the Court later upheld the appeals court decision and struck down the Texas law in *Texas v. Johnson* (1990). Within weeks, Congress attempted to reverse the Court by passing the Flag Protection Act, which would have subjected

to arrest anyone who "knowingly mutilates, defaces, physically defiles, burns, maintains on the floor or ground, or tramples upon any flag."

Since that time, Congress has proposed amendments to the Constitution that would outlaw flag burning. In 2005, the House of Representatives approved such a measure. However, the following year, the Senate rejected the proposal, which fell one vote short of the required two-thirds majority.

See also: Freedom of Speech; Symbolic Speech.

Foreign Affairs and the Supreme Court

Supreme Court decisions dealing with relations between the United States and other nations. To the framers of the Constitution, foreign policy meant making treaties and waging war. They divided these responsibilities: Congress would declare war, and the president would conduct war with armies raised and maintained by Congress. The president would negotiate treaties; Congress would approve treaties. Challenges to the foreign policy decisions of Congress and the president come to the Court infrequently, and the Court rarely has overruled Congress in the conduct of foreign affairs.

Congress has declared war formally only five times: the War of 1812 (1812–1814); the Mexican War (1846–1848); the Spanish-American War (1898); World War I (1914–1918); and World War II (1939–1945). The rest of America's foreign wars have been undeclared. From time to time the absence of a formal declaration of war has been challenged before the Supreme Court. In 1800, the Court held that Congress need not declare full-scale war but could provide for a limited conflict.

Members of the 1787 Constitutional Convention considered giving the Senate sole authority to make treaties with foreign countries. Ultimately, that power was shared with the president, who had the "Power, by and with the Advice and

Consent of the Senate, to make Treaties." How equal a partner this phrasing made the Senate in the actual negotiation of treaties was debated for several decades. The Court laid this argument to rest in 1936, declaring, "The President alone negotiates. Into the field of negotiation the Senate cannot intrude, and Congress itself is powerless to invade it."

Since 1795, the Senate has claimed the right to amend and modify treaties submitted for approval by the president. Twice the Supreme Court has reviewed and approved this power. In 1869, and again in 1901, the Court ruled that the Senate may make approval conditional upon adoption of amendments to the treaty. The Court has also ruled that a treaty may supersede a prior act of Congress, and that an act of Congress may in effect repeal prior treaties or parts of them.

The Supreme Court also has supported a number of other congressional powers concerning foreign affairs. These include the power to regulate foreign imports through **tariffs,** to acquire territory through conquest or treaty, and to acquire territory through discovery. In a series of cases in the early 1900s, the Court left it up to Congress to determine whether to incorporate a territory into the United States. In 1840, the Court recognized an absolute right by Congress to dispose of federal property.

See also: War Power and the Supreme Court.

Fourth Amendment

See Search Warrants.

Frankfurter, Felix (1882–1965)

Influential liberal Supreme Court Justice whose opinions advanced the cause of civil rights in the United States. Felix Frankfurter had served in numerous government positions before being nominated to the Court by President Franklin D. Roosevelt (1933–1945) on January 5, 1939, to replace Benjamin Cardozo, who had died. Frankfurter was confirmed by the Senate on January 17, 1939, by a voice vote. He served on the Court until he retired in 1962.

An Austrian Jew, Felix Frankfurter came to the United States with his parents, Leopold and Emma Winter Frankfurter, in 1894 and was brought up amid the poverty of New York City's Lower East Side. He attended City College in New York and, after an impressive three years at the Harvard University School of Law, took a job with a New York law firm. He soon was recruited away, however, by Henry L. Stimson, the U.S. attorney for the Southern District of New York.

Stimson had been appointed by President Theodore Roosevelt (1901–1909), and at the end of the Roosevelt administration, Stimson went into private practice and brought Frankfurter with him. Stimson was later named secretary of war under President William Howard Taft (1909–1913). Frankfurter then accompanied his mentor to Washington, D.C., and was appointed legal officer in the War Department's Bureau of Insular Affairs.

In 1913, Harvard University offered Frankfurter a teaching post in the law school, and he happily returned to his alma mater. Passionate about teaching, Frankfurter trained two generations of students devoted to the law and public service. He also became involved in the Zionist movement, argued a number of minimum and maximum wage cases for the National Consumers League, and helped found the New Republic.

Frankfurter returned to Washington, D.C., in 1917 as an assistant to Secretary of War Newton D. Baker. That same year, President Woodrow Wilson (1913–1921) named a mediation commission to handle the rash of strikes obstructing the defense industry. Frankfurter was named its secretary and counsel. While serving on the commission, Frankfurter investigated the handling of the case of Tom Mooney, the alleged Preparedness Day Parade bomber, and the Bisbee, Arizona, deportation case wherein approximately one thousand miners were taken roughly from their labor camps in Arizona and dropped in a deserted town in New Mexico. In both instances,

Frankfurter found that the rights of the individuals involved had been violated. These cases, as well as his work with the NAACP, and the fact that he was a founding member of the American Civil Liberties Union, earned him a reputation as a die-hard liberal which would follow him throughout his career.

He also served as chairman of the War Labor Policies Board. This position first introduced him to Franklin D. Roosevelt, who, as assistant secretary of the Navy, sat on the board.

At the end of World War I (1914–1918), Frankfurter attended the Paris Peace Conference as a representative of the American Zionist movement and then returned to Cambridge, Massachusetts, where he took a teaching position at Harvard. At Harvard, Frankfurter enjoyed a growing reputation as an expert on the U.S. Constitution and the Supreme Court. He was offered a seat on the Massachusetts Supreme Court in 1932, which he declined. His friendship with Franklin Roosevelt grew closer, and in 1933, the newly elected president asked him to be solicitor general, another post that Frankfurter declined. He remained, however, a close adviser to the president.

Named to the Court in 1939 to replace Justice Cardozo, Frankfurter was Roosevelt's third appointment. Despite his support for liberal causes, Frankfurter's voting on the Court was considered conservative. He joined with the majority in *Korematsu v. United States* (1944), upholding the exclusion of Japanese Americans from the West Coast. He argued that the country was engaged in a world war against horrific foes, and he believed the claims of the nation were stronger than those of individuals. He dissented in *Board of Education v. Barnette* (1943), the case that overturned an earlier ruling that had said children could be expelled from school for declining to salute the flag for religious reasons. As an immigrant to the United States, Frankfurter felt it was important to show patriotism.

Frankfurter continued to advise the president on a number of issues until Roosevelt's death in 1945. Frankfurter remained on the Court until he suffered a debilitating stroke in 1962. He died in Washington, D.C., in 1965.

See also: Korematsu v. United States (1944).

Freedom of Assembly

The right of individuals to peaceably assemble for lawful purposes. Although the First Amendment to the U.S. Constitution guarantees freedom of assembly, it was not until 1876 that the Supreme Court first ruled that freedom of assembly was a privilege of national citizenship. Almost sixty years later, in *DeJonge v. Oregon* (1937), the Court recognized that the right of assembly was on an equal status with the rights of free speech and free press. It also ruled that the Fourteenth Amendment protected this right from infringement by the states.

Parades and Demonstrations

Parading and demonstrating have always been subject to greater regulation than exercises of pure speech and assembly. To preserve the freedoms of speech and assembly, the Court has insisted that parade and demonstration regulations be precisely worded and applied in nondiscriminatory fashion.

Civil rights protestors gather to pray outside a city government building in Alabama in the early 1960s. Freedom of assembly is an essential right guaranteed by the First Amendment to the U.S. Constitution. (Library of Congress, Prints and Photographs Division)

JUSTICE FOR ALL

A Right to Loiter?

Laws against loitering and vagrancy date to colonial times, but they came under challenge during the civil rights movement. In *Shuttlesworth v. Birmingham* (1965), the Court ruled that the police may not use their peacekeeping power to harass or arrest people peacefully going about their business. Fred Shuttlesworth, a black minister in Birmingham, Alabama, was arrested under a city code that made it "unlawful for any person to stand or loiter upon any street or sidewalk of the city after having been requested by any police officer to move on." Justice Potter Stewart said the Constitution does not give a city the total power to permit persons "to stand on a public sidewalk . . . only at the whim of any police officer." To act otherwise "bears the hallmark of a police state."

In *Papachristou v. City of Jacksonville* (1972), the Court swept aside the remnants of vagrancy and loitering laws. It declared unconstitutional a Jacksonville, Florida, ordinance that stated, "Rogues and vagabonds or dissolute persons" as well as "common drunkards, common nightwalkers, lewd, wanton and lascivious persons . . . habitual loafers (and) disorderly persons . . . shall be deemed vagrants" and arrested. The Court ruled that because these laws are so vague, they "cannot be squared with our constitutional standards." The Court reaffirmed this principle in Chicago v. Morales, striking down a Chicago law that allowed police officers to arrest anyone who is "reasonably believe[d] to be a criminal street gang member loitering in any public place" and who fails to disperse when warned. The justices declared the ordinance unconstitutional because it failed to spell out the "forbidden conduct" and because it gave police too much power to interfere with the innocent.

A - Z

To preserve the public welfare, the Court has held that not all public places are appropriate sites for public protests. In *Cox v. New Hampshire* (1941), the Court ruled that a locality may deny a parade permit if the parade would interfere with others using the streets.

In 1992, the Court ruled that parade regulations must be neutral and not give local officials too much discretion in enforcing such regulations. Three years later, the Court held that state law cannot force parade organizers to include participants with whom they disagree. Boston veterans wanted to exclude marchers whose main purpose was to proclaim their homosexual identity. When a parade is privately organized, the Court said, it is a form of private expression protected by the First Amendment's guarantee of free speech.

Labor Picketing

Unlike other sorts of parades and demonstrations, picketing also uses economic pressure and coercion to bring about better working conditions. Since this activity is considered conduct, government may regulate it.

Initially, the courts considered all labor picketing illegal. It was not until 1940 when the Court gave picketing First Amendment protection. In *Thornhill v. Alabama* (1940), the Court declared an Alabama anti-picketing law to be a violation of the rights of free speech, assembly, and petition.

The following year, in *AFL v. Swing* (1941), the Court ruled that a state could not pass a law limiting picketing to cases where union members had a dispute with their employer.

Exceptions to Free Assembly

The Court has placed limits on assembly that may lead to violence or constitute illegal conduct. In *Milk Wagon Drivers Union v. Meadowmoor Dairies Inc.* (1941), the Court ruled that the First Amendment did not prevent government from preventing picketing in the interest of public safety. In this case, the majority upheld a lower court order forbidding a union of milk wagon drivers to engage in picketing because their past picketing had resulted in violence.

The Court further weakened protection for picketing in *Giboney v. Empire Storage and Ice Co.* (1949). It ruled that picketing as "conduct" may in some circumstances be so intertwined with illegal labor practices that states may prohibit it. Starting with *Giboney* and ending with three decisions in 1950, the Court effectively reversed *Thornhill*. It denied First Amendment protection if the purpose of the picketing could be considered opposed to state laws or policies. Nevertheless, in *Brotherhood of Teamsters, Local 695 v. Vogt* (1957), the Court argued that *Thornhill* was still valid, even though states may restrict the right to assemble under certain conditions.

See also: Bill of Rights; Freedom of Speech.

Freedom of Association

The freedom to hold any political belief and to associate with others sharing that belief. Although the First Amendment guarantees freedom of association, the Court did not formally recognize it for more than 125 years.

Freedom of association is not absolute. The Court has approved restricting it, especially during times of perceived or real national emergency. Although this freedom is still ill defined, the Court is firm on one point: a person must not be found guilty of a crime simply because he or she belongs to a particular group.

Establishing the Right

Almost from the beginning of the republic, the federal government tested the limits of freedom of association. In 1798, Congress passed the Alien and Sedition Acts, which severely penalized individuals for criticizing the government or government officials. These widely unpopular laws expired before they were ever challenged before the Court. During the Civil War (1861–1865), military officials imposed restrictions on individual rights and expression. Once again, however, no one ever challenged the constitutionality of those actions before the Court.

The Espionage Cases

The Supreme Court first ruled upon freedom of association in a series of espionage cases decided after World War I (1914–1918). At that time, the Court was faced by the need to balance protection for free speech with the government's need to protect itself against internal political threats. In these cases, the Court upheld laws that penalized persons who spoke or published statements intended to interfere with the nation's military success, bring the government or military into disrepute, or promote the cause of the enemy. Nevertheless, the Court began to establish legal tests to determine when such restriction of speech and expression was permissible and when it was not.

Guilt by Association

In *Whitney v. California* (1927), the majority of the Court appeared to allow persons to be punished simply for associating with groups that espoused potentially illegal acts. The Court upheld the conviction of Anita Whitney under a 1919 California law that made it illegal to organize or participate in Communist Party activities.

In the 1930s, the Court backed away from the guilt-by-association rule it seemed to adopt in *Whitney*. In a series of cases during this decade, the Court focused upon the actions of the individual rather than his or her political beliefs, emphasizing personal guilt rather than guilt by association. In the Court's opinion in *DeJonge v. Oregon* (1937), Chief Justice Charles Evans Hughes wrote that the state could not punish a person making a lawful speech simply because the speech was sponsored by an allegedly "subversive" organization.

JUSTICE FOR ALL

Private Clubs

Private clubs with racially discriminatory admissions policies are generally considered beyond the reach of the Fourteenth Amendment to the U.S. Constitution. In *Moose Lodge 107 v. Irvis* (1972), the Supreme Court found that issuing a state liquor license to a private club that discriminates against blacks does not amount to discrimination by the state in violation of the Fourteenth Amendment.

The majority ruled that the degree of involvement necessary to constitute state infringement of basic rights varies from case to case. In this situation, the liquor regulations, with one exception, did not promote discrimination and therefore did not involve the state in the private discriminatory policy. The exception was the liquor board's requirement that all club bylaws be obeyed. The Court found that in cases where the bylaws restricted membership by race, the state regulation amounted to enforcement of a discriminatory practice.

In *Tillman v. Wheaton-Haven Recreation Association* (1973), the Court rejected the claim of a community recreation association that it was a private club exempt from the Civil Rights Act of 1964. The association limited membership in its swimming pool to white residents of the community and their white guests. The Court ruled that the association was not entitled to the exemption because it had no selection criteria for membership other than race and residence in the community.

A-Z

Communism and Association

Concern about the threat of **communism** intensified after World War II (1941–1945), leading Congress to pass federal laws intended to protect the nation against communist subversion. These laws restricted the freedom of political belief, expression, and association for those who held certain political views.

Congress passed three major federal laws to discourage the growth of communist organizations in the United States. The Smith Act of 1940 made it a crime to advocate the violent overthrow of the government or to organize or to belong to any group advocating such revolutionary action. The McCarran Act of 1950 required all communist-action groups or communist-front groups to register with the Justice Department and disclose their membership lists. It also prohibited their members from holding government or defense-related jobs or using U.S. passports. The Communist

Control Act of 1954 declared the Communist Party a "treasonable conspiracy" against the U.S. government and, thus, an illegal organization.

The Court's Position Evolves

During the first decade of the **cold war**, from about 1947 to 1957, the Court generally upheld these laws. As the cold war thawed, the Court began to restrict how the government could apply these laws. It began to insist that such laws be used only to penalize persons who knowingly and actively sought to promote communist revolution in the United States.

From 1957 through 1967, the Court forced the government to stop enforcing of these laws and prosecuting people under the Smith Act. The main case was *Yates v. United States* (1957), which imposed strict standards of proof upon the government to prosecute members of the Communist

Party under the Smith Act. In *Yates*, the Court required the government to show a direct connection between participation in the Communist Party and forcible overthrow of the government.

In *Albertson v. Subversive Activities Control Board* (1965), the Court held that the registration requirements of the McCarren Act violated the Fifth Amendment privilege against self-incrimination. The Court held unanimously that the information sought in the registration forms from Communist Party officers included material that was self-incriminating. Thus, forcing them to register did violate the officers' Fifth Amendment privilege. This ruling effectively ended government efforts to force registration of the Communist Party.

Restricting Political Association: A Contemporary View

In the early 1970s, the Court set out its view of restrictions a state might place on voters' or candidates' association with a particular political party. These rulings touched upon the question of who was allowed to vote in a party primary election. In 1973, the Court upheld a state requirement that voters who wish to vote in a party's primary enroll in that party at least 30 days before the last general election.

In *California Democratic Party v. Jones* (2000), the Court struck down a California law that opened primary elections to all voters, regardless of whether they belonged to a party. The Court ruled that political parties and their faithful members have a right to choose their own candidates and to exclude independents from the process. "Representative democracy . . . is unimaginable without the ability of citizens to band together in promoting among the electorate candidates who espouse their political views," said Justice Antonin Scalia. "[A] corollary of [this] right to associate is the right not to associate."

See also: Bill of Rights; Freedom of Speech.

Freedom of Religion

Supreme Court rulings that deal with the First Amendment guarantees of free exercise of religion and separation of church and state. Both of these protections stemmed from the American **colonial** experience, which included both flight from religious persecution in Europe and the establishment of state religions in several colonies. The colonies that eventually formed the United States represented a wide variety of religious sects whose memebers held differing attitudes about state involvement in religion. By the time of the American Revolution (1775–1783), **religious toleration** was well established in most states. In the Bill of Rights, added to the Constitution in 1791, religious freedom led the list of individual rights protected from government interference.

The Establishment Clause

The Supreme Court has struggled to give precise meaning to the First Amendment's limits on the government. What, after all, is meant by an "establishment of religion"? Is it simply a ban on the official proclamation of a "national religion," as Chief Justice William H. Rehnquist suggests in *Wallace v. Jaffree* (1985)? Does it speak more broadly, erecting "a wall of separation between church and state," as President Thomas Jefferson (1801–1809) wrote in a letter to a Danbury Baptist Congregation in 1802?

These questions took on a new urgency after World War II (1939–1945). Until then, the federal legislature rarely passed laws that dealt with churches and the faithful, so the ban on laws "respecting an establishment of religion" had little practical significance. By the middle decades of the twentieth century, however, the Court had decided that the ban on an "establishment of religion" applied to states, cities, and local school boards. In *Everson v. Board of Education* (1947), the Court struck down the common practice of using taxpayer money to pay the cost of busing children to **parochial schools** (as well as public schools).

Since *Everson*, a debate has raged among constitutional scholars and religious activists as to whether the Constitution's framers indeed intended to erect a wall of separation between church and state. The doctrine of strict separation between church and state reached its peak during the 1960s and 1970s, when the Court struck down state-sponsored prayer and Bible readings in public schools. In recent years, the Court has made clear that private prayer or religious activity is permitted on a public school campus. Students have a free speech

JUSTICE FOR ALL

Jehovah's Witnesses

The Jehovah's Witnesses, followers of a religion founded in the late 1860s and early 1870s, have been at the forefront of many important Supreme Court cases dealing with freedom of religion. According to constitutional historian Robert F. Cushman, since 1938, members of the sect have brought some thirty major cases testing the principles of religious freedom to the Supreme Court. In most of those cases, the Court has ruled in their favor.

The first such case was *Lovell v. Griffin* (1938), in which the Court held that religious handbills were entitled to protection of freedom of the press. In another important case, *Cantwell v. Connecticut* (1940), the Court held that the Fourteenth Amendment prohibited states from abridging the free exercise of religion. It also ruled that public officials did not have the authority to determine that some causes were religious and others were not. In other significant decisions, the Court upheld the right of Witnesses to solicit from door to door and to ring homeowners' doorbells, to refuse to salute the flag, and to be exempt from peddler's fees on sales of their literature. In *Watchtower Bible & Tract Society of New York v. Village of Stratton* (2002), the Court reaffirmed that the Jehovah's Witnesses have rights under the First Amendment to go door to door to solicit donations without obtaining a city permit in advance.

right to pray on their own, to read the Bible at school, or to talk about their faith. In a series of rulings, the justices upheld the principle of "equal access" to public school facilities for religious students and Christian groups.

The conservative wing of the Court also has shifted the law in favor of allowing tax money to flow to religious schools. In *Agostini v. Felton* (1997), the Court ruled that federal funds can be used to pay public school tutors to teach remedial reading classes in parochial schools. In *Zelman v. Simmons-Harris* (2002), the Court upheld Ohio's use of state vouchers or tuition grants to pay for children in Cleveland to attend religious schools. On this frontier, the wall of separation erected during the 1960s has been thoroughly breached.

Free Exercise

Unlike the Establishment Clause, the First Amendment's protection for the "free exercise of religion"

has led to minimal conflicts in the Court. The few cases have grown out of clashes between state or local governments and minority religions such as the Mormons, Jehovah's Witnesses, the Amish, and Hare Krishnas.

Many of the Court's landmark free speech decisions of the 1940s arose when local and state authorities tried to prevent Jehovah's Witnesses from going door-to-door to solicit contributions. In *West Virginia State Board of Education v. Barnette* (1943), the Court ruled that the children of Jehovah's Witnesses cannot be compelled to salute the flag at school. In the 1960s and 1970s, the Court continued to rule in general in favor of religious freedom in clashes with government authorities. However, the Court has ruled that religious followers are not entitled to an exemption from "neutral, generally applicable laws." This 5-4 decision, handed down in *Employment Division, Department of Human Resources of Oregon v.*

Smith (1990), touched off sharp criticism. Both supporters and opponents of state support for religion argued that the Court's watered-down standard would not protect religious liberty. Critics eventually went on to win passage of a law to overturn the decision, but the Court struck down the new law as unconstitutional in *City of Boerne v. Flores* (1997).

See also: Bill of Rights; Freedom of Speech; School Prayer and Bible Readings.

Further Reading

Head, Tom. *Freedom of Religion.* New York: Facts On File, 2005.

Waldman, Steven. *Founding Faith: How Our Founding Fathers Forged a Radical New Approach to Religious Liberty.* New York: Random House, 2009.

Freedom of Speech

Supreme Court rulings that deal with the First Amendment guarantee that, "Congress shall make no law . . . abridging the freedom of speech. . . ." Speech is the basic vehicle for communicating ideas, thoughts, and beliefs. The right to speak freely is necessary to the free flow of ideas that is considered so crucial to the success of representative government in the United States. Although the First Amendment states its protection absolutely, few contend that the right it protects is without limit. The forms of speech that merit no First Amendment protection include **libel** and **obscenity.** The speech-related cases before the Court repeatedly come down to two questions: What is protected speech? When may such speech be curbed?

Types of Speech

The Court approaches speech that stands alone— or pure speech—in a manner different from speech that is accompanied by a course of conduct, such as picketing. It also considers some actions, such as wearing armbands as form of protest, to be protected as speech under the Constitution.

Pure Speech

Verbal expression of thought and opinion, whether spoken calmly in the privacy of one's home or delivered passionately in public, is the purest form of speech. Because pure speech does not interfere with or inconvenience others, it is subject to the least amount of government control. The Court, however, recognizes the right of government to curb pure speech that threatens the national security or public safety. It also acknowledges that government has a right to regulate pure speech that interferes with the rights of others.

The broadest official restrictions on pure speech have come during times of war, when the Court has upheld federal and state controls on **seditious** and **subversive** speech. It has sustained punishment of speech that causes a violent and hostile reaction by those who hear it. Because the Court considers the varying circumstances attending each free speech case, it has been unable to develop and apply consistently a standard for determining when the threat to national security or public safety warrants a restriction on or punishment of the speech.

Certain forms of pure speech and expression fall outside the protection of the First Amendment because they are not essential to the communication of ideas and have little social value. "Fighting words"—public insults calculated to elicit a violent response—fall into this category, as does obscenity. Here again, however, the Court has had great difficulty settling on a standard by which to define the obscene. Initially, the Court placed speech that advertised products and services outside the protection of the First Amendment. Since 1975, however, it has recognized that advertisements convey ideas and information of substantial value to the public and so has brought commercial speech under First Amendment coverage.

Symbolic Speech

The Court has ruled expression that makes a symbolic statement to be pure speech. For example, the justices upheld the right of students to wear armbands and to fly the flag upside down in symbolic protest of the Vietnam War. Although such symbolism may make itself felt on an involuntary audience, it, like pure speech, relies for effect primarily on its power to evoke an idea or emotion. The Court has also held, however, that symbolic speech, like pure speech, may be so intertwined with conduct that the state may regulate both.

The Ku Klux Klan, a racist organization, marches in Washington, D.C., in 1926. Later, in a case that concerned the Klan, *Brandenburg v. Ohio* (1969), the Supreme Court held that it is unconstitutional to punish a person who calls for violence as a means of achieving political reform. (Library of Congress, Prints and Photographs Division)

A – Z

When speech is combined with conduct, such as parading, demonstrating, or picketing, the Court is more open to allowing government regulation.

Speech Plus Conduct

The Court has upheld the right of persons to engage in speech plus conduct. At the same time, however, it has given government the right to regulate the conduct aspect to ensure public safety and order. Such regulation must be precisely drawn and applied in a nondiscriminatory fashion. The government also must have a legitimate and substantial interest to justify the regulation, and the regulation must restrict the speech aspect as little as possible. Picketing is one area of speech plus conduct that the Court has held to have almost no First Amendment protection. Peaceful labor picketing is, however, protected under federal labor law.

Because the First Amendment bars only government action abridging speech, it generally does not affect speech on private property. Here, too, there are exceptions. The First Amendment applies to privately owned company towns that provide all services to its residents that a municipally owned town would. The owners of private property dedicated to specific public purposes—for example, a shopping mall—may restrict speech on their property that is not directly related to its public use.

Government Restraints

Government can restrain free speech rights either by suppressing an utterance before it is spoken or by punishing the speaker afterward. Prohibiting the prior restraint of speech through censorship, severe taxation, or licensing systems, for example, is particularly important to ensure freedom of the press. Although the First Amendment is stated absolutely—"Congress shall make no law . . ."—few contend that the amendment is an absolute ban on government restriction of speech. Most justices and constitutional scholars distinguish between pure expression and expression that is in itself conduct or that incites conduct. The first, with a few exceptions, is absolutely protected against governmental infringement; the second is not. The Court explained this distinction in *Cantwell v. Connecticut* (1940). Although it was speaking specifically of the freedom of religion, the ruling

Public Speech on Private Property: The First Amendment Restricted

The Company Town. The Court first confronted this issue in *Marsh v. Alabama* (1946). Chickasaw, Alabama, a suburb of Mobile, was wholly owned by a private corporation. A Jehovah's Witness, Grace Marsh, passed out handbills on a Chickasaw street in violation of a regulation forbidding such distribution. She challenged her subsequent arrest and conviction, claiming that her First Amendment rights had been infringed. A majority of the Supreme Court agreed. Save for its private ownership, wrote Justice Hugo L. Black, Chickasaw had all the characteristics of any other American town, and its residents had the same interest as residents of municipally owned towns in keeping channels of communication open. "There is no more reason for depriving these people of the liberties guaranteed by the First and Fourteenth Amendments than there is for curtailing these freedoms with respect to any other citizens," Black said.

Picketing and Private Malls. In 1968, the Court relied on *Marsh v. Alabama* when it forbade the owner of a private shopping mall to prohibit union picketing of a store in the mall. A nonunion supermarket in a privately owned mall near Altoona, Pennsylvania, was picketed by members of a food employees union who wished to point out that the supermarket did not employ union workers or abide by union pay and working condition requirements. The owners of the store and the shopping center won an injunction against picketing in the mall and its private parking lots.

By a 6-3 vote, the Supreme Court declared the injunction invalid in *Amalgamated Food Employees Union Local 590 v. Logan Valley Plaza* (1968). Noting the similarities between the shopping center and the business district in the company town involved in *Marsh,* Justice Thurgood Marshall observed that the general public had unrestricted access to the mall and that it served as the functional equivalent of a town business district. These circumstances, the majority said, rendered the mall public for purposes of the First Amendment, and consequently its owners could not invoke state trespass laws to prohibit picketing that advanced the communication of ideas. Marshall noted the narrowness of the ruling:

> All we decide here is that because the shopping center serves as the community business block "and is freely accessible and open to the people in the area and those passing through" . . . the State may not delegate the power, through the use of its trespass laws, wholly to exclude those members of the public wishing to exercise their First Amendment rights on the premises in a manner and for a purpose generally consonant with the use to which the property is actually put.

Justice Black dissented, contending that the majority erred in its reliance on *Marsh* as a precedent. *Marsh* held that the First Amendment applied when the private property had taken on *all* of the aspects of a town, he said, adding,

> I can find nothing in Marsh which indicates that if one of these features is present, e.g., a business district, this is sufficient for the Court to confiscate a part of an owner's private property and give its use to people who want to picket on it.

Handbill Protests in Shopping Centers. Within four years, a majority of the Court qualified the ruling in *Logan Valley Plaza,* holding that owners of a private shopping mall could prohibit the distribution of leaflets unrelated to business conducted in the mall. The circumstances in *Lloyd Corporation, Ltd. v. Tanner* (1972) were similar to those in *Marsh* with one major difference. The Lloyd Center was not a company town but a privately owned and operated shopping mall that prohibited the circulation of handbills. Inside the mall, several people attempted to distribute handbills inviting the general public to attend a meeting to

Public Speech on Private Property: The First Amendment Restricted, *continued*

protest the Vietnam War. When asked to desist, they did, but then brought suit charging they had been denied their right to free speech. By a 5-4 vote the Supreme Court rejected the charge. Writing for the majority, Justice Lewis F. Powell Jr. held that although the shopping mall served the public, it still maintained its private character:

> The invitation is to come to the Center to do business with the tenants. There is no open-ended invitation to the public to use the Center for any and all purposes, however incompatible with the interests of both the stores and the shoppers whom they serve. This Court has never held that a trespasser or an uninvited guest may exercise general rights of free speech on property privately owned and used nondiscriminatorily for private purposes only.

Writing for the dissenters, Justice Marshall saw nothing to distinguish this case from the Court's holdings in *Marsh* and *Logan Valley Plaza*.

Picketing and Private Malls II. In 1976, the Court moved a step closer to divesting speech on private property used for specific public purposes of any First Amendment protection, but a majority of the Court still refused to overturn the *Logan Valley Plaza* decision, leaving the issue unsettled. *Hudgens v. National Labor Relations Board* (1976) arose after striking employees of a shoe company warehouse decided also to picket the company's retail stores. One of these was situated in a shopping mall whose owners threatened to have the pickets arrested for trespassing if they did not desist. The pickets withdrew but challenged the owners' threat as an unfair labor practice under the National Labor Relations Act.

Before answering that question, the Supreme Court majority felt it necessary to determine whether the picketing was entitled to any First Amendment protection. A majority concluded it was not. Three of the members of the majority held that the *Lloyd* decision had in effect overruled the *Logan Valley Plaza* decision and that, consequently, uninvited speech on private property was not protected. The three other justices comprising the majority did not believe that the *Logan Valley Plaza* decision had been overruled, but they distinguished between the pickets in that case, who conveyed information about the operation of a store actually located in the mall, and the pickets in *Hudgens,* who tried to convey information about a warehouse located away from the mall.

Justices Marshall and William J. Brennan Jr. dissented. Marshall insisted that when an owner of a private shopping mall invited the public onto his property to conduct business he gave up a degree of privacy to the interests of the public. One public interest was "communicating with one another on subjects relating to businesses that occupy" the shopping center. "As far as these groups are concerned," said Marshall, "the shopping center owner has assumed the traditional role of the state in its control of historical First Amendment forums." Just four years later, however, the Court seemed to move again on this question, holding unanimously that a state could require the owner of a shopping mall to permit students to collect signatures on a petition to Congress within his mall.

The First Amendment prohibits only government action abridging the freedom of speech. Most First Amendment cases therefore involve situations in which speech occurs or is abridged in a public forum or on public property. Some private property is dedicated to public use, however, and there the question arises whether the property owner becomes subject to the First Amendment prohibition. If that is so, then a private owner may no more restrict exercise of First Amendment freedoms on his property than may a government.

SPOTLIGHT

Fighting Words and Hate Crimes

"Fighting words" —words so insulting that they provoke violence from the person to whom they are addressed—are generally unprotected by the First Amendment. However, the Court has not looked favorably on laws criminalizing "hate speech," which targets persons because of their race, religion, or sexual orientation.

In *Chaplinsky v. New Hampshire* (1942), a Jehovah's Witness provoked a public disturbance when he publicly assailed another religion as "a racket," and called a police officer "a God damned racketeer" and "a damned Fascist." He was convicted of violating a state statute making it a crime to call another person "offensive and derisive names" in public. The Court upheld the conviction, arguing that to "[R]esort to epithets or to personal abuse is not in any proper sense communication of information or opinion safeguarded by the Constitution."

During the 1980s, many states and localities passed laws forbidding "hate speech" and "hate crimes." In the early 1990s, two of these laws were challenged before the Supreme Court as violations of free speech rights. In *R.A.V. v. City of St. Paul,* the justices struck down a city ordinance prohibiting cross burning as a form of hate speech. The Court ruled that the law unconstitutionally singled out specific types of "hate speech" for criminal punishment.

The second ruling, in 1993, upheld a law that required enhanced penalties for crimes committed because of prejudice. Chief Justice Rehnquist wrote that judges traditionally have been permitted to consider "a wide variety of factors" in sentencing a defendant, including the motive for the crime.

may be applied to all First Amendment freedoms: "[T]he Amendment embraces two concepts— freedom to believe and freedom to act. The first is absolute but, in the nature of things, the second cannot be. Conduct remains subject to regulation for the protection of society."

Unprotected Speech

Some forms of expression that fall outside protection of the First Amendment are fairly obvious. Few would apply First Amendment protection to a person who encourages murder or, as Justice Oliver Wendell Holmes Jr. said, to "falsely shouting fire in a theatre and causing a panic." Few would argue that publishers are free to print deliberately false and defamatory material about public or private individuals.

The outer bounds of First Amendment protection are not fixed. The Court once ruled that libelous statements were unprotected. It has since held that false and defamatory statements about public officials and figures are protected unless the subject of the statements can show that the speaker acted with actual **malice**. Obscenity is still outside the scope of First Amendment protection, but even there the standards for determining what is obscene and what is not have undergone significant change in recent decades.

Speech and Conduct

Commercial speech, libel, and obscene material are examples of pure expression. The Court has found it more difficult to determine the point at which expression becomes conduct that falls outside the bounds of First Amendment. Assume, for example, that a man is making a heated speech on a controversial issue on a public street corner. Does the First Amendment protect him against punishment for any consequences his speech might have? If not, must the government wait to stop the speech until his listeners take action either against the speaker or the object of his speech? May it stop him at the point that it thinks his words will lead to a breach of the peace, or can the government, knowing from past experience that the speaker is a rabble-rouser, prevent him from speaking at all? Finding answers to these questions is made more difficult by the emotional response generated by many forms of expression. As Justice Robert H. Jackson once observed, the "freedom to differ is not limited to things that do not matter much."

The voicing of a popular opinion rarely raises a First Amendment challenge. Unpopular minority opinions on matters of crucial concern are most likely to draw hostility from the majority upon whose goodwill the rights of the minority depend. If the majority sees the unpopular opinion as a threat, it may ask the government to suppress that opinion. Such suppression is just what the First Amendment was designed to prevent.

See also: Bill of Rights; Censorship; Flag Burning; Freedom of the Press; Gag Rules; Libel; Obscenity; Sit-Ins; Speech, Unprotected; Symbolic Speech.

Further Reading

Farish, Leah. *The First Amendment: Freedom of Speech, Religion, and the Press.* Berkeley Heights, NJ: Enslow Publishers, 1998.

Icenoggle, Jodi. *Schenk v. United States and the Freedom of Speech Debate.* Berkeley Heights, NJ: Enslow Publishers, 2005.

Leinwand, Gerald. *Freedom of Speech.* New York: Facts On File, 1990.

Freedom of the Press

Supreme Court rulings that deal with the First Amendment guarantee that "Congress shall make no law . . . abridging the freedom of . . . the press." Although the First Amendment is usually thought of in terms of individual freedoms, the societal value of a free press is what the Supreme Court has stressed in its decisions. At the least, the guarantee of freedom of the press means freedom from prior restraint or censorship by the government before publication. At the most, the guarantee also means that governments may not punish the press for what it publishes.

As is true of many other constitutional guarantees, however, only a few Supreme Court justices have advocated this absolute view of free press. Most justices have viewed freedom of the press as subject to certain restrictions. With the rise of methods of "publication" unforeseen by the Framers—for instance, via radio, television, and the Internet—the Court's search for the proper balance between a free press and governmental interests has become more complicated.

Prior Restraint

The Supreme Court has struck down a number of laws as prior restraints on the press. This list includes statutes that forbade continued publication of malicious criticisms of government officials, prohibited circulation of noncommercial handbills, or placed a discriminatory tax on newspapers. The first such case was *Near v. Minnesota* (1931), in which the Court struck down a state law that prevented publication of malicious or scandalous material only if it were made with "good motives" and for "justifiable ends." The justices ruled this an unconstitutional prior restraint on publication.

In 1971, the Supreme Court rejected a request by the Nixon administration (1969–1974) to stop publication of the Pentagon Papers, articles revealing the content of classified government documents about U.S. involvement in Vietnam. The Court said the government had failed to show sufficient justification for restraining continued publication of the documents. In that case and in others, however, the Court has strongly implied that prior restraint might be permissible under certain, extreme circumstances. The Court also has upheld the right of government to regulate certain aspects of publishing, including labor and business practices, and the manner and place of distribution of circulars and handbills. These regulations may operate from time to time as prior restraints on the press.

A - Z

Punishment After Publication

The Court has not guarded the press quite so rigorously against punishment after publication as against prior restraint of publication. During World War I, it upheld the convictions of several people for publication of articles the Court found to be in violation of the Espionage Act of 1917 and the Sedition Act of 1918. Sedition consists of advocating rebellion against, or the overthrow of, government.

Libel, or defaming an individual in print, was long thought by the Court to be outside the protection of the First Amendment. In the 1960s, however, the Court began to reverse this stance, extending to publishers considerable protection against libel suits brought by public officials and public figures. In *New York Times v. Sullivan* (1964), the Supreme Court determined that a statement about a public official constitutes libel only if the libeled party proves that the statement was made with "actual malice"—that is, with knowledge that it was false, or with reckless disregard of whether it was false or not. The Court has held that the First Amendment affords the press less protection from libel suits brought by private individuals and little, if any, when the case does not involve a matter of public concern.

A related issue concerns whether the First Amendment protects the press against claims that published articles or broadcast reports have interfered with individual privacy. In the few cases it has decided involving this issue, the Court has ruled against the privacy claims unless a claimant could prove that a publisher acted with actual malice or displayed reckless disregard for the truth of the report.

The Court still considers "obscene" publications to be outside the protection of the First Amendment and subject to prior restraint as well as subsequent punishment. Child pornography, for instance, is considered obscene and outside the bounds of First Amendment protection. The justices, however, have had great difficulty in defining what else is obscene, and the standard, which has been changed many times, continues to evolve as societal values change.

Free Press vs. a Fair Trial

In the mid-twentieth century, freedom of the press collided upon occasion with the right to impartial and fair administration of justice. Comprehensive reporting of the workings of the justice system is crucial to its fair administration, but news reports—especially of sensational crimes—may injure a defendant's rights to a fair trial by negatively prejudicing the community. Gag rules are one response of trial judges to this situation. With such orders, the trial court judge restricts the information the press may report about the trial in question. In *Nebraska Press Association v. Stuart* (1976), the Court reviewed such a gag order and found it an unconstitutional prior restraint. But the Court has upheld several contempt citations against reporters who defied court-ordered gag rules. To protect a defendant's right to a fair trial, some judges have excluded the press and the public from pretrial hearings. In *Gannett Co. Inc. v. DePasquale* (1979), the Supreme Court upheld such an exclusion order. A year later, however, in *Richmond Newspapers Inc. v. Commonwealth of Virginia*, the Court read the First Amendment to guarantee both the press and the public the right to attend trials.

Privileged Access

Does the role of the press in a representative government entitle reporters to special protection to sources? The Court has ruled against journalists' arguments that the First Amendment gives them special privileges. Gag rules are just one aspect of this access question. Another aspect—access to prisons to view conditions and interview inmates—has been answered negatively by a majority of the Court.

Confidentiality is a more troubling area. Can reporters be required to divulge their anonymous sources to court officials and other law enforcement officers investigating alleged criminal activity? Reporters contend that their relationships with news sources should be privileged, as are the relationships between doctor and patient, lawyer and client, and husband and wife. The Court has, however, so far rejected this argument at the federal level. In *Branzburg v. Hayes, in re Pappas, United States v. Caldwell* (1972), it held that a reporter has no more constitutional right to withhold information that might help resolve a crime than does an ordinary citizen. In another ruling disappointing to the press, *Zurcher v. The Stanford Daily* (1978), the Court held that the First Amendment does not require police to use subpoenas instead of search warrants when it seeks evidence of a crime from newspaper offices and files.

See also: Bill of Rights; Censorship; Freedom of Speech; Gag Rules; Libel; *New York Times v. Sullivan* (1974); Obscenity; Pentagon Papers; Speech, Unprotected.

Further Reading

Cohen, Henry. *Freedom of Speech and Press: Exceptions to the First Amendment.* Hauppauge, NY: Novinka Books, 2008.

Herbert, David L., ed. *The Bill of Rights–Freedom of the Press.* Farmington Hills, MI: Greenhaven Press, 2005.

Freedom to Petition

The First Amendment right of citizens to request that the government right a perceived wrong. The right "to petition the Government for a redress of grievances" has its origins in the Magna Carta of 1215, the medieval English **charter**, or founding document, of political and civil liberties. Although the modern notion of a petition typically involves signing a written form or statement, political petition can take a variety of forms. Protests and demonstrations, for example, are also considered forms of petition. In addition, petitioners are not restricted to seeking redress of grievances only from Congress; they may petition administrative agencies and the courts.

Historical Petitions

One of the earliest exercises of the right to petition in the United States occurred in the 1830s, when Congress received scores of petitions seeking to abolish slavery in the District of Columbia. However, the most noteworthy exercises of the right have arisen over economic issues. The roughly 500 members of "Coxey's army," an Ohio group led by businessman Jacob S. Coxey, invoked the right of petition in their march on Washington in 1894. Coxey's followers, protesting unemployment caused by a financial panic the previous year, called for the government to create public works jobs that would put people back to work.

A similar but much larger-scale petition march took place in 1932, when some 15,000 World War I (1914–1918) veterans known as the "Bonus Army" marched on Washington. The group demanded that the government immediately redeem bonus certificates given the veterans for their war service, even though the certificates were not due to be paid until 1945. Neither Coxey's army nor the Bonus Army achieved their goals. The government actually resorted to military force to disperse the Bonus Army, killing several and wounding hundreds more.

In 1968, the Reverend Martin Luther King Jr. started a movement known as the Poor People's Campaign, which also planned a mass march on Washington, D.C. King intended to demand Congress pass an Economic Bill of Rights to help the working poor. Although King was assassinated on April 4, 1968, the marchers continued, reaching Washington in May. Despite two weeks of protests and lobbying with government agencies, the marchers failed to win support for the bill.

Applications of the Right to Petition

Congress has used the **due process clause** of the Fourteenth Amendment to protect freedom of petition from infringement by state governments. In addition, petition of government is not limited solely to seeking a redress of grievances: petitioners may seek benefits. Individuals, citizen groups, and corporations all lobby government to persuade it to adopt policies that will benefit their particular interests. The major decision defining lobbyists' right to petition came in *United States v. Harriss* (1954), when the Court upheld the authority of Congress to require certain lobbyists to register.

In *Brown v. Glines* (1980), the Court ruled that military personnel must receive the approval of the base commander before they may send a petition to Congress. The majority declared that such approval did not infringe upon the right of petition. However, a person who exercises this right may still sued for libel for any false claims they make in their petition. In *Walters v. National Association of Radiation Survivors* (1995), the Court upheld a ten dollar limit on what a veteran can pay an attorney for representation in pursuing claims with the Veterans Administration. The Court ruled that the limit did not abridge a veteran's right to effectively petition the government for redress of grievances.

See also: Bill of Rights; Freedom of Speech.

A – Z

Gag Rules

Court orders that bar the press from publishing articles containing certain types of information about pending court cases. Refusal to comply with the order may result in being held in **contempt of court.** Gag rules are clearly a prior restraint on publication, and the press has repeatedly challenged their constitutionality.

In the Court's first full-scale review of a gag rule, *Nebraska Press Association v. Stuart* (1976), all nine justices held the order to be an unconstitutional prior restraint of publication. The case arose from the arrest of Erwin Charles Simants for the murder of a Nebraska family. Because the crime occurred in a rural area with a relatively small number of potential jurors, the judge issued a gag rule on the day of the preliminary hearing. He feared that that excessive publicity would make it impossible to assemble an unbiased jury and conduct a fair trial. Although the hearing took place in open court, the judge forbade the press to report any of the testimony given or the evidence presented. The order remained in effect until the jury was chosen.

Writing the Court's opinion, Chief Justice Warren Burger said the judge could have used less drastic means than the gag rule to ensure a fair trial. "[P]rior restraints on speech and publication are the most serious and the least tolerable infringement on First Amendment rights," Burger wrote. "A prior restraint . . . has an immediate and irreversible sanction. If it can be said that a threat of criminal or civil sanctions after publication 'chills' speech, prior restraint 'freezes' it at least for the time." Furthermore, said Burger, the right to report evidence given in an open courtroom is a settled principle. "[O]nce a public hearing had been held, what

transpired there could not be subject to prior restraint."

Burger and four of his colleagues refused to prohibit gag rules in all circumstances, however. Burger wrote, "This Court has frequently denied that First Amendment rights are absolute and has consistently rejected the proposition that a prior restraint can never be employed."

Three justices, although concurring with the ruling, felt that all gag rules were unconstitutional. "The right to a fair trial by a jury of one's peers is unquestionably one of the most precious and sacred safeguards enshrined in the Bill of Rights," wrote Justice Brennan in a concurring opinion joined by Justices Marshall and Stewart. Brennan, however, added, "I would hold . . . that resort to prior restraints on the freedom of the press is a constitutionally impermissible method for enforcing that right." Judges have less drastic means of ensuring fair trials than by prohibiting press "discussion of public affairs."

See also: Freedom of the Press.

Gibbons v. Ogden (1824)

Supreme Court case that established Congress's power to regulate interstate commerce. Article I, Section 8, of the U.S. Constitution states: "The Congress shall have Power to . . . regulate commerce with foreign Nations, and among the several States, and with the Indian Tribes." However, it makes no mention of what powers, if any, the states have with respect to the federal government when it comes to controlling state commerce. *Gibbons v. Ogden* not only settled that question but also opened the door for increased federal intervention in state affairs in a variety of matters.

The lawsuit of one-time business partners Aaron Ogden (left) and Thomas Gibbons (right) led to a landmark ruling in the case *Gibbons v. Ogden* (1824). Chief Justice John Marshall's opinion defined commerce and stated that Congress has the power to regulate interstate commerce. (New York Historical Society) (Georgia Historical Society)

A - Z

Basis of the Case

The case arose from a dispute between two steamship operators, Aaron Ogden and Thomas Gibbons. Ogden operated steamboats in New York under a state **monopoly.** Gibbons, his former partner, was competing with Ogden—and the monopoly—by running steamboats between New York and New Jersey. Although Gibbons was not licensed by the New York monopoly, his ships were licensed under the federal law governing the coasting trade. Ogden obtained an order from the New York courts directing Gibbons to stop his operation. Gibbons took the case to the Supreme Court.

The Court's Ruling

On March 2, 1824, the Court struck down the state monopoly, ruling that it conflicted with the broad federal power to regulate interstate commerce. Speaking for the Court, Chief Justice Marshall defined commerce as intercourse, not simply traffic or buying and selling alone. Commerce also included navigation, the

Landmark Decision Highlights: *Gibbons v. Ogden* (1824)

Issue: Whether the State of New York exercised a power reserved exclusively to Congress—the regulation of interstate commerce

Opinion: The Court found that the New York law was invalid by virtue of the Supremacy Clause. In his opinion, Chief Justice John Marshall developed a clear definition of the word commerce, which included navigation on interstate waterways. He also gave meaning to the phrase "among the several states" in the Commerce Clause. Marshall's was one of the earliest and most influential opinions concerning this important clause. He concluded that regulation of navigation by steamboat operators to conduct interstate commerce was a power reserved to and exercised solely by Congress.

particular subject at hand. Marshall explained, "The power over commerce, including navigation, was one of the primary objects for which the people of America adopted their government, and must have been contemplated in forming it." Furthermore, Marshall wrote:

Commerce among the states cannot stop at the external boundary line of each state, but may be introduced into the interior . . . The power of Congress, then, comprehends navigation within the limits of every state in the Union; so far as that navigation may be, in any manner, connected with "commerce with foreign nations, or among the several states, or with the Indian tribes."

Aftermath and Significance

Much has been written about the significance of this decision. Felix Frankfurter, later to sit on the Court, wrote that the theme Marshall first sounded in *Gibbons v. Ogden* became the focal point of the constitutional system—"the doctrine that the commerce clause, by its own force, and without national legislation, puts it into the power of the Court to place limits upon state authority." "Marshall's use of the commerce clause," he continued, "gave momentum to the doctrine that state authority must be subject to such limitations as the Court finds it necessary to apply for the protection of the national community."

In addition to the case's importance in the constitutional development of the United States, the ruling had a considerable effect on its economic development, as two historians observe:

Steamboat navigation, freed from the restraint of state-created monopolies . . . increased at an astonishing rate. Within a few years steam railroads, encouraged by the freedom of interstate commerce from state restraints, were to begin a practical revolution of internal transportation. The importance of national control of commerce in the rapid economic development is almost incalculable. For many years after 1824 Congress enacted but few important regulatory measures, and commerce was thus free to develop without serious monopolistic or governmental restraint.

Another scholar, emphasizing the latter point, notes:

Like most of the important cases decided by Chief Justice Marshall, [*Gibbons v. Ogden*] involved, not the assertion of the power of the federal government over interstate commerce, but acted rather as a prohibition against state activity. Apart from granting coasting licenses, the federal government was not interested in the commerce involved. The decision was an act in defense of laissez-faire, rather than of positive federal control.

For thirty years after the *Gibbons* ruling, a debate raged over whether Congress had an exclusive power to regulate commerce or whether the states retained some authority in that area. Underlying this debate was the issue of slavery. Historian Charles Warren wrote that:

. . . throughout the long years when the question of the extent of the Federal power over commerce was being tested in numerous cases in the Court, that question was, in the minds of Southerners, simply coincident with the question of the extent of the Federal power over slavery. So the long-continued controversy as to whether Congress had exclusive or concurrent jurisdiction over commerce was not a conflict between theories of government, or between Nationalism and State-Rights, or between differing legal construction of the Constitution, but was simply the naked issue of State or Federal control of slavery. It was little wonder, therefore, that the Judges of the Court prior to the Civil War displayed great hesitation in deciding this momentous controversy.

See also: *Gibbons v. Ogden,* 1824, in the **Primary Source Library**.

Further Reading

Levinson, Isabel Simone. *Gibbons v. Ogden: Controlling Trade Between States.* Berkeley Heights, N.J.: Enslow Publishers, 1999.

Gideon v. Wainwright (1963)

Supreme Court case establishing the principle that the state is obliged to provide legal assistance at no charge to criminal defendants who cannot afford an attorney. Prior to the ruling in *Gideon v. Wainwright*, states were not required to provide counsel to defendants. The Court first declared in *Betts v. Brady* (1942) that "appointment of counsel is not a fundamental right" for such state defendants. Under *Betts*, the Court considered the special circumstances of each case to determine if denial of counsel denied the defendant fair treatment under the law.

With *Gideon*, the Supreme Court unanimously discarded this case-by-case approach. The Court

held that the right to the assistance of counsel was so fundamental that the Fourteenth Amendment's due process clause extended the Sixth Amendment right of counsel guarantee to state defendants. States would thereafter be required to provide counsel for all defendants charged with felonies and unable to pay a lawyer.

Basis of the Case

Clarence Earl Gideon, an **indigent,** was tried and convicted in a Florida state court of felony breaking and entering. He requested but was denied a court-appointed attorney. The judge based the refusal on the fact that Gideon's offense was not a capital crime. Gideon conducted his own defense but was convicted and sentenced to five years in prison. Gideon later prepared his own petitions asking a federal court to declare his conviction invalid. He argued that the state obtained the conviction in violation of his constitutional right to counsel, and asked the Court to order his release. The Court agreed to hear Gideon's case and appointed a well-known Washington attorney, Abe Fortas, to argue on his behalf. The Court also requested that both sides

JUSTICE FOR ALL

The Right to Refuse Counsel

In a case that seemed to turn inside out the series of rulings expanding the right of defendants to have the assistance of an attorney, the Court in the mid-1970s held that defendants also have the right to *refuse* legal assistance. In *Faretta v. California* (1975), the Court ruled that individuals have the right to conduct their own defense and to reject counsel appointed to represent them.

Justice Potter Stewart acknowledged that recognition of this right seemed "to cut against the grain of this court's decisions holding that the Constitution requires that no accused can be convicted and imprisoned unless he has been accorded the right to the assistance of counsel." Stewart noted, however, that "it is one thing to hold that every defendant, rich or poor, has the right to the assistance of counsel, and quite another to say that a state may compel a defendant to accept a lawyer he does not *want.*"

A - Z

A - Z

In The Supreme Court of The United States
Washington D.C.

Clarence Earl Gideon
    Petitioner

vs.

H.G. Cochran Jr, as
Director, Divisions
of corrections State
of Florida

Petition for a writ
of Certiorari Directed
to The Supreme Court
State of Florida.

No. 890 Misc.

OCT. TERM 1961

U.S. Supreme Court

To: The Honorable Earl Warren, Chief
Justice of the United States
    Comes now the petitioner, Clarence
Earl Gideon, a citizen of The United states
of America, in proper person, and appearing
as his own counsel. Who petitions This
Honorable Court for a Writ of Certiorari
directed to The Supreme Court of The State
of Florida. To review the order and Judge-
ment of the court below denying The
petitioner a writ of Habeus Corpus.
    Petitioner submits That The Supreme
Court of The United States has The authority
and jurisdiction to review the final Judge-
ment of The Supreme Court of The State
of Florida The highest court of The State
Under sec. 344(B) Title 28 U.S.C.A. and
Because The "Due process clause" of the

Clarence Earl Gideon, a penniless convict who was unable to hire a defense attorney, sent a handwritten petition to the Supreme Court to hear his case. The Court granted his petition and ruled unanimously, in *Gideon v. Wainwright* (1963), that every state must provide an attorney to poor individuals charged with a felony. (National Archives)

Landmark Decision Highlights: *Gideon v. Wainwright* (1963)

Issue: Did the Florida state court's failure to appoint counsel for Clarence Earl Gideon violate his right to a fair trial and due process of law, as protected by the Sixth and Fourteenth Amendments?

Opinion: In a unanimous opinion, the Supreme Court held that Gideon had a right to be represented by a court-appointed attorney. In doing so, the Court overruled its decision in *Betts v. Brady* (1942). In this case, the Court found that the Sixth Amendment's guarantee of counsel was a fundamental right, essential to a fair trial, which should be made applicable to the states through the Due Process Clause of the Fourteenth Amendment.

in the case argue an additional question: Should *Betts v. Brady* be reconsidered?

The Court's Ruling

The Supreme Court reversed the ruling in *Betts*, unanimously declaring that the state had denied Gideon his constitutional right to counsel. Justice Hugo Black, who had dissented from *Betts*, wrote the Court's opinion in *Gideon*. He wrote:

> The fact is that the Court in *Betts v. Brady* made an abrupt break with its own well-considered precedents. In returning to these old precedents, sounder we believe than the new, we but restore constitutional principles established to achieve a fair system of justice. Not only these precedents but also reason and reflection require us to recognize that in our adversary system of criminal justice, any person haled into court, who is too poor to hire a lawyer, cannot be assured a fair trial unless counsel is provided for him. This seems to us to be an obvious truth . . . Lawyers to prosecute are everywhere deemed

essential to protect the public's interest in an orderly society . . .

> That government hires lawyers to prosecute and defendants who have the money hire lawyers to defend are the strongest indications of the widespread belief that lawyers in criminal courts are necessities, not luxuries.

See also: 📖 *Gideon v. Wainwright,* 1963, in the **Primary Source Library;** Right to Legal Counsel.

Further Reading

Fridell, Ron. *Gideon v. Wainwright: The Right to Free Counsel.* New York: Benchmark Books, 2006.

Lewis, Anthony. *Gideon's Trumpet.* New York: Vintage Books, 1989.

Ginsburg, Ruth Bader (1933–)

Associate justice of the U.S. Supreme Court, appointed by President Bill Clinton (1993–2001) and confirmed by Congress on August 3, 1993. She is the 107th justice to serve on the Court, but only the second woman to do so, after Sandra Day O'Connor. Ginsburg has proved herself to be a liberal-leaning justice on a conservative-leaning Court.

Born into a Jewish family of modest means in Brooklyn, New York, Bader attended Cornell University and graduated first among the women in her class. There, she also met and married Martin Ginsburg. She subsequently entered Harvard Law School, where she made the law review, cared for an infant daughter, and helped her husband complete his law studies after he was diagnosed with cancer. Ginsburg then completed her own degree, graduating tied for first place in her class.

Ginsburg won a two-year clerkship with a federal district court judge and later accepted a research position at Columbia University. She taught at Rutgers University Law School in New Jersey from 1963 to 1972, and in 1972 became the

In 1993, President Bill Clinton (1993–2001) chose Ruth Bader Ginsburg as his first nominee to the Supreme Court. Ginsburg was sworn in as the 107th justice on August 9, 1993. Ginsburg, the second female Supreme Court justice, is also the first Jewish woman to serve on the Court. (Collection of the Supreme Court of the United States)

moderate judicial record, following the letter of the law and advocating judicial restraint. In 1993, President Bill Clinton nominated Ginsburg to replace retiring Supreme Court Justice Byron White. Clinton said he was moved by Ginsburg's nontraditional life and predicted she would bring consensus to the Court.

Ginsburg was the first Supreme Court justice appointed by a Democratic president since Lyndon Johnson (1963–1969) appointed Thurgood Marshall in 1967. At the time, she was the only member of the Court not appointed by a Republican president. She was joined a year later by Stephen Breyer, whom Clinton named to replace outgoing Justice Harry Blackmun.

Ginsburg has supported the separation of church and state, civil rights, and the right to abortion. She also dissented from the series of states' rights rulings that began in the mid-1990s. In one of her most important opinions, *United States v. Virginia* (1996), she spoke for the Court in striking down state policies that exclude individuals from state universities based on their sex. Ginsburg asserted that such gender discrimination is unconstitutional and violates the Fourteenth Amendment's **equal protection clause**.

See also: Associate Justice Ruth Bader Ginsburg on *Brown v. Board of Education*, October 21, 2004 in the **Primary Source Library**; Associate Justices; Confirmation of Justices and Judges; O'Connor, Sandra Day; Sex Discrimination.

first woman to hold a tenured position on the Columbia Law School faculty.

At this time, she also worked for the American Civil Liberties Union (ACLU), where her caseload included several early sex discrimination complaints. Ginsburg gained nationwide attention for developing the legal strategy that established constitutional principles against sex discrimination. Cases she handled as director of the ACLU's Women's Rights Project led the Supreme Court to require greater scrutiny of legal classifications based on sex. Ginsburg won five of the six cases she argued before the Court.

In 1980, President Jimmy Carter (1977–1981) named Ginsburg to the U.S. Court of Appeals for the District of Columbia. She developed a

Grand Jury

See Right to a Jury Trial.

Grandfather Clauses

State laws, once widely enforced throughout the South, that required all voters to pass a literacy test *or* to show that their ancestors had been entitled to vote prior to a certain date. These clauses were used routinely to deny blacks the right to vote.

In *Guinn v. United States* (1915), the Court ruled unconstitutional Oklahoma's combined use of a literacy test and a "grandfather" clause. The voting requirement was challenged as a violation of the Fifteenth Amendment to the U.S. Constitution, because it exempted most white males from the literacy test. This permitted voting officials to test primarily blacks, most of whose ancestors were not eligible to vote in 1866. The state argued that the clause did not deny blacks the right to vote; it simply required them all to take the literacy tests. The Fifteenth Amendment, the state continued, did not give all blacks the right to vote. It merely prevented states from denying them the right to vote on purely racial grounds.

With *Guinn*, the Court began moving toward its modern view of the Fifteenth Amendment. The Court unanimously struck down Oklahoma's system as an unconstitutional evasion of the amendment. Chief Justice Edward D. White wrote the Court's opinion. In it, however, the Court continued to affirm state power to require voters to demonstrate some measure of literacy. *Guinn* had a limited effect on black voting rights in the South because it dealt only with the grandfather clause.

In a second Oklahoma case decided the same day in 1915, the Court upheld the federal indictments of county election officials who refused to count certain persons' votes. The Court, in *United States v. Mosely*, declared that "the right to have one's vote counted is as open to protection by Congress as the right to put a ballot in a box." Oklahoma subsequently adopted a requirement that all voters register within a twelve-day period but exempted those who had voted in the 1914 elections, prior to *Guinn*. In 1939, the Court held that this, too, was an unconstitutional attempt to disenfranchise blacks in violation of the Fifteenth Amendment. Justice Felix Frankfurter, writing for the majority, said that the Fifteenth Amendment "nullifies sophisticated as well as simple-minded modes of discrimination."

See also: Right to Vote.

Griswold v. Connecticut (1965)

Landmark case in which the Supreme Court determined that the right to privacy is protected by the U.S. Constitution. In *Griswold v. Connecticut* (1965), the Court struck down a state law forbidding all use of birth control devices. Although Justice William O. Douglas, writing the majority opinion, was careful not to rest the conclusion upon the due process clause, Justice Hugo L. Black, in dissent, found the ruling a direct descendant of *Lochner v. New York* (1905). This too was substantive due process, he warned, and it was "no less dangerous when used to enforce this Court's views about personal rights than those about economic rights."

Eight years later, Justice William H. Rehnquist sounded the same complaint, dissenting from the Court's decision in *Roe v. Wade* (1973), which struck down state laws banning abortion. "As in *Lochner* and similar cases applying substantive due process standards," Rehnquist wrote, the standard adopted in *Roe v. Wade* "will inevitably require this Court to examine the legislative policies and pass on the wisdom of these policies."

In the 1990s, the Court narrowly affirmed the essential holding of *Roe*, voting 5-4 in *Planned Parenthood of Southeastern Pennsylvania v. Casey* (1992). The three justices whose votes effectively preserved the right to abortion wrote in their plurality opinion:

> Neither the Bill of Rights nor the specific practices of the States at the time of the adoption of the Fourteenth Amendment marks the outer limits of the substantive sphere which the Fourteenth Amendment protects . . . It is settled now, as it was when the Court heard arguments in *Roe v. Wade*, that the Constitution places limits on a State's right to interfere with a person's most basic decisions about family and parenthood."

A – Z

The Court again invoked the liberty and due process clauses to strike down homosexual sodomy laws. The Fourteenth Amendment's liberty clause "gives substantial protection to adult persons in deciding how to conduct their private lives in matters pertaining to sex," the Court said in *Lawrence v. Texas* (2003).

See also: Due Process; Right to Privacy; *Roe v. Wade* (1973).

Further Reading

Baum, Lawrence. *The Supreme Court.* Washington, D.C.: CQ Press, 2009.

Crawford, Jan Greenburg. *Supreme Conflict: The Inside Story of the Struggle for Control of the United States Supreme Court.* New York: Penguin, 2008.

Irons, Peter. *A People's History of the Supreme Court: The Men and Women Whose Cases and Decisions Have Shaped Our Constitution.* New York: Penguin, 2005.

Habeas Corpus

See Writ of Habeas Corpus.

Harlan, John Marshall I (1833–1911)

Supreme Court justice noted for his solitary dissent in *Plessy v. Ferguson* (1896), which upheld the doctrine of "separate but equal." John Marshall Harlan was nominated to the Court by President Rutherford B. Hayes (1877–1881) on October 17, 1877, to replace David Davis, who had resigned. Harlan was confirmed by the Senate on November 29, 1877, by a voice vote. He took the judicial oath on December 10, 1877, and served until his death on October 14, 1911.

John Marshall Harlan was born into a prominent Kentucky political family. Both his ancestors and his descendants played important roles in public life. His mother was Eliza Davenport Harlan. His father, James Harlan, an admirer of Henry Clay's patriotism and Chief Justice John

Marshall's leadership on the Supreme Court, was a U.S. representative from Kentucky and also served as attorney general and secretary of state of Kentucky. Justice Harlan's son, John Maynard Harlan, became a prominent Chicago lawyer and was the unsuccessful Republican nominee for mayor of Chicago in 1897 and 1905. His grandson and namesake, John Marshall Harlan II, was himself a Supreme Court justice, serving from 1955 to 1971.

Young Harlan studied law at Transylvania University in Kentucky, known as the "Harvard of the West," and then completed his legal education in his father's law office. He was admitted to the bar in 1853.

Harlan's only judicial experience before his appointment to the Court was his first office, Franklin County judge, from 1858 to 1859. After that one-year experience on the bench, Harlan turned to politics. He ran for the U.S. House of Representatives in 1859 as the candidate of a coalition of anti-Democratic groups, including the Whigs and Know-Nothings, but lost by sixty-seven votes.

As a slaveholder and a member of the Southern aristocracy, Harlan had difficulty following many of the nation's Whigs into the new Republican Party. In the presidential election of 1860, he backed the Constitutional Union Party, which stood for a compromise settlement of the increasingly bitter sectional conflict. When the Civil War (1861–1865) was fought, however, Harlan chose to stay loyal to the Union and served as an officer in the Northern forces.

When his father died in 1863, Harlan resigned his commission and ran successfully for attorney general of Kentucky on the pro-Union ticket. Although he was opposed to many policies of the Lincoln administration—he supported Democrat George B. McClellan against Lincoln in 1864—and believed that the postwar constitutional amendments ending slavery and attempting to guarantee the rights of blacks were a mistake, Harlan eventually joined the Republican Party and was its nominee for governor of Kentucky in 1875.

The major impact Harlan had on the national political scene came in 1876, when he headed the Kentucky delegation to the Republican National Convention. At a critical moment during the deadlocked proceedings, Harlan swung the state's votes to Ohio Governor Rutherford B. Hayes, helping to start a bandwagon moving in Hayes's direction. Hayes was nominated and elected. President Hayes (1877–1881) acknowledged his debt to Harlan by considering him for appointment as attorney general.

Although other political considerations intervened so that no cabinet post was open for Harlan, Hayes kept him in mind. The new president appointed him to head a commission to settle the rival claims of two factions for control of Louisiana in the spring of 1877. Then, when Supreme Court Justice David Davis resigned to enter the U.S. Senate, Hayes nominated Harlan to fill the vacancy.

Harlan's tenure, almost 34 years, was one of the longest in the Court's history, exceeded by only four other justices. During his service on the Court, he was called on by President Benjamin Harrison (1889–1893) in 1892 to serve as the U.S. representative in the arbitration of the Bering Sea controversy with Great Britain.

He had a lively temperament, often delivering his opinions extemporaneously, in the style of an old-fashioned Kentucky stump speech. His vigorous attacks on several famous majority decisions earned him the title of "Great Dissenter." Most notable was his eloquent dissent in *Plessy v.*

Ferguson (1896), the case that upheld Louisiana's "separate but equal" law with respect to public accommodations.

See also: Plessy v. Ferguson (1896).

Harlan, John Marshall II (1899–1971)

Supreme Court justice nominated by President Dwight D. Eisenhower (1953–1961) on November 8, 1954, to replace Robert Jackson, who had died. John Marshall Harlan II was confirmed by the Senate on March 16, 1955, by a 71-11 vote. He took the judicial oath on March 28, 1955, and retired on September 23, 1971.

The namesake and grandson of Supreme Court Justice John Marshall Harlan, who served from 1877 to 1911, he was born in Chicago, Illinois, where his father, John Maynard Harlan, was a prominent attorney. John Maynard Harlan was also engaged in politics, running two losing races for mayor of Chicago near the turn of the century. The future justice's mother was Elizabeth Palmer Flagg Harlan.

The younger Harlan, who went by John M. Harlan to distinguish himself from his famous forebear, attended Princeton University, graduating in 1920. Awarded a Rhodes Scholarship, he spent the next three years studying jurisprudence in Great Britain at Balliol College, Oxford. Returning to the United States, he earned his law degree in 1924 from the New York Law School.

For the next twenty-five years, Harlan was a member of a prominent Wall Street law firm, but he took periodic leaves to serve in various public positions. In 1925, he became an assistant U.S. attorney for the Southern District of New York. He returned to private practice but soon left again, this time to serve as one of the special prosecutors in a state investigation of municipal graft.

During World War II (1939–1945), Harlan served as head of the Operational Analysis Section of the Eighth Air Force, even though he was well past the usual age of service. After the war he returned to private practice but was again called to public service. From 1951 to 1953, he was chief counsel to the New York State Crime Commission, which Governor Thomas E. Dewey had appointed to investigate the relationship between organized crime and state government. A lifelong Republican, Harlan was nominated in January 1954 by President Dwight D. Eisenhower to the U.S. Court of Appeals for the Second Circuit. Harlan had hardly begun his work there, however, when the president named him in November 1954 to the Supreme Court.

Harlan did not share the activist views of the Warren Court. He allied himself with Felix Frankfurter—they agreed in more than 80 percent of the cases they heard together—but he was much more of a moderate than an inflexible conservative. In First Amendment cases, his views were more liberal. In *NAACP v. Alabama ex rel. Patterson* (1958), he upheld the right of the organization to keep its membership lists private. In *Cohen v. California* (1971), he wrote the majority opinion, which extended to a rude message on the back of a jacket the constitutional protection afforded to speech. Suffering from cancer of the spine, Harlan resigned from the Court in September 1971 and died on December 29 of that year.

See also: Frankfurter, Felix.

Landmark Decision Highlights: *Hazelwood School District v. Kuhlmeier* (1988)

Issue: Did principal Robert E. Reynolds's deletion of the articles that he deemed inappropriate in the school newspaper violate the students' rights under the First Amendment?

Opinion: No. The Court held that the First Amendment did not require schools to promote particular types of student speech. The Court held that schools must be able to set high standards for student speech, and that schools had the right to refuse to sponsor speech that was "inconsistent with 'the shared values of a civilized social order.'" Educators do not violate the First Amendment by exercising editorial control over the content of student speech as long as their actions are "reasonably related to legitimate . . . concerns." The Court held that actions of principal Reynolds met this test.

Hazelwood School District v. Kuhlmeier (1988)

Supreme Court decision in which school officials were allowed to exercise control over the content of a school-sponsored newspaper. The case was key in defining the extent to which First Amendment rights of freedom of the press applied to students in a school venue.

Basis of the Case

Students at Hazelwood East High School near St. Louis, Missouri, wrote and edited *Spectrum*, the school newspaper, as part of a journalism class. In May 1983, the principal deleted two pages of the six-page paper, pages that contained stories on teen pregnancies, the impact of divorce, and references to unnamed students at the school. Principal Robert Reynolds said the material was

not appropriate for younger students, and he worried that the content would invade the privacy of some persons. Three students sued, arguing that the school violated the free press rights of the students by censoring the paper. The students won a ruling from the U.S. Court of Appeals in St. Louis.

The Court's Ruling

Upon appeal, however, the Court disagreed, 6-3. "School officials retained ultimate control over what constituted 'responsible journalism' in a school-sponsored newspaper," wrote Justice Byron White in *Hazelwood School District v. Kuhlmeier* (1988). He characterized the school newspaper as part of the curriculum, and therefore properly regulated by school authorities. Moreover, most of the money to fund the paper came from the school, and the journalism instructor was charged with editing the paper. In this instance, the principal stepped in because the teacher had left to take a new job. "We conclude that Principal Reynolds act[ed] reasonably in requiring the deletion" of the two articles, White said.

The Court established three tests to determine whether a publication is school-sponsored and thus covered by the decision:

(1) Is it supervised by a faculty member?

(2) Is it designed to impart particular knowledge or skills to student participants or audiences?

(3) Does it use the school's name or resources?

In two subsequent cases, lower courts ruled that extracurricular publications may not be subject to restrictions under *Hazelwood*. Even some school-sponsored student publications that are part of the curriculum may be exempt from *Hazelwood* if they are "public forums" for student expression. A public forum exists when school officials open a publication for unrestricted student use. In the *Hazelwood* case, the school never labeled the student newspaper as a "forum" or gave any evidence that it intended to designate the newspaper as a forum. The Court, therefore, ruled that a forum did not exist. This marked the first time a court declared that a student newspaper did not constitute a forum for student expression.

Dissent and Commentary

In dissent, Justices William J. Brennan Jr., Thurgood Marshall, and Harry A. Blackmun contended that school officials had broken a promise to "not restrict free expression or diverse viewpoints" in the school paper. "In my view, the principal broke more than just a promise. He violated the First Amendment's prohibitions against censorship of any expression that neither disrupts classwork nor invades the rights of others," Brennan wrote.

Brennan sharply criticized the ruling, saying that it showed "how readily school officials (and courts) can camouflage viewpoint discrimination as the 'mere' protection of students from sensitive topics." He went on to remark, "Such unthinking contempt for individual rights is intolerable from any state official. It is particularly insidious from one to whom the public entrusts the task of inculcating in its youth an appreciation for the cherished democratic liberties that our Constitution guarantees."

Other observers agreed. The Student Press Law Center, which is an advocate for student free press rights, has also condemned the decision in *Hazelwood*:

The Supreme Court's decision in *Hazelwood School District v. Kuhlmeier* struck a potentially devastating blow for scholastic journalism. The Court significantly cut back the First Amendment protections public high school students have been afforded for years. Even those who are not facing censorship problems today should be concerned about the implications of this decision for student journalists now and in the future. At some schools, censorship has become standard operating procedure; at any school it is a threat.

See also: Censorship; Freedom of the Press; 📖 *Hazelwood School District v. Kuhlmeier*, 1988, in the **Primary Source Library**.

Further Reading

Phillips, Tracy A. *Hazelwood v. Kuhlmeier And the School Newspaper Censorship Debate: Debating Supreme Court Decisions*. Berkeley Heights, N.J.: Enslow Publishers, 2006.

Heart of Atlanta Motel v. United States (1964)

Landmark Supreme Court case in which racial segregation in public accommodations was declared unconstitutional. In its ruling, the Court rejected a challenge to Title II of the 1964 Civil Rights Act. That act barred discrimination in public accommodations on grounds of race, color, religion, or national origin if the discrimination was supported by state law or other official action, if lodgings or other service were provided to interstate travelers, or if a substantial portion of the goods sold or entertainment provided moved in interstate commerce.

A – Z

Moreton Rolleston Jr., owner of the Heart of Atlanta Motel, challenged the constitutionality of the Civil Rights Act of 1964. In *Heart of Atlanta Motel v. United States (1964)*, the Supreme Court unanimously upheld the law. The Court declared that Congress may use its powers to regulate interstate commerce to prohibit racial discrimination in privately owned accommodations. (© Bettmann, Corbis)

Landmark Decision Highlights: *Heart of Atlanta Motel v. United States* (1964)

Issue: Whether Congress, by passing the 1964 Civil Rights Act, exceeded its Commerce Clause powers by depriving motels, such as the Heart of Atlanta, of the right to choose their own customers

Opinion: The Supreme Court held that the Commerce Clause allowed Congress to regulate local aspects of commerce, and that the Civil Right Act of 1964 was constitutional. The Court concluded that places of public accommodation had no "right" to select guests as they saw fit, free from governmental regulation.

Basis of the Case

The case of *Heart of Atlanta Motel v. United States* (1964) involved a motel in downtown Atlanta that refused to serve blacks in defiance of the new federal civil rights law. The motel owner charged that Congress had exceeded its authority under the commerce clause when it enacted Title II. He also claimed that Congress denied him his Fifth Amendment rights by depriving him of the freedom to choose his customers.

The Court's Ruling

Writing for a unanimous Court, Justice Tom C. Clark rejected the motel owner's argument. Clark noted that the motel was accessible to interstate travelers, that it sought out-of-state business by advertising in national publications, and that 75 percent of its guests were interstate travelers.

Clark then cited testimony from congressional hearings that showed that blacks were frequently discouraged from traveling because of the difficulty encountered in obtaining accommodations. Congress had reasonably concluded that discrimination was an impediment to interstate travel, the Court said. Clark next turned to the commerce power of Congress. He found that Congress had the authority not only to regulate interstate commerce but also to regulate intrastate matters that affected interstate commerce:

> [T]he power of Congress to promote interstate commerce includes the power to regulate the local incidents thereof, including local activities in both the States of origin and destination, which might have a substantial and harmful effect upon that commerce. One need only examine the evidence . . . to see that Congress may—as it has—prohibit racial discrimination by motels serving travelers, however "local" their operations may appear.

The Court also said that it made no difference that Congress had used its power under the commerce clause to achieve a moral goal. That fact, wrote Clark,

> does not detract from the overwhelming evidence of the disruptive effect that racial discrimination has had on commercial intercourse. It was this burden which empowered Congress to enact appropriate legislation, and, given this basis for the exercise of its power, Congress was not restricted by the fact that the particular obstruction to interstate commerce with which it was dealing was also deemed a moral and social wrong.

The Court also rejected the claim that Title II violated the motel owner's Fifth Amendment rights. Congress acted reasonably to prohibit racial discrimination, the Court said. Clark noted that thirty-two states had civil rights laws that were similar to the 1964 federal law. Furthermore, "in a long line of cases this Court has rejected the claim that the prohibition of racial discrimination in public accommodations interferes with personal liberty."

Aftermath

The Court's decision upholding the constitutionality of the use of the commerce power to bar private discrimination seemed to conflict with its decision in the *Civil Rights Cases* (1883). At that time, the Court ruled that Congress lacked the power to enforce the Thirteenth and Fourteenth Amendments by barring private acts of discrimination in public accommodations. The Court said in its 1964 ruling that it found the 1883 decision "without precedential value" since Congress in 1875 had not limited prohibition of discrimination to those businesses that impinged on interstate commerce. Clark wrote about that case:

> Since the commerce power was not relied on by the Government and was without support in the [trial] record it is understandable that the Court narrowed its inquiry and excluded the Commerce Clause as a possible source of power. In any event, it is clear that such a limitation renders the opinion devoid of authority for the proposition that the Commerce Clause gives no power to Congress to regulate discriminatory practices now found substantially to affect interstate commerce.

See also: Civil Rights Act of 1964; Civil Rights and the Supreme Court; *Civil Rights Cases* (1883).

Hill, Anita (1950–)

University of Oklahoma law professor who testified to prevent the confirmation of Clarence Thomas to the Supreme Court in 1991. Hill submitted a statement to the Senate Judiciary Committee accusing Thomas of having made unwelcome sexual advances to her when she worked with him in the early 1980s at the Department of Education and at the Equal Employment Opportunity Commission (EEOC). The events provided some of the most emotionally charged moments in any Court confirmation hearings.

Thomas was the head of EEOC under President Ronald Reagan (1981–1989) and then a federal appeals judge. Over his career, Thomas had amassed a large body of conservative writings: he was personally opposed to affirmative action and favored narrow interpretations of constitutional individual rights and congressional power. In 1991, President George H.W. Bush (1989–1993) nominated Thomas to fill the Court vacancy left by the retirement of Justice Thurgood Marshall.

Thomas completed the Senate Judiciary Committee hearings in early October 1991 and appeared headed for confirmation. Then, the weekend before the full Senate vote on the nomination, word of sexual harassment allegations against Thomas leaked to several media outlets. The disclosure of the allegations—and the committee's failure to investigate them thoroughly—touched off a storm of criticism and demands for a delay in the Senate vote. The Senate Judiciary Committee reluctantly held a second round of hearings to air Hill's complaint and Thomas's defense.

When the hearings opened on October 11, the accuser and accused delivered some of the most extraordinary public testimony ever offered to a congressional committee. Thomas declared his innocence and "categorically" denied that he had ever harassed Hill or even tried to date her. He lashed out at the committee, calling the episode a "high-tech lynching."

Then Dr. Hill spent seven hours calmly telling her story, how Thomas had humiliated her with lewd comments and unwanted advances. She said she believed he had wanted to have sexual intercourse with her. She provided embarrassing details of what she said were Thomas's comments to her on the job. "It is only after a great deal of agonizing consideration that I am able to talk of these unpleasant matters to anyone except my closest friends," she testified.

In the end, the Senate voted 52-48 to confirm Thomas. Most senators said Dr. Hill's charges and Thomas's defense did not affect their final decisions.

See also: Associate Justices; Confirmation of Justices and Judges; Thomas, Clarence.

Holmes, Oliver Wendell Jr. (1841–1935)

Associate justice of the U.S. Supreme Court, appointed by President Theodore Roosevelt (1901–1909) and confirmed by Congress on December 8, 1902. He was the fifty-eighth justice to serve on the Court and one of the longest sitting, spending nearly thirty years on the Court. Holmes was one of the most influential and widely quoted justices.

Nominated to the Supreme Court by President Theodore Roosevelt (1901–1909) in 1902, Associate Justice Oliver Wendell Holmes Jr. sat on the bench for almost thirty years, retiring in early 1932. Among Justice Holmes's best remembered majority opinions is his test noted in *Schenck v. United States* (1919). According to the test, a law that attempts to limit a citizen's free speech is constitutional if that language poses a "clear and present danger," such as provoking violence. (Library of Congress, Prints and Photographs Division)

Early Life

Holmes was the son of Dr. Oliver Wendell Holmes Sr., a physician and an anatomy professor at Harvard Medical School who was also a poet, essayist, and novelist. The elder Holmes was a member of the New England literary circle that included Henry Wadsworth Longfellow, Ralph Waldo Emerson, James Russell Lowell, and James Greenleaf Whittier. Dr. Holmes's wife, Amelia Lee Jackson Holmes, was the third daughter of Justice Charles Jackson of the Massachusetts Supreme Court. Their son attended a private school in Cambridge, Massachusetts, and later attended Harvard, graduating as class poet in 1861.

The Civil War (1861–1865) had just begun, and upon graduation Holmes was commissioned as a second lieutenant in the Massachusetts Twentieth Volunteer Regiment. He was wounded in three battles in three years, leaving the Army in 1864 with the rank of captain. After the war, Holmes returned to Harvard to study law despite his father's belief that "a lawyer can't be a great man."

Holmes was admitted to the Massachusetts bar in 1867 and practiced in Boston for fifteen years. During his legal career, he taught constitutional law at Harvard, edited the *American Law Review*, and lectured on common law at the Lowell Institute. His twelve lectures were compiled in a volume titled *The Common Law* and published shortly before his fortieth birthday. The London *Spectator* praised Holmes's writings as the most original work of legal speculation in decades. *The Common Law* was translated into German, Italian, and French.

Supreme Court Career

In 1882, the governor of Massachusetts appointed Holmes an associate justice of the Massachusetts Supreme Court. Holmes served on the state court for twenty years, the last three as chief justice. He wrote more than a thousand opinions, many of them involving labor disputes.

Although Holmes's progressive labor views drew criticism from railroad and corporate interests, they were helpful in securing his place on the Supreme Court. In 1902, President Theodore Roosevelt was looking for someone to fill the "Massachusetts seat" on the Court, which had been vacated by the death of Justice Horace Gray.

Roosevelt, also an opponent of large corporations, found Holmes's views compatible with his own. Roosevelt nominated the 61-year-old Holmes, and the Senate confirmed him without objection two days later.

Although a lifelong Republican, Holmes did not fulfill Roosevelt's expectations as a loyal party man. Shortly after his appointment, he dissented from the Court's decision in 1904 to break up the railroad trust of the Northern Securities Company. His opinion surprised the nation and angered the president.

Holmes's twenty-nine years of service on the Supreme Court spanned the tenures of Chief Justices Melville Weston Fuller, Edward Douglass White, William Howard Taft, and Charles Evans Hughes, and the administrations of Presidents Theodore Roosevelt, William Howard Taft (1909–1913), Woodrow Wilson (1913–1921), Warren G. Harding (1921–1923), Calvin Coolidge (1923–1929), and Herbert Hoover (1929–1933). For twenty-five years, Holmes never missed a court session; he walked daily the two and a half miles from his home to the Court building. At the suggestion of Chief Justice Hughes and his colleagues on the bench, Holmes retired on January 12, 1932, at the age of ninety.

Legacy

In his years on the Court, Holmes wrote 873 opinions and, although he is known as one of the great dissenters, he wrote proportionately fewer dissents than many other justices. His reputation rests on the clear writing and forcefulness of his dissents. In 1905, Holmes dissented in *Lochner v. New York*. Holmes argued for the right of a state to regulate working hours, in this case for bakers, some of whom were required to work one hundred hours per week.

Holmes is also known for the "clear and present danger" test for seditious speech in *Schenck v. United States* (1919). This unanimous decision upheld the conviction of a Socialist Party member who printed and distributed anti-draft pamphlets at a time when the country was preparing for war. In the case, Holmes wrote that Congress could prohibit language that presents "a clear and present danger" to public safety. He compared the danger to that presented by shouting "Fire!" in a crowded theater.

A – Z

A–Z

However, in *Abrams v. United States*, decided seven months later, Holmes dissented in a similar situation. In this case, the offensive material was a leaflet protesting American intervention in Russia. Holmes declared that the First Amendment protected speech unless it posed such a threat that an immediate response was necessary.

See also: Associate Justices; Confirmation of Justices and Judges.

Further Reading

Littlefield, Sophie, and William M. Wiecek. *Oliver Wendell Holmes, Jr.: The Supreme Court and American Legal Thought.* New York: PowerPlus Books, 2005.

Hughes, Charles Evans (1862–1948)

Chief Justice of the United States, appointed by President William Howard Taft (1909–1913) as an associate justice and confirmed by Congress on May 2, 1910. He was the sixty-second justice to serve on the Court. In 1930, President Herbert Hoover (1929–1933) named Hughes to become the eleventh chief justice. In an ironic twist, the person whom Hughes succeeded as chief justice was Taft, who had assumed the position several years after leaving the presidency.

Hughes was the only child of an antislavery minister in New York State. His parents schooled him at home until age fourteen, when he enrolled in Madison College (now Colgate University). He graduated from Columbia University in 1884 and passed the bar exam at age twenty-two. Hughes entered private law practice for the next twenty years, with an interim of three years teaching law at Cornell University.

In 1905, Hughes won statewide recognition by investigating illegal rate-making practices and fraudulent insurance activities in New York. The following year, he was elected the state's governor; he won reelection two years later. In 1910, President William Howard Taft appointed Hughes to the Court to fill the vacancy left by Justice David Brewer's death.

After six years on the Court, Hughes ran for president, endorsed by both the Republican Party and the Progressive Party. After losing the 1916 election by only twenty-three electoral votes, he returned to private practice.

When Warren G. Harding became president in 1921, he appointed Hughes secretary of state, a post Hughes also held during the administration of President Calvin Coolidge (1923–1929). Hughes played a critical role in brokering international arms and diplomatic agreements at the Washington Armament Conference in 1921. In 1930, President Herbert Hoover nominated Hughes to replace William Taft as chief justice. Although the appointment met considerable opposition in the Senate, Hughes was confirmed by a 52-26 vote.

As chief justice, Hughes wrote the Court's opinion in several of the cases that overturned much of President Roosevelt's (1933–1945) New Deal legislation. He is also the author of the landmark freedom of the press case *Near v. Minnesota* (1931). In *Near*, the Court struck down as unconstitutional a law barring future publication of a newspaper that prints malicious or defamatory material.

In 1941, Hughes informed President Franklin Roosevelt of his wish to retire due to "considerations of health and age." The following year, Hughes was awarded the American Bar Association medal for conspicuous service to jurisprudence.

See also: Associate Justices; Chief Justice of the United States; New Deal and the Supreme Court; Taft, William Howard.

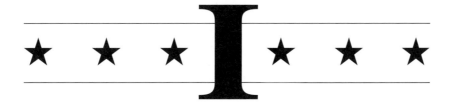

Impeachment of Justices

The trial and possible removal of a judge from office for offenses committed while serving in the judiciary. The U.S. Constitution states that Supreme Court justices, like all other federal judges, are appointed for life "during good behavior." A judge may die in office or retire, but the only method specified by the Constitution for forcible removal of a federal judge is through impeachment in the House of Representatives and conviction by a two-thirds vote of the Senate.

Article II of the Constitution states that "all Civil Officers of the United States shall be removed from office on Impeachment for, and conviction of, Treason, Bribery, or other high Crimes and Misdemeanors." "Treason" and "bribery" are well-defined terms, but much debate centers on what the Constitution's authors meant by "high crimes and misdemeanors." Did they intend it to be read narrowly to mean that a judge could be removed from office only if he or she committed some indictable offense? Or did the Framers intend that the phrase be construed broadly so that impeachment might be used as a political weapon?

The only successful impeachment of a Supreme Court justice occurred in 1804, when Democratic-Republican members of the House of Representatives impeached **Federalist** justice Samuel Chase for misconduct. They hoped to impeach other Federalist members of the Court after Chase, but the Senate failed to convict Chase on largely politically motivated charges, and the Democratic-Republicans abandoned their plan.

The Chase trial probably proved that impeachment and conviction could not succeed if the motivations were primarily partisan ones. Yet the episode did not resolve the fundamental constitutional question of whether only indictable offenses can lead to impeachment. On two separate occasions, the House investigated politically motivated impeachment charges against Justice William O. Douglas. The first happened in 1953 after Douglas granted a temporary stay of execution of two convicted spies. Conservative Republican senators conducted another investigation in 1970 for a variety of perceived political slights from the Court in general and Douglas in particular. In neither instance did proceedings progress beyond the inquiry stage. In the latter case, the leader of the movement to impeach Douglas argued "an impeachable offense is whatever a majority of the House of Representatives considers it to be at a given moment in history."

Only one other justice has faced a serious impeachment threat. Abe Fortas resigned from the Court in 1969 after the House threatened to begin an impeachment inquiry into his association with an industrialist convicted of financial irregularities.

Implied Powers

Authority granted to Congress to carry out its functions but which is not specifically enumerated, or named, in the Constitution. The first seventeen clauses of Article I, Section 8, of the Constitution specifically enumerate the powers granted to Congress. The eighteenth clause is a general grant to Congress of the power "To make all laws which shall be necessary and proper for carrying into Execution the Foregoing Powers, and all other Powers vested by this Constitution in the Government of the United States, or in any

Department or Officer thereof." A major question facing the early Court was whether this so-called "elastic" clause restricts or expands the enumerated powers of Congress.

Secretary of State Thomas Jefferson (1801–1809) and Secretary of the Treasury Alexander Hamilton argued this question after Congress passed legislation establishing the First National Bank in 1791. Jefferson viewed the legislation as invalid; the Constitution did not specifically give Congress the power to incorporate a bank. He said the phrase "necessary and proper" meant Congress only could enact those laws that were *indispensable* to carrying out one of the other enumerated powers.

Hamilton, on the other side, contended that Congress had two sorts of implied powers. One set derived from the fact of the national government's sovereignty, and one derived from the "necessary and proper" clause. The criterion for determining if an act of Congress is constitutional, Hamilton said:

> . . . is the end, to which the measure relates as a mean. If the end be clearly comprehended within any of the specified powers, and if the measure have an obvious relation to that end and is not forbidden by any particular provision of the Constitution, it may safely be deemed to come within the compass of the national authority.

Under Chief Justice John Marshall, the Court early on indicated that it would adopt Hamilton's broader view. In 1805, the Court upheld a federal law that gave payment priority to the United States in cases of **bankruptcies.** It "would produce endless difficulties if the opinion should be maintained that no law was authorized which was not indispensably necessary to give effect to a specified power," Marshall said. "Congress must possess the choice of means and must be empowered to use any means which are in fact conducive to the exercise of a power granted by the Constitution."

Marshall's view on this point would not be fully developed until 1819, when it emerged in the case of *McCulloch v. Maryland. McCulloch*

involved the second national bank. Rechartered in 1816, the Second Bank of the United States was extremely unpopular, particularly in the Eastern and Southern states. Nevertheless, the Court upheld the power of Congress to incorporate the bank. Although the Constitution said nothing about the power to establish a bank and create corporations, Marshall argued that it did grant the government "great powers" and "ample means for their execution." This broader view of implied powers greatly strengthened the federal government at the expense of state power.

See also: McCulloch v. Maryland (1819).

Injunctions

Judicial orders directing someone to halt a course of action. A judge orders an injunction when he or she decides that an action will cause irreparable injury to another person, and that a subsequent lawsuit will not provide adequate compensation for the injury. Injunctions are issued under the federal courts' equity power—their general responsibility to ensure fairness and justice—rather than under their more specific **jurisdiction,** or official authority, over matters arising from the Constitution and laws.

Injunctions may be temporary, simply preserving the status quo until the parties involved resolve the dispute, or they may be permanent bans on certain courses of action. A federal judge may issue a preliminary or temporary injunction even before deciding whether he or she has jurisdiction over a case. The order must be obeyed until it is reversed or lifted.

Some people consider the power to issue injunctions to be inherent in the nature of the federal courts. The Court, however, traditionally has held that Congress must authorize the federal courts to issue such orders. Congress issued such statutory authority in 1789 and has steadily exercised its power to limit the circumstances in which federal courts may issue injunctions.

The Judiciary Act of 1789 made clear that equity suits were to be brought only when no legal remedy existed to resolve a dispute. More specific limitations followed quickly. In 1793, Congress forbade the courts to use injunctions to temporarily halt state court proceedings. The Anti-Injunction Act, which set out the fundamental policy of federal noninterference with state judicial proceedings, remains in effect today.

In 1867, Congress forbade federal courts to use injunctions to interfere with the assessment or collection of federal taxes. One result of this ban is the landmark case *Pollock v. Farmers' Loan and Trust Co.* (1895), which challenged the constitutionality of the peacetime income tax. *Pollock* was a suit seeking an injunction directing a bank *not* to pay its federal income taxes.

In the late 1800s and early 1900s, federal courts used injunctions widely to protect property owners and employers, and to curtail the activities of organized labor. In response, Congress passed laws in 1914 and 1932 limiting such "government by injunction." Similarly, Congress also passed legislation requiring that a panel of three judges—not just a single judge—grant injunctions halting enforcement of state laws or acts of Congress. Appeals from the decisions of these panels could be taken directly to the Court. These provisions were repealed in 1976.

See also: Writ of Mandamus.

Interstate Relations

Constitutional principles specifying the legal, political, and economic relationship between the states. The differences between the early states were many, economically and socially. To facilitate smooth relationships between the newly linked states, the framers of the U.S. Constitution adopted some of the principles of international relations and converted them into provisions governing the relationships of the states.

Article IV requires that each state give "full faith and credit" to the public acts of the other states. The "full faith and credit" clause means that, in civil cases, one state must treat the final judgment of the courts of another state as conclusive. However, one state's judgment can be challenged in another state, and one state's courts can usually block implementation of another state's orders.

Article IV also states, "The citizens of each state shall be entitled to all privileges and immunities of citizens in the several states." The primary purpose of this clause was to require each state to treat the citizens of other states in the same way as their own. The privileges and immunities a state is bound to grant all states' citizens are general ones, such as the right to be protected by the government, the right to property, the right to travel through or live in a state, and the right to bring lawsuits.

The Constitution provides that "no state shall, without the consent of Congress . . . enter into any Agreement or Compact with another state." The Supreme Court, however, has never invalidated any interstate agreement on the basis that it lacked congressional approval. Agreements that do not tend to increase the power of the states relative to that of the national government, or otherwise infringe on federal prerogatives, are assumed to have congressional consent unless specifically challenged by Congress.

When two states sue each other, the Supreme Court hears the case. The first case between states (New York and Connecticut) arrived at the Court in 1799 but was dismissed before it was decided. In 1846, the Court settled its first boundary dispute, between the states of Rhode Island and Massachusetts. Only months before the onset of the Civil War (1861–1865), the states acknowledged the Court's power over interstate matters when Alabama and Georgia asked the Court to settle a boundary dispute.

After the war, boundary disputes multiplied, but by this time the Court's authority to resolve such matters was so generally accepted that they came naturally to the justices for settlement. With this acceptance, the variety of interstate issues coming to the Court increased greatly. Many of these have involved water-related disputes, beginning with one between New York and New Jersey in 1829. Through the end of the twentieth century, disputes over water rights continued to be a staple of the Court's calendar.

See also: Constitution of the United States.

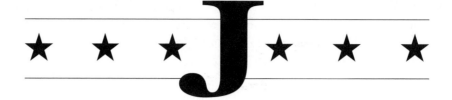

Jay, John (1745–1829)

First Chief Justice of the United States, appointed by President George Washington (1789–1797) and confirmed by Congress on September 26, 1789. Jay officially was the first justice to serve on the Court.

Jay, the youngest of eight children, grew up on his family's farm at Rye, New York. Following education at home and in a private boarding school, he entered King's College (now Columbia University) and graduated at the age of nineteen. He was admitted to the bar four years later.

Jay represented New York at both the First and Second Continental Congresses. In December 1778, he was elected president of the First Continental Congress. The following September, he went to Spain in an attempt to win diplomatic recognition and economic aid for the United States, which, at the time was fighting Great Britain for its independence. In 1783, Jay helped negotiate the Treaty of Paris, which formally ended the Revolutionary War (1775–1783).

While organizing his first administration, George Washington first offered Jay the position of secretary of state. When Jay declined, the president named him chief justice. In this position, Jay helped pave the way for a strong, independent national judiciary.

In 1794, Jay, while still chief justice, was sent to England in an effort to ease growing hostilities between that country and the United States. The result was the controversial Jay Treaty, which outraged many at home who felt it surrendered too many American rights. When he returned from the treaty negotiations, Jay discovered he had been elected governor of New York. He promptly resigned as chief justice and served as governor for two three-year terms.

As governor, Jay supported the gradual freeing of slaves and instituted a revision of the state criminal code. He became interested in prisoner welfare and recommended the construction of a model penitentiary. He also reduced the number of crimes carrying the death penalty.

In December 1800, following the resignation of Chief Justice Oliver Ellsworth, President John Adams (1797–1801) nominated Jay for a second term as chief justice. Although the Senate immediately confirmed him, Jay refused the office. He cited both health reasons and what he saw as the powerlessness of the Court. He wrote Adams that the Court lacked "the energy, weight, and dignity which are essential to its affording due support to the national government." Jay lived in retirement on his eight hundred-acre estate in Westchester County, New York, until his death at age eighty-three in 1829.

See also: Chief Justice of the United States; Confirmation of Justices and Judges.

Jehovah's Witnesses

See Freedom of Religion.

Johnson, Andrew

See Presidency and the Supreme Court.

Judicial Activism

See Judicial Restraint.

Judicial Restraint

The application of rules and doctrines that limit the authority of the Supreme Court. The Court faces a dilemma that is apparent in its very name: It is supreme in the field of law, standing at the peak of the U.S. legal system, but it is also a court. Its members are not elected by the people and therefore cannot claim the ultimate decision-making power in a democracy. Nonetheless, nearly every governmental dispute can be characterized as a legal or constitutional matter. As a result, the Court's legal power could in theory become limitless. The guidelines and principles of judicial restraint act as a self-imposed check on the Court. Judges differ, however, in the degree to which they view those principles and apply those guidelines.

Judicial Restraint and Judicial Activism

Judicial restraint is characterized by a reluctance to strike down existing laws and a broad respect for **precedent,** or earlier legal decisions used as guides for deciding future cases. Judges who exercise judicial restraint feel that the Court should become involved only in cases that involve clear and indisputable constitutional questions. They also prefer that legal decisions be limited whenever possible to the case at hand, and not applied broadly to other cases.

The philosophy of judicial activism, by contrast, is marked by a greater willingness to use the law to achieve certain outcomes. *Black's Law Dictionary* defines judicial activism as "a philosophy of judicial decision-making whereby judges allow their personal views about public policy, among other factors, to guide their decisions, usu(ally) with the suggestion that adherents of this philosophy tend to find constitutional violations and are willing to ignore precedent." So-called "activist judges" are less bound by precedent or previously established legal interpretations.

Principles of Judicial Restraint

The single most basic restriction on the work of the federal courts is the requirement that they decide only "cases" or "controversies." As interpreted by the Court, those words limit the power of federal courts to resolving disputes between parties whose legal interests collide, for which federal courts may have a remedy.

The Court's insistence on hearing only actual "cases" and "controversies" has not stopped it from hearing so-called "friendly" suits. In these cases, there is no real or substantial controversy; each side agrees to pursue the suit in order to attain a mutually desired judicial resolution.

Some of the landmark decisions in the Court's history have come in friendly cases, including *Dred Scott v. Sandford* (1857). Similarly, the Court does not automatically dismiss "test cases"—cases that have been selected by the administration or some pressure group as a means to test a law. The Court's decision to hear or dismiss a test case usually depends on whether it presents an actual conflict of legal rights that can be resolved by the courts.

Mootness

Another aspect of judicial restraint is the rule that the Court will not decide a case that is "moot." Mootness occurs when time or events alter the circumstances of a case enough to remove the dispute. Such cases are then dead, or "moot." For example, in *DeFunis v. Odegaard* (1974), Marco DeFunis charged that he had been denied admission to a state university under an affirmative action program. However, by the time his case was argued before the Court, he was in his final year of law school at another university. The Court held the case to be moot.

Legal Standing

To bring a case to the Court, a party also must have standing to sue, or legal standing. That is, the party must be directly involved in or affected by the dispute. In most private disputes, the injury or interest asserted is clear. Issues of legal standing are more controversial when laws or other government action are challenged as unconstitutional. In these cases, the relationship between the **plaintiff**—the person filing the lawsuit—and the challenged action is more remote than it is in cases involving private disputes.

Political Questions

In *Marbury v. Madison* (1803), the Court ruled that "Questions in their nature political, or which

A–Z

are, by the constitution and laws, submitted to the executive, can never be made in this court." Since that time, the Court has employed the "political question" doctrine as a convenient device for avoiding head-on collisions with Congress, the president, or the states. For example, the Court generally has left questions of foreign policy and foreign affairs to the political branches. Similarly, the Court has used the political question doctrine to refuse to intervene in questions of legislative process or procedure, including issues concerning constitutional amendments. It has left the resolution of those matters to Congress or the states.

Precedent

Supreme Court decisions are final, unless Congress overrules them by statute, Congress and the states amend the Constitution to reverse the Court, or the Court decides to overturn precedent. The doctrine of *stare decisis*–"let the decision stand"–binds the Court to adhere to the decisions of an earlier day. The doctrine has a practical basis: the need for stability in law. Even so, from 1810 to 2003, the Court made more than 230 exceptions to the doctrine of *stare decisis* in more than 170 situations and expressly overruled earlier decisions. The Court of the twentieth century clearly has felt free to overrule previous decisions. Some three out of four of the Court's reversals have come since 1900.

Comity

The existence of both state and federal court systems in the United States imposes certain restraints upon the federal judiciary. When someone asks a federal judge to intervene in state matters, the Court often counsels restraint, based on the demands of *comity*. Under this principle, different courts exercise a mutual restraint in order to prevent interference with each other. The demands of comity require that individuals who challenge state actions in federal courts first "exhaust" all possible state remedies for their complaint. Comity also involves the "abstention" doctrine, which requires federal judges to refrain from acting on a matter until state courts have had the opportunity to correct the situation. The application of these rules by the Court has led to much debate on and off the bench, particularly since the Court has applied most of the procedural guarantees of the Bill of

Rights to state court proceedings. In the 1960s, the Court tended to find or create new exceptions to these rules of restraint. Under more conservative leadership since, the Court has tended to narrow such exceptions. The process of adjustment continues.

See also: Federalism.

Further Reading

Powers, Stephen P., and Rothmann, Stanley. *The Least Dangerous Branch? Consequences of Judicial Activism*. New York: Praeger, 2002.

Judicial Review

Principle that states the Supreme Court can review laws passed by Congress and strike down those the Court finds unconstitutional. Most constitutional scholars agree that a majority of the Framers of the Constitution expected the Court to enforce some limitations on congressional power. However, the question of whether the Court could actually **nullify** an act of Congress as unconstitutional remained unanswered until 1803. In that year, the Court issued its decision in *Marbury v. Madison*, noting that it was "the province and duty of the judicial department, to say what the law is."

Constitutional Basis

The U.S. Constitution does not expressly grant the Court the power of judicial review. The implicit justification for this judicial role lies in the supremacy clause (Article VI, Section 2):

> This Constitution, and the Laws of the United States which shall be made in Pursuance thereof; and all Treaties made, or which shall be made, under the Authority of the United States, shall be the supreme Law of the Land; and the Judges in every State shall be bound thereby, any Thing in the Constitution or Laws of any State to the Contrary notwithstanding.

Few constitutional scholars believe that the Framers intended to deny the Court the power of judicial review. The concept of judicial review was relatively well established in the colonies, and several state courts had struck down state laws that they had found inconsistent with their state constitutions.

The Constitutional Convention of 1787 considered and rejected the proposal that the Court share the **veto** power over acts of Congress with the president. The major reason this idea was voted down seems to have been the feeling that the Court should not be involved in enacting a law that it might later be required to enforce. According to the records of the Constitutional Convention compiled by Max Farrand, only two of the Framers expressed reservations about judicial review, although other scholars feel that the number of opponents was larger. During the ratification period, James Madison and Alexander Hamilton supported the concept in the *Federalist Papers.* Future Supreme Court Chief Justices Oliver Ellsworth and John Marshall endorsed the principle at their state ratification conventions.

The First Congress, in Section 26 of the Judiciary Act of 1789, specifically granted the Supreme Court the right of judicial review over state court decisions

> . . . where is drawn in question the validity of a treaty or statute of, or an authority exercised under, the United States and the decision is against their validity; or where is drawn in question the validity of a statute of, or an authority exercised under any State, on the ground of their being repugnant to the constitution, treaties, or laws of the United States, and the decision is in favor of their validity, or where is drawn in question the construction of any clause of the constitution, or of a treaty, or statute of, or commission held under the United States, and the decision is against the title, right, privilege, or exemption, specially set up or claimed by either party, under such clause of the said constitution, treaty, statute or commission.

Early Exercise

Most of the early Court justices seemed to believe that they enjoyed a similar power of judicial review over federal statutes. Several of the justices, sitting as circuit court judges, refused to administer a 1792 federal pension law. They argued that the administrative duties it required of them were not judicial and so were in conflict with the constitutional separation of powers. Sitting as the Court in 1796, the justices assumed that they had this power of judicial review when they upheld a federal tax on carriages. The ruling, since it upheld the law rather than nullified it, drew little comment. A few days later, the Court for the first time invalidated a state law because it conflicted with a federal treaty. By the time of *Marbury v. Madison,* the Court already had exercised judicial review without specifically declaring it possessed that power. With the decision in *Marbury,* the Court formally established the extent of its power by declaring an act of Congress unconstitutional.

See also: Congress and the Supreme Court; Judiciary Act of 1789; Jurisdiction of the Supreme Court; *Marbury v. Madison* (1803).

Further Reading

Forsyth, Christopher, ed. *Judicial Review and the Constitution.* Oxford, UK: Hart Publishing, 2000.

Judicial System, U.S.

See Jurisdiction of the Supreme Court.

Judiciary Act of 1789

Congressional legislation that established the federal judicial system of the United States. Although the Constitution created the Supreme Court and gave Congress the authority to establish lower courts, it did not specify the structure or procedures of such courts. The Judiciary Act of 1789 laid out the basics of the federal court system, filling in the gaps left by the Constitution.

Key Provisions of the Judiciary Act of 1789

- Established that the Supreme Court be composed of one chief justice and five associate justices

- Established the meeting times of the Court—twice each year

- Determined the jurisdiction of the Court

- Established the circuit court system

- Determined the oath for each justice: "I, _____, do solemnly swear (or affirm), that I will administer justice without respect to persons, and do equal right to the poor and to the rich, and that I will faithfully and impartially discharge and perform all the duties incumbent on me as, according to the best of my abilities and understanding, agreeably to the constitution, and laws of the United States. So help me God."

The Judiciary Act of 1789 set up the basic structure of the United States court system. Although Congress has modified this law many times over the years, the overall plan of the nation's judicial system has remained the same.

Main Provisions

The Judiciary Act of 1789 addressed issues of both the structure and function of federal courts. For example, it specified the size of the Court for the first time: one chief justice and five associate justices. At a larger level, it created thirteen judicial districts—geographic areas, each under the **jurisdiction,** or authority, of a separate federal court.

District and Circuit Courts

Two of the "inferior courts" that Congress created in 1789 under its constitutional authority were district courts and circuit courts. District courts are trial courts that hear both criminal and civil cases involving the federal government. Each state fell under the jurisdiction of a single district court, except for Massachusetts and Virginia. These larger and more populous states were each divided into two federal judicial districts, each with its own district court.

In addition to judicial districts, the act divided the nation into three judicial circuits, each under the jurisdiction of a federal circuit court. These served as trial courts for cases involving citizens from different states as well as major federal crimes. However, circuit courts also could hear appeals from the federal district courts. The Judiciary Act of 1789 required the Supreme Court justices to "ride circuit." Under the terms of the act, two justices sat with one district court judge at circuit courts in each of three circuits. In 1792, the six justices were required to attend a total of twenty-seven circuit courts a year and two sessions of the Court.

District courts have remained substantially the same since their creation in 1789, but the circuit courts changed dramatically. As the country expanded westward, circuit-riding duties grew more burdensome. Finally, in 1891, Congress established a separate system of circuit courts of appeals. Twenty years later, Congress finally relieved Court justices of all circuit court duties. Today, the former circuit courts are known as federal courts of appeal.

Jurisdiction

The Judiciary Act of 1789 spelled out what types of cases the Court had the power to try as a court of original jurisdiction, and which ones it could hear on **appeal.** Congress gave the Court original jurisdiction over all civil actions between states, those between a state and the United States, all lawsuits brought by or against ambassadors and diplomatic personnel, and all cases in which a state was a party. The Court was given appellate jurisdiction over decisions of the federal circuit courts as well as certain decisions by state courts. These included state decisions invalidating federal laws or treaties; decisions upholding laws challenged as unconstitutional; or decisions rejecting claims made by a party under a provision of the federal constitution, treaties, or laws.

The act gave the Court the power to review state court rulings rejecting federal claims. However, it also made clear that most cases would be resolved in state courts. The Judiciary Act of 1789 left to the state courts all cases arising within the states, even if they involved a federal question.

To ensure that constitutional principles and federal law were uniformly applied, however, in such cases the act granted the right of appeal to the Court under the much-debated Section 25. This section authorized the Court to reexamine and reverse or uphold the final judgment of the highest court in a state when the state court decided against the federal claim in cases involving the Constitution, federal laws, or federal treaties.

Other Provisions

The act also established several other fundamental aspects of the federal justice system. It created the office of the Attorney General of the United States, who serves as the nation's chief law enforcement officer. It also provided for marshals and district attorneys for each federal judicial district.

One provision of the act was later famously struck down as unconstitutional. The act granted the Court the power to issue writs of mandamus to courts hearing cases that did not fall under the Court's appellate jurisdiction. A writ of mandamus is an order by a superior court to a lower court directing the lower court to perform its duties properly. In the landmark case of *Marbury v. Madison* (1803), the Court declared this provision of the act unconstitutional. The justices ruled that the Court had no authority to exert such power in cases over which they had no jurisdiction.

See also: Appellate Jurisdiction; Jurisdiction of the Supreme Court; *Marbury v. Madison* (1803); Writ of Mandamus.

Jurisdiction of the Supreme Court

The areas in which the Court may exercise its authority as the nation's highest court. The Court is primarily an appeals court; its main responsibility is to review the decisions of lower courts. However, the Court does have original jurisdiction—the power to hear a case for the first time—in some types of cases.

Original Jurisdiction

The Constitution grants the Court original jurisdiction in "all cases affecting Ambassadors, other public Ministers and Consuls, and those in which a State shall be a Party." This original jurisdiction may be exclusive (held by the Court only) or concurrent (shared with other federal courts or with state courts). Cases brought under the Court's original jurisdiction comprise a very small portion of the modern Court's caseload, and most of those cases involve interstate controversies. Few original cases have been brought involving foreign diplomats.

In the case of *Marbury v. Madison* (1803), the Court ruled that Congress may not expand or curtail the Court's original jurisdiction. Congress, however, has successfully asserted the power to decide whether the Court's original jurisdiction over certain matters is exclusive or concurrent with the jurisdiction of other courts.

The Judiciary Act of 1789 gave the Court exclusive jurisdiction over all civil suits between a state and the United States or between two states. Lawsuits between a state and an individual might be heard in other courts and only later before the Court. In addition, the act gave the Court exclusive jurisdiction over all suits against ambassadors, public ministers, or their domestics. It did not, however, give the Court jurisdiction over all cases brought by ambassadors or public ministers, nor over all cases involving consuls.

The Court is not obliged to hear cases that fall under its original jurisdiction. Just before the Civil War (1861–1865), for example, Kentucky came to the Court asking for an order directing the governor of Ohio to return a fugitive free black man indicted in Kentucky for helping a slave to escape. The Court reaffirmed its jurisdiction over such a case, and then declined to issue the requested order.

Appellate Jurisdiction

Article III of the Constitution grants the Court appellate jurisdiction—the right to hear appeals of cases tried in lower courts. It also gave Congress the power to make exceptions to the Court's appellate jurisdiction. Congress quickly exercised this power. The Judiciary Act of 1789 granted the Court jurisdiction over appeals from the decisions of the circuit courts in civil cases, so long as more than two thousand dollars was at stake. Not until 1889 did the Court have the jurisdiction to hear appeals in criminal cases. Perhaps most important, the act granted the Court authority to take appeals from rulings of high state courts upholding state laws or

A–Z

A–Z

How a Case Reaches the Supreme Court

- **Original jurisdiction**
The Court must hear cases that may set a precedent (ruling that can later be used to justify a similar case) and other legal disputes that involve a state or the federal government.

- **Appellate jurisdiction**
The Court must hear appeals that seek to declare a federal or state law unconstitutional. The Court can accept or reject other cases from lower federal or state courts. The Court accepts cases only if four or more justices agree to grant a *writ of certiorari*.

Article III, Section 2, of the U.S. Constitution outlines the jurisdiction of the nation's court system.

state actions against challenges that they conflict with the U.S. Constitution, federal laws, or treaties.

Defining the Court's Appellate Jurisdiction

In 1866, the Court declared, "(I)t is for Congress to determine how far, within the limits of the capacity of this court to take, appellate jurisdiction shall be given. . . ." The full truth of this statement was brought home three years later after Congress expanded the availability of the writ of habeas corpus to persons who felt they were illegally detained by state or federal authorities. The writ is an order to authorities to produce a person accused of crime in public court. The purpose of the law was to provide protection from state prosecution and detention for federal officials enforcing Reconstruction laws in the South.

Ironically, the first major test of the law came in *Ex Parte McCardle* (1868). The case involved a Southern newspaper editor who had been arrested by a military tribunal charged with impeding Reconstruction through his newspaper articles. The first question under consideration was whether the Court had jurisdiction to hear an appeal of a lower court's refusal to issue the writ. The unanimous Court held that it did.

Before the Court had a chance to address the second question, Congress repealed the portion of the 1867 Habeas Corpus Act extending the Court's appellate jurisdiction over cases arising under it. When the Court resumed its hearings on *McCardle*, it held that Congress had eliminated the Court's jurisdiction over the case. Chief Justice Salmon P. Chase spoke for the Court (there was no dissenting opinion):

The provision of the Act of 1867, affirming the appellate jurisdiction of this court in cases of habeas corpus, is expressly repealed. It is hardly possible to imagine a plainer instance of positive exception.

We are not at liberty to inquire into the motives of the Legislature. We can only examine into its power under the Constitution; and the power to make exceptions to the appellate jurisdiction of this court is given by express words.

What, then, is the effect of the repealing Act upon the case before us? We cannot doubt as to this. Without jurisdiction the court cannot proceed at all in any cause. . . .

It is quite clear, therefore, that this court cannot proceed to pronounce judgment in this case, for it has no longer jurisdiction of the appeal.

Later in the year, Chase would comment, in another opinion, that such a repeal of jurisdiction was "unusual and hardly to be justified except upon some imperious public exigency." As historian Charles L. Black Jr. notes, however, the McCardle case "marks the extent of the vulnerability of the Judiciary to congressional control, and hence underlines the significance of Congress's never (except for this case and perhaps one or two other ambiguous and minor instances) having tried to employ this power to hamper judicial review even of its own acts."

See also: Appellate Jurisdiction; Congress and the Supreme Court; Judiciary Act of 1789; *Marbury v. Madison* (1803).

Further Reading
Baum, Lawrence. *The Supreme Court.* Washington, D.C.: CQ Press, 2009.

Juveniles, Rights of

Legal protections granted to minors by the U.S. judicial system. State and federal laws recognize a difference between adults and juveniles and treat them differently in a variety of situations. Historically, juveniles have not enjoyed the same basic guarantees of the Bill of Rights with respect to court proceedings as adults. In recent years, however, the Court has expanded the scope of juvenile rights, particularly in the area of due process, the guarantee that defendants are entitled to the protection of all the laws of the land.

General Rights

While the Court has granted greater legal protections to juveniles in some areas, it has been more reluctant to do so in others. Some of the privileges it has extended to juveniles include the right of juveniles to be notified of charges against them, to have the aid of counsel, to confront witnesses against them, to be informed of their right to remain silent, and to be found guilty—or delinquent—beyond a reasonable doubt.

The Court has refused, however, to extend the right to a jury trial to juvenile court proceedings, which by their nature are less formal than regular criminal court proceedings. To require a jury trial, the Court reasoned, would make the operations of the juvenile courts unnecessarily rigid and formal. In the case of *In re Gault* (1967), the Court upheld a New York law permitting pretrial detention of juveniles when there is a high risk that they may commit serious crimes before trial.

Due Process Rights

Juveniles, the Court has ruled, possess some but not all of the due process rights assured to adults by the Fifth Amendment's due process clause and the Sixth Amendment. The **due process clause** guarantees that no one will be deprived of life or liberty without having access to the formal legal process.

Juvenile court proceedings are considered civil, not criminal, hearings. They are designed to shelter young offenders from the exposure of a public trial, giving them the opportunity to

begin anew without the handicap of publicity or a criminal record. Until 1967, only general elements of due process and fair treatment were applied to these proceedings, but in *In re Gault* (1967), the Court held that juveniles charged with violating the law did have the right to confront and cross-examine persons presenting the evidence against them. Furthermore, the Court declared that juveniles had the same rights as adults to notice, aid of counsel, and protection against self-incrimination.

In *In re Winship* (1970), the Court ruled that juveniles must be found delinquent by proof beyond a reasonable doubt rather than by any lesser standard. In this case, the justices held that Samuel Winship, a twelve-year-old found guilty by a preponderance of the evidence of stealing money from a woman's pocketbook, had been denied his due process rights. The stricter standard of proof of guilt, beyond a reasonable doubt, was an essential element of due process and fair treatment applicable to juvenile as well as adult proceedings, said the Court. The following year, however, in *McKeiver v. Pennsylvania* and *In re Burrus* (1971), the Court refused to extend the right to trial by jury to juvenile court proceedings. Justice Harry A. Blackmun explained:

> **I**f the jury trial were to be injected into the juvenile court system as a matter of right, it would bring with it into that system the traditional delay, the formality and the clamor of the adversary system and, possibly, the public trial . . .
>
> If the formalities of the criminal adjudicative process are to be superimposed upon the juvenile court system, there is little need for its separate existence. Perhaps that ultimate disillusionment will come one day, but for the moment we are disinclined to give impetus to it.

Four years later, in *Breed v. Jones* (1975), the Court extended the Fifth Amendment protection against double jeopardy to minors. The justices ruled that a defendant found in juvenile court to have violated the law could not subsequently be tried for the same act as an adult.

See also: Due Process.

Kennedy, Anthony M. (1936–)

Associate justice of the U.S. Supreme Court, appointed by President Ronald Reagan (1981–1989) and confirmed by Congress on February 18, 1988. He is the 104th justice to serve on the Court.

Kennedy graduated from McClatchy High School in Sacramento, California, and went on to Stanford University, graduating in 1958. He spent his final undergraduate year at the London School of Economics before entering Harvard Law School, earning his degree in 1961. Upon his father's death in 1963, Kennedy returned to Sacramento and took over his father's law practice. He also taught part time at the McGeorge School of Law at the University of the Pacific.

Kennedy's legal abilities brought him to the attention of Ronald Reagan, then governor of California. That connection won Kennedy a nomination by President Gerald R. Ford (1974–1977) to a seat on the Ninth Circuit Court of Appeals in 1975. He took the seat in 1976 and remained on the court for a dozen years, earning a reputation as a conservative, diligent, and even-handed jurist. Kennedy became President Ronald Reagan's choice for the Court in 1987 after the Senate had rejected the nomination of Robert H. Bork, and Douglas Ginsburg's name was withdrawn.

From the start, Kennedy joined Chief Justice William H. Rehnquist to form a conservative majority limiting federal power, upholding the principle of state "sovereign immunity," allowing limited public aid to religious schools, and prohibiting race-based redistricting. Kennedy was credited with being the author of the Court's unsigned opinion in *Bush v. Gore* (2000), which ended the Florida recount and delivered the White House to George W. Bush.

Kennedy has, however, proven to be independent and unpredictable in other areas. A strong advocate of free speech, he joined the opinion of Justice William J. Brennan Jr. to strike down a Texas law forbidding flag burning. He also joined with Justices David H. Souter and Sandra Day O'Connor to write the Court's opinion in *Planned Parenthood of Southeastern Pennsylvania v. Casey* (1992), which upheld the basic right to abortion while permitting certain state regulations.

In *U.S. Term Limits v. Thornton* (1995), Kennedy cast the decisive fifth vote to strike down state term limits on federal officeholders. Though a defender of religious rights, Kennedy spoke for the Court in outlawing school-sponsored prayers and invocations at graduation ceremonies in *Lee v. Weisman* (1992). In perhaps his most powerfully written opinion—in *Lawrence v. Texas* (2003)—Kennedy spoke for the Court in striking down state anti-sodomy laws.

See also: Associate Justices; *Bush v. Gore* (2000); O'Connor, Sandra Day; Souter, David.

Korematsu v. United States (1944)

Supreme Court case that upheld President Franklin D. Roosevelt's (1933–1945) decision to detain Japanese Americans in internment camps during World War II (1939–1945). Forty years later, Congress would issue a formal apology to the detainees and their families for their treatment during the war.

Basis of the Case

On December 7, 1941, Japanese aircraft attacked the U.S. naval base at Pearl Harbor, Hawaii, touching off war between Japan and the United States.

After the United States's entry into World War II (1939–1945), Japanese American citizens living on the nation's West Coast were relocated to detention centers across the country. In 1944, the Supreme Court upheld the constitutionality of the detention camps as a military necessity during the war. (AP Photo)

The attack also set off a wave of anti-Japanese feeling in the United States, particularly since it came before Japan had formally declared war. To many Americans, the large number of Japanese Americans on the West Coast represented a security threat and possible source of enemy spies and saboteurs.

On February 19, 1942, President Franklin D. Roosevelt issued Executive Order No. 1066, which placed Japanese Americans living on the West Coast under rigid curfew laws and restricted their movements. A congressional resolution of March 21, 1942, supported the president's action. Roosevelt subsequently ordered the removal of all Japanese Americans, both citizens and non-citizens, from the coastal region for the duration of the war to protect against sabotage. The removal program made no distinction between citizens and **aliens.** Japanese Americans suffered great economic and psychological distress. By spring 1942, the War Relocation Authority had moved more than one hundred thousand Japanese Americans to internment camps. Seventy thousand

U.S. citizens of Japanese ancestry were detained in camps for up to four years, subjected to forcible confinement, and then resettled in areas away from the Pacific Coast.

Landmark Decision Highlights: *Korematsu v. United States* (1944)

Issue: Whether the president and Congress went beyond their war powers by implementing exclusion and restricting the rights of Americans of Japanese descent during World War II (1939–1945)

Opinion: The Supreme Court held that the need to protect against espionage during wartime outweighed Korematsu's rights. Justice Hugo Black argued that compulsory exclusion, though constitutionally suspect, is justified during circumstances of "emergency and peril."

The Court's Ruling

The constitutionality of the curfew, exclusion, and relocation programs came before the Court in three cases decided in 1943 and 1944. The effect of all three decisions was to uphold this extraordinary exercise of the war power by Congress and the president.

In *Hirabayashi v. United States* (1943), the Court unanimously upheld the curfew order as applied to U.S. citizens as "within the boundaries of the war power." The Court's opinion, written by Chief Justice Harlan Fiske Stone, made clear, however, that the Court was not considering "whether the President, acting alone, could lawfully have made the curfew order." Because Congress had **ratified,** or approved Roosevelt's executive order by law, the issue became that of "the constitutional power of the national government through the joint action of Congress and the executive to impose this restriction as an emergency war measure." The Court held that the curfew order was within that jointly exercised power. Eighteen months later, in *Korematsu v. United States* (1944), with a 6-3 vote, the Court upheld the exclusion of Japanese Americans from their West Coast homes. The majority relied heavily upon the reasoning in *Hirabayashi* in concluding that it was not outside the power of Congress and the executive, acting together, to impose this exclusion.

The same day, however, the Court granted a writ of habeas corpus to Mitsuye Endo, a Japanese American girl, freeing her from one of the detention centers. These centers were intended as "interim places of residence" for persons whose loyalty was being ascertained. After one was determined to be loyal, the intent was that loyal persons be re-settled outside the centers. Endo's loyalty had been determined, but she was still being held, so the Court ordered her release.

Aftermath

In 1988, Congress approved and President Ronald Reagan (1981–1989) signed legislation offering a formal apology to Japanese Americans held in U.S. camps during the war. The bill promised the sixty thousand surviving internees twenty thousand dollars each, with payments spread over ten years. Original estimates of the number of survivors was too low, and Congress did not **appropriate,** or set aside, enough money for the program. In 1992, Congress expanded the fund to compensate all seventy-eight thousand estimated claimants.

See also: 📖 *Korematsu v. United States,* 1944, in the **Primary Source Library**; War Power and the Supreme Court; Writ of Habeas Corpus.

Further Reading

Alonso, Karen. *Korematsu v. United States: Japanese-America Internment Camps.* Berkeley Heights, N.Y.: Enslow Publishers, 1998.

Chin, Steven A. *When Justice Failed: The Fred Korematsu Story.* Orlando, Fla.: Steck-Vaughn, 1992.

Legislative Veto

Controversial provision in a law that allows Congress to block action by the executive branch, with or without presidential approval. The legislative veto, which originated during the administration of President Herbert Hoover (1929–1933), was intended to enable Congress to exercise some control over how the president executed laws passed by the legislature.

Article I of the Constitution states that for a bill to become law the House and the Senate must

Jagdish Rai Chadha, a Kenyan, overstayed his student visa but persuaded the Immigration and Naturalization Service (INS) to suspend his deportation. The U.S. House of Representatives then used a legislative veto to reject Chadha's stay of deportation. Chadha challenged the law and won; in *INS v. Chadha* (1983), the Court ruled that the legislative veto was unconstitutional. (*The New York Times*)

a Kenyan East Indian who had overstayed his student visa, persuaded the Immigration and Naturalization Service (INS) to suspend his deportation. Congress, however, had amended the Immigration and Nationality Act of 1952 to give either of its chambers the power to veto an INS decision to suspend an individual's deportation. In December 1975, the House exercised its power to veto Chadha's stay of deportation. Chadha contested the House veto, arguing that it was unconstitutional for the House to overrule the INS in this way. In 1980, the U.S. Court of Appeals for the Ninth Circuit agreed, holding the one-house veto unconstitutional.

The Court heard arguments to appeal that ruling in February 1982. On the last day of that term, the Court ordered a second round of arguments, which were held on the opening day of the October 1982 term. Chadha, in the meantime, had married an American, fathered a child, and settled down in the United States. It took the Court all term to reach a decision. On June 23, 1983, it held the legislative veto unconstitutional by a 7-2 vote. The majority found the device an impermissible violation of the procedure that required that bills be passed by both houses and then presented to the president for signature.

See also: Checks and Balances; Separation of Powers.

Libel

sign it and then present it to the president for signature. The legislative veto was first used as part of the 1933 legislative appropriations bill. Over the next fifty years, legislative veto provisions were included, in one form or another, in more than two hundred laws. Some permitted a veto by a single House or even a committee; others required action by both Houses.

Presidents from Hoover on protested the veto as an encroachment on their power. It was not until the early 1980s, however, during President Ronald Reagan's (1981–1989) first term, that a challenge to this device reached the Court. The case of *Immigration and Naturalization Service v. Chadha* began in 1974, when Jagdish Rai Chadha,

Publication or broadcast of statements that defame the character or reputation of an individual. The courts have established different standards for judging libel cases brought by private and public figures. In addition, some public figures have more leeway to make possibly libelous public statements. Judges, legislators, and executive officials, for example, enjoy absolute immunity from libel suits. Some professionals, such as doctors and lawyers, enjoy a more limited immunity. By contrast, publishers historically have been liable to damage suits.

In the United States, truth is an absolute defense to libel. However, when the truth involves a matter of judgment, as in a political opinion, it may be impossible to prove. In the landmark case of *New York Times v. Sullivan* (1964), the Court laid out the standard for determining when a statement about a public official rises to the level of libel:

> **T**he constitutional guarantees require, we think, a federal rule that prohibits a public official from recovering damages for a defamatory falsehood relating to his official conduct unless he proves that the statement was made with "actual malice"—that is, with knowledge that it was false or with reckless disregard of whether it was false or not.

Two years after *New York Times Co. v. Sullivan,* the Court further defined the category of "public official." In *Rosenblatt v. Baer* (1966), the Court defined "public officials" as "those among the hierarchy of government employees who have, or appear to the public to have, substantial responsibility for or control over the conduct of governmental affairs. . . .

In *Rosenbloom v. Metromedia Inc.* (1971), the Court considered for the first time whether private individuals must prove actual malice to win damages for libel. Chief Justice Warren Burger and Justices William Brennan and Harry Blackmun agreed that the actual malice rule should be applied to all discussion of public issues, even discussion including defamatory statements about private individuals. Justice Hugo Black concurred, maintaining that the guarantee of a free press protected publishers against all libel suits.

Three years later, in *Gertz v. Robert Welch Inc.,* the Court shifted gears and declared that the actual malice rule did not apply in libel cases brought by private individuals. The majority argued that private citizens lack the access of public officials and public figures to "channels of effective communication" to combat allegations about their conduct. Furthermore, private individuals, unlike public officials and figures, have not voluntarily subjected themselves to public scrutiny.

See also: Freedom of the Press.

Line Item Veto

Provision that allows the president to "cancel" specific spending items and tax benefits contained in bills presented for signing. Throughout U.S. history, the president has had an all-or-nothing option when presented with a bill passed by Congress: either sign it into law or veto it. In 1996, however, Congress passed the Line Item Veto Act, granting the president the power to veto parts of legislation while passing the remainder.

Lawmakers who opposed the line item veto filed a lawsuit to challenge the act in 1997. The Court rejected their claim, stating that members of Congress had no standing, or legal basis, to sue. The justices argued that one must suffer a personal injury from a law to have standing, and denied that the lawmakers had suffered such damages.

A year later, however, in the case of *Clinton v. City of New York* (1998), the Court struck down the Line Item Veto Act. In this case, President Bill Clinton (1993–2001) used the line item veto to cancel spending and tax breaks for two special interests. The first would have saved the city of New York and the state of New York as much as $2.6 billion for having violated federal rules concerning their financing of the Medicaid program. Rather than repaying the Treasury, New York got approval of an item in the Balanced Budget Act of 1997 to spare it. Clinton eliminated this provision because, he said, "preferential treatment" for one state could not be justified. He also canceled a special tax exemption for farm cooperatives that was included in the Tax Relief Act of 1997. The city of New York and the Snake River Potato Growers of Idaho sued to challenge the constitutionality of the veto.

In striking down the line item veto, the Court argued that the Constitution provides the president only two options when presented with a bill passed by Congress: to sign it or to veto it. The justices relied on a strict reading of Article I, Section 7, also known as the presentment clause: "Every Bill which shall have passed the House of Representatives and the Senate shall, before it become a Law, be presented to the President of

President Bill Clinton (1993–2001) signed the Line Item Veto Act into law on April 9, 1996, providing the president with new powers in shaping tax and spending legislation. However, in *Clinton v. City of New York* (1998), the Supreme Court declared the law unconstitutional, requiring that the president accept or reject all bills in their entirety. (Reuters)

the United States; If he approve [sic] he shall sign it, but if not he shall return it." The first president, George Washington, believed this meant he must either "approve all the parts of a Bill or reject it in toto," a line quoted by Justice John Paul Stevens in his opinion for the 6-3 majority.

See also: Checks and Balances.

Loving v. Virginia (1967)

Supreme Court case in which the Court struck down as unconstitutional laws that punished a person for marrying someone of a different race. The Virginia law at the center of the case, the **unanimous** Court held, violated the Fourteenth Amendment's **equal protection clause** and denied those it affected due process of the law.

Basis of the Case

The case arose from the marriage of a black woman, Mildred Jeter, and a white man, Richard Perry Loving, in June 1958. The couple left Virginia to marry in order to avoid a Virginia state law that banned interracial marriages. Soon after the couple

returned to Virginia, police raided their home, hoping to find them engaged in sex; interracial sex also was a crime in the state. The Lovings produced their marriage certificate, but for an interracial couple, even marrying out of state and returning to Virginia was a crime. They were charged with two violations of the Virginia Code prohibiting interracial relations. In January 1959, the Lovings pleaded guilty and received a suspended sentenced upon the condition that they leave Virginia.

In November 1963, the American Civil Liberties Union (ACLU) filed an appeal to overturn the decision based on violation of Fourteenth Amendment protections. After another year and a half in state courts, the Virginia Supreme Court upheld the conviction in early 1965. In April 1967, the Court agreed to hear an appeal.

The Court's Ruling

In a unanimous decision, the Court overturned the convictions and ruled that Virginia's laws prohibiting interracial marriage violated both the due process clause and the equal protection clause of

---

Landmark Decision Highlights:
Loving v. Virginia (1967)

Issue: Did Virginia's law against interracial marriages violate the equal protection clause of the Fourteenth Amendment?

Opinion: In a unanimous decision, the Court held that distinctions drawn according to race were generally "odious to a free people" and were subject to "the most rigid scrutiny" under the equal protection clause. The Virginia law, the Court found, had no legitimate purpose " independent of invidious racial discrimination."

the Fourteenth Amendment. In its decision, the court wrote:

> **T**he freedom to marry has long been recognized as one of the vital personal rights essential to the orderly pursuit of happiness by free men . . . To deny this fundamental freedom on so unsupportable a basis as the racial classification embodied in these statutes . . . is surely to deprive all the State's citizens of liberty without due process of law. The Fourteenth Amendment requires that the freedom of choice to marry not be restricted by invidious racial discriminations. Under our Constitution, the freedom to marry or not marry a person of another race resides with the individual and cannot be infringed by the State.

Despite the Court's decision in *Loving*, so-called "anti-miscegenation" laws remained on the books in a number of states. It would be more than thirty years before the state of Alabama repealed the nation's last law banning mixed-race marriages in 2000.

See also: Due Process; Equal Protection of the Law; 📖 *Loving v. Virginia,* 1967, in the **Primary Source Library.**

Further Reading

Alonso, Karen. *Loving v. Virginia: Interracial Marriage.* Berkeley Heights, NJ: Enslow Publishers, 2000.

Gold, Susan Dudley. *Loving v. Virginia: Lifting the Ban Against Interracial Marriage.* New York: Benchmark Books, 2007.

Loyalty Oaths

Supreme Court rulings that deal with laws that require individuals to swear or affirm their loyalty to the United States. At one time or another, such oaths have been required of many government employees and even private citizens. The Court now considers most such laws unconstitutional, with some exceptions.

The first widespread use of loyalty oaths in the United States occurred after the Civil War (1861–1865). Several states passed laws requiring people to take so-called "test oaths" to swear their loyalty to the Union before they could take part in many activities. These activities included voting, practicing law, running for office, and even serving as teacher or member of the clergy. In *Cummings v. Missouri* (1867), the Court ruled such state laws unconstitutional. It also declared any federal test oath invalid.

The issue of loyalty oaths did not come before the Court again until the late 1940s and 1950s. At this time, fears of communism led state, local, and federal governments to impose a new set of loyalty oaths. In 1951, the Court upheld state laws requiring loyalty oaths from city employees (*Gardner v. Board of Public Works of Los Angeles*) and candidates running for public office (*Gerende v. Board of Supervisors of Elections*). A year later, it upheld a New York law providing for dismissal of any public employee belonging to a list of proscribed organizations (*Adler v. Board of Education, City of New York*).

In addition to public employees, many states required officers of labor unions to swear they were not members of or affiliated with the **Communist Party.** The Court supported this practice in *American Communications Association v. Douds* (1950).

A new set of justices came to the Court in the 1960s, however, and they revisited many of these decisions. The rulings in *Elfbrandt v. Russell* (1966) and *Keyishian v. Board of Regents of the State University of New York* (1967) effectively overturned the 1950s decisions in *Gerende, Gardner,* and *Adler* that banned public employees from membership in specific political parties. The justices did uphold the constitutionality of loyalty oaths that require public employees to "oppose the overthrow of the government by force, violence, or by any illegal or unconstitutional measure."

The Court, however, struck down similar laws concerning political parties in *Communist Party of Indiana v. Whitcomb* (1974). In that case, it held that a party cannot be banned from the ballot for advocating forcible overthrow of the government, "except where such advocacy is directed to inciting or producing imminent lawless action and is likely to incite or produce such action."

Mandamus

See Writ of Mandamus.

Mapp v. Ohio (1961)

Supreme Court case in which the exclusionary rule was extended to the states. The exclusionary rule states that evidence seized by federal agents in violation of the Fourth Amendment to the U.S. Constitution ban against unreasonable search and seizure may not be used in federal courts. In *Mapp v. Ohio,* the Court finally declared, "the exclusionary rule is an essential part of both the Fourth and Fourteenth Amendments."

The case involved a situation in which Cleveland, Ohio, police officers broke into a house without a search warrant, suspecting that a criminal was hiding inside. The officers manhandled the female resident, Dollree Mapp, and searched the entire premises, finding a trunk containing obscene materials. Mapp later was tried and convicted

for possession of obscene materials. The Court overturned Mapp's conviction because the evidence used against her had been unconstitutionally seized. Writing for the majority, Justice Tom C. Clark stated:

Nothing can destroy a government more quickly than its failure to observe its own laws, or worse, its disregard of the charter of its own existence . . .

The ignoble shortcut to conviction left open to the State [by allowing use of illegally obtained evidence] tends to destroy the entire system of constitutional restraints on which the liberties of the people rest. Having once recognized that the right to privacy embodied in the Fourth Amendment is enforceable against the States, and that the right to be secure against rude invasions of privacy by state officers is, therefore, constitutional in origin, we can no longer permit that right to remain an empty promise.

The Court held, however, that the *Mapp* decision would not be retroactively applied to

---

Landmark Decision Highlights: *Mapp v. Ohio* (1961)

Issue: Dollree Mapp was convicted of possessing obscene materials after an illegal search of her home. She appealed her conviction, based on two issues: whether or not the confiscated materials were protected by the First Amendment and whether or not evidence obtained through a search in violation of the Fourth Amendment may be admitted in a state criminal proceeding.

Opinion: The Court ignored the First Amendment issue and declared that "all evidence obtained by searches and seizures in violation of the Constitution is, under the Fourth Amendment, inadmissible in a state court." Thus, the Court ruled that Mapp had been convicted on the basis of illegally obtained evidence. This was a historic—and controversial—decision, because the Court determined that illegally obtained evidence may not be used in state as well as federal courts.

overturn state criminal convictions that had occurred before the new standard was established. In *Linkletter v. Walker* (1965), the Court stated that *Mapp* applied only to cases on direct review at the time of the 1961 ruling and to later cases. The Court in the 1970s limited the use of the exclusionary rule to overturn convictions, reflecting the lack of enthusiasm of some members of the Court for the rule. Chief Justice Warren Burger said, in *Bivens v. Six Unknown Named Agents* (1971), that he preferred an alternative remedy, perhaps a damage suit against the offending officials.

See also: Search Warrants.

Marbury v. Madison (1803)

Supreme Court case that formally established the principle of judicial review, the concept that the Court could rule on the constitutionality of laws passed by Congress. Many scholars consider *Marbury v. Madison* to be the single most important ruling in the Court's history.

Basis of the Case

In 1800, Republican Thomas Jefferson defeated **incumbent Federalist** John Adams (1797–1801)

On his last night in office, President John Adams (1797–1801) (right) appointed several judicial officers, who have come to be known as the "midnight judges." Several of the appointees, including William Marbury, did not receive their commissions, and, after Thomas Jefferson (1801–1809) took office, Jefferson forbade Secretary of State James Madison to deliver the judges' commissions. In turn, Marbury sued, leading to the landmark case of *Marbury v. Madison* (1803). The Supreme Court clearly asserted its power of judicial review in this case. (National Geographic Society)

intended to deprive Jefferson of a quick appointment to the Court.

On Adams's last day in office, he signed the commissions for the new justices of the peace. The commissions were then taken to Marshall, who was to attach the Great Seal of the United States and have the commissions delivered to the appointees. Marshall affixed the seal but somehow failed to see that all the commissions were actually delivered. William Marbury, an aide to the secretary of the Navy, was one of the appointees who did not receive his commission. With three other men in the same position, he asked Jefferson's secretary of state, James Madison, to give him the commission. When Madison, at Jefferson's direction, refused, Marbury asked the Court to issue a writ of mandamus to Madison to give the four men their commissions. A writ of mandamus is an order by a higher court ordering a lower court to carry out its duties. In December 1801, Chief Justice Marshall asked Madison to show cause at the next session of the Court why he should not comply with the order.

If the Court ordered delivery of the commission, Madison might refuse to obey the order, which the Court had no means to enforce. If the Court did not issue the writ, it would be surrendering to Jefferson's point of view. Either way, the Court would be admitting its lack of power.

William Marbury, a Georgetown businessman and member of the Federalist Party, was appointed justice of the peace of the District of Columbia by John Adams on the day before the president left office. The secretary of state, John Marshall, was unable to deliver all of Adams's commissions. Marbury then asked the Supreme Court to issue a writ of mandamus compelling the new secretary of state, James Madison, to award Marbury his commission. The Court ruled that, while Marbury was legally entitled to the position, the Court had no authority to order the secretary of state to deliver the paperwork because part of the Judiciary Act of 1789 was unconstitutional. This decision established the Supreme Court's right of judicial review. Marbury never got his commission. (The Granger Collection, New York)

for the presidency. Before leaving office, however, Adams appointed his secretary of state, John Marshall, a committed Federalist, as Chief Justice of the United States. He also pushed legislation creating sixteen new circuit court judgeships, authorizing Adams to appoint as many justices of the peace for the newly created District of Columbia as he deemed necessary, and reducing the number of Supreme Court justices from six to five with the next vacancy. This last measure was

Landmark Decision Highlights:
Marbury v. Madison (1803)

Issue: Whether or not the Supreme Court has the power, under Article III, Section 2, of the U.S. Constitution, to interpret the constitutionality of a law passed by Congress

Opinion: The Court decided that William Marbury's request for a *writ of mandamus* was based on a law that the Court held to be unconstitutional. The Court unanimously decided that the federal law contradicted the Constitution, and because the Constitution is the Supreme Law of the Land, it must reign supreme. Through this case, Chief Justice John Marshall established the power of judicial review.

Chief Justice Marshall resolved this problem with a remarkable decision that has been called a "masterwork of indirection, a brilliant example of Marshall's capacity to sidestep danger while seeming to court it, to advance in one direction while his opponents are looking in another."

The Court's Healing

Marshall ruled that once the president had signed the commissions and the secretary of state had recorded them, the appointments were complete. He also ruled that a writ of mandamus was the proper tool to use to require the secretary of state to deliver the commissions.

Marshall then addressed the question of whether or not the Court had the authority to issue the writ. He concluded that it did not. Congress had unconstitutionally expanded the Court's original **jurisdiction,** or area of authority, when it authorized the Court to issue such writs to officers of the federal government under the Judiciary Act of 1789.

Finally, he turned to the question of whether or not the judiciary had the authority to determine when acts of Congress conflicted with the Constitution:

> It is, emphatically, the province and duty of the judicial department to say what the law is. . . . The judicial power of the United States is extended to all cases arising under the constitution. Could it be the intention of those who gave this power, to say, that in using it, the constitution should not be looked into? That a case arising under the constitution should be decided, without examining the instrument under which it arises? This is too extravagant to be maintained.

Aftermath and Significance

While refusing the power to issue writs of mandamus in such cases, Marshall claimed for the Court the far more significant power of judicial review. Marshall's claim of authority, however, was not generally viewed by his contemporaries with the same importance that future scholars would confer on it. In fact, Jefferson, who believed that the legislature was the only branch capable of

determining the validity of its actions, apparently did not find Marshall's claim of power particularly significant. According to historian Charles Warren, "Jefferson's antagonism to Marshall and the Court at that time was due more to his resentment at the alleged invasion of his Executive prerogative than to any so-called 'judicial usurpation' of the field of Congressional authority."

See also: Judicial Review; Jurisdiction of the Supreme Court; 📖 *Marbury v. Madison*, 1803, in the **Primary Source Library**; Marshall, John; Writs of Mandamus.

Further Reading

Devillers, David. *Marbury v. Madison: Powers of the Supreme Court.* Berkeley Heights, N.J.: Enslow Publishers, 1998.

Maritime and Admiralty Law

Laws dealing with situations that arise from the activities of shipping and navigation on the nation's waterways. The U.S. Constitution gives Congress no specific authority over admiralty and maritime matters. The only mention of the subject is in Article III, Section 2, which states that the "judicial power shall extend . . . to all Cases of admiralty and maritime jurisdiction." This phrase implies the existence of a body of admiralty and maritime law, but the question remained whether Congress had any power to modify this law.

In *Gibbons v. Ogden* (1824), the Court cited Congress's power to regulate **interstate commerce** to strike down a steamboat monopoly operating between two states. The ruling established the principle that the federal government could override state laws that interfered with interstate commerce. The opinion in that case also settled a second issue: navigation was commerce. The question then became one of state power: Was the federal power over navigation exclusive, or were there some situations in which states could regulate traffic on the waterways?

In the next major navigation case, *Pennsylvania v. Wheeling and Belmont Bridge Co.* (1852), the

Court held that Congress could use its commerce power to override state law affecting interstate navigation. In the same period, the Court held that Congress could not regulate navigation on a river wholly in one state and involving commerce that was not connected to interstate or foreign commerce

In 1866, the Court reaffirmed Congress's complete control over navigable waters "which are accessible from a State other than those in which they lie." Five years later, it permitted federal regulation of a boat that transported goods in interstate commerce even though the boat operated solely on waters entirely within one state. In *The Lottawanna* (1875), the Court asserted that the framers of the Constitution could not have meant to leave changes in maritime law to the states.

Congressional power over the nation's waterways was made virtually complete in 1940, when the Court held that federal authority even extended to some waters that were not at the time navigable. In *United States v. Appalachian Electric Power Co,.* the Court ruled that the Federal Power Commission had the authority to regulate dam construction on a portion of Virginia's New River that might be made navigable by the dam.

See also: Gibbons v. Ogden (1824).

The fourth Chief Justice of the United States, John Marshall was a firm believer in the power of the federal government, and the hundreds of cases decided during his tenure significantly increased the supremacy of the central government. Among the landmark cases decided during his tenure are *Marbury v. Madison* (1803); *McCulloch v. Maryland* (1819); and *Gibbons v. Ogden* (1824). (Library of Congress, Prints and Photographs Division)

Marshall, John (1755-1835)

Chief Justice of the United States, appointed by President John Adams (1797–1801) and confirmed by Congress on February 4, 1801. He was the thirteenth justice to serve on the Court and the fourth to serve as chief justice. Marshall, who also served as secretary of state and as a member of the U.S. House of Representatives, was the longest-serving of any chief justice. During his tenure, he presided over some of the most important decisions in the Court's early history.

Early Life and Career

John Marshall was the eldest of fifteen children born in a log cabin on the Virginia frontier. His father was an assistant surveyor to George Washington and member of the Virginia House of Burgesses, the state's legislature. His mother was the daughter of an educated Scottish clergyman. As a youth, Marshall was tutored by two clergymen, but his primary teacher was his father, who introduced him to the study of English literature and law.

During the Revolutionary War (1775–1783), young Marshall participated in the siege of Norfolk as a member of the Culpeper Minutemen. He was present at the battles of Brandywine, Monmouth, Stony Point, and Valley Forge as a member of the Third Virginia Regiment. In 1779, he returned home to await another assignment but was never recalled. He left the Continental Army with the rank of captain in 1781.

Marshall's only formal instruction in the law came in 1780 when he attended a course of law lectures at the College of William and Mary. He was later admitted to the Virginia bar and developed a lucrative law practice. Marshall was elected to the Virginia House of Delegates from Fauquier County in 1782 and 1784. He reentered the House in 1787 and was instrumental in Virginia's **ratification,** or formal approval, of the new U.S. Constitution. At the state ratifying convention, his primary attention was directed to the need for judicial review. By 1789, Marshall was considered to be a leading **Federalist** in the state.

National Service

Marshall refused many appointments in the Federalist presidential administrations of George Washington (1789–1797) and John Adams (1797–1801). The posts he turned down included U.S. attorney general, associate justice of the Supreme Court, and secretary of war. In 1796, he refused an appointment by President Adams as minister to France, but the following year he agreed to serve as one of three special envoys sent to smooth relations with that country. This mission, known as the XYZ Affair, failed when French diplomats demanded a bribe as a condition for negotiation. Congress, however, was greatly impressed by the stubborn resistance of the American emissaries, and Marshall received a generous grant as a reward for his participation.

In 1799, Washington persuaded Marshall to run for the U.S. House of Representatives as a Federalist from Richmond, Virginia. Marshall's career in the House was brief, however, for in 1800 President Adams named him secretary of state. When Adams retired to his home in Massachusetts for a few months that year, Marshall served as the effective head of government.

Chief Justice

When Oliver Ellsworth resigned as chief justice in 1800, Adams initially offered the position to John Jay, who had been the Court's first chief justice. Jay declined, and the Federalists urged Adams to elevate Associate Justice William Paterson. Adams instead nominated Marshall.

Marshall was the primary founder of the American system of constitutional law, including the doctrine of judicial review. He participated in more than one thousand Court decisions, writing more than five hundred of them himself. These included landmark decisions such as *Marbury v. Madison (1803); McCulloch v. Maryland* (1819); and

Gibbons v. Ogden (1824). In 1807, he presided over the treason trial of Aaron Burr in the Richmond Circuit Court, locking horns with Jefferson, who sought an absolute conviction. Burr was acquitted.

In 1831, at age seventy-six, Marshall underwent successful surgery in Philadelphia for the removal of kidney stones. By this time, he had served more than thirty years as chief justice during six different presidential administrations. Three years later, he developed an enlarged liver, and his health declined rapidly. When Marshall died on July 6, 1835, three months short of his eightieth birthday, it is said that the Liberty Bell cracked as it tolled in mourning.

See also: Chief Justice of the United States; *Gibbons v. Ogden* (1824); Judicial Review; *Marbury v. Madison* (1803); *McCulloch v. Maryland* (1819).

Further Reading

Simon, James. F. *What Kind of Nation: Thomas Jefferson, John Marshall, and the Epic Struggle to Create a United States*. New York: Simon and Schuster, 2003.

Smith, Jean Edward. *John Marshall: Definer of a Nation*. New York: Henry Holt, 1996.

Marshall, Thurgood (1908–1993)

Associate justice of the U.S. Supreme Court, appointed by President Lyndon B. Johnson (1963–1969) and confirmed by the Senate on August 30, 1967. He was the ninety-sixth justice to serve on the Court and the first African American to do so.

Marshall was the son of Norma Williams Marshall, a primary school teacher, and William Canfield Marshall, a club steward. In 1926, he left Baltimore to attend the all-black Lincoln University in Chester, Pennsylvania, where he developed a reputation as an outstanding debater. After graduating in 1930, Marshall entered Howard University in Washington, D.C., to study law.

While he was in college, Marshall developed a lifelong interest in civil rights. After graduating first in his law school class in 1933, he began a

Associate Justice Thurgood Marshall holds the distinction of having been the first African American to serve on the U.S. Supreme Court. Before serving, he had a noteworthy career as chief counsel for the National Association of Colored People (NAACP) and was the organization's lawyer in *Brown v. Board of Education* (1954), the landmark case that overturned the "separate but equal" doctrine, which had provided the legal basis for racial discrimination in the United States. (Library of Congress, Prints and Photographs Division)

In 1961, President John F. Kennedy (1961–1963) appointed Marshall to the Second Circuit Court of Appeals. Opposition from Southern Democratic senators delayed his confirmation for a year. Four years later, President Lyndon B. Johnson chose Marshall to be the nation's first black solicitor general. The government's chief advocate before the Court, Marshall scored impressive victories in the areas of civil and constitutional rights, including winning Court approval of the 1965 Voting Rights Act.

On June 13, 1967, President Johnson chose Marshall to become the first black justice of the Court. He is known for his majority opinion in *Stanley v. Georgia* (1969), which held that the Constitution protects a person's right to read anything he chooses in the privacy of his home. In *Benton v. Maryland* (1969), he wrote the opinion that applies the double jeopardy clause of the Constitution to state actions. Opposed to the death penalty, Marshall joined his colleague William Brennan in dissenting in every case that upheld it. After nearly a quarter century of service on the Court, Marshall retired on October 1, 1991.

See also: Associate Justices; *Brown v Board of Education* (1954); Civil Rights and the Supreme Court; Right to Vote.

McCulloch v. Maryland (1819)

Supreme Court ruling that established the principle that Congress could pass laws in areas where the Constitution did not give it specific power to act. In its decision, the Court ruled that Congress enjoys implied powers to implement the powers expressly granted it by the Constitution. The Court stated that Congress has the power to pass laws "necessary and proper" to exercise its constitutional powers. The justices also decided that states may not take actions that block the federal government from exercising its authority under the Constitution.

Basis of the Case

In 1816, Congress incorporated a national bank that was extremely unpopular, particularly in the

long involvement with the National Association for the Advancement of Colored People (NAACP). In 1940, he became the head of the newly formed NAACP Legal Defense and Education Fund, a position he held for more than twenty years.

Marshall coordinated the fund's attack on segregation in voting, housing, public accommodations, and education. The culmination of his career as a civil rights attorney came in 1954 as chief counsel in a series of cases grouped under the title *Brown v. Board of Education*. In that historic case, which Marshall argued before the Supreme Court, civil rights advocates convinced the Court to declare segregation in public schools unconstitutional.

Southern states. Many of these states tried to keep it from opening branches at all or, failing that, tried to tax branches out of existence. Maryland chose the latter strategy, imposing a hefty tax on the notes issued by the bank's Baltimore branch.

James McCulloch, a bank cashier, refused to pay the tax. He claimed the state tax was an unconstitutional infringement on the federally chartered bank. For its part, Maryland argued that Congress had exceeded its powers when it chartered the bank. The state also claimed that in any event it had the power to tax the bank within its borders.

The Court's Ruling

Writing for the majority, Chief Justice John Marshall first upheld the power of Congress to incorporate the bank. He noted that the national government is "one of enumerated powers," but asserted that "though limited in its powers [it] is supreme within its sphere of action." The Constitution said nothing about the power to establish a bank and create corporations, Marshall acknowledged, but it did grant Congress "great powers"—to tax, to regulate commerce, to declare war, and to support and maintain armies and navies. It also gave Congress "ample means for their execution." Incorporation, Marshall said, was one of these means.

In the remainder of the opinion, Marshall developed the now-famous doctrine that "the power to tax involves the power to destroy." Therefore, the state tax on the federal bank threatened the supremacy of the federal government.

Aftermath and Significance

In the eyes of constitutional scholar Robert G. McCloskey, *McCulloch v. Maryland* was "by almost any reckoning the greatest decision John Marshall ever handed down—the one most important to the future of America, most influential in the court's own doctrinal history, and most revealing of Marshall's unique talent for stately argument." It should be noted that the Jeffersonians were furious over this decision. Virginians Spencer Roane and John Taylor of South Carolina wrote lengthy attacks on it. Marshall responded anonymously as "A Friend of the Constitution" in the *Alexandria Gazette*.

McCulloch forcefully upheld the supremacy of federal law over conflicting state law. It reaffirmed the Court's judicial review powers, and espoused a broad construction of the "necessary and proper" clause in particular and congressional power in general that has been in use ever since. Hardly a bill passed by Congress does not rely to some extent on the "necessary and proper" clause for its validity. It has been especially significant to congressional control over fiscal affairs and to the establishment of the vast network of regulatory agencies. As Marshall pointed out, it is the basis of the federal power to punish violations of the law. It is also the foundation for the doctrine of eminent domain. All these powers have in one way or another touched the life of every citizen of the United States. Marshall's contribution was summarized by R. Kent Newmyer:

> As in *Marbury v. Madison*, the genius of the *McCulloch* opinion lay not in its originality but in its timing, practicability, clarity and eloquence. Original it was not. . . . Marshall did not create these nationalist principles. What he did do was seize them at the moment when they were most relevant to American needs and congenial to the American mind, and (aided by the rhetoric of Alexander Hamilton) he translated them gracefully and logically into the law of the Constitution. Basing his interpretation of the law on the needs and spirit of the age, Marshall gave it permanence. Hamilton himself was unable to do as much.

See also: Implied Powers; 📖 *McCulloch v. Marykand*, 1819, in the **Primary Source Library.**

Further Reading

Crompton, Samuel Willard. *McCulloch V. Maryland: Implied Powers of the Federal Government*. New York: Chelsea House Publications, 2007.

Gold, Susan Dudley. *McCulloch V. Maryland: State v Federal Power*. New York: Benchmark Books, 2007.

Miranda v. Arizona (1966)

Supreme Court case that established formal guidelines for the interrogation practices of state and local police. The ruling required that police inform suspects of their constitutional rights at the time of arrest, what are now referred to as one's "Miranda rights." These include the right to remain silent and the right to be represented by counsel.

Basis of the Case

Ernesto Miranda was convicted of kidnapping and rape in Arizona. Miranda made statements to police during his interrogation that the prosecution later used as evidence against him. Police did not notify Miranda of his rights to remain silent and to consult an attorney. Miranda challenged his conviction, claiming that police obtained it in violation of the Fifth Amendment guarantee against self-incrimination.

The Court's Ruling

In a 5-4 vote, the Court upheld Miranda's challenge. It ruled that interrogators must make a suspect aware of his or her constitutional rights to remain silent and to have the aid of an attorney. If they fail to do so, prosecutors may not use incriminating statements obtained during interrogation as evidence in court. "The presence of

Law enforcement officials carry cards similar to this one to inform arrested persons of their rights. The landmark ruling in *Miranda v. Arizona* (1966) guarantees that persons accused of a crime have the right to remain silent and to meet with an attorney. (The Granger Collection, New York)

Landmark Decision Highlights: *Miranda v. Arizona* (1966)

Issue: Does the practice of interrogating individuals without notifying them of their right to counsel and their protection against self-incrimination violate the Fifth Amendment?

Opinion: In its ruling, the Court specifically outlined the necessary aspects of police warnings to suspects, including warnings of the right to remain silent and the right to have counsel present during questioning. The Court ruled that prosecutors could not use statements stemming from the interrogation of defendants unless they demonstrated the use of procedural safeguards "effective to secure the privilege against self-incrimination."

counsel," stated Chief Justice Earl Warren for the majority, was "the adequate protective device" to "insure that statements made in the government-established atmosphere are not the product of compulsion."

Warren explained that the Fifth Amendment requires that all interrogation must cease whenever a suspect indicates a desire to remain silent. "At this point he has shown that he intends to exercise his Fifth Amendment privilege," wrote the chief justice. Therefore, "any statement taken after the person invokes his privilege cannot be other than the product of compulsion, subtle or otherwise."

Dissent and Aftermath

Justices Tom C. Clark, John Marshall Harlan II, Byron R. White, and Potter Stewart dissented. They felt the Court should continue to look at the "totality of the circumstances" when determining the admissibility of confessions. Justice Harlan criticized the ruling as "poor constitutional law," while White argued that the majority had misread the Fifth Amendment prohibition against self-incrimination:

Confessions and incriminating admissions, as such, are not forbidden evidence; only those which are compelled are banned. I doubt that the Court observes these distinctions today. . . .

The obvious underpinning of the Court's decision is a deep-seated distrust of all confessions. . . . There is, in my view, every reason to believe that a good many criminal defendants, who otherwise would have been convicted on what this Court has previously thought to be the most satisfactory kind of evidence, will now, under this new version of the Fifth Amendment, either not be tried at all or will be acquitted if the State's evidence, minus the confession, is put to the test of litigation."

The decision in *Miranda v. Arizona* was one of a series of rulings by the court in the 1950s and 1960s that extended the specific protections of the Bill of Rights to state defendants. This brought criticism of the Court to a peak in the late 1960s. One of the major themes of the 1968 presidential campaign was "law and order"—a phrase that the winning candidate, Richard M. Nixon (1969–1974), used to criticize the Court's rulings.

Many members of Congress also were persuaded that the Court was encouraging crime by impeding law enforcement officers in their duties. In the Crime Control and Safe Streets Act of 1968, Congress included provisions intended to blunt or overrule the effect of *Miranda*. The law stated that confessions could be used in federal courts whenever the judge found them voluntary. The 1968 law, however, affected only federal trials, not state trials. The states remained bound by the *Miranda* requirements.

Despite opposition to *Miranda*, the Court stood by the decision. Early in 1969, the Court held that *Miranda* required that police must warn suspects of their constitutional rights before questioning them, even when the interrogation takes place in the suspect's home. Over the next twenty-five years, however, the Court declined to extend *Miranda* protections further. It also allowed a number of indirect uses of statements and other evidence obtained from persons not warned of their rights.

See also: Confessions; 📖 *Miranda v. Arizona,* 1966, in the **Primary Source Library**; Self-Incrimination.

Further Reading

Kelly-Gangi, Carol. *Miranda V. Arizona And the Rights of the Accused: Debating Supreme Court Decisions.* Berkeley Heights, N.J.: Enslow Publishers

Vanmeter, Larry A. *Miranda V. Arizona.* New York: Chelsea House Publications, 2006.

Wice, Paul B. *Miranda V. Arizona: "You Have the Right to Remain Silent . . .".* London, UK: Franklin Watts, 1996.

New Deal and the Supreme Court

Supreme Court rulings on President Franklin D. Roosevelt's (1933–1945) "New Deal" economic legislation during the **Great Depression** of the 1930s. The Court's rejection of many early New Deal programs led Roosevelt to consider packing the Court with judges sympathetic to his plans. In the end, however, the president and the Court avoided a direct confrontation, and much of the New Deal legislation went into effect.

Sources of the Conflict

The stock market crash of 1929 and the ensuing Great Depression were economic crises of proportions unprecedented in U.S. history. Herbert C. Hoover (1929–1933), who was president at the time of the crash, felt that the economy would correct itself. He did not believe in broad governmental relief or social reform programs. The public was calling for action, however, and in 1932, they elected Franklin D. Roosevelt president by a wide margin.

In his first one hundred days in office, Roosevelt led the Congress in attacking the Great Depression on all fronts through his plan called the New Deal. Congress passed a series of bills that regulated banking and involved government heavily in agriculture and industry. To keep farmers from going bankrupt, the government offered farmers payments to control production, agricultural practices, and prices. The National Industrial Recovery Act (NIRA) established "codes of fair competition" for wages, prices, and trade practices in industry. In addition, the NIRA stipulated that labor had the right to organize workers for collective bargaining.

Roosevelt maintained that the New Deal had its constitutional basis in the president's emergency executive powers, and the Congress's power to provide for the general welfare and to regulate interstate commerce. At the time, it was the most far-reaching assertion of the power of the federal government.

The Supreme Court of 1933 was not receptive to revolutionary uses of federal power. Nevertheless, in 1934, the Court seemed to hint that it would take a favorable attitude toward the "emergency" exercise of extraordinary power in the New Deal statutes. The Court rejected two challenges to New Deal programs in 1934. Between January 1935 and June 1936, however, the Court ruled against the administration in eight out of ten cases involving New Deal statutes.

Roosevelt's Counterattack

Unlike the Court, the American public overwhelmingly approved of Roosevelt's economic plans, reelecting him in a landslide in 1936. The Court's opposition to such a popular program and equally popular president began to produce a view of the Court as an obstacle to reform. Members of Congress even recommended that Congress curtail the Court's **jurisdiction,** or area of authority. It was Roosevelt, though, who led the counterattack.

On February 5, 1937, Roosevelt sent Congress a message proposing a judicial "reorganization." According to Roosevelt's plan, for every Supreme Court justice age seventy and a half or above, the president could appoint another one, up to a maximum of six. The measure would have increased the number of Court justices to as many as fifteen. Roosevelt also called for adding new judges to the federal courts and changing the procedures for hearing constitutional challenges to acts of Congress. He presented the plan as a bill to relieve the justices' workload. It was, however, a "Court-packing" scheme to get Roosevelt-appointed justices on the bench to reverse the Court's anti-New Deal stance.

Conflict and Compromise

The plan touched off a widespread and bitter debate in Congress and in the nation. Even some of the president's political allies were opposed to the plan. The public also expressed displeasure with the proposed "reorganization." The Court itself dealt the death blow to the Court-packing plan with a series of decisions announced between late March and late May 1936 upholding New Deal measures. In several 5-4 decisions, Justice Owen Roberts abandoned the four conservatives with whom he had voted in previous decisions, and cast the deciding vote in support of the New Deal programs.

Other developments also spelled defeat for the plan. Arkansas Senator "Joe" Robinson, who led the Senate fight on behalf of Roosevelt's plan, died of a heart attack on July 14, 1937. The president eventually accepted a watered-down bill that reformed lower court procedures but left the number of Supreme Court justices unchanged. Retirements also allowed Roosevelt to make four appointments to the Court between 1937 and 1940, which helped ensure the success of his New Deal legislation.

See also: Presidency and the Supreme Court; Roosevelt's 1937 Court Reform Plan.

New York Times v. Sullivan (1964)

Supreme Court decision that declared public officials suing for libel must prove "actual malice" upon the part of the defendant. The Court ruled that factual errors made about a public official's actions were not sufficient grounds for libel. Only if the defendant made false charges knowingly and with ill intent could an official sue for libel.

Basis of the Case

L.B. Sullivan was an elected commissioner of Montgomery, Alabama, responsible for the police department. He sued the *New York Times* and four black clergymen for libel as a result of an advertisement the clergymen had placed in the newspaper on March 29, 1960. The advertisement called attention to the violence with which the civil rights movement in the South had been met. Sullivan's libel suit was based on the following two paragraphs:

In Montgomery, Alabama, after students sang "My Country, 'Tis of Thee" on the State Capitol steps, their leaders were expelled from school, and truckloads of police armed with shotguns and tear-gas ringed the Alabama State College Campus. When the entire student body protested to state authorities by refusing to re-register, their dining hall was padlocked in an attempt to starve them into submission . . .

Again and again the Southern violators have answered Dr. King's peaceful protests with intimidation and violence. They have bombed his home almost killing his wife and child. They have assaulted his person. They have arrested him seven times—for "speeding," "loitering" and similar "offenses." And now they have charged him with "perjury"—a felony under which they could imprison him for ten years.

The advertisement did not refer to Sullivan personally, but Sullivan claimed that the references to police included him. The two paragraphs also

SPOTLIGHT

Group Libel

States occasionally have sought to quiet racial and religious intolerance and unrest by enacting laws that make it illegal to defame groups of people. Although such laws clearly restrain the freedom of the press to discuss public issues, the Court upheld them in the only case it has heard on the validity of group libel laws. The justices held that the First Amendment offered no protection for such statements.

Beauharnais v. Illinois (1952) concerned a man who headed an organization called the White Circle League. He distributed leaflets making clearly racist statements about blacks and calling on the mayor and city council to protect white residents and neighborhoods against harassment by blacks. Beauharnais was convicted of violating an Illinois group libel statute that made it illegal to publish anything defamatory or derogatory about "a class of citizens of any race, color, creed or religion." The Court upheld the conviction.

For the majority, Justice Felix Frankfurter observed that "if an utterance directed at an individual may be the object of criminal sanctions, we cannot deny to a State power to punish the same utterance directed at a defined group." Frankfurter declared that the First Amendment was irrelevant to this case because the Court had ruled earlier that the amendment afforded no protection for libel. Later Court decisions found that both civil and criminal libels are within the scope of the First Amendment protections, but the Court has not reconsidered its decision in *Beauharnais*.

contained errors. The students sang the national anthem, not "My Country, 'Tis of Thee." Several students were expelled from the school for demanding service at an all-white lunch counter, but not for leading the demonstration at the capitol. Students protested by boycotting classes for a day, not by refusing to re-register. The campus dining room was never padlocked; the only students denied access to it were those who did not have meal tickets. King had been arrested four times, not seven times. The suit was tried under Alabama libel law, and Sullivan was awarded damages of five hundred thousand dollars.

The Court's Ruling

The *Times* appealed the decision to the Court, which unanimously reversed it. Writing for six justices, Justice William Brennan stated that courts have recognized that "erroneous statement is inevitable in free debate, and that it must be

protected if the freedoms of expression are to have the 'breathing space' that they 'need . . . to survive.'" This was true of speech about public officials as well as public issues, Brennan noted. Brennan then set out the standard for determining whether defamatory statements about public officials are protected by the First Amendment:

The constitutional guarantees require, we think, a federal rule that prohibits a public official from recovering damages for a defamatory falsehood relating to his official conduct unless he proves that the statement was made with "actual malice"—that is, with knowledge that it was false or with reckless disregard of whether it was false or not.

This standard became known as the *New York Times* rule or actual malice rule. In applying that rule to the circumstances of the Sullivan case, the Court discovered no evidence that the individual clergymen knew their statements to be false or were reckless. Although the *Times* had information in its news files that would have corrected some of the errors, the Court did not find that the *Times* personnel had acted with any actual malice.

Aftermath and Significance

In a series of subsequent decisions, the Court elaborated on its *New York Times* rule. In *Herbert v. Lando* (1979), the Court rejected a television producer's claim that the First Amendment protected him from having to answer questions about the editorial process of a certain story. Since that time, the Court has been seriously divided in determining against what category of person the *New York Times* rule operates. All the justices have agreed that public officials and public figures must show actual malice to win damages. After a brief period when the Court seemed to apply the actual malice standard to suits brought by private individuals involving matters of public concern, it now allows states to set less stringent standards of proof for private citizens alleging libel.

See also: 📖 *New York Times v. Sullivan*, 1964, in the **Primary Source Library;** Freedom of the Press; Libel.

Landmark Decision Highlights: *New York Times v. Sullivan* (1964)

Issue: To what extent do the First Amendment protections for speech and press limit a state's power to award damages in a libel action brought by a public official against critics of his official conduct?

Opinion: In its ruling, the Court held that the First Amendment protects the publication of all statements, even false ones, about the conduct of public officials except when statements are made with actual malice—with knowledge that they are false or in reckless disregard of their truth.

Further Reading

Gold, Susan Dudley. *New York Times Co. v. Sullivan: Freedom of the Press or Libel?.* New York: Benchmark Books, 2006.

Ninth Amendment

See Right to Privacy.

Obscenity

Words, acts, or expressions considered lewd or indecent. Although this category of material can be very broad, the Court has consistently agreed that to be considered obscene, material must deal with sex.

The Court has never considered obscenity to be protected by the First Amendment. Obscenity is one category of expression that is unprotected, because it is "no essential part of any exposition of ideas, and of . . . slight social value as a step to truth." Perhaps the major difficulty in dealing with obscenity as a legal concept is defining it. That challenge has proved frustrating. As Justice Potter Stewart famously stated, while obscenity is hard to define, "I know it when I see it."

The Court did not express any opinion on a definition of obscenity until *Roth v. United States* (1957).

Obscenity: An Elusive Definition and a Changing Standard

The *Roth* Standard

The Court did not express any opinion on a definition of obscenity until the 1950s, when, in one ruling, it considered a federal and a state obscenity law. *Roth v. United States* (1957) concerned a federal statute making it a crime to mail materials that were "obscene, lewd, lascivious or filthy." *Alberts v. California* (1957) concerned a state law making it illegal to publish, sell, distribute, or advertise any "obscene or indecent" material. The majority relied heavily on Judge Learned Hand's test in establishing what became known as the "*Roth* standard." Obscene matter, declared the Court, has no First Amendment protection. Justice William J. Brennan Jr. wrote:

> All ideas having even the slightest redeeming social importance—unorthodox ideas, controversial ideas, even ideas hateful to the prevailing climate of opinion—have the full protection of the guaranties, unless excludable because they encroach upon the limited area of more important interests. But implicit in the history of the First Amendment is the rejection of obscenity as utterly without redeeming social importance.

Brennan then proposed a definition of obscenity:

> [S]ex and obscenity are not synonymous. Obscene material is material which deals with sex in a manner appealing to prurient interest. The portrayal of sex, e.g., in art, literature, and scientific works is not itself sufficient reason to deny material the constitutional protection of freedom of speech and press. . . . It is therefore vital that the standards for judging obscenity safeguard the protection of freedom of speech and press for material which does not treat sex in a manner appealing to prurient interest.

The standard for making this determination, Brennan said, was "whether to the average person, applying contemporary standards, the dominant theme of the material taken as a whole appeals to the prurient interest." Finding that the trial courts in *Roth* and *Albert* had applied this standard to hold the material in question obscene, the majority upheld convictions under both the federal and state laws.

After *Roth*, the Court grew increasingly fragmented on what makes material obscene. In *Manual Enterprises v. Day* (1962), Justice John Marshall Harlan II held that to be obscene, material must not only appeal to prurient interest but also be patently offensive. That is, he wrote, obscene materials are those "so offensive on their face as to affront current community standards of decency." Because the case involved a federal obscenity statute, Harlan thought the community and the standards of decency should be national in scope. Two years later, in *Jacobellis v. Ohio* (1964), Justice Brennan added the requirement that the materials in question must be found "utterly without redeeming social importance." Justice Potter Stewart added in a concurrence in *Jacobellis* that while obscenity is hard to define, "I know it when I see it."

The height of confusion over a definition of obscenity was reached one day in 1966, when the Court, deciding three cases, issued fourteen separate opinions. In one case, the Court ruled that the book *Fanny Hill* was not obscene. The threefold test to be applied was that the dominant theme of the book must appeal to prurient interest, that the book must be found patently offensive when judged by contemporary community standards, and that it must be found utterly without redeeming social value. Because the trial court had found that the book might have "some minimal literary value," it was not obscene.

(continued on next page)

Obscenity: An Elusive Definition and a Changing Standard, *continued*

The *Miller* Standard

In the early 1970s, for the first time since the 1957 *Roth* decision, a slim majority of the Court endorsed a standard for determining what was obscene. This new standard gave governments at all levels much more latitude to ban obscene materials than did the *Roth* test. Writing for the five-justice majority in *Miller v. California* (1973), Chief Justice Warren E. Burger held that states could regulate:

> . . . works which depict or describe sexual conduct. That conduct must be specifically defined by the applicable state law, as written or authoritatively construed. A state offense must also be limited to works which, taken as a whole, appeal to the prurient interest in sex, which portray sexual conduct in a patently offensive way, and which, taken as a whole, do not have serious literary, artistic, political or scientific value.

Under this standard, Burger said, the majority intended to exclude only hardcore materials from First Amendment protection. As a guideline, he suggested that such materials were those that included "patently offensive representations or descriptions of ultimate sexual acts, normal or perverted, actual or simulated" and "patently offensive representations or descriptions of masturbation, excretory functions, and lewd exhibition of the genitals."

The majority specifically rejected the *Jacobellis* test that to be obscene, materials must be "utterly without redeeming social value." It also rejected the idea that the community standard must be national in scope. "It is neither realistic nor constitutionally sound to read the First Amendment as requiring that the people of Maine or Mississippi accept public depiction of conduct found tolerable in Las Vegas or New York City," Burger wrote.

The majority stressed that First Amendment values would be adequately protected by this standard. Burger noted that appellate courts had the authority to "conduct an independent review of constitutional claims when necessary." The Court did just that when it overturned a Georgia jury's finding that the movie *Carnal Knowledge* was obscene. Holding that local juries did not have "unbridled discretion" to determine what is patently offensive, the Court in *Jenkins v. Georgia* (1974) found nothing in the movie that fit its *Miller* standards for what might constitute hardcore obscenity. The Court subsequently upheld state laws prohibiting the promotion of sexual performances by children but struck down a state law banning material just because it incited lust. That covered material that did no more than "arouse 'good, old-fashioned, healthy' interest in sex."

In 1982, the Court held that the First Amendment limited the power of public school officials to take books off the library shelves because some parents found the contents objectionable. Four years later, the Court held that the First Amendment was not abridged when school officials suspended a student for a lewd speech at a school assembly. "It is a highly appropriate function of public school education to prohibit the use of vulgar and offensive terms in public discourse," the Court declared.

In *Pope v. Illinois* (1987), the Court revisited the *Miller* test for "literary, artistic, political, or scientific value." The justices declared that local community standards should not be used in deciding whether an allegedly obscene book or film has any such value. Instead, an objective, national standard should be used, with the overriding question being whether a reasonable person would find value in the material, taken as a whole.

The Supreme Court has never considered obscenity to be protected by the First Amendment. Obscenity is one category of expression that is unprotected because it is "no essential part of any exposition of ideas, and of . . . slight social value as a step to truth." The only criterion the Court has consistently agreed upon is that to be obscene, material must deal with sex.

This case concerned a federal statute making it a crime to mail materials that were "obscene, lewd, lascivious or filthy." The majority relied heavily on Judge Learned Hand's test in establishing what became known as the "*Roth* standard." Obscene matter, declared the Court, has no First Amendment protection.

Justice William J. Brennan also proposed a definition of obscenity as "material which deals with sex in a manner appealing to prurient interest." The standard for making this determination, Brennan said, was "whether to the average person, applying contemporary standards, the dominant theme of the material taken as a whole appeals to the prurient interest."

After *Roth,* the Court grew increasingly fragmented on what makes material obscene. However, in the early 1970s, a slim majority of the Court endorsed a standard for determining obscenity. This new standard gave governments at all levels much more latitude to ban obscene materials than did the *Roth* test. Writing for the five-justice majority in *Miller v. California* (1973), Chief Justice Warren E. Burger held that states could regulate works that depict or describe sexual conduct "in a patently offensive way, and which, taken as a whole, do not have serious literary, artistic, political or scientific value."

In *Pope v. Illinois* (1987), the Court revisited the *Miller* test for "literary, artistic, political, or scientific value." The justices declared that local community standards should not be used in deciding whether an allegedly obscene book or film has any such value. Instead, an objective, national standard should be used, with the overriding question being whether a reasonable person would find value in the material, taken as a whole.

See also: Freedom of the Press.

O'Connor, Sandra Day (1930–)

Associate justice of the U.S. Supreme Court, appointed by President Ronald Reagan (1981–1989) and confirmed by the Senate on September 25, 1981. She was the 102nd justice to serve on the Court and the first woman to do so. During her

twenty-five years on the Court, O'Connor was frequently the deciding vote in many 5-4 decisions. For this reason, her retirement in 2006 led to a spirited battle over her replacement.

Early Life and Education
O'Connor was born Sandra Day, in El Paso, Texas, and spent summers on the 162,000-acre (65,559-hectare) ranch that her grandfather had founded in southeastern Arizona. After graduating from high school at age sixteen, Day earned a degree in economics from Stanford University in 1950. She received her law degree from Stanford two years later. She was an editor of the *Stanford Law Review* and a member of Order of the Coif, a legal honorary society.

As a woman, O'Connor had difficulty finding work as an attorney, and she turned to public service. She served as deputy county attorney of San Mateo County, California, from 1952–1953. She also worked as a civilian attorney for Quartermaster Market Center, Frankfurt, Germany, where her husband, John Jay O'Connor III, was stationed from 1954–1957. After returning to the United States, she finally had the opportunity to practice law as an attorney in Phoenix, Arizona.

Public Career
In 1965, O'Connor became an assistant attorney general of Arizona, the first woman to hold the position. After four years, she was appointed to the state senate, and the following year she won election to that body. During her six years as a state senator, she served for two years as majority leader—the first woman in the nation to hold such a post of legislative leadership.

In 1974, O'Connor was elected to the superior court of Maricopa County, and, five years later, Arizona Governor Bruce Babbitt appointed her to the Arizona Court of Appeals. In 1981, President Reagan chose her as his first nominee to the Supreme Court. Once again, Sandra Day O'Connor was "the first woman"—this time, the first to sit on the U.S. Supreme Court.

Supreme Court Justice
On the Court, O'Connor was at first solidly in the conservative wing, but over time she moved to the center. After the retirement of Justice Lewis F. Powell Jr. in 1987, O'Connor became the Court's pivotal justice, the one whose vote decided

A – Z

Sandra Day O'Connor, the first woman to serve on the Supreme Court, takes the oath of office from Chief Justice Warren Burger (left) on September 25, 1981. Justice O'Connor's husband, John J. O'Connor III, holds the family's bibles. (AP Photo, Michael Evans)

the crucial cases. She defined the Court's position in areas such as religion, abortion, affirmative action, and the death penalty. In 1992, O'Connor joined David Souter, who announced his retirement in 2009, and Anthony Kennedy in a plurality opinion that affirmed *Roe v. Wade* (1973), which guarantees a woman's right to have an abortion. While states may regulate abortion, they may not place an "undue burden" before women who seek an abortion prior to the time a fetus may live on its own, O'Connor decided.

As an advocate of federalism, O'Connor played a key role in the long line of decisions that limited federal power and upheld states' rights. In 2000, she cast the deciding fifth vote in *United States v. Morrison* to strike down the federal Violence Against Women Act. She believed that the law crossed the line by authorizing federal courts to decide state and local offenses. In *Kimel v. Florida* (2000) and *Board of Trustees of the University of*

Alabama v. Garrett (2001), O'Connor also spoke for the Court in shielding states from being sued by state employees who alleged that they were victims of discrimination because of their age or disability.

O'Connor usually supported the death penalty, but in 2002, she cast a key vote to outlaw its use against mentally retarded defendants. Her crucial role was apparent in 2003, when the Court narrowly upheld affirmative action in colleges and university admissions. "In a society, like our own, in which race unfortunately still matters," universities may give extra consideration to qualified minority applicants, she said for the 5-4 majority in *Grutter v. Bollinger*.

On July 1, 2005, O'Connor announced she planned to retire, saying she wanted to spend more time caring for her husband, John, who was suffering from Alzheimer's disease. However, when Chief Justice William C. Rehnquist died in

September of that year, she agreed to stay on for several more months until President George W. Bush (2001–2009) could appoint a new chief justice to succeed Rehnquist and a new associate justice to replace her. Bush's nominee, Harriet Miers, eventually withdrew her name following widespread criticism of her qualifications. Samuel Alito eventually filled O'Connor's seat in January 2006.

See also: 📖 Associate Justice Sandra Day O'Connor's Letter of Resignation, July 1, 2005, in the **Primary Source Library;** Associate Justices; Confirmation of Justices and Judges.

One Person, One Vote

The principle that each person's vote in a statewide election should have the same weight as every other person's vote. The Court first set forth the one person, one vote principle in *Gray v. Sanders* (1963), when the Court found Georgia's county-unit primary system for electing state officials denied voters the equal protection of the laws. The system weighted votes to give rural districts greater influence than urban districts in statewide primary elections

The following year, in *Wesberry v. Sanders* (1964), the Court applied the one person, one vote principle to congressional districts. Voters in Georgia's Fifth Congressional District complained that the population of their congressional district was more than twice the ideal state average of 394,312 persons per district, but the state refused to create new districts to reflect the increased population. They argued that this failure denied them equal protection of the laws. In the majority opinion, Justice Hugo Black wrote:

To say that a vote is worth more in one district than in another would not only run counter to our fundamental ideas of democratic government, it would cast aside the principle of a House of Representatives elected "by the People."

While it may not be possible to draw congressional districts with mathematical precision, that is no excuse for

ignoring our Constitution's plain objective of making equal representation for equal numbers the fundamental goal of the House of Representatives.

In *Reynolds v. Sims* (1964), the Court ruled that the Fourteenth Amendment required equally populated electoral districts for both houses of state legislatures. The Court rejected the suggestion that a state might choose one house of its legislature on the basis of population and the other on an area basis. Chief Justice Warren explained that, unlike the federal government, political subdivisions of states, like cities and countries were never considered "sovereign entities." The Fourteenth Amendment's **equal protection clause** required substantially equal representation of all citizens. The Court did not provide any precise formula for defining "substantially equal" and left it to lower courts to work out a useful standard. Chief Justice Earl Warren set forth the reasoning behind the one person, one vote rule with clarity and firmness:

Legislators represent people, not trees or acres. Legislators are elected by voters, not farms or cities or economic interests. As long as ours is a representative form of government, and our legislatures are those instruments of government elected directly by and directly representative of the people, the right to elect legislators in a free and unimpaired fashion is a bedrock of our political system. . . .

See also: Baker v. Carr (1962).

Original Jurisdiction

See Jurisdiction of the Supreme Court.

Opinions

Written statements, issued by one or more justices after the conclusion of a Court case, that explain the legal reasoning behind the authors' decision.

A–Z

There are three basic types of opinions: the majority opinion, dissenting opinions, and concurring opinions. The majority opinion is the most important of the three, because it reflects the reasoning of most of the justices. Dissenting and concurring opinions, however, also are significant because they may form the basis for future rulings on the same or related matters.

Forming and Assigning Opinion

Opinions on a case first take shape at the conclusion of oral arguments before the Court. At this time, the justices meet "in conference" to discuss the matters of law raised by the case. Beginning with the most junior justice and continuing in ascending order of seniority, each justice states how he or she would rule in the case and explains the legal reasoning behind that decision.

After counting the votes and deciding which party has prevailed, one justice who voted with the majority is chosen to write the majority opinion. The most senior justice among the majority determines who will write the opinion. If the chief justice votes with the majority, he or she assigns the opinion. In the rare case of a tie vote, the decision of the lower court stands and no opinions are written. Only justices who are on the Court from the time it hears oral arguments in a case to the time the Court issues its decision may take part in writing an opinion.

Majority Decisions

Although one justice serves as lead author of the majority opinion, the final opinion does not reflect his or her reasoning alone. The process of writing an opinion comprises several stages and involves all of the justices in the majority.

The justice assigned to write the opinion starts by creating a first draft that he or she then circulates to the other justices. Often the justice chosen to write the opinion assigns this task to a law clerk. After the other judges review the draft, they may suggest changes to the opinion. It is up to the assigned author to determine whether to accept or reject these suggestions. Authoring justices typically are less likely to include changes that do not align with their own judicial philosophy.

Another consideration in the drafting process is the fact that votes at this stage of the trial are not final. Justices may still change their minds

and vote with the previous minority. This may swing the balance of the vote, changing the final decision. The fewer justices who voted in the majority, the more likely the writer is to consider their views when crafting the opinion.

The majority opinion typically is signed by the author on behalf of the other members of the majority, who are named in the opinion. Occasionally, however, the majority issues an unsigned, or *per curiam,* opinion. Perhaps the most prominent recent example of a *per curiam* opinion is *Bush v. Gore* (2000), which ended the presidential vote recount in Florida and effectively awarded the presidency to George W. Bush (2001–2009).

Dissenting Opinions

A justice who votes with the minority may issue a dissenting opinion, which explains the reasoning behind his or her disagreement with the majority opinion. Because dissenting opinions reflect the judicial philosophy of a specific justice, they do not go through the same process of drafting and circulation to other justices as does the majority opinion.

Although dissenting opinions do not have the weight of law, they serve significant functions in the operation of the court. Perhaps the most important of these is to serve as the basis for deciding future cases. No Court decision is set in stone; some of the most famous decisions in the Court's history were overturned by later Courts, often using reasoning based on dissents from the earlier decisions. More immediately, a well-argued dissent may be enough to persuade a member of the majority to switch his or her vote before the final decision is announced.

Concurring Opinions

In many cases, a justice will vote with the majority but disagree with the legal reasoning the other justices used to decide the case. In these instances, the first justice will write what is known as a concurring opinion. The opinion expresses the author's agreement with the decision itself, but also outlines where the author disagrees with the legal reasoning of his or her colleagues in the majority. As with dissenting opinions, the reasoning set forth in concurring opinions may form the basis for decisions in future cases.

Pentagon Papers

Series of articles printed in the *The New York Times* in June 1971, concerning U.S. involvement in the Vietnam War (1959–1975), which led to an unprecedented legal confrontation between the U.S. government and the press. The administration of President Richard M. Nixon (1969–1974) asked the Court to prohibit the *Times* from publishing the articles, arguing that publication would cause "irreparable injury to the defense interests of the U.S."

Basis of the Case

The Pentagon Papers were based upon a forty-seven-volume, seven thousand-page classified history of U.S. involvement in Vietnam from the late 1940s to the late 1960s. They indicated that the U.S. government was more involved in the Vietnamese civil war at almost every stage than U.S. officials had ever publicly admitted. Daniel Ellsberg, a defense analyst who had helped prepare the history, provided copies to the press.

The New York Times was the first newspaper to publish articles based on the papers; the first installment appeared in its June 13, 1971, edition. The following day, after the second installment appeared, the Justice Department asked the *Times* to return the documents and to halt publication of the series. The *Times* refused to comply.

On June 15, U.S. District Court Judge Murray I. Gurfein ordered the *Times* to halt publication temporarily. After hearing the government's arguments, Gurfein ruled on June 19 that the government was not entitled to a permanent **injunction,** or court order, forbidding publication of further articles. The government appealed the decision, and the appeals court on June 23 returned the case to the lower court for further hearings. It also extended until June 25 an order preventing

the *Times* from publishing more articles in the meantime. The *Times* then asked the Supreme Court to review the order by the court of appeals.

The Court's Decision

The Court heard arguments in the *Pentagon Papers Case* (1971) on June 26 and announced its decision four days later. In a 6-3 vote, the Court ruled that the government had failed to meet "the heavy burden of showing justification" for restraining further publications of the Pentagon Papers. Each of the nine justices wrote a separate opinion. Taken together, these opinions covered the wide range of sentiment that exists when a First Amendment right must be weighed against national security claims.

In separate concurring opinions, Justices Hugo Black and William O. Douglas maintained that freedom of the press was absolute and could not be abridged by the government under any circumstances. Justice William J. Brennan Jr. thought the government might properly restrain the press in certain clear emergencies, but the circumstances of this case did not present such an emergency, according to him. The government sought the injunction on the grounds that the publication "could," "might," or "may" damage national security, Brennan said, "But the First Amendment tolerates absolutely no prior judicial restraints of the press predicated upon surmise or conjecture that untoward consequences may result."

Justices Potter Stewart and Byron R. White both also thought that prior restraints might be permissible under certain conditions. They also believed that disclosure of some of the information in the Pentagon Papers might be harmful to national interests. "But I cannot say that disclosure of any of [the papers] will surely result in direct, immediate, and irreparable damage to our Nation or its people," concluded Stewart. "That being so, there can under the First Amendment be

In 1971, Daniel Ellsberg (center), a former Department of Defense researcher, reports to a House of Representatives panel concerning allegations that he leaked top-secret reports, called the Pentagon Papers, to the press. The Pentagon Papers revealed that the United States had increased its bombing on targets in Laos and Cambodia, as well as coastal attacks on North Vietnam. (AP Photo)

but one judicial resolution of the issues before us." White said, "I am quite unable to agree that the inherent powers of the Executive and the courts reach so far as to authorize remedies having such a sweeping potential for inhibiting publications by the press."

The critical factor for Justice Thurgood Marshall was that Congress had twice refused to give the president authority to prohibit publications disclosing matters of national security or to make such disclosures criminal. It would be a violation of the doctrine of separation of powers, he said, for the Court to use its power to prevent behavior that Congress specifically declined to prohibit.

Dissent and Aftermath

Chief Justice Warren E. Burger and Justices John Marshall Harlan II and Harry A. Blackmun dissented. All three lamented the haste with which the cases had been decided. Justice Harlan listed a number of questions that he said should and would have been considered if the cases had been deliberated more fully. The three dissenters and Stewart and White from the majority indicated that they believed the newspapers might be subject to subsequent criminal penalties for publishing classified government documents, but the question never arose.

See also: Freedom of the Press.

Further Reading

Ellsberg, Daniel. *Secrets: A Memoir of Vietnam and the Pentagon Papers.* New York: Penguin, 2003.

Herring, George. *The Pentagon Papers.* New York: McGraw-Hill, 1993.

Plessy v. Ferguson (1896)

Supreme Court case that upheld the constitutionality of legally enforced racial segregation. *Plessy* was a landmark decision that represented a major reversal for the cause of civil rights. The Court's ruling allowed state-ordered segregation to stand for another sixty years.

Basis of the Case

The case was a deliberate test of the constitutionality of a Louisiana law requiring separate but equal railroad accommodations for the races. Louisiana was one of six states that by 1896 had enacted such "Jim Crow" laws segregating blacks from whites in public accommodations. Homer Plessy, a Louisiana resident who was one-eighth black and appeared white, bought a first-class train ticket from New Orleans to Covington, Louisiana. He took a seat in the coach reserved for whites. When Plessy refused to move to the black coach, he was arrested.

Plessy appealed the conviction, arguing that the state law segregating blacks and whites violated his rights under the Thirteenth and Fourteenth Amendments. He also claimed that the

A – Z

The Supreme Court's decision in *Plessy v. Ferguson* (1896) allowed states to segregate whites from blacks, as long as facilities, such as schools or bus terminals, were of equal quality. In reality, facilities for black Americans were consistently inferior. The doctrine of "separate but equal" was overturned by the Court's landmark decision in *Brown v. Board of Education* (1954). (Library of Congress, Prints and Photographs Division)

Landmark Decision Highlights: *Plessy v. Ferguson* (1896)

Issue: Was Louisiana's law mandating racial segregation on its trains an unconstitutional infringement of the equal protection clause of the Fourteenth Amendment?

Opinion: The Court ruled that the Louisiana law was constitutional. In an opinion authored by Justice Henry Billings Brown, the Court upheld state-imposed racial segregation. The justices based their decision on the "separate but equal" doctrine, which said that separate facilities for blacks and whites satisfied the Fourteenth Amendment as long as they were equal.

law unconstitutionally infringed upon Congress' power to regulate interstate commerce. After losing his appeal at the state level, Plessy appealed to the Supreme Court.

The Court's Ruling

Writing for the majority, Justice Henry B. Brown said the state law did not infringe on congressional authority over commerce because interstate commerce was not involved. "In the present case," said Brown, "no question of interference with interstate commerce can possibly arise, since the East Louisiana Railway appears to have been purely a local line, with both its termini within the State." The state statute also did not violate the Thirteenth Amendment:

A statute which implies merely a legal distinction between the white and colored races—a distinction which is founded in the color of the two races, and which must always exist so long as white men are distinguished from the other race by color—has no tendency to destroy the legal equality of the two races, or reestablish a state of involuntary servitude.

Plessy's challenge to the law as a violation of the Fourteenth Amendment also failed. The majority ruled that the amendment guaranteed only

political equality and did not encompass what the Court considered social distinctions:

The object of the [Fourteenth] Amendment was undoubtedly to enforce the absolute equality of the two races before the law, but in the nature of things it could not have been intended to abolish distinctions based upon color, or to enforce social, as distinguished from political equality, or a commingling of the two races upon terms unsatisfactory to either. Laws permitting, and even requiring, their separation in places where they are liable to be brought into contact do not necessarily imply the inferiority of either race to the other, and have been generally recognized as within the competency of the state legislatures in the exercise of their police powers.

The question then, was whether the law was an unreasonable use of the state's police power. The Court judged it reasonable for the state to consider the traditions and customs of its people. Brown wrote,

[W]e consider the underlying fallacy of [Plessy's] argument to consist in the assumption that the enforced separation of the two races stamps the colored race with a badge of inferiority. If this be so, it is not by reason of anything found in the act, but solely because the colored race chooses to put this construction upon it. . . . If the civil and political rights of both races be equal one cannot be inferior to the other civilly, or politically. If one race be inferior to the other socially, the Constitution of the United States cannot put them upon the same plane.

Dissent and Aftermath

In a lone dissent, Justice John Marshall Harlan I harshly criticized the decision. Harlan acknowledged that whites were the dominant race in prestige, education, wealth, and power, "[b]ut in view of the Constitution," he declared, "in the eye of the law, there is in this country no superior, dominant, ruling class of citizens. There is no caste here. Our Constitution is colorblind and neither knows nor tolerates classes among citizens." He charged that the majority had ignored the fact that the Louisiana law segregated blacks because whites considered them inferior. "The thin disguise of 'equal' accommodations for passengers in railroad coaches will not mislead any one, nor atone for the wrong this day done."

In the years after *Plessy,* segregation laws multiplied throughout the South. Twenty years after the decision, the federal government even reimposed racial segregation upon itself under President Woodrow Wilson (1913–1921). Only with the rise of the civil rights movement in the 1950s would a later Court reverse *Plessy* and protect all citizens from state infringement upon their constitutional rights.

See also: Brown v. Board of Education (1954); Civil Rights and the Supreme Court; *Heart of Atlanta Motel v. United States* (1964); 📖 *Plessy v. Ferguson,* 1896, in the **Primary Source Library.**

Further Reading

McNeese, Tim. *Plessy v. Ferguson: Separate but Equal.* Berkeley Heights, NJ: Chelsea House Publications, 2006.

Medley, Keith Weldon. *We As Freemen: Plessy v. Ferguson.* Gretna, La.: Pelican Publishing Company, 2003.

Thomas, Brooks. *Plessy v. Ferguson.* New York: Bedford/St. Martin's, 1996.

Powell v. Alabama (1932)

The first modern Court ruling on the right to counsel. In this case, also known as the Scottsboro Boys case, the Court established the principle that defendants are entitled to have the opportunity to consult with a lawyer and prepare a defense.

In the case, nine young illiterate black teenagers were charged with the rape of two white girls on a freight train passing through Tennessee and Alabama. Their trial was held in Scottsboro, Alabama, where community hostility toward the defendants was intense. The trial judge appointed all the members of the local bar to serve as defense counsel, but when the trial began, no attorney appeared to represent the defendants. The judge then appointed a local lawyer, who undertook the task with reluctance. The defendants were convicted.

The defendants challenged their convictions, arguing that they were effectively denied aid of counsel. The Court agreed. The action of the judge in appointing all members of the local bar as defense counsel was merely a gesture that resulted in no aid to the defendants in the critical pretrial period, the Court said. It ruled that the right to the aid of counsel is so fundamental that denying it to a defendant deprives that individual of due process of the law. In making its decision, the Court leaned heavily upon the circumstances of the case and the characteristics of the defendants:

In the light of the facts . . . the ignorance and illiteracy of the defendants, their youth, the circumstances of public hostility, the imprisonment and the close surveillance of the defendants by the military forces, the fact that their friends and families were all in other states and communication with them necessarily difficult, and above all that they stood in deadly peril of their lives—we think the failure of the trial court to give them reasonable time and opportunity to secure counsel was a clear denial of due process.

But . . . even if opportunity had been given, to employ counsel . . . we are of opinion that, under the circumstances just stated, the necessity of counsel was so vital and imperative that the failure of the trial court to make an effective appointment of counsel was likewise a denial of due process within the meaning of the Fourteenth Amendment . . . [W]here the defendant is unable to employ counsel, and is incapable adequately of making his own defense because of ignorance, feeblemindedness, illiteracy or the like, it is the duty of the court, whether requested or not, to assign counsel for him as a necessary requisite of due process of law.

A – Z

The plight of the nine "Scottsboro boys," arrested in rural Alabama for allegedly raping two white women, resulted in numerous court cases, including *Powell v. Alabama* (1932). This Supreme Court case expanded the rights of defendants to legal representation. Samuel Leibowitz (center), a prominent attorney and later a judge, handled the defendants' case after their initial conviction. (Brown Brothers)

Landmark Decision Highlights: *Powell v. Alabama* (1932)

Issue: Did the hasty trials of nine young, illiterate African American youths accused of raping two white women violate the due process clause of the Fourteenth Amendment?

Opinion: The Court held that the trials denied due process because the defendants were not given reasonable time and opportunity to secure counsel in their defense. Associate Justice George Sutherland also implicated the Sixth Amendment's guarantee of the right to counsel.

See also: Due Process; Right to Legal Counsel.

Power, Origins of Judicial

See Appellate Jurisdiction; Constitution of the United States; Judicial Review; Judiciary Act of 1789; Jurisdiction of the Supreme Court; *Marbury v. Madison* (1803); Supreme Court, History of the.

Presidency and the Supreme Court

Supreme Court rulings that deal with the powers of the president of the United States. Presidential power developed virtually unchecked by the Court until the 1930s. The gradual alteration in the balance of power from the states to the federal government broadened the scope and range of executive authority. Thirty years of continuous crisis, from the **Great Depression** through World War II (1939–1945) and the cold war that followed, further accelerated the expansion of presidential power. Today, presidential power far exceeds the limits of the executive role set out by the Constitution.

Challenging Presidential Authority

Two factors contribute to the infrequency of Court rulings on the authority of the chief executive. The constitutional language outlining the powers of the president is phrased in very general terms. The president holds the executive power, is commander in chief, and is directed to take care that the laws are faithfully executed. Because of this language, the basis for constitutional challenges to presidential action is uncertain.

The aura that surrounds the office of the president also protects its occupant from court challenges. Political scientist Louis Koenig remarked that even if the president "lags in donning monarchic trappings, others will put them on him . . ." Justice Robert Jackson has pointed out that "Executive power has the advantage of concentration in a single head in whose choice the whole Nation has a part . . . No other personality in public life can begin to compete with him in access to the public mind through modern methods of communications. By his prestige as head of state and his influence upon public opinion he exerts a leverage upon those who are supposed to check and balance his power which often cancels their effectiveness." As a result, the Court has been cautious in battling the chief executive on matters that deal with the president's constitutional powers.

In foreign and military matters, the Court has upheld the almost unrestrained use of presidential power. Even when the Court blocked many of Franklin D. Roosevelt's (1933–1945) economic programs to address the Great Depression in the 1930s, it upheld his virtually unlimited authority to conduct the nation's foreign affairs. Although the Constitution grants Congress the power to declare war, only a handful of the nation's conflicts have been accompanied by a formal declaration of war by Congress. Most have occurred as a result of presidential actions, orders, or resolutions later supported by Congress.

The Court, on the other hand, has not been reluctant to deny the president broad power in domestic affairs. When President Harry S. Truman (1945–1953) imposed government control over the steel mills during the Korean War (1950–1953), the Court rejected the president's claim of the power to take such action. Twenty years later, the Court later specifically recognized the need to

President Barack Obama (2009–) announced the retirement of Associate Justice David Souter on May 1, 2009. Later that month, the president nominated Judge Sonia Sotomayor as Souter's replacement. Sotomayor was sworn in as the 111th justice on August 8, 2009. She is the third woman justice and the first Hispanic to serve on the Court. (Ron Sachs, UPI, Landov)

limit the president's privilege to protect documents and information related to foreign affairs. In *United States v Nixon* (1974), it denied President Richard M. Nixon (1969–1974) an absolute executive privilege to withhold tapes made in the White House that were sought for use as evidence in a trial.

The Veto Power

The Court has made few rulings on the president's veto power. The major ruling in this area was *Okanogan Indians, et al. v. United States* (1929), also known as the *Pocket Veto Case*. Here, the Court ruled that the president must return a bill he rejects to Congress while it is in session. Formerly, presidents could simply hold onto bills approved late in the session of Congress, refusing to sign them while Congress was still in session.

This allowed the president to overturn a law passed by Congress without having to issue a formal veto. Subsequent rulings, however, have undercut this decision. The executive branch and Congress still remain at odds over what constitutes a congressional adjournment and permits the use of the pocket veto.

Throughout U.S. history, the president has had an all-or-nothing option when presented with a bill passed by Congress—either sign it into law or veto it. Many presidents, however, have wanted to veto part of a bill rather than the bill in its entirety. For example, President Ronald Reagan (1981–1989) wanted a "line item veto" so he could strike what he considered wasteful spending items from bills. Many state governors had this power, Reagan noted. His successor, President George H.W. Bush (1989–1993), also favored the idea. Republican legislators took up the case and in 1996 won passage of the Line Item Veto Act, which President Bill Clinton (1993–2001) signed into law. The act authorized the president to "cancel" certain spending items and tax benefits contained in bills presented for signing.

Challenges to the law arose when Clinton used the line item veto to cancel spending and tax breaks for two special interests, the city of New York and the Snake River Potato Growers of Idaho. The Court took up the case of *Clinton v. City of New York* (1998) and struck down the Line Item Veto Act. The Court agreed that the Constitution provides the president only two options when presented with a bill passed by Congress: to sign it or to veto it.

Presidential Pardons

The Constitution gives the president the power "to grant Reprieves and Pardons for Offenses against the United States" to all persons excepting those who have been impeached. A pardon is an exemption from a sentence and guilt; a reprieve is the suspension of a sentence or other legally imposed penalties for a temporary period.

The Court has supported the president's discretion to exercise the pardon power against all challenges. A pardon may be full or partial, absolute or conditional, or general. The president may attach conditions to a pardon, the Court has held, so long as they are not contrary to the Constitution or federal laws. A full pardon, the Court has held,

SPOTLIGHT

The Solicitor General

When the White House wants the Supreme Court to take a certain position on an issue, it is the solicitor general, or one of the solicitor general's staff, who argues the administration's case to the Court. When the government is a party to a case, the solicitor general argues the government's side. When it is not a party, but nevertheless wishes to make its views known on the issue, the solicitor general files an *amicus curiae* ("friend of the court") brief.

The government has been very successful in arguing cases before the Court. One study of the Court's opinions shows that the government won more than 60 percent of its cases in the eighteenth and nineteenth centuries. From 1953 through 1983, it won almost 70 percent of its cases. Subsequent studies have found that success rate continuing through the late 1980s, but dropping off slightly in the 1990s. Since 2000, the solicitor general's success rate has risen back to more than 70 percent.

The government's record in cases where it filed as *amicus curiae* is even better. The position endorsed by the government prevailed in as many as 87 percent of the cases in some terms after World War II (1939–1945). For the terms between 1958 and 1967, the government's rate of success in such cases averaged 71 percent.

ends the punishment and blots out the guilt "so that in the eyes of the law the offender is as innocent as if he had never committed the offence."

Ex parte Garland (1866) is the leading case defining the effect and the reach of a presidential pardon. In that case, the majority concluded:

The power thus conferred is unlimited, with the exception stated [impeachment]. It extends to every offence known to the law, and may be exercised at any time after its commission, either before legal proceedings are taken, or during their pendency, or after conviction and judgment. This power of the President is not subject to legislative control. Congress can neither limit the effect of his pardon, nor exclude from its exercise any class of offenders. The benign prerogative of mercy reposed in him cannot be fettered by any legislative restrictions.

The question of placing conditions on a presidential pardon came before the Court after the Civil War (1861–1865). During the war, President Abraham Lincoln (1861–1865) offered pardons to all Confederates who swore allegiance to the Constitution and the Union. Lincoln's offer, if accepted, would have restored to former Confederates any property taken from them during the war. In *United States v. Klein* (1872), the Court upheld the president's right to offer the pardon and property restoration in exchange for allegiance.

Presidents and Justices

The Constitution grants the president the power to appoint Court justices, with the "advice and consent" of the Senate. This potentially gives the president a large measure of influence over the Court's judicial philosophy. However, presidents can never be certain that the individuals they appoint to the Court will support their views when faced with a challenge to the exercise of presidential power. Thomas Jefferson (1801–1809) made several appointments to the bench whom he hoped would counteract Chief Justice John Marshall's control over the Court's decisions. However, Jefferson's effort to reduce Marshall's effectiveness failed. Truman appointed three members of the majority who ruled against him in the steel seizure case. One, Justice Tom C. Clark, was a close friend of the president. President Nixon appointed Warren E. Burger chief justice in large part because Burger opposed earlier Court rulings that limited prosecutors' efforts to convict criminals. In an ironic turn of events, Burger wrote the opinion in *United States v. Nixon,* which left Nixon with the option of resigning his office or facing impeachment. He was forced to resign.

See also: Checks and Balances; Federalism; Fiscal and Monetary Power and the Supreme Court; Foreign Affairs and the Supreme Court; Line Item Veto; New Deal and the Supreme Court; Nomination and Confirmation of Justices and Judges; Roosevelt's 1937 Court Reform Plan; *United States v. Nixon* (1974); War Powers and the Supreme Court.

Further Reading

Ellis, Richard J., ed. *Judging Executive Power: Sixteen Supreme Court Cases That Have Shaped the American Presidency.* New York: Rowman and Littlefield, 2009.

Jantzen, Steven. *The Presidency, Congress, and the Supreme Court.* New York: Scholastic, 1989.

Principles of U.S. Government

See Jurisdiction of the Supreme Court.

Prior Restraint

See Censorship.

Probable Cause

Legal term referring to the minimum standard of evidence needed for a magistrate to issue a search warrant. There are various legal definitions for the term, but probable cause requires "belief that the law was being violated on the premises to be searched; and . . . the facts . . . are such that a reasonably discreet and prudent man would be led to believe that there was a commission of the offense charged."

In *Nathanson v. United States* (1933), the Court ruled that a sworn statement not adequately supported by facts, does not constitute probable cause to issue a warrant:

U nder the Fourth Amendment, an officer may not properly issue a warrant to search a private dwelling unless he can find probable cause therefore from facts or circumstances presented to him under oath or affirmation. Mere affirmance of belief or suspicion is not enough.

The Court has held valid warrants based on hearsay, and it has not required direct personal observation of the facts or circumstances justifying the warrant by the individual who seeks it. The magistrate, however, must be satisfied that the informant is credible or the information reliable.

Only if an individual cannot or does not consent to a search are police required to obtain a warrant. Voluntary consent of the individual who owns or occupies the place to be searched validates the search. The Court, however, has held that the individual who is asked to consent to a search need not be informed that he or she may refuse. In *Schneckloth v. Bustamonte* (1973), the Court discussed the elements of voluntary consent:

V oluntariness is a question of fact to be determined from all the circumstances, and while the subject's knowledge of a right to refuse is a factor to be taken into account, the prosecution is not required to demonstrate such knowledge as a prerequisite to establishing a voluntary consent.

The following year, in *United States v. Matlock* (1974), the Court held that when one occupant of a house consents to a search of the premises, the search is proper, and evidence uncovered in it may be used against another occupant. In 1990, in another case involving multiple occupants of a residence, the Court ruled that an overnight houseguest has a legitimate expectation of privacy and is entitled to Fourth Amendment protection against police intrusion at the house. By a vote of 7-2, the justices said the guest has sufficient interest in the home to challenge the legality of his warrantless arrest there.

See also: Search Warrants.

Property Rights

See Eminent Domain; Fair Housing.

Race and Redistricting

Supreme Court decisions concerning the practice of drawing election district boundaries in such a way as to affect African American voting strength in a single district. For the purposes of voting in federal elections, every state is divided into several different districts, or geographical regions. Periodically, state legislatures redraw the boundaries of voting districts to reflect changes in local populations. Occasionally, they have drawn these boundaries in such a way as to increase or decrease the influence of black voters.

Keeping Blacks From the Polls

Until the mid-1900s, many Southern states used a variety of devices such as **literacy tests** and **poll taxes** to disenfranchise black voters. One of the last such tactics that the Court declared unconstitutional was the racial gerrymander—the practice of drawing election district boundaries to dilute or eliminate concentrations of black voting strength in a single district. *Gomillion v. Lightfoot* (1960) brought this practice before the Court, which found it a clear violation of the Fifteenth Amendment.

In *Thornburg v. Gingles* (1986), the Court held that a state could not divide large blocs of minority voters among several mostly white districts because it diluted the electoral strength of the minority. This concept of "vote dilution" was not precise or obvious in all circumstances, but the thrust of the law was clear. As the 1990 census began, state officials believed that where it was possible to do so, they should draw electoral districts that would favor the election of black and Hispanic representatives. The pressure to carve out black majority districts in the Southern states set off a backlash that would reach the Court a few years later.

In *Shaw v. Reno* (1993), the Court condemned "racial **gerrymandering**" as a threat to the Constitution's guarantee of equal treatment for all because it relied on the use of race as a decision-making factor. At issue was a district that wound around in a snake-like fashion for 160 miles in central North Carolina, picking up black neighborhoods in four metropolitan areas. The Court agreed with a group of white voters who alleged that North Carolina had set up "a racially discriminatory voting process" and deprived them of the right to vote in "a color-blind" election.

Voting Rights Act

The following year, the Court ruled that the Voting Rights Act does not require legislative districting plans to maximize the number of districts in which minority groups are in the majority. Instead, the Court said state legislatures usually can satisfy the Voting Rights Act if minority voters form "effective voting majorities in a number of districts roughly proportional to the minority voters' respective shares in the voting-age population."

See also: One Person, One Vote; Voting Rights.

Rehnquist, William H. (1924–2005)

Chief Justice of the United States, first appointed to the Court by President Richard M. Nixon (1969–1974) and confirmed by Congress on December 10, 1971. In 1986, President Ronald Reagan (1981–1989) named, and Congress confirmed, Rehnquist as successor to retiring Chief Justice Warren Burger. Rehnquist served in that office until his death in 2005. He was the one hundredth justice to serve on the Court and the sixteenth to serve as chief justice.

President Richard Nixon (1969–1974) appointed William H. Rehnquist as associate justice in 1972. In 1986, President Ronald Reagan (1981–1989) elevated Rehnquist to Chief Justice of the United States. Rehnquist died in September 2005 and was replaced by Chief Justice John Roberts. (AP Photo, APTN)

Early Life and Career

William Rehnquist was born and grew up in Milwaukee, Wisconsin. After World War II (1939–1945) service in the Air Force, he attended Stanford University and received both bachelor's and master's degrees in political science in 1948. He later graduated first in his class at Stanford Law School in 1952. One of his classmates was Sandra Day, who later joined him on the Court.

After law school, Rehnquist clerked for Supreme Court Justice Robert H. Jackson. In 1952, he wrote a memorandum for Jackson supporting separate but equal schools for blacks and whites. When the Senate Judiciary Committee asked him about those views during his 1971 confirmation hearings, Rehnquist renounced them. He said the views were Jackson's, not his own.

During the 1964 presidential campaign, Rehnquist campaigned for Barry Goldwater, the **Republican** candidate. He also worked with Richard G. Kleindienst, who later became President Nixon's deputy attorney general. After Nixon won the presidency in 1968, Kleindienst appointed Rehnquist to head the Justice Department's Office of Legal Counsel.

Rehnquist quickly became one of the Nixon administration's chief spokesmen on Capitol Hill. It was his job to review the legality of all presidential executive orders and other constitutional law questions in the executive branch. He frequently testified before congressional committees in support of the administration's policies, most of which matched his own conservative philosophy.

Court Service

In 1971, President Nixon nominated Rehnquist to the Court as an associate justice; he was confirmed by the Senate by a 68-26 vote on December 10, 1971. He took his seat as associate justice on January 7, 1972. Rehnquist voted consistently in favor of law enforcement over the rights of suspects and for **states' rights** over the power of the federal government. After fifteen years as an associate justice, he was picked by President Ronald Reagan to replace retiring Chief Justice William Burger.

Controversy surrounded his nomination as chief justice, as many senators questioned his views on civil rights. In the end, the Senate approved the nomination by a vote of 65-33. At the time, the thirty-three nay votes were the most received by a Court nominee in the twentieth century.

As chief justice, Rehnquist was the Court's unquestioned leader and its most dominant figure. He has made the Court into a reliable supporter of law enforcement and of the death penalty. He also edged the Court toward greater support for public aid to religious schools and restrictions on the use of affirmative action and race-based redistricting.

Rehnquist led a revival of states' rights and breathed new life into the principle that the Court has a duty to limit the power of Congress and the federal government. Rehnquist believed that the states are "sovereign entities" whose core powers cannot be infringed by the federal government.

In 1999, Rehnquist presided over the impeachment trial of President Bill Clinton (1993–2001) and announced his acquittal on all the charges. An amateur historian, he wrote four books while serving as chief justice: *The Supreme Court: How It Was, How It Is* (1988); *Grand Inquests: The Historic Impeachments of Justice Samuel Chase and President Andrew Johnson* (1992); *All the Laws but One: Civil Liberties in Wartime* (1998); and *The Centennial Crisis: The Disputed Election of 1876* (2004).

In October 2004, Rehnquist announced he was being treated for thyroid cancer. Rehnquist returned to the Court in spring 2005 and, to the surprise of many, did not announce his retirement when the term ended. He died at his home on Labor Day weekend of that year. Three days later, President George W. Bush (2001–2009) nominated John G. Roberts Jr., a former law clerk to Rehnquist, to succeed him as chief justice.

See also: Associate Justices; Burger, Warren E.; Chief Justice of the Supreme Court; O'Connor, Sandra Day; Roberts, John G.

Further Reading

Dean, John W. *The Rehnquist Choice: The Untold Story of the Nixon Appointment That Redefined the Supreme Court.* New York: Free Press, 2002.

Hudson, David L. *The Rehnquist Court: Understanding Its Impact and Legacy.* New York: Praeger Press, 2006.

Ricci v. DeStefano (2009)

Supreme Court case that may have long-lasting impact on affirmative action and how race may be used in determining job promotions, admission to universities, and other situations in which affirmative action guidelines have been used. The Court's 5-4 decision in *Ricci v. DeStefano* determined that the city of New Haven, Connecticut, violated the rights of white and Hispanic firefighters when it threw out a promotions test because no blacks had passed it. The Ricci decision is complex, stretching for about ninety pages, with a majority opinion, two concurring opinions, and a dissent. The ruling's meanings and ultimate effect on affirmative action will likely be argued for years to come.

After the Court issued its ruling, the case was sent back to the court of appeals for further consideration. Justice Anthony Kennedy delivered the opinion of the Court:

In the fire department of New Haven, Connecticut—as in emergency-service agencies throughout the Nation—firefighters prize their promotion to and within the officer ranks. An agency's officers command respect within the department and in the whole community; and, of course, added responsibilities command increased salary and benefits. Aware of the intense competition for promotions, New Haven, like many cities, relies on objective examinations to identify the best qualified candidates.

In 2003, 118 New Haven firefighters took examinations to qualify for promotion to the rank of lieutenant or captain. Promotion examinations in New Haven (or City) were infrequent, so the stakes were high. The results would determine which firefighters would be considered for promotions during the next two years, and the order in which they would be considered. Many firefighters studied for months, at considerable personal and financial cost.

When the examination results showed that white candidates had outperformed minority candidates, the mayor and other local politicians opened a public debate that turned rancorous. Some firefighters argued the tests should be discarded because the results showed the tests to be discriminatory. They threatened a discrimination lawsuit if the City made promotions based on the tests. Other firefighters said the exams were neutral and fair. And they, in turn, threatened a discrimination lawsuit if the City, relying on the statistical racial disparity, ignored the test results and denied promotions to the candidates who had performed well. In the end the City took the side of those who protested the test results. It threw out the examinations.

Certain white and Hispanic firefighters who likely would have been promoted based on their good test performance sued the City and some of its officials. Theirs is the suit now before us. The suit alleges that, by discarding the test results, the City and the named officials discriminated against the plaintiffs based on their race, in violation of both Title VII of the Civil Rights Act of 1964 and the Equal Protection Clause of the Fourteenth Amendment . . .

We conclude that race-based action like the City's in this case is impermissible under Title VII unless the employer can demonstrate a strong basis in evidence that, had it not taken the action, it would have been liable under the disparate-impact statute. The respondents, we further determine, cannot meet that threshold standard. As a result, the City's action in discarding the tests was a violation of Title VII. In light of our ruling under the statutes, we need not reach the question whether respondents' actions may have violated the Equal Protection Clause. . . .

Our holding today clarifies how Title VII applies to resolve competing expectations under the disparate treatment and disparate-impact provisions. If, after it certifies the test results, the City faces a disparate-impact suit, then in light of our holding today it should be clear that the City would avoid disparate-impact liability based on the strong basis in evidence that, had it not certified the results, it would have been subject to disparate treatment liability.

Petitioners are entitled to summary judgment on their Title VII claim, and we therefore need not decide the underlying constitutional question. The judgment of the Court of Appeals is reversed, and the cases are remanded for further proceedings consistent with this opinion.

See also: Affirmative Action; Equal Protection of the Law.

Right to a Jury Trial

Supreme Court rulings that deal with the constitutional right to a trial by jury. Article III of the Constitution states that "the Trial of all Crimes, except in Cases of Impeachment, shall be by Jury." In *Patton v. United States* (1930), the Court held that a jury in a federal criminal case must consist of twelve people, must be supervised by a judge, and must reach a unanimous verdict.

It was not until 1968, however, that the Court applied the right to trial by jury to the states. Nearly a century earlier, in *Walker v. Sauvinet* (1876), the Court held that the Seventh Amendment right to trial by jury in civil cases was not protected against state action. In *Maxwell v. Dow* (1900), the Court ruled that neither the Fifth nor Fourteenth Amendments required that state juries consist of twelve persons. "Trial by jury has never been affirmed to be a necessary requisite of due process of law," declared the Court.

In *Duncan v. Louisiana* (1968), decided one hundred years after adoption of the Fourteenth Amendment, the Court finally applied the right to trial by jury to the states. According to the Court, the Sixth

Amendment right to a jury trial is a necessary ingredient of due process. Gary Duncan, charged with **battery** in Louisiana courts, had been denied a jury trial. He was convicted and sentenced to a fine and two years in prison. Duncan appealed to the Court, arguing that this denial of a jury trial violated his right to due process. The Court agreed.

By applying the right to jury trial to the states, the Court created two new questions. Were states now required to use only twelve-person juries? Must all state jury verdicts be unanimous? In *Williams v. Florida* (1970) the Court held it proper for states to use juries composed of as few as six persons in noncapital cases. In 1978, the Supreme Court made plain that juries must consist of at least six persons, rejecting Georgia's use of a five-person jury.

In the early 1970s, the Court held that state juries need not reach their verdicts unanimously. This ruling came in *Johnson v. Louisiana* (1972) and *Apodaca v. Oregon* (1972). In the Louisiana case, the Court rejected the defendant's argument that the lack of a unanimous decision amounted to reasonable doubt about the defendant's guilt. In the Oregon case, the Court upheld an Oregon law requiring that juries reach their verdicts by no less a majority than 10-2.

See also: Due Process.

Right to a Public Trial

Supreme Court rulings that deal with the Sixth Amendment guarantee to a public trial for persons charged with crimes. In the late 1970s, the Court held that the Sixth Amendment guarantee is solely for the benefit of the defendant, not for the public in general or the press.

In *Gannett Co. v. DePasquale* (1979), the Court held that a trial judge could close a pretrial hearing to the press and the public if he or she felt it necessary to protect the defendant's right to a fair trial. "To safeguard the due process rights of the accused, a trial judge has an affirmative constitutional duty to minimize the effects of prejudicial pretrial publicity," wrote Justice Potter Stewart. He noted that one of the most effective means of minimizing publicity is to close pretrial proceedings to the public and to the press.

A series of subsequent decisions have established a growing presumption that trial proceedings should be open. In *Richmond Newspapers v. Virginia* (1980), the Court overturned the decision of a trial judge to close a murder trial to the press and public. "We hold that the right to attend criminal trials is implicit in the guarantees of the First Amendment," wrote Chief Justice Warren E. Burger. "[W]ithout the freedom to attend such trials, which people have exercised for centuries, important aspects of freedom of speech and 'of the press could be eviscerated [gutted].'" Burger acknowledged that in some situations the only way to preserve the right to a fair trial is to limit the access of press and public to the courtroom. If such limitations are necessary, however, they must be outlined clearly and backed by written findings on the part of the judge that closure is essential to preserve an overriding state interest.

In *Waller v. Georgia* (1984), the Court held that a judge may close pretrial hearings to the public only if an open hearing will prejudice some overriding interest in the case. Two years later, in still another case on these points, Chief Justice Warren Burger declared that the defendant's right to a fair trial need not be in conflict with the public's right to access. In *Press-Enterprise Co. v. Superior Court* (1986) the justices ruled that a newspaper could have access to the transcript of a preliminary hearing in a criminal case. Burger wrote to emphasize that one important way to assure the defendant's right to a fair trial is to keep the process open to neutral observers.

See also: Due Process.

Right to a Speedy Trial

Supreme Court rulings that deal with the Sixth Amendment guarantee of a quick trial. The Court has made clear that the right to a speedy trial is a relative matter, "consistent with delays and depend[ent] upon circumstances." The Court has adopted a balancing approach in cases alleging that a defendant has been denied this right. The justices weigh the particular facts to determine the reasons for the delay as well as the effect of the delay on the defendant.

A - Z

SPOTLIGHT

Enemy Combatants at Guantánamo

In response to the September 11, 2001, terror attacks on the United States, the administration of George W. Bush invaded first Afghanistan, and later Iraq. Prisoners captured in these conflicts who were suspected of terrorist activity were detained at the U.S. Naval Base at Guantánamo Bay, Cuba. The administration declared that since these detainees were not uniformed soldiers, they were not subject to the normal protections afforded to prisoners of war.

The administration also declared that the detainees did not enjoy the constitutional rights guaranteed to prisoners, such as the writ of habeas corpus, the right to a public trial, and the right to a speedy trial. A writ of habeas corpus (a Latin phrase meaning "I have the body") is a court order compelling authorities to produce a prisoner in court and state the charges against him or her. Many detainees have spent years in Guantánamo Bay without being formally charged with any crime.

In 2006, the Court ruled in *Hamdan v. Rumsfeld* that the administration did not have the authority to set up the system of military tribunals that tried the detainees held at Guantánamo Bay. In January 2009, President Barack Obama signed an executive order suspending the activities of the military tribunals and calling for the closing of the detention facility in 2010.

The right to a speedy trial does not apply to delays before a person is accused of a crime, only to the interval between arrest and trial. The Court reaffirmed this point in its decision in *United States v. Lovasco* (1977). It rejected the argument that a defendant was denied due process by a good-faith investigative delay between the time the offense was committed and the time of his **indictment.**

In *Klopfer v. North Carolina* (1976), the Court held guaranteed the right to a speedy trial against abridgment by the states. The Court struck down a North Carolina law that allowed the state to postpone a criminal prosecution indefinitely without dismissing the charges against the defendant. Under this law, the defendant would remain free, but the prosecutor could bring the case to court any time a judge agreed such action was appropriate.

In *Barker v. Wingo* (1972), the Court rejected the argument that a defendant who fails to demand a speedy trial has forever waived that right. *Barker v. Wingo* prompted Congress to pass the Speedy

Trial Act of 1974 to reduce delays in federal trials. The act established a deadline of one hundred days between arrest or indictment and trial. Failure to meet the deadline would result in dismissal of the charges.

In *United States v. MacDonald* (1982), the Court further defined the right to a speedy trial, ruling that this guarantee applied to the period between arrest and indictment. In 1990, the Court said an eight-year delay between indictment and arrest violated the Sixth Amendment right to a speedy trial. The defendant was indicted on federal drug charges in 1980 but left the country, apparently unaware of his indictment, before he could be arrested. After several years, he returned to the United States, married, earned a college degree, found steady employment, and lived under his own name. He was arrested after a routine credit check. The Court ruled that he could not be tried after such a long delay.

See also: Due Process.

Right to Die

Supreme Court rulings that deal with the rights of persons to end their own lives. Since about the 1970s, advances in medicine have allowed the "human body [to be kept] alive for longer than any reasonable person would want to inhabit it," as Justice Antonin Scalia put it. As a result, a growing movement formed around the concept that dying persons had the right to decide to hasten their death. This was referred to generally as the "right to die." The Court has taken a cautious approach to this newly asserted right.

In 1990, the Court took up the case of Nancy Beth Cruzan, the victim of an auto accident who had suffered irreversible brain damage. Her parents said their daughter would not want to exist that way and asked state hospital officials to remove the water and feeding tube that kept her alive. The officials refused, citing Missouri's strong "right to life" policy. The Cruzans went to court and sought an order to remove the life-sustaining tubes. A trial judge ruled for the parents, but the Missouri Supreme Court reversed that decision.

The Court upheld Missouri authorities—but the ruling was not a total loss for advocates of the right to die. "We assume the United States Constitution would grant a competent person a constitutionally protected right to refuse lifesaving hydration and nutrition," said Chief Justice William H. Rehnquist in *Cruzan v. Missouri Department of Health* (1990). If so, a dying or disabled person may choose to die by starvation and dehydration. All nine justices agreed that there was a basic right to refuse unwanted medical treatment. The Court split, however, on whether one person or persons—in this case, Nancy's parents—could decide for another to end his or her life.

In 1997, the Court took up two cases in which physicians challenged state laws banning assisted suicide for mentally competent terminally ill patients. In a pair of 9-0 decisions announced on the same day, the Court ruled for the states, rejecting the claim that the assisted suicide laws were unconstitutional. Chief Justice William Rehnquist stressed that the legal bans on suicide were time-honored and traditional. The Court argued that

there is a clear difference between a doctor's withdrawing a breathing tube and giving medication that causes death. "When a patient refuses life sustaining medical treatment, he dies from an underlying fatal disease or pathology, but if a patient ingests lethal medication prescribed by a physician, he is killed by that medication," Chief Justice Rehnquist wrote. "The two acts are different, and New York may therefore, consistent with the Constitution, treat them differently," he concluded.

Right to Legal Counsel

Supreme Court cases dealing with the Sixth Amendment guarantee that all accused criminals have the right to legal assistance. "In all criminal prosecutions," the Sixth Amendment states, "the accused shall enjoy the right . . . to have the assistance of counsel for his defense." Nevertheless, throughout American history, only persons charged with federal crimes punishable by death have been guaranteed this right. The right of all other defendants to the legal counsel traditionally has depended upon their ability to hire and pay their own lawyer.

Beginning in the 1930s, however, the Court vastly enlarged the class of persons who have the right to legal counsel. The Court's first modern ruling on the right to counsel came in the first Scottsboro Boys case, *Powell v. Alabama* (1932). In this case, the trial judge appointed all the members of the local bar to serve as defense counsel for nine young black boys accused of raping two white girls. When no attorney appeared to represent the defendants, the judge appointed a local lawyer on the morning of the trial, who only reluctantly took the case. The defendants were convicted but challenged the decision, arguing that they were effectively denied aid of counsel because they did not have the opportunity to consult with their lawyer and prepare a defense. The Court agreed.

Since 1790, federal law has required that persons charged with capital crimes in federal courts be provided an attorney. Nearly 150 years later, the Court held that the Sixth Amendment required this assurance for *all* federal defendants in *Johnson v. Zerbst* (1938). In this case, John Johnson, a Marine,

POINT/COUNTERPOINT

PRIVACY FOR CONSENTING ADULTS: *Lawrence v. Texas* (2003)

A "right to privacy" clause is nowhere to be found in the U.S. Constitution or any of its amendments. Yet, over the years, the Court has expanded the right of individuals to be secure in their own homes and has extended the rights of consenting adults. In *Lawrence v. Texas* (2003), the Court noted that "the most intimate and personal choices a person may make in a lifetime, choices central to personal dignity and autonomy, are central to the liberty protected by the Fourteenth Amendment."

Justice Anthony Kennedy

The question before the Court is the validity of a Texas statute making it a crime for two persons of the same sex to engage in certain intimate sexual conduct.

In Houston, Texas, officers of the Harris County Police Department were dispatched to a private residence in response to a reported weapons disturbance. They entered an apartment where one of the petitioners, John Geddes Lawrence, resided. The right of the police to enter does not seem to have been questioned. The officers observed Lawrence and another man, Tyron Garner, engaging in a sexual act. The two petitioners were arrested, held in custody over night, and charged and convicted before a Justice of the Peace. . . .

The petitioners exercised their right to a trial de novo in Harris County Criminal Court. They challenged the statute as a violation of the Equal Protection Clause of the Fourteenth Amendment and of a like provision of the Texas Constitution. Those contentions were rejected. The petitioners, having entered a plea of *nolo contendere* [no contest], were each fined $200 and assessed court costs of $141.25.

We [the Supreme Court] granted certiorari, to consider three questions:

1. Whether Petitioners' criminal convictions under the Texas "Homosexual Conduct" law—which criminalizes sexual intimacy by same-sex couples, but not identical behavior by different-sex couples—violate the Fourteenth Amendment guarantee of equal protection of laws?
2. Whether Petitioners' criminal convictions for adult consensual sexual intimacy in the home violate their vital interests in liberty and privacy protected by the Due Process Clause of the Fourteenth Amendment?
3. Whether *Bowers v. Hardwick* (1986), should be overruled?"

The petitioners were adults at the time of the alleged offense. Their conduct was in private and consensual.

At the outset it should be noted that there is no long-standing history in this country of laws directed at homosexual conduct as a distinct matter. . . . The absence of legal prohibitions focusing on homosexual conduct may be explained in part by noting that according to some scholars the concept of the homosexual as a distinct category of person did not emerge until the late 19th century . . . ("The modern terms homosexuality and heterosexuality do not apply to an era that had not yet articulated these distinctions"). Thus early American sodomy laws were not directed at homosexuals as such but instead sought to prohibit non-procreative sexual activity more generally....

Laws prohibiting sodomy do not seem to have been enforced against consenting adults acting in private. A substantial number of sodomy prosecutions and convictions for which there are surviving records were for predatory acts against those who could not or did not consent, as in the case of a minor or the victim of an assault . . . But far from possessing "ancient roots," American laws targeting same-sex couples did not develop until the last third of the 20th century . . . It was not until the 1970's that any State singled out same-sex relations for criminal prosecution, and only nine States have done so . . .

The issue is whether the majority may use the power of the State to enforce these views on the whole society through operation of the criminal law. "Our obligation is to define the liberty of all, not to mandate our own moral code..."

Persons in a homosexual relationship may seek autonomy for these purposes, just as heterosexual persons do. The decision in Bowers would deny them this right.

Justice Antonin Scalia

I begin with the Court's surprising readiness to reconsider a decision rendered a mere 17 years ago in *Bowers v. Hardwick*. I do not myself believe in rigid adherence to *stare decisis* in constitutional cases; but I do believe that we should be consistent rather than manipulative in invoking the doctrine. . . .

(1) *Bowers*, the Court says, has been subject to "substantial and continuing [criticism], disapproving of its reasoning in all respects, not just as to its historical assumptions." Exactly what those nonhistorical criticisms are, and whether the Court even agrees with them, are left unsaid. . . .

(2) It seems to me that the "societal reliance" on the principles confirmed in *Bowers* and discarded today has been overwhelming. Countless judicial decisions and legislative enactments have relied on the ancient proposition that a governing majority's belief that certain sexual behavior is "immoral and unacceptable" constitutes a rational basis for regulation. . . . The impossibility of distinguishing homosexuality from other traditional "morals" offenses is precisely why *Bowers* rejected the rational-basis challenge. "The law," it said, "is constantly based on notions of morality, and if all laws representing essentially moral choices are to be invalidated under the Due Process Clause, the courts will be very busy indeed."

DOCUMENT-BASED QUESTION

How does Justice Anthony Kennedy describe the growth of a right to privacy among consenting adults? What criticisms of the Lawrence v. Texas ruling does Justice Antonin Scalia identify?

A – Z

was charged with passing **counterfeit money.** He was tried and convicted in civil court without the aid of an attorney to act in his defense. He challenged his conviction as obtained in violation of his constitutional rights. The Court upheld his claim.

This expansion of the Sixth Amendment right to counsel continued during the 1960s and 1970s. At that time, the Court ruled that the amendment guaranteed the aid of an attorney to all state defendants charged with crimes that could be considered serious. In the 1980s, the Court further expanded the right to include a guarantee that **indigents** defending themselves with a claim of insanity are entitled to the aid of a court-appointed and publicly paid psychiatrist.

See also: Powell v. Alabama (1932).

Right to Privacy

Supreme Court rulings that deal with the constitutional right of individuals to be free from state interference in their personal lives. The Court over the decades has struggled with its constitutional foundation; nevertheless, a majority of the justices has accepted that right. As a result, the Court has struck down state laws prohibiting the use of contraceptives as well as those criminalizing abortions, the possession of obscene material at home, and private, consensual sex between homosexual adults.

In *Griswold v. Connecticut* (1965), the Court struck down a Connecticut law forbidding anyone in the state to use or counsel the use of contraceptives. The justices cited the **due process guarantee** of the Fourteenth Amendment, as well as provisions of the First, Third, Fourth, Fifth, and Ninth Amendments in support of their ruling.

Four years later, the Court held that a state could not forbid the possession of obscene material. The holding was based in part upon the "right to be free, except in very limited circumstances, from unwanted governmental intrusions into one's privacy." The state had no right to control the content of a person's thoughts, held the Court.

In *Roe v. Wade* (1973), the Court used the right of privacy as the basis to strike down state laws banning abortion. Writing the Court's opinion,

Justice Harry A. Blackmun took note of the conflicting views on the foundation of the right and declared firmly that "[t]his right of privacy, whether it be founded in the Fourteenth Amendment's concept of personal liberty and restrictions upon state action, as we feel it is, or . . . in the Ninth Amendment's reservation of rights to the people, is broad enough to encompass a woman's decision whether or not to terminate her pregnancy."

The issue of homosexual rights and privacy first came before the Court in *Bowers v. Hardwick* (1986). A divided Court found that the right of privacy did not prevent the state from forbidding or punishing private, consensual homosexual activity. The Court overruled this decision in *Lawrence v. Texas* (2003), holding that the privacy right shields gays and lesbians from being prosecuted for private sexual behavior. The 6-3 decision voided the remaining thirteen state laws that made sodomy a crime. Justice Anthony M. Kennedy said the Court has recognized that "the most private human conduct, sexual behavior, and in the most private of places, the home" is off-limits to meddling by the government.

See also: Abortion, Constitutional Debate; *Roe v. Wade* (1973).

Right to Vote

Supreme Court cases dealing with the ability of citizens to cast ballots in elections. Although the right to vote is the cornerstone of the democratic political system, the Constitution, until 1868, made almost no mention of that right. Until that time, the Court ruled that state citizenship, not federal citizenship, was the source of the right to vote.

In the earliest years of the United States, only free white adult males who owned property could vote. All states eventually dropped property qualifications, although some continued to require voters to pay a **poll tax.** The Civil War (1861–1865) and the amendments that marked its close seemed to promise a new era of broadened political participation. The Fourteenth Amendment, **ratified** in 1868, appeared to guarantee all citizens—female as well as male, black as well as white—the right to vote. Within a decade, however, the Court made clear that the Fourteenth Amendment had no such practical effect. The Constitution of the United States, declared the Court, still granted no one the right to vote. That was a state prerogative.

The Fifteenth Amendment, ratified in 1870, prohibited states from denying anyone the right to vote on account of race, color, or "previous condition of servitude." Nevertheless, Court decisions continued to support the view that voter qualifications and election regulations were exclusively state responsibilities. State officials, protected from federal action by these decisions, successfully employed **literacy tests,** grandfather clauses, poll taxes, and **white primaries** to limit black political participation.

It was not until 1915 that the Court began to edge toward a new view of the amendments and the protection they intended to provide for the right to vote. However, it was Congress, spurred by the civil rights movement of the 1960s, which ultimately led the way in fulfilling the promise of the Fifteenth Amendment. The Voting Rights Act of 1965 at last secured for the nation's black

citizens the right to vote. To do so, the act asserted federal authority over electoral matters traditionally left in the hands of state officials.

Once Congress acted, the Court steadily backed its power to ensure the right to vote. A series of rulings in the 1960s gave the broadest possible reading to the Fifteenth Amendment, the power of Congress to enforce it, and to the 1965 act, making it the most effective civil rights law ever enacted.

See also: Grandfather Clauses.

Rights, Personal

See Abortion, Constitutional Debate on; Bill of Rights; Due Process; Equal Protection of the Law; Right to Die; Right to Privacy; Search Warrants; Writ of Habeus Corpus.

Amendments That Extended Voting Rights

- In 1868, the Fourteenth Amendment appeared to guarantee the right to vote to all citizens—including women and blacks—by forbidding any state to abridge the privileges and immunities of U.S. citizens.
- In 1870, the Fifteenth Amendment explicitly enfranchised former slaves.
- In 1920, the Nineteenth Amendment granted women the right to vote.
- In 1961, the Twenty-third Amendment granted residents of Washington, D.C., the right to vote in presidential elections.
- In 1964, the Twenty-fourth Amendment prohibited use of a poll tax as a reason to deny anyone the right to vote in federal elections.
- In 1971, the Twenty-sixth Amendment lowered the voting age to eighteen.

Throughout the years, amendments to the U.S. Constitution have enabled more American citizens to participate in the nation's democratic processes.

Roberts, John G. (1955-)

Current Chief Justice of the United States, appointed by President George W. Bush (2001–2009) and confirmed by Congress on September 29, 2005. He is the 109th justice to serve on the Court and the seventeenth chief justice.

Roberts was born in Buffalo, New York, but grew up in Indiana. He earned his bachelor's degree at Harvard University in 1976 and his law degree there three years later. Following graduation, Roberts practiced law in Washington, D.C. He first came to the Court in 1980 to work as a law clerk for Associate Justice William H. Rehnquist. At the time, Rehnquist was considered the most conservative member of the Supreme Court.

Roberts's timing could not have been better. That fall, Ronald Reagan (1981–1989) defeated Jimmy Carter (1977–1981) in the presidential election, launching an era of Republican dominance. After Roberts completed his one-year clerkship, he took a job as a top assistant to

In a historic ceremony, Chief Justice John Roberts (right) administers the presidential oath of office to Barack Obama (2009–), the 44th president and the first African American president, on a frigid Inauguration Day, January 20, 2009. Roberts is the seventeenth Chief Justice of the United States. (Reuters, Rick Wilking, Landov)

President Reagan's attorney general, William French Smith. A year later, Roberts moved to the White House counsel's office. There he played a behind-the-scenes role in making legal policy for the Reagan administration.

In 1986, Roberts left the White House to join the law firm of Hogan and Hartson. He returned to government service in 1989, when Solicitor General Kenneth W. Starr chose Roberts as his chief deputy. Roberts served four years in that post and was nominated for the U.S. Court of Appeals for the District of Columbia, but the Senate refused to confirm him. Roberts returned to private practice at Hogan and Hartson in 1992.

In 2003, President George W. Bush named Roberts to the appeals court, and this time Roberts won confirmation. Two years later, Roberts was at the top of the president's list for a Court nomination, but it was unclear which seat he would fill. On July 19, 2005, President Bush named Roberts to replace retiring Associate Justice Sandra Day O'Connor. Before the Senate could take up his nomination, however, Chief Justice Rehnquist died, and Bush quickly selected Roberts to fill Rehnquist's seat instead. Roberts won Senate confirmation by a 78-22 vote.

Observers consider Roberts one of the more conservative members of the Court. He has, for example, issued opinions opposing assisted suicide and supporting restrictions on abortion. Nevertheless, Roberts has sided in a number of instances with liberal justices, in particular on cases dealing with police searches and seizures.

See also: Associate Justices; Chief Justice of the Supreme Court; Rehnquist, William H.

Roe v. Wade (1973)

Supreme Court case that struck down most anti-abortion laws in the United States as a violation of the constitutional right to privacy. It is one of the most controversial of all Court cases and one that has influenced Court politics since its announcement. Few Court rulings have had such a wide impact or been as extensively and heatedly debated.

Basis of the Case

In 1970, Texas resident Norma L. McCorvey claimed she had become pregnant the result of rape and sought to have an abortion. Texas, however, like many states at the time, had laws banning abortion. McCorvey filed a lawsuit under the name "Jane Roe," asking the U.S. District Court in Texas to grant an injunction, or court order, preventing enforcement of the state's law banning abortion. Texas District Attorney Henry Wade was named the defendant in the suit.

Although the district court ruled in McCorvey's favor on the merits of the case, it refused to grant the injunction. In 1971, the case of *Roe v. Wade* reached the Court on appeal. Following the first round of arguments in the case, Justices John Marshall Harlan II retired, and Justice Hugo Black died. After William Rehnquist and Lewis F. Powell

Jr. filled the vacant seats, the case was reargued in late 1972.

The Court's Decision

On January 22, 1973, the Court announced its decision. By a vote of 7-2, it found in favor of McCorvey, declaring the Texas law unconstitutional. The Court found that a woman's decision to terminate a pregnancy was protected from government infringement as a fundamental right. The majority asserted that the "right of privacy, whether it be founded in the Fourteenth Amendment's concept of personal liberty and restrictions upon state action, as we feel it is, or, as the District Court determined, in the Ninth Amendment's reservation of rights to the people, is broad enough to encompass a woman's decision whether or not to terminate her pregnancy."

In previous cases, the Court had located the basis for privacy rights in several provisions of the Bill of Rights as well as the Fourteenth Amendment. In *Roe,* the Court identified a right of privacy located in the due process clause of the Constitution. The majority refused to find, however, that the state had no legitimate interest in passing a law that prohibited abortion. The Court thus concluded that "the right of personal privacy includes the abortion decision, but that this right is not unqualified and must be considered against important state interests in regulation."

Definitions and Restrictions

The Court did not directly address the most sensitive issues raised by the ruling: When does the unborn fetus become a person and thus acquire constitutional rights? The majority ruling treated these as separate questions. While the justices declared themselves "not in a position to speculate as to the answer" of the first, it offered a qualified response to the second.

The Court adopted a test to determine the state's interest in regulating abortion based on a system of trimesters, or three-month periods. In the first trimester of a pregnancy, according to the Court, the state has no legitimate interest in a woman's pregnancy and cannot restrict a woman's right to an abortion at all. During the second trimester, the state can regulate abortion

---

Landmark Decision Highlights: *Roe v. Wade* (1973)

Issue: Does the Constitution include a woman's right to terminate her pregnancy by abortion?

Opinion: The Court held that a woman's right to an abortion fell within the right to privacy, previously recognized in *Griswold v. Connecticut* (1965), and was protected by the Fourteenth Amendment. The decision gave a woman total autonomy over the pregnancy during the first trimester and determined levels of state interest for the second and third trimesters.

A – Z

in a way that protects the health of the mother. In the third trimester, the state can restrict or prohibit abortion as it chooses. The Court did grant exceptions to prohibition during the third trimester where necessary "for the preservation of the life or health of the mother."

Dissent and Reaction

The two dissenting justices, Byron R. White and William H. Rehnquist, wrote passionately against the decision. Criticizing the constitutional basis of the decision, Rehnquist remarked "To reach its result, the Court necessarily has had to find within the scope of the Fourteenth Amendment a right that was apparently completely unknown to the drafters of the Amendment." Justice White agreed: "I find nothing in the language or history of the Constitution to support the Court's judgment. The Court simply fashions and announces a new constitutional right for pregnant mothers and, with scarcely any reason or authority for its action, invests that right with sufficient substance to override most existing state abortion statutes." Many Americans agreed with White and Rehnquist that there is no specific right to privacy in the Constitution that privileges the federal government to regulate abortion. They believe that the issue is properly left to the states to decide.

Supporters of the decision see it as an important milestone in the path to equality for women and a safeguard for the right of privacy. They argue that laws prohibiting abortion deny women control over their bodies. Some advocates have argued that these laws are the equivalent of forced servitude, which is prohibited by the Thirteenth Amendment.

Current Impressions

Nearly forty years after the *Roe* decision, abortion remains a controversial political issue. Since 1973, many states have enacted laws to place limits on abortion, such as parental consent and notification laws, and laws banning the use of public money for abortions. In 1976, Congress passed the Hyde Amendment, which prohibited federal funding of abortions through Medicaid. The Court ultimately struck down some of the state restrictions, but upheld state and federal laws restricting public funding of abortions.

Public opinion polls show general support for the *Roe* decision. In a 2007 Harris poll, 56 percent of respondents felt that the Court was correct in ruling that the state could not regulate abortion during the first trimester; 40 percent felt the Court's ruling was incorrect. Polls, however, do not reflect the intensity of feeling stirred up by the *Roe* decision, which some view as vital to women's rights while others condemn as legalized murder of the unborn.

The issue of support for *Roe* has imposed itself on the nomination and confirmation of Supreme Court justices. During confirmation hearings, nominees are certain to be questioned about their position on *Roe,* and careful to phrase their answers in a way that offends neither supporters nor opponents of abortion. No potential justice wishes to jeopardize his or her chances of confirmation by declaring unqualified support for or opposition to what is perhaps the most contentious Court decision of the last half century.

See also: Abortion, Constitutional Debate on; Due Process; Right to Privacy; 📖 *Roe v. Wade,* 1973, in the **Primary Source Library.**

Further Reading

Faux, Marian. *Roe v. Wade, Updated Edition: The Untold Story of the Landmark Supreme Court Decision that Made Abortion Legal.* New York: Cooper Square Press, 2000.

Herda, D.J. *Roe V. Wade: The Abortion Question.* Berkeley Heights, N.J.: Enslow Publishers, 1994.

Romaine, Deborah. *Famous Trials - Roe v. Wade.* San Diego, Calif.: Lucent Books, 1998.

Roosevelt's 1937 Court Reform Plan

Efforts by President Franklin D. Roosevelt (1933–1945) to expand the size of the Court in order to appoint justices sympathetic to his New Deal economic legislation. Although Roosevelt's plan ultimately failed, it played a part in convincing the justices to abandon their opposition to the New Deal.

Background

In 1932, with the United States suffering through the **Great Depression,** voters elected Franklin D. Roosevelt president. Roosevelt ran on a promise

In 1932, members of the Supreme Court opposed the growing power of the federal government under President Franklin D. Roosevelt's New Deal. Shown in this 1932 photograph are (seated from left) Justices Louis D. Brandeis, and Willis Van Devanter, Chief Justice Charles Evans Hughes, Justices James C. McReynolds, and George Sutherland, and (standing from left) Justices Owen J. Roberts, Pierce Butler, Harlan Fiske Stone, and Benjamin N. Cardozo. (Library of Congress, Prints and Photographs Division)

to restore the economy by offering Americans a "New Deal." This involved a significant expansion of public works and government assistance programs, including Social Security. In 1936, the voters overwhelmingly elected Roosevelt to a second term.

Although very popular with the public, the New Deal met with opposition from the Court. The Court's opposition to a program and a president with such an overwhelming mandate caused the public to view the Court as an obstacle to reform. Members of Congress offered several proposals to curb the Court's authority. It was Roosevelt, however, who led the charge against the Court.

On February 5, 1937, President Roosevelt sent Congress a message proposing a judicial "reorganization." The measure would have increased the number of Court justices to as many as fifteen. It proposed creating one new seat for each justice who, upon reaching the age of seventy and a half, declined to retire. Thus, for every justice age seventy or above, the president could appoint another one, up to a maximum of six. The measure also called for other changes, such as adding fifty new judges to the federal courts. Roosevelt presented the plan as a bill to relieve the justices' workload, but it was in fact a "Court-packing" scheme to get liberal justices on the bench to reverse the Court's anti-New Deal stance.

Public Reaction

Roosevelt miscalculated public reaction to such a proposal. He had not prepared the public or obtained the advice of Senate leaders before introducing the measure. The plan touched off a

A - Z

By 1940, several of the justices who had ruled New Deal legislation to be unconstitutional had retired, thus allowing President Roosevelt to nominate members who were inclined to support his plans. Seated from left are Justices Owen J. Roberts and James C. McReynolds, Chief Justice Charles Evans Hughes, Justices Harlan Fiske Stone and Hugo L. Black, and standing (from left) are Justices William O. Douglas, Stanley F. Reed, Felix Frankfurter, and Frank Murphy. (Library of Congress, Prints and Photographs Division)

widespread and bitter debate in Congress and in the nation. At a Democratic victory dinner March 4, 1937, Roosevelt criticized the Court for rendering the nation powerless to deal with the problems of economic recovery. In a radio "fireside chat" broadcast a few days later, Roosevelt told the American people that the Court had "cast doubts on the ability of the elected Congress to protect us against catastrophe by meeting squarely our modern social and economic conditions."

Nevertheless, the public strongly opposed the idea of tampering with the Court. The public still regarded the Court as the guardian of the Constitution, free from political influence. The proposal not only angered the public, it also split the

Democrats in Congress. By early March, several Democratic Senators led opposition to the bill.

The Court Reverses Itself

Ironically, it was the Court itself that dealt the death blow to the Court-packing plan with a series of decisions upholding New Deal measures. On March 29, by a 5-4 vote in *West Coast Hotel Co. v. Parrish* (1937), the Court upheld Washington State's minimum wage law for women. The law was nearly identical to another state law the Court struck down ten months earlier. The same day, the Court unanimously upheld a farm mortgage bill that was virtually the same as one they struck down in 1935.

On April 12, again by a 5-4 vote, the Court upheld the National Labor Relations Act. On May 24, by votes of 5-4 and 7-2, the Court upheld the unemployment compensation and the old-age benefits of the Social Security Act. In each 5-4 decision, Justice Owen Roberts—now in favor of the New Deal—cast the deciding vote, abandoning the four conservatives with whom he had voted in previous terms. Justice Roberts's "switch in time" was long assumed to be a direct response to the Court-packing threat, but it actually occurred before Roosevelt presented his plan. The first case indicating Roberts's shift to the left was *West Coast Hotel Co. v. Parrish* in June 1936. In this case,

VIEWPOINTS

HISTORICAL FIGURES

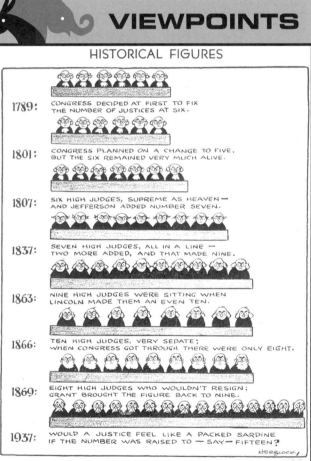

A 1937 political cartoon pokes fun at President Franklin D. Roosevelt's (1933–1945) proposal to increase the number of Supreme Court justices from nine to fifteen. Ultimately, Roosevelt's recommendation died in a Senate committee, and the number of justices remains at nine. (A 1937 Herblock cartoon, copyright by **The Herb Block Foundation**)

VIEWPOINTS

Many political cartooonists of the day were skeptical of President Franklin D. Roosevelt's recommendation to increase the number of Supreme Court justices. Critics of the president noted that his recommendation was aimed at six of the most conservative justices, namely those who had challenged the president's New Deal legislation. (Library of Congress, Prints and Photographs Division)

Roberts reversed his earlier opposition to state minimum wage laws and voted to uphold New York's minimum wage law.

Other developments also spelled defeat for the plan. The Supreme Court Retirement Act approved by Roosevelt in March 1937 permitted justices to retire without resigning, retaining pension and other benefits, at age seventy and a half. Justice Willis Van Devanter, a New Deal foe, announced on May 18 that he would retire at the end of the term. This gave Roosevelt his first opportunity to appoint a new justice to the Court. The administration later accepted a watered-down reorganization measure that reformed lower court procedure but included no provision for additional justices on the Court.

See also: New Deal and the Supreme Court.

Salaries and Benefits of the Justices

Compensation provided to the members of the Supreme Court for their service. In addition to an annual salary, Court justices enjoy a generous retirement program.

Congress historically has been slow to raise the salaries of federal judges. On September 23, 1789, Congress set the salary of an associate justice at $3,500 a year, and for the chief justice at $4,000 a year. That salary remained the same until 1819. In 1989, Chief Justice William H. Rehnquist broke with tradition to appear before a congressional committee, meet privately with congressional leaders, and hold a press conference to urge Congress to increase the salaries of federal judges. In 1990, Congress granted the judges a raise.

From the establishment of the Court and for almost a century, many justices were caught in a dilemma: low salaries and no retirement plan. Many solved the problem by leaving the bench to accept employment elsewhere. Until 1869, justices who were unable to carry out their duties because of age or disability often hesitated to submit their resignations because there were no retirement benefits. The Judiciary Act of April 10, 1869, changed that. It provided that any judge who was seventy years old and held his commission for at least ten years would receive the same salary for life that he or she earned at the time of resignation.

Before 1937, justices who left the Court for any reason had to resign rather than retire. This meant that their pensions were subject to changing civil service guidelines. That policy was changed with the Supreme Court Retirement Act of 1937. This act stated that any judge age sixty-five with fifteen years of service would receive an annuity equal to the salary he was receiving at the time he or she retired.

A justice of the Court who is unable to perform his or her duties cannot be forced to resign. Congress, however, has provided that the president can replace other federal judges deemed to be "unable to discharge efficiently all the duties of his office by reason of permanent mental or physical disability" with Senate approval.

Scalia, Antonin (1936–)

Associate justice of the U.S. Supreme Court, appointed by President Ronald Reagan (1981–1989) and confirmed by the Senate on September 17, 1986. Justice Scalia (1986–) is the 103rd justice to serve on the Court and the first Italian American to do so. Most observers consider Scalia to be the most conservative member of the current Court.

Antonin Scalia was born in Trenton, New Jersey, and grew up in Queens, New York, where he attended Jesuit religious schools. He graduated from Georgetown University in 1957 and Harvard Law School three years later. In the late 1960s, after seven years in private practice in Cleveland, Ohio, he left to teach law at the University of Virginia Law School. Early in his career, he developed a strong individual style marked by a keen legal intellect and a certain whimsical nature. He made playful use of language, would sometimes sing at public appearances, and liked to entertain friends with his piano playing.

In 1971, Scalia became general counsel of the White House Office of Telecommunications Policy under President Richard Nixon (1969–1974). Three years later, he joined the Justice Department as assistant attorney general in charge of the Office of Legal Counsel. Scalia remained in that position until 1977, when he returned to teaching.

In 1982, President Reagan named Scalia to the U.S. Court of Appeals for the District of Columbia Circuit. Scalia developed a reputation as an outspoken conservative with very definite views of the law. He believed the power of the courts was limited. He also took a strong interest in the interpretation of laws. He argued that the only legitimate guide for judges is the actual text of a statute and its related provisions.

In 1986, Reagan promoted Scalia to the Supreme Court. True to his reputation, Scalia has established himself as the most consistently conservative and outspoken member of the Court. Even so, he has written few important opinions. Rather, he is best known for his dissents. In his most biting dissents, he has accused his colleagues of taking their cues from "elite" opinion. "Today's opinion is the product of a Court, which is the product of a law-profession culture, that has largely signed on to the so-called homosexual agenda," he said, dissenting from the ruling in *Lawrence v. Texas* (2003) which struck down anti-sodomy laws.

See also: Associate Justices; Judicial Activism; Judicial Restraint; ▢ Memorandum of Associate Justice Antonin Scalia, 2004, in the **Primary Source Library.**

School Prayer and Bible Readings

Supreme Court rulings that deal with the intersection of church and state in public schools. Before the 1960s, prayer was a common occurrence in classrooms across the country. Cases involving prayer and Bible reading in schools had been appealed to the Supreme Court, but the Court had never ruled directly on the constitutionality of such practices. That situation changed dramatically in 1962.

School Prayer
The case of *Engel v. Vitale* (1962) involved a state recommendation that students in New York schools recite a nondenominational prayer at the beginning of each school day. Not all schools in the state, however, required students to say the prayer. Parents

of ten pupils in the New Hyde Park school district, in Long Island, New York, which had adopted the recommended prayer, brought suit to stop the practice. They claimed that the prayer was contrary to their religious beliefs and practices and that its adoption and use violated the Establishment Clause, which prohibits state sponsorship of any religion.

The Court held that the prayer was "wholly inconsistent with the Establishment Clause." The fact that the prayer was nondenominational and that students who did not wish to participate could remain silent or leave the room did not free the prayer "from the limitations of the Establishment Clause."

Bible Readings
A year later, the Court reached similar conclusions in two cases concerning the practice of daily Bible readings in public school classrooms: *School District of Abington Township v. Schempp* (1963) and *Murray v. Curlett* (1963).

Schempp concerned a Pennsylvania statute that required the reading of at least ten verses from the Bible each day, followed by recitation of the Lord's Prayer and the Pledge of Allegiance. Pupils were excused from participating at the request of their parents. The Schempps asserted that certain literal Bible readings were contrary to their Unitarian religious beliefs, and they sued to stop the readings. In *Murray*, the plaintiffs, Madalyn Murray and her student son, William, were atheists. They contended that the daily religious exercises placed "a premium on belief as against non-belief and subject[ed] their freedom of conscience to the rule of the majority." They asked that the readings be stopped.

The Court held that the Bible readings in both cases were unconstitutional. The readings were clearly religious exercises prescribed as part of the school curriculum for students compelled by law to attend school. They were held in state buildings and supervised by teachers paid by the state. By these actions, the state abandoned the neutrality toward religion demanded by the establishment clause.

Reaction and Later Developments
Public opposition to the decisions in *Schempp* and *Murray* ran high. Both chambers of Congress even considered passing constitutional amendments to

overrule the Court's decisions. Neither the House nor the Senate, however, was able to produce the two-thirds votes needed to send a proposed amendment to the states for **ratification,** or formal approval.

The Court steered clear of school prayer cases for more than twenty years, until *Wallace v. Jaffree* (1985). At this time, the justices decided to take a long, hard look at the new version of school prayer—a "moment of silence." Twenty-three states had passed laws that permitted public school teachers to set aside a moment in class each day for students to engage in quiet meditation. When a state appeals court struck down Alabama's law, the state asked the Court to overturn the decision. The Court refused, agreeing with the appeals court that the law violated the establishment clause.

In 1989, a rabbi gave a nondenominational message to the graduates at the Nathan Bishop Middle School: "God of the Free, Hope of the Brave: For the Legacy of America where diversity is celebrated and the rights of minorities are protected, we thank You," he began. He spoke of the importance of liberty and justice and made no overly religious comments, except to repeat the phrase, "We thank You." Deborah Weisman and her father challenged the rabbi's address in court as a violation of the establishment clause. In *Lee v. Weisman* (1992), the Court ruled the school's action in allowing the rabbi to deliver the invocation unconstitutional because it forced students to participate in "state-sponsored religious activity."

While the Court prohibited school officials and clergy from leading prayers, in 1990 it ruled that students retain a free speech right to pray on their own at school. When some school officials designated students as prayer leaders at school events, however, the issue came before the court. In this case, the Santa Fe, Texas, school board had authorized members of the senior class to elect one student each year to deliver a pregame prayer over the public address system at football games.

In *Santa Fe Independent School District v. Doe* (2000), the Court struck down the school board's policy, emphasizing that "school sponsorship of a religious message is impermissible." Justice John Paul Stevens wrote "the delivery of such a message—over the school's public address system, by a speaker representing the student body, under the supervision of the school faculty and pursuant

to a school policy that explicitly and implicitly encourages public prayer—is not properly characterized as "private speech."

See also: Engle v. Vitale; Freedom of Religion.

Further Reading

Andryszuski, Tricia. *School Prayer: A History of the Debate.* Berkeley Heights, NJ: Enslow Publishers, 1997.

Gold, Susan Dudley, *Engel v. Vitale: Prayer in the Schools.* New York: Benchmark Books, 2006.

Search Warrants

Supreme Court rulings that dealt with court orders allowing law enforcement officials to search for objects or people involved in the commission of a crime and to produce them in court. The Fourth Amendment guarantees the "right of the people to be secure in their persons, houses, papers and effects, against unreasonable searches and seizures." The requirement that officials obtain written permission to conduct searches of private property was intended to protect the individual against arbitrary invasion of privacy by police or other authorities.

The second portion of the amendment spells out requirements for obtaining a search warrant. It underscores the "reasonableness" requirement: that "no Warrants shall issue, but upon probable cause, supported by Oath or affirmation, and particularly describing the place to be searched and the person or things to be seized." The warrant must be sufficiently specific to remove the element of discretion from those persons who are to execute it.

The Court has recognized two primary exceptions to search warrant requirements: a search related to a lawful arrest, or a search of a moving vehicle that has been halted by police. Although the Court generally has resisted arguments for new exceptions to the warrant requirement, it has held that neither aerial surveillance nor police searches of privately owned open fields need be authorized by warrant. It has steadily lengthened the list of situations in which police are permitted to search cars without first obtaining warrants.

JUSTICE FOR ALL

Private Search

The Fourth Amendment protects individuals only against searches and seizures by government agents, not by private individuals. The Court set out this rule in *Burdeau v. McDowell* (1921). After J.C. McDowell was dismissed from his corporate job, his former employers blew open the lock on his private office safe, broke the lock on his desk drawer, and delivered the contents of the desk and safe to the Justice Department, which was investigating McDowell's role in a mail fraud scheme. McDowell challenged the seizure of the evidence as a violation of his right to be secure in his "papers and effects" against unreasonable search and seizure.

The Court rejected McDowell's challenge, holding that the Fourth Amendment reached only government action. Acts committed by private individuals, as in McDowell's case, were outside the protection of that guarantee. McDowell could, however, the Court noted, institute a private suit against those individuals who took his papers and turned them over to the government.

A - Z

The Court has adopted the "exclusionary rule" as a method of enforcing the Fourth Amendment guarantee. In effect in federal courts since 1914, this rule provides that evidence obtained in violation of the Fourth Amendment rights of a defendant may not be used as evidence against the defendant at trial. In *Mapp v. Ohio* (1961), the Court extended this protection to defendants in state as well as federal courts.

The Court has interpreted the Constitution to require that search and arrest warrants be issued by a neutral and detached magistrate. The Court emphasized the importance of this requirement in the 1970s. In *Coolidge v. New Hampshire* (1971), the Court forbade the use of evidence obtained in a police search based on a warrant issued by the state official who was the chief investigator and prosecutor in the case. The following year, however, the Court ruled that municipal court clerks may issue search warrants in cases involving the breach of municipal laws. There was no Fourth Amendment "commandment that all warrant authority must reside exclusively in a lawyer or judge."

See also: Mapp v. Ohio (1960).

Segregation

See Brown v. Board of Education (1954); Equal Protection of the Law; Fair Housing; *Heart of Atlanta Motel v. United States* (1964); *Plessy v. Ferguson* (1896).

Self-Incrimination

Supreme Court rulings that deal with the Fifth Amendment guarantee that no one "shall be compelled in any criminal case to be a witness against himself." One may not be forced to confess, required to testify, or provide evidence that could convict oneself. The Court has affirmed repeatedly that innocent persons as well as guilty ones may invoke this privilege. In doing so, it rejected the assumption that anyone who "takes the Fifth" must be guilty. A defendant, however, must claim the protection against self-incrimination. It is considered waived unless invoked, and when it is claimed, a judge decides whether the claim is justified. The accused waives the guarantee by agreeing to testify in his or her own defense.

In *Hale v. Henkel* (1906), the Court ruled that only "natural" persons, not corporations, labor unions, or other organizations, may invoke the privilege. Individuals in possession of public records, or those of an organization, cannot claim the Fifth Amendment privilege to protect those records, even if the records contain information incriminating to the witness. In *Wilson v. United States* (1911), the Court found that only purely personal and private documents in the possession of the owner are protected.

The Court has declared it unconstitutional for a state to punish employees who refuse to testify about employment-related activities after being ordered to waive their privilege against self-incrimination. In *Garrity v. New Jersey* (1967), it reversed convictions of public employees based on testimony obtained through such coercion. It also ruled that states may not fire persons just because they invoke this privilege.

Congress has passed a number of federal laws requiring individuals to keep detailed records, reports, registration, and tax payments related to membership in some groups, as well as to drug and firearms transactions, and to gambling. Opponents of such laws argued that they effectively forced people engaged in such activities to incriminate themselves. Until the 1960s, however, the Court generally upheld these kinds of registration and tax provisions. Beginning with its decision in *Albertson v. Subversive Activities Control Board* (1965), involving Communist Party registration, the Court held that such requirements violated the Fifth Amendment. In the late 1960s and early 1970s, the Court struck down many of these registration provisions on Fifth Amendment grounds. Congress subsequently rewrote some of the offending laws and omitted the self-incriminatory provisions.

See also: Bill of Rights; Confessions; *Miranda v. Arizona* (1966).

Separation of Powers

See Checks and Balances; Federalism; Legislative Veto; Line Item Veto.

Sex Discrimination

Supreme Court rulings that deal with equal rights and legal treatment for men and women. Although the Fourteenth Amendment guaranteed all citizens equal protection under the law, it was more than a century later before the Court extended that guarantee to women. Although the Court has taken important steps toward placing men and women on an equal footing before the law, it continues to uphold some laws based on traditional beliefs about the respective roles of men and women.

Historical Backgrounds
The Court's attitude toward women has tended to reflect the prevailing societal attitudes of the time. Early on, the Court adopted a philosophy described as "romantic paternalism" to justify discrimination against women. In *Bradwell v. Illinois* (1873), the Court relied on the view of woman as wife, mother, and homemaker to uphold a state law barring women from practicing law.

The Court held the same view when it came to allowing women to vote, serve on juries, or work outside the home. For example, in 1904, the Court upheld a Denver ordinance prohibiting the sale of liquor to women and barring women from working in bars or stores where liquor was sold. In the early 1900s, the Court upheld state laws setting maximum hours and minimum wages for women while holding similar regulations for men a violation of the right to contract their labor.

Challenging Sex Discrimination
All the modern cases challenging discrimination on the basis of sex have occurred since 1969. In the earliest of those cases, the Court applied the traditional standard of review and more often than not found that the state had a rational basis to justify treating women differently from men. In a line of cases in the 1970s, however, the Court held that classification by sex was impermissible. The laws struck down in these cases presumed that all men behaved in one way and all women in another, failing to allow for any variation from this unproved assumption. The Court found such assumptions arbitrary, too broad, and unjustified.

In 1971, the Court began to apply the equal protection test more strictly against state laws

SPOTLIGHT

Women in the Military

The Court has heard few cases concerning the admission of women into the military or the roles they may perform in the armed forces. The national military policy that bars women from combat roles also plays a central part in the most significant Court ruling concerning women in the military, *Rostker v. Goldberg* (1981). In that case, the Court ruled that only men were required to register for the military draft. A 6-3 majority argued that because women could not fill combat roles, there was no need to include them in a draft. To date, *Rostiker* is the last case concerning women's service in the military that has come before the Supreme Court.

that discriminated simply on the basis of gender. In *Reed v. Reed* (1971), the Court struck down an Idaho law that gave preference to male relatives over female relatives in executing a will. Four years later, the Court declared unconstitutional state laws exempting women from jury duty. That same year, the Court also overturned a Utah law that set different ages at which men and women were considered adults. In 1976, it struck down an Alabama law that set minimum height and weight requirements for prison guards, arguing that the law effectively denied such jobs to most women in the state.

Nevertheless, there were some instances in which the Court still held the view that women should be treated differently. After striking down the height and weight requirements for prison guards in Alabama, the Court upheld a state regulation excluding women from certain prison guard jobs. The justices held that females were more vulnerable to attack than males in all-male prisons, and this disqualified them for the job of preserving security there. In 1974, the Court overturned an Ohio law that required pregnant women to leave their jobs at a specified time but upheld laws that allowed employers to exclude pregnancy from coverage under workplace disability insurance.

Current Developments

In the late twentieth century, this area of the law was still evolving. Justice Ruth Bader Ginsburg, who as a lawyer had urged the Court to be more aggressive in its scrutiny of gender classifications,

wrote in 1994, "[E]ven under the Court's equal protection jurisprudence, which requires 'an exceedingly persuasive justification,' it remains an open question whether 'classifications based upon gender are inherently suspect.'" In 1996, Ginsburg was the author of a decision against the men-only admissions policy of the state-funded Virginia Military Institute.

In 1986, the Court ruled that sexual harassment in the workplace should be considered a form of illegal sex discrimination under the 1964 Civil Rights Act. In 1998, it applied this finding in the case of *Faragher v. City of Boca Raton,* finding that an employer can be held liable for sexual harassment committed by a supervisor.

See also: Civil Rights Act of 1964; Equal Protection of the Law.

Sit-Ins

Refers to Supreme Court rulings that deal with a non-violent form of protest in which protesters refuse to move from a public place until they are forcibly removed. This form of protest was pioneered in the 1960s by black students and other individuals speaking out against racial segregation of public facilities. Protesters requested service at "whites only" lunch counters in the South and remained there quietly until ejected or arrested. At least one justice believed that these "sit-ins" were

In this 1963 photograph, opponents of equal rights for African Americans pour condiments on the participants of a sit-in who demanded service at a "whites-only" lunch counter. Although the sit-in, a non-violent means of protest, was used successfully during the American civil rights movement of the 1950s and early 1960s, participants were often mistreated or arrested. (AP Photo)

the two ministers who had urged participation in that sit-in. "It is generally recognized that there can be no conviction for aiding and abetting someone to do an innocent act," the majority wrote in *Shuttlesworth v. Birmingham* (1965).

In *Lombard v. Louisiana* (1963), there was no law requiring segregated eating places in New Orleans. Nonetheless, the Court found that public statements of the city mayor and police chief effectively "required" that public eating facilities be segregated. If it is constitutionally impermissible for a state to enact a law segregating the races, "the State cannot achieve the same result by an official command which has at least as much coercive effect as an ordinance," the justices said.

See also: Equal Protection of the Law; Freedom of Speech.

a form of expression that was guaranteed constitutional protection under some circumstances.

The Court ruled on such actions in series of five cases commonly known as the *Sit-In Cases* (1962). In the first case, *Peterson v. City of Greenville* (1963), an eight-justice majority overturned the convictions of ten protestors who attempted to desegregate a department store lunch counter in Greenville, South Carolina. A city ordinance required racial segregation of public eating places. Arresting the protestors, the Court argued, amounted to state enforcement of the city ordinance denying equal protection. It was no defense that the store managers would have brought criminal trespass charges in the absence of the ordinance.

Peterson became the rule for overturning similar criminal trespass convictions in *Gober v. City of Birmingham* (1963) and *Avent v. North Carolina* (1963). In both cases, city ordinances required separation of the races in eating places. Having overturned trespass convictions in *Gober,* the Court also overturned aiding and abetting convictions of

Sixth Amendment

See Right to a Fair Trial.

Slaughterhouse Cases (1873)

Supreme Court cases that refused to guarantee citizens the full protections of the Bill of Rights against actions by state governments. The Fourteenth Amendment, **ratified** in 1869, guaranteed all citizens equal protection for their constitutional rights under the law. It was unclear, however, whether this guarantee protected individual rights only from federal laws, or from state laws as well. The ruling in the *Slaughterhouse Cases* represented a significant obstacle to disadvantaged groups, including minorities and women, who sought to secure their civil rights during this era.

In 1869, a group of New Orleans butchers charged that the state of Louisiana had violated the Fourteenth Amendment by granting one company the exclusive right to operate a slaughterhouse in the city. By law, all other slaughterhouses in the area were to be closed. The butchers argued that the state-ordered monopoly deprived them of the right to carry on their business. This was one of the rights specifically guaranteed by the Fourteenth Amendment.

On April 14, 1873, the Court ruled against the butchers. The majority argued that the monopoly did not forbid the butchers from practicing their trade; rather, it merely required that they do so at a particular slaughterhouse. Considering the citizenship section of the amendment, Justice Samuel F. Miller made an important distinction:

It is quite clear, then, that there is a citizenship of the United States and a citizenship of a State, which are distinct from each other . . . Of the privileges and immunities of the citizens of the United States, and of the privileges and immunities of the citizens of the State. . . . it is only the former which are placed by this clause under the protection of the Federal Constitution, and that the latter, whatever they may be, are not intended to have any additional protection by this paragraph of the Amendment."

Thus, the butchers' challenge to the monopoly failed, for "the privileges and immunities relied on in the argument are those which belong to citizens of the States as such . . . and are left to the state governments for security and protection, and not by this article placed under the special care of the Federal Government."

In dissent, Justice Stephen Field argued that the Fourteenth Amendment did extend protection to citizens against the loss of their common rights due to state legislation:

The fundamental rights, privileges and immunities which belong to him as a free man and a free citizen, now belong to him as a citizen of the United States, and are not dependent upon his citizenship of any State. . . . They do not derive their existence from its legislation, and cannot be destroyed by its power.

Slavery Issues

Supreme Court rulings that concerned the institution of slavery and the rights of slaves under the U.S Constitution. Although neither the Preamble to the Constitution nor any of the first twelve amendments specifically mentions slavery or slaves, the document alludes to the practice in Article 2, Section I. That article gives each state a number of representatives in Congress based on the number of "free Persons" and "three-fifths of all other Persons." Because the total includes "those bound to Service for a Term of Years," the term "other Persons" is clearly a reference to permanent slaves, primarily black slaves in the Southern United States.

The Court's first significant ruling concerning slavery was *Dred Scott v. Sanford* (1856). The case involved Scott, a slave who had lived for a number of years with his owner in northern states where slavery was illegal. After Scott's original owner died, the owner's widow sold Scott to a man named Sanford. Scott sued for his freedom based on his residence in states in which slavery was illegal. The Court, however, rejected Scott's argument. A majority of justices ruled that as a slave, Scott was the property of his owners to do with as they chose. Under the federal Fugitive Slave Law, the state of Missouri and its citizens were required to return runaway slaves to their owners.

It took the Civil War (1861–1865) to end slavery in practice, and two amendments to end it as a legal institution. In 1865, the states **ratified,** or formally approved, the Thirteenth Amendment, which outlawed the practice of slavery "except as the punishment for a crime whereof the party shall have been duly convicted." This amendment, however, did little to protect freed slaves from legal discrimination in former slave states.

SPOTLIGHT

The *Amistad*

In 1841, antislavery forces won a victory when they persuaded the Court to free fifty-three Africans who had been held as slaves aboard the schooner *Amistad*. After leaving port in Havana, Cuba, the Africans broke their shackles and killed most of the crew. The two Spaniards who held them as slaves, Don Jose Ruiz and Don Pedro Montez, steered the ship on a zigzag course until it ran aground near Montauk Point on Long Island. U.S. officials took custody of the ship and brought it to New London, Connecticut.

The federal courts had jurisdiction over maritime and salvage disputes and therefore the authority to decide the fate of these Africans. Were they slaves and murderers or free men who had been kidnapped? Former President John Quincy Adams (1825–1829) argued the case on behalf of the Africans. He proved the men were not native-born Cuban slaves, as the two Spaniards claimed. Rather, they were Africans who had been captured and held as slaves, in violation of Spanish law. The U.S. government intervened to argue that the slaves and the ship should be returned to Spanish custody.

The Court rejected the government's argument in *United States v. Claimants of the Schooner Amistad* (1841). "These Negroes never were the lawful slaves of Ruiz or Montez or of any other Spanish subjects. They are natives of Africa, and were kidnapped there, and were unlawfully transported to Cuba," wrote Justice Joseph Story. He ordered "said Negroes be declared free and be dismissed from the custody of the court and go without delay."

The Fourteenth Amendment, ratified in 1868, sought to remedy that situation. It stated that

> **N**o State shall make or enforce any law which shall abridge the privileges or immunities of the United States; nor shall any State deny any person of life, liberty, or property, without due process of law; nor deny to any persons under its jurisdiction the equal protection of the laws.

While the Civil War amendments effectively ended slavery in the United States, it would be many years before former slaves enjoyed the full protections of the Bill of Rights. Although they no longer had to struggle for physical freedom, former black slaves and their descendants faced almost a century of continued legal segregation and discrimination with little help from the Supreme Court.

Sotomayor, Sonia (1954–)

First Hispanic and the third woman to serve on the Supreme Court. Nominated by President Barack Obama (2009–) on May 26, 2009, and confirmed by the Senate on August 6, 2009, by a 68-31 vote, Sonia Sotomayor took the judicial oath of office on August 8. She is the 111th justice to serve on the Court.

Sonia Sotomayor, who is of Puerto Rican descent, was born in the Bronx in New York City. Her father died when she was nine years old, and she and a younger brother were reared by her mother, a nurse. Sotomayor excelled in school and graduated at the head of her class at Blessed Sacrament School and at Cardinal Spellman High School. She won a scholarship and attended Princeton University in New Jersey. At Princeton, she continued to excel and then went on to Yale Law School. At Yale, Sotomayor served as an editor of the *Yale Law Journal* and as managing editor of the *Yale Studies in World Public Order.*

Sotomayor was nominated to the U.S. District Court for the Southern District of New York by President George H.W. Bush (1989–1993) in 1991, and the Senate confirmed her nomination in 1992. In 1997, President Bill Clinton (1993–2001) nominated her to the U.S. Court of Appeals for the Second Circuit. On the Second Circuit, where she served for eleven years, Sotomayor heard appeals in more than three thousand cases and personally wrote almost four hundred opinions. She also taught law at the New York University School of Law and Columbia Law School.

After Justice David Souter announced his resignation in early 2009, President Obama selected Judge Sotomayor as his nominee to the high court. When introducing he nominee, the president noted:

Of the many responsibilities granted to a President by our Constitution, few are more serious or more consequential than selecting a Supreme Court justice. The members of our highest court are granted life tenure, often serving long after the Presidents who appointed them. And they are charged with the vital task of applying principles put to paper more than 20 [sic] centuries ago to some of the most difficult questions of our time.

So I don't take this decision lightly. I've made it only after deep reflection and careful deliberation. While there are many qualities that I admire in judges across the spectrum of judicial philosophy, and that I seek in my own nominee, there are few that stand out that I just want to mention.

First and foremost is a rigorous intellect—a mastery of the law, an ability to hone in on the key issues and provide clear answers to complex legal questions. Second is a recognition of the limits of the judicial role, an understanding that a judge's job is to interpret, not make, law; to approach decisions without any particular ideology or agenda, but rather a commitment to impartial justice; a respect for precedent and a determination to faithfully apply the law to the facts at hand . . .

The process of reviewing and selecting a successor to Justice Souter has been rigorous and comprehensive . . . After completing this exhaustive process, I have decided to nominate an inspiring woman who I believe will make a great justice: Judge Sonia Sotomayor of the great state of New York. (Applause.)

Over a distinguished career that spans three decades, Judge Sotomayor has worked at almost every level of our judicial system, providing her with a depth of experience and a breadth of perspective that will be invaluable as a Supreme Court justice.

Along the way she's faced down barriers, overcome the odds, lived out the American Dream that brought her parents here so long ago. And even as she has accomplished so much in her life, she has never forgotten where she began, never lost touch with the community that supported her.

What Sonia will bring to the Court, then, is not only the knowledge and experience acquired over a course of a brilliant legal career, but the wisdom accumulated from an inspiring life's journey.

It's my understanding that Judge Sotomayor's interest in the law was sparked as a young girl by reading the Nancy Drew series—(laughter)—and that when she was diagnosed with diabetes at the age of eight, she was informed that people with diabetes can't grow up to be police officers or private investigators like Nancy Drew. And that's when she was told she'd have to scale back her dreams.

Well, Sonia, what you've shown in your life is that it doesn't matter where you come from, what you look like, or what challenges life throws your way— no dream is beyond reach in the United States of America.

A–Z

Souter, David (1939–)

Associate justice of the U.S. Supreme Court, appointed by President George H.W. Bush and confirmed by Congress on October 2, 1990. Justice Souter (1990–2009) is the 105th justice to serve on the Court. Although expected to be a reliable conservative vote on the Court when he was appointed, Souter has often voted with the more liberal justices.

Souter was born in Melrose, Massachusetts, the only child of a banker. He attended Harvard College, where he graduated with honors in 1961. Souter attended Oxford University on a Rhodes Scholarship from 1961 to 1963. He then attended Harvard Law School, graduating in 1966 and then working for two years in a private law firm.

Early Career

In 1968, Souter became an assistant attorney general for the New Hampshire criminal division. He rose to deputy attorney general in 1971 and in 1976 was appointed attorney general. Under Governor Meldrim Thomson Jr., Souter defended a number of controversial orders. These included the lowering of state flags to half-staff on Good Friday to commemorate the death of Jesus. He prosecuted Jehovah's Witnesses who obscured the state motto "Live Free or Die" on their license plates. He also was responsible for the prosecution of protesters who took over the Seabrook nuclear power plant in 1977.

Souter served as attorney general until 1978, when he was named to the state's trial court. Five years later, Governor John H. Sununu selected Souter for the state supreme court. Sununu later become President Bush's chief of staff. When Bush had the opportunity to name a successor to retiring justice William J. Brennan Jr., Sununu suggested Souter's name.

Decisions

Initially part of the conservative bloc, Souter has moved to the left of center on the modern conservative Court. By the mid-1990s, he voted more often with President Bill Clinton's (1993–2001) appointees, Ruth Bader Ginsburg and Stephen G. Breyer, than with the justices appointed by

Presidents Ronald Reagan (1981–1989) and George H.W. Bush (1989–1993). He dissented from the series of rulings that diminished the power of Congress and endorsed states' rights. Souter argued that the Constitution gave Congress broad power to shape national law.

Souter has been devoted to the principle of church-state separation. He dissented when the Court's conservative majority upheld the flow of taxpayers' money to religious schools. He also played a key role in defending the principle that the government can limit the effect of big money in politics, speaking for the Court in 2000 and 2001 in rulings that upheld state and federal campaign contribution limits. His opinions formed the basis for the Court's decision in 2003 to uphold the McCain-Feingold Act, which banned the unregulated flow of money to the political parties.

Speech, Unprotected

Court rulings that concern what types of speech do not merit protection under the First Amendment to the U.S. Constitution. Although the First Amendment guarantees freedom of speech, some forms of expression clearly fall outside protection of the amendment. The Court has applied different standards, however, at different times to determine what speech should be protected.

The first standard that the Supreme Court proposed to test the extent of government limits on speech was Justice Oliver Wendell Holmes Jr.'s "clear and present danger test." In *Schenck v. United States* (1919), involving espionage and anti-government speech during World War I, Holmes stated,

> The question in every case is whether the words are used in such circumstances and are of such a nature as to create a clear and present danger that they will bring about the substantive evils that Congress has a right to prevent.

With the country engaged in a war, the justices argued that the defendant's efforts to obstruct military recruitment represented a clear and present danger punishable under federal law. The doctrine was little used after *Yates v. United States* (1957), however.

The clear and present danger test was replaced for a time by the so-called balancing doctrine. Here, the Court weighed the value of preserving free speech against the value of preserving whatever governmental interest that speech might adversely affect. Throughout the cold war period—roughly, the late 1940s to the late 1980s—the Court applied the balancing test to state and federal laws restricting the speech and actions of individuals associated with the Communist Party and other allegedly subversive organizations. The Court disposed of some of the cold war cases by using the "incitement test." This standard distinguished between promoting unlawful conduct (such as the violent overthrow of the government) as an abstract principle, and doing so in a way that actually incited action. The first was protected by the First Amendment; the second was not.

The three standards most frequently employed today are "statutory vagueness," "facial overbreadth," and the "least restrictive means test." They are based on the notions that laws imposing restrictions that are too broad, or vague, might inhibit some persons from exercising their constitutionally protected freedoms. Under the least restrictive means test, government may restrain expression only as much as necessary to achieve its purpose.

Statutes lacking in any of these respects may be challenged, even by persons whose speech may in fact be punishable under the law. In 2003, for example, the Court struck down a Virginia law that made all cross burnings a crime, even as it said some cross burnings may be banned. Because burning a cross on the property of an African American family sends a message of terror and intimidation, states may make such acts a crime, said Justice Sandra Day O'Connor. Burning a cross at a Ku Klux Klan rally on private property, however, may be a symbol of group solidarity. Such "symbolic expressions" are generally protected by the First Amendment, she said.

See also: Freedom of Speech.

States' Rights Issues

See Civil Rights and the Supreme Court; Equal Protection of the Law; Federalism; Implied Powers.

Stevens, John Paul (1920–)

Associate justice of the U.S. Supreme Court, appointed by President Gerald R. Ford (1974–1977) and confirmed by Congress on December 19, 1975. He is the 101st justice to serve on the Court and is the oldest current member of the Court.

Stevens is the youngest of the four sons of a prominent Chicago family. He graduated Phi Beta Kappa from the University of Chicago in 1941, and then served in the Navy during World War II, earning the Bronze Star. After graduating from Northwestern University Law School in 1947, he served as a law clerk to Justice Wiley B. Rutledge before joining a well-known Chicago law firm. Three years later, Stevens formed his own law firm, where he remained until President Richard M. Nixon appointed him to the Seventh Circuit Court of Appeals in 1970.

President Ford nominated Stevens to the Supreme Court when Justice William O. Douglas retired in 1975. Observers considered Stevens neither liberal nor conservative but a centrist whose well-crafted scholarly opinions made him a "judge's judge." Stevens has proven the observations correct; he has been **pragmatic** and independent rather than ideological.

With the conservative appointments of Presidents Ronald Reagan (1981–1989), George H.W. Bush (1989–1993), and George W. Bush (2001–2009), Stevens is considered one of the Court's more liberal justices. He wrote the Court's 1995 decision throwing out state term limits for members of Congress, saying that permitting such restrictions would lead to a patchwork of state qualifications and undermine the uniformity and national character of the U.S. government.

Stevens strongly dissented from rulings that curbed the powers of Congress and revived what he referred to as the discredited doctrine of states' rights. He mocked his conservative colleagues for having invented the principle of state "sovereign immunity," which the Framers of 1787 had forgotten to mention in the text of the Constitution. In 2002, Stevens spoke for the Court in *Atkins v. Virginia,* declaring an end to the execution of mentally retarded defendants. He has also

A – Z

been a longtime advocate of the separation of church and state and a more recent convert to the cause of affirmative action and gay rights. At age ninety, Stevens remained a lively presence during the Court's oral arguments. However, in April 2010, he announced his retirement.

See also: Judicial Activism; Judicial Restraint.

Stop-and-Frisk Searches

Supreme Court rulings that deal with the police practice of stopping suspicious persons and "frisking" them for weapons. According to the justices, such searches are reasonable within the boundaries of the Fourth Amendment, even without a search warrant or enough information to constitute probable cause for arrest.

In *Terry v. Ohio* (1968), Chief Justice Earl Warren announced the Court's policy but also emphasized the limited nature of this authority. It is not a general or unlimited power to stop every pedestrian. Rather, it is triggered whenever the officer has some specific reason to suspect wrongdoing by a pedestrian, the Court said. The brief search itself consists "solely of a limited patting of the outer clothing of the suspect for concealed weapons," Warren stated. It is not to be used as a pretext to search the suspect for drugs or other illegal items. Nonetheless, the Court has been reluctant to restrain officers further by second-guessing their reason for stopping a suspect or by rejecting evidence that was found after an initial frisk.

In *United States v Sokolow* (1989), the Court upheld the use of "drug courier" profiles by federal agents operating at airports and train stations. Persons who fit the profiles sometimes are stopped for questioning, even if agents have no other reason to suspect them of a crime. Just as "nervous, evasive behavior" at an airport counter may give agents reason to detain a traveler, "unprovoked flight upon noticing the police" gives officers good reason to pursue and stop the individual, Chief Justice Rehnquist said in *Illinois v. Wardlow* (2002).

The Court has, however, refused to give officers broader authority to search presumably innocent pedestrians and seize evidence from them.

In *Minnesota v. Dickerson* (1993), the Court ruled that police cannot feel around in a detained person's pockets and clothing in hopes of finding drugs. The justices also insisted in *Florida v. J.L.* (2000) that police must have "reliable" evidence of wrongdoing before they stop someone. The Court said that stop-and-frisk based entirely on an "anonymous tip" was unreasonable because police had no way to judge the reliability of the tipster. If anonymous tips were enough to justify police stops, said Justice Ruth Bader Ginsburg, vengeful persons could harass their enemies by subjecting them to unwarranted, unreasonable, and embarrassing searches by the police.

See also: Automobile Searches; Search Warrants.

Story, Joseph (1779–1845)

Long-serving and influential Supreme Court justice nominated in 1811 by President James Madison (1809–1817). Joseph Story was confirmed by the Senate on November 18, 1811, by a voice vote. He took the judicial oath on February 3, 1812, and served until his death on September 10, 1845. Today, he is considered one of the foremost of American legal writers. It was Story who delivered the majority opinion in the historic *Amistad* case.

Joseph Story was descended on both sides from old New England families. His father, Elisha Story, was a participant in the Boston Tea Party in 1773. His mother was Mehitable Pedrick Story.

After graduating second in his class from Harvard University in Cambridge, Massachusetts, in 1798, Story began reading law, sometimes for fourteen hours a day, in the Marblehead law office of Samuel Sewall. Sewall later served as chief justice of the Massachusetts Supreme Court. Admitted to the bar in 1801, Story began practice in the town of Salem.

Story was an ardent poetry lover throughout his life. He was known by his hometown friends as "the poet of Marblehead." In 1805, he published "The Power of Solitude," a long, effusive poem written in heroic couplets. When his father and his wife of only seven months both died that year, Story, in a fit of sorrow, burned all copies of the poem he could find. He experienced further tragedy losing five of his seven children by his second marriage.

An avid conversationalist, Story enjoyed music, drawing, and painting. In addition to being a writer, Story was an able public speaker. He delivered the annual Fourth of July oration in Salem in 1804 and in 1826 delivered the Phi Beta Kappa oration at Harvard.

Story served for three years in the Massachusetts legislature and then entered the U.S. Congress in 1808. During his one term of service in the House, he was blamed by President Thomas Jefferson (1801–1809) for the repeal of Jefferson's foreign trade **embargo,** and he lost favor within the Democratic-Republican Party by calling for a plan to strengthen the U.S. Navy. In January 1811, Story returned to the Massachusetts legislature and was elected Speaker of the House. By November of that year, he had become one of the youngest men ever to sit on the Court.

Only thirty-two years old and with no court experience, Story had not been Madison's first choice for the job, but Levi Lincoln and John Quincy Adams had both declined, and Alexander Wolcott had been rejected by the Senate. Although he had a few financial reservations about taking the job, Story accepted the position as a great honor.

A supporter of higher learning for women, Story retained an active interest in education for most of his life. In 1819, he was elected to the Harvard Board of Overseers and became a fellow of the Harvard Corporation six years later. In 1829, Story moved from Salem to Cambridge, Massachusetts, to become professor of law at his alma mater. He played a major role in the foundation of Harvard Law School. He is also credited, along with Chancellor James Kent of New York, with founding the equity system of jurisprudence as practiced in the United States today.

While at Harvard, Story wrote his famous nine *Commentaries* on the law. Each of these works went through many editions, and one–*Commentaries on the Constitution* (1833)–was published in French, Spanish, and German, enhancing Story's international reputation.

In addition to the *Commentaries,* Story wrote legal essays for the *North American Review* and the *American Law Review,* and contributed unsigned articles to the *Encyclopedia Americana.* His Court opinions, though often accused of being tedious, are seminal works in the history of American national law.

On the Court, Story rarely broke from the strong nationalism of Chief Justice John Marshall. In fact, it was Story's opinion in *Martin v. Hunter's Lessee* (1816) that established the appellate supremacy of the Supreme Court over state courts in civil cases involving federal statutes and treaties.

When Marshall died in 1835, Story undoubtedly wanted the chief justiceship, and his colleagues generally agreed he should be appointed. Story, however, was strongly disliked by President Andrew Jackson (1829–1937). Jackson once called Story the "most dangerous man in America." Roger Taney received the chief justice nomination instead.

Story's nine years on the Taney Court were spent largely in dissent, and by the beginning of the 1845 term, he was prepared to resign. He refused to leave until he had attended to all his unfinished business, however. He died on September 10, 1845, after a sudden illness.

See also: Slavery Issues.

Sturges v. Crowninshield (1819)

Early Supreme Court case in which two constitutional issues were addressed: first, the relative lawmaking powers of Congress and the states; and second, the passing of laws that violate the Constitution's contract clause. The Court's ruling ultimately was vague and did not fully settle all the matters the case presented.

Sturges v. Crowninshield involved a bankruptcy law passed by the New York state legislature intended to ease the difficulties of debtors in **default.** The case raised a question about whether the law violated Article I, Section 8, of the Constitution, which gives Congress power to establish "uniform laws of the subject of bankruptcies throughout the United States." It was unclear whether the language in the Constitution meant that Congress has the sole power to establish bankruptcy laws or whether the states may do so as well.

The law also allowed for the discharge of debts incurred before its passage. Opponents of the law pointed out that the Constitution forbids states to pass any law that impairs the obligations of legal contracts. In this case, creditors faced the possibility that contracts they signed with borrowers before the law was passed would be worthless and unenforceable.

A unanimous Court voted to strike down the law, but Justice John Marshall stated in his opinion that the mere existence of Congress's power to pass a federal bankruptcy law did not, in itself, deny the states the right to pass their own bankruptcy laws. At the same time, Marshall's opinion did not address what would happen if the Congress and a state passed conflicting bankruptcy laws. Since Congress had not yet exercised its power to pass bankruptcy laws, the Court's silence on this issue was matter of concern to the states.

While the Court's stance on the issue of bankruptcy was unclear, the justices found unanimously that the law was unconstitutional because of the provision forgiving prior debts. The Court considered this to be a clear violation of the contract clause.

Eight years later, however, the Court upheld a new version of the New York bankruptcy law in *Gibbons v. Ogden* (1827), which represented a weakening of the protection from state action afforded by the contract clause. Marshall warned that the latter decision threatened to turn the contract clause into "an inanimate, inoperative, unmeaning" phrase.

See also: Bankruptcy and Bankruptcy Laws; *Gibbons v. Ogden* (1827); 📖 *Sturges v. Crowninshield,* (1819), in the **Primary Source Library.**

Supreme Court, History of the

A chronological account of the formation and development of the Supreme Court of the United States. In *The Federalist Papers,* Alexander Hamilton

Shown in this 1865 photograph (from left) are Court Clerk Daniel W. Middleton, Justices David Davis, Noah H. Swayne, Robert C. Grier, James M. Wayne, Chief Justice Salmon P. Chase, Justices Samuel Nelson, Nathan Clifford, Samuel F. Miller, and Stephen J. Field. President Abraham Lincoln (1861–1865) appointed five of these justices—Swayne, Miller, and Davis in 1862; Field in 1863; and Chase in 1864. (Library of Congress, Prints and Photographs Division)

referred to the Court as the "least dangerous" branch of government because it possessed neither the "power of the purse" nor that of "the sword." Indeed, in its early days, the Court was the least influential and most obscure branch of government. Over time, however, the Court has expanded its influence to touch on almost every aspect of civic life.

The Early Court

The Constitution vests the judicial power of the nation in a Supreme Court and defines some of the limits of its **jurisdiction,** or area of legal authority. However, it offers no specifics as to the Court's composition, and the most important types of cases the Court hears—those ruling on the constitutionality of legislative acts—are not specifically mentioned in the Constitution. The principle of judicial review, or the idea that the Court has the authority to judge the constitutionality of laws, was not formally established until the case of *Marbury v. Madison* (1803).

Congress has power to create lower courts, a power it used to fill in many of the gaps in the Constitution concerning the structure of the federal judiciary. The Judiciary Act of 1789 set the size of the Court at six justices—a chief justice and five associate justices. Later, judiciary acts would increase the Court to its present size of nine. The act also more specifically defined the types of cases that fell under the Court's original jurisdiction, as well as which ones it could hear on appeal. Although

it gave the Court the power of judicial review over state laws, it made no mention of the Court's authority to rule on federal laws.

The First Courts

The first Court, led by Chief Justice John Jay, was most notable for its low profile. The Court heard very few cases compared to its later counterparts. Its most significant decision was *Chisholm v. Georgia* (1793), which upheld the right of individuals to sue states in federal court. Congressional opposition to the ruling in *Chisholm* led to passage of the Eleventh Amendment in 1795. This amendment prohibits federal courts from hearing certain types of lawsuits against states.

The Marshall Court (1801–1835)

The Court continued to be only a minor force in the nation's political life throughout the remainder of the eighteenth century. The succession of John Marshall as chief justice in 1801, however, marked the beginning of a period of significant expansion of the Court's power.

Early in his term, Marshall announced his intention to establish the Court's independence from Congress. *Marbury v. Madison* (1803) marked the first time that the Court overturned an act of Congress as unconstitutional. In this case, Congress had tried to expand the jurisdiction of the Court unconstitutionally. The Court's ruling, and its refusal to comply with Congress,

Changes in the Size of the Supreme Court

Terms	Act of Congress	Seats
1789–1801	Judiciary Act of 1789	6
1801–1802	Circuit Court Act of 1801	5
1802–1807	Repeal of Circuit Court Act of 1801	6
1807–1837	Judiciary Act of 1807	7
1837–1863	Congressional addition (1837)	9
1863–1866	Judiciary Act of 1863	10
1866–1869	Congressional reduction (1866)	8
1869–Present	Judiciary Act of 1869	9

The Judiciary Act of 1869 mandates, "That the Supreme Court of the United States shall hereafter consist of the Chief Justice of the United States and eight associate justices."

left no doubt that the Court was not as weak as it had first appeared.

Under Marshall, the Court expanded the power of the federal government at the expense of state power. In the landmark cases of *McCulloch v. Maryland* (1819) and *Gibbons v. Ogden* (1824), the Court upheld the use of Congress's power to regulate interstate commerce to establish a national bank and regulate private businesses engaged in interstate navigation. By contrast, essentially the same Court ruled in *Barron v. Baltimore* (1833) that the protections afforded by the Bill of Rights applied only to actions by the federal government and not to actions take by state government.

The Taney Court (1836–1864)

Under Marshall's successor, Roger B. Taney, the Court took a more sympathetic view of states' rights, particularly the rights of Southern slaveholders. The Taney Court is best known for its decision in *Dred Scott v. Sandford* (1857), which declared that slaves were property and had "no rights which the white man is bound to respect." Under Taney, the Court also declared unconstitutional the Missouri Compromise of 1820, an act of Congress prohibiting slavery in certain territories. The Court's decisions contributed to the political tensions between North and South that led eventually to the Civil War (1861–1865).

Post Civil-War Courts

Northern victory in the war ended slavery in practice, and the passage of the Thirteenth and Fourteenth Amendments after the war promised to end unequal treatment of former slaves. However, in the cases that came before the Court in the decades after the war, the justices consistently refused to prohibit discriminatory practices against blacks by individuals or state governments. In one of its most infamous decisions, the Court, in *Plessy v. Ferguson* (1896), ruled that racial segregation of public facilities was legal, as long as both races were provided with "substantially equal" facilities. The ruling in *Plessy* gave legal sanction to discrimination by state governments for another sixty years.

The Court at this time was a solidly conservative institution that was principally concerned with protecting business from government intervention.

In the early twentieth century, the Court opposed legislation to shorten the work week, provide for a minimum wage, or impose minimal workplace safety standards. The Court was also hostile to the interest of unions and labor groups. Still, despite its basic conservatism, the Court struck one of the most sweeping blows for expansion of civil rights with its decision in *Gitlow v. New York* (1925). This case introduced the doctrine of incorporation, which applied the restrictions of the Bill of Rights to state governments as well as the federal government.

The Court Under Franklin D. Roosevelt

The 1930s saw a Court divided into recognizably liberal and conservative wings. With one more member, the conservative bloc on the Court typically formed a majority opposing the expansion of federal power. During the 1930s, this became a point of conflict between the Court and President Franklin D. Roosevelt (1933–1945).

Roosevelt, who took office at the depth of the **Great Depression** of the 1930s, wanted to pass legislation to expand the federal government's involvement in many areas of the economy. The Court consistently struck down what was known as Roosevelt's New Deal legislation, leading the president to propose a bill to add more justices of his choosing to the Court. In the end, Roosevelt never had to make good on this threat to "pack" the Court with justices of his own selection. By the late 1930s, the Court, now containing members appointed by Roosevelt, had finally abandoned its opposition to the New Deal expansion of federal government.

Compulsory Retirement?

There have been repeated—if so far unsuccessful—suggestions that a constitutional amendment be enacted to require justices of the Court to retire at age seventy or seventy-five. Justice Owen J. Roberts expressed his support for such a proposal more than thirty years ago:

> believe it is a wise provision. First of all, it will forestall the basis of the last attack on the Court, the extreme age of the justices, and the fact that superannuated

SPOTLIGHT

Mandatory Retirement?

Concerning the tenure of justice of the Supreme Court, the U.S. Constitution states only that the "judges . . . shall hold their offices during good behavior." In other words, justices may hold their office for life, no matter how old or ill they might become. In practice, however, this generous provision of the Constitution led to problems. For the first eighty years of the Court's existence, Congress made no pension provisions for justices who wished to retire. As a result, several stayed on the Court until death, even though they were physically and mentally incapable of performing their duties.

That situation was somewhat remedied by the congressional passage on April 10, 1869, of an act that provided that any federal justice who reached seventy years of age and had ten years of service could resign and receive a pension equal to his salary at the time of resignation.

In 1936, President Franklin D. Roosevelt announced a plan to rid the Court of aged conservatives who were blocking implementation of most of his economic recovery program. At the time, all members of the federal judiciary, except Supreme Court justices, were allowed to retire from regular service rather than resign. Judges who retired were still entitled to the salary of the office, including the increases in salary given to active judges.

Supreme Court justices, however, had to resign, and their pensions were subject to the same fluctuations as other retired government officials. When Justice Oliver Wendell Holmes, Jr., was prevailed upon to resign in 1932, for example, his pension was ten thousand dollars a year—half his annual pay as a justice—because the Herbert Hoover (1929–1933) administration, aiming to economize, set that amount as the maximum pension for former government employees.

Chief Justice Charles Evans Hughes thought later that two of the more conservative members of the Court would have joined Holmes and retired if Congress had not been so miserly. As it was, Justices Willis Van Devanter and George Sutherland remained on the Court, forming the nucleus of the conservative majority that struck down one New Deal law after another.

In response to Roosevelt's "Court-packing" proposal, which it opposed, Congress quickly approved the Supreme Court Retirement Act of 1937, which permitted justices age seventy, with ten years of service—or at age 65, with 15 years of service—to retire at full salary rather than resign. The law quickly proved effective. Roosevelt signed it into law March 1, 1937, and on May 18, Justice Van Devanter announced his retirement.

A - Z

old gentlemen hung on there long after their usefulness had ceased. More than that, it tends to provide for each administration an opportunity to add new personnel to the Court, which, I think, is a good thing.

Charles Fairman, a political scientist, wrote in the *Harvard Law Review* that "there are two distinct reasons for urging some scheme for compulsory retirement" of Supreme Court justices:

There is, first, the actual impairment of mental and physical powers . . . A second reason for insuring renewal of the Court involves considerations of a different order. Rigidity of thought and obsolescence of social outlook, though more objective, may be no less real than the waning of bodily powers. When a majority of the Court cling to views of public policy no longer entertained by the community or shared by the political branches of government, a conflict arises which must be resolved.

Cold War Courts

By the end of World War II (1939–1945), eight of the nine justices were Roosevelt appointees, the sole exception being Owen Roberts. Over the next twenty-five years, they would pass some of the most notable and controversial decisions in the Court's history.

The Warren Court (1953–1969)

When President Dwight David Eisenhower (1953–1961) appointed Earl Warren to be chief justice in 1953, the president was fulfilling a campaign promise he had made to Warren during the campaign, when he was seeking Warren's support. Later, however, Eisenhower declared this to be the biggest mistake he made as president. Under Warren, the Court took a decidedly more activist turn. Its first major decision, and arguably its most significant, was *Brown v. Board of Education* (1954), which overturned *Plessy* and declared segregation in public schools unconstitutional. In the early 1960s, the Court issued a series of rulings to protect the rights of criminal defendants. These included finding that

illegally seized evidence cannot be used in a trial, that the state must provide an attorney to any defendant who cannot otherwise afford one, and that police must inform suspects of their rights before being questioned. It was under Warren that the first black Justice, Thurgood Marshall, joined the Court in 1967.

The Burger Court (1969–1986)

The Court led by Warren E. Burger is best known for upholding the legality of abortion in some circumstances in *Roe v Wade* (1973). Its other notable ruling was in *United States v. Nixon* (1974), where it found that the president's claim of **executive privilege** to withhold documents from Congress is not absolute. The ruling led ultimately to the resignation of President Richard Nixon (1969–1974). The Burger Court also witnessed the appointment of the first female justice, Sandra Day O'Connor, in 1981.

Recent Courts

The Court under Chief Justice William H. Rehnquist (1986–2005) reached several controversial decisions in the areas of free speech and privacy. It declared flag burning a form of speech protected by the First Amendment, while ruling student-led school prayers unconstitutional. The Court overturned bans on late-term abortions in *Stenberg v. Carhart* (2000), as well as anti-sodomy laws in *Lawrence v. Texas* (2003). It drew a great deal of criticism for its ruling in *Bush v. Gore* (2000), which ended the presidential election recount in Florida and awarded George W. Bush (2001–2009) the presidency. Since 2005, John Roberts has served as chief justice and has presided over a generally conservative Court.

See also: Associate Justices; Chief Justice of the United States; Jurisdiction of the Supreme Court; Salaries and Benefits of the Justices; Supreme Court Building; Term of the Supreme Court; Supreme Court, Traditions of the.

Further Reading

Baum, Lawrence. *The Supreme Court.* Washington, D.C.: CQ Press, 2009.

Patrick, John J. *The Supreme Court of the United States: A Student Companion.* New York: Oxford University Press USA, 2006.

Supreme Court, Traditions of the

Practices and principles that shape the way the Court operates and its relations with the other branches of government. The Court is the most traditional of the three major branches of government. Some traditional aspects of the Court seem merely quaint, such as the quill pens available as mementos to attorneys who argue before the Court. Others, such as mandatory retirement of justices or televising Court sessions, continue to generate debate.

Continuity and Change

The main factor in the continuity of the Court is that its justices are appointed for life. The majority of justices have either died while still on the bench or retired near the end of their lives. None has been removed from the bench involuntarily, although several have resigned under pressure. Just as change is central to Congress and the presidency through periodic elections, continuity is built into the Court through longevity of service. The average length of service of all justices of the Court, including sitting members, has been about fifteen years.

With a new member added only every two years or so on average, successive Courts assume their own collective identity as the same justices work together over the space of decades. Each new member, however different in ideology and temperament from his or her associates, can make only a small difference.

The membership of the Court is determined in large part by slowly evolving circumstances: by the political party in power as vacancies occur; by the length of time a Court has sat together; and, finally, by the durability of each justice, surviving changes in the Court and in the times.

Precedent

Another factor in the Court's essential continuity is its reliance on precedent in arriving at decisions. Except in rare cases, any decision is based primarily on earlier relevant opinions of the Court or lower courts as interpreted in light of the case under consideration. Whether the Court upholds, modifies, or reverses an earlier Court's judgment, the decision is rooted in precedent.

Other Traditions

Among the Court's most important traditions is secrecy. No one except the justices is allowed in the conference room while the justices are deliberating. The justices believe they have good reason to maintain the veil of secrecy that surrounds their conference deliberations and their personal relations with other members of the Court. Widespread disclosure of what goes on in conference could reduce public esteem for the Court and its rulings. When leaks occur, the Court refuses to confirm or deny their accuracy, and the justices are reluctant to reveal instances of infighting and conflict among themselves.

Seniority

The system of seniority affects Court procedures such as conference discussion and voting, announcement of opinions, and seating in the courtroom. It is also a determining factor in assignment of office space. Only the chief justice is exempt from the rules of seniority. During conferences, discussion of cases begins with the chief justice and proceeds down the line of seniority to the junior associate justice. The junior justice has the task of sending for and receiving documents or other information the Court may need. When opinions are announced in the courtroom, the justices who wrote the opinions announce them in reverse order of seniority.

The offices of the justices also are assigned according to seniority. Because there were only six suites inside the so-called "golden gates"—the large bronze doors that seal the justices off from the public—the three junior justices usually occupy the offices on the corridor just outside.

Formality

Both in and out of Court, the justices seek to present an image of formality and courtesy. Before they go into the courtroom and at the beginning of their private conferences, the justices shake hands with each other. This practice began in the late nineteenth century when Chief Justice Melville Fuller decided that it was a good idea to remind the justices that differences of opinion did not preclude overall harmony of purpose. In court and in their

POINT/COUNTERPOINT

SHOULD SUPREME COURT HEARINGS BE TELEVISED?

Many political observers, as well as some members of Congress, have called for the sessions of the U.S. Supreme Court to be televised, much like the daily coverage of sessions of the House of Representatives and the Senate. Others, however, including many judges and most Supreme Court justices, are opposed to the idea, citing privacy issues and noting that television cameras will destroy the solemn deliberations of the Court.

Bruce Peabody, assistant professor of political science at Fairleigh Dickinson University in Madison, New Jersey, believes that televising Court sessions would help Americans understand how the court system works. Lorraine H. Tong, a government policy analyst who works for the Congressional Research Service, presents opposing views for members of Congress to consider.

Professor Bruce Peabody

[In 2006, Congress considered] a bill proposed by Senator Arlen Specter of Pennsylvania mandating that the court "permit television coverage" of all its "open sessions." The measure would allow the court to shut off the cameras if a majority of justices objected on the grounds that this coverage would cause unfairness to the parties of a case. . . .

What benefits will "we the people" get out of greater Supreme Court coverage? While television does not clearly shift people's views about public policy, it can change what we look at. This spotlight effect could bring greater attention to the court, which remains one of our least understood and publicized institutions

But even if it's a good idea, would Specter's legislation be constitutional? Could the justices—some of whom have vocally opposed the measure—eventually invalidate the bill if it became law?

One constitutional argument against the proposed law is that it would threaten the separation of powers. Mandating television coverage smacks of congressional meddling in the details of the court's internal operations. . . .

There is a second, stronger objection to the proposed legislation. Ours is supposed to be a Constitution of listed, or enumerated, national powers. Congress cannot pass a law unless the Constitution authorizes it to act.

The Constitution does give Congress authority to "make all laws which shall be necessary and proper for carrying into execution" the powers given to the federal government. So can Congress plausibly argue that televising Supreme Court proceedings is "necessary and proper" to advancing the "judicial power" which the Constitution vests "in one Supreme Court" and in whatever lower courts Congress chooses to create? At first glance, this argument seems a stretch. Whatever its shortcomings, the Supreme Court has operated well enough over the past two hundred-plus years without appearing on "C-SPAN3."

For better or worse, it's ultimately up to American citizens to gather, sift, and interpret the information about public affairs made available to them. Certainly, we all make mistakes and misjudgments in our efforts to do this. But enhancing the flow of information from the court can only help us to better understand and monitor the most powerful judiciary in the world.

Lorraine H. Tong

The Supreme Court has noted that pretrial publicity can cause "tensions [to] develop between the right of the accused to trial by an impartial jury and the rights guaranteed others by the First Amendment." This suggests the possibility that excessive publicity could give rise to due process problems in particular situations, and to permit cameras in a courtroom during trial would arguably cause excessive publicity in some cases. The Judicial Conference of the United States has opposed televising federal court proceedings due to concerns that the fundamental right of citizens to a fair trial might be impaired, and because of the intimidating effect it might have on litigants, witnesses, and jurors in both civil and criminal trial proceedings. . . .

At the April 4, 2006, House hearing on the Supreme Court's budget request for FY [fiscal year] 2007, Justice Clarence Thomas was asked his views on televising the Court's proceedings. Justice Thomas expressed concerns that doing so would risk undermining the manner in which the court considers cases. He noted that while some Justices felt more strongly than others, the "general consensus" was "not one of glee." The integrity of court proceedings, in some opponents' estimation, would be jeopardized if cameras gained access to the courtroom. Justice Antonin Scalia said in October 2005, "We don't want to become entertainment. I think there's something sick about making entertainment out of real people's legal problems. I don't like it in the lower courts, and I particularly don't like it in the Supreme Court." During the Senate Judiciary Committee [meetings] on March 30, 2006, several Senators expressed strong reservations about or opposition to televising court proceedings. Expressing concerns about "grandstanding," Senator Orrin Hatch said, "Judges are not politicians—they should not be making speeches from the bench."

Potential for Misinterpretation. Some believe that televising oral arguments, or a portion of the proceedings, could lead to misinterpretation of the way the courts operate. Justice Kennedy and others have said that oral arguments do not give the complete picture of the Supreme Court's work, and constitute only a small portion of its decision-making process. The Justices do most of their work in solitude—reading, writing, considering voluminous documents—before deliberating with the other Justices in conference. Justice Scalia expressed similar concerns that even if proceedings were televised gavel-to-gavel, the vast majority of the public would not see the entire proceedings, and sound bites would misinform, rather than inform, the public. . . .

DOCUMENT-BASED QUESTION:

What positive outcome does Professor Bruce Peabody anticipate from televised Supreme Court sessions? What concerns does the article by Lorraine Tong identify?

written opinions, the justices traditionally addressed each other as "my brother" or "my dissenting brothers." In contemporary courts, with women justices, members refer to each other simply as "Justice." Still, the image of harmony is occasionally undermined by personal, ideological, and legal differences among justices with strong views and even stronger egos.

Despite the occasional sharp comments in their opinions, the justices regularly say they enjoy a friendly and collegial relationship with all the members of the Court. Justices Clarence Thomas and Stephen G. Breyer rarely agree in major cases, but the two sit together on the bench and can often be seen talking and joking together. Both have made nearly identical statements in speeches attesting to the fact they have never heard a harsh personal comment or a raised voice in the private conferences of the justices.

Meeting Locations of the Supreme Court

Merchant's Exchange Building, New York City	1790
Independence Hall, Philadelphia	1790–1791
Old City Hall, Philadelphia	1791–1800
U.S. Capitol, Washington, D.C.	1800–1935
Supreme Court Building, Washington, D.C.	1935–present

Although the Supreme Court was always a coequal branch of the federal government, it did not move into its own quarters until 1935. In 1929, Chief Justice William Howard Taft finally persuaded Congress to allocate the funds to construct a permanent home for the Court.

Supreme Court Building

The history of the Court's accommodations since the nation's founding and that of the structure that houses the current Court. When the federal government moved from Philadelphia to Washington, D.C., in 1800, the Supreme Court had no accommodations whatsoever. Today, its impressive quarters are a symbol of the stability and permanence of the U.S. justice system.

Early Accommodations

Congress assigned the Court a small room on the first-floor entrance hall of the Capitol in which to conduct its business. There, the Court held its first session in Washington on February 2, 1801. It was the first of a series of often makeshift, hand-me-down quarters assigned by Congress to the Court before the completion of its present building in 1935.

The need for repairs to the space forced the Court to move into the Capitol library in 1808, but "the Library became so inconvenient and cold that the Supreme Court preferred to sit at Long's Tavern" during the February 1809 term. The Court returned to the Capitol in 1810 and met in a courtroom especially designed for it. It remained in the new courtroom until the British burned the Capitol on August 24, 1814, during the War of 1812. The British are said to have used Supreme

Court documents to start the fire. The Court returned to its regular courtroom beneath the Senate chamber in 1819 and remained there until moving to new chambers on the first floor of the Capitol in 1860.

None of the justices had individual office space in the Capitol; each had to provide for his own and his staff's working quarters at a time when spacious housing in Washington was difficult to find. Nevertheless, the justices held sessions in these quarters for seventy-five years, with only two exceptions.

New Court Building

President William Howard Taft (1909–1913) began promoting the idea of a separate building for the Supreme Court around 1912. Congress finally authorized funds for the construction of a permanent dwelling for the Court in 1929. On October 7, 1935, the Court held its first session at the new building at One First Street, Northeast, across the plaza from the Capitol.

The building, built in the Greek Revival style, measures 385 feet by 304 feet and rises four stories above ground level. Marble is the primary building material: Almost a third of the building's cost was spent on domestic and foreign marble. Most of the floors in the building are oak, and the doors and walls of most offices are American-quartered white oak. Bronze and mahogany were also used. The roof was made from cream-colored Roman tile set

The Supreme Court Building was completed in 1935. Cass Gilbert, the architect who designed the building, chose the Neoclassical style used in ancient Rome to reflect the United States's democratic ideals. (AP Photo, Kenneth Lambert)

A – Z

on bronze strips over lead-coated copper on a slab of watertight concrete.

Since its completion in 1935, the Supreme Court building has been a subject of both praise (a "marble palace") and outspoken criticism (a "marble mausoleum"). Its admirers speak in terms of structural simplicity, austerity, beauty, and dignity. For them, it is a fitting monument epitomizing the words on the front entrance of the building: "Equal Justice under Law." At the time it was built, however, it had many detractors. In the 1930s, the authors of the Federal Writers' Project, in their *Guide to Washington,* wrote that "the building has a cold, abstract, almost anonymous beauty but is lacking in that power which comes from a more direct expression of purpose."

Layout and Design

The building was designed so that the justices need not enter public areas except when hearing oral arguments and announcing their opinions. A private elevator connects the underground garage with the corridor, closed to the public, where the justices' offices are located.

The basement of the Supreme Court building contains a garage, the offices of the facilities manager and maintenance staff, a carpentry shop, a laundry, and a police roll-call room. The ground floor contains the Public Information Office, the Clerk's Office, the publications unit, police "headquarters," and other administrative offices, in addition to the exhibit halls, cafeteria, and gift shop.

The first floor contains the courtroom, the conference room, and all of the justices' chambers except that of Ruth Bader Ginsburg, who has offices on the second floor. The second floor contains the justices' dining room and library, the office of the reporter of decisions, the legal office, and law clerks' offices. On the third floor is the library, and on the fourth floor there is a gymnasium and storage area. The public is allowed to see only the ground floor and part of the first floor.

A - Z

Little has changed in the physical appearance of the Court building since 1935, although the courtroom was renovated in 1992. In 2003, the Court underwent a $122 million modernization project to make improvements including updating the wiring and electrical systems throughout the building, and constructing a two-story underground annex to house the Court police.

Swann v. Charlotte-Mecklenburg County Board of Education (1971)

Supreme Court case in which the Court held that school officials could choose from a broad range of tools to eliminate segregation in their district. In a unanimous decision, the Court ruled that busing, racial quotas, and **gerrymandered** school districts were all appropriate methods of eliminating the remnants of school segregation.

Background of the Case

The case arose from controversy over the desegregation of the Charlotte-Mecklenburg County, North Carolina, school system. In the 1969–1970 school year, the system had eighty-four thousand students—71 percent white and 29 percent black. In that year, almost twenty-nine thousand of those students were bused to school in an effort to desegregate the school system.

Of the twenty-four thousand black students, twenty-one thousand lived within the city of Charlotte. Because of the smaller number and dispersed residences of black pupils in the rural part of the county, there were no all-black schools in that part of the system. In the city, however, most schools remained racially identifiable, and two of every three of the city's black students attended one of twenty-five schools that were ninety-eight percent to one hundred percent black. Three of every four of the area's white students attended schools that were primarily white. In February 1970, a federal district judge ordered thirteen thousand additional students bused; more than nine thousand of these pupils were elementary school children.

Landmark Decision Highlights:
Swann v. Charlotte-Mecklenburg County Board of Education (1971)

Issue: Whether or not federal courts are constitutionally authorized to oversee and produce remedies for state-imposed segregation

Opinion: In a unanimous decision, the Court held that once violations of previous mandates directed at desegregating schools had occurred, the scope of district courts' equitable powers to remedy past wrongs were broad and flexible. The Court ruled that:

(1) remedial plans were to be judged by their effectiveness, and the use of ratios or quotas were legitimate "starting points" for solutions;

(2) mostly or exclusively black schools required close scrutiny by the courts;

(3) non-contiguous attendance zones, as corrective measures, were within the courts' remedial powers;

(4) no rigid guidelines could be established concerning busing of students to particular schools.

Under the order, no school remained all black, and the effort was made to reach a 71:29 white-black ratio in each school, reflecting the overall white-black ratio in the system. The Fourth Circuit Court of Appeals overturned the elementary school part of the plan as imposing an unreasonable burden upon the school board. The NAACP Legal Defense Fund, representing the black parents concerned, appealed to the Supreme Court, arguing that the order should have been left intact.

The Court's Ruling

The Court held that the federal district court had properly used mathematical ratios of whites and blacks as "a starting point in the process of shaping a remedy." Chief Justice Warren Burger argued, however, that a court could not require a specific degree of racial mixing. The Court also acknowledged that residential patterns often result in schools that are attended only by children of one race. The presence of such schools does not necessarily indicate a system that is still segregated, but, wrote Burger, school authorities or the district court "should make every effort to achieve the greatest possible degree of actual desegregation and will thus necessarily be concerned with the elimination of one-race schools."

The Court endorsed plans that allowed a child attending a school where his or her race was a majority to transfer to a school where the child's race was a minority. To be successful, the justices added, such plans must ensure the transferring pupil available space in the school and free transportation. To overcome the effects of segregated residential patterns, the Court endorsed drastic gerrymandering of school districts and pairing, clustering, and grouping of schools that were not necessarily adjacent to one another.

Bus transportation of students had been an "integral part of the public education system for years," Burger wrote, and was a permissible technique to help achieve desegregation. The limits to busing would vary with many factors, "but probably with none more than the age" of the children, the Court said. The Court acknowledged that some of these remedies might be "awkward, inconvenient and even bizarre in some situations and may impose burdens on some; but all awkwardness and inconvenience cannot be avoided in the interim period when the remedial adjustments are being made to eliminate the dual school systems."

The Court was careful to say that its decision did not deal with discrimination resulting from factors other than state law. Nor did it address the question of what action might be taken against schools that were segregated as a result of "other types of state action, without any discriminatory action by the school authorities." In reference to the potential problem of resegregation, the Court concluded that "neither school authorities nor district courts are constitutionally required to make year-by-year adjustments of the racial composition of student bodies once the affirmative duty to desegregate has been accomplished and racial discrimination through official action is eliminated from the system."

See also: Brown v. Board of Education (1954); Education, Schools, and the Supreme Court; 📖 *Swann v. Mecklenburg County Board of Education,* 1971, in the **Primary Source Library.**

Symbolic Speech

Supreme Court cases dealing with the expression of ideas and beliefs through symbols rather than words. Generally, symbolic speech is considered to be protected by the First Amendment. Depending upon its context, however—how it is used and in what setting—symbolic speech may not enjoy constitutional protection.

The Court first dealt with the issue in 1931, when it found California's "red flag" law unconstitutional. The statute had made it a crime to raise a red flag as a symbol of, among other things, "opposition to organized government." In *Stromberg v. California,* the Court found this clause to be an unconstitutional restriction of free speech. The justices ruled that the law could not penalize an individual for advocating a change in government through peaceful means.

The fullest exposition of symbolism as a form of communication protected by the First Amendment came in *West Virginia State Board of Education v. Barnette* (1943). In this case, known as the second "flag salute" case, the Court ruled that states could not compel schoolchildren to pledge allegiance to the American flag. The majority said that the First Amendment did not permit a state to compel allegiance to a symbol of the organized government.

Another form of symbolic speech reviewed by the Court was the sit-in of the early 1960s. To protest racial **discrimination** in public accommodations, black students and others requested service at "whites only" lunch counters and remained there quietly until ejected or arrested. In *Garner v. Louisiana* (1961), the Court found these sit-ins were a form of expression guaranteed constitutional protection under some circumstances.

The unpopularity of the Vietnam War (1959–1975) generated several symbolic speech cases. In *United States v. O'Brien* (1968), the Court refused to view draft card burning, an expression of protest against the war and the draft, as symbolic speech protected by the First Amendment. "We cannot accept the view that an apparently limitless variety of conduct can be labeled 'speech' whenever the person engaging in the conduct intends thereby to express an idea," the majority said.

A – Z

Cross burning is another form of symbolic speech that the Court found to be protected by the First Amendment in certain instances. The government may prosecute those who burn a cross to "intimidate" or terrorize others. However, in *Virginia v. Black* (2003), the Court struck down a Virginia law banning all cross burnings as crimes because the First Amendment protects even hateful expressions of symbolic speech. Justice Sandra Day O'Connor wrote, "It is true that a cross burning, even at a political rally, arouses a sense of anger or hatred among the vast majority of citizens who see a burning cross. But this sense of anger or hatred is not sufficient to ban all cross burnings."

See also: Flag Burning; Sit-Ins; Speech, Unprotected.

Taft, William Howard (1857–1930)

Chief Justice of the United States, appointed by President Warren G. Harding (1921–1923) and confirmed by Congress on July 11, 1921. Taft was the sixty-ninth justice to serve on the Court and the tenth chief justice. He is also the only member of the Court to have served as president of the United States.

Early Life and Political Career

Taft was born on September 15, 1857, in Cincinnati, Ohio, the son of an Ohio Superior Court judge. His father also served as secretary of war and attorney general under President Ulysses S. Grant, and as ambassador to Austria-Hungary and Russia under President Chester A. Arthur. Taft's brother, Charles, served a term in the U.S. House of Representatives from 1895 to 1897.

Taft graduated in 1878 from Yale University, where he was the **salutatorian** of his graduating class. He received a law degree from Cincinnati Law School in 1880. During the 1880s, Taft held a series of positions in county government, including assistant county prosecutor and assistant county solicitor for Hamilton County. In 1887, barely thirty years old, he was appointed to the Ohio Superior Court. Five years later, President

William Howard Taft is the only person in U.S. history to have served as president (1909–1913) and chief justice (1921–1930), and in both roles, Taft strongly advocated for a permanent Supreme Court building, which was finally approved in 1929. (Library of Congress, Prints and Photographs Division)

DECISION MAKERS

Taft and the Supreme Court Building

William Howard Taft is the only person to have served as president and chief justice of the United States. During his time on the Court, he personally wrote an opinion in 256 cases. In addition, he worked to make the judiciary more effective. His studies of the British and American judicial systems led to the passage of the Judiciary Act of 1925, which allowed the Court to try cases in order of national importance. In this way, the court could more efficiently move through cases of the highest priority. Also included in this act was the granting by the Court of supervisory power over the lower federal courts. Thus, the entire judicial branch finally began to operate under a single entity, with the chief justice at its head.

One of Taft's most noteworthy achievements was his successfully arguing for the construction of a Supreme Court building. He convinced Congress that the separation of powers would be better exemplified if the Court met somewhere other than in the Capitol. Taft took an active interest in the planning and construction of the building. For example, he insisted that the new building provide chambers, or offices, for each justice—something the justices had never enjoyed. Though the Supreme Court building would not be completed until 1935, five years after Taft's death, it remains his most visible legacy of the nation's judicial system. The Supreme Court building was designated a National Historical Landmark on May 4, 1987.

Benjamin Harrison (1889–1893) named him solicitor general. In 1892, Taft sought and received appointment to the Sixth Circuit Court, where he served for eight years.

In 1900, President William McKinley (1897–1901) asked Taft to head a commission overseeing the Philippines' transition from military to civilian government following the Spanish-American War (1898). In 1901, Taft became governor general of the Philippines, a position he held until McKinley's successor, Theodore Roosevelt, named him secretary of war in 1904. Taft became one of Roosevelt's closest advisers; the president increasingly relied on Taft to handle important matters for the administration, such as the Panama Canal project.

Taft As President

In 1908, Taft ran for and won the presidency as the **Republican Party** nominee. However, the presidency was a post that Taft did not particularly

desire; he ran at the urging of his wife, his close friend President Theodore Roosevelt (1901–1909), and other Republican Party backers. His single term in office was not controversial. It saw the institution of the postal savings system and the Tariff Board, the intervention of American troops in the Dominican Republic, the **ratification** of the Sixteenth Amendment to the Constitution, and a continuation of the breakup of large business monopolies called trusts, begun under Theodore Roosevelt.

Taft named six men to the Supreme Court, including a chief justice, Edward D. White. The others were Horace H. Lurton, Charles Evans Hughes (who eventually would replace Taft as chief justice), Willis Van Devanter, Joseph R. Lamar, and Mahlon Pitney. By the time Taft was named chief justice in 1921, only two of his appointees, Van Devanter and Pitney, were still on the bench.

Soon after he was elected president, Taft began to fall out of favor with former President Roosevelt. The two men came to represent opposing sides of a division within the Republican Party. When Taft was renominated in 1912, Roosevelt ran for president under the banner of the Bull Moose Party and effectively splintered the Republican vote. After the election, won by Democrat Woodrow Wilson, Taft described Roosevelt as "the most dangerous man that we have had in the country since its origin."

Chief Justice

After leaving the White House, Taft taught law at Yale University, wrote magazine articles, and gave frequent lectures. He served as the joint chairman of the National War Labor Board (1918–1919) and undertook a fifteen-state tour in an attempt to rally support for President Wilson's proposed League of Nations, a forerunner to the United Nations.

Taft achieved his greatest ambition when President Warren Harding named him to replace Chief Justice Edward Douglass White in 1921. He is credited with modernizing procedures at the Court and cutting down on its workload. He created the Judicial Conference of the United States, which fosters cooperation among the federal judiciary's many courts. He secured passage of the Judiciary Act of 1925, giving the Court greater power to decide which cases to hear. He also lobbied Congress to provide funds for the Supreme Court building, but he did not live to see it completed. The only person in U.S. history to hold both the presidency and the chief justiceship, Taft died on March 8, 1930.

See also: Chief Justice of the United States; Circuit Court of Appeals.

Taney, Roger B. (1777–1864)

Chief Justice of the United States, appointed by President Andrew Jackson (1829–1837) and confirmed by Congress on March 28, 1836. Taney was the twenty-fourth justice to serve on the Court and the first Roman Catholic to do so. He served as the Court's fifth chief justice. Taney is best known for his opinion in *Dred Scott v. Sandford* (1857), in

Chief Justice Roger B. Taney is best remembered for his ill-advised decision in *Dred Scott v. Sanford* (1857). Taney had hoped the ruling would put an end to the slavery issue. Instead, the ruling inflamed sectional differences in the nation. (Library of Congress, Prints and Photographs Division)

which he held that slaves had no legal rights and could not become citizens.

Life and Career

Taney was born in Calvert County, Maryland, on his father's tobacco plantation. He was educated in local rural schools and privately tutored by a Princeton student. In 1795, at age eighteen, he graduated first in his class from Dickinson College in Pennsylvania. He then served three years as an apprentice lawyer in Annapolis before being admitted to the bar in 1799.

Taney began his political career as a member of the Federalist Party, serving one term in the Maryland legislature from 1799 to 1800. After being defeated for reelection, he moved to Frederick, where he developed a profitable law practice and became active in county politics. In 1816, he won election to the Maryland senate and became a

SPOTLIGHT

A Right To Travel

The Taney Court's rulings on the connected issues of commerce and slavery were confusing, to say the least. In the December 1846 term, the Court upheld the federal fugitive slave law, but in the same term it backed state power to regulate commerce in intoxicating liquor. The diversity of reasoning among the justices in these latter cases—known as the *License Cases*—from Massachusetts, Rhode Island, and New Hampshire reflected the Court's increasing division over the proper allocation of state and federal power over commerce. Six justices wrote nine opinions. In 1849, this uncertainty flowered into complete confusion with the Court's ruling in the so-called *Passenger Cases*.

These two cases, from New York and Boston, involved challenges to state laws that required masters of vessels to post bonds and to pay a tax for each immigrant who landed in the state. Opponents claimed that the laws infringed upon federal power to regulate foreign commerce. Supporters—including Taney—felt the laws were a proper exercise of the state's police power to protect public health and welfare. After hearing each case argued three times, the Court found that these laws conflicted with federal power over foreign commerce and were therefore unconstitutional.

Beyond that, however, the Court was splintered. Eight justices wrote separate opinions that took seven hours to read from the bench. In the end, the justices could not agree on whether the federal power over foreign commerce was exclusive, leaving no room for state regulation, or whether there might be such room if Congress had not exercised its power in a particular area. Court reporter Benjamin C. Howard declined to summarize the ruling beyond the fact that it struck down the challenged laws.

dominant figure in party politics. Taney's senate term expired in 1821.

In 1828, while serving as Maryland attorney general, Taney led Andrew Jackson's successful presidential campaign in the state. When his term as Maryland attorney general expired in 1831, Jackson named Taney U.S. attorney general. In this position, Taney helped to lead Jackson's efforts to revoke the **charter,** or founding document, of the Second Bank of the United States. When Treasury Secretary William Duane refused to withdraw federal deposits from the bank, Jackson replaced him temporarily with Taney. However, the Senate refused to confirm Taney

as permanent treasury secretary and he was forced to resign in 1834.

In 1835, Jackson nominated Taney to replace aging Supreme Court Justice Gabriel Duvall. An anticipated close vote in the Senate, however, indefinitely postponed the nomination. When Chief Justice John Marshall died the following year, Jackson once again nominated Taney to fill the vacant seat. This time, the Senate confirmed the choice.

Dred Scott v. Sandford

Taney's reputation rests almost entirely on his opinion in *Dred Scott v. Sandford,* in which he referred to blacks as "an inferior order . . . altogether unfit to associate with the white race, either in social or political relations." This decision hastened the Civil War (1861–1865) and damaged the standing of the Court. Taney is also, however, responsible for a much earlier and more socially responsible decision in *Charles River Bridge v. Warren Bridge* (1837), in which the Court asserted that contracts made by a state legislature should benefit the public good.

See also: Chief Justice of the United States; *Dred Scott v. Sandford* (1856).

Term of the Supreme Court

The formal schedule of the Supreme Court for the year. By law, the Court begins its regular annual term on the first Monday in October. The regular session, known as the October term, lasts nine months. The summer recess, which is not determined by statute or Court rules, generally begins in late June or early July of the next year, just after the Court has taken action on the last case argued during the term. The Court's growing caseload has resulted in longer terms.

Until 1979 the Court actually **adjourned,** or formally ended, its session when the summer recess began. Since 1979, however, the Court has been in continuous session throughout the year, marked by periodic recesses. This system avoids the need to hold a special term to deal with matters arising in the summer.

The Constitution gives Congress the power to set the term of the Court and, over the years, the annual sessions of the Court have changed several times. Until 1801, the Court met twice a year, in February and August. The justices had few cases during these years, and the early sessions were devoted largely to organization and discussions of lawyers' qualifications. The Judiciary Act of 1801 called for Court terms beginning in June and December. The Judiciary Act of 1802 restored the February term of the Court but not the August term, which resulted in a fourteen-month adjournment, from December 1801 until February 1803.

Over the next one hundred years, the opening day of the annual session changed a number of times. Since 1917, terms have begun on the first Monday in October.

The Court's annual schedule reflects both continuity and change. During its formal annual sessions, certain times are set aside for oral argument, for conferences, for writing opinions, and for announcing decisions. Because of the ever-increasing number of petitions arriving at the Court each year, the justices are confronted with a tremendous—some say excessive—amount of work during the regular term, which now lasts nine months.

Their work does not end when the session is finished, however. During the summer recess, the justices receive new cases to consider. About one-fourth of the applications for review filed during the term are read by the justices and their law clerks during the summer interim.

Thomas, Clarence (1948–)

Associate justice of the U.S. Supreme Court, appointed by President George H.W. Bush (1989–1993) and confirmed by Congress on October 23, 1991. Thomas is the 106th justice to serve on the Court and the second African American to do so. Thomas's confirmation hearings were marked by controversy over charges of sexual harassment by a former colleague, University of Oklahoma law professor Anita Hill.

Thomas was born in a settlement of five hundred inhabitants south of Savannah, Georgia. His father abandoned the family when Thomas was two years old, and his mother struggled to provide for her three children, working as a maid. Thomas attended an all-black school run by white nuns, and he initially decided to become a priest. He enrolled in a Missouri seminary in 1967 but left after experiencing prejudice from other students. He transferred to Holy Cross College, where he graduated in 1971 with honors. In 1974, he graduated from Yale Law School.

Thomas then joined the staff of John C. Danforth, Missouri's attorney general. After three

DECISION MAKERS

Senate Judiciary Committee

One of the most powerful players in the process of confirming Supreme Court justices is the Senate Judiciary Committee. This body, composed of members of the Senate from both major political parties, has the task of reviewing the president's nominees to the Court. After holding investigations and hearings into the background and qualifications of a nominee, the Judiciary Committee votes to determine whether the nominee deserves to face a vote in the full Senate. Particularly in recent years, the committee has approved the vast majority of nominees who come before it.

The process of investigation is not without its difficulties and controversies, including the problem of information leaks. Although the deliberations of the committee are supposed to be confidential, information about them often leaks to the media. In the case of Clarence Thomas, information about the sexual harassment charges made against him by Anita Hill were first made public through leaks to newspaper and radio reporters. Despite the storm of protest from Hill's supporters—and calls for a delay to the Senate vote—Thomas eventually won confirmation. Congress later appointed a special counsel to investigate the source of the leaks but was unable to identify how Hill's charges reached the media.

A – Z

years as an assistant attorney general, Thomas worked as a staff attorney for Monsanto Company from 1977 to 1979. From 1979 to 1981, he served as a legislative assistant to Danforth, who had been elected to the U.S. Senate. Thomas then accepted a position in the administration of President Ronald Reagan (1981–1989) as assistant secretary for civil rights. In 1982, Reagan named Thomas to chair the Equal Employment Opportunity Commission.

President George H.W. Bush appointed Thomas to the Court of Appeals for the District of Columbia Circuit in 1990. Eighteen months later, Bush selected Thomas, whose judicial record was notably conservative, for the Supreme Court. Thomas was critical of abortion rights and opposed affirmative action. Those positions and controversy over other substantive issues, however, were eclipsed during the televised confirmation hearings by the allegations of Anita Hill, a University of Oklahoma law professor and former employee of Thomas's, that he had sexually harassed her.

Although Dr. Hill's charges were never proved, Thomas claimed that the ordeal, which set off a media frenzy, dramatically changed him. The Senate's 52-48 vote on Thomas was the closest Supreme Court confirmation vote in more than a century. Thomas succeeded Thurgood Marshall, the Court's first black justice, whose six-decade legal career had shaped the country's civil rights struggle.

From the start, Thomas became a member of the conservative bloc, opposing abortion rights and favoring law enforcement, states' rights, and a more accommodating approach to religion. He has voted most often with Justice Antonin Scalia and Chief Justice William H. Rehnquist. He joined them in rulings that curbed federal antidiscrimination laws, and he dissented with them when the Court prohibited school-sponsored prayers at graduation ceremonies and football games. Thomas also has been a strong voice against race-based remedies for past discrimination, including affirmative action and "majority-minority" voting districts.

A–Z

Anti-War Protests

The unpopularity of the Vietnam War among the American people generated several freedom of speech cases. In *United States v. O'Brien* (1968), the Court refused to view draft card burning, an expression of protest against the war and the draft, as symbolic speech protected by the First Amendment. "We cannot accept the view that an apparently limitless variety of conduct can be labeled 'speech' whenever the person engaging in the conduct intends thereby to express an idea," the majority said. Even if that view were adopted, the majority continued, the First Amendment would not protect draft card burning:

> This Court has held that when "speech" and "nonspeech" elements are combined in the same course of conduct, a sufficiently important governmental interest in regulating the nonspeech element can justify incidental limitations on First Amendment freedoms.

Here, the majority said Congress had a substantial interest in maintaining the draft registration system as part of its duty to raise and maintain armies. Almost thirty years later, in *Barnes v. Glen Theater* (1991), the Court cited this idea of a substantial public interest that permits some restriction on freedom of expression when it upheld a state law that forbade nude dancing.

In yet another form of protest against the Vietnam War, an actor wore an Army uniform while he and others performed a protest play on a sidewalk outside an Army induction center in Houston. The play depicted U.S. soldiers killing Vietnamese women and children. The actor was arrested and convicted of violating a federal law that made it a crime to wear an official military uniform in a theatrical production unfavorable to the armed forces. The Court unanimously overturned that conviction in *Schacht v. United States* (1970), concluding that the wearing of the uniform was part of the actor's speech. "An actor, like everyone else in our country, enjoys a constitutional right to freedom of speech, including the right openly to criticize the Government during a dramatic performance," the Court said.

In *Holder v. Hall* (1994), Thomas wrote that the Court's earlier cases upholding racially designated voting districts disserved the country: "In doing so we have collaborated in what may aptly be termed the racial balkanization of the Nation." In 2003, he dissented when the Court upheld the limited use of affirmative action at the nation's colleges and universities.

See also: Hill, Anita; Marshall, Thurgood; Rehnquist, William H.; Scalia, Antonin.

Tinker v. Des Moines (1969)

Supreme Court case that established the principle that the First Amendment's protection for freedom of speech extended into school classrooms. The Court upheld students' rights to exercise free speech as long as doing so did not constitute a disruption to the class.

Basis of the the Case

In December 1965, three students in Des Moines, Iowa—John and Mary Beth Tinker and Christopher Eckhardt—wore black armbands with peace symbols on them to school. The armbands were to protest the Vietnam War and support a Christmastime cease fire proposed by Senator Robert F. Kennedy. To prevent what they felt would be a disruptive act, school board members passed a policy that banned the wearing of armbands to school. When the three students violated the policy, they were suspended.

With the help of the Iowa Civil Liberties Union (ICLU), the children's parents filed suit to overturn the school board's policy, but a U.S. District Court ruled against them. The families' appeal eventually reached the Supreme Court in November 1968.

The Court's Decision

On February 24, 1969, the Court announced its decision, ruling 7-2 in favor of the students. The justices found that the wearing of armbands to school was a form of "symbolic speech" that is a constitutionally protected. They also declared that school administrators needed to show constitutionally valid reasons for any attempt to regulate or prohibit specific forms of speech in the classroom. Justice Hugo Black disagreed with the majority

> **Landmark Decision Highlights:**
> *Tinker v. Des Moines* (1969)
>
> **Issue:** Does the prohibition against the wearing of armbands in public school, as a form of symbolic protest, violate the First Amendment's protection of freedom of speech?
>
> **Opinion:** The Court determined that the wearing of armbands was "closely akin to 'pure speech'" and protected by the First Amendment. The school principals failed to show that the forbidden conduct would substantially interfere with appropriate discipline.

view that "symbolic speech" is constitutionally protected. He also believed that the Tinkers' behavior did constitute a disruption to the class. The other dissenter, Justice John Marshall Harlan II, argued that the regulation prohibiting armbands should not be overturned because it was made by the school board in good faith.

Later Rulings

Subsequent Court decisions have placed certain limitations on free speech by students in the classroom or school-sponsored events. In *Hazelwood School District v. Kuhlmeier* (1988), for example, the Court ruled that schools have the right to regulate the content of school-sponsored publications. Schools may, in some instances, regulate student speech even at school-sponsored events that occur off school grounds. In *Morse v. Frederick,* the Court upheld the suspensions of students who held up a banner promoting drug use at a public gathering for the Olympic Torch relay in Eugene, Oregon. The Court ruled that the government had a compelling interest in preventing drug use by students, which gave it the right to regulate speech in this instance.

See also: Censorship; Freedom of Speech; *Hazelwood School District v. Kuhlmeier* (1988); Symbolic Speech; ▭ *Tinker v. Des Moines,* 1969, in the **Primary Source Library.**

A – Z

United States v. Nixon (1974)

Supreme Court case in which the justices rejected the claim that the president had an absolute privilege to refuse judicial demands for information. The Court ordered President Richard M. Nixon (1969–1974) to surrender to a special prosecutor tapes of White House conversations between the president and his aides. The release of the tapes, which revealed the president's criminal involvement in a break-in at Democratic National Headquarters, led to Nixon's resignation.

Background of the Case

In June 1972, five men broke into the headquarters of the Democratic National Committee in Washington, D.C.'s Watergate Hotel. The men had been hired by aides to President Nixon, who also carried

---

Landmark Decision Highlights: *United States v. Nixon* (1974)

Issue: Is the president's right to safeguard certain information, using "executive privilege" confidentiality power, entirely immune from judicial review?

Opinion: The Court ruled that neither the doctrine of separation of powers, nor a general need for confidentiality of high-level communications, can support an absolute presidential privilege. The Court granted that there was a limited executive privilege in areas of military or diplomatic affairs, but gave preference to "the fundamental demands of due process of law in the fair administration of justice."

VIEWPOINTS

A 1974 political cartoon pokes fun at President Richard Nixon's (1969–1974) claim that his taped conversations could be kept from the public. The Supreme Court, in *United States v. Nixon* (1974), ruled that the president has no absolute claim to "executive privilege." Nixon resigned from the presidency in 1974, rather than face certain impeachment. (Guernsey Le Pelley © 1974 *The Christian Science Monitor* [www.csmonitor.com]. All rights reserved.)

out a wide range of other illegal activities that included wiretapping political foes of the president. The burglars were caught, and over time the president's involvement became clear to investigators.

In April 1974, special prosecutor Leon Jaworski obtained a **subpoena**, or court order, calling for delivery of certain tapes, memoranda, and papers related to specific meetings of the president with particular White House aides. The president claimed executive privilege to refuse to honor the subpoena. When the district court ordered the president to deliver the requested materials, Nixon appealed to the Supreme Court.

The Court's Decision

On July 24, 1974, the justices rejected Nixon's claim of privilege. Chief Justice Warren E. Burger explained the derivation of executive privilege:

> Whatever the nature of the privilege of confidentiality of presidential communications in the exercise of Article II (of the Constitution) powers, the privilege can be said to derive from the supremacy of each branch within its own assigned area of constitutional duties . . . (N)either the doctrine of separation of powers, nor the need for confidentiality of high level communications, without more, can sustain an absolute, unqualified presidential privilege of immunity from judicial process under all circumstances. . . . Absent a claim of need to protect military, diplomatic or sensitive national security secrets, we find it difficult to accept the argument that even the very important interest in confidentiality of presidential communications is significantly diminished by protection of such material for in camera inspection with all the protection that a district court will be obliged to provide.

In rejecting this particular claim of privilege, however, the Court for the first time acknowledged a constitutional basis for executive privilege:

> A President and those who assist him must be free to explore alternatives in the process of shaping policies and making decisions and to do so in a way many would be unwilling to express except privately. These are the considerations justifying a presumptive privilege for presidential communications. The privilege is fundamental to the operation of government and inextricably rooted in the separation of powers under the Constitution. . . . Nowhere in the Constitution . . . is there any explicit reference to a privilege of confidentiality, yet to the extent this interest relates to the effective discharge of a President's powers, it is constitutionally based.

Reaction and Aftermath

When the decision came down, the nation's newspapers overwhelmingly supported it. The *Wall Street Journal,* for example, saw the ruling as "a common sense resolution of the immediate problems involved" rather than the rescue of the republic. "Surely it is healthier," the *Journal* observed, "to have the President's arguments based not in defiance of the courts but in compliance with them." The paper expressed editorial gratitude for President Nixon's announcement that he would surrender the tapes, on behalf of "those of us who have been struggling to keep an open mind."

Similarly, the *Washington Star* called the decision "historic, definitive and above all correct" and was able to take some comfort from the Court's recognition, for the first time, of the existence of executive privilege in the White House. That recognition will make for "a more careful and cleaner presidency"; otherwise, the courts "would have required the President and his advisors to conduct the nation's business in a fishbowl, a situation that would be intolerable and unworkable."

The New York Times praised the Court for reaffirming "the supremacy of law over Presidential pretensions" and establishing that "the presidency cannot be used as a sanctuary for miscreants." The *Times* said, "If this nation was to remain the Republic established by the authors of the Constitution, the court could only have ruled as it did."

The Washington Post paid one of its relatively rare tributes to Chief Justice Warren E. Burger, for "a particularly sound and skillful opinion . . . nicely reconciling the conflicting interests of confidentiality for the President and the right of due process for criminal defendants." The paper concluded, regretfully, that "it is a measure of how far we have come when a President of the United States can hope to earn favor by not defying a decision by the Supreme Court."

See also: Presidency and the Supreme Court.

Further Reading

Herda, D.J. *United States v. Nixon: Watergate and the President*. Berkeley Heights, N.J.: Enslow Publishers, 1996.

Van Meter, Larry A. *United States v. Nixon: The Question of Executive Privilege*. New York: Chelsea House Publications, 2007.

University of California Regents v. Bakke (1978)

Supreme Court case that dealt with reverse discrimination, specifically, whether state universities may set aside a certain number of openings in each class for members of minority groups. The Court ultimately found itself divided over the issue. On one hand, it ruled that state universities may not set aside a fixed quota of seats in each class for minority group members. However, a different five-justice majority held that admissions officers do not violate the equal protection guarantee when they consider race as one of many factors that determine which applicant is accepted and which rejected.

Basis of the Case

Allan Bakke, a thirty-eight-year-old white engineer, was twice denied admission to the medical school at the University of California at Davis. To ensure minority representation in the student body, the university had set aside sixteen seats for minority applicants in each medical school class of one hundred students. Bakke challenged the set-aside as a violation of his constitutional right to equal protection of the laws. In each year his application was rejected, the school had accepted some minority applicants with qualifications inferior to his. He contended that he would have been admitted had it not been for this rigid preference system.

the Court's Ruling

Justice Lewis Powell was the key to the *Bakke* decision: He was the only justice who was in both majorities. On the first point—the decision to strike down the Davis quota system—Powell voted with Chief Justice Warren E. Burger and Justices William H. Rehnquist, Potter Stewart, and John

---

Landmark Decision Highlights:
University of California Regents v. Bakke (1978)

Issue: Whether or not the University of California violated the Fourteenth Amendment's equal protection clause and the Civil Rights Act of 1964 by practicing an affirmative action policy that resulted in the repeated rejection of Allan Bakke's application for admission to its medical school.

Opinion: Four of the justices contended that any racial quota system supported by government violated the Civil Rights Act of 1964. Justice Lewis F. Powell Jr. agreed, casting the deciding vote ordering the medical school to admit Bakke. However, in his opinion, Powell argued that the rigid use of racial quotas at the school violated the equal protection clause of the Fourteenth Amendment. The other four justices held that the use of race in admissions decisions in higher education was constitutionally permissible.

Paul Stevens. This group saw *Bakke* as a controversy between litigants that could be settled by applying the Civil Rights Act of 1964 without involving constitutional issues. Title VI of the act, they pointed out, barred any discrimination on the grounds of race, color, or national origin in any program receiving federal financial assistance. When that ban was placed alongside the facts of the case, it was clear to them that the university had violated the statute. Stevens explained:

> The University, through its special admissions policy, excluded Bakke from participation in its program of medical education because of his race. The University also acknowledges that it was, and still is, receiving federal financial assistance. . . . The meaning of the Title VI ban on exclusion is crystal clear: Race cannot be the basis of excluding anyone from participation in a federally funded program.

Powell's reasoning on this point differed from the view of the four dissenters. Where they found no constitutional involvement, he found the scope of the Title VI ban and the equal protection clause of the Fourteenth Amendment identical: What violated one therefore violated the other, so he based his vote against the university's preference system on both the law and the Constitution.

The Davis admissions program used an explicit racial classification, Powell noted. Such classifications were not always unconstitutional, he continued, "[b]ut when a state's distribution of benefits or imposition of burdens hinges on . . . the color of a person's skin or ancestry, that individual is entitled to a demonstration that the challenged classification is necessary to promote a substantial state interest." Powell could find no substantial interest that justified establishment of the university's specific quota system. Not even the desire to remedy past discrimination was a sufficient justification, he said.

Powell did not believe, however, that all racial classifications were unconstitutional. He voted with Justices William J. Brennan Jr., Thurgood Marshall, Byron R. White, and Harry A. Blackmun to approve the use of some race-conscious affirmative action programs. These four contended that the university's wish to remedy past societal discrimination was sufficient justification. For the four, Brennan wrote:

> Government may take race into account when it acts not to demean or insult any racial group, but to remedy disadvantages cast on minorities by past racial prejudice, at least when appropriate findings have been made by judicial, legislative, or administrative bodies with competence to act in this area.

The four endorsed the broad remedial use of race-conscious programs, even in situations where no specific constitutional violation had been found.

See also: Affirmative Action.

Further Reading

McPherson, Stephanie. *The Bakke Case and the Affirmative Action Debate: Supreme Court Decisions.* Berkeley Heights, NJ: Enslow Publishers, 2005.

Stefoff, Rebecaa. *The Bakke Case: Challenge to Affirmative Action.* New York: Benchmark Books, 2006.

Unreasonable Search and Seizure

See Exclusionary Rule; *Mapp v. Ohio* (1961).

U.S. District Courts

Trial courts in the United States federal court system. The district courts are the first of the three levels of courts in the federal judicial system. They hear both civil and criminal cases and have original **jurisdiction,** which means that they hear cases the first time such cases are brought to trial.

Origins and Structure

The Constitution established the Supreme Court as the highest court in the land but also authorized Congress to create "inferior courts" as necessary. Congress first exercised this power when it passed the Judiciary Act of 1789. This act created a three-tier system of federal courts consisting of district district courts, federal appeals courts, and the Supreme Court.

The act also required that Supreme Court justices travel through the districts each year to hear cases that fell within the district courts' jurisdiction. In the days before rapid transit, this typically was a long and burdensome task. Justices would travel thousands of miles on horseback, carriage, and even sometimes on foot, spending months "riding the circuit." Congress abolished circuit riding in 1801, but the incoming administration of President Thomas Jefferson restored the practice. The Judiciary Act of 1869 established a separate set of judges to hear cases in circuit courts, ending the need for traveling justices to preside over the courts. Even so, Congress did not officially end the practice of riding circuit until 1911.

The Judiciary Act of 1789 established thirteen judicial districts, one for each of the original states

A – Z

except Virginia and Massachusetts. Each of those states was divided into two districts. As the nation expanded, Congress added more districts. Today, the United States is divided into ninety-four judicial districts—eighty-nine in the states themselves, and five more in U.S. territories such as Guam and Puerto Rico. As in the earliest days of the nation, every state contains least one judicial district. In addition to the federal trial courts, each district also includes a bankruptcy court

Jurisdiction

District courts exercise original jurisdiction in the following types of cases:

- Civil lawsuits arising under the Constitution, laws, and treaties of the United States
- Some lawsuits between citizens of different states
- Cases dealing with admiralty or maritime law

- Criminal prosecutions in which the United States is the plaintiff
- Civil lawsuits to which the United States is a party

In most of these cases, the federal district court in a state shares jurisdiction with state courts. A party can choose to file suit in either a federal district court or a state court. Parties may "remove" a case from a state to a federal court, as long as the federal court also has original jurisdiction. In addition to their original jurisdiction, the district courts have appellate jurisdiction over certain judgments and court orders.

The losing party in a case heard in district court may appeal the decision to the United States court of appeals in the circuit in which the district court is located. In rare instances, cases tried in district court may be appealed directly to the U.S. Supreme Court.

See also: Circuit Court of Appeal; Judiciary Act of 1789.

Wallace v. Jaffree (1984)

Supreme Court case dealing with the constitutionality of so-called "moment of silence" laws. Such laws permit public school teachers to set aside a moment in class each day for students to engage in quiet meditative activity. The Court's ruling did not make all such laws unconstitutional, but it set limits on how they could be implemented.

At the time of the ruling, twenty-three states had passed "moment of silence" laws. When an Alabama appeals court upheld a lower court order striking down the law, the state asked the Court to reinstate the law. The Court refused, 6-3, agreeing with the appeals court that the law violated the establishment clause of the Constitution.

Some moment of silence laws might pass muster, said the majority, but not one that was so clearly just an excuse to return prayer to the public schools. Writing for the majority, Justice John Paul Stevens declared that it was "established principle that the government must pursue a course of complete neutrality toward religion." Chief Justice Warren E. Burger dissented, joined by Justices Byron R. White and William H. Rehnquist, who said it was time for the Court to reassess its precedents on this issue.

The broadest and most significant dissent in *Wallace v. Jaffree* was by Rehnquist, who challenged the separation of church and state doctrine as wrong-headed and based on a misreading of history. The establishment clause was "designed to prohibit the establishment of a national religion, and perhaps to prevent discrimination among sects. [The founders] did not see it as requiring neutrality on the part of government between religion and irreligion," Rehnquist continued.

"The 'wall of separation between church and state' is a metaphor based on bad history. . . . It should be frankly and explicitly abandoned," he concluded.

Rehnquist's dissent signaled the possibility of a significant change in the law. President Ronald Reagan (1981–1989) and the Republican Party platform had called for a return to prayer in the public schools. A year after *Wallace v. Jaffree,* Reagan selected Rehnquist as chief justice. In addition to elevating Rehnquist, Reagan appointed three new justices: Sandra O'Connor, Antonin Scalia, and Anthony M. Kennedy. Reagan's successor, George H.W. Bush (1989–1993), added two more: David H. Souter and Clarence Thomas. By 1992, there appeared to be a solid bloc of conservative justices who were ready to cast aside the strict separation of church and state and to allow, at a minimum, religious invocations at school ceremonies. This has not come to pass, however, as the Court has consistently refused to expand the reach of religion into the schools.

See also: Education, Schools, and the Supreme Court; Freedom of Religion; School Prayer and Bible Readings.

War Power and the Supreme Court

Supreme Court decisions outlining the powers and responsibilities of the other branches of government related to declaring and fighting wars. The Constitution divides responsibility for waging war between the president and Congress. While the president is commander in chief of the army and navy when they are called into actual service, Congress has the power to declare war, raise and support armies, provide and maintain a navy, and make rules and regulations to govern the armed forces. Over time, however, the respective roles of the president and Congress have become blurred. As a result, the Court has been called upon to help define those roles.

The Court has been reluctant limit the war powers of either Congress or the president. The Court has permitted Congress to delegate substantial amounts of power to the executive branch during wartime. It has also supported invasions of other

states' sovereignty as well the rights of private citizens and corporations. "In short," constitutional scholar Robert E. Cushman states, "what is necessary to win the war Congress may do, and the Supreme Court has shown no inclination to hold void new and drastic war measures."

Declaring War

Congress has formally declared war five times: the War of 1812, the Mexican War, the Spanish-American War, World War I, and World War II. In both of its most recent foreign wars, Congress authorized the use of force against Iraq in 1991 and 2003 at the president's request. Although far more limited than earlier declarations of war, these resolutions put the political and constitutional weight of the legislative branch behind the president as the nation prepared for battle.

From time to time, the absence of a formal declaration of war has been challenged before the Court. In 1800, the Court held that Congress need not declare full-scale war but could provide for a limited conflict. The Court has ruled in several cases that if Congress approves of an executive action or appropriation of money to carry out that action, it is the same as approving the action beforehand. The Court in 1947 ruled that "the appropriation by Congress of funds for the use of such agencies stands as confirmation and ratification of the action of the Chief Executive."

Debate surrounding the Vietnam War led to passage of the War Powers Resolution by Congress in 1973. This act required the president to seek congressional authority before committing U.S. troops to combat. Presidents have argued that it represents an unconstitutional infringement upon the president's powers as commander-in-chief. The Court refused to inject itself in the argument over whether the war in Vietnam should have been formally declared, and it has never heard a case concerning the constitutionality of the War Powers Resolution.

Raising Armies

The government's authority to raise armies through a compulsory draft remained untested in federal courts until Congress adopted the Selective Service Act of 1917. Opponents challenged the law on several grounds, including the charge that it violated the Thirteenth Amendment's prohibition against involuntary servitude. In 1918, the Court unanimously

A–Z

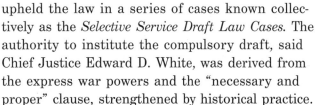

SPOTLIGHT

The Court, Congress, and Cambodia

The Court's reluctance to become involved in disagreements between the president and Congress over the war power is clearly demonstrated in a series of events in 1973. Despite signing cease-fire agreements concerning the war in Vietnam, the United States continued to bomb Cambodia. That year, Congress voted to cut off funds for further bombing operations. In July, U.S. District Court Judge Orrin G. Judd issued an order halting all military operations in Cambodia after July 27.

The same day, at the request of the government, the Court of Appeals for the Second Circuit delayed the Judd order and agreed to hear the government's appeal. On August 4, the Court of Appeals for the Second Circuit reversed the district court's original ruling halting military operations in Cambodia. The Supreme Court refused to review that decision.

upheld the law in a series of cases known collectively as the *Selective Service Draft Law Cases*. The authority to institute the compulsory draft, said Chief Justice Edward D. White, was derived from the express war powers and the "necessary and proper" clause, strengthened by historical practice.

The Court has never ruled on whether a "peacetime" draft is constitutional. Lower federal courts, however, have upheld the draft in the absence of declared war. The draft continues to be a source of many legal questions, however. In 1981, the Court upheld the power of Congress to exclude women from the military draft. In *Rostker v. Goldberg* (1981) the Court held, 6-3, that because women were barred by law and policy from combat, they were not "similarly situated" with men for the purposes of draft registration. Three years later, the Court held that Congress did not violate the ban on bills of attainder when it denied federal student aid to male college students who had failed to register for the military draft.

See also: Foreign Affairs and the Supreme Court.

Warren, Earl (1891–1974)

Chief Justice of the United States, appointed by President Dwight D. Eisenhower (1953–1961) and confirmed by Congress on March 1, 1954. He was

the eighty-eighth justice to serve on the Court and the fourteenth chief justice. During his tenure, Warren presided over some of the Court's more notable and controversial decisions. The Warren Court was considered a high point in judicial activism for the Court.

Earl Warren was born in Los Angeles, the son of Scandinavian immigrant parents. He worked his way through college and law school at the University of California. After receiving his law degree in 1914, he worked in private law offices in San Francisco and Oakland.

Early Career

In 1919, Warren was named deputy city attorney for Oakland and later became a deputy district attorney for Alameda County. In 1925, Warren was appointed district attorney when the **incumbent** resigned; he was later reelected to the post three times. Warren developed a reputation as a crime fighter, sending a city manager and several councilmen to jail on graft charges and smashing a crooked deal on garbage collection.

In 1942, Warren made the first of three consecutive successful runs for governor of California. At first viewed as a conservative, Warren developed a **progressive** image after World War II. In 1945, he proposed a state program of prepaid medical insurance and later championed liberal pension and welfare benefits. Warren made two unsuccessful bids for national political office while governor. In 1948, he ran for vice president on

The fourteenth Chief Justice of the United States, Earl Warren, served on the Court from 1953 until 1969. Among the landmark cases that were decided under his tenure are *Brown v. Board of Education* (1954); *Gideon v. Wainwright* (1963); *Miranda v. Arizona* (1966); and *Loving v. Virginia* (1967). (Library of Congress, Prints and Photographs Division)

the Republican ticket with Governor Thomas E. Dewey of New York. In 1952, he sought the Republican presidential nomination. With little chance to win, however, he supported Dwight D. Eisenhower, helping him win the nomination.

Eisenhower repaid Warren's support in 1953, nominating him to replace recently deceased Chief Justice Fred M. Vinson. Reflecting on his choice years later in light of the Warren Court's liberal record, Eisenhower reportedly said that the appointment of Warren was the biggest mistake he made as president.

Landmark Cases

The Warren Court is credited with a large number of landmark decisions, many written by the chief justice. Best known is the Court's unanimous decision in *Brown v. Board of Education* (1954), which said that separate schools for blacks and whites were inherently unequal and violated the equal protection guarantee of the Fourteenth Amendment. Warren also wrote the majority opinion in *Miranda v. Arizona* (1966). Here, the Court said that those held in police custody must be told of their constitutional rights before they can be questioned. In addition to his work on the Court, Warren headed the commission that investigated the 1963 assassination of President John F. Kennedy.

In 1968, Warren submitted his resignation, but the Senate became bogged down a fight over who would succeed Warren on the bench. Warren agreed to serve another year, resigning in 1969 when President Richard M. Nixon chose Warren E. Burger as the new chief justice.

See also: Brown v. Board of Education (1954); Judicial Activism; *Miranda v. Arizona* (1966).

White Primaries

Supreme Court rulings that deal with state practices that denied blacks the right to vote in primary elections. Southern politics was completely dominated by the **Democratic Party** during the first half of the twentieth century. The party was often organized on a statewide or county basis as a private club or association that could freely exclude blacks. Texas's use of the white primary to shut blacks out of participation in the political process came before the Court five times.

In 1923, the Texas legislature passed a law forbidding blacks to vote in the state Democratic primary. Dr. L.A. Nixon, a black resident of El Paso, challenged the law, arguing that it clearly violated the Fourteenth and Fifteenth Amendments. In *Nixon v. Herndon* (1927), the Court agreed with Nixon's claim. "A more direct and obvious infringement" of the equal protection guarantee would be hard to imagine, wrote Justice Oliver Wendell Holmes Jr. for a unanimous Court. After *Herndon*, the Texas legislature authorized state political parties' executive committees to establish their own qualifications for voting in the primary. Nixon again sued, challenging the law as racially discriminatory. The Court again found in Nixon's favor.

Nevertheless, the Texas Democratic Party voted to limit membership to whites. This was permissible, the justices agreed in *Grovey v. Townsend.* (1933). The Court unanimously held that the political party was not acting as a creature of the state and that its action was thus unreachable under either the Fourteenth or Fifteenth Amendments. The Court in this case viewed the political party as a private club, a voluntary association of private individuals, whose actions were not restricted by the Constitution.

A–Z

In 1944, the Court overturned *Grovey* and held the all-white primary unconstitutional. *Smith v. Allwright* arose out of the refusal of S.S. Allwright, a county election official, to permit Lonnie E. Smith, a black man, to vote in the 1940 Texas Democratic primary. Smith sued Allwright for damages. Lower federal courts denied Smith the right to bring suit. *Grovey v. Townsend,,* they said, placed this sort of discrimination beyond federal control. The Court, however, held the white primary unconstitutional as a violation of the Fifteenth Amendment. The majority found state action evident in the number of state laws regulating primary elections.

In 1953, the relentless effort to maintain the white primary finally came to an end. Since 1889, the Jaybird Party, an all-white Democratic organization in one Texas county, had declared itself a private club and had submitted political candidates' names in an unofficial county primary for whites only. The successful candidate in the Jaybird primary invariably entered and won the following Democratic primary and general election. The Court invalidated the results, finding this use of racially exclusive private clubs as a political caucus a violation of the Fifteenth Amendment. Justice Hugo Black wrote in *Terry v. Adams*:

> The Jaybird primary has become an integral part, indeed the only effective part, of the elective process that determines who shall rule and govern in the county. The effect of the whole procedure . . . is to do precisely that which the Fifteenth Amendment forbids—strip Negroes of every vestige of influence in selecting the officials who control the local county matters that intimately touch the daily lives of citizens.

Writ of Habeas Corpus

Judicial order compelling the government to produce a prisoner so that he or she may appear before a court to argue his or her case. Loosely translated from the Latin, it means "you have the body." The writ is used by a court to inquire into the reasons for a person's detention by government authority. Habeas corpus, the Court has noted, "has time and again played a central role in national crises, wherein the claims of order and of liberty clash most acutely."

Since the nation's founding, the federal courts have gradually expanded the use of the writ into a major instrument for the reform of federal and state criminal procedures. Federal courts have broad discretion in determining when the issuance of this writ is appropriate to order release of a prisoner. There is no time limit within which a prisoner must seek a writ of habeas corpus as a remedy for errors at his trial, and it may be issued to military or civilian authorities. The Court has declared that the power of federal courts to issue this writ must be given by written law, as it always has been. The writ has been used in modern times to challenge a lack of jurisdiction of the sentencing court or to charge constitutional error. If such charges are proved, the entire detention is illegal, regardless of the guilt of the person detained.

For most of the nineteenth century, the writ was used only to challenge the jurisdiction of the sentencing court, and only in cases involving federal prisoners. In 1867, the Court began to expand the use of the writ. However, the modern federal use of the writ of habeas corpus to question the detention of state prisoners can be traced to the Court's decision in *Frank v. Mangum* (1915). Here, the Court refused to order the release of a man convicted of murder by a state court, although he alleged that he had been denied a fair trial because the court was dominated by a mob. In an opinion written by Justice Mahlon Pitney, however, the Court enlarged its traditional view of the responsibility of a federal court to examine state convictions.

The Court denied habeas corpus relief in this case because the defendant's claim of mob domination had been reviewed fully—and rejected—by a state appeals court. Eight years later, in *Moore v. Dempsey* (1923), the Court granted a similar plea. Subsequently, the Court has broadened the power of federal courts, when considering state prisoners' petitions for habeas corpus, to review matters already considered and resolved by state courts. Since 1970, however, the Court has narrowed the number of situations in which prisoners can obtain writs of habeus corpus.

Writ of Mandamus

A court order requiring a government official to take some action related to his or her post. The writ may be an absolute and unqualified command, or it may give the individual the opportunity to show why he or she should not comply with the writ. Companion to the mandamus is the writ of prohibition, which bars a government official or lower court from taking certain action, instead of ordering action.

In modern times, the Court issues few writs of mandamus, even when it finds the person seeking them entitled to such an order. It customarily rules that the party is entitled to that remedy, but it withholds the issuance of the writ assuming that the official or the lower court will act in conformity with its ruling. In *Marbury v. Madison* (1803), the Court made clear that this writ was to be used only in cases over which the issuing court already had **jurisdiction,** or authority.

The **separation of powers** has limited the issuance of these writs from federal courts to federal executive officials. In *Marbury* the Court distinguished between the types of action that a court might order an executive branch official to take and those in which the separation of powers forbids judicial interference. Only ministerial acts, wrote Chief Justice John Marshall, could be the subject of writs of mandamus.

The extraordinary nature of these writs in the federal system has been further underscored by the Court's insistence that such writs be issued only to persons who lack any other legal remedy.

In general, only final judgments are eligible for review by a higher court. In keeping with this policy, the Court has resisted most efforts by parties to obtain a writ of mandamus to review or undo an interim ruling of a lower court. The Court also has insisted that the writ of mandamus is not to be used as a substitute for a direct appeal from a ruling.

The most frequent modern use of writs of mandamus is by an appellate court to confine a lower court "to a lawful exercise of its prescribed jurisdiction" or to compel it "to exercise its authority when it is its duty to do so." The Court also has the power to issue the writ to a state court, so long as the case involved is within the appellate jurisdiction of the Court.

The Court has held that the writ of mandamus should not be used to order a trial judge to reinstate certain pleas, because the judge's decision to dismiss them can be reviewed on appeal. On the other hand, the Court has upheld the use of the writ to override trial judges' decisions to appoint a special master to hear a case, to deny a jury trial, and to reverse a federal judge's decision that in order to avoid delay in hearing a case, it should be tried in state, rather than federal, court.

Zavelo v. Reeves (1913)

See Bankruptcy and Bankruptcy Laws.

PART THREE

Judiciary Act, Chapter XX, Sections 1–4, 9, 11, 14, 1789

This very early act of Congress described the first structure of the federal court system. It provided for district (trial) courts, circuit (appeals) courts, and described the minimum requirements for various cases to be heard under federal jurisdiction, instead of by state courts. The Act expressly gave the Supreme Court jurisdiction over writs of habeas corpus. For centuries, habeas corpus has been invoked to prevent the jailing of individuals for indefinite terms without these individuals having been convicted in a court of law.

Judiciary Act of 1789

CHAP. XX. – An Act to establish the Judicial Courts of the United States.

SEC. 1. *Be it enacted by the Senate and House of Representatives of the United States of America in Congress assembled,* That the supreme court of the United States shall consist of a chief justice and five associate justices, any four of whom shall be a quorum, and shall hold annually at the seat of government two sessions, the one commencing the first Monday of February, and the other the first Monday of August. That the associate justices shall have precedence according to the date of their commissions, or when the commissions of two or more of them bear date on the same day, according to their respective ages.

SEC. 2. *And be it further enacted,* That the United States shall be, and they hereby are divided into thirteen districts, to be limited and called as follows, to wit: one to consist of that part of the State of Massachusetts which lies easterly of the State of New Hampshire, and to be called Maine District; one to consist of the State of New Hampshire, and to be called New Hampshire District; one to consist of the remaining part of the State of Massachusetts, and to be called Massachusetts district; one to consist of the State of Connecticut, and to be called Connecticut District; one to consist of the State of New York, and to be called New York District; one to consist of the State of New Jersey, and to be called New Jersey District; one to consist of the State of Pennsylvania, and to be called Pennsylvania District; one to consist of the State of Delaware, and to be called Delaware District; one to consist of the State of Maryland, and to be called Maryland District; one to consist of the State of Virginia, except that part called the District of Kentucky, and to be called Virginia District; one to consist of the remaining part of the State of Virginia, and to be called Kentucky District; one to consist of the State of South Carolina, and to be called South Carolina District; and one to consist of the State of Georgia, and to be called Georgia District.

SEC. 3. *And be it further enacted*, That there be a court called a District Court, in each of the afore mentioned districts, to consist of one judge, who shall reside in the district for which he is appointed, and shall be called a District Judge, and shall hold annually four sessions. . . .

SEC. 4. *And be it further enacted*, That the before mentioned districts, except those of Maine and Kentucky, shall be divided into three circuits, and be called the eastern, the middle, and the southern circuit. That the eastern circuit shall consist of the districts of New Hampshire, Massachusetts, Connecticut and New York; that the middle circuit shall consist of the districts of New Jersey, Pennsylvania, Delaware, Maryland and Virginia; and that the southern circuit shall consist of the districts of South Carolina and Georgia, and that there shall be held annually in each district of said circuits, two courts, which shall be called Circuit Courts, and shall consist of any two justices of the Supreme Court, and the district judge of such districts, any two of whom shall constitute a quorum: *Provided*, That no district judge shall give a vote in any case of appeal or error from his own decision; but may assign the reasons of such his decision. . . .

SEC. 9. *And be it further enacted*, That the district courts shall have, exclusively of the courts of the several States, cognizance of all crimes and offences that shall be cognizable under the authority of the United States, committed within their respective districts, or upon the high seas; where no other punishment than whipping, not exceeding thirty stripes, a fine not exceeding one hundred dollars, or a term of imprisonment not exceeding six months, is to be inflicted; and shall also have exclusive original cognizance of all civil causes of admiralty and maritime jurisdiction, including all seizures under laws of impost, navigation or trade of the United States, where the seizures are made, on waters which are navigable from the sea by vessels of ten or more tons burthen, within their respective districts as well as upon the high seas; saving to suitors, in all cases, the right of a common law remedy, where the common law is competent to give it; and shall also have exclusive original cognizance of all seizures on land, or other waters than as aforesaid, made, and of all suits for penalties and forfeitures incurred, under the laws of the United States. And shall also have cognizance, concurrent with the courts of the several States, or the circuit courts, as the case may be, of all causes where an alien sues for a tort only in violation of the law of nations or a treaty of the United States. And shall also have cognizance, concurrent as last mentioned, of all suits at common law where the United States sue, and the matter in dispute amounts, exclusive of costs, to the sum or value of one hundred dollars. And shall also have jurisdiction exclusively of the courts of the several States, of all suits against consuls or vice-consuls, except for offences above the description aforesaid. And the trial of issues in fact, in the district courts, in all causes except civil causes of admiralty and maritime jurisdiction, shall be by jury. . . .

SEC. 11. *And be it further enacted*, That the circuit courts shall have original cognizance, concurrent with the courts of the several States, of all suits of a civil nature at common law or in equity, where the matter in dispute exceeds, exclusive of costs, the sum or value of five hundred dollars, and the United States are plaintiffs, or petitioners; or an alien is a party, or the suit is between a citizen of the State where the suit is brought, and a citizen of another State. And shall have exclusive cognizance of all crimes and offences cognizable under the authority of the United States, except where this act otherwise provides, or the laws of the United States shall otherwise direct, and concurrent jurisdiction with the district courts of the crimes and offences cognizable therein. But no person shall be arrested in one district for trial in another, in any civil action before a circuit or district court. . . .

SEC. 14. *And be it further enacted,* That all the before-mentioned courts of the United States, shall have power to issue writs of *scire facias, habeas corpus,* and all other writs not specially provided for by statute, which may be necessary for the exercise of their respective jurisdictions, and agreeable to the principles and usages of law. And that either of the justices of the supreme court, as well as judges of the district courts, shall have power to grant writs of *habeas corpus* for the purpose of an inquiry into the cause of commitment.—*Provided,* That writs of *habeas corpus* shall in no case extend to prisoners in gaol, unless where they are in custody, under or by colour of the authority of the United States, or are committed for trial before some court of the same, or are necessary to be brought into court to testify. . . .

Marbury v. Madison, 1803

On its face, this case is about the failure by the new administration of Thomas Jefferson (1801–1809) to deliver to Mr. Marbury his seal as a newly commissioned notary public. However, Chief Justice John Marshall crafted the opinion in the case to firmly establish the power of the federal judiciary, centered on the principle of judicial review. After Marbury, *the power of the Supreme Court as final interpreter of the U.S. Constitution became an essential feature of American government.*

Chief Justice Marshall carefully describes the limits of the Court's power but also asserts the Court's ability to limit the powers of Congress and of the president. The decision relies upon a basic idea of constitutional governance: that any unlimited power is by its nature unconstitutional. He carefully explains, however, that the Court may only review the decisions of the executive branch when the president is acting under a duty to faithfully execute the law and the rights of an individual are at stake. In contrast, the political functions of the executive (the president) are never within the Court's power to review.

Marbury v. Madison

Opinion of the court.

At the last term on the affidavits then read and filed with the clerk, a rule was granted in this case, requiring the secretary of state to shew cause why a mandamus should not issue, directing him to deliver to William Marbury his commission as a justice of the peace. . . .

No cause has been shewn [shown], and the present motion is for a mandamus. The peculiar delicacy of this case, the novelty of some of its circumstances, and the real difficulty attending the points which occur in it, require a complete exposition of the principles, on which the opinion to be given by the court, is founded.

In the order in which the court has viewed this subject, the following questions have been considered and decided.

obligatory upon the States by the Fourteenth Amendment. We think the Court in Betts was wrong, however, in concluding that the Sixth Amendment's guarantee of counsel is not one of these fundamental rights. Ten years before Betts v. Brady, this Court, after full consideration of all the historical data examined in Betts, had unequivocally declared that "the right to the aid of counsel is of this fundamental character."

[R]eason and reflection require us to recognize that in our adversary system of criminal justice, any person haled into court, who is too poor to hire a lawyer, cannot be assured a fair trial unless counsel is provided for him. This seems to us to be an obvious truth. Governments, both state and federal, quite properly spend vast sums of money to establish machinery to try defendants accused of crime. Lawyers to prosecute are everywhere deemed essential to protect the public's interest in an orderly society. Similarly, there are few defendants charged with crime, few indeed, who fail to hire the best lawyers they can get to prepare and present their defenses. That government hires lawyers to prosecute and defendants who have the money hire lawyers to defend are the strongest indications of the wide-spread belief that lawyers in criminal courts are necessities, not luxuries. The right of one charged with crime to counsel may not be deemed fundamental and essential to fair trials in some countries, but it is in ours. From the very beginning, our state and national constitutions and laws have laid great emphasis on procedural and substantive safeguards designed to assure fair trials before impartial tribunals in which every defendant stands equal before the law. This noble ideal cannot be realized if the poor man charged with crime has to face his accusers without a lawyer to assist him.

Escobedo v. Illinois, 1964

A person accused of a crime needs the advice of a lawyer to ensure that a fair outcome is achieved, whether a trial ever takes place or not. The case below addresses when in the process the accused person has the right to an attorney. The Court held that once a person knows that she or he is specifically suspected of a particular crime, the accused has the right to an attorney present for questioning by the police, even if the accused has not yet been indicted. An indictment is the formal written charge of a crime. Once indicted, a suspect knows that he or she must face a trial or seek a plea bargain.

Escobedo v. Illinois

It is argued that if the right to counsel is afforded prior to indictment, the number of confessions obtained by the police will diminish significantly, because most confessions are obtained during the period between arrest and indictment, and "any lawyer worth his salt will tell the suspect in no uncertain terms to make no statement to police under any circumstances." This argument, of course, cuts two ways. The fact that many confessions are obtained during this period points up its critical nature as a "stage when legal aid and advice" are surely needed. The right to counsel would indeed be hollow if it began at a period when few confessions were obtained. There is necessarily a direct relationship between the importance of a stage to the police in their quest for a confession and the criticalness of that stage to the accused in his need for legal advice. Our Constitution, unlike some others, strikes the balance in favor of the right of the accused to be advised by his lawyer of his privilege against self-incrimination. We have learned the lesson of history, ancient and modern, that a system of criminal law enforcement which comes to depend on the 'confession' will, in the long run, be less reliable and more subject to abuses than a system which depends on extrinsic evidence independently secured through skillful investigation. As Dean Wigmore so wisely said:

"(A)ny system of administration which permits the prosecution to trust habitually to compulsory self-disclosure as a source of proof must itself suffer morally thereby. The inclination develops to rely mainly upon such evidence, and to be satisfied with an incomplete investigation of the other sources. The exercise of the power to extract answers begets a forgetfulness of the just limitations of that power. The simple and peaceful process of questioning breeds a readiness to resort to bullying and to physical force and torture. If there is a right to an answer, there soon seems to be a right to the expected answer—that is, to a confession of guilt. Thus the legitimate use grows into the unjust abuse; ultimately, the innocent are jeopardized by the encroachments of a bad system. Such seems to have been the course of experience in those legal systems where the privilege was not recognized."

This Court also has recognized that "history amply shows that confessions have often been extorted to save law enforcement officials the trouble and effort of obtaining valid and independent evidence . . ."

We have also learned the companion lesson of history that no system of criminal justice can, or should, survive if it comes to depend for its continued effectiveness on the citizens' abdication through unawareness of their constitutional rights. No system worth preserving should have to fear that if an accused is permitted to consult with a lawyer, he will become aware of, and exercise, these rights. If the exercise of constitutional rights will thwart the effectiveness of a system of law enforcement, then there is something very wrong with that system.

We hold, therefore, that where, as here, the investigation is no longer a general inquiry into an unsolved crime but has begun to focus on a particular suspect, the suspect has been taken into police custody, the police carry out a process of interrogations that lends itself to eliciting incriminating statements, the suspect has requested and been denied an opportunity to consult with his lawyer, and the police have not effectively warned him of his absolute constitutional right to remain silent, the accused has been denied "The Assistance of Counsel" in violation of the Sixth Amendment to the Constitution as "made obligatory upon the States by the Fourteenth Amendment" [*Gideon v. Wainwright*] and that no statement elicited by the police during the interrogation may be used against him at a criminal trial.

New York Times v. Sullivan, 1964

The First Amendment to the U.S. Constitution preserves freedom of speech and of the press. Restrictions upon freedom of speech have been controversial throughout the nation's history. The Court has upheld the view that government does not have the power to determine what ideas are false; therefore, it cannot restrict views and opinions by labeling them "false." False statements of fact are trickier, but in the case below, the Court holds that public officials cannot use bad facts as grounds to restrict speech.

New York Times v. Sullivan

We are required in this case to determine for the first time the extent to which the constitutional protections for speech and press limit a State's power to award damages in a libel action brought by a public official against critics of his official conduct.

Background of the Case

Respondent L.B. Sullivan is one of the three elected Commissioners of the City of Montgomery, Alabama. He testified that he was "Commissioner of Public Affairs and the duties are supervision of the Police Department, Fire Department, Department of Cemetery and Department of Scales." He brought this civil libel action against the four individual petitioners, who are Negroes and Alabama clergymen, and against petitioner the New York Times. . . . A jury in the Circuit Court of Montgomery County awarded him damages of $500,000 . . . and the Supreme Court of Alabama affirmed.

Respondent's complaint alleged that he had been libeled by statements in a full-page advertisement that was carried in the New York Times on March 29, 1960. Entitled "Heed Their Rising Voices," the advertisement began by stating that "As the whole world knows by now, thousands of Southern Negro students are engaged in widespread non-violent demonstrations in positive affirmation of the right to live in human dignity as guaranteed by the U.S. Constitution and the Bill of Rights." It went on to charge that [the students faced a "wave of terror" in response to their activism].

The text appeared over the names of 64 persons, many widely known for their activities in public affairs, religion, trade unions, and the performing arts. Below these names . . . appeared the names of the four individual petitioners and of 16 other persons, all but two of whom were identified as clergymen in various Southern cities. The advertisement was signed at the bottom of the page by the "Committee to Defend Martin Luther King and the Struggle for Freedom in the South," and the officers of the Committee were listed.

Of the ten paragraphs of text in the advertisement, the third and a portion of the sixth were the basis of respondent's claim of libel. They read as follows:

Third paragraph:

"In Montgomery, Alabama, after students sang 'My Country, 'Tis of Thee' on the State Capitol steps, their leaders were expelled from school, and truckloads of police armed with shotguns and tear-gas ringed the Alabama State College Campus. When the entire student body protested to state authorities by refusing to re-register, their dining hall was padlocked in an attempt to starve them into submission."

Sixth paragraph:

"Again and again the Southern violators have answered Dr. King's peaceful protests with intimidation and violence. They have bombed his home almost killing his wife and child. They have assaulted his person. They have arrested him seven times-for 'speeding,' 'loitering' and similar 'offenses.' And now they have charged him with 'perjury'—a felony under which they could imprison him for ten years."

Although neither of these statements mentions respondent by name, he contended that the word "police" in the third paragraph referred to him as the Montgomery Commissioner who supervised the Police Department, so that he was being accused of "ringing" the campus with police. He further claimed that the paragraph would be read as imputing to the police, and hence to him, the padlocking of the dining hall in order to starve the students into submission. As to the sixth paragraph, he contended that since arrests are ordinarily made by the police, the statement "They have arrested (Dr. King) seven times" would be read as referring to him; he further contended that the "They" who did the arresting would be equated with the "They" who committed the other described acts and with the "Southern violators." Thus, he argued, the paragraph would be read as accusing the Montgomery police, and hence him, of answering Dr. King's protests with "intimidation and violence," bombing his home, assaulting his person, and charging him with perjury. Respondent and six other Montgomery residents testified that they read some or all of the statements as referring to him in his capacity as Commissioner.

Inaccuracies

It is uncontroverted that some of the statements contained in the two paragraphs were not accurate descriptions of events which occurred in Montgomery. Although Negro students staged a demonstration on the State Capital steps, they sang the National Anthem and not "My Country, 'Tis of Thee." Although nine students were expelled by the State Board of Education, this was not for leading the demonstration at the Capitol, but for demanding service at a lunch counter in the Montgomery County Courthouse on another day. Not the entire student body, but most of it, had protested the expulsion, not by refusing to register, but by boycotting classes on a single day; virtually all the students did register for the ensuing semester. The campus dining hall was not padlocked on any occasion . . . Although the police were deployed near the campus in large numbers on three occasions, they did not at any time "ring" the campus . . . Dr. King had not been arrested seven times, but only four; and although he claimed to have been assaulted some years earlier in connection with his arrest for loitering outside a courtroom, one of the officers who made the arrest denied that there was such an assault.

On the premise that the charges in the sixth paragraph could be read as referring to him, respondent was allowed to prove that he had not participated in the events described. Although Dr. King's home had in fact been bombed twice when his wife and child were there, both of these occasions antedated respondent's tenure as Commissioner, and the police were not only not implicated in the bombings, but had made every effort to apprehend those who were. Three of Dr. King's four arrests took place before respondent became Commissioner. Although Dr. King had in fact been indicted (he was subsequently acquitted) on two counts of perjury, each of which carried a possible five-year sentence, respondent had nothing to do with procuring the indictment.

Respondent made no effort to prove that he suffered actual pecuniary loss as a result of the alleged libel. . . .

Opinion of the Court

We reverse the judgment. We hold that the rule of law applied by the Alabama courts is constitutionally deficient for failure to provide the safeguards for freedom of speech and of the press that are required by the First and Fourteenth Amendments in a libel action brought by a public official against critics of his official conduct. We further hold that under the proper safeguards the evidence presented in this case is constitutionally insufficient to support the judgment for respondent.

See also: Freedom of the Press in **Supreme Court A to Z**; *New York Times v. Sullivan* in **Supreme Court A to Z**.

Miranda v. Arizona, 1966

The phrase "You have the right to remain silent" has become a necessary ingredient in television police dramas. It is the best-known portion of the "Miranda rights," the list of constitutional protections that must be stated to a criminal suspect when she or he is taken into police custody. Miranda was in fact one of four cases addressed in the 1966 opinion. The Court sometimes groups cases that revolve around the same issue in order to better explain the meaning of a decision. Here, the Court clarified the rules for how police may get information from suspects. Failure to follow the rules means that any information the police may receive from the subject will not be usable in court and therefore may weaken as a criminal case.

Miranda v. Arizona

The cases before us raise questions which go to the roots of our concepts of American criminal jurisprudence: the restraints society must observe consistent with the Federal Constitution in prosecuting individuals for crime. More specifically, we deal with the admissibility of statements obtained from an individual who is subjected to custodial police interrogation and the necessity for procedures which assure that the individual is accorded his privilege under the Fifth Amendment to the Constitution not to be compelled to incriminate himself.

Our holding will be spelled out with some specificity in the pages which follow but briefly stated it is this: the prosecution may not use statements, whether **exculpatory [evidence favorable to the defendant in a criminal trial]** or inculpatory **[evidence that shows, or tends to show, a person's involvement in an act],** stemming from custodial interrogation of the defendant unless it demonstrates the use of procedural safeguards effective to secure the privilege against self-incrimination. By custodial interrogation, we mean questioning initiated by law enforcement officers after a person has been taken into custody or otherwise deprived of his freedom of action in any significant way. As for the procedural safe-guards to be employed, unless other fully effective means are devised to inform accused persons of their right of silence and to assure a continuous opportunity to exercise it, the following measures are required. Prior to any questioning, the person must be warned that he has a right to remain silent, that any statement he does make may be used as evidence against him, and that he has a right to the presence of an attorney, either retained or appointed. The defendant may waive effectuation of these rights, provided the waiver is made voluntarily, knowingly and intelligently. If, however, he indicates in any manner and at any stage of the process that he wishes to consult with an attorney before speaking there can be no questioning. Likewise, if the individual is alone and indicates in any manner that he does not wish to be interrogated, the police may not question him. The mere fact that he may have answered some questions or volunteered some statements on his own does not deprive him of the right to refrain from answering any further inquiries until he has consulted with an attorney and thereafter consents to be questioned . . .

An understanding of the nature and setting of this in-custody interrogation is essential to our decisions today. The difficulty in depicting what transpires at such interrogations stems from the fact that in this country they have largely taken place incommunicado. From extensive factual studies undertaken in the early 1930's, including the famous Wickersham Report to Congress by a Presidential Commission, it is clear that police violence and the 'third degree' flourished at that time. In a series of cases decided by this Court long after these studies, the police resorted to physical brutality-beatings, hanging, whipping-and to sustained and protracted questioning incommunicado in order to extort confessions. The Commission on Civil Rights in 1961 found much evidence to indicate that 'some policemen still resort to physical force to obtain confessions' . . . The use of physical brutality and violence is not, unfortunately, relegated to the past or to any part of the country. Only recently in Kings County, New York, the police brutally beat, kicked and placed lighted cigarette butts on the back of a potential witness under interrogation for the purpose of securing a statement incriminating a third party.

The examples given above are undoubtedly the exception now, but they are sufficiently widespread to be the object of concern. Unless a proper limitation upon custodial interrogation is achieved-such as these decisions will advance-there can be no assurance that practices of this nature will be eradicated in the foreseeable future. . . .

Today, then, there can be no doubt that the Fifth Amendment privilege is available outside of criminal court proceedings and serves to protect persons in all settings in which their freedom of action is curtailed in any significant way from being compelled to incriminate themselves. We have concluded that without proper safeguards the process of in-custody interrogation of persons suspected or accused of crime contains inherently compelling pressures which work to undermine the individual's will to resist and to compel him to speak where he would not otherwise do so freely. In order to combat these pressures and to permit a full opportunity to exercise the privilege against self-incrimination, the accused must be adequately and effectively apprised of his rights and the exercise of those rights must be fully honored.

It is impossible for us to foresee the potential alternatives for protecting the privilege which might be devised by Congress or the States in the exercise of their creative rule-making capacities. Therefore we cannot say that the Constitution necessarily requires adherence to any particular solution for the inherent compulsions of the interrogation process as it is presently conducted. Our decision in no way creates a constitutional straitjacket which will handicap sound efforts at reform, nor is it intended to have this effect. We encourage Congress and the States to continue their laudable search for increasingly effective ways of protecting the rights of the individual while promoting efficient enforcement of our criminal laws.

The Fifth Amendment privilege is so fundamental to our system of constitutional rule and the expedient of giving an adequate warning as to the availability of the privilege so simple, we will not pause to inquire in individual cases whether the defendant was aware of his rights without a warning being given. Assessments of the knowledge the defendant possessed, based on information as to his age, education, intelligence, or prior contact with authorities, can never be more than speculation; a warning is a clearcut fact. More important, whatever the background of the person interrogated, a warning at the time of the interrogation is indispensable to overcome its pressures and to insure that the individual knows he is free to exercise the privilege at that point in time. . . .

Loving v. Virginia, 1967

The Lovings were an African American woman and a white man who were married in the District of Columbia. While residing in Virginia, they were convicted under state law of the felony crime of "miscegenation"—interracial marriage or interracial sexual relations. The equal protection clause of the Constitution's Fourteenth Amendment says that the states may only make and enforce laws that impact the rights and privileges of all citizens equally. Only in 1967 did the Court hold that laws banning interracial marriage violated the equal protection clause. The Court overturned the Lovings' criminal convictions.

The Loving decision was also important because it helped establish the "strict scrutiny" test for laws involving racial classifications. Under strict scrutiny, a law must not merely have some rational relationship to a legitimate state power. The challenged law, to survive, must meet the test of the equal protection clause.

Loving v. Virginia

This case presents a constitutional question never addressed by this Court: whether a statutory scheme adopted by the State of Virginia to prevent marriages between persons solely on the basis of racial classifications violates the Equal Protection and Due Process Clauses of the Fourteenth Amendment. For reasons which seem to us to reflect the central meaning of those constitutional commands, we conclude that these statutes cannot stand consistently with the Fourteenth Amendment.

[T]he State [of Virginia] argues that the meaning of the Equal Protection Clause, as illuminated by the statements of the Framers, is only that state penal laws containing an interracial element as part of the definition of the offense must apply equally to whites and Negroes in the sense that members of each race are punished to the same degree. Thus, the State contends that, because its miscegenation statutes punish equally both the white and the Negro participants in an interracial marriage, these statutes, despite their reliance on racial classifications do not constitute an invidious discrimination based upon race . . .

Because we reject the notion that the mere 'equal application' of a statute containing racial classifications is enough to remove the classifications from the Fourteenth Amendment's proscription of all invidious racial discriminations, we do not accept the State's contention that these statutes should be upheld if there is any possible basis for concluding that they serve a rational purpose. The mere fact of equal application does not mean that our analysis of these statutes should follow the approach we have taken in cases involving no racial discrimination . . .

[T]he Equal Protection Clause requires the consideration of whether the classifications drawn by any statute constitute an arbitrary and invidious discrimination. The clear and central purpose of the Fourteenth Amendment was to eliminate all official state sources of invidious racial discrimination in the States.

There can be no question but that Virginia's miscegenation statutes rest solely upon distinctions drawn according to race. The statutes proscribe generally accepted conduct if engaged in by members of different races. Over the years, this Court has consistently repudiated "(d)istinctions between citizens solely because of their ancestry" as being "odious to a free people whose institutions are founded upon the doctrine of equality." At the very least, the Equal Protection Clause demands that racial classifications, especially suspect in criminal statutes, be subjected to the "most rigid scrutiny," and, if they are ever to be upheld, they must be shown to be necessary to the accomplishment of some permissible state objective, independent of the racial discrimination which it was the object of the Fourteenth Amendment to eliminate.

There is patently no legitimate overriding purpose independent of invidious racial discrimination which justifies this classification. The fact that Virginia prohibits only interracial marriages involving white persons demonstrates that the racial classifications must stand on their own justification, as measures designed to maintain White Supremacy. We have consistently denied the constitutionality of measures which restrict the rights of citizens on account of race. There can be no doubt that restricting the freedom to marry solely because of racial classifications violates the central meaning of the Equal Protection Clause.

Tinker v. Des Moines, 1969

American government divides power between the federal government and the states. Each state possesses so-called police powers, giving it the ability to make and enforce laws necessary for the safety, health, and welfare of the state's citizens. This broad power, necessary for the provision of many basic services of government (including public education), can sometimes clash with individual rights. This case concerns the rights of public school students to express themselves and what measures, if any, school authorities may take to restrict such expression. Tinker *identifies the basic tension between freedom of individual expression and the maintenance of discipline in school and holds that public school authorities cannot restrict student expression where such expression would not materially and substantially interfere with the school's operation and maintenance of basic discipline.*

Tinker v. Des Moines

Petitioner John F. Tinker, 15 years old, and petitioner Christopher Eckhardt, 16 years old, attended high schools in Des Moines, Iowa. Petitioner Mary Beth Tinker, John's sister, was a 13-year-old student in junior high school.

In December 1965, a group of adults and students in Des Moines held a meeting at the Eckhardt home. The group determined to publicize their objections to the hostilities in Vietnam and their support for a truce by wearing black armbands during the holiday season and by fasting on December 16 and New Year's Eve.

On December 16, Mary Beth and Christopher wore black armbands to their schools. John Tinker wore his armband the next day. They were all sent home and suspended from school until they would come back without their armbands. They did not return to school until after the planned period for wearing armbands had expired—that is, until after New Year's Day.

First Amendment rights, applied in light of the special characteristics of the school environment, are available to teachers and students. It can hardly be argued that either students or teachers shed their constitutional rights to freedom of speech or expression at the schoolhouse gate. This has been the unmistakable holding of this Court for almost 50 years. . . . On the other hand, the Court has repeatedly emphasized the need for affirming the comprehensive authority of the States and of school officials, consistent with fundamental constitutional safeguards, to prescribe and control conduct in the schools. . . .

The problem posed by the present case does not relate to regulation of the length of skirts or the type of clothing, to hair style, or deportment. It does not concern aggressive, disruptive action or even group demonstrations. Our problem involves direct, primary First Amendment rights akin to "pure speech."

The school officials banned and sought to punish petitioners for a silent, passive expression of opinion, unaccompanied by any disorder or disturbance on the part of petitioners. There is here no evidence whatever of petitioners' interference, actual or nascent, with the schools' work or of collision with the rights of other students to be secure and to be let alone. Accordingly, this case does not concern speech or action that intrudes upon the work of the schools or the rights of other students.

Only a few of the 18,000 students in the school system wore the black armbands. Only five students were suspended for wearing them. There is no indication that the work of the schools or any class was disrupted. Outside the classrooms, a few students made hostile remarks to the children wearing armbands, but there were no threats or acts of violence on school premises.

The District Court concluded that the action of the school authorities was reasonable because it was based upon their fear of a disturbance from the wearing of the armbands. But, in our system, undifferentiated fear or apprehension of disturbance is not enough to overcome the right to freedom of expression. Any departure from absolute regimentation may cause trouble. Any variation from the majority's opinion may inspire fear. Any word spoken, in class, in the lunchroom, or on the campus, that deviates from the views of another person may start an argument or cause a disturbance. But our Constitution says we must take this risk, and our history says that it is this sort of hazardous freedom—this kind of openness—that is the basis of our national strength and of the independence and vigor of Americans who grow up and live in this relatively permissive, often disputatious, society.

In order for the State in the person of school officials to justify prohibition of a particular expression of opinion, it must be able to show that its action was caused by something more than a mere desire to avoid the discomfort and unpleasantness that always accompany an unpopular viewpoint. Certainly where there is no finding and no showing that engaging in the forbidden conduct would "materially and substantially interfere with the requirements of appropriate discipline in the operation of the school," the prohibition cannot be sustained.

In the present case, the District Court made no such finding, and our independent examination of the record fails to yield evidence that the school authorities had reason to anticipate that the wearing of the armbands would substantially interfere with the work of the school or impinge upon the rights of other students. Even an official memorandum prepared after the suspension that listed the reasons for the ban on wearing the armbands made no reference to the anticipation of such disruption.

In our system, state-operated schools may not be enclaves of totalitarianism. School officials do not possess absolute authority over their students. Students in school as well as out of school are "persons" under our Constitution. They are possessed of fundamental rights which the State must respect, just as they themselves must respect their obligations to the State. In our system, students may not be regarded as closed-circuit recipients of only that which the State chooses to communicate. They may not be confined to the expression of those sentiments that are officially approved. In the absence of a specific showing of constitutionally valid reasons to regulate their speech, students are entitled to freedom of expression of their views.

From the Harry A. Blackmun Papers, 1970

Associate Justice Harry A. Blackmun was appointed to the Court in 1970 by President Richard Nixon (1969–1974). He served until his retirement in 1994 at the age of eighty-five. In May 1997, Blackmun gave his papers to the Library of Congress. Blackmun was a contemporary, for varying amounts of time, of several of the current associate justices who sit on the Court: John Paul Stevens, Antonin Scalia, Anthony M. Kennedy, Clarence Thomas, and Ruth Bader Ginsburg. In this excerpt from 1970, Blackmun described his feelings about his introduction to the Court.

From the Harry A. Blackmun Papers

The first time I joined everybody in my robe must have been the ninth day of June 1970, when I came down and was sworn in. I remember walking into the conference room, and there were these eight black-robed figures standing around with names like Hugo Lafayette Black, and William Orville Douglas, and William James Brennan Jr., and John Marshall Harlan and all the rest. Names that any law student, or any lawyer in those days knew well, knew about. Made me wonder what I was doing there. They were very kind at the time and made me feel welcome.

Swann v. Mecklenburg County Board of Education, 1971

The first Brown v. Board of Education *decision, in 1954, found racially separate public schools unconstitutional. The second* Brown *decision, in 1955, provided remedial measures to correct segregation. Segregated schooling, however, had a long history in too many parts of the country, and desegregation efforts often faced sharp opposition, leading local school officials to move slowly and by half-measures.* Swann *discussed four controversial tactics for working toward desegregation. At the time, a frustrated Court was willing to permit courts to use broad powers to prod school authorities into action. Later decisions tended to limit these powers rather than extend them.*

Swann v. Mecklenburg County Board of Education

The objective today remains to eliminate from the public schools all vestiges of state-imposed segregation. Segregation was the evil struck down by Brown I as contrary to the equal protection guarantees of the Constitution. That was the violation sought to be corrected by the remedial measures of Brown II . . . If school authorities fail in their affirmative obligations under these holdings, judicial authority may be invoked. Once a right and a violation have been shown, the scope of a district court's equitable powers to remedy past wrongs is broad, for breadth and flexibility are inherent in equitable remedies.

In seeking to define even in broad and general terms how far this remedial power extends it is important to remember that judicial powers may be exercised only on the basis of a constitutional violation. Remedial judicial authority does not put judges automatically in the shoes of school authorities whose powers are plenary. Judicial authority enters only when local authority defaults.

The central issue in this case is that of student assignment, and there are essentially four problem areas:

(1) to what extent racial balance or racial quotas may be used as an implement in a remedial order to correct a previously segregated system;

(2) whether every all-Negro and all-white school must be eliminated as an indispensable part of a remedial process of desegregation;

(3) what the limits are, if any, on the rearrangement of school districts and attendance zones, as a remedial measure; and

(4) what the limits are, if any, on the use of transportation facilities to correct state-enforced racial school segregation.

(1) Racial Balances or Racial Quotas.

In this case it is urged that the District Court has imposed a racial balance requirement of 71%-29% on individual schools . . . As the voluminous record in this case shows, the predicate for the District Court's use of the 71%-29% ratio was twofold: first, its express finding, approved by the Court of Appeals and not challenged here, that a dual school system had been maintained by the school authorities at least until 1969; second, its finding, also approved by the Court of Appeals, that the school board had totally defaulted in its acknowledged duty to come forward with an acceptable plan of its own, notwithstanding the patient efforts of the District Judge who, on at least three occasions, urged the board to submit plans.

We see therefore that the use made of mathematical ratios was no more than a starting point in the process of shaping a remedy, rather than an inflexible requirement. Awareness of the racial composition of the whole school system is likely to be a useful starting point in shaping a remedy to correct past constitutional violations. In sum, the very limited use made of mathematical ratios was within the equitable remedial discretion of the District Court.

(2) One-race Schools.

The record in this case reveals the familiar phenomenon that in metropolitan areas minority groups are often found concentrated in one part of the city. In some circumstances certain schools may remain all or largely of one race until new schools can be provided or neighborhood patterns change. Schools all or predominantly of one race in a district of mixed population will require close scrutiny to determine that school assignments are not part of state-enforced segregation.

In light of the above, it should be clear that the existence of some small number of one-race, or virtually one-race, schools within a district is not in and of itself the mark of a system that still practices segregation by law. The district judge or school authorities should make every effort to achieve the greatest possible degree of actual desegregation and will thus necessarily be concerned with the elimination of one-race schools . . . Where the school authority's proposed plan for conversion from a dual to a unitary system contemplates the continued existence of some schools that are all or predominately of one race, they have the burden of showing that such school assignments are genuinely nondiscriminatory. The court should scrutinize such schools, and the burden upon the school authorities will be to satisfy the court that their racial composition is not the result of present or past discriminatory action on their part.

(3) Remedial Altering of Attendance Zones.

The maps submitted in these cases graphically demonstrate that one of the principal tools employed by school planners and by courts to break up the dual school system has been a frank *and sometimes drastic* gerrymandering of school districts and attendance zones . . . As an interim corrective measure, this cannot be said to be beyond the broad remedial powers of a court.

No fixed or even substantially fixed guidelines can be established as to how far a court can go, but it must be recognized that there are limits. The objective is to dismantle the dual school system. "Racially neutral" assignment plans proposed by school authorities to a district court may be inadequate; such plans may fail to counteract the continuing effects of past school segregation resulting from discriminatory location of school sites or distortion of school size in order to achieve or maintain an artificial racial separation. When school authorities present a district court with a "loaded game board," affirmative action in the form of remedial altering of attendance zones is proper to achieve truly non-discriminatory assignments. In short, an assignment plan is not acceptable simply because it appears to be neutral.

(4) Transportation of Students.

The importance of bus transportation as a normal and accepted tool of educational policy is readily discernible in this and the companion case Davis, supra. The Charlotte school authorities did not purport to assign students on the basis of geographically drawn zones until 1965 and then they allowed almost unlimited transfer privileges. The District Court's conclusion that assignment of children to the school nearest their home serving their grade would not produce an effective dismantling of the dual system is supported by the record.

Thus the remedial techniques used in the District Court's order were within that court's power to provide equitable relief; implementation of the decree is well within the capacity of the school authority . . . In these circumstances, we find no basis for holding that the local school authorities may not be required to employ bus transportation as one tool of school desegregation. Desegregation plans cannot be limited to the walk-in school.

Roe v. Wade, 1973

The "right to privacy" appears nowhere in the Constitution. However, in cases leading up to Roe, *the Court found that the explicit inclusions in the Bill of Rights must not be read so narrowly as to eliminate implicit rights. Also, the Ninth Amendment states that the inclusion of certain explicit rights does not deny other rights to the citizens merely because those rights are unnamed.*

In this context, the Court took up Roe. *The legal status of abortion was a bitter question. Despite the intense philosophical differences and the emotions they stir up, the Court attempted to balance the history of abortion laws in the United States, the privacy right of a pregnant woman contemplating or undertaking the termination of a pregnancy, and the interest a state legitimately has in ensuring that any medical procedure be performed safely. Since 1973, the decision in* Roe, *with certain permitted restrictions, has made abortion legal in the United States. Still, abortion is often a deeply divisive political issue and has been a major point of contention in the confirmation hearings of new justices.*

Roe v. Wade

We forthwith acknowledge our awareness of the sensitive and emotional nature of the abortion controversy, of the vigorous opposing views, even among physicians, and of the deep and seemingly absolute convictions that the subject inspires. One's philosophy, one's experiences, one's exposure to the raw edges of human existence, one's religious training, one's attitudes toward life and family and their values, and the moral standards one establishes and seeks to observe, are all likely to influence and to color one's thinking and conclusions about abortion.

It perhaps is not generally appreciated that the restrictive criminal abortion laws in effect in a majority of States today are of relatively recent vintage. Those laws, generally proscribing abortion or its attempt at any time during pregnancy except when necessary to preserve the pregnant woman's life, are not of ancient or even of common-law origin. Instead, they derive from statutory changes effected, for the most part, in the latter half of the 19th century.

Gradually, in the middle and late 19th century the quickening distinction disappeared from the statutory law of most States and the degree of the offense and the penalties were increased. By the end of the 1950s a large majority of the jurisdictions banned abortion, however and whenever performed, unless done to save or preserve the life of the mother. The exceptions, Alabama and the District of Columbia, permitted abortion to preserve the mother's health. Three States permitted abortions that were not "unlawfully" performed or that were not "without lawful justification," leaving interpretation of those standards to the courts. In the past several years, however, a trend toward liberalization of abortion statutes has resulted in adoption, by about one-third of the States, of less stringent laws. . . .

It is thus apparent that at common law, at the time of the adoption of our Constitution, and throughout the major portion of the 19th century, abortion was viewed with less disfavor than under most American statutes currently in effect. Phrasing it another way, a woman enjoyed a substantially broader right to terminate a pregnancy than she does in most States today. At least with respect to the early stage of pregnancy, and very possibly without such a limitation, the opportunity to make this choice was present in this country well into the 19th century. Even later, the law continued for some time to treat less punitively an abortion procured in early pregnancy.

The Constitution does not explicitly mention any right of privacy. In a line of decisions . . . the Court has recognized that a right of personal privacy, or a guarantee of certain areas or zones of privacy, does exist under the Constitution . . . This right of privacy, whether it be founded in the Fourteenth Amendment's concept of personal liberty and restrictions upon state action, as we feel it is, or, as the District Court determined, in the Ninth Amendment's reservation of rights to the people, is broad enough to encompass a woman's decision whether or not to terminate her pregnancy. The detriment that the State would impose upon the pregnant woman by denying this choice altogether is apparent. Specific and direct harm medically diagnosable even in early pregnancy may be involved. Maternity, or additional offspring, may force upon the woman a distressful life and future. Psychological harm may be imminent. Mental and physical health may be taxed by child care. There is also the distress, for all concerned, associated with the unwanted child, and there is the problem of bringing a child into a family already unable, psychologically and otherwise, to care for it. In other cases, as in this one, the additional difficulties and continuing stigma of unwed motherhood may be involved. All these are factors the woman and her responsible physician necessarily will consider in consultation.

We, therefore, conclude that the right of personal privacy includes the abortion decision, but that this right is not unqualified and must be considered against important state interests in regulation.

Where certain 'fundamental rights' are involved, the Court has held that regulation limiting these rights may be justified only by a 'compelling state interest,' and that legislative enactments must be narrowly drawn to express only the legitimate state interests at stake.

The pregnant woman cannot be isolated in her privacy. She carries an embryo and, later, a fetus, if one accepts the medical definitions of the developing young in the human uterus. The situation therefore is inherently different from marital intimacy, or bedroom possession of obscene material, or marriage, or procreation, or education. . . .

[W]e do not agree that, by adopting one theory of life, Texas may override the rights of the pregnant woman that are at stake. We repeat, however, that the State does have an important and legitimate interest in preserving and protecting the health of the pregnant woman, whether she be a resident of the State or a non-resident who seeks medical consultation and treatment there, and that it has still another important and legitimate interest in protecting the potentiality of human life. These interests are separate and distinct. Each grows in substantiality as the woman approaches term and, at a point during pregnancy, each becomes "compelling."

To summarize and to repeat:

1. A state criminal abortion statute of the current Texas type, that excepts from criminality only a life-saving procedure on behalf of the mother, without regard to pregnancy stage and without recognition of the other interests involved, is violative of the Due Process Clause of the Fourteenth Amendment.(a) For the stage prior to approximately the end of

the first trimester, the abortion decision and its effectuation must be left to the medical judgment of the pregnant woman's attending physician.

(b) For the stage subsequent to approximately the end of the first trimester, the State, in promoting its interest in the health of the mother, may, if it chooses, regulate the abortion procedure in ways that are reasonably related to maternal health.

(c) For the stage subsequent to viability, the State in promoting its interest in the potentiality of human life may, if it chooses, regulate, and even proscribe, abortion except where it is necessary, in appropriate medical judgment, for the preservation of the life or health of the mother.

2. The State may define the term 'physician,' as it has been employed in the preceding paragraphs of this Part XI of this opinion, to mean only a physician currently licensed by the State, and may proscribe any abortion by a person who is not a physician as so defined.

Norma McCorvey (left), the Jane Roe in *Roe v. Wade* (1973), and Gloria Allred, her attorney, hold hands as they leave the Supreme Court building in 1989 after the Court listened to arguments in a Missouri abortion case. The Court's 1973 decision in *Roe v. Wade* remains controversial. (AP Photo, J. Scott Applewhite)

Hazelwood School District v. Kuhlmeier, 1988

Hazelwood *quotes the most famous lines from the earlier case,* Tinker v. Des Moines. *This is done to distinguish the new case from the earlier precedent. Judges build new decisions upon past decisions; this often requires explaining how a new case is different from an old case. Here, the issue is slightly different from the issue in* Tinker, *because the nature of student expression is different. Justice Byron A. White's opinion concludes that while* Tinker *is correct in strictly limiting when school officials can restrict student expression, schools have much more room to decide simply not to support particular student speech.*

Hazelwood School District v. Kuhlmeier

This case concerns the extent to which educators may exercise editorial control over the contents of a high school newspaper produced as part of the school's journalism curriculum.

Petitioners are the Hazelwood School District in St. Louis County, Missouri; various school officials; Robert Eugene Reynolds, the principal of Hazelwood East High School; and Howard Emerson, a teacher in the school district. Respondents are three former Hazelwood East students who were staff members of Spectrum, the school newspaper. They contend that school officials violated their First Amendment rights by deleting two pages of articles from the May 13, 1983, issue of Spectrum.

Spectrum was written and edited by the Journalism II class at Hazelwood East. . . .

The Board of Education allocated funds from its annual budget for the printing of Spectrum. These funds were supplemented by proceeds from sales of the newspaper. The practice at Hazelwood East during the spring 1983 semester was for the journalism teacher to submit page proofs of each Spectrum issue to Principal Reynolds for his review prior to publication. On May 10, [journalism instructor] Emerson delivered the proofs of the May 13 edition to Reynolds, who objected to two of the articles scheduled to appear in that edition. One of the stories described three Hazelwood East students' experiences with pregnancy; the other discussed the impact of divorce on students at the school.

Reynolds was concerned that, although the pregnancy story used false names "to keep the identity of these girls a secret," the pregnant students still might be identifiable from the text. He also believed that the article's references to sexual activity and birth control were inappropriate for some of the younger students at the school. In addition, Reynolds was concerned that a student identified by name in the divorce story had complained that her father "wasn't spending enough time with my mom, my sister and I" prior to the divorce, "was always out of town on business or out late playing cards with the guys," and "always argued about everything" with her mother. Reynolds believed that the student's parents should have been given an opportunity to respond to these remarks or to consent to their publication. He was unaware that Emerson had deleted the student's name from the final version of the article. **[Reynolds decided to print the paper without the two pages affected by the pregnancy and divorce stories.]**

Students in the public schools do not "shed their constitutional rights to freedom of speech or expression at the schoolhouse gate." They cannot be punished merely for expressing their personal views on the school premises-whether "in the cafeteria, or on the playing field, or on the campus during the authorized hours," unless school authorities have reason to believe that such expression will "substantially interfere with the work of the school or impinge upon the rights of other students."

We have nonetheless recognized that the First Amendment rights of students in the public schools "are not automatically coextensive with the rights of adults in other settings," and must be "applied in light of the special characteristics of the school environment." A school need not tolerate student speech that is inconsistent with its "basic educational mission," even though the government could not censor similar speech outside the school. Accordingly, we held in *Fraser* that a student could be disciplined for having delivered a speech that was "sexually explicit" but not legally obscene at an official school assembly, because the school was entitled to "disassociate itself" from the speech in a manner that would demonstrate to others that such vulgarity is "wholly inconsistent with the 'fundamental values' of public school education." We thus recognized that "[t]he determination of what manner of speech in the classroom or in school assembly is inappropriate properly rests with the school board," rather than with the federal courts. It is in this context that respondents' First Amendment claims must be considered.

The question whether the First Amendment requires a school to tolerate particular student speech the question that we addressed in *Tinker* is different from the question whether the First Amendment requires a school affirmatively to promote particular student speech. The former question addresses educators' ability to silence a student's personal expression that happens to occur on the school premises. The latter question concerns educators' authority over school-sponsored publications, theatrical productions, and other expressive activities that students, parents, and members of the public might reasonably perceive to bear the imprimatur of the school. These activities may fairly be characterized as part of the school curriculum, whether or not they occur in a traditional classroom setting, so long as they are supervised by faculty members and designed to impart particular knowledge or skills to student participants and audiences.

Educators are entitled to exercise greater control over this second form of student expression to assure that participants learn whatever lessons the activity is designed to teach, that readers or listeners are not exposed to material that may be inappropriate for their level of maturity, and that the views of the individual speaker are not erroneously attributed to the school. Hence, a school may in its capacity as publisher of a school newspaper or producer of a school play "disassociate itself," not only from speech that would "substantially interfere with [its] work . . . or impinge upon the rights of other students," but also from speech that is, for example, ungrammatical, poorly written, inadequately researched, biased or prejudiced, vulgar or profane, or unsuitable for immature audiences. A school must be able to set high standards for the student speech that is disseminated under its auspices-standards that may be higher than those demanded by some newspaper publishers or theatrical producers in the "real" world-and may refuse to disseminate student speech that does not meet those standards. In addition, a school must be able to take into account the emotional maturity of the intended audience in determining whether to disseminate student speech on potentially sensitive topics, which might range from the existence of Santa Claus in an elementary school setting to the particulars of teenage sexual activity in a high school setting. A school must also retain the authority to refuse to sponsor student speech that might reasonably be perceived to advocate drug or alcohol use, irresponsible sex, or conduct otherwise inconsistent with "the shared values of a civilized social order," or to associate the school with any position other than neutrality on matters of political controversy.

Accordingly, we conclude that the standard articulated in *Tinker* for determining when a school may punish student expression need not also be the standard for determining when a school may refuse to lend its name and resources to the dissemination of student expression. Instead, we hold that educators do not offend the First Amendment by exercising editorial control over the style and content of student speech in school-sponsored expressive activities so long as their actions are reasonably related to legitimate pedagogical concerns.

George W. Bush, et. al., petitioners, v. Albert Gore Jr., et. al., 2000

The 2000 presidential campaign between George W. Bush (2001–2009) and then Vice President Al Gore was one of the closest—and most bitterly contested—races in American history. Ultimately, the election's outcome hinged on Florida's twenty-five electoral votes. Because the margin of difference between the two candidates was so narrow, the ballots were subject to an automatic recount. This tally, too, was contested, and subjected to a partial manual recount. On December 12, 2000, the Supreme Court ruled that employing various means of recounting ballots violated the equal protection clause *of the U.S. Constitution, thereby awarding the election to Bush, despite Gore's having won the popular vote.*

George W. Bush, et. al., petitioners, v. Albert Gore, Jr., et. al.

. . . On November 8, 2000, the day following the Presidential election, the Florida Division of Elections reported that petitioner, Governor Bush, had received 2,909,135 votes, and respondent, Vice President Gore, had received 2,907,351 votes, a margin of 1,784 for Governor Bush. Because Governor Bush's margin of victory was less than "one-half of a percent . . . of the votes cast," an automatic machine recount was conducted under §102.141(4) of the election code, the results of which showed Governor Bush still winning the race but by a diminished margin. Vice President Gore then sought manual recounts in Volusia, Palm Beach, Broward, and Miami-Dade Counties, pursuant to Florida's election protest provisions. A dispute arose concerning the deadline for local county canvassing boards to submit their returns to the Secretary of State. The Secretary declined to waive the November 14 deadline imposed by statute. The Florida Supreme Court, however, set the deadline at November 26. We granted certiorari and vacated the Florida Supreme Court's decision, finding considerable uncertainty as to the grounds on which it was based (Bush I).

On November 26, the Florida Elections Canvassing Commission certified the results of the election and declared Governor Bush the winner of Florida's 25 electoral votes. On November 27, Vice President Gore, pursuant to Florida's contest provisions, filed a complaint in Leon County Circuit Court contesting the certification. He sought relief pursuant to §102.168(3)(c), which provides that "[r]eceipt of a number of illegal votes or rejection of a number of legal votes sufficient to change or place in doubt the result of the election" shall be grounds for a contest. The Circuit Court denied relief, stating that Vice President Gore failed to meet his burden of proof. He appealed to the First District Court of Appeal, which certified the matter to the Florida Supreme Court.

Accepting jurisdiction, the Florida Supreme Court affirmed in part and reversed in part. The court held that the Circuit Court had been correct to reject Vice President Gore's challenge to the results certified in Nassau County and his challenge to the Palm Beach County Canvassing Board's determination that 3,300 ballots cast in that county were not, in the statutory phrase, "legal votes."

The right to vote is protected in more than the initial allocation of the franchise. Equal protection applies as well to the manner of its exercise. Having once granted the right to vote on equal terms, the State may not, by later arbitrary and disparate treatment, value one person's vote over that of another . . .

There is no difference between the two sides of the present controversy on these basic propositions. Respondents say that the very purpose of vindicating the right to vote justifies the recount procedures now at issue. The question before us, however, is whether the recount procedures the Florida Supreme Court has adopted are consistent with its obligation to avoid arbitrary and disparate treatment of the members of its electorate.

Much of the controversy seems to revolve around ballot cards designed to be perforated by a stylus but which, either through error or deliberate omission, have not been perforated with sufficient precision for a machine to count them. In some cases a piece of the card—a chad—is hanging, say by two corners. In other cases there is no separation at all, just an indentation.

The record provides some examples. A monitor in Miami-Dade County testified at trial that he observed that three members of the county canvassing board applied different standards in defining a legal vote. And testimony at trial also revealed that at least one county changed its evaluative standards during the counting process. Palm Beach County, for example, began the process with a 1990 guideline which precluded counting completely attached chads, switched to a rule that considered a vote to be legal if any light could be seen through a chad, changed back to the 1990 rule, and then abandoned any pretense of a per se rule, only to have a court order that the county consider dimpled chads legal. This is not a process with sufficient guarantees of equal treatment . . .

The State Supreme Court ratified this uneven treatment. It mandated that the recount totals from two counties, Miami-Dade and Palm Beach, be included in the certified total. The court also appeared to hold sub silentio that the recount totals from Broward County, which were not completed until after the original November 14 certification by the Secretary of State, were to be considered part of the new certified vote totals even though the county certification was not contested by Vice President Gore. Yet each of the counties used varying standards to determine what was a legal vote. Broward County used a more forgiving standard than Palm Beach County, and uncovered almost three times as many new votes, a result markedly disproportionate to the difference in population between the counties. . . .

That brings the analysis to yet a further equal protection problem. The votes certified by the court included a partial total from one county, Miami-Dade. The Florida Supreme Court's decision thus gives no assurance that the recounts included in a final certification must be complete. Indeed, it is respondent's submission that it would be consistent with the rules of the recount procedures to include whatever partial counts are done by the time of final certification, and we interpret the Florida Supreme Court's decision to permit this. This accommodation no doubt results from the truncated contest period established by the Florida Supreme Court in *Bush I,* at respondents' own urging. The press of time does not diminish the constitutional concern. A desire for speed is not a general excuse for ignoring equal protection guarantees.

In addition to these difficulties the actual process by which the votes were to be counted under the Florida Supreme Court's decision raises further concerns. That order did not specify who would recount the ballots. The county canvassing boards were forced to pull together ad hoc teams comprised of judges from various Circuits who had no previous training in handling and interpreting ballots. Furthermore, while others were permitted to observe, they were prohibited from objecting during the recount.

The recount process, in its features here described, is inconsistent with the minimum procedures necessary to protect the fundamental right of each voter in the special instance of a statewide recount under the authority of a single state judicial officer. Our consideration is limited to the present circumstances, for the problem of equal protection in election processes generally presents many complexities.

The question before the Court is not whether local entities, in the exercise of their expertise, may develop different systems for implementing elections. Instead, we are presented with a situation where a state court with the power to assure uniformity has ordered a statewide recount with minimal procedural safeguards. When a court orders a statewide remedy, there must be at least some assurance that the rudimentary requirements of equal treatment and fundamental fairness are satisfied. . . .

Upon due consideration of the difficulties identified to this point, it is obvious that the recount cannot be conducted in compliance with the requirements of equal protection and due process without substantial additional work. It would require not only the adoption (after opportunity for argument) of adequate statewide standards for determining what is a legal vote, and practicable procedures to implement them, but also orderly judicial review of any disputed matters that might arise. In addition, the Secretary of State has advised that the recount of only a portion of the ballots requires that the vote tabulation equipment be used to screen out undervotes, a function for which the machines were not designed. If a recount of overvotes were also required, perhaps even a second screening would be necessary. Use of the equipment for this purpose, and any new software developed for it, would have to be evaluated for accuracy by the Secretary of State, as required by Fla. Stat. §101.015 (2000).

The Supreme Court of Florida has said that the legislature intended the State's electors to "participat[e] fully in the federal electoral process . . ." That statute, in turn, requires that any controversy or contest that is designed to lead to a conclusive selection of electors be completed by December 12. That date is upon us, and there is no recount procedure in place under the State Supreme Court's order that comports with minimal constitutional standards. Because it is evident that any recount seeking to meet the December 12 date will be unconstitutional for the reasons we have discussed, we reverse the judgment of the Supreme Court of Florida ordering a recount to proceed. . . .

The judgment of the Supreme Court of Florida is reversed, and the case is remanded for further proceedings not inconsistent with this opinion. . . .

It is so ordered.

Lawrence v. Texas, 2003

In Lawrence v. Texas, *the Court declared unconstitutional, in a 6-3 decision, a Texas law that prohibited sexual acts between same-sex couples. Justice Anthony Kennedy, writing for the majority, held that the right to privacy protects a right for consenting adults to engage in private homosexual activity. Justice Kennedy's opinion expressly overruled the Court's decision in* Bowers v. Hardwick *(1986), in which the justices had come to an opposite conclusion.*

Lawrence v. Texas

Liberty protects the person from unwarranted government intrusions into a dwelling or other private places. In our tradition the State is not omnipresent in the home. And there are other spheres of our lives and existence, outside the home, where the State should not be a dominant presence. Freedom extends beyond spatial bounds. Liberty presumes an autonomy of self that includes freedom of thought, belief, expression, and certain intimate conduct. The instant case involves liberty of the person both in its spatial and more transcendent dimensions.

I

The question before the Court is the validity of a Texas statute making it a crime for two persons of the same sex to engage in certain intimate sexual conduct.

In Houston, Texas, officers of the Harris County Police Department were dispatched to a private residence in response to a reported weapons disturbance. They entered an apartment where one of the petitioners, John Geddes Lawrence, resided. The right of the police to enter does not seem to have been questioned. The officers observed Lawrence and another man, Tyron Garner, engaging in a sexual act. The two petitioners were arrested, held in custody over night, and charged and convicted before a Justice of the Peace . . .

The petitioners exercised their right to a trial de novo in Harris County Criminal Court. They challenged the statute as a violation of the Equal Protection Clause of the Fourteenth Amendment and of a like provision of the Texas Constitution. Those contentions were rejected. The petitioners, having entered a plea of nolo contendere [no contest], were each fined $200. . . .

We granted certiorari to consider three questions:

"1. Whether Petitioners' criminal convictions under the Texas 'Homosexual Conduct' law–which criminalizes sexual intimacy by same-sex couples, but not identical behavior by different-sex couples–violate the Fourteenth Amendment guarantee of equal protection of laws?

"2. Whether Petitioners' criminal convictions for adult consensual sexual intimacy in the home violate their vital interests in liberty and privacy protected by the Due Process Clause of the Fourteenth Amendment?

"3. Whether Bowers v. Hardwick, 478 U.S. 186 (1986) [a Supreme Court decision that the constitutionality of a George law criminalizing homosexual relations in private between consenting adults[, should be overruled?"

II

We conclude the case should be resolved by determining whether the petitioners were free as adults to engage in the private conduct in the exercise of their liberty under the Due Process Clause of the Fourteenth Amendment to the Constitution. For this inquiry we deem it necessary to reconsider the Court's holding in Bowers. . . .

The Court began its substantive discussion in Bowers as follows: "The issue presented is whether the Federal Constitution confers a fundamental right upon homosexuals to engage in sodomy and hence invalidates the laws of the many States that still make such conduct illegal and have done so for a very long time." That statement, we now conclude, discloses the Court's own failure to appreciate the extent of the liberty at stake. To say that the issue in Bowers was simply the right to engage in certain sexual conduct demeans the claim the individual put forward, just as it would demean a married couple were it to be said marriage is simply about the right to have sexual intercourse. The laws involved in Bowers and here are, to be sure, statutes that purport to do no more than prohibit a particular sexual act. Their penalties and purposes, though, have more far-reaching consequences, touching upon the most private human conduct, sexual behavior, and in the most private of places, the home. The statutes do seek to control a personal relationship that, whether or not entitled to formal recognition in the law, is within the liberty of persons to choose without being punished as criminals.

This, as a general rule, should counsel against attempts by the State, or a court, to define the meaning of the relationship or to set its boundaries absent injury to a person or abuse of an institution the law protects. It suffices for us to acknowledge that adults may choose to enter upon this relationship in the confines of their homes and their own private lives and still retain their dignity as free persons. When sexuality finds overt expression in intimate conduct with another person, the conduct can be but one element in a personal bond that is more enduring. The liberty protected by the Constitution allows homosexual persons the right to make this choice. . . .

The longstanding criminal prohibition of homosexual sodomy upon which the Bowers decision placed such reliance is as consistent with a general condemnation of nonprocreative sex as it is with an established tradition of prosecuting acts because of their homosexual character. . . . It was not until the 1970s that any State singled out same-sex relations for criminal prosecution, and only nine States have done so . . . In summary, the historical grounds relied upon in Bowers are more complex than the majority opinion and the concurring opinion by Chief Justice Burger indicate. Their historical premises are not without doubt and, at the very least, are overstated.

It must be acknowledged, of course, that the Court in Bowers was making the broader point that for centuries there have been powerful voices to condemn homosexual conduct as immoral. The condemnation has been shaped by religious beliefs, conceptions of right and acceptable behavior, and respect for the traditional family. For many persons these are not trivial concerns but profound and deep convictions accepted as ethical and moral principles to which they aspire and which thus determine the course of their lives. These considerations do not answer the question before us, however. The issue is whether the majority may use the power of the State to enforce these views on the whole society through operation of the criminal law. "Our obligation is to define the liberty of all, not to mandate our own moral code."

Chief Justice Burger joined the opinion for the Court in Bowers and further explained his views as follows: "Decisions of individuals relating to homosexual conduct have been subject to state intervention throughout the history of Western civilization. Condemnation of those practices is firmly rooted in Judeao-Christian moral and ethical standards." As with Justice White's assumptions about history, scholarship casts some doubt on the sweeping nature of the statement by Chief Justice Burger as it pertains to private homosexual conduct between consenting adults. In all events we think that our laws and traditions in the past half century are of most relevance here. These references show an emerging awareness that liberty gives substantial protection to adult persons in deciding how to conduct their private lives in matters pertaining to sex. . . .

The sweeping references by Chief Justice Burger to the history of Western civilization and to Judeo-Christian moral and ethical standards did not take account of other authorities pointing in an opposite direction. A committee advising the British Parliament recommended in 1957 repeal of laws punishing homosexual conduct. Parliament enacted the substance of those recommendations 10 years later. Of even more importance, almost five years before Bowers was decided the European Court of Human Rights considered a case with parallels to Bowers and to today's case. An adult male resident in Northern Ireland alleged he was a practicing homosexual who desired to engage in consensual homosexual conduct. The laws of Northern Ireland forbade him that right. He alleged that he had been questioned, his home had been searched, and he feared criminal prosecution. The court held that the laws proscribing the conduct were invalid under the European Convention on Human Rights. Authoritative in all countries that are members of the Council of Europe (21 nations then, 45 nations now), the decision is at odds with the premise in Bowers that the claim put forward was insubstantial in our Western civilization.

In our own constitutional system the deficiencies in Bowers became even more apparent in the years following its announcement. The 25 States with laws prohibiting the relevant conduct referenced in the Bowers decision are reduced now to 13, of which 4 enforce their laws only against homosexual conduct. In those States where sodomy is still proscribed, whether for same-sex or heterosexual conduct, there is a pattern of nonenforcement with respect to consenting adults acting in private. . . .

In *Planned Parenthood of Southeastern Pa. v. Casey,* the Court reaffirmed the substantive force of the liberty protected by the Due Process Clause. The Casey decision again confirmed that our laws and tradition afford constitutional protection to personal decisions relating to marriage, procreation, contraception, family relationships, child rearing, and education. In explaining the respect the Constitution demands for the autonomy of the person in making these choices, we stated as follows:

"These matters, involving the most intimate and personal choices a person may make in a lifetime, choices central to personal dignity and autonomy, are central to the liberty protected by the Fourteenth Amendment. At the heart of liberty is the right to define one's own concept of existence, of meaning, of the universe, and of the mystery of human life. Beliefs about these matters could not define the attributes of personhood were they formed under compulsion of the State."

Persons in a homosexual relationship may seek autonomy for these purposes, just as heterosexual persons do. The decision in Bowers would deny them this right. . . .

The central holding of Bowers has been brought in question by this case, and it should be addressed. Its continuance as precedent demeans the lives of homosexual persons. . . .

The rationale of Bowers does not withstand careful analysis. . . . Bowers was not correct when it was decided, and it is not correct today. It ought not to remain binding precedent. Bowers v. Hardwick should be and now is overruled.

The present case does not involve minors. It does not involve persons who might be injured or coerced or who are situated in relationships where consent might not easily be refused. It does not involve public conduct or prostitution. It does not involve whether the government must give formal recognition to any relationship that homosexual persons seek to enter. The case does involve two adults who, with full and mutual consent from each other, engaged in sexual practices common to a homosexual lifestyle. The petitioners are entitled to respect for their private lives. The State cannot demean their existence or control their destiny by making their private sexual conduct a crime. Their right to liberty under the Due Process Clause gives them the full right to engage in their conduct without intervention of the government. "It is a promise of the Constitution that there is a realm of personal liberty which the government may not enter." The Texas statute furthers no legitimate state interest which can justify its intrusion into the personal and private life of the individual. . . .

Had those who drew and ratified the Due Process Clauses of the Fifth Amendment or the Fourteenth Amendment known the components of liberty in its manifold possibilities, they might have been more specific. They did not presume to have this insight. They knew times can blind us to certain truths and later generations can see that laws once thought necessary and proper in fact serve only to oppress. As the Constitution endures, persons in every generation can invoke its principles in their own search for greater freedom. . . .

Memorandum of Associate Justice Antonin Scalia, 2004

In 2004, lawyers for the environmental group Sierra Club, as well as other groups, requested that Associate Justice Antonin Scalia step aside from ruling in a case involving Vice President Dick Cheney and the Bush administration's (2001–2009) energy task force. The lawyers noted that the two men's recent duck-hunting trip had created the appearance that the justice was likely to favor the vice president in the dispute. Justice Scalia decided not to remove, or recuse, himself from the case in a twenty-one-page memorandum, excerpts from which are cited here.

Memorandum of Associate Justice Antonin Scalia

Memorandum of JUSTICE SCALIA.

I have before me a motion to recuse in these cases consolidated below. The motion is filed on behalf of respondent Sierra Club. The other private respondent, Judicial Watch, Inc., does not join the motion and has publicly stated that it "does not believe the presently-known facts about the hunting trip satisfy the legal standards requiring recusal. . . ."

I

The decision whether a judge's impartiality can "reasonably be questioned" is to be made in light of the facts as they existed, and not as they were surmised or reported. . . . The facts here were as follows: For five years or so, I have been going to Louisiana during the Court's long December-January recess, to the duck-hunting camp of a friend whom I met through two hunting companions from Baton Rouge, one a dentist and the other a worker in the field of handicapped rehabilitation. The last three years, I have been accompanied on this trip by a son-in-law who lives near me. Our friend and host, Wallace Carline, has never, as far as I know, had business before this Court. He is not, as some reports have described him, an "energy industry executive" in the sense that summons up boardrooms of ExxonMobil or Con Edison. He runs his own company that provides services and equipment rental to oil rigs in the Gulf of Mexico.

During my December 2002 visit, I learned that Mr. Carline was an admirer of Vice President Cheney. Knowing that the Vice President, with whom I am well acquainted (from our years serving together in the Ford administration), is an enthusiastic duck-hunter, I asked whether Mr. Carline would like to invite him to our next year's hunt. The answer was yes; I conveyed the invitation (with my own warm recommendation) in the spring of 2003 and received an acceptance (subject, of course, to any superseding demands on the Vice President's time) in the summer. The Vice President said that if he did go, I would be welcome to fly down to Louisiana with him. (Because of national security requirements, of course, he must fly in a Government plane.) That invitation was later extended—if space was available—to my son-in-law and to a son who was joining the hunt for the first time; they accepted. The trip was set long before the Court granted certiorari in the present case, and indeed before the petition for certiorari had even been filed.

We departed from Andrews Air Force Base at about 10 a.m. on Monday, January 5, flying in a Gulfstream jet owned by the Government. We landed in Patterson, Louisiana, and went by car to a dock where Mr. Carline met us, to take us on the 20-minute boat trip to his hunting camp. We arrived at about 2 p.m., the 5 of us joining about 8 other hunters, making about 13 hunters in all; also present during our time there were about 3 members of Mr. Carline's staff, and, of course, the Vice President's staff and security detail. It was not an intimate setting. The group hunted that afternoon and Tuesday and Wednesday mornings; it fished (in two boats) Tuesday afternoon. All meals were in common. Sleeping was in rooms of two or three, except for the Vice President, who had his own quarters. Hunting was in two- or three-man blinds. As it turned out, I never hunted in the same blind with the Vice President. Nor was I alone with him at any time during the trip, except, perhaps, for instances so brief and unintentional that I would not recall them—walking to or from a boat, perhaps, or going to or from dinner. Of course we said not a word about the present case. The Vice President left the camp Wednesday afternoon, about two days after our arrival. I stayed on to hunt (with my son and son-in-law) until late Friday morning, when the three of us returned to Washington on a commercial flight from New Orleans.

My recusal is required if, by reason of the actions described above, my "impartiality might reasonably be questioned. . . ." Why would that result follow from my being in a sizable group of persons, in a hunting camp with the Vice President, where I never hunted with him in the same blind or had other opportunity for private conversation? The only possibility is that it would suggest I am a friend of his. But while friendship is a ground for recusal of a Justice where the personal fortune or the personal freedom of the friend is at issue, it has traditionally not been a ground for recusal where official action is at issue, no matter how important the official action was to the ambitions or the reputation of the Government officer.

A rule that required Members of this Court to remove themselves from cases in which the official actions of friends were at issue would be utterly disabling. Many Justices have reached this Court precisely because they were friends of the incumbent President or other senior officials—and from the earliest days down to modern times Justices have had close personal relationships with the President and other officers of the Executive [branch]. John Quincy Adams hosted dinner parties featuring such luminaries as Chief Justice Marshall, Justices Johnson, Story, and Todd, Attorney General Wirt, and Daniel Webster. Justice Harlan and his wife often 'stopped in' at the White House to see the Hayes family and pass a Sunday evening in a small group, visiting and singing hymns. Justice Stone tossed around a medicine ball with members of the Hoover administration mornings outside the White House. Justice Douglas was a regular at President Franklin Roosevelt's poker parties; Chief Justice Vinson played poker with President Truman. A no-friends rule would have disqualified much of the Court in Youngstown Sheet & Tube Co. v. Sawyer, the [1952] case that challenged President Truman's seizure of the steel mills. Most of the Justices knew Truman well, and four had been appointed by him. . . .

It is said, however, that this case is different because the federal officer (Vice President Cheney) is actually a named party. That is by no means a rarity. At the beginning of the current Term, there were before the Court (excluding habeas actions) no fewer than 83 cases in which high-level federal Executive officers were named in their official capacity—more than 1 in every 10 federal civil cases then pending. That an officer is named has traditionally made no difference to the proposition that friendship is not considered to affect impartiality in official-action suits. Regardless of whom they name, such suits, when the officer is the plaintiff, seek relief not for him personally but for the Government; and, when the officer is the defendant, seek relief not against him personally, but against the Government.

Associate Justice Ruth Bader Ginsburg on *Brown v. Board of Education*, October 21, 2004

In an address at New York's Columbia University School of Law in 2004, Associate Justice Ruth Bader Ginsburg spoke about the importance of the decision in Brown v. Board of Education *(1954), not only to the United States but also to the entire world. She notes that the decision inspired women and minorities, as well as the oppressed in the international community, in their quest for equal treatment.*

Associate Justice Ginsburg on Brown

Although the Brown decision did not refer to the international stage, there is little doubt that the climate of the era explains, in significant part, why apartheid in America began to unravel after World War II. Recall that the United States and its allies had fought, successfully, to destroy Hitler's Holocaust Kingdom and the rank racism that prevailed during the years of Nazi ascendancy in Europe. Yet our own troops, when we entered that War, were racially segregated. In the midst of the War, in 1942, Swedish economist Gunnar Myrdal published The American Dilemma in which he observed: "America, for its international prestige, power and future security, needs to demonstrate to the world that American Negroes can be satisfactorily integrated into its democracy."

Illustrative of the growing awareness as the War progressed, a young Rabbi, Roland B. Gittelsohn, then a service chaplain, delivered a eulogy over newly-dug graves of U.S. Marines on the Pacific Island of Iwo Jima. In words preserved at the Harry S. Truman Library, Rabbi Gittelsohn spoke of the way it was, and the way it should be:

"Here lie men who loved America because their ancestors, generations ago, help[ed] in her founding, and other men, who loved her with equal passion because they themselves or their [parents] escaped from oppression to her blessed shores. Here lie officers and men, Negroes and whites, rich men and poor, together. . . . Here no man prefers another because of his faith, or despises him because of his color. . . . Among these men there is no discrimination, no prejudice, no hatred. Theirs is the highest and purest democracy. . . . Whoever of us . . . thinks himself superior to those who happen to be in the minority, makes of this ceremony, and of the bloody sacrifice it commemorates, [a] . . . hollow mockery.

To this, then, as our solemn, sacred duty do we, the living, now dedicate ourselves, to the right of Protestants, Catholics and Jews, of white men and Negroes alike, to enjoy the democracy for which all of them have here paid the price. . . ."

On a personal note, Brown and its forerunners, along with the movement for international human rights that came later, powerfully influenced the women's rights litigation in which I was engaged in the 1970s. Thurgood Marshall and his co-workers sought to educate the Court, step by step, about the pernicious effects of race discrimination. Similarly, advocates for gender equality sought to inform the Court, through a series of cases, about the injustice of laws ordering or reinforcing separate spheres of human activity for men and women. The ACLU's Women's Rights Project, which I helped to launch and direct, was among the organizations inspired by the NAACP Legal Defense and Education Fund's example.

Brown figured four years ago in a courageous decision by Israel's Chief Justice, Aharon Barak. The Israel Land Administration had denied the asserted right of Arabs to build their homes on land in Israel open to the general public for home construction. The Administration defended the denial on the ground that it would allocate land to establish an exclusively Arab communal settlement. Citing Brown, the Israeli Supreme Court ruled that such allegedly separate-but-equal treatment constituted unlawful discrimination on the basis of national origin. . . .

To sum up, Brown both reflected and propelled the development of human rights protection internationally. It was decided with the horrors of the Holocaust in full view, and with the repression of Communist regimes in the Soviet Union and Eastern Europe a current reality. It propelled an evolution yet unfinished toward respect, in law and in practice, for the human dignity of all the world's people.

Primary Source Library

Associate Justice Sandra Day O'Connor's Letter of Resignation, July 1, 2005

Nominated by President Ronald Reagan (1981–1989) in 1981, Sandra Day O'Connor became the first woman to serve on the Court. After twenty-four terms on the Court, she gave her letter of resignation to President George W. Bush (2001-2009) in July 2005. She noted that she would continue to serve, however, until the confirmation of her successor (who would be Judge John Roberts).

Associate Justice O'Connor's Letter of Resignation

This is to inform you of my decision to retire from my position as an associate justice of the Supreme Court of the United States, effective upon the nomination and confirmation of my successor. It has been a great privilege indeed to have served as a member of the court for 24 terms. I will leave it with enormous respect for the integrity of the court and its role under our constitutional structure.

Sincerely,

Sandra Day O'Connor

Supreme Court of the United States
Washington, D. C. 20543

CHAMBERS OF
JUSTICE SANDRA DAY O'CONNOR

July 1, 2005

Dear President Bush:

This is to inform you of my decision to retire from my position as an Associate Justice of the Supreme Court of the United States effective upon the nomination and confirmation of my successor. It has been a great privilege, indeed, to have served as a member of the Court for 24 Terms. I will leave it with enormous respect for the integrity of the Court and its role under our Constitutional structure.

Sincerely,

Sandra Day O'Connor

The President
The White House
Washington, D. C.

President George W. Bush Nominates Judge John Roberts as Chief Justice, September 5, 2005

In the summer of 2005, President George W. Bush (2001–2009) nominated Judge John Roberts as associate justice of the Court to replace Justice Sandra Day O'Connor, who had announced her retirement. After Chief Justice William H. Rehnquist died on September 3 of that year, the president chose to elevate Judge Roberts to the chief justice position. Roberts was confirmed by the Senate on September 29 by a vote of 78-22.

President Bush Nominates Judge Roberts as Chief Justice

Morning. This summer I announced the nomination of Judge John Roberts to be associate justice of the Supreme Court of the United States. I choose Judge Roberts from among the most distinguished jurists and attorneys in the country because he possesses the intellect, experience and temperament to be an outstanding member of our nation's Highest Court.

For the past two months, members of the United States Senate and the American people have learned about the career and character of Judge Roberts. They like what they see. He's a gentleman. He's a man of integrity and fairness. And throughout his life, he has inspired the respect and loyalty of others. John Roberts has built a record of excellence and achievement, and a reputation for goodwill and decency toward others.

In his extraordinary career, Judge Roberts has argued 39 cases before the nation's Highest Court. When I nominated him to the U.S. Court of Appeals for the District of Columbia, he was confirmed by unanimous consent. Both those who've worked with him and those who have faced him in the courtroom speak with admiration of his striking ability as a lawyer and his natural gifts as a leader. Judge Roberts has earned the nation's confidence and I'm pleased to announce that I will nominate him to serve as the 17th chief justice of the Supreme Court.

The passing of Chief Justice William Rehnquist leaves the center chair empty just four weeks left before the Supreme Court reconvenes. It is in the interest of the Court and the country to have a chief justice on the bench on the first full day of the fall term. The Senate is well along in the process of considering Judge Roberts's qualifications. They know his record and his fidelity to the law. I'm confident that the Senate can complete hearings and confirm him as chief justice within a month. As a result of my decision to nominate Judge Roberts to be chief justice, I also have the responsibility to submit a new nominee to follow Justice Sandra Day O'Connor. I will do so in a timely manner.

Twenty-five years ago, John Roberts came to Washington as a clerk to Justice William Rehnquist. In his boss, the young law clerk found a role model, a professional mentor, and a friend for life. I'm certain that Chief Justice Rehnquist was hoping to welcome John Roberts as a colleague, and we're all sorry that day didn't come. Yet it's fitting that a great chief justice be followed in office by a person who shared his deep reverence for the Constitution, his profound respect for the Supreme Court, and his complete devotion to the cause of justice.

Congratulations.

Judge Sonia Sotomayor on Her Nomination to the Supreme Court, May 26, 2009

President Barack Obama (2009–), the first African American U.S. president, made a historic choice when he nominated Judge Sonia Sotomayor to replace Associate Justice David H. Souter. On May 26, 2009, the president introduced his nominee to the press and the public. After the president's introduction, Judge Sotomayor responded, talking about her life experiences and thanking the president. Sotomayor became the first Hispanic and the third woman to serve on the Court after she was confirmed by the U.S. Senate in August 2009. Sotomayor, with degrees from both Princeton and Yale, brings vast judicial experience to the Court, having been nominated to the U.S. District Court in 1992 by President George H.W. Bush (1989–1983) and then elevated to the federal court of appeals by President Bill Clinton (1993–2001) in 1998.

Judge Sotomayer's Speech

I was just counseled not to be nervous.

(LAUGHTER)

That's almost impossible.

Thank you, Mr. President, for the most humbling honor of my life. You have nominated me to serve on the country's highest court, and I am deeply moved.

I could not, in the few minutes I have today, mention the names of the many friends and family who have guided and supported me throughout my life, and who have been instrumental in helping me realize my dreams.

I see many of those faces in this room. Each of you, whom I love deeply, will know that my heart today is bursting with gratitude for all you have done for me.

The president has said to you that I bring my family. In the audience is my brother Juan Sotomayor—he's a physician in Syracuse, New York; my sister-in-law, Tracey; my niece Kylie—she looks like me.

Primary Source Library

(LAUGHTER)

My twin nephews, Conner and Corey.

I stand on the shoulders of countless people, yet there is one extraordinary person who is my life aspiration. That person is my mother, Celina Sotomayor.

(APPLAUSE)

My mother has devoted her life to my brother and me. And as the president mentioned, she worked often two jobs to help support us after dad died. I have often said that I am all I am because of her, and I am only half the woman she is.

Sitting next to her is Omar Lopez, my mom's husband and a man whom I have grown to adore. I thank you for all that you have given me and continue to give me. I love you.

(APPLAUSE)

I chose to be a lawyer and ultimately a judge because I find endless challenge in the complexities of the law. I firmly believe in the rule of law as the foundation for all of our basic rights.

For as long as I can remember, I have been inspired by the achievement of our founding fathers. They set forth principles that have endured for than more two centuries. Those principles are as meaningful and relevant in each generation as the generation before.

It would be a profound privilege for me to play a role in applying those principles to the questions and controversies we face today.

Although I grew up in very modest and challenging circumstances, I consider my life to be immeasurably rich. I was raised in a Bronx public housing project, but studied at two of the nation's finest universities.

I did work as an assistant district attorney, prosecuting violent crimes that devastate our communities. But then I joined a private law firm and worked with international corporations doing business in the United States.

I have had the privilege of serving as a federal district court trial judge, and am now serving as a federal appellate circuit court judge.

This wealth of experiences, personal and professional, have helped me appreciate the variety of perspectives that present themselves in every case that I hear. It has helped me to understand, respect and respond to the concerns and arguments of all litigants who appear before me, as well as to the views of my colleagues on the bench.

I strive never to forget the real world consequences of my decisions on individuals, businesses and government.

It is a daunting feeling to be here. Eleven years ago, during my confirmation process for appointment to the Second Circuit, I was given a private tour of the White House. It was an overwhelming experience for a kid from the South Bronx.

Yet, never in my wildest childhood imaginings did I ever envision that moment, let alone did I ever dream that I would live this moment.

Mr. President, I greatly appreciate the honor you are giving me, and I look forward to working with the Senate in the confirmation process. I hope that as the Senate and American people learn more about me, they will see that I am an ordinary person who has been blessed with extraordinary opportunities and experiences. Today is one of those experiences.

Thank you again, sir.

(APPLAUSE)

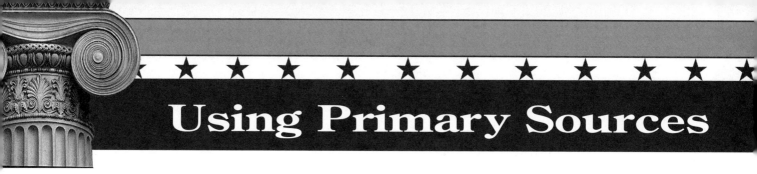

Using Primary Sources

Researching with Primary and Secondary Sources

A primary source is firsthand information or data. A primary source has not been subject to analysis by someone else. Typical primary sources—such as the Judiciary Act of 1789, *Marbury v. Madison* (1803), and an image of the Supreme Court Chamber—are eyewitness accounts of events, letters, diary entries, photographs, and documents. In the Primary Source Library, Part Three of this volume, there is a variety of primary sources, especially useful when researching how the U.S. Supreme Court was formed and how it operates.

In contrast, a secondary source is information that has been reviewed and analyzed by someone else. For example, a biography of Thurgood Marshall, the first African American to serve on the Court, is a secondary source. The author of such a biography has reviewed and analyzed a variety of primary and secondary sources to present a biography of the subject (Marshall). Most magazine articles, books, and Internet sources are secondary sources.

Developing Research Questions

When you are assigned a report and select a topic for research, it is important to begin with a clear sense of direction. Ask yourself several questions that will help you limit your topic. For example, for a report on judicial review, you will likely be able to find hundreds of primary and secondary sources. However, to help narrow the topic, ask yourself the following questions:

● What is judicial review?

● How did judicial power come about?

● Who can exercise this power?

● Under what circumstances would the Supreme Court use its power of judicial review?

● When has this power been used in the past?

● In what ways has this power been exercised recently?

● What is the impact of judicial review on American society today?

With answers to these questions, you will have the focus you need to begin further research.

Identifying Sources of Information

You likely will begin looking for information in your school or local library. You can also locate other sources of information within your community, such as local government sources, newspaper offices, historical societies, and museums. All of these sources can provide valuable information. However, you

331

must determine if the information will be useful to your research topic. Evaluate and decide on the usefulness of the source. Useful sources should have the following characteristics:

- **Pertinent and appropriate**
  Is the information related to your topic? Skim the book, and check the table of contents and the index.

- **Trustworthy and dependable**
  Is the source objective? Does it seem accurate? What sources did the author of the book or article use?

- **Current and recent**
  How old is the source? Is the information out of date? Keep in mind that historical documents such as the U.S. Constitution and topics such as *Marbury v. Madison* (1803) are researched and evaluated by political scientists and historians. Be sure that some of your sources are current analyses.

- **Typical and representative**
  Be certain to find balanced or unbiased sources. If you are writing about a controversial topic, such as *Bush v. Gore* (2000), be sure to use sources that represent both sides of the issue.

Planning and Organizing

As you gather various primary and secondary sources, you begin to develop a plan for your report. This might include a preliminary outline with headings and subheadings that will help you organize your resources and report. With this plan you can decide what information to include in your notes.

Thorough note-taking is essential; you will want to document all the information you have gathered for your report. Following are useful tips for taking notes:

- Use ruled index cards.
- Use a separate card for each item of information.
- Use a separate card for each source.
- Use the following techniques to record information:
- **Quote**
  Copy the information exactly as it appears in the source. Use quotation marks to indicate a direct quote.
- **Paraphrase**
  Rewrite the information in your own words.
- **Summarize**
  Condense the information, noting essential material and key ideas.

Documenting Sources for the Bibliography

On index cards, keep a record of the books, newspaper or magazine articles, Internet sites, and other sources you have consulted. As you locate useful sources, record the publishing data on your index cards, so you can easily find the information later. This data will be essential for compiling the bibliography at the end of your report.

Citing Sources

All writers must identify the sources of the words, facts, and thoughts that they find in other works. Noting your sources allows you reader to check those sources and determine how reliable or important a particular piece of information is.

What You Should Document

- Someone's exact words
- A close paraphrase of another's ideas or several ideas
- Information on the topic which is not found in most books on the subject or which is not generally known

What You Do Not Have To Document

- Simple definition, commonly used sayings, or famous quotations
- Information that is common knowledge or that is easily found in most sources

Author and Publication Information

Author information should always appear at the beginning of your citation, with the author's last name first.

- For books with two authors, reverse only the first author's name, followed by a comma and the second author's name.
- If no author is noted, list the editor; if no editor is identified, start with the title of the work.
- Should you use more than one work by the same author, you do not need to list the author information each time. Use three hyphens followed by a period to begin the line.
- The name of the work (underlined or in italic type) appears next, followed by a period.

Publication information follows the author and title of the work. You also may need to include the editor's name, volume or edition number, and a series name.

Citing Online Sources

When citing online sources, you likely will not be able to include all the information in the list that follows. Many online sources do not provide all this information. Therefore, provide as much information as possible.

- Author or editor of the source
- Title of a book (underlined or in italic type)
- Title of an article, short work, or poem (in quotation marks)
- Publication information for any print version of the source
- Title of the database, scholarly project, periodical, or professional site (underlined)
- Version number of the source or journal; volume number, issue number, or other identifier
- Date of the electronic version or last update

Using the Primary Source Library in This Volume

In Part Three of this volume, you will find a wealth of primary sources useful for various research topics. In chronological order, important source documents appear that are related to the establishment, development, and daily functioning of the U.S. Supreme Court. To help you find out how the powers of the Court have grown over time, for example, the following primary sources would be useful:

- The Judiciary Act of 1789
- *Marbury v. Madison* (1803)
- *McCulloch v. Maryland* (1819)
- *Gibbons v. Ogden* (1824)

For more information about doing research with authoritative sources, consult your local librarian, teacher, or one of numerous available publications.

Glossary

adjourned Delayed until a stated later time or indefinitely

alienage Being from a foreign country

aliens Those belonging or owing allegiance to another country or government

amendments Changes to the U.S. Constitution

appeal The transfer of a case from a lower to a higher court for a new hearing; a case thus transferred; a request for a new hearing

appropriate To set aside something, such as funds, for a specific use

appropriation Resource or fund set apart for a particular use

bankruptcies Proceedings in a federal court in which a debtor's assets are sold or surrendered and the debtor is relieved of further liability

battery An intentional unpermitted act causing harmful or offensive contact with the "person" of another

charter A founding document

class action suit A lawsuit brought by one or a few individuals on behalf of an entire class of people

colonial Of or relating to colonies, those lands that are dependent on a parent country for trade and military protection

communism The economic and social philosophy based on the holding of all property in common, with actual ownership being held by the community as a whole or the state

Communist Party A worldwide political organization that advocates the principles of communism through a communist form of government

contempt of court Situation that occurs when someone disobeys a court order, shows disrespect for the judge, or disrupts judicial proceedings; contempt can be either direct (occurs in the judge's presence and disrupts court proceedings) or indirect (occurs outside the presence of the judge)

counterfeit money Fake coins or currency passed off as genuine

default Failure to do something required by law; failure to satisfy the terms of a loan obligation or to pay back a loan

Democratic Party One of the two major political parties in the United States; the Democratic Party originated in the late 1820s

discrimination Treating, considering, or making a distinction in favor of or against a person based on the group, class, race, or religion to which that person belongs rather than on individual merit

due process The principle that the government must respect all of the legal rights that are owed to a person according to the law of the land

due process clause Clause of the Fourteenth Amendment, which guarantees that no one will be deprived of life or liberty without having access to the formal legal process

due process guarantee Assurance that no one will be deprived of life or liberty without having access to the formal legal process

equal protection clause Clause of the Fourteenth Amendment, which guarantees to all persons equal protection under the law

establishment clause Clause of the First Amendment, which prohibits the government from passing legislation to establish an official religion or preferring one religion over another

executive privilege The power claimed by the president of the United States and other members of the executive branch to resist subpoenas and other interventions by the legislative and judicial branches of government

Federalist A member of the Federalist Party, one of the first political parties in the United States; Federalists believed in a strong central government and, in foreign policy, favored Great Britain

gerrymandered The condition (of a voting district) of having been designed to give one group an unfair advantage in an election

gerrymandering The division of a geographical area into voting districts designed to give an unfair advantage to one party in elections

Great Depression In United States history, a serious economic downturn that began with the crash of the stock market in 1929 and ended after the nation entered World War II (1939–1945)

incumbent Politician running for the office that she or he is currently holding

indicted Formally charged with a serious crime

indictment The filing of a formal charge against anyone accused of a capital or otherwise serious crimes

indigent Lacking food, clothing, and other necessities of life because of poverty

injunction A court order prohibiting a party from a specific course of action

interstate commerce The trading of goods across state lines

jurisdiction The right and power of a court to interpret and apply the law

lame-duck A politician who, at the end of his or her current term, will be succeeded either due to choice or to term limits

libel Written or printed words or images that defame a person, as opposed to spoken words or gestures

literacy tests Exams given to determine how well educated an individual is; often used to prevent minority groups from voting

lynchings Illegal executions, by hanging, of individuals by a mob

malice A legal term referring to a party's intention to do injury to another party; malice may be either expressed or implied

monopoly A situation in which a business or individual has sufficient control over a market to prevent any meaningful competition

naturalization The process by which a foreign-born person becomes a citizen

nullify To make something of no consequence or value

obscenity Words, acts, or images designed to incite lust or depravity; language, images, or actions that are offensive in polite society

parochial schools Private schools usually organized by a religious group

plaintiff The person who brings charges in a court of law

poll taxes Money paid in order to vote

pragmatic Practical; concerned with facts

precedents Established courses of action in a given situation

progressive Wanting social, economic, and governmental reforms, especially in the late 1800s and early 1900s

ratification A formal approval or confirmation (of an amendment or treaty)

ratified Approved

ratify To approve

reapportionment The redistribution of representation in a legislative body, especially the periodic reallotment of U.S. congressional seats as required by the U.S. Constitution

religious toleration Accepting or permitting others' religious beliefs and practices that disagree with one's own

Republican Relating to a republic

Republican Party Founded in 1854, one of the two major political parties in the United States

restrictive covenants a deed restriction that limits the property rights of the owner; in urban centers, restrictive covenants, which first became popular in the late nineteenth century, created segregated neighborhoods

salutatorian In the United States and Canada, an academic title given to the second-highest graduate of an educational institution

seditious Disloyal; in opposition to civil authority or government

separation of powers The division of authority among different branches of government

standing Legal right

states' rights The concept that the rights and laws of individual states override the powers of the federal government

statutory law Written law (as opposed to oral law or traditions)

subpoena A writ summoning a person to court to give testimony

subversive A person who secretly works to overthrow a government or political system

tariffs Taxes on imported goods

test cases Lawsuits filed to determine the courts' position on a matter of law

treason A crime against one's nation

unanimous Having the agreement or consent of all persons involved

veto Rejection of a bill

white primaries Primary elections in which only whites could cast ballots for candidates; now illegal

writ of certiorari An order issued by an appeals court to a lower court to review that court's findings

Selected Bibliography

Alonso, Karen. *Korematsu v. United States: Japanese-American Internment Camps.* Berkeley Heights, N.J.: Enslow Publishers, 1998.

Alonso, Karen. *Loving v. Virginia: Interracial Marriage.* Berkeley Heights, N.J.: Enslow Publishers, 2000.

Baum, Lawrence. *The Supreme Court.* Washington, D.C.: CQ Press, 2009.

Chin, Steven A. *When Justice Failed: The Fred Korematsu Story.* Orlando, Fla.: Steck-Vaughn, 1992.

Cohen, Henry. *Freedom of Speech and Press: Exceptions to the First Amendment.* Hauppauge, N.Y.: Novinka Books, 2008.

Colby, William H. *Long Goodbye: The Deaths of Nancy Cruzan.* Carlsbad, Calif.: Hay House, 2003.

Crompton, Samuel Willard. *McCulloch v. Maryland: Implied Powers of the Federal Government.* New York: Chelsea House Publications, 2007.

Cromwell, Sharon. *Dred Scott v. Sandford: A Slave's Case for Freedom and Citizenship.* Mankato, Minn.: Compass Point Books, 2009.

Curry, George. *The Affirmative Action Debate.* New York: Basic Books, 1996.

Davis, Abraham L., and Barbara L. Graham. *The Supreme Court, Race, and Civil Rights: From Marshall to Rehnquist.* Belmont, Calif.: Sage, 1996.

Dean, John W. *The Rehnquist Choice: The Untold Story of the Nixon Appointment That Redefined the Supreme Court.* New York: Free Press, 2002.

Devillers, David. *Marbury v. Madison: Powers of the Supreme Court.* Berkeley Heights, N.J.: Enslow Publishers, 1998.

Drewry, Gavin, et al. *The Court of Appeal.* Oxford, UK: Hart Publishing, 2007.

Ellis, Richard J., ed. *Judging Executive Power: Sixteen Supreme Court Cases That Have Shaped the American Presidency.* New York: Rowman and Littlefield, 2009.

Ellsberg, Daniel. *Secrets: A Memoir of Vietnam and the Pentagon Papers.* New York: Penguin, 2003.

Farish, Leah. *The First Amendment: Freedom of Speech, Religion, and the Press.* Berkeley Heights, N.J.: Enslow Publishers, 1998.

Faux, Marian. *Roe v. Wade, Updated Edition: The Untold Story of the Landmark Supreme Court Decision that Made Abortion Legal.* New York: Cooper Square Press, 2000.

Findlaw. http://lp.findlaw.com/

Finkelman, Martin. *Dred Scott v. Sandford: A Brief History with Documents.* New York: Bedford/St. Martin's, 1997.

Fireside, Harvey, and Sarah Fuller. *Brown v. Board of Education: Equal Schooling for All.* Berkeley Heights, N.J.: Enslow Publishers, 1994.

Fisher, Louis. *The Supreme Court and Congress: Rival Interpretations.* Washington, D.C.: CQ Press, 2008.

Foley, Michael A. *Arbitrary and Capricious: The Supreme Court, the Constitution, and the Death Penalty.* New York: Praeger, 2003.

Forsyth, Christopher, ed. *Judicial Review and the Constitution.* Oxford, UK: Hart Publishing, 2000.

Fridell, Ron. *Gideon v. Wainwright: The Right to Free Counsel.* New York: Benchmark Books, 2006.

Friedman, Leon. *Abortion.* New York: Facts On File, 1995.

Gold, Susan Dudley. *Brown v. Board of Education: Separate But Equal?.* New York: Benchmark Books, 2004.

——. *Loving v. Virginia: Lifting the Ban Against Interracial Marriage.* New York: Benchmark Books, 2007.

——. *McCulloch v. Maryland: State v. Federal Power.* New York: Benchmark Books, 2007.

Graham, Gene S. *One Man, One Vote: Baker v. Carr and the American Levellers.* New York: Little Brown, 1972.

Head, Tom. *Freedom of Religion.* New York: Facts On File, 2005.

Herbert, David L., ed. *The Bill of Rights– Freedom of the Press.* Farmington Hills, Mich.: Greenhaven Press, 2005.

Herda, D.J. *The Dred Scott Case: Slavery and Citizenship.* Berkeley Heights, N.J.: Enslow Publishers, 1994.

——. *Roe v. Wade: The Abortion Question.* Berkeley Heights, N.J.: Enslow Publishers, 1994.

——. *United States v. Nixon: Watergate and the President.* Berkeley Heights, N.J.: Enslow Publishers, 1996.

Herring, George. *The Pentagon Papers.* New York: McGraw-Hill, 1993.

Hudson, David L. *The Rehnquist Court: Understanding Its Impact and Legacy.* New York: Praeger Press, 2006.

Icenoggle, Jodi. *Schenk v. United States and the Freedom of Speech Debate.* Berkeley Heights, N.J.: Enslow Publishers, 2005.

Jantzen, Steven. *The Presidency, Congress, and the Supreme Court.* New York: Scholastic, 1989.

Kelly-Gangi, Carol. *Miranda v. Arizona and the Rights of the Accused: Debating Supreme Court Decisions.* Berkeley Heights, N.J.: Enslow Publishers, 2006.

Keursten, Ashlyn. *Decisions on the U.S. Courts of Appeals.* London: Routledge, 2001.

Kowalski, Kathiann M. *Affirmative Action (Open for Debate).* New York: Benchmark Books, 2006.

Leinwand, Gerald. *Freedom of Speech.* New York: Facts On File, 1990.

Levinson, Isabel Simone. *Gibbons v. Ogden: Controlling Trade Between States.* Berkeley Heights, N.J.: Enslow Publishers, 1999.

Lewis, Anthony. *Gideon's Trumpet.* New York: Vintage Books, 1989.

Littlefield, Sophie, and William M. Wiecek. *Oliver Wendell Holmes, Jr.: The Supreme Court and American Legal Thought.* New York: PowerPlus Books, 2005.

Martin, Waldo. *Brown v. Board of Education: A Brief History with Documents.* New York: St. Martin's Press, 2007.

McNeese, Tim. *Plessy v. Ferguson: Separate but Equal.* New York: Chelsea House Publications, 2006.

McPherson, Stephanie. *The Bakke Case and the Affirmative Action Debate: Supreme Court Decisions.* Berkeley Heights, N.J.: Enslow Publishers, 2005.

Medley, Keith Weldon. *We As Freemen: Plessy v. Ferguson.* Gretna, La.: Pelican Publishing Company, 2003.

Meter, Larry A. *United States v. Nixon: The Question of Executive Privilege.* New York: Chelsea House Publications, 2007.

Neubauer, David W., and Stephen S. Meinhold. *Battle Supreme: The Confirmation of Chief Justice John Roberts and the Future of the Supreme Court.* New York: Wadsworth, 2005.

Patrick, John J. *The Supreme Court of the United States: A Student Companion.* New York: Oxford University Press USA, 2006.

Perl, Lila. *Cruzan v. Missouri: The Right to Die.* Tarrytown, N.Y.: Marshall Cavendish, 2007.

Phillips, Tracy A. *Hazelwood v. Kuhlmeier And the School Newspaper Censorship Debate: Debating Supreme Court Decisions.* Berkeley Heights, N.J.: Enslow Publishers, 2006.

Pickering, Charles W. *Supreme Chaos: The Politics of Judicial Confirmation & the Culture War.* Macon, Ga.: Stroud and Hall, 2006.

Powers, Stephen P., and Rothmann, Stanley. *The Least Dangerous Branch? Consequences of Judicial Activism.* New York: Praeger, 2002.

Quirk, William. *Courts and Congress: America's Unwritten Constitution.* Piscataway, N.J.: Transaction Publishers, 2008.

Romaine, Deborah. *Famous Trials–Roe v. Wade.* San Diego, Calif.: Lucent Books, 1998.

Rubin, Eva R., ed. *The Abortion Controversy.* New York: Praeger, 1993.

Savage, David G. *The Supreme Court and Individual Rights.* Washington, DC: CQ Press, 2009.

Sergis, Diana G. *Bush v. Gore: Controversial Presidential Election Case.* Berkeley Heights, N.J.: Enslow Publishers, 2003.

Silverstein, Mark. *Judicious Choices: The Politics of Supreme Court Confirmations, Second Edition.* New York: W.W. Norton, 2007.

Simon, James. F. *What Kind of Nation: Thomas Jefferson, John Marshall, and the Epic Struggle to Create a United States.* New York: Simon and Schuster, 2003.

Smith, Jean Edward. *John Marshall: Definer of a Nation.* New York: Henry Holt, 1996.

Steffoff, Rebecca. *Furman V. Georgia: Debating the Death Penalty.* New York: Benchmark Books, 2007.

Stefoff, Rebecca. *The Bakke Case: Challenge to Affirmative Action.* New York: Benchmark Books, 2006.

Supreme Court of the United States. http://www.supremecourt.gov.

Thomas (Library of Congress). http://thomas.loc.gov/.

Thomas, Brooks. *Plessy v. Ferguson.* New York: Bedford/St. Martin's, 1996.

Toobin, Jeffrey. *Too Close to Call: The Thirty-Six Day Battle to Decide the 2000 Election.* New York: Random House, 2002.

United States Government Manual. http://www.gpoaccess.gov/gmanual/.

U.S. Supreme Court Building. http://www.nps.gov/nr/travel/wash/dc78.htm.

Vanmeter, Larry A. *Miranda v. Arizona.* New York: Chelsea House Publications, 2006.

Waldman, Steven. *Founding Faith: How Our Founding Fathers Forged a Radical New Approach to Religious Liberty.* New York: Random House, 2009.

Warren, Charles. *Congress, the Constitution, & the Supreme Court.* Buffalo, N.Y.: William S. Hein, 1994.

Wice, Paul B. *Miranda v. Arizona: "You Have the Right to Remain Silent . . . ."* London, UK: Franklin Watts, 1996.

Case Index

Page numbers in *italics* indicate illustrations.

A

Abrams v. United States (1919), 152
Adair v. United States (1908), *86*
Adarand v. Pena (1995), 14
Adler v. Board of Education, City of New York (1952), 170
AFL v. Swing (1941), 124
Agostini v. Felton (1997), 127
Albermarle Paper Co. v. Moody (1975), 75
Alberts v. California (1957), *185*
Albertson v. Subversive Activities Control Board (1965), 126, 222
Allgeyer v. Louisiana (1897), 103
American Communications Association v. Douds (1950), 170
Apodaca v. Oregon (1972), 205
Argersinger v. Hamlin (1972), *49*
Arizona v. Evans (1995), 113
Atkins v. Virginia (2002), 229
Avent v. North Carolina (1963), 224

B

Bailey v. Drexel Furniture Co. (1922), 69–70, *86*
Baker v. Carr (1962), 45, *46*, 47, 53, 294–295
Barker v. Wingo (1972), 206
Barnes v. Glen Theatre (1991), *250*
Barron v. Baltimore (1833), 48, 234
Baze v. Rees (2008), 97
Beauharnais v. Illinois (1952), *183*
Benton v. Maryland (1969), *49*, 99, 177
Betts v. Brady (1942), 139, *141*, 296–297
Bivens v. Six Unknown Named Agents (1971), 172
BMW v. Gore (1996), 15
Board of Education v. Barnette (1943), 122
Board of Regents of the University of California v. Bakke (1978), 60, *254–255*
Board of the Trustees of the University of Alabama v. Garrett (2001), 188
Bowers v. Hardwick (1986), *208–209*, 210, 318, 319, 321
Bradwell v. Illinois (1873), 222
Brandenburg v. Ohio (1969), *129*
Branzburg v. Hayes, in re Pappas, United States v. Caldwell (1972), 134
Breed v. Jones (1975), 163
Brotherhood of Railroad Trainmen v. Howard (1952), 108
Brotherhood of Teamsters, Local 695 v. Vogt (1957), 124
Brown v. Board of Education (1954), 11, 23, *55–59*, 77, 78, 110, *177*, *193*, 236, *259*, *284–285*, 290–291, 307, 324–325
Brown v. Glines (1980), 135
Buchanan v. Warley (1917), 114
Bullington v. Missouri (1981), 99
Burdeau v. McDowell (1921), *221*
Bush v. Gore (2000), 61–*64*, 164, 190, 236, 315–318, 332

C

Calder v. Bull (1798), 113
California Democratic Party v. Jones (2000), 126
Cantwell v. Connecticut (1940), *49, 127,* 129
Carlson v. Landon (1952), 45
Carroll v. United States (1925), 43
Central Hudson Gas & Electric Co. v. Public Service Commission of New York (1980), *109*
Chaplinsky v. New Hampshire (1942), *132*
Charles River Bridge v. Warren Bridge (1837), 105, 248
Chicago, Burlington and Quincy R. Co. v. Chicago (1897), *49*
Chicago V. Morales (1999), *123*
Chisholm v. Georgia (1793), 4, *67*, 233
City of Boerne v. Flores (1997), 128
Civil Rights Cases (1883), *78*, 149
Clinton v. City of New York (1998), 168, *169*, 198
Cohen v. California (1971), 146
Cole v. Arkansas (1948), *49*
Coleman v. Miller (1939), *50*
Colorado Anti-Discrimination Commission v. Continental Airlines (1963), 108
Communist Party of Indiana v. Whitcomb (1974), 170
Coolidge v. New Hampshire (1971), 221
Corrigan v. Buckley (1926), 114
Cox v. New Hampshire (1941), 123
Craig v. Boren (1976), *109*
Cramer v. United States (1945), *61*
Crist v. Bretz (1978), *49*
Cruzan v. Missouri Department of Health (1990), *92–93*, 207
Cummings v. Missouri (1867), 170

D

Dartmouth College v. Woodward (1819), *94–95*, 269–273
DeFunis v. Odegaard (1974), 157
DeJonge v. Oregon (1937), *49*, 122, 124
Dillon v. Gloss (1921), *50*
Dred Scott v. Sandford (1857), 73, *85*, 87, 99, *100*–102, 157, 225, 234, *246–248*
Duncan v. Louisiana (1968), *49*, 204–205

E

Eisenstadt v. Baird (1972), 53
Elfbrandt v. Russell (1966), 170
Employment Division, Department of Human Resources of Oregon v. Smith (1990), 127–128
Engle v. Vitale (1962), 105–*107*, 219
Escobedo v. Illinois (1964), 12, 79, 110, *111*, 112, 297–298
Everson v. Board of Education (1947), *49*, 126–127
Ex parte Garland (1866), 50, *85*, 113, 199
Ex parte McCardle (1868), 162

Ex parte Milligan (1866), 6, 113
Ex parte Quirin (1942), 10

Faragher v. City of Boca Raton (1998), 223
Faretta v. California (1975), *139*
Florida v. J.L. (2000), 230
Frank v. Mangum (1915), 260
Franks v. Bowman Transportation Co. Inc. (1976), 75
Furman v. Georgia (1972), 92, 96
Furnco Construction Corp. v. Waters (1978), 75

Gannett Co. Inc. v. DePasquale (1979), 134, 205
Gardner v. Board of Public Works of Los Angeles
   (1951), 170
Garner v. Louisiana (1961), 243
Garrity v. New Jersey (1967), 222
Gerende v. Board of Supervisors of Elections (1951), 170
Gertz v. Robert Welch Inc. (1974), 168
Gibbons v. Ogden (1824), 83, 116, 136–138, 174, *175*, 176,
   232, 234, 279–280
Giboney v. Empire Storage and Ice Co. (1949), 124
Gideon v. Wainwright (1963), 11, 23, *49*, 111, 139, *140, 141*,
   259, 295–297, 298
Gitlow v. New York (1925), 11, 48, *49*, 77, 104, 234
Gober v. City of Birmingham (1963), 224
Gomillion v. Lightfoot (1960), 201
Gompers v. Buck's Stove and Range Co. (1911), 91
Gonzales v. Carhart (2007), 36
Grady v. Corbin (1990), 99
Gratz v. Bollinger (2003), 37
Gray v. Sanders (1963), 189
Gregg v. Georgia (1976), 92, 97
Griggs v. Duke Power Co. (1971), 75
Griswold v. Connecticut (1965), 34, *49*, 53, 143–144,
   210, *213*
Grosjean v. American Press Co. (1936), 65
Grovey v. Townsend (1933), 259–260
Grutter v. Bollinger (2003), 37, 188
Guinn v. United States (1915), 143

Hague v. CIO (1939), *49*
Hale v. Henkel (1906), 222
Hamdan v. Rumsfeld (2006), *206*
Hammer v. Dagenhart (1918), 69–70, *86*
Haupt v. United States (1947), *61*
Hazelwood School District v. Kuhlmeier (1988), *146*–147,
   251, 313–315
Heart of Atlanta Motel v. United States (1964), 147–149
Helvering v. Davis (1937), *86*
Hepburn v. Griswold (1870), *85*, 119
Herbert v. Lando (1979), 184
Herring v. United States (2009), 30–32
Hills v. Gautreaux (1976), 115
Hirabayahsi v. United States (1943), 166
Holder v. Hall (1994), 250
Hudgens v. National Labor Relations Board (1976), *131*

Illinois v. Wardlow (2002), 230
Immigration and Naturalization Service v. Chadha (1983), *167*
In re Burrus (1971), *103*, 163
In re Gault (1967), 163
In re Oliver (1948), *49*
In re Winship (1970), *103*, 163

Jacobellis v. Ohio (1964), *185, 186*
Jenkins v. Georgia (1974), *186*
Johnson v. Louisiana (1972), 205
Johnson v. Zerbst (1938), 207
Jones v. Alfred H. Mayer Co. (1968), 115
Jurek v. Texas (1976), 97

Katz v. United States (1967), 104
Kawakita v. United States (1952), *61*
Kelo v. City of New London (2005), 105
Keyishian v. Board of Regents of the State University
   of New York (1967), 170
Kimel v. Florida (2000), 188
Klopfer v. North Carolina (1967), *49*, 206
Knox v. Lee (1871), *85*, 119
Korematsu v. United States (1944), 10, *109*, 122, 164–166,
   288–289
Kotch v. Board of River Port Pilot Commissioners (1947), *109*

★ ★ ★ L ★ ★ ★

Lawrence v. Texas (2003), 144, 164, *208–209*, 210, 219,
   236, 318–321
Lee v. Weisman (1992), 14, 164, 220
Legal Tender Cases, Hepburn v. Griswold (1870), 22
Lindsley v. Natural Carbonic Gas Co. (1911), *109*
Linkletter v. Walker (1965), 172
Lloyd Corporation Ltd. v. Tanner (1972), *130, 131*
Lochner v. New York (1905), 103, 143, 151
Lombard v. Louisiana (1963), 224
Louisiana ex rel. Francis v. Resweber (1947), *49*
Lovell v. Griffin (1938), *127*
Loving v. Virginia (1967), 23, *109, 169*–170, *259*, 303–304
Luther v. Borden (1849), 46

★ ★ ★ M ★ ★ ★

Malloy v. Hogan (1964), *49*, 110–111
Manual Enterprises v. Day (1962), *185*
Mapp v. Ohio (1961), 11, 30–31, *49*, 112, *171*–172, 221
Marbury v. Madison (1803), 4, 5, 27, 67, 83, *86*, 157–159, 161,
   172–174, *175*, 176, 178, 233, 261, 264–269, 294, 331, 332
Marsh v. Alabama (1946), *130*
Martin v. Hunter's Lessee (1816), 231
Massiah v. United States (1964), 79, 110
Maxwell v. Dow (1900), 204
McClesky v. Kemp (1987), 97
McCulloch v. Maryland (1819), 5, 116, 154, *175*, 176, 177–178,
   234, 273–275
McDonnell Douglas Corp. v. Green (1973), 75
McGowan v. Maryland (1961), *109*

McKeiver v. Pennsylvania (1971), *103,* 163
McNabb v. United States (1943), 79
Milk Wagon Drivers Union v. Meadowmoor
    Dairies Inc. (1941), 124
Miller v. California (1973), *186,* 187
Minnesota v. Dickerson (1993), 230
Miranda v. Arizona (1966), 12, 23, 79, *179–180, 259,* 301–303
Mississippi University for Women v. Hogan (1982), *109*
Missouri v. Jenkins (1995), 14
Moore v. Dempsey (1923), 260
Moose Lodge 107 v. Irvis (1972), *125*
Morehead v. New York ex rel. Tipaldo (1936), 9
Morse v. Frederick (2007), 251
Mulford v. Smith (1939), *86*
Murray v. Curlett (1963), 219

NAACP v. Alabama ex rel. Patterson (1958), 146
Nathanson v. United States (1933), 200
Near v. Minnesota (1931), 65, 133, 152
Nebraska Press Association v. Stuart (1976), 134, 136
New York Times v. Sullivan (1964), 53, 134, 168, 182–184,
    293, 299–301
New York Times v. United States (1971), 66
Nix v. Hedden (1893), *118*
Nixon v. Herndon (1927), 259

Okanogan Indians et al. v. United States (1929), 198
Olmstead v. Unites States (1928), 104

Palko v. Connecticut (1937), 77
Panama Refining Co. v. Ryan (1935), 9, *86*
Papachristou v. City of Jacksonville (1972), *123*
Patton v. United States (1930), 204
Pennsylvania v. Wheeling and Belmont Bridge Co. (1852),
    174–175
Pentagon Papers Case (New York Times v. United States
    (1971), 66 Peterson v. City of Greenville (1963), 224
Planned Parenthood of Southeastern Pennsylvania v. Casey
    (1992), 14, 35, 143, 164, 321
Plessy v. Ferguson (1896), 8, 11, 55, 56, 76, 77, 144, 145,
    193–195, 234, 282–283, *284*–286, 290–291
Plyler v. Dow (1982), *109*
Pointer v. Texas (1965), *49*
Pollock v. Farmers' Loan and Trust Co. (1895), 8, *85,* 118, 155
Pope v. Illinois (1987), *186,* 187
Powell v. Alabama (1932), 195, *196–197,* 207
Press-Enterprise Co. v. Superior Court (1986), 205
Proffitt v. Florida (1976), 97

Railroad Retirement Board v. Alton Railway Co. (1935), 9
Rakas v. Illinois (1978), 44
R.A.V. v. City of St. Paul (1992), *132*
Reed v. Reed (1971), 223
Regents of the University of California v. Bakke (1978), 37
Reitman v. Mulkey (1967), 115

Reynolds v. Sims (1964), 189
Ricci v. DeStefano (2009), 203–204
Richmond Newspapers Inc. v. Commonwealth of Virginia
    (1980), 134, 205
Robinson v. California (1962), 11
Robinson v. Memphis and Charleston Railroad Co. (1883), 78
Roe v. Wade (1973), 12–14, 34–36, 60, 143, 188, 210, *213*–214,
    236, 310-*313*
Rosenberger v. University of Virginia (1995), 15
Rosenblatt v. Baer (1966), 168
Rosenbloom v. Metromedia Inc. (1971), 168
Rostker v. Goldberg (1981), *223,* 258
Roth v. United States (1957), 184 *185, 186,* 187

Sante Fe Independent School District v. Doe (2000), 220
Schacht v. United States (1970), *250*
Schechter Poultry Corp. v. United States (1935), 9, *86*
Schenck v. United States (1919), *150,* 151, 228, 286
Schneckloth v. Bustamonte (1973), 200
School District of Abington Township v. Schempp (1963), 219
Seminole Tribe of Florida v. Florida (1996), 14
Shaw v. Reno (1993), 201
Shelley v. Kraemer (1948), 114–115
Shuttlesworth v. Birmingham (1965), *123,* 224
Silverthorne Lumber Co. v. United States (1920), 112
Simon & Schuster Inc. v. Members of New York State Crime
    Victims Board (1991), 65
Sit-In Cases (1962), 224
Skinner v. Oklahoma (1942), *109*
Slaughterhouse Cases (1873), 224–225
Smith v. Allwright (1944), 260
Smith v. Goguen (1974), 120
Spence v. Washington (1974), 120
Stack v. Boyle (1951), 45
Stanley v. Georgia (1969), 177
Steele v. Louisville and Nashville Railroad Co. (1944), 108
Stengberg v. Carhart (2000), 36, 236
Steward Machine Co. v. Davis (1937), *86*
Street v. New York (1969), 120
Stromberg v. California (1931), 243
Sturges v. Crowninshield (1819), 231–232, 276–277
Swann v. Charlotte-Mecklenburg County Board of Education
    (1971), 242–243, 307–309

Terry v. Adams (1953), 260
Terry v. Ohio (1968), 30, 230
Texas v. Johnson (1990), 120
Thornburg v. Gingles (1986), 201
Thornhill v. Alabama (1940), 123, 124
Tillman v. Wheaton-Haven Recreation Association
    (1973), 115, *125*
Tinker v. Des Moines (1969), *251,* 305–306, 313

Union Local 590 v. Logan Valley Plaza (1968), *130, 131*
United Sates v. Salerno (1987), 45
United States v. Appalachian Electric Power Co. (1940), 175

United States v. Brown (1965), 51

United States v. Butler (1936), *86*, 118

United States v. Calandra (1974), 30

United States v. Carolene Products Co. (1938), 77, *109*

United States v. Claimants of the Schooner Amistad (1841), *226*

United States v. Darby (1941), 70, *86*

United States v. Harriss (1954), 135

United States v. Klein (1872), 199

United States v. Lopez (1995), 14, 116

United States v. Lovasco (1977), 206

United States v. MacDonald (1982), 206

United States v. Matlock (1974), 201

United States v. Morrison (2000), 188

United States v. Mosely (1915), 143

United States v. Nichols (1883), 78

United States v. Nixon (1974), 22, 200, 236, *252–254*

United States v. O'Brien (1968), 243, *250*

United States v. Ryan (1883), 78

United States v. Singleton (1883), 78

United States v. Sokolow (1989), 230

United States v. Stanley (1883), 78

United States v. Virginia (1996), *109*, 142

United States v. Vuitch (1971), 35

United States v. Whren (1996), 44

United States v. Wong Kim Ark (1898), 73

University of California Regents v. Bakke (1978), 60, *254–255*

U.S. Term Limits v. Thornton (1995), 164

Veazie Bank v. Fenno (1869), 119

Village of Arlington Heights v. Metropolitan Housing Development Corporation (1977), 115

Virginia v. Black (2003), 244

Walker v. Sauvinet (1876), 204

Wallace v. Jaffree (1985), 126, 220, 256–257

Waller v. Georgia (1984), 205

Walters v. National Association of Radiation Survivors (1995), 135

Washington v. Texas (1967), *49*

Watchtower Bible & Tract Society of New York v. Village of Stratton (2002), *127*

Webster v. Reproductive Health Services (1989), 13, 35

Weeks v. United States (1914), 30–31, 112

Wesberry v. Sanders (1964), 189

West Coast Hotel Co. v. Parrish (1937), 10, 216–217

West River Bridge Company v. Dix (1848), 105

West Virginia State Board of Education v. Barnette (1943), 127, 243

Whitney v. California (1927), 124

Williams v. Florida (1970), 205

Williams v. Mississippi (1898), 8

Williamson v. Lee Optica of Oklahoma (1955), *109*

Wilson v. United States (1911), 222

Wolf v. Colorado (1949), *49*

Wygant v. Jackson Board of Education (1986), *109*

Yates v. United States (1957), 125–126, 228

Yick Wo v. Hopkins (1886), 38

Youngstown Sheet & Tube Co. v. Sawyer (1952), 323

Zelman v. Simmons-Harris (2002), 127

Zurcher v. The Stanford Daily (1978), 134

Zwickler v. Koota (1967), 98

General Index

Note: Page numbers in **bold italic** type indicate main encyclopedia entries. Page numbers in *italic* type indicate illustrations, figures, tables, or maps. Page numbers in **bold** type refer to terms that are highlighted in bold in the text and are also defined in the Glossary.

★ ★ ★A★ ★ ★

Abolitionists, 102
Abortion, *See also* Due Process; Rights
   ban on, 13
   constitutional debate on, ***34–36***
   late-term, 35, 36
   Laws against, 35
   Planned Parenthood of Southeastern Pennsylvania v. Casey (1992) and, 14, 164
   privacy and, 12
   Roe v. Wade (1973) and, 60, 213
Abrams v. United States (1919), 152
Absention Doctrine, 158
Act of 1873, *89*
Act to Improve the Administration of Justice (1988), *89*
Adair v. United States (1908), *86*
Adams, John
   appointing Justices and, 4, 67, *172, 173,* 175, 176
Adarand v. Pena (1995), 14
Adjourned, 3, **248**
Adler v. Board of Education, City of New York (1952), 170
Affirmative Action, ***36–37,*** *See also* Equal Employment Opportunity
Affirmed, **31**
AFL v. Swing (1941), 124
African Americans
   affirmative action, 36
   Clarence Thomas, 248
   Homer Plessy, 55, 76
   Thurgood Marshall, 25, 57
   voting and, 201
Agostini v. Felton (1997), 127
Agricultural Adjustment Act (1933), *86*
Alabama, 46, 51
Albermarle Paper Co. v. Moody (1975), 75
Albetson v. Subversive Activities Control Board (1965), 126, 222
Alberts v. California (1957), *185*
Alien and Sedition Acts, 124
Alien Registration Act (1940), 45
Aliens, 114, *See also* Citizenship; Naturalization
   description of, **110, 165**
   protection of, ***37–38***

United States v. Wong Kim Ark (1898), 73
Alito, Samuel A., 26, ***38–39,*** *See also* Associate Justices
Allgeyer v. Louisiana (1897), 103
Allred, Gloria, *312*
All the Laws but One: Civil Liberties in Wartime (Rehnquist), 203
Amendments, **7, 90,** *See also* Constitution of the United States
   First, 32, 48, *49,* 65, 66, 77, 83, 98, 104, 105, 122, 124, *130–131,* 132–133, 184, 186, 243
   Second, 32, 48
   Third, 48
   Fourth, 29, 30, 31, 32, *44,* 48, *49,* 105, 112, 171, 201, 220, *221*
   Fifth, 12, 48, *49,* 95, 98, 101, 102–103, 105, 110, 112, 163, 180, 221–222
   Sixth, 48, *49,* 110, 111, 112, 139, 163, 205, 207, 210
   Seventh, 48, 204
   Eighth, 11, 32, 45, 48, 92, 96
   Ninth, 48, *49,* 90
   Tenth, 48, 90
   Eleventh, 4, 233
   Twelfth, 64
   Thirteenth, 7, 55, 76, 78, 91, 99, 193
   Fourteenth, 7, 8, 32, 34, 35, 38, 46, 48, *49,* 55, 57, 59, 64, 65, 73, 76, 77, 78, 87, 91, 95, 99, 103, 104, 115, 122, *125,* 139, 189, 193, 194, 195, 204–205, 222, 224–225, 282–286
   Fifteenth, 7, 201, 211
   Sixteenth, 8, 117
   Twenty-Third, 74
   Twenty-Seventh, 50–51
American Bar Association, 152
American Civil Liberties Union (ACLU), 38, 122, 142, 169
American Communications Association v. Douds (1950), 170
American Law Review, 151, 231
American Revolution, 40
Amicus Curiae, 199
Amistad, 226
Anarchists, 73
Antidiscrimination Laws, 13

Anti-Injunction Act, 155
Antislavery, 152
Anti-Sodomy Laws, 164
Anti-War Protests, *250*
Apodaca v. Oregon (1972), 205
Appeals Court, **15,** 55, **160**
Appellate Court, **28,** *40,* 159, 161–162
Appellate Jurisdiction, *See* Circuit Court of Appeals
Apportionments, 8
Appreciable Deterrence, **31**
Appropriation, **51,** 167
Argersinger v. Hamlin (1972), *49*
Arizona v. Evans (1995), 113
Armbands, 251
Arrest Warrants, 30, 221
Articles of Confederation, 20, ***40–41,*** 276–277, *See also* Constitutional Convention; Constitution of the United States
Assembly, freedom of, 49
Associate Justices, ***41–43,*** *See also* Chief Justice of the United States; Confirmation of Justices and Judges; Nominations
Association, freedom of, 75
Atheists, 219
Atkins v. Virginia (2002), 229
Attorney General, 161
Automobile Searches, ***43–44,*** *See also* Probable Cause; Search Warrants; Unreasonable Search and Seizure
Avent v. North Carolina (1963), 224

★ ★ ★B★ ★ ★

Badger, George E.
   nomination of, *80*
Bail, **45,** 48, *See also* Constitution of the United States
Bailey v. Drexel Furniture Co. (1922), 69–70, *86*
Bail Reform Act (1966), 45
Baker v. Carr (1962), 45, ***45–47,*** *46,* 47, 53, 294–295, ***294–295***
Bakke, Allan, 37
Balanced Budget Act, 168
Baldwin, Henry
   congressional service of, *88*
Ballinger, Richard A., 52
Ballots, Recounting, 15

Bankruptcy, *47,* **154**
Bankruptcy Abuse Prevention, 47
Banner, Stuart, 97
Barbour, Philip B.
    congressional service of, *88*
Barker v. Wingo (1972), 206
Barnes v. Glen Theatre (1991), *250*
Barron, Clarence W., 52
Barron, John, 48
Barron v. Baltimore (1833), 48, 234
Battery, **205**
Baze v. Rees (2008), 97
Bearing Arms, 48
Beauharnais v. Illinois (1952), *183*
Becker, Frank J., *106–107*
Benton v. Maryland (1969), *49,* 99, 177
Betts v. Brady (1942), 139, *141,* 296–297
Bill of Rights, 12, **47–50,** *See also*
    Aliens; Constitution of the United
    States; Due Process; Equal Protec-
    tion; Freedom of Association; Free-
    dom of Religion; Freedom of the
    Press; Freedom to Petition
    application of, 104, 158
    Constitution of the United States
        and, 90
    due process and, 77
    Eighth Amendment, 92
    Fourth Amendment and, 29
    granting bail and, 45
    James Madison and, 51
    juveniles and, 163
    meaning of, 27
    protections from, 180, 224, 226, 234
Bills of Attainder, **50–51,** *See also* Ex
    Post Facto Laws
bin Laden, Osama, 15–16
Birth Control, 143–144
Bivens v. Six Unknown Named Agents
    (1971), 172
Black, Hugo L., 143
    congressional service of, *88*
    Gideon v. Wainwright (1963) and, 141
    Jehovah's Witnesses and, *130*
    Ku Klux Klan, 82
    One Person, One Vote, 189
    Pentagon Papers and, 191
    retirement of, 35
    Rosenbloom v. Metromedia Inc.
        (1971), 168
    Terry v. Adams, 260
Black, Jeremiah S., 23
    nomination of, *80*
Black Codes, 107, 108
Blackmun, Harry A., 55
    *Cruzan v. Missouri Department of
        Health* (1990) and, 93
    nomination of, 21
    Papers of, **307**

Planned Parenthood v. Casey (1992)
    and, 36
    rights of juveniles and, 163
    right to privacy and, 210
    Warren E. Burger and, 60
Black's Law Dictionary, 157
Blair, John, 20
Blatchford, Samuel, *82*
BMW v. Gore (1996), 15
Board of Education v. Barnette
    (1943), 122
*Board of Regents of the University of
    California v. Bakke* (1978), 60,
    254–255
*Board of the Trustees of the University of
    Alabama v. Garrett* (2001), 188
Bollinger, Lee, 37
Bonus Army, 135
Bootlegging, 104
Bork, Robert H., 25, 81, 164
    nomination of, *80*
Boston Subway System, 52
Bowers v. Hardwick (1986), *208–209,*
    210, 318, 319, 321
Bradford, Edward A.
    nomination of, *80*
Bradley, Joseph P., *63,* 76, 78
Bradwell v. Illinois (1873), 222
Brandeis, Louis D., 22, 24, **51–53,** 81,
    215, 287
Brandenburg v. Ohio (1969), 129
*Branzburg v. Hayes, in re Pappas,
    United States v. Caldwell* (1972), 134
Breed v. Jones (1975), 163
Brennan, William J., **53–54,** 183
    appointment of, 19, 20
    Baker v. Carr (1962) and, 46
    *Cruzan v. Missouri Department of
        Health* (1990) and, 93
    Furman v. Georgia (1972), 96
    obscenity and, 187
    Pentagon Papers Case (1971)
        and, 191
    Roth v. United States (1957), 185
    Warren E. Burger and, 60
Brewer, David, 42
Breyer, Stephen G., **54–55,** 64
Bribery, 153
Brotherhood of Locomotive
    Firemen, 108
*Brotherhood of Railroad Trainmen v.
    Howard* (1952), 108
*Brotherhood of Teamsters, Local 695 v.
    Vogt* (1957), 124
Brown, Henry B., 194
Brown, Linda, 56, *58*
Brown, Oliver, 56
Brown Foundation for Educational
    Equity, Excellence, and Research, 58

Brown v. Board of Education (1954), 11,
    23, **55–57,** *55–59,* 77, 78, 110, *177,*
    193, 236, *259, 284–285, 285,*
    290–291, **290–291,** 307, 324–325,
    324–325, *See also* Segregation
Brown v. Board of Education National
    Historic Site Act of 1992, *58*
Brown v. Glines (1980), 135
Buchanan, James, 100–101
Buchanan, Patrick, 62
Buchanan v. Warley (1917), 114
Bullington v. Missouri (1981), 99
Bull Moose Party, 246
Bullying, 29
Burdeau v. McDowell (1921), *221*
Bureau of Insular Affairs, 121
Burger, Warren E., **59–60**
    appointment of, 22, 200
    Bivens v. Six Unknown Named Agents
        (1971), 172
    child labor and, 69
    executive privilege and, 253
    Miller v. California (1973) and,
        186, 187
    racial mixing and, 242
    retirement of, 82
    Richmond Newspapers v. Virginia
        (1980), 205
Burger Court (1969-1986), 236
Burr, Aaron, **60–61,** 176
Burton, Harold H., 20
    congressional service of, *88*
Bush, George H.W., 25, 38, 83, 228
Bush, George W.
    Bush v. Gore (2000), 61–64, 164, 190,
        315–318
    election of 2000 and, 15, 16
    Harriet Miers and, 26, 81, 189
    John G. Roberts and, 211–212, **327**
    Samuel A. Alito and, 38
Bush v. Gore (2000), **61–64,** *61–64,*
    164, 190, 236, **315–318,** 332,
    See also Judicial Restraint;
    Jurisdiction; One Person, One Vote;
    Presidency and the Supreme Court
Businesses, 7–8
Butchers, 76
Butler, Pierce, 20, *215,* 287
Butterfly Ballots, 62
Butterworth, Robert, 62
Byrnes, James F.
    congressional service of, *88*

★ ★ ★ **C** ★ ★ ★

Calder v. Bull (1798), 113
California Assembly, 116
California Democratic Party v. Jones
    (2000), 126
Campbell, John A., 21

Cantwell v. Connecticut (1940), *49,*
  127, 129
Capital Punishment, *See* Death Penalty
Capitol, The, 4
Cardozo, Benjamin N., 20, 22, 112,
  121, *215*
Carlson v. Landon (1952), 45
Carnal Knowledge, 186
Carpetbaggers, 21
Carriage Tax, 117
Carroll, George, 43–44
Carroll v. United States (1925), 43
Carswell, G. Harrold, 21, 81
  nomination of, *80*
Carter, Jimmy, 54
Censorship, **65–66,** 129, *See also*
  Freedom of the Press; Libel;
  Obscenity
Center for Individual Rights, 37
Central Hudson Gas & Electric Co. v.
  Public Service Commission of New
  York (1980), *109*
Chadha, Jagdish Rai, *167*
Chaplinsky v. New Hampshire
  (1942), *132*
Charles River Bridge Company, 105
Charles River Bridge v. Warren Bridge
  (1837), 105, 248
Charters, **5, 135, 247**
Chase, Salmon P., 22, *232*
  congressional service of, *88*
Chase, Samuel, 20, 153
Checks and Balances, **66–67,** *See also*
  Judicial Review
Cheney, Richard, 62, 322–324
Chicago, Burlington and Quincy R. Co.
  v. Chicago (1897), *49*
Chicago Housing Authority (CHA), 115
Chicago v. Morales (1999), *123*
Chief Justice of the United States,
  67–69, *See also* Associate Justices
Child Labor Laws, *70,* 84, *86,* 87
Child Pornography, 134
Chisholm v. Georgia (1793), 4, *67,* 233
Church Groups, 14
Circuit Court of Appeals, **71–73,**
  280–282, *See also* Judicial System
Circuit Courts (1789), *71*
Circuit Courts (2009), *72*
Citizens, 27–33
Citizenship, **73–75,** 76, 87, *See also*
  Aliens; Naturalization
City of Boerne v. Flores (1997), *128*
Civil Liberties, 11
Civil Rights, 11, 48, 50
  amendments and, 47
  cruel and unusual punishment
    and, 92
  Felix Frankfurter and, 121

following the Civil War, 76
  groups, 82
  protestors, *122*
  and the Supreme Court, **75–77**
  Thurgood Marshall and, 176–177
  William H. Rehnquist and, 202
Civil Rights Act
  (1865), 78
  (1866), 114, 115
  (1875), *85*
  (1964), **75,** 77, 108, 110, *125,* 147,
    223, 254
Civil Rights Cases (1883), **78,** *78,* 149
Civil War
  Augustus H. Garland and, 114
  developments following, 76
  Ex Parte Milligan (1866) and, 113
  Fifth Amendment and, 103
  John Marshall Harlan II and, 145
  Jurisdiction of the Supreme Court
    and, 161
  national currency and, 119
  nomination of Lucius Q.C. Lamar
    and, 24
  Oliver Wendell Holmes Jr., 151
  Pentagon papers and, 199
  presidential power and the, 5–7
  right to vote and, 210
  Scott v. Sandford (1857) and, 87
  slavery and, 91
  slavery and the, 20
Clark, Tom C., 12, 22, 171, 200
Class Action Suit, **56**
Cleveland, Grover, 21, 24, *82,* 117
Clifford, Nathan, *63, 232*
  congressional service of, *88*
Clinton, William J., 54, 55, 168, *169,*
  203, *See also* Presidency and the
  Supreme Court
Clinton v. City of New York (1998), 168,
  169, 198
Cohen v. California (1971), 146
Coining Money, 118, *119*
Cold War, **125,** 229
Cold War Courts, 236
Coleman v. Miller (1939), *50*
Cole v. Arkansas (1948), *49*
College Admissions, 37
Colonial, **126**
Colonists, 1
Colorado Anti-Discrimination Commission
  v. Continental Airlines (1963), 108
Colorado Anti-Discrimination
  Commission, 108
Columbus, Christopher, 74
Comity, 158
Commentaries (Story), 231
Commerce, 137–138
Common Law, The, 151

Communist Control Act (1954), 125
Communist Party, 51, 73, **125, 170,**
  229, *292*
Communist Party of Indiana v.
  Whitcomb (1974), 170
Communist Threat, **292**
Company Town, The, *130*
Compelling Interest, 35
Confederates, 24, 40, 91
Confessions, **78–79,** *See also*
  Self-Incrimination
Confirmation of Justices and Judges,
  79–83
Congress and the Supreme Court,
  83–90
Conservative Party, 14–15, 24,
  30, 81, 219
Constitutional Convention, 2, 3,
  120, 159
Constitutional Requirements, 17–22
Constitutional Rights, 27
Constitutional Union Party, 144–145
Constitution of the United States, 1, 27,
  90–91, 158–159, *See also*
  Amendments; Bill of Rights
  Article I, 2, 50, 113, 118, 153,
    166, 168
  Article II, 2, 17, 43, 79
  Article III, 40, 43, 46, 47, 71,
    153, 161
  Article IV, 46, 116, 155
  Article VI, 116
  Preamble, 225
  provisions of, 2
Consumer Debts, 47
Consumer Protection Act, 47
Contempt of Court, **91, 136**
Counterfeit Money, **210**
Contraceptives, 34, 53
Coolidge v. New Hampshire (1971), 221
Corrigan v. Buckley (1926), 114
Court of Appeals, **28**
Court-Packing, 87, 182, 215, 235
Cox, Archibald, 54
Coxey, Jacob S., 135
Coxey's Army, 135
Cox v. New Hampshire (1941), 123
Craig v. Boren (1976), *109*
Cramer v. United States (1945), *61*
Credit Cards, 47
Crime, prevention of, 30
Crime Control and Safe Streets Act
  (1968), 180
Criminal Laws, 13
Crist v. Bretz (1978), *49*
Crittenden, John J.
  nomination of, *80*
Cronyism, 25, 26
Cross Burnings, 243–244

Cruel and Unusual Punishment, *91–92,* *See also* Death Penalty
Cruzan, Nancy Beth, 92–93, 207
Cruzan v. Missouri Department of Health (1990), *92–93,* 92–93, 207
Culpeper Minutemen, 175
Cummings v. Missouri (1867), 170
Curfew Order, 165–166
Currencies, 119
Curtis, Benjamin R., 19
Cushing, Caleb, 81
   nomination of, *80*
Cushing, William, 20
Cushman, Robert E., 257

★ ★ ★ D ★ ★ ★

Dartmouth College v. Woodward (1819), *94–95,* 94–95, 269–273, *269–273*
Davis, David, *63, 232*
   congressional service of, *88*
Davis, John W., 57
Death Penalty, 32, 92, *95–98,* 99, *See also* Cruel and Unusual Punishment
Death with Dignity, 93
Debts, 47
Decision Makers
   Senate Judiciary Committee, *249*
   Senatorial Courtesy, *82*
   Taft and the Supreme Court Building, *245*
Declaration of Independence, 101
Declaratory Judgments, *98*
Default, **231**
DeFunis, Marco, 157
DeFunis v. Odegaard (1974), 157
DeJonge v. Oregon (1937), *49,* 122, 124
Delinquents, *103*
Democratic Party, **259**
Denaturalization, 74–75
Dennis, Eugene, *292*
Deportation, 167
Dies, Martin, 51
Dillon v. Gloss (1921), *50*
Direct Taxation, 117–118
Dirksen, Everett, *106–107*
Discrimination, *See also* Segregation; Sex Discrimination
   aliens, 38
   Colorado Anti-Discrimination Commission and, 108
   Corrigan v. Buckley (1926) and, 114
   job, 75
   laws against, 13
   minorities, 37
   race and, **7,** 149, 234, **243**
   sex and, 110, 222–223
Disputed Election of 1876 (Rehnquist), 203
Dissent, **32,** 147, 180, 192, 219

District Courts, 71
Diversity, 37
Dominican Republic, 245
Donations, 32
Double Jeopardy, *98–99,* 163
Douglas, William O., 60, 153, *216*
Dred Scott v. Sandford (1857), 73, *85,* 87, 99, *99–102,* 100–102, 157, 225, 234, *246–248,* 247–248
Driscoll, Alfred E., 53
Drugs, possession of, 31
Due Process, *102–104, See also* Bill of Rights
   abortion and, 34
   Bill of Rights and, 48, *49*
   Bush v. Gore (2000) and, 64
   Cruzan v. Missouri Department of Health (1990) and, 93
   Federalism and, **116**
   Gideon v. Wainwright (1963) and, 139
   juveniles and, **163**
   minimum wage laws and, **9**
   Palko v. Connecticut (1937) and, 77
   Powell v. Alabama (1932) and, 195
   right to petition and, **135**
   right to privacy and, **210**
Duncan, Gary, 205
Duncan v. Louisiana (1968), *49,* 204–205
Duvall, Gabriel, *247*
   congressional service of, *88*

★ ★ ★ E ★ ★ ★

East Louisiana Railroad, 55, 76, 194
Eavesdropping, *104–105*
Eckhardt, Christopher, 251
Economic Bill of Rights, 135
Education, Schools, and the Supreme Court, *See Hazelwood School District v. Kuhlmeier* (1988); *Tinker v. Des Moines* (1969)
Eighth Air Force, 145
Eighth Amendment, *See* Amendments
Eisenhower, Dwight D., 20, 22, 53, 60
Eisenstadt v. Baird (1972), 53
Elections
   1876, *63*
   2000, 15, 61–64, *63*
Electoral Vote Count Act, 64
Electric Chair, *97*
Electronic Eavesdropping, *104–105, See also* Unreasonable Search and Seizure
Elfbrandt v. Russell (1966), 170
Ellsberg, Daniel, *192*
Ellsworth, Oliver, 20, 176
   congressional service of, *88*

Embargo, **231**
Emerson, John, 99
Eminent Domain, *105*
Employment Division, Department of Human Resources of Oregon v. Smith (1990), 127–128
Encyclopedia Americana, 231
Endo, Mitsuye, 166
Engle v. Vitale (1962), *105–107,* 105–107, 219, *See also* Freedom of Religion; School Prayer and Bible Readings
Equal Employment Opportunity, 75, *107–109,* 149–150, *See also* Affirmative Action; Civil Rights Act (1964)
Equal Protection, *57,* 64, *109,* *110,* **142,** 169, *See also* Due Process
Equal Protection Clause, **189**
Equal Rights, 50–51, 222, *224*
Ervin, Sam, *106–107*
Escobedo v. Illinois (1964), 12, 79, 110, *110–112,* 111, 112, 297–298, *297–298*
Espionage Act (1917), 134, 286
Espionage Cases, 124
Establishment Clause, **38,** 106, 126, 127, 219, 256
Everson v. Board of Education (1947), *49,* 126–127
Evidence, illegally obtaining, 112
Exclusionary Rule, 29–31, 31–32, *111–113,* 221, *See also* Writ of Habeas Corpus
Executive Branch, 1, 66
Executive Order No. 1066, 165
Executive Privilege, **236**
Ex parte Garland (1866), 50, *85,* 113, 199
Ex parte McCardle (1868), 162
Ex parte Milligan (1866), 6, *113*
Ex parte Quirin (1942), 10
Ex Post Facto Laws, 50, 51, *113–114, See also* Bills of Attainder; Loyalty Oaths

★ ★ ★ F ★ ★ ★

Fair Employment Laws, 108
Fair Housing, 77, *114–115, See also* Equal Protection
Fair Labor Standards Act, *70*
Falsifying Documents, 32, 92
Fanny Hill, 185
Faragher v. City of Boca Raton (1998), 223
Faretta v. California (1975), *139*
Farrand, Max, 159
Federal Declaratory Judgment Act (1934), 98

Federal Farm Bankruptcy Act, 9
Federal Income Tax, *85*
Federalism, ***115–116,*** *See also* Due
  Process; Equal Protection; Interstate
  Commerce
Federalist #78, The, 2
Federalist Papers, The, 3, 19, 159
Federalist Party, 24, **153,** 173, **176,** 188
Federal Judicial Center, 69
Federal Power Commission, 18, 175
Federal Rules of Criminal Procedure, 45
Federal Writers' Project, 241
Field, Stephen J., 19, ***116–117,*** *232*
Fifth Amendment, *See* Amendments;
  Self-Incrimination
Fifth Circuit, 21
Fighting Words, 128, *132*
Firefighters, 203
Fireside Chat, 216
Firing Squads, *97*
First Circuit Court of Appeals, 54
First National Bank, 154
Fiscal and Monetary Power and the
  Supreme Court, ***117–119***
Flag Burning, ***120,*** 164, *See also*
  Freedom of Speech; Symbolic Speech
Flag Protection Act, 120
Flags, 128, 243
Florida, elections in, 61–64
Florida Supreme Court, 62–63
Florida v. J.L. (2000), 230
Ford, Gerald R., 164
Foreign Affairs, 90, ***120–121***
Formality, 237
Fortas, Abe, 25, 60, 139
  nomination of, *80*
Founders, 66
Fourth Amendment, *See* Amendments;
  Search Warrants
Framers, 1, 57, 133, 153, 158
Frankfurter, Felix, 42, ***121–122,*** 138,
  143, 183, *216*
*Franks v. Bowman Transportation Co.
  Inc.* (1976), 75
Frank v. Mangum (1915), 260
Freedom of Assembly, ***122–124,*** 125
Freedom of Association, ***125–126***
Freedom of Religion, ***126–128,*** *See
  also* School Prayer and Bible
  Readings
Freedom of Speech, ***128–133,*** 228, 251,
  299–301, *See also* Flag Burning; Gag
  Rules; *Hazelwood School District v.
  Kuhlmeier* (1988); Sit-Ins; Symbolic
  Speech; *Tinker v. Des Moines* (1969)
Freedom of the Press, 65–66, ***133–135,***
  146–147
Freedom to Petition, ***135***
Free Exercise, 127

Free Press *vs.* a Fair Trial, 134
Fuller, Melville W., 117
Furman v. Georgia (1972), 92, 96
Furnco Construction Corp. v. Waters
  (1978), 75

★ ★ ★G★ ★ ★

Gag Rules, 134, *136, See also* Freedom
  of Speech; Freedom of the Press
Gambling, 14
Gannett Co. Inc. v. DePasquale (1979),
  134, 205
*Gardner v. Board of Public Works of Los
  Angeles* (1951), 170
Garland, Augustus H., 50, 114
Garner v. Louisiana (1961), 243
Garrity v. New Jersey (1967), 222
Gender Discrimination, 142, 222–223
Geneva Conventions, 15–16
Geography, 20–21
*Gerende v. Board of Supervisors of
  Elections* (1951), 170
Gerrymandering, **201, 242**
Gertz v. Robert Welch Inc. (1974), 168
Gibbons, Thomas, *137*
Gibbons v. Ogden (1824), 83, 116,
  136–138, ***136–138,*** 174, *175,* 176,
  232, 234, 279–280, ***279–280***
*Giboney v. Empire Storage and Ice
  Co.* (1949), 124
Gideon, Clarence Earl, 139, *140*
Gideon v. Wainwright (1963), 11, 23, *49,*
  111, 139, ***139–141,*** *140, 141,* 259,
  295–297, ***295–297,*** 298
Ginsburg, Ruth Bader, ***141–142,***
  324–325
  appointment of, 55
  Bush v. Gore (2000) and, 64
  dissent, 32
  gender classifications and, 223
  Supreme Court Building and, 241
Gitlow, Benjamin, 77
Gitlow v. New York (1925), 11, 48, *49,*
  77, 104, 234
Gober v. City of Birmingham (1963), 224
Goebel, Julius, Jr., 2, 4
Gold, 117
Goldberg, Arthur, 54
Gomillion v. Lightfoot (1960), 201
*Gompers v. Buck's Stove and Range
  Co.* (1911), 91
Gonzales v. Carhart (2007), 36
Good Faith Exceptions, 112
Gore, Al, 15, 315–318
  Bush v. Gore (2000), 61–64
Government Neutrality, 14
Government Restraints, 129
Grady v. Corbin (1990), 99
Grandfather Clauses, ***142–143***

*Grand Inquests: The Historic
  Impeachments of Justice Samuel
  Chase and President Andrew Johnson*
  (Rehnquist), 203
Grand Jury, 142, *See also* Right to a
  Jury Trial
Grant, Ulysses S., 81
Gratz, Jennifer, 37
Gratz v. Bollinger (2003), 37
Gray v. Sanders (1963), 189
Great Depression, 8, 9, 82, 87, **197,**
  214, 234
Great Dissenter, 145
Green, Marion, 108
Gregg v. Georgia (1976), 92, 97
Grier, Robert C., 117, *232*
Griggs v. Duke Power Co. (1971), 75
Griswold v. Connecticut (1965), 34, *49,*
  53, 143–144, ***143–144,*** 210, *213*
Grosjean v. American Press Co.
  (1936), 65
Grovey v. Townsend (1933), 259–260
Grutter, Barbara, 37
Grutter v. Bollinger (2003), 37, 188
Guantanamo Bay, 15–16
Guide to Washington, 241
Guilt by Association, 124
Guinn v. United States (1915), 143
Gun-Free School Zones Act of 1990, 14
Guns, 32
Gurfein, Murray I., 191

★ ★ ★H★ ★ ★

Hague v. CIO (1939), *49*
Hale v. Henkel (1906), 222
Hamdan v. Rumsfeld (2006), *206*
Hamilton, Alexander, 1, 2–3, 19, 154,
  159, 232–233
Hammer v. Dagenhart (1918),
  69–70, *86*
Handbill Protests, *130*
Hanging, *97*
Harding, Warren G., 20
Harlan, John Marshall, II, 12, 35, 46,
  78, ***144–146,*** 185, 194–195
Harris, Katherine, 62
Harrison, Benjamin, 19–20, *66*
Harvard Law Review, 236
Hate Crimes, *132*
Haupt v. United States (1947), *61*
Hawaii, 73
Hayes, Rutherford B., 21, *63,* 117
Haynsworth, Clement F., Jr.
  nomination of, 21, *80*
Hazelwood School District v. Kuhlmeier
  (1988), ***146–147,*** *146*–147, 251,
  313–315, ***313–315***
Heart of Atlanta Motel v. United States
  (1964), 147–149, ***147–149***

Helvering v. Davis (1937), *86*
Hepburn v. Griswold (1870), *85*, 119
Herbert v. Lando (1979), 184
Herring, Bennie Dean, 31
Herring v. United States (2009),
    30–32
Hill, Anita, 25, *149–150*
Hill, Arthur, 52
Hill, David B., *82*
Hills v. Gautreaux (1976), 115
Hirabayahsi v. United States (1943), 166
Hoar, Ebenezer R.
    nomination of, *80*
Holder v. Hall (1994), 250
Holmes, Oliver Wendell, Jr., 132, *150*,
    150–152, 235, 259, *287*
Home Rule Act, 74
Homosexuality, 144, 208, 210, 318–321
Hoover, Herbert C., 18, 20, 22,
    152, 181
Hornblower, William B., *82*
    nomination of, *80*
House of Representatives, 83, 153, 175
*Hudgens v. National Labor Relations
    Board* (1976), *131*
Hughes, Charles Evans, 10, 82, *152*,
    215, 216
Hyde Amendment, 214

★ ★ ★ I ★ ★ ★

Illinois v. Wardlow (2002), 230
Immigrants, 38
Immigration and Nationality Act
    (1952), 74
Immigration and Naturalization Service
    (INS), 167
*Immigration and Naturalization Service
    v. Chadha* (1983), *167*
Immigration Quotas, 38
Impeachment, 2, 43, 91, *153*
Implied Powers, *153–154*
Income Taxes, 8, 117
Incumbent, **258**
Incumbent Federalist, **172–173**
Indians, *73*
Indian Treaty, 17
Indictment, **45, 48, 95, 206,** 297
Indigents, **139, 210**
Indirect Taxes, 117
Injunctions, *154–155,* **191,** *See also*
    Writ of Mandamus
In re Burrus (1971), *103,* 163
In re Gault (1967), 163
In re Oliver (1948), *49*
In re Winship (1970), *103,* 163
Interest Groups, 17
Internal Affairs, 90
Interracial Marriage, 169, 303–304
Interracial Sex, 169–170

Interrogation Practices, 179
Interstate Commerce, 83, 84, **174,** 194
Interstate Relations, *154,* 161
Interstate Travelers, 147–149, 148–149
Intoxication, 43
Iowa Civil Liberties Union (ICLU), 251
Iowa Republican Party, 21
Iredell, James, 20, 42

★ ★ ★ J ★ ★ ★

Jackson, Howell E., 20
    congressional service of, *88*
Jackson, Robert H., 9, 133
Jacobellis v. Ohio (1964), *185, 186*
Jane Roe, 213, *312*
Japanese Americans, 122, 164–166,
    165, 288–289
Jay, John, 4, 19, 20, 24, *67,* **156,** 233
Jaybird Party, 260
Jay Treaty, 156
Jefferson, Thomas, 4, 22, 60, 67, 200
Jehovah's Witnesses, **127,**
    130, 132
Jenkins v. Georgia (1974), *186*
Jeter, Mildred, 169–170
Jews, 22, 24, 51, 52, 54, 121
Jim Crow Laws, 55–57, 76, 193
Johnson, Andrew, 81, 113, 114
Johnson, Gregory, 120
Johnson, Lyndon B., 25, 60, 176, 177
Johnson, Thomas, 20
Johnson v. Louisiana (1972), 205
Johnson v. Zerbst (1938), 207
Jones v. Alfred H. Mayer Co. (1968), 115
Joseph H. Hirshhorn Museum and
    Sculpture Garden, 69
Judicial, **67, 83**
Judicial Activism, *See Bush v. Gore*
    (2000); Judicial Restraint
Judicial Branch, **27**
Judicial Conference, 69
Judicial Restraint, 13, **157–158**
Judicial Review, 4–5, *67,* **158–159**
Judicial System, U.S., *See* Jurisdiction
Judicial Usurpation, 174
Judiciary Act
    (1789), 4–5, 20, 43, *71, 89,* 91, 154–155,
        159–161, 233, **262–264**
    (1801), 248
    (1802), 248
    (1807), *89*
    (1837), *89*
    (1863), *89*
    (1866), *89*
    (1869), *89,* 218, 255
    (1891), *89,* 280
    (1925), *89,* 246
Judiciary Code
    (1911), *89*

Judiciary Committee, 82, 83
Jurek v. Texas (1976), 97
Jurisdiction, 40, **160,** *161–162*
    Baker v. Carr (1962), **45**
    branches of government and, 1
    Circuit Courts and, **72**
    citizenship and naturalization, **73**
    Constitution of the United States
        and, **90**
    injunctions and, **154**
    judicial review and, **83**
    Marbury v. Madison (1803)
        and, **174**
    New Deal and, **182**
    Supreme Court history and, **233**
    U.S. District Court and, **255,** 256
    Writ of Mandamus and, **261**
Jury Trials, 48
Justice Department, 60
Justice for All
    Brown v. Board of Education
        (1954), *58*
    Due Process, *103*
    Jehovah's Witnesses, **127**
    Loitering, *123, 124*
    Private Clubs, *125*
    private searches, *221*
    Right to Refuse Counsel, *139*
    Treason, *61*
Justices
    requirements for, 79
Justices and the Supreme Court
    Building (1929), *287*
Justices Who Served in Congress, *88*
Justiciable, 46
Juveniles, *See also* Due Process
    rights of, *163*

★ ★ ★ K ★ ★ ★

Kansas City Schools, 14
Katz v. United States (1967), 104
Kawakita v. United States (1952), *61*
Kelo v. City of New London (2005), 105
Kennedy, Anthony M., 26, 35, 63, 93,
    164, 188, 208
Kennedy, John F., 177
*Keyishian v. Board of Regents of
    the State University of New York*
    (1967), 170
Kidnapping, 179
Kimel v. Florida (2000), 188
King, Edward
    nomination of, *80*
King, Martin Luther, Jr., 135, 293
Klopfer v. North Carolina (1967), *49,*
    206
Know-Nothings, 144
Knox v. Lee (1871), *85,* 119
Koenig, Louis, 197

Korematsu v. United States (1944), 10, *109*, 122, 164–166, **164–166,** 288–289, **288–289**
Kotch v. Board of River Port Pilot Commissioners (1947), *109*
Ku Klux Klan, 82, *129*, 229

★ ★ ★ L ★ ★ ★

Labor Management and Reporting Act (1959), 51
Labor Unions, 87
Lamar, Joseph R., 20, 52
Lamar, Lucius Q.C., 21, 24
  congressional service of, *88*
Lame Duck, 81
Landmark Decision Highlights
  Baker v. Carr (1962), *46*
  Brown v. Board of Education (1954), *55*
  Bush v. Gore (2000), *64*
  Civil Rights Cases (1883), *78*
  Cruzan v. Missouri Department of Health (1990), *92*
  Dartmouth College v. Woodward (1819), *94*
  Dred Scott v. Sandford (1857), *101*
  Engle v. Vitale (1962), *107*
  Escobedo v. Illinois (1964), *111*
  Gibbons v. Ogden (1824), *137*
  Gideon v. Wainwright (1963), *141*
  Hazelwood School District v. Kuhlmeier (1988), *146*
  Heart of Atlanta Motel v. United States (1964), *148*
  Korematsu v. United States (1944), *165*
  Loving v. Virginia (1967), *169*
  Mapp v. Ohio (1961), *171*
  Marbury v. Madison (1803), *173*
  Miranda v. Arizona (1966), *180*
  New York Times v. Sullivan (1964), *184*
  Plessy v. Ferguson (1896), *194*
  Powell v. Alabama (1932), *197*
  Roe v. Wade (1973), *213*
  Swann v. Charlotte-Mecklenburg County Board of Education (1971), *242*
  Tinker v. Des Moines (1969), *251*
  United States v. Nixon (1974), *252*
  University of California Regents v. Bakke (1978), *254*
Lawrence v. Texas (2003), 144, 164, *208–209,* 210, 219, 236, 318–321, **318–321**
League of Women Voters, 54
Lee v. Weisman (1992), 14, 164, 220
Legal Assistance, 139–141
Legal Defense Fund, 57

Legal Standing, 157
Legal Tender Acts, 22, *85,* 117
Legal Tender Cases, *Hepburn v. Griswold* (1870), 22
Legislative, **83**
Legislative Branch, 1, 66
Legislative Veto, **166–167**
Lethal Injection, *96, 97*
Lewis, John L., 91
Lewis, Terry, 62
Libel, **128,** *167–168, 183,* 184
Liberty Bell, 176
License Cases, *247*
Lieberman, Joseph, 62
Lincoln, Abraham, 5, 6, 19, 21, 113, 116, 199
Lindsley v. Natural Carbonic Gas Co. (1911), *109*
Line Item Veto, *168–169,* 198
Line of Cases, 28
Linkletter v. Walker (1965), *172*
Liquor Licenses, *125*
Literacy Tests, 143, **201, 211**
Living Wills, 93
Lloyd Center, *130*
Lloyd Corporation Ltd. v. Tanner (1972), *130, 131*
Lochner v. New York (1905), 103, 143, 151
Loitering, *123*
Lombard v. Louisiana (1963), 224
Long, Huey, 65
Lottery Tickets, 84
Louisiana ex rel. Francis v. Resweber (1947), *49*
Louisiana Purchase, 101
Lovell v. Griffin (1938), *127*
Loving, Richard Perry, 169–170
Loving v. Virginia (1967), 23, *109,* **169–170,** *259,* **303–304**
Loyalty Oaths, 19–20, **170**
Lurton, Horace, 20
Luther v. Borden (1849), 46
Lynchings, 95

★ ★ ★ M ★ ★ ★

Madison, James, 4, 19, 51, 159, 173
Magna Carta, 135
Mail Fraud, *221*
Malice, 132
Malloy v. Hogan (1964), *49,* 110–111
Mandamus, *See* Writ of Mandamus
Manual Enterprises v. Day (1962), *185*
Mapp, Dollree, 171
Mapp v. Ohio (1961), 11, 30–31, *49,* 112, **171–172,** *171–172,* 221
Marbury, Thomas, 67
Marbury, William, 4, 173, *173*

Marbury v. Madison (1803), 4, 5, 27, 67, 83, *86,* 157–159, 161, *172–174,* **172–174,** *175,* 176, 178, 233, 261, 264–269, **264–269,** 294, 331, 332
Maritime and Admiralty Law, **174–175**
Marshall, John, **175–176**
  Aaron Burr and, 60
  appointment of, 4
  banks and, 178
  congressional service of, *88*
  control and, 22, 200
  Dartmouth College v. Woodward (1819) and, 94
  death of, 231, 247
  implied powers and, 154
  Judiciary Act (1789) and, 5
  Marbury v. Madison (1803) and, 27, 83, 172–174, 264, 294
  McCulloch v. Maryland (1819) and, 273–275
  Sturges v. Crowninshield (1819) and, 232
  Writ of Mandamus and, 261
Marshall, Thurgood, 25, 57, 93, 96, **176–177,** 192
Marshall Court (1801-1835), 233–234
Marsh v. Alabama (1946), *130*
Martin v. Hunter's Lessee (1816), 231
Maryland Supreme Court, 5
Massachusetts Supreme Court, 122
Massachusetts Twentieth Volunteer Regiment, 151
Massiah v. United States (1964), 79, 110
Matthews, Stanley, 23
  congressional service of, *88*
  nomination of, *80*
Maximum Work-Hour Laws, 76
Maxwell v. Dow (1900), 204
McCain-Feingold Act, 228
McCarran Act (1950), *125*
McCleskey, Warren, 97
McCleskey v. Kemp (1987), 97
McCloskey, Robert G., 3
McCorvey, Norma "Jane Roe," 35, *312*
McCulloch, James, 178
McCulloch v. Maryland (1819), 5, 116, 154, *175,* 176, 177–178, **177–178,** 234, 273–275, **273–276**
McDonnell Douglas Corp. v. Green (1973), 75
McDowell, James, *221*
McGowan v. Maryland (1961), *109*
McKeiver v. Pennsylvania (1971), *103,* 163
McKenna, Joseph
  congressional service of, *88*

McKinley, John
congressional service of, 88
McKinley, William, 245
McLean, John
congressional service of, 88
McNabb v. United States (1943), 79
McReynolds, James C., 215, 216
Medicaid, 168
Medical Devices, regulation of, 33
Medical Treatment, 93
Memorandum of Associate Justice
Antonin Scalia (2004), 322–324
Meredith, James, 120
Mexican War, 120
Micou, William C.
nomination of, 80
Middleton, Daniel W., 232
Midnight Judges, 172
Miers, Harriet, 26, 38, 81, 189
Military Draft, 258
Milk Products, 77
Milk Wagon Drivers Union v.
Meadowmoor Dairies Inc.
(1941), 124
Miller, Samuel F., 21, 232
Miller Standard, 186
Miller v. California (1973), 186, 187
Milligan, L.P., 113
Minimum Wage Laws, 9, 216
Minnesota v. Dickerson (1993), 230
Minorities, 36, 37
Minority Religions, 127
Minors, 163
Minton, Sherman, 22, 53
congressional service of, 88
Miranda v. Arizona (1966), 12, 23, 79,
179, 179–180, 179–181, 259,
301–303, 301–303
Misconduct, 153
Mississippi University for Women v.
Hogan (1982), 109
Missouri Compromise (1820), 85
Missouri Supreme Court, 93, 100
Missouri v. Jenkins (1995), 14
Moment of Silence, 256
Monopoly, 52, 84, 137, 225
Monsanto Company, 249
Moody, William H.
congressional service of, 88
Moore v. Dempsey (1923), 260
Moose Lodge 107 v. Irvis (1972), 125
Mootness, 157
Morehead v. New York ex rel. Tipaldo
(1936), 9
Morse v. Frederick (2007), 251
Mulford v. Smith (1939), 86
Municipal Laws, 221
Murphy, Frank, 216
Murray v. Curlett (1963), 219

NAACP v. Alabama ex rel. Patterson
(1958), 146
Nathan Bishop Middle School, 220
Nathanson v. United States
(1933), 200
National Anthem, 183
National Association for the Advance-
ment of Colored People (NAACP), 55,
57, 58, 97, 122, 177, 242
National Banks, 5, 177–178
National Gallery of Art, 69
National Industrial Recovery Act
(NIRA), 9, 86, 181
National Labor Relations Act, 131, 217
National War Labor Board, 246
Nationality Act (1952), 73, 167
Naturalization, 38, 73–75, 101, 114, See
also Aliens; Citizenship
Navigation, 137–138
Near, J.M., 65
Near v. Minnesota (1931), 65, 133, 152
Nebraska Press Association v. Stuart
(1976), 134, 136
Nelson, Samuel, 19, 232
New Deal, 14, 181–182
Franklin D. Roosevelt and, 8, 10, 215,
216, 234
Great Depression and, 87
Robert H. Jackson and, 9
Willis Van Devanter and, 217
New Federalism, 116
New Haven Railroad, 52
New York Civil Liberties Union, 106
New York State Board of Regents, 106
New York State Crime Commission,
145–146
New York Times, 13, 53, 66, 183–184,
191, 253, 293
New York Times v. Sullivan (1964), 53,
134, 168, 182–184, 293, 299–301,
299–301
Ninth Amendment, See Amendments;
Right to Privacy
Ninth Circuit Court of Appeals, 164
Nix v. Hedden (1893), 118
Nixon, Richard M.
G. Harrold Carswell and, 81
Lewis F. Powell Jr. and, 20
New York Times and, 191
Pentagon Papers Case and, 66
resignation of, 54
Senate and, 21
United States v. Nixon (1974) and,
198, 252–253
Warren E. Burger and, 22, 59
William H. Rehnquist and, 202
Nixon v. Herndon (1927), 259
Nominations, 17–26, 23

Nominations Not Confirmed by the
Senate, 80
Nominees, 19, 24–26
Noncapital Offenses, 45
Norris-LaGuardia Act, 108
North American Review, 231
Nullify, 158

Obama, Barack, 198, 212, 226, 227, 328
Obscenity, 128, 184–187, 185, 186, See
also Freedom of the Press
O'Connor, Sandra Day, 187–189, 326
appointment of, 25
Bush v. Gore (2000) and, 63
Cruzan v. Missouri Department of
Health (1990) and, 93
Due Process and, 16
Planned Parenthood v. Casey (1992)
and, 35
retirement of, 81
Samuel A. Alito and, 38
Office of Legal Counsel, 218
Ogden, Aaron, 137
Okanogan Indians et al. v. United States
(1929), 198
Olmstead v. Unites States (1928), 104
One Person, One Vote, 47, 189
Opinions, 189–190
Oppression, 37
Original Jurisdiction, See Jurisdiction

Palko v. Connecticut (1937), 77
Panama Refining Co. v. Ryan (1935),
9, 86
Papachristou v. City of Jacksonville
(1972), 123
Paris Peace Conference, 122
Parker, John J.
nomination of, 80
Parochial Schools, 126
Paterson, William, 20, 42, 176
congressional service of, 88
nomination of, 80
Patterson, Robert B., 53
Patton v. United States (1930), 204
Peabody, Bruce, 239
Pearl Harbor, 164–166
Peck, James H., 91
Peckham, Wheeler H., 82
nomination of, 80
Pennsylvania v. Wheeling and Belmont
Bridge Co. (1852), 174–175
Pentagon Papers, 133, 191–192
Pentagon Papers Case (1971), 66
Personal Safety, 30
Peterson v. City of Greenville (1963), 224
Petition, freedom of, 48

Philadelphia Convention, 19
Photo Identification, voting and, 32
Picketing, 123–124, 129, *130, 131*
Pierce, Franklin, 21
Pitney, Mahlon, 260
    congressional service of, *88*
Plaintiff, **56**, 157
Planned Parenthood, 35, 143–144
Planned Parenthood of Southeastern
    Pennsylvania v. Casey (1992), 14, 35,
    143, 164, 321
Plessy, Homer, 55, 76
Plessy v. Ferguson (1896), 8, 11, 55, 56,
    76, 77, 144, 145, **193–194,** *193–195,*
    234, 282–283, **282–286,** *284*–286,
    290–291
Plyler v. Dow (1982), *109*
Point/Counterpoint
    Brown v. Board of Education
        (1954), *285*
    Plessy v. Ferguson (1896), *284*
    Privacy for Consenting Adults, *208*
    Supreme Court hearings and
        television, *238–239*
Pointer v. Texas (1965), *49*
Political Association, 126
Political Campaigns, donations, 32
Political Cartoons, *36, 66, 252, 286*
Polk, James K., 81
Pollock v. Farmers' Loan and Trust Co.
    (1895), 8, *85,* 118, 155
Poll Taxes, 76, **201, 210**
Polygamists, 114
Pope v. Illinois (1987), *186,* 187
Post Civil-War Courts, 234–236
Post-Revolutionary Americans, 29
Powell, Lewis F., Jr., 20, 35, 81
Powell v. Alabama (1932), 195,
    195–197, *196–197,* 207
Power, Origins of Judicial, *See* Appellate
    Jurisdiction; Constitution; Judicial
    Review; Judiciary Act of 1789; Juris-
    diction; *Marbury v. Madison* (1803);
    Supreme Court, History of
Pragmatic, **229**
Prayer in School, 14, 105–107
Precedent, **28, 55, 56, 73, 157,** 158
Preemption, 33
Pregnancy, 213
Preparedness Day Parade, 121
Prescription Drugs, regulation of, 33
Presidency and the Supreme Court,
    197–200
Presidential Authority, Challenging, 197
Presidential Pardons, 198–199
Presidential Power, 5–7
Press, freedom of, 48
Press-Enterprise Co. v. Superior Court
    (1986), 205

Prior Restraint, 133, **200,** *See also*
    Censorship
Prisoner Welfare, 156
Prison Guards, 223
Pritchett, C. Herman, 117
Privacy, 12, 30, 34, 35, 201, 310–312
Private Property, *131–132*
Private Searches, *221*
Probable Cause, 29–30, **200–201**
Pro-Choice, 34
Proffitt v. Florida (1976), 97
Progressive, **52,** 258
Property Rights, *See* Eminent Domain;
    Fair Housing
Protections, 32
Protesting, 120, *122,* 123
Protests, 223–224, *250*
Public Officials, 168
Public Schools, 11
    minorities and, 38
    segregation in, 48, 57, 77, 177
Public Speech on Private Property,
    130–131
Public Transportation, 48
Puerto Rico, 73
Punishment After Publication, 134
Pure Speech, 128

★ ★ ★R★ ★ ★

Race and Redistricting, **201–202**
Race-Blind Admissions Systems, 37
Racism, 48, 50, 97, 98, 149
Railroad Retirement Board v. Alton
    Railway Co. (1935), 9
Railroads, 8, 84, 108, 193
Railway Labor Act, 108
Rakas v. Illinois (1978), 44
Rape, 95, 179, 195, 207
Ratification, **40, 76,** *100,* **103, 176,**
    220, 245
Ratified, **166, 210, 225**
R.A.V. v. City of St. Paul (1992), *132*
Read, John M.
    nomination of, *80*
Reagan, Ronald
    Anthony M. Kennedy and, 164
    conservatives and, 16, 82
    David Souter and, 228
    G. Harrold Carswell and, 81
    judicial activism and, 12–13
    line item vetoes and, 198, 202
    New Federalism and, 116
    nominations of, 25
    Sandra Day O'Connor and, 187
Reapportionment, **38, 45,** 46
Recess of the Senate, 18–19
Reconstruction, 162
Reconstruction Era, 21
Recordkeeping, 32

Recounting Ballots, 61–64
Red Flag, 243
Reed, Stanley F., 45, *216*
Reed v. Reed (1971), 223
Reform Party, 62
Regents of the University of California v.
    Bakke (1978), 37
Regulations, 9, 11, 33, 84
Rehnquist, William H., 143, **202–203**
    abortion and, 35, 36
    assistant of, 69
    Bush v. Gore (2000) and, 63, 64
    Cruzan v. Missouri Department of
        Health (1990) and, 93, 207
    Gun-Free School Zones Act of 1990
        and, 14, 87
    nomination of, 82
    Sandra Day O'Connor and, 188
    United States v. Salerno (1987)
        and, 45
    Wallace v. Jaffree (1984) and,
        256–257
    Webster v. Reproductive Health
        Services (1989) and, 13
Reitman v. Mulkey (1967), 115
Religion
    freedom of, 48
    minority, 127
    rights, 14
    toleration of, **126**
Reorganization, 182
Republican National Convention, 120, 145
Republican Party, *202,* **245,** 257
Restrictive Covenants, **114**
Retirement, 234, *235*
Revolutionary War, 156, 175
Reynolds, Robert, 146–147
Reynolds v. Sims (1964), 189
Ricci v. DeStefano (2009), 203–204,
    203–204
Richmond Newspapers Inc. v. Common-
    wealth of Virginia (1980), 134, 205
Ride Circuit, 71
Rights
    to Die, **207**
    to a Jury Trial, **204–205**
    to Legal Counsel, **207–210**
    Personal, *See* Abortion; Due Process;
        Equal Protection; Right to Die;
        Right to Privacy; Search War-
        rants; Writ of Habeas Corpus
    to Privacy, 143–144
    to a Public Trial, **205**
    to Remain Silent, 79
    to a Speedy Trial, **205–206**
    to Vote, **210–211**
Roberts, John G., 30, 31, 32, **211–212,**
    327–328
Roberts, Owen J., 10, *215, 216,* 217

Robinson v. California (1962), 11
Robinson v. Memphis and Charleston Railroad Co. (1883), 78
Rock Island Railroad, 47
Roe v. Wade (1973), 12–14, 34–36, 60, 143, 188, 210, *213*–214, **213–214,** 236, **310–312,** *310–313*
Rolleston, Moreton, Jr., *148*
Roman Catholics, 53, 246
Roosevelt, Franklin D.
  1937 Court Reform Plan, **214–217**
  Felix Frankfurter and, 121
  Great Depression and, 197, 234
  Harlan Stone and, 20
  liberals and, 16
  New Deal and, 8, 10, 87
  proposals of, 43
  retirement and, 235
Roosevelt, Theodore, 245
Roosevelt's 1937 Court Reform Plan, **214–217**
Rosenberger v. University of Virginia (1995), 15
Rosenblatt v. Baer (1966), 168
Rosenbloom v. Metromedia Inc. (1971), 168
Rostker v. Goldberg (1981), *223*, 258
Roth Standard, *185*, 187
Roth v. United States (1957), 184 *185*, *186*, 187
Rumsfeld, Donald, 15–16
Rutledge, John, 3–4, 19, 20, 24, 25
  nomination of, *80*

★ ★ ★ **S** ★ ★ ★

Salaries and Benefits of the Justices, **218**
Salutatorian, **244**
Sanford, John F.A., 100
Sante Fe Independent School District v. Doe (2000), 220
Scalia, Antonin, **218–219**
  Bowers v. Hardwick (1986) and, *209*
  Bush v. Gore (2000) and, 63, 64
  Constitution of the United States and, 55
  Cruzan v. Missouri Department of Health (1990) and, 93
  memorandum of, 322–324
  nomination of, 25
  right to die and, 207
  Roe v. Wade (1973) and, 36
  Samuel A. Alito and, 38
Schacht v. United States (1970), *250*
Schechter Poultry Corp. v. United States (1935), 9, *86*
Schenck v. United States (1919), *150*, 151, 228, 286
Schneckloth v. Bustamonte (1973), 200

School District of Abington Township v. Schempp (1963), 219
School Prayer and Bible Readings, 14, 105–107, **219–220,** *See also* Freedom of Religion
Scott, Dred, *99*, 99–102, *100*, *101*–102
Scottsboro Boys, *196*
Search Warrants, 134, **220–221**
Second Bank of the United States, 154
Second Constitutional Convention, 41
Securities and Exchange Commission (SEC), 33
Seditious Speech, **128**
Segregation, *See also* Discrimination
  Brown v. Board of Education (1954) and, 55–57
  Jim Crow laws and, 193
  in public schools, 11, *56*, 59, 77, 177
  races and, 48, 50, 76, 81, 114, 195, 224, 242, 290–291
Selective Service Draft Laws Case, 258
Self-Incrimination, 110, 112, 163, 180, **221–222,** *See also* Confessions; Fifth Amendment
Seminole Tribe of Florida v. Florida (1996), 14
Senate Judiciary Committee, 23, 25, 39, 43, 52, 54, 83, 150, *249*
Senatorial Courtesy, 82
Seniority, 237
Separate but Equal, 282–286
Separation of Church and State, 126
Separation of Powers, **261**
September 11th Terrorist Attacks, 206
Sex Discrimination, 142, **222–223,** *See also* Discrimination
Sexual Harassment, 25, 83, 249
Shaw v. Reno (1993), 201
Shays's Rebellion, 40–41
Shelley v. Kraemer (1948), 114–115
Sherman Antitrust Act, 7
Shuttlesworth, Fred, *123*
Shuttlesworth v. Birmingham (1965), *123*, 224
Sierra Club, 322–324
Silver Platter Doctrine, 112
Silverthorne Lumber Co. v. United States (1920), 112
Simants, Erwin Charles, 136
Simon & Schuster Inc. v. Members of New York State Crime Victims Board (1991), 65
Sit-In Cases (1962), 224
Sit-Ins, **223–224,** *See also* Freedom of Speech
Sixth Amendment, *See* Amendments
Skinner v. Oklahoma (1942), *109*
Slaughterhouse Cases (1873), 76, 224–225, **224–225,** 284–285

Slavery, 7, 20, 76, 91, 99–102, 135, 138, 156, **225–226**
Smith, George O., 18
Smith Act, 126
Smithsonian Institution, 69
Smith v. Allwright (1944), 260
Smith v. Goguen (1974), 120
Social Regulation, 84
Social Security Act, 87, *215*, 217
Social Status Quo, 8
Sotomayor, Sonia, *84*, **226–227, 328**
Souter, David H., 64, 92, 188, 227, **228**
Sovereign Entities, 203
Sovereign Immunity, 164
Spanish-American War, 120
Spectator, 151
Spectrum, 146–147
Speech
  freedom of, 48, 75, 251, 299–301
  Unprotected, **228–229**
Speech Plus Conduct, 129
Speedy Trial Act (1974), 206
Spellman, Francis Cardinal, *106–107*
Spencer, John C.
  nomination of, *80*
Spence v. Washington (1974), 120
Spotlight
  1876 Election, *63*
  2000 Election, *63*
  Amistad, The, 226
  Anti-War Protests, *250*
  Citizenship, *74*
  Court, Congress, and Cambodia, *258*
  Enemy Combatants at Guantanamo, *206*
  fighting words, *132*
  Fourteenth Amendment, *100*
  Group Libel, *183*
  hate crimes, *132*
  lethal injection, *97*
  mandatory retirement, *235*
  Right to Travel, *247*
  School Prayer, *106–107*
  Solicitor General, *199*
  tomatoes, *118*
  Twenty-Seventh Amendment, *50–51*
  Women in the Military, *223*
Stack v. Boyle (1951), 45
Stanbery, Henry, 81
  nomination of, *80*
Standard of Weights and Measures, 118–119
Standing, **46**
Stanford Law Review, 187
Stanley v. Georgia (1969), 177
Stare Decisis, 158
States' Rights, **202**
Statutory Law, **40**
Steamboats, 137–138

Steele v. Louisville and Nashville Rail-road Co. (1944), 108
Stenberg v. Carhart (2000), 36, 236
Stevens, John P., 36, 61, 64, 93, **229–230**
Steward Machine Co. v. Davis (1937), *86*
Stewart, Potter
  appointment of, 19
  Establishment Clause and, 106
  Gannett Co. v. DePasquale (1979) and, 205
  Jacobellis v. Ohio (1964) and, 185
  Katz v. United States (1967) and, 104–105
  Miranda v. Arizona (1966) and, 12
  Pentagon Papers Case (1971) and, 191
  Shuttlesworth v. Birmingham (1965) and, *123*
Stimson, Henry L., 121
Stock Market Crash (1929), 181
Stone, Harlan Fiske, 20, 70, 77, 81, *215, 216, 287*
Stop-and-Frisk Searches, **230,** *See also* Automobile Searches; Search Warrants
Story, Joseph, 95, **230–231**
  congressional service of, *88*
Street v. New York (1969), 120
Stromberg v. California (1931), 243
Strong, William
  congressional service of, *88*
Student Press Law Center, 147
Sturges v. Crowninshield (1819), 231–232, **231–232,** 276–277, **276–277**
Subpoenas, **60,** 134, **252**
Substantive Due Process, 34–35
Subversive Speech, **128**
Subway Systems, 52
Suicide, 207
Sullivan, L.B., 182, 293
Supreme Court, *18*
  building, *6, 240,* **240–242,** *241*
  and the Communist Threat (1951), **292**
  History of the, **232–236**
  Size of, *233*
  terms, **248**
  Traditions of the, **237–240**
Supreme Court Chamber (1860-1935), **278**
Supreme Court: How It Was, How It Is, The (Rehnquist), 203
Supreme Court of Missouri, 115
Supreme Court Retirement Act (1937), 217, 218
Surveillance, 104
Sutherland, George, 42, 66, *215, 287*
  congressional service of, *88*

Swann v. Charlotte-Mecklenburg County Board of Education (1971), **242–243,** *242–243,* **307–309**
Swayne, Noah H., *232*
Swindler, William, 11
Symbolic Speech, 128–129, **243–244,** *See also* Flag Burning; Freedom of Speech; Sit-Ins

★ ★ ★ T ★ ★ ★

Taft, William Howard, **244–246,** *287*
  Bailey v. Drexel Furniture Co. (1922) and, 69–70
  Charles Evans Hughes and, 152
  nominations of, 20
  Olmstead v. United States (1928) and, 104
  Richard A. Ballinger and, 52
  Supreme Court Chamber and, 278
Taliban, 15–16
Tampering, 216
Taney, Roger B., 6, 80, 101, 102, 231, *246,* **246–248**
Taney Court (1836-1864), 234
Tariffs, *118,* **121**
Taxation, 65–66
Tax Breaks, 168
Taxes, 178, 247
Tax Relief Act (1997), 168
Teen Pregnancies, 146
Terrorists, 15–16
Terry v. Adams (1953), 260
Terry v. Ohio (1968), 30, 230
Test Cases, **35, 55,** 157
Test Oath Law (1865), *85,* 114, 170
Texas Court of Criminal Appeals, 120
Texas Democratic Party, 259
Texas v. Johnson (1990), 120
Third Virginia Regiment, 176
Thomas, Clarence, 25–26, 38, 63, 64, 83, 92, **248–250**
Thornberry, Homer
  nomination of, *80*
Thornburg v. Gingles (1986), 201
Thornhill v. Alabama (1940), 123, 124
Tilden, Samuel J., *63*
Tillman v. Wheaton-Haven Recreation Association (1973), 115, *125*
Tinker, Mary Beth, 251
Tinker v. Des Moines (1969), **251,** **305–306,** 313
Toll Bridges, 105
Tomatoes, *118*
Tong, Lorraine H., *239*
Traffic Violations, 44
Transportation, 243
Treason, **60,** 153, 176
Treasonable Conspiracy, 125

Treaty of Paris, 156
Truman, Harry S., 20, 22, 197–198
Tyler, John, 19, 81

★ ★ ★ U ★ ★ ★

Unanimous, **169**
Uncle Sam Anti-Alien Cartoon (1918), **286**
Unconstitutional Acts, 5, 6, 8, 11, 15, *85–86*
Undue Burdens, 35, 36
Union Local 590 v. Logan Valley Plaza (1968), *130, 131*
Unions, 91, 125, *130*
Unitarians, 219
United Mine Workers of America, 91
United States v. Appalachian Electric Power Co. (1940), 175
United States v. Brown (1965), 51
United States v. Butler (1936), *86,* 118
United States v. Calandra (1974), 30
United States v. Carolene Products Co. (1938), 77, *109*
United States v. Claimants of the Schooner Amistad (1841), *226*
United States v. Darby (1941), 70, *86*
United States v. Harriss (1954), 135
United States v. Klein (1872), 199
United States v. Lopez (1995), 14, 116
United States v. Lovasco (1977), 206
United States v. MacDonald (1982), 206
United States v. Matlock (1974), 201
United States v. Morrison (2000), 188
United States v. Mosely (1915), 143
United States v. Nichols (1883), 78
United States v. Nixon (1974), 22, 200, 236, **252–254**
United States v. O'Brien (1968), 243, *250*
United States v. Ryan (1883), 78
United States v. Salerno (1987), 45
United States v. Singleton (1883), 78
United States v. Sokolow (1989), 230
United States v. Stanley (1883), 78
United States v. Virginia (1996), *109,* 142
United States v. Vuitch (1971), 35
United States v. Whren (1996), 44
United States v. Wong Kim Ark (1898), 73
University of California at Davis, 37
University of California Regents v. Bakke (1978), 60, 254–255, **254–255**
University of Michigan, 37
University of Virginia, 14
Unprotected Speech, 132
Unreasonable Search and Seizure, 29–33, 43–44, 48, 104, 112, 171, 212
U.S. Capitol, *See* Capitol, The

U.S. Circuit Court of Appeals, 28, 60,
142, 146, 167, 219
U.S. District Courts, 28, **255–256**
U.S. Term Limits v. Thornton
(1995), 164

★ ★ ★ V ★ ★ ★

Vacancies, 18
Vanderbilt, Arthur T., 53
Van Devanter, Willis, *215, 217, 287*
Veazie Bank v. Fenno (1869), 119
Veterans Administration, 135
Vetoes, 66, **159,** 198
Vietnam, 191
Vietnam War, 66, 128, 191,
250, 251
Viewpoints
Affirmative Action, *36*
Benjamin Harrison, *66*
Executive Privilege, *252*
Supreme Court justices, *217*
*Village of Arlington Heights v.
Metropolitan Housing Development
Corporation* (1977), 115
Vinson, Fred M.
congressional service of, *88*
Violence Against Women Act, 188
Virginia Code, 169
Virginia House of Delegates, 176
Virginia Military Institute, 223
Virginia v. Black (2003), 244
Virgin Islands, 73
Voting, 32, 126, 143, 201
Voting Rights, 76
Voting Rights Act, 77, 91, 177,
202, *211*

★ ★ ★ W ★ ★ ★

Wade, Henry, 213
Wagner Labor Act (1935), 53
Waite, Morrison, 117
Walker v. Sauvinet (1876), 204
Wallace v. Jaffree (1985), 126, 220,
256–257
Waller v. Georgia (1984), 205
Wall Street Journal, 52, 253
Walsh, Thomas J., 52
*Walters v. National Association of
Radiation Survivors* (1995), 135
Walworth, Reuben H.
nomination of, *80*
War Labor Policies Board, 122
War of 1812, 120, 240
War on Terror, 15–16

War Power and the Supreme Court,
257–258
War Relocation Authority, 165
Warren, Charles, 95
Warren, Earl, **258–259**
appointment of, 19
Brown v. Board of Education (1954)
and, 59, 77, 284–285
Miranda v. Arizona (1966) and, 79
retirement of, 25
Reynolds v. Sims (1964) and, 189
United States v. Nixon (1974) and,
22–23
Warren, Samuel D., 52
Warren Court (1953-1969), 236
Washington, D.C., 4, *6*
Washington, George, 17, 19, 24, 74, 156,
169, 176
Washington Armament
Conference, 152
Washington Post, 253
Washington Star, 253
Washington v. Texas (1967), *49*
*Watchtower Bible & Tract Society of
New York v. Village of Stratton*
(2002), *127*
Watergate, 54
Watergate Hotel, 252
Water Rights, 155
Wayne, James M., *232*
congressional service of, *88*
Weapons, 31, 32, 43
Webster, Daniel, 94
Webster v. Reproductive Health Services
(1989), 13, 35
Weddington, Sarah, 35
Weeks v. United States (1914),
30–31, 112
Weisman, Deborah, 220
Welfare Benefits, 38
Wesberry v. Sanders (1964), 189
West Coast Hotel Co. v. Parrish (1937),
10, 216–217
West River Bridge Company v. Dix
(1848), 105
*West Virginia State Board of Education
v. Barnette* (1943), 127, 243
Wheeler, Burton, 82
Whig Party, 19, 81, 144
White, Byron R., 12, 13–14, 35, 55,
93, 191
White, Edward D., 20, 82, 143
congressional service of, *88*
White Circle League, *183*

White House Office of Telecommunica-
tions, 218
White Primaries, **211,** *259–260*
Whitney v. California (1927), 124
Williams, George H., 81
nomination of, *80*
Williamson v. Lee Optica of Oklahoma
(1955), *109*
Williams v. Florida (1970), 205
Williams v. Mississippi (1898), 8
Wills, Living, 93
Wilson, James, 20, 42
Wilson, Woodrow, 24, 51–52
Wilson v. United States (1911), 222
Winship, Samuel, 163
Wiretaps, 104
Wolcott, Alexander
nomination of, *80*
Wolf v. Colorado (1949), 49
Women's Rights, 60, 81, 142, 222–223
Woodbury, Levi
congressional service of, *88*
Woods, William B., 21, 24
Woodward, George W.
nomination of, *80*
World War I, 120, 122
World War II, 10, 38, 53, 120, *165,
199,* 236
Writ of Certiorari, **73**
Writ of Habeas Corpus, 113, **144,** 162,
166, **260**
Writ of Mandamus, 161, 173, **261,** *See
also* Injunctions
Wygant v. Jackson Board of Education
(1986), *109*

★ ★ ★ X ★ ★ ★

XYZ Affair, 176

★ ★ ★ Y ★ ★ ★

Yates v. United States (1957),
125–126, 228
Yellow-Dog Contracts, *86*
Yick Wo v. Hopkins (1886), 38
Youngstown Sheet & Tube Co. v. Sawyer
(1952), 323

★ ★ ★ Z ★ ★ ★

Zavelo v. Reeves (1913), *See* Bankruptcy
Zelman v. Simmons-Harris (2002), 127
Zionist Movement, 53, 121, 122
Zurcher v. The Stanford Daily
(1978), 134
Zwickler v. Koota (1967), 98